THE HUGUENOTS

AND

THE REVOCATION OF THE EDICT OF NANTES

AMS PRESS
NEW YORK

MEDAL STRUCK AT ROME TO COMMEMORATE THE
REVOCATION OF THE EDICT OF NANTES

THE HUGUENOTS

AND

THE REVOCATION OF THE EDICT OF NANTES

BY

HENRY M. BAIRD

PROFESSOR IN THE UNIVERSITY OF THE CITY OF NEW YORK; AUTHOR OF THE
HISTORY OF THE RISE OF THE HUGUENOTS OF FRANCE, AND
OF THE HUGUENOTS AND HENRY OF NAVARRE

WITH MAPS

VOL. II.

NEW YORK
CHARLES SCRIBNER'S SONS
1895

Library of Congress Cataloging in Publication Data

Baird, Henry Martyn, 1832-1906.
   The Huguenots and the revocation of the Edict of
Nantes.

   Conclusion of the narrative begun in the author's
Rise of the Huguenots and continued in his Huguenots
and Henry of Navarre.
   1. Huguenots in France. 2. Edict of Nantes.
3. France--History--Bourbons, 1589-1789. I. Title.
DC111.B265 1972   284'.5'0944   76-161752
ISBN 0-404-08003-0

Reprinted from the edition of 1895, New York
First AMS edition published in 1972
Manufactured in the United States of America

International Standard Book Number:
Complete Set: 0-404-08003-0
Volume II: 0-404-08005-7

AMS PRESS INC.
NEW YORK, N.Y.   10003

CONTENTS

OF

VOLUME SECOND

BOOK IV

THE REVOCATION AND THE SEQUEL (1685-1702)

CHAPTER XI

1685

CHAPTER XII

1685

CHAPTER XIII

1685–1702

CHAPTER XIV

1685–1702

BOOK V.

THE CAMISARDS (1702-1710).

CHAPTER XV

1702-1703.

CHAPTER XVI

1703–1704

CONTENTS xiii

CHAPTER XVII

1704-1710

BOOK VI

THE DESERT AND THE RE-ESTABLISHMENT OF PROTESTANTISM
(1715–1802)

CHAPTER XVIII

1715–1787

CHAPTER XIX

1763–1787

BOOK FOURTH

THE REVOCATION AND THE SEQUEL (1685–1702)

BOOK FOURTH

THE REVOCATION AND THE SEQUEL (1685–1702)

CHAPTER XI

THE RECALL OF THE EDICT

A JUNCTURE had been reached at which the persecution of the Huguenots could not stand still; it must either advance or re-

Persecution must advance or recede. cede. In a period of profound peace, with no foreign enemy to give alarm, France was everywhere the scene of such acts as belong exclusively to the reign of war. A portion of the population, respectable for its numbers, more worthy of consideration by reason of the virtue, intelligence, and social standing of those of whom it was composed—it may be a million and a quarter, it may be a million and a half of souls, adherents of a religion recognized, certainly tolerated by the law, were receiving, through no fault of their own, such treatment as vanquished enemies receive at the hands of the conqueror. Scarcely could the royal troops have been more actively employed in declared war. For they were perpetually in motion, marching and countermarching, quartered now in this town or city, now in that; but always occupying the houses of the Huguenots and sparing the houses of the Roman Catholics. And, since the Huguenots were, with rare exceptions, the most decorous, the most upright, the most intelligent and most frugal citizens, and therefore the men and women that were

growing most steadily in wealth, everywhere, by the havoc
which they wrought in Huguenot homes, the soldiers of the
king delighted the rabble, the idle and thriftless, in other
words, that part of the populace which is ever on the alert for
opportunities for pillage rather than anxious to secure the
rewards of honest industry.

Such a state of things must come to an end. The law professed to protect the Huguenots in their homes, in their persons, in their industries, even in their religious worship. Louis
the Fourteenth had never dropped the mask of respect for the
Edict of Nantes, which he had repeatedly ratified, even
though each effort ostensibly made to execute it had
proved a blow aimed at its very existence. Yet a proscribed sect could hardly be treated with greater injustice than was this recognized communion. Meanwhile, the
authors and abettors of the prevalent system of persecution
continued for years to maintain, with unrivalled effrontery,
that they had done, and were doing, nothing harsh or unkind.
Paul Pélisson having at one time written a treatise on "Religious Differences," requested an expression of opinion regarding
it from his nephew, the historian Rapin Thoyras. Thereupon
the latter observed that he highly approved the principles of
mildness established in the work, but thought them quite inopportune at a season when clearly maxims of an opposite character were followed in France. "I seem," he humorously remarked, "to hear Sganarelle addressing his wife, 'My dear
heart, I'll thrash you!' 'Dear object of my eyes, I'll beat you
to death!'"[1] Such a contradiction was there between professions and acts.

Every official in France, from the king down, seemed to have a
lie in his right hand. The minister of war who issued the order
for the Dragonnades studiously avoided reference to force and
violence, and acted as if the mere presence, or even the fear of

The lying pretence of respecting the Edict of Nantes.

---

[1] Letter of Rapin Thoyras to Le Duchat, May, 1722, in which the historian relates the incident.   Bulletin, etc., vi. 75 ; Cazenove, Rapin Thoyras, sa famille,
sa vie et ses œuvres, App., p. xxiv.   I need scarcely say that the reference of
Rapin Thoyras is to the Sganarelle of the first scene of Molière's comedy Le Méde-
cin malgre lui, which appeared in 1666; but Rapin Thoyras does not quote exactly.
Molière's "Doux objet de mes vœux" becomes " doux objet de mes yeux," etc.

troops deporting themselves in an orderly manner, exacting no more than was their due, constituted the sum of the pressure brought to bear upon the Protestants to induce them to lend an obedient ear to the king's request, conveyed to them by the intendants, that they should adopt the religion which he favored.

It was as though a general compact had been entered into by all the principals and all the accomplices of the undertaking, not to see, not to hear, not to take the slightest cognizance of any violence that might be exercised—while, at that very moment, from all parts of the realm, there arose to high heaven a piteous wail of distress coming from thousands and tens of thousands of throats. The king saw and heard nothing of it, Louvois nothing, Père de la Chaise nothing. The cry of distress did not reach Louis, for access to him was well guarded. If a stray complaint now and then by chance penetrated the barrier thrown up about his Majesty and claimed his notice, it was made the occasion of earnest remonstrance on the part of the minister of war. Louvois was unspeakably distressed. In apparent surprise he writes to Foucault:

Louvois's affected surprise.

"His Majesty has been annoyed to learn that a company and a half of dragoons have been quartered upon a woman at Poitiers, in order to compel her to be converted. I have sent you word so often that these acts of violence are not to his Majesty's taste, that I cannot but be greatly astonished that you do not conform to his orders, which have been so often reiterated to you." [1] At another time he adds to his remonstrance this sentence: "If this does not induce you to restrain yourself, I shall be compelled to beg his Majesty to instruct some one else to write you his intentions in whom you have more confidence." [2] What messages Louvois sent the intendants in private, what assurances of protection he gave or hinted at, we are not told; but it is not difficult to conjecture. The Dragonnades had long been in progress, and if the minister of war, whose authority was well nigh supreme in the conduct of these operations, affected not to know or not to be obeyed, it would be fair to ap-

---

[1] Louvois to Foucault, October 16, 1685, Mémoires de Foucault, 517.

[2] Louvois to Foucault, November, 1685, in A. Michel, Louvois et les Protestants, 63.

ply to him a remark similar to that which he himself addressed
to Marillac, a few years before,[1] and say : "When a minister of
war gives an order, he is obeyed without an answer." Yet
before the publication of the revocatory edict, Louvois did not
often drop the mask. He was less scrupulous afterward. A
month had passed and his indignation knew no bounds when
he was informed of the obstinacy of the Huguenots of
His subse-
quent brutal- Dieppe. "Since these fellows are the only persons
ity.   in the kingdom that have distinguished themselves
by their refusal to submit to what the king wants of them," he
wrote to the intendant Beaupré, "you are not, as regards them,
to keep within the bounds that have been prescribed. You cannot make the maintenance of the troops in their houses too hard
and burdensome ; that is to say, you should augment the number of men quartered upon them as much as you think it possible to do without relieving the Protestants of Rouen. And
instead of twenty *sous* apiece and their food, you may allow ten
times as much to be exacted of them, and permit the troopers
to commit whatever disorder may be necessary to remove the
people from the state in which they are, and to make of them an
example that shall be as useful for the conversion of the other
Protestants as their example would be injurious were their obstinacy to go unpunished."[2]

The assembly of the clergy likewise simulated ignorance,
seeing nothing, knowing nothing of these horrors, understanding to all appearance as little what was taking place in
The clergy
closes its   every part of France as the officiating priest or inquis-
eyes.   itor when handing over a deposed ecclesiastic or heretic to the secular arm with the words, "Lord Judge, we entreat
you as affectionately as we can, as well by the love of God, as
from pity and compassion, and out of respect for our prayers,
that you do this wretched man no injury tending to death or
the mutilation of his body," knew that this was a direct consignment to the gallows or to the flames.[3] It is convenient

[1] Above, volume i., page 510.
[2] Louvois to Beaupré, November 17, 1685. Rulhière MSS. in National Lib.,
printed in F. Waddington, Le Protestantisme en Normandie (Paris, 1862), p. 2,
and Bulletin de la Soc. de l'hist. du Prot. fr., xi. 385.
[3] See the service for the degradation of priests in the Pontificale Romanum (ed.

not to see too much. One of the regular convocations of the clergy was held in Versailles this very year, at which the usual gifts of money were voted to the crown, the price of the crown's acquiescence in the demands for new measures disadvantageous to the Protestants ; but no word of the church's orators betrayed a consciousness that any severity had been exercised toward the Protestants. One of these orators, Daniel de Cosnac, Bishop of Valence, could scarcely find words strong enough to express his appreciation of the greatness of the monarch whom he addressed in the name of his colleagues. "This new grandeur, Speeches of Bishop Cosnac of Valence, Sire," he said, "comes not from the number of your conquests, from the provinces reduced to subjection to you, from Europe of which you have become the arbiter. It comes from that zeal and that unintermitting application which have always made you prefer the purpose to bring back the pretended reformers into the churches to all human considerations, to all political reasons. It comes from that innumerable crowd of conversions that have been effected by your orders, by your solicitude, by your liberality. It is to this single portion of your admirable life that I confine myself ; for you are too great, Sire, to be exhibited entire !"[1] Finding in Louis's religious achievements a title to imperishable renown, a fame that would last "when time shall be no more," the bishop waxed eloquent in depicting the delight with which former kings, could they come back to the earth, would view the humiliation of the Protestant religion (whose votaries were once the intellectual, the powerful, the finest geniuses of the court), "now despised, abased, and henceforth reduced to seeing itself abandoned by all rational persons, and all this—without violence, without arms, and even much less by the force of your edicts than by your exemplary piety."[2] In a similar strain, the other spokes-

---

Venice, 1836) page 362, and Rise of the Huguenots, i. 115. The Latin text is : "Domine Judex, rogamus vos cum omni affectu, quo possumus, ut amore, pietatis et misericordiæ intuitu, et nostrorum interventu precaminum, miserrimo huic nullum mortis vel mutilationis periculum inferatis."

[1] This is such a choice bit of flattery that I must give it in the original. "C'est à ce seul endroit de votre admirable vie que je m'arrête, car vous êtes trop grand, Sire, pour être montré tout entier."

[2] Harangue adressée au roi, à Versailles, le 14 juillet, 1685. Mémoires de Daniel de Cosnac (Paris, 1852), ii. 316 et seq.

man of the clergy, the coadjutor of the Archbishop of Rouen,
a son of the great Colbert, congratulated Louis the Fourteenth
on having tamed the obstinacy of the heretics by first
gaining their hearts, and suggested that perhaps they
might never have returned to the bosom of the church
in any other way than "*by the path strewn with flowers*" offered
to them by the king.[1]

*and the
Coadjutor
of Rouen.*

All this was consummate acting, and there was no great
difficulty in keeping it up for a time by common consent.

It was not so easy to impose upon foreign nations, particularly upon nations that were Protestant, whose inhabitants regarded the persecuted Huguenots as their brethren in the faith.
The attempt, however, had to be made, and it was this that
rendered the position of a French envoy at some courts almost
as uncomfortable as La Mothe Fénélon found his stay at the
court of Queen Elizabeth, in 1572, after the Massacre of Saint
Bartholomew's Day.

The Count d'Avaux, French minister to Holland, soon discovered that to keep silent or to give only vague and evasive
replies to troublesome inquiries and reports was his
best policy. "The Amsterdam gentlemen" withstood
all the Prince of Orange's representations, but were
shaken in their minds when they heard of the treatment of the Protestant places of worship at Saumur and elsewhere ; and the count states that he avoided a discussion of the
matter, contenting himself with telling them in general that
things were not as the Dutch tried to make them believe.[2]
But such shuffling would not answer. "I am bound to inform
your Majesty," D'Avaux wrote to Louis, shortly after, "that the
preachers and the narratives of facts sent from France em-
bitter them [the States] so much, that I do not know what will
come of it in the sequel."[3]   By and by the Dutch met the poor
envoy with dire reports of the treatment of the Huguenots of
Bordeaux, a seaport much frequented by sailors from the Low
Countries, and complained that they had heard that the royal

*Embarrass-
ment of
Count
d'Avaux in
Holland.*

[1] Benoist, v. 794.
[2] Négociations de M. le comte d'Avaux en Hollande depuis 1679 jusqu'en
1688 (Paris, 1754), iv. 145, under date of March 8, 1685.
[3] March 22, 1685, ibid., iv. 160.

troops were employed to force the Protestants to embrace the Roman Catholic religion. And yet D'Avaux was compelled, by the king's express instructions, to deny notorious facts, and assure the body of Amsterdam's sturdy magistrates, that there had been no trouble at all in Bordeaux, that everything was quiet and trade was carried on as usual. The conversions were effected simply by the intendant's persuasion.[1]

But the position was vexatious and humiliating. It is humiliating and vexatious to pursue for any length of time a system of mendacity—yes, even for a great king and his overbearing envoys.

Great was the relief when the formal Edict of Revocation appeared, and there was no further need of the lying pretence of the equitable treatment of the Huguenots in France.

Intelligent contemporaries busied themselves with speculations respecting the reasons why, on the one hand, the final measures of severity against the Huguenots did not come earlier, and, on the other, why they came so soon or at all.

Why the edict was not sooner issued.   The philosophic Benoist finds three causes of delay— in the fear entertained at Versailles lest extreme persecution of the French Protestants should rekindle foreign war, in the fear lest Charles the Second of England might show his displeasure at the injuries and insults done to the Prince of Orange, and in the fear of the loss of money and of population which the Revocation might entail. The first ground of apprehension was removed by the truce of 1684, the second by the death of Charles and the succession of James the Second, an avowed Roman Catholic, to the throne of Great Britain. As for the third, it was hoped that the measures adopted to prevent emigration and the export of wealth would prove effectual.[2]

The Venetian ambassadors were shrewd observers, and their opinions always merit respectful consideration. Girolamo

Girolamo Venier's reasons for the recall.   Venier, when bemoaning, four years later, the disastrous results that had flowed from Louis's rash act, laid the blame for the recall of the Edict of Nantes, first, upon the lack of foresight respecting the great losses that ·

---

[1] Louis XIV. to Count d'Avaux, September 20, 1685, etc., ibid., v. 81, 82.
[2] Histoire de l'Édit de Nantes, v. 787, 788.

might be involved; next, upon the king's great zeal; thirdly, upon the ever-increasing number of the Protestants, and, finally, upon the success attending the first attempts at conversion that were made. These things it was that enlisted the ardor of the ministers and the religious genius of the monarch in the great undertaking. Sloth seemed intolerable at a time when so many princes were active in labor for the interests of Christianity, and when France was plunged in a bitter dispute with the court of Rome. Hence was ambition stimulated, hence was awakened an eager desire to do some great thing for Religion, and the court resolved upon the total destruction of the Huguenots. The interests of the state appeared to point in the same direction as did the dictates of piety. For, as all of the Huguenots married, these wretched people were increasing to such an extent that fears were entertained lest they might presently come to constitute the majority of the citizens. Yet it would seem, remarks the envoy, that it had been better to treat the religious disease, spread though it was throughout the principal parts of this great body politic, with palliatives, and so avoid producing increased irritation. But in that case the ministers of state must needs have been changed in the temper of their minds. Moreover, the success attending their first attempts spurred them on ever to acts of greater violence.[1]

It is no less interesting than important to trace, as far as this is possible, the personal influence brought to bear upon Louis the Fourteenth to induce him at this moment to recall the edict for which, in time past, he had professed profound regard. The royal confessor, Père de la Chaise, Harlay, Archbishop of Paris—members of the famous Council of Conscience—the Marquis of Louvois, Minister of State for War, and Madame de Maintenon, the king's confidante, are the persons who have been most commonly credited with a principal share in the matter.

The " Council of Conscience" was not established and regu-

---

[1] Relation of Girolamo Venier, sent from Vienna, July 4, 1689, in the documents of the fifth volume of Ranke, Französische Geschichte. See, also, the Revocation of the Edict of Nantes, illustrated from state papers in the Archives of Venice. By Sir Henry Austen Layard (Proceedings of the Huguenot Society of London, ii. 115, etc.).

lated by letters-patent, after the model of the other councils concerned in the administration of government, nor were its functions precisely defined by law. It was a creature of the king's good pleasure. Its office was to give the monarch advice respecting all matters of religion, including the disposal of benefices or church livings. The royal confessor, Père de la Chaise, uniformly left Paris for Versailles on Friday afternoon, to be present at a conference, for which Saturday was regularly set apart by the king. The Archbishop of Paris was most frequently there also. The council seems at this time to have been composed of those two alone. With no other ecclesiastics did Louis think that he could better consider the plans which he had formed for the entire overthrow of Protestantism. For, although very different in mental qualities and in external deportment, the prelate and the confessor were at one in their purpose to further the great scheme which the king had long since come to view as destined to be the crowning glory of his reign. Harlay, when Archbishop of Rouen, had been regarded even by Protestants as a mild and reasonable churchman, and his methods and manners met with praise.

There was less that was favorable to be said of his private morals, either before or since his promotion. The scandals of his fine house at Conflans were matters of public notoriety; nor did the pamphlets of the day spare the names of abbesses and women high in rank who frequented it.[1] If Harlay did not become a better man, he renounced, on assuming the see of Paris, the part of moderation which he had hitherto played, and showed himself the persecutor indifferently of Jansenists and of Protestants. No measure that would recommend him to the support of Père de la Chaise and the Jesuits, no measure for the conversion of the Reformed, however violent and dishonest, that would further the design of the king, failed to receive his approbation. Père de la Chaise was

The "Council of Conscience."

Harlay, Archbishop of Paris.

---

[1] Inasmuch as Louis XIV., however dissolute himself, was known to be a severe censor of the morals of the clergy, men were perplexed to account for the undiminished favor he showed to Harlay, despite the prelate's well-known character, and to discover the reasons for the erection of the see of Paris, some three years after Harlay was transferred to it, into a duchy and "pairie." See the Relation of Spanheim, 249.

a more decorous priest. He, too, had at first advocated moderation in the treatment of the adherents of the Reformed doctrines. But his importance in the Order of Jesus was small and his influence limited, until, almost by accident, he was chosen by Louis to be his confessor. From that moment, despite the fact that he possessed neither great native genius, nor commanding intellect, nor learning, nor the gift of preaching, his credit became almost boundless. And now the gentleness of his deportment toward the Huguenots was exchanged for a harshness and indeed an unrelenting ferocity, which spared neither age nor sex, and pursued the objects of his aversion even to the galleys and to death. It was held by the well-informed and able envoy of the Elector of Brandenburg to be a proof positive that Père de la Chaise was greatly responsible for the systematic persecution of the Protestants, that being the confessor of a king not a tyrant by nature, nor a lover of cruelty, and, as confessor, the master of the royal conscience, he could, had he so pleased, have deterred Louis from the course of persecution that cost the blood of such numbers of his faithful subjects.[1]

Père de la Chaise, the king's confessor.

Besides the Père de la Chaise and the Archbishop of Paris, who, it cannot reasonably be doubted, "had the best part in those fatal counsels devoted to the ruin of the Reformed religion in France,"[2] the Marquis of Louvois must certainly be reckoned among the most active promoters of the measures that led to the Recall of the Edict of Nantes and of the Recall itself.

The Marquis of Louvois.

---

[1] I do not know where the Council of Conscience and the characters and the attitude of the archbishop and the confessor are better treated than in the Relation of Ezéchiel Spanheim, one of the most valuable documents of the time. I have drawn freely upon it (pages 243-254). Constructed after the model of those "relations" which the Venetian ambassadors had long been in the habit of drawing up, at the close of their diplomatic missions, for the benefit of the doge and the senate of the republic, it scarcely falls short, in accuracy, fulness, and discrimination, of the best of those famous productions. Supplementing his almost daily despatches, and conveying general views which could not find a place in these hurried communications, the Relation of Spanheim proves him to have well deserved the high reputation which he earned as a wise and skilful diplomatist, first, in the service of the Palatine and, afterward, in that of the Great Elector.

[2] Spanheim, 244.

The son of Chancellor Le Tellier had inherited his father's great abilities, but neither his bodily appearance nor his manners. He was so heavy and lumpish that he seemed to be unfitted for activity and vigilance. He looked rough and thoughtless. Never were appearances more deceptive. In reality he was energetic, watchful, full of life and vigor, laborious, persevering, patient. His leading fault was that he was too quick in the formation of the plans which, having adopted them with too little consideration, he subsequently pursued without swerving. He worked out the details with a wonderful care and with untiring application. Thus it was that the objects at which he aimed were often ill-judged and ignoble, the means by which he sought to attain those objects well calculated to the end, but in themselves mean, dishonest, and reckless. No man was more selfish and unscrupulous, none could be more inhuman. The action which, next to the Revocation, is the greatest blot upon the reign of Louis the Fourteenth, was the result of Louvois's direct instigation. It was Louvois who, not only by his pernicious counsels, precipitated France into the unnecessary war in which Louis was confronted by the emperor, the kings of Spain and Sweden, and the electors of Bavaria, Saxony, and the Palatinate, allied by the League of Augsburg (1686), but, two years later, during the course of that war, ordered, as we have seen, the wanton devastation of the entire Palatinate, that the once fertile district, now turned into a desolate wilderness, might serve as a formidable barrier to the enemy's advance.[1]

We have seen in a previous chapter that Louvois was directly responsible for the resumption of the Dragonnades in Béarn, after the four years of suspension, more or less complete, since the exploits of Marillac in Poitou.[2] The truculent author, or abettor, of the most outrageous form of compulsory conversion ever known, could not but advocate the formal repeal of the law

---

[1] Spanheim, writing in 1690, declares that it is beyond all doubt and that he has the proofs. "Je veux dire que c'est aux seuls conseils de M. de Louvois que le public doit imputer l'engagement de la guerre présente et de toutes les suites funestes qu'elle peut avoir eues jusqu'ici et pourra avoir dans la suite." Relation, 191.

[2] Supra, vol. i. p. 549.

which had hitherto stood in the way of the complete execution of his designs. Moreover, it was no small relief to be freed from the necessity of according the semblance of respect to a law the spirit of which was flagrantly violated every day. The revocation signified the continuance of the policy adopted by Louis. The revocation involved also the growth of the power wielded by the family of which Louvois was the most influential member. Until 1683, the entire direction of the government—the administration of justice, war, trade, public buildings, all affairs foreign and domestic—was divided equally between two families. On the one side were a father and a son, Chancellor Le Tellier, at the head of the judicial, and Louvois, at the head of the war department. On the other side were two brothers, Colbert, the controller general or minister for finance, and Croissy, minister for foreign relations. But Colbert dying in the year I have just named, the chancellor secured the vacant position for his own relative and intimate friend, Le Peletier. Thus the equipoise was destroyed; and from two to two, the ministers of the leading families came to stand as three to one. Not to speak of the notorious fact that even now the Marquis of Croissy asserted himself far less imperiously in his own department than did Louvois in his, there was a fair prospect that the ambitious war minister might by adroit management secure the removal of his weaker rival, and thus engross the entire administration of public affairs. Personally a great favorite with the king, whose age was nearly the same as that of the minister of war, Louvois might hope, by the hearty advocacy of a measure so coincident with Louis's great design as the formal recall of the Edict of Nantes, to gain a yet firmer hold upon the place which he occupied, being the most powerful subject, and, according to common report, the most wealthy personage in France, if not in all Europe.[1] It was the influence of Madame de Maintenon, no friend of Louvois, that prevented the consummation of his hopes by re-establishing the equilibrium between the Colberts and the Le Telliers.[2]

The four ministers of state.

---

[1] Spanheim, 160–163. According to this author (p. 200), Louvois was reputed "le plus riche particulier de l'Europe."

[2] Louvois's father dying in 1685, the king saw fit, while conferring the chan-

The active participation of the Archbishop of Paris, of the Père de la Chaise, and of Marquis Louvois in procuring the revocatory edict being beyond controversy, an interesting inquiry remains regarding the complicity of Madame de Maintenon.

Françoise d'Aubigné was a granddaughter of that eminent Huguenot hero, statesman, and historian, whose striking figure attracts so much of the attention of the student of Protestantism during the reigns of Henry the Third and Henry the Fourth. Doubtless, with the name, Françoise had inherited much of the keen wit and intellectual vigor of Theodore Agrippa d'Aubigné. The descent was not, however, in a line that promised much for the inheritance of the best moral traits. Her father was that same dissolute Constant d'Aubigné, of whom the author of the "Histoire Universelle," letting posterity into his confidence, said at the close of his great work : "God, who does not attach His graces to flesh and blood, having humbled me by means of a degenerate son, to whom in the preface of the entire work I had reserved the honor of laying this capstone, has raised me up by the hand and lengthened the days of my old age, to consecrate this last gift on His own altar."[1] Posterity, by a strange conceit of the author, became the recipient of the dedication intended for the unworthy son.[2]

Françoise was born at Niort on the twenty-seventh of November, 1635. Her mother was the daughter of the governor of

(marginal note: Françoise d'Aubigné, Madame de Maintenon.)

cellorship on Louis Boucherat, to leave the seat in the ministry of state unfilled. Four or five years later, he appointed to it the Marquis of Seignelay, the great Colbert's son. Thus there were again two ministers of state of the one family and two of the other. Spanheim, ubi supra. The great elector's envoy highly appreciates, in another place (p. 23), the particular skill with which Madame de Maintenon "a su balancer le crédit et l'ascendant du Marquis de Louvois sur l'esprit du Roi, et empêcher qu'il ne restât seul maître des affaires et du gouvernement. C'est dans cette vue qu'elle a su relever la famille Colbert, qui parut d'abord déchue de considération par la mort du ministre de ce nom, soutenir le Marquis de Seignelay, son fils, lui conserver la direction en chef de la marine, et le porter enfin au poste qu'il remplit aujourd'hui de ministre d'État," etc.

[1] Histoire Universelle, iii. 537.

[2] Not only does the title-page of the first volume bear the words " Dediée à la Postérité," but in the appendix she is apostrophized : " Reçois donc et retiens, chere postérité, un abregé des faveurs du ciel," etc.

the prison of Château Trompette, at Bordeaux, to whose cus-
tody her father was intrusted when confined for the crime of
murdering his first wife and her paramour. The second wife
was sprung of a good family, but her imprudent marriage to an
unprincipled adventurer boded no good fortune. It was during
a second imprisonment of Constant for ten years, as a member
of a band of counterfeiters, that Françoise and her brother
Charles, her senior by somewhat over a year, were born.
When Françoise was ten years old, she sailed with her parents
to the French West Indies, where her father had an appointment, under the French Company for the American Islands, as
governor of the little island of Marie Galande. On his arrival
Constant found his new domain inhabited only by savages, and,
after a brief residence at Martinique, he returned to France
and ended his varied and disreputable existence in the city of
Orange, on the last day of August, 1647. He had changed to
and fro, from the Protestant to the Roman Catholic religion
and back again, so frequently that it could scarcely be said to
which faith he belonged. A sentiment seems to have determined him to die a Protestant in a Protestant town. His wife
was a Roman Catholic, and had had Françoise baptized by a
priest. A Roman Catholic the daughter remained, until coming
into the home of her aunt, Madame de Villette, a favorite
daughter of Theodore Agrippa, she heartily embraced the Reformed faith, which was commended to her not only by instructions but by a pious example. A few months later an order of
Conversion   the government, obtained by a relative of her mother,
to the Ro-   removed her to a convent of the Ursulines. It was
man Catho-
lic religion. from this place, and when nearly fourteen years old,
that Françoise wrote a piteous little note, which is the first
thing we have from her pen, begging Madame de Villette to
rescue her from a place "where life," she says, "is worse
than death." "Ah, madame and aunt," she adds, "you have
no conception what a hell this so-called house of God is to me,
nor the ill-treatment, harshness, and cruel actions of the women
who have been constituted guardians of my body—not my soul,
however, for that they cannot reach."[1] Yet after a determined

---

[1] Françoise d'Aubigné to Madame de Villette, Paris, October 12 (1649), in
Haag, France protestante, ii. 528 ; Geffroy, Mad. de Maintenon, i. 4.

resistance, of which some traces remain, she succumbed and abjured a religion to which she never afterward showed any disposition to return. It was not, however, the severity of the nuns that accomplished the result; for by her obstinacy, as she used afterward to relate, she tired out, Bible in hand, the priests that undertook to instruct her.[1] Her conversion was effected by the gentler measures to which, seeing their mistake, the Ursulines subsequently resorted.

When less than seventeen years old (in May, 1652), Françoise was married to a comic poet, Paul Scarron, deformed in body and twenty-five years her senior, who, in compassion for her dependent position and penury, generously offered either to make her his wife or to furnish a sum of money that would enable her to enter a convent. Eight years later, at Scarron's death, she was left a widow in destitute circumstances, but with rare charms of conversation, bred or fostered by intercourse with polite society.

An interval of ten years elapsed, during which her main dependence for support was a small annual pension enjoyed by her husband and continued to her after his death. At length (in 1669 or 1670) the king's favorite, Madame de Montespan, whose kind offices Françoise d'Aubigné had sought in this matter, either took pity upon her or saw in her a person that might become serviceable to her; and the widow of Scarron received the delicate and responsible appointment of governess to the illegitimate children, the fruit of the king's adulterous union. This was the beginning of Françoise d'Aubigné's singular elevation. The demure and retiring widow, who is said at first to have excited repugnance in the breast of Louis the Fourteenth, by a gravity of speech and deportment contrasting in too marked a degree with the levity and license of the ladies of his court, slowly but steadily grew in favor with his Majesty, as a consequence of the propriety with which she comported herself in a difficult position.

The favorite's occasional coldness, and even her violent temper, leading to "terrible scenes," which the king was occasionally compelled to witness,[2] were probably more endurable

---

[1] La France protestante, i. 528.

[1] "Il se passe ici des choses terribles entre Madame de Montespan et moi ; le

to Françoise than were Madame de Montespan's patent efforts
to make mischief between her and the monarch.[1] For in the
character of Agrippa d'Aubigné's granddaughter, as she herself
admitted to her confessor, the passion for distinction and
love of self were the chief ingredients.[2] In good time she
reaped the reward of her patience and adroitness in the shape
of liberal gifts from the public treasury. With two hundred
and fifty thousand francs thus obtained, she bought the handsome estate of Maintenon, with its castle and substantial income, fourteen leagues distant from Paris, and ten from Versailles.[3] Additional gifts enabled her to beautify the place
beyond recognition. More than all, Louis was pleased to confer upon Françoise a territorial designation of nobility, and in
less than five years from the time that she became governess
of the king's children, the widow Scarron found herself Marquise of Maintenon.[4] Such rapid advancement was the pre-
sage of still greater good fortune. In 1683 the queen died.
Not long after—the precise date is unknown, but it must have
been early in 1684—Louis married Madame de Maintenon.
Her marriage to Louis XIV., 1684. The ceremony was performed with the utmost secrecy, in midwinter, and at dead of night, in a small
chamber of the palace of Versailles. The king's
confessor, the Père de la Chaise, said the mass. The sole witnesses were Harlay, Archbishop of Paris, as diocesan; Bon-
tems, first valet de chambre and governor of Versailles, the
Marquis of Montchevreuil, and Louvois, minister of war.[5] The

Roi en fut hier témoin, et ces demêlés-là, joints aux maux continuels de ces enfans, me mettent dans un état que je ne pourrai soutenir longtemps." Letter
to the Abbé Gobelin, February, 1675, Geffroy, i. 58.

[1] Letter to the same, August, 1674, ibid., i. 45.

[2] "L'estime des gens d'aussi bon goût ne sauroit être indifférente et ne flatte
que trop la vanité d'une personne pétrie de gloire et d'amour propre." Letter
to the same, August 1, 1674, ibid., i. 44.

[3] "Elle est belle, noble, et vaut dix à onze mille livres de rente." Letter to
M. d'Aubigné, her brother, November 10, 1674, ibid., i. 55.

[4] Letter to the Abbé Gobelin, January 15, 1675, ibid., i. 57.

[5] Mémoires du Duc de Saint Simon (Paris, 1853), xxiv. 171. The archbishop
and Louvois, according to current report, had gotten a promise from Louis that
he would never make the marriage public. The time was "quelque temps
après le retour du Roi de Fontainebleau, et au milieu de l'hiver qui suivit la
mort de la reine." As Maria Theresa died July 30, 1683, the statement of Saint

marriage was never publicly acknowledged, but it was soon understood by every one in the court to have taken place. Whether Madame de Maintenon accepted the situation with good grace, or made two or three abortive attempts to obtain recognition as Louis the Fourteenth's second queen, is a question in dispute. That marrying a fickle and self-willed monarch, when he was about forty-six years of age, and she herself not much short of fifty, she retained her influence over him undiminished for a period of more than thirty years to the day of his death, is a fact about which there is no question.

It was apparently in the course of the second year of the marriage of Madame de Maintenon to Louis the Fourteenth that the Edict of Nantes was revoked. Had she a leading part in bringing about the great event? She had for many years been a Roman Catholic. Her intimate correspondence with her confessor, the Abbé Gobelin, gives the impression that she was a devotee honestly seeking to obey the directions of her spiritual adviser. Her attachment to her adopted faith was presumably sincere, as it was certainly ostentatious. Her intelligence was undoubted. Writers who, like Saint Simon, regarded her as deceitful and given to intrigue, admitted that the fault was rather the result of circumstances than her natural bent of character. As against the dissolute Madame de Montespan, whose fascinating influence she came to antagonize, and whom she ultimately supplanted in the king's regard, she attempted to recall Louis from a disgraceful course of double adultery; and she found it to her advantage to become an auxiliary, if not an ally, of the monarch's religious advisers in leading him to a more decorous life, and a deportment more becoming his title of "Very Christian." Much more than this has been affirmed. The assertion has been made so often and so confidently as to pass for certain fact, that there was a secret compact between the marquise and the king's confessor, and that her successful

[margin note:] Did she instigate the Revocation?

Simon would fix the date of the marriage with Madame de Maintenon in January or February, 1684, or more than a year and a half before the Revocation. If this be so, I scarcely need remark how completely it discredits the story that Madame de Maintenon's instigation of the revocatory edict was a condition to her marriage with the king.

urgency in favor of the repeal of the Edict of Nantes was the price exacted by the Jesuits for their consent to her union with Louis the Fourteenth. It is freely admitted that Madame de Maintenon sedulously avoided the appearance of participating in the conduct of affairs of state, but at the same time it is positively affirmed that both the recall of the Edict of Nantes and the continued persecutions of the Huguenots were mainly due to the instigation of this woman—"the unfaithful Esther of her race."

This is the representation of the clever Saint Simon, not, indeed, strictly speaking, a contemporary historian of the events (for he was but ten years of age at the date of the Revocation and he consequently treated of the matters that led to it from hearsay), yet a writer so near to the events and so favorably situated, if not for obtaining an original view, yet, at least, for gathering the current story, as always to be entitled to respectful attention. Madame de Maintenon, he tells us, found Louis the Fourteenth possessed of the notion that he was an apostle, because all his life long he had been persecuting Jansenism, or what he had been taught to believe was Jansenism. The field appeared free and open for her to turn her own zeal to good account with the king and to gain influence everywhere. The fate of Protestantism was considered in secret by three persons—Père de la Chaise, the king's confessor, Louvois, who as minister of war had since Colbert's death almost engrossed all the power of his colleagues, and Madame de Maintenon, the monarch's new and cherished wife. With a mind that never soared above intrigue, neither the birth nor the training of the latter was such as that she could fail to seize with ardor so excellent an opportunity to please the king and to strengthen her position more and more by her devotion.[1]

The letters that have passed current as hers have seemed to confirm this view of the active participation of Madame de Maintenon. Thus a letter dated four years before the Revocation (the twenty-fourth of August, 1681), contains the words : "The king begins to think seriously of his salvation and that of his subjects. If God spares his

Saint Simon's representation.

Letters of Madame de Maintenon.

---

[1] Mémoires du Duc de Saint Simon, xxiv., 176–180.

life for us, there will be only one religion in his kingdom. This is the view of M. de Louvois, and I am more inclined to believe him on this point than M. Colbert, who thinks only of his finances and scarcely ever of religion." [1] And another letter, ostensibly written after the publication of the revocatory edict, informs us: "The king is very glad to have put the finishing touch to the great work of the reunion of the heretics to the church. Père de la Chaise has promised that it will not cost a single drop of blood, and M. de Louvois says the same thing." [2]

These and other expressions of supreme satisfaction with the edict of recall might well be taken to corroborate the assertions of Saint Simon, were it not that the letters from which they are taken have been proved beyond a doubt to be forgeries from the pen of the clever but unscrupulous La Beaumelle. Unfortunately, the gap in the authentic correspondence of Madame de Maintenon which La Beaumelle undertook to fill by drawing upon his imagination to supply what she must have written under the circumstances, still remains, and probably always will remain. Her own destruction of her correspondence with the king, obscure as its motives must ever be, has put it out of our power to explain fully the character of one who was quite ready to remain a riddle to posterity. Recent investigation has raised fresh doubts, not so much concerning the disposition, as concerning the ability of Madame de Maintenon to exercise a controlling influence in hastening the Revocation; and it would seem not unlikely that Voltaire was virtually correct when, more than a century ago, he wrote: "Why do you say that Madame de Maintenon had a great part in the Revocation of the Edict of Nantes? She tolerated this persecution, as she tolerated that of the Cardinal of Noailles and that of Racine; but assuredly she had no part at all in it: that is a certainty. She never dared to contradict Louis the Fourteenth." [3] If, however, it be improbable that her hand

Forgeries of La Beaumelle.

---

[1] Rulhière, Éclaircissemens historiques, i. 206. [2] Ibid., i. 325, 326.

[3] Voltaire to Formey, January 17, 1753. Correspondance de Voltaire (Œuvres complètes. Paris, 1830), viii. 154. Voltaire illustrates Madame de Maintenon's position by the position of Madame de Pompadour in his own times. "Madame de Pompadour," he says, "would not dare to speak against the former bishop of Mirepoix, whom she detests as much as I despise him."

directed the current that swept away the rights and privileges of those for whom birth and education might have been expected to cause her to entertain at least some lingering affection,[1] there is, at least, no doubt that she fell in with it, uttering no protest, offering no remonstrance that might have weakened her position with the king. There is, indeed, no evidence that she had any inclination either to protest or to remonstrate. The king's delight at the multiplication of converts from Protestantism was her delight also. Her satisfaction at the progress of the work of Pélisson and at the success of the dragoons was as unmingled with qualms as to the methods that were followed as was the satisfaction of Louis himself. " Think of it and rejoice," she wrote, less than a month before the publication of the fatal edict, "that one hundred thousand more souls have been converted in Guyenne ; that the town of Saintes has been converted by deliberation [of its citizens]; that my brother harangued the town of Cognac to induce the people to copy this example, and that everybody yielded ; that the king is expending very large sums in order to send money to augment the churches, that he writes to the bishops every day to despatch missionaries everywhere to instruct and console, and that he causes books on the mass to be distributed, which have a wonderful effect upon people who have always been told that there is no need of our understanding what the priest says ; that his Majesty gives instructions everywhere that no expense be spared for conversions ; that all the converts are relieved of the *taille*, and at his expense, in order that the burden of the Catholics should not be increased ; and that news is sent from all quarters that what is taking place in this regard is miraculous. Is not this, my very dear friend,

Marginal note: Madame de Maintenon approves Louis's course.

---

[1] For a discussion of this subject see the Mémoires inédits sur Mme. de Maintenon par Languet de Gergy, Archev. de Sens, which are preceded by Théophile Lavallée's monograph on La Famille d'Aubigné, etc.; the long series of articles by M. Charles Read, in the Bulletin de la Soc. de l'hist. du Prot. fr., xxxvi. and xxxvii. (1887 and 1888), entitled La Petite-fille d'Agrippa d'Aubigné devant la légende et l'histoire ; especially the article of A. Geffroy in the Revue des Deux Mondes, January 15, 1869, De l'authenticité des lettres de Mme. de Maintenon, xxxix. 362-398, and his recent book, Madame de Maintenon d'après sa correspondance authentique, 2 vols., Paris, 1887.

matter for rejoicing?"[1] With no less satisfaction she wrote to her confessor, a few days later: "I believe that you want me to write you news from the king. He is very well, thanks to God, and rejoices at the arrival of all the couriers that give us tidings of millions of conversions."[2] Nowhere a word of sympathy with her former fellow-believers; nowhere a regret expressed for the cruel treatment by which they were driven to make profession of a religion which they detested at heart. Nor is this strange. It is quite in keeping with the cold-blooded indifference with which, four years previously, she had advised her spendthrift brother to lay out his means in the purchase of lands in Poitou or in the neighborhood of Cognac, where they would shortly go for nothing in consequence of the flight of the Huguenots.[3]

and utters no word of pity for her former fellow-believers.

Nor must I fail to add, anticipating the course of events, that Madame de Maintenon showed no signs of relenting as the years went on. She never entertained the thought of a possible re-enactment of the Edict of Nantes which Vauban and others showed to be the only hope of restoring prosperity to the realm. She opposed even the repeal of the new legislation that made the condition of the Protestants worse than that which the revocatory edict contemplated. Consulted, in 1697, regarding the best mode of treating the Huguenots, now that the lapse of twelve years had demonstrated the impotence of the attempt to convert them by force, she was not willing to grant them the right to exist in France even without the restoration of public worship. To restore this, however, would, she held, be to increase their insolence and prepare them to take advantage of any mishap befalling the royal arms. The return of the exiles would, in her opinion, rather enfeeble than strengthen the state. Liberty of conscience would not satisfy them without public worship. Liberty of conscience being conceded, how deny to parents the right to educate their children, and, this right once granted, a powerful body of men would be perpetuated whom their religion would always render antagonistic to the interests

---

[1] Madame de Maintenon to Madame de Brinon, September 20, 1685. Geffroy, i. 164, 165.

[2] Madame de Maintenon to Abbé Gobelin, September 26, 1685. Ibid., i. 166.

[3] The same to M. d'Aubigné, September 27, 1681. Ibid., i. 133.

of France. "Moreover," she added frankly, "so far as the king is concerned, I feel repugnance to such a change as is proposed. To abandon an enterprise which he has pressed so resolutely, on which he has permitted so much praise to be given him, and in which his enemies have always published that he would fail, it seems to me, would affect his reputation and be contrary to the usual wisdom and firmness of his resolutions." [1]

I cannot, in fine, present to the reader a more just appreciation of the attitude of this singular woman, in regard to the persecution of the people from whom she had herself sprung, than in the words of a wise and well-informed contemporary, contained in the Relation which Spanheim laid before his master the great Elector, in 1690, shortly after his return from the French court where he had been for nine years an envoy extraordinary :

"I ought here to add a few reflections on the fatal participation that is ascribed to her in the unhappy and cruel persecution Spanheim's raised against the Protestants in France : a thing that view of Mme. has appeared the more strange, because she and her de Mainte-non's share whole family were born and reared in the same religion ; in the perse-cution. because her grandfather, of whom mention has been made, signalized his zeal, his pen, and his courage in its defence ; because almost all her kindred were still in it, and were not sheltered from these same persecutions. Nothing can be said, no cause can be guessed, save that she sacrificed everything to the inclination of the king and to the resolution which he adopted long since with regard to this matter ; that she wished to make of it a special ground of merit with him ; that she may even for a while have flattered herself that this great design might be accomplished without resorting to such extraordinary and violent means as were employed in the sequel ; that she had not at that time the ability or the disposition to avert them ; and that bigotry finally came to the support of prejudice, and moreover, of her entire resignation to the humors of the king and the course to which he was pledged. Such was the state of affairs at the time of my departure from France, a year since ; such

---

[1] Réponse de Mme. de Maintenon à un Mémoire touchant la manière la plus convenable de travailler à la conversion des Huguenots, 1697. Ibid., i. 293–299.

it still is, so far as I know. The course of events has transformed a plain lady, old and poor, the widow of a writer of bur-
lesques, the follower of the mistress of the king, and in a court,
moreover, the most gallant in Europe, into the confidant, the
mistress, and, as is believed, even the wife of a great monarch,
and this at a time when that monarch was still in the vigor of
his age and at the height of his glory." [1]

The final blow was struck at the existence of Protestantism in
France on the seventeenth day of October, 1685,[2] when Louis
the Fourteenth, then temporarily sojourning in the
castle of Fontainebleau, affixed his signature to the
Edict revoking the Edict of Nantes. The draft of this
decree had for some days been in course of preparation.

*Louis signs
the revoca-
tory edict,
October 17,
1685.*

The Marquis of Châteauneuf, as the secretary of state to whom
the affairs of the Reformed were specially intrusted, is known to
have given the law its final shape ; but other hands also had a part
in drawing it up. The aged Chancellor Le Tellier, once a friend
of moderation, but of late an advocate of extreme measures, was
accorded the principal credit of the work by the most distinguished pulpit orator of France.[3] It is not improbable that, as

---

[1] E. Spanheim, Relation de la Cour de France, 24.

[2] The document itself is dated only October, 1685. That the true date of the
signature by the king is the 17th, appears from the letters of Louis XIV. himself
(countersigned by Le Tellier), and of Louvois to Foucault, forwarding a copy of
the revocatory edict (Mémoires de Foucault, 135–137), as well as from the
secret registers of the Parliament of Metz : " Le lundi 22 octobre, le procureur
général, étant entré en la chambre, presenta à la cour les lettres de cachet du
roy datées du 17 octobre. Les dites lettres de cachet lues au bureau, ensemble
l'Édit du roy donné à Fontainebleau au mois d'octobre, présent mois . . .
portant suppression des Edits de Nantes et de Nismes," etc.—F. Puaux (in the
Bulletin de la Soc. de l'hist. du Prot. fr., xxxiv., 1885, 497), states the matter
correctly when he says that Louis XIV. signed the edict on the 17th, and that
it was taken to the Great Seal on the next day, Thursday the 18th.

[3] See Bossuet's eulogy of Le Tellier. On the 15th of October, Louvois wrote
from Fontainebleau to his father the chancellor, then lying ill at his castle of
Chaville near Meudon, that the king had heard with pleasure the reading of the
law of which the latter had sent him the draft, and returned it with some articles added, upon which he desired Le Tellier's opinion at the earliest moment
(Rulhière, Éclaircissemens historiques, i. 323). On the other hand, three weeks
later, November 5th, the same minister wrote to the Duke of Noailles, referring
to the last article, which certainly was one of the additions : " I do not doubt
that some quarterings of troops, tolerably severe, upon the remaining nobles and

it is reported, Le Tellier's anxiety to witness the enactment of
the law before his approaching death, was the reason of the
hurried promulgation of a document which in more than one
article betrays marks of inconsiderate precipitancy.

Of the revocatory edict, so momentous in its consequences
both for the Huguenots and for the fortunes of France down
to our own times, it is now necessary to give a brief account.
The new law is not a long document. It probably does not
cover one-tenth of the number of pages taken up by the Edict
of Nantes, including the public and the particular or secret
articles, which, together with the letters-patent of Henry the
Fourth, are commonly embraced by that name.

The preamble is specially worthy of notice. It ascribed the
origin of the Edict of Nantes to the desire of Henry the Great,
Preamble   of glorious memory, grandfather of the present mon-
of the edict. arch, to prevent the peace which he had procured for
his subjects from being disturbed by reason of the Pretended
Reformed Religion, as it was disturbed in the reigns of the
kings Henry's predecessors. In arranging the provisions of
that edict the legislator aimed at maintaining tranquillity and
diminishing the mutual aversion of the adherents of the two religions, in order the better to labor for the reunion with the
church of those who had strayed from it. The untimely death
of Henry, it was alleged, interfered with the execution of his
design, and the unlawful undertakings of the Protestants, during the minority of his successor, led to the withdrawal of some
of the privileges accorded to them. But Louis the Thirteenth,
in his clemency, vouchsafed to grant the Protestants a new
treaty at Nismes, in 1629, by which quiet having been restored
to the kingdom, his majesty purposed to apply himself to compassing the same pious ends. Foreign wars, however, arose.
From 1635 until the truce concluded with the European princes
in 1684, France enjoyed only brief intervals of repose. Noth-

---

members of the third estate of the Protestants, will disabuse them of the error
they are in respecting the edict drawn up for us by Monsieur de Châteauneuf.
And his Majesty desires you to express yourself very harshly against those that
may wish to be the last to profess a religion that displeases him and of which he
has forbidden the worship throughout all his kingdom." Ibid., i. 345. See.
also, Benoist, v. 865.

ing could be done in the interest of religion, save to diminish
the number of the Protestant places of worship by abolishing
such as had been established contrary to the prescriptions of
the edicts, and to suppress the *chambres mi-parties* which had
only been erected provisionally. God had, however, at length
permitted France to obtain perfect peace. The attention of the
king was no longer engrossed in protecting his subjects from
the enemy. He could henceforth use the truce for the purpose
of giving himself wholly to the task of securing the success of
the plan of his grandfather and father—a plan which had also
been his own since his accession to the crown. And now he
saw, with due gratitude to God, that his solicitude had accomplished the end at which he aimed, since *the best and the greater
part of his subjects of the Pretended Reformed Religion had embraced the Roman Catholic Religion.*[1] "Inasmuch, therefore,"
said Louis, "as thereby the execution of the Edict of Nantes
and of everything that has been ordained in favor of the said
Pretended Reformed Religion has become needless, we have
judged that we could do nothing better, in order to blot out entirely the memory of the troubles, confusion, and disasters
which the progress of that false religion occasioned in our realm,
and which gave birth to the said edict, and to so many other
edicts and declarations that preceded it, or have been made in
consequence of it, than to revoke entirely the said Edict of
Nantes, and the particular articles accorded as its sequel, and
all that has since been done in favor of the said religion."
    The first article of the law itself was naturally devoted to the
formal recall of the legislation favorable to the Huguenots. By

---

[1] "Puisque la meilleure et la plus grande partie de nos sujets de ladite R. P. R.
ont embrassé la Catholique."—In a letter to Barrillon, his ambassador to
James II., written on October 19, Louis XIV. states that the number of conversions reported to him amounts to nearly fifty thousand. "Je suis bien
aise de vous dire que Dieu ayant donné tout le bon succèz que je pouvois dé-
sirer aux soins que j'apporte depuis longtemps à ramener tous mes sujets au
giron de l'Église, et les avis que je reçois tous les jours d'un nombre infini de
conversions qui se montent déjà à près de cinquante mille personnes, ne me
laissant plus lieu de douter que mesme les plus opiniastres ne suivent l'exemple des autres, j'ai interdit tout exercice de la R. P. R.," etc. MS. Archives
des affaires étrangeres, in Schickler, Les Églises du Refuge en Angleterre, ii.
358.

the present "perpetual and irrevocable edict," Louis the Fourteenth suppressed and revoked not only the Edict of Nantes in all its extent, including the secret articles and the letters-patent that accompanied it, but the Edict of Nismes, of July, 1629, and every grant of whatsoever nature that had been made to the Protestants through these edicts or otherwise. These laws and grants were to be as though they had never been. As a consequence, it was the king's pleasure that all the "temples" of the Protestants within his dominions should immediately be torn down.

All edicts of toleration repealed.

The second article forbade all gatherings of Protestants for the services of their religion. The third forbade noblemen of all ranks to hold services in their houses or upon their lands. The penalty in either case was the same : confiscation of body and of goods, that is, banishment or death and loss of property.[1]

Abolition of public worship.

The three following articles had reference to the Protestant ministers. Those that refused to embrace the Roman Catholic religion were enjoined to leave France within fifteen days from the publication of the edict, and, meantime, neither to preach nor to perform any other ministerial function, on pain of the galleys. To those, on the other hand, that became converts the king promised that they should enjoy the same exemptions from taxation and from the obligation to lodge troops quartered upon them that they had heretofore enjoyed, and they were to receive an annual stipend larger by one-third than they had received as ministers. A pension of a half of this sum was to be secured after their death to their widows. Moreover, the king dispensed any ministers that might elect to become barristers or to take degrees in law, from the three years of study prescribed by the royal statutes, and relieved them of one-half of the customary fees for examination exacted at the universities.

Protestant ministers exiled.

The seventh article abolished all private schools for the instruction of Protestant children, and, in general, any and all things that might imply any concession in favor of the Protestant religion.

Schools closed.

---

[1] See the next note.

The eighth article prescribed that all children hereafter born

Children to be baptized by the priests. of Protestant parents should be baptized by the parish priests and brought up in the Roman Catholic religion. Recalcitrant parents incurred a fine of five hundred livres or more.

By the ninth article all refugees were invited to return within

Refugees recalled and emigration forbidden. four months to the enjoyment of the property they had forsaken, which otherwise would remain confiscated in accordance with a recent law.

In the tenth article the king issued "very express and repeated prohibitions" to all his Protestant subjects against leaving his kingdom, or allowing their wives and their children to leave it, and against exporting their goods and chattels. The penalty was the galleys for men, and confiscation of body and goods for women.[1]

An eleventh article proclaimed the monarch's intention that

Relapsed persons. the laws heretofore made against relapsed persons be executed according to their form and tenor.

Last of all came this remarkable provision: "As for the rest, the said adherents of the Pretended Reformed religion, while awaiting the time when it may please God to enlighten them as he has enlightened the others, shall be permitted to dwell in the

Pretended toleration. towns and places of our kingdom and regions and lands subject to us, and therein to prosecute their trades and enjoy their property, without let or hinderance on account of their religion, upon the condition, as aforesaid, that they do

---

[1] It seems to me strange and almost inexplicable that the penalty, twice threatened in this edict, of "confiscation of body and goods" should not have had a definite and unmistakable meaning. Actually, lawyers themselves were divided in opinion. Many thought that it meant *death*, others that it was synonymous with *banishment for life*. The latter was Foucault's view, which he supported by showing the absurdity that would follow from the former interpretation: the women would be condemned to a more severe penalty than the men for the same offence. The curious reader will be pleased to read his words: "On a voulu dire que la confiscation de corps et de biens, qui est la peine indite par l'édit de révocation de celui de Nantes contre les religionnaires qui quitteroient le royaume, étoit la *mort;* mais elle ne peut être entendue que du *bannissement perpétuel*, qui est une véritable confiscation de corps et de biens, la peine de mort demandant une prononciation plus expressive, et qui ne doit point être équivoque ; autrement les femmes seroient condemnées à des peines plus fortes que les hommes." Mémoires de Foucault, 157.

not hold services nor assemble under pretext of prayers or worship of any kind of the said religion, under the penalties above prescribed of confiscation of body and goods."

The whole was signed by Louis, as a thing that should for ever be firm and stable, at Fontainebleau in the month of October—the day of the month was not given—1685. It was sealed with the great seal of green wax, on strings of red and green silk. It bore the *visa* of Le Tellier, as Chancellor, and the additional attesting signature of "Colbert," that is, of the Marquis of Croissy, the brother, or the Marquis of Seignelay, the son, of the great Colbert, both of whom were accustomed to sign thus.

The Parliament of Paris not being in session, the document was endorsed as registered in the *Chambre des Vacations*, October the twenty-second, 1685.[1]

Such was the famous edict of recall, the most famous of all the laws issued by Louis the Fourteenth, as untruthful in its treacherous assurances of security to the peaceful Huguenot, as it was mendacious in the premiss upon which it rested—a tissue of deceit and falsehood from beginning to end. This was in keeping with the circumstances

A tissue of falsehood and treachery.

---

[1] The Edict revoking the Edict of Nantes has often been printed. I refer the reader to the Édits, Déclarations et Arrests (Paris, 1885), 239–245, to Benoist, Histoire de l'Édit de Nantes, v. (pièces just.) 184–186, etc. A fac-simile of the original document, still preserved in the French national archives, was published by the Société de l'hist. du Prot. franç. in connection with its Bulletin on the occasion of the Bi-centenary of the Revocation in 1885. Translations into English and other languages are numerous, *e.g.*, in Mrs. Ann Maury's Memoirs of a Huguenot Family (Autobiography of James Fontaine), New York, 1853, 506–510, in David Dundas Scott's Suppression of the Reformation in France (London, 1840), 341–344, and in Dr. Philip Schaff's Progress of Religious Toleration (Papers of Amer. Soc. of Church Hist., i. 113–115). A slight but important mistake is made by one or two of these in translating the beginning of the last article : " Pourront au surplus lesdits de la R. P. R. en attendant qu'il plaise à Dieu les éclairer comme les autres, demeurer dans les villes," etc. Mrs. Maury makes this, " *The remainder* of those of the pretended Ref. rel., . . . may remain," etc. Dr. Schaff, " With regard to *the remainder* of the said R. P. R.," etc. Scott translates more accurately, " *As for the rest*, liberty is granted," etc. So, also, Sander, Die Huguenotten und das Edikt von Nantes (Breslau, 1885), 285–290, " *Im übrigen* konnen sie von der genannten v. r. Rel. . . . bleiben," u. s. w. The treacherous article gives assurance not to a part but to *all* members of the Reformed Church, that they may dwell in France unmolested so long as they shall abstain from religious gatherings for divine worship.

in which the abrogation of the Edict of Nantes had its birth. The assertion of the clergy that, in insisting, through a long course of years, upon the repeal of the privileges accorded to the Protestants, it was moved by a love of the souls of heretics, is a pretence too transparent to impose upon any person of common sense. The thorough worldliness of almost the entire episcopate of France, the notorious dissoluteness of the most strenuous advocates of repeal, including such prelates as the Archbishop of Paris, effectually dispose of the allegation. Men absorbed in the pursuit of pleasure or power, and, above all, notorious libertines, cannot be conceived of by a sane mind as actuated in any course of conduct by a love of souls. Equally erroneous would it be to imagine that the government followed the suggestions of the French clergy through any sincere love for the church. If the king may possibly have regarded the salvation of his own soul as dependent upon the prosecution of the work of converting his Protestant subjects, and thus have pursued that work from motives which he mistook for piety, it was otherwise both with the clergy and with the secular advisers of his majesty. The government wanted the grants of money which the clergy had in its power to make, and which the clergy was quite willing to make, for the purpose of securing undisputed sway over the consciences of men. The affair was purely a matter of barter and sale. If it was veiled under a decorous show of interest in the spiritual welfare of those that dissented from the established church, the hypocritical claim cheated nobody. The farce was too grotesque, the tone assumed by the actors was too little in harmony with their known characters, to deceive any intelligent spectator.[1]

The reader who has carefully noted the progress of events in France for the quarter of a century preceding the publication of the revocatory edict, needs scarcely to be informed that the document to which Louis the Fourteenth set his hand, and which he ordered the parliaments of France to register as the law of the land, in the month of October, 1685, does not in the contemporaneous records mark so sudden and abrupt a change as possibly he may have expected. There was

The edict makes general the reign of violence,

---

[1] See the remarks of Paul de Félice, Mer : son Église Réformée, 166.

no strange and startling transformation. Persecution was not now to begin ; it had long since begun, and was raging with fury in various parts of the realm. The edict only made general and uniform the reign of violence that had hitherto been partial and spasmodic, and threw the mantle of the law about the lawless acts of iniquity. Emigration, too, the emigration to foreign lands that was to deplete France of its best blood, had not now and the em- to begin ; the Huguenots had for months been pouring igration. out of the country in an ever-increasing stream, which not all the king's efforts, not all the barbarous laws he might publish, and the inhuman punishments he might visit upon those that failed to make good their escape, could sensibly retard. Over the borders the Protestants that were so fortunate as to inhabit the provinces touching upon Switzerland, Germany, or the Low Countries had been passing into districts more hospitable to religious freedom. A week before the Revocation of the Edict of Nantes was published, a news-letter sent to a journal of Harlem from Maastricht, stated that there were in that friendly town already more than two thousand refugees from Sedan. They had come a distance of over eighty miles. The Archbishop of Rheims, after ineffectually trying to proselyte the Reformed of Sedan, had sent the dragoons to accomplish what his persuasions had failed to do, and almost the entire Protestant population had taken to flight. Stragglers—men, women, and children—that had wandered in the woods, daily came in to swell the numbers of the fortunate fugitives.[1] The chief difference that is noticeable from this time forward is, that the movement now takes on colossal dimensions. The rivulets become torrents. The flood-gates are opened.

On the part of the government there was every sign of impatient haste. The very day that the fatal law was signed, and Impatient five days before it was to be given to the public, copies haste of the were despatched to every intendant, to every parlia- government. ment. The letters that accompanied these copies impressed upon intendants and parliaments alike that they must see that the law be very exactly observed. The Protestant

---

[1] See the important series of extracts from the Gazette of Harlem, 1679 to 1685, published by the Bulletin, etc., xxix. 262.

"temples" must be torn down. The Protestant laymen must be prevented from emigrating. On the contrary, the ministers that refused to be converted must be provided with certificates to insure that they be not detained upon the frontiers and must be sent out of the kingdom at once. It was the thing upon which the king had set his heart above everything else.[1] An explanatory letter from Louvois stated that the Huguenot pastor might take with him his wife and any of his children under seven years old, none above that age. He must not dispose of his real estate. The ministers heretofore established for the purpose of administering baptism and celebrating marriages were to share the lot of the rest of their brethren.[2]

The work is entered upon with feverish anxiety at Paris itself; yet the date of the publication is adjourned until Monday in order that a plot worthy of those that concocted it may be carried out on Sunday. This is nothing less than a preconcerted arrangement to entrap the Huguenots of the capital in their great church at Charenton and force them into an appearance of conversion.[3] A cordon of archers is to be drawn around the building when the worshippers shall have assembled. A prelate—the Archbishop of Paris or the Bishop of Meaux—with an imposing retinue of robed ecclesiastics, will displace the pastors, and from the pulpit will deliver as a sermon a warm exhortation to the Huguenots to be converted and enter the fold of Mother Holy Church. Conspirators judiciously posted in different parts of the edifice will accept his exhortations with loud cries of "*Reunion! Reunion!*" and will seem to pledge the whole con-

Trick to surprise the worshippers of Charenton.

---

[1] "Ne doutant pas que vous ne vous appliquiez avec un soin particulier et selon que l'affaire le mérite à tout ce que je vous recommande par la présente, comme la chose du monde que j'ai le plus à cœur." Louis XIV. to Foucault, October 17, 1685. (A circular letter.) Mémoires de Foucault, 135, 136.

[2] Louvois to Foucault, same date. Ibid., 136, 137.

[3] Benoist, Hist. de l'Édit de Nantes, v. 904, 905, gives the story of the plot. See, also, Douen, Destruction du Temple de Charenton, in Bulletin, xxxiv., 1885, 388, and in his history of the Revocation at Paris, i. 571, 572. The title-page of Allix's sermon, when printed at Amsterdam, 1688, confirms the statement. The discourse "devait être prononcé à Charenton par M'. Allix . . . le jour qu'on abattit le temple, mais pour des raisons importantes on ne jugea pas à propos de faire aucun exercice ce jour, ainsi il ne fut pas prononcé."

course to reconciliation with the Roman Catholic and Apostolic religion. The bishop will pronounce the assembly absolved of heresy. It will go forth to France and to the world that Charenton itself has dutifully yielded to the summons of the Very Christian king. In order to lull the Parisian Huguenots into a false and fatal security, they receive the assurance, on Saturday, that, although the edict is signed, it will not be registered in parliament until Monday, and they may therefore gather in perfect safety for their last service. Fortunately Jean Claude obtains an intimation of· the plan. Foreseeing the blow impending over the heads of his devoted flock, he has already taken leave of them, at a previous service, in a discourse of rare and moving eloquence.[1] Ménard, one of his colleagues has followed his example. Another colleague, Pierre Allix, has prepared himself to speak his own farewell in a sermon based upon the appropriate words of Saint Paul when taking leave of the elders of Ephesus. He is persuaded by Claude to forego the delivery of his address.[2] The Huguenots, forewarned of their danger, do not come together. The walls of the grand old temple will never again resound to the voice of a Huguenot minister or to the melodies of the psalms of Marot and Beza.

Jean Claude's farewell.

Disappointed in their expectation of seeing the principal Huguenot church of France dragooned into apparent conversion, the court and the clergy vented their spite upon the min-

---

[1] This seems to have been on October 7, for Ménard occupied the pulpit October 14. There has been an animated discussion between Messrs. O. Douen and Daniel Benoit respecting the authenticity of the sermon said to have been preached by Claude on this occasion, which was printed subsequently at Geneva. See Bulletin, etc., xxxvi. (1887) 147-160. The fervid eloquence of the discourse is incontestable, but M. Douen's reasons for suspecting the genuineness seem to me to be stronger than the reasons alleged by M. Benoit in its defence. An advice from Paris, October 12th in the Gazette of Harlem is our authority for the deep impression which Claude's farewell produced. Bulletin, etc., xxix. 1880, 263.

[2] Pierre Allix, who was subsequently naturalized in England and founded a French church in London in conformity with the established church, was an able and voluminous author. He became canon and treasurer of Salisbury cathedral, and both of the universities conferred upon him the doctorate in theology. See Haag, La France Protestante (2d ed.), i. 147, etc.

ister who had given wise counsel and upon the edifice of wood
and stone where he had preached. Jean Claude received notice to leave France within twenty - four hours. He
must not even be allowed the fortnight which the edict
of revocation seemed to grant for preparation. La-
querre, the king's *valet de pied*, was sent to see him out

He is given
twenty-four
hours to
leave
France.

of the kingdom, and did not quit him until Claude was well over
the border.[1] If there were two matters upon which the narrow-
minded king had set his heart more than upon anything else,
they were the instant demolition of the Protestant "temples"
and the instant exile of such Protestant pastors as rejected the
tempting bribes offered them for apostasy. Without ministers
to conduct their devotions and houses in which to worship, he
made sure that the Huguenot laity would easily succumb. His
zeal for the destruction of the "temples" was positively childish. He was at first inclined to give the Protestant
churches (which did not belong to him) for Roman
Catholic purposes; but now nothing would do but

Louis's fe-
verish anx-
iety.

that they should be razed to the ground. Two days before
signing the edict, Louvois wrote to Basville: "The king is
persuaded that it is unadvisable to think of converting the
'temples' into churches; they must all be razed as fast as the
inhabitants of the places in which they are situated are converted. His majesty urges you to attend to this matter." [2]
And when orders had been issued for tearing down the building
at Charenton, in such hot haste was Louis to learn the particulars, that one of his ministers wrote to La Reynie, superin-
tendent of police, who had the matter in charge : " I beg you
urgently to notify me at once of everything that occurs at the
demolition of the 'temple' of Charenton ; for his Majesty has
asked me more than four times to-day, whether I had not had
tidings of what had happened at the time of the registry of the
edict. He is very attentive to what respects the sequel of this
affair." [3] With such encouragement, the enterprise was accom-

---

[1] See Seignelay's order, October 21, 1685. Puaux, Notice sur Jean Claude,
prefaced to his edition of the Plaintes, p. xxxix.

[2] Louvois to Basville, October 15, 1685. Bulletin, etc., xiii. 233.

[3] Seignelay to La Reynie, October 22, 1685. The same minister wrote in like
manner to the attorney-general : " I must tell you that the king seemed to me

plished by the close of the week, too slowly to satisfy the impatience of the king and of the populace of Paris, who had done

The "temple" of Charenton torn down. much quicker work, when in 1621, they burned the edifice that previously stood on the same spot,[1] but none too carefully for the prudent corporations that were to profit by robbery of the Huguenots. I have not discovered that the managers of either of those orthodox institutions, the hospital general of Paris or the "Nouvelles Catholiques," between which the king divided the site of the Protestant church and the neighboring consistory house and cemetery, testified any scruples to taking possession of the proceeds of the theft. I have, however, found that a zealous Roman Catholic, the feudal lord of the place, two years later, gave it as his opinion that Charenton, since the suppression of the Protestant religion and the overthrow of the "temple," was no appropriate place for an institution for making Roman Catholics out of the daughters of Huguenot parents. "The tombs of their fathers and the ruins of the 'temple' are objects that counteract all the pains that may be taken for their instruction."[2]

From Paris the effects of the Revocation spread with the speed of lightning to the provinces. It was not a question, as I have said, of beginning a persecution, but of intensifying it. Only one circumstance threatened to delay the work. The king

Embarrassment arising from the last article of the new edict. had uttered a needless falsehood and embarrassed his trusty servants. Had he not gone out of his way, in the last article of the new edict, to assure the Protestants that might still be unconverted that they should be unmolested, so long as they remained quiet in their homes and abstained from public worship? It was an act of fatuity such as unprincipled men are apt to commit whose perceptions

---

to be so desirous of being informed of the slightest particulars, that I think it will be needful for you to be pleased to despatch a special courier in case anything occur with which it is worth while to acquaint his Majesty." Depping, Correspondance administrative sons le règne de Louis XIV., iv. 346, 364.

[1] Supra, vol. i. p. 202.

[2] "Les tombeaux de leurs pères et la ruine du temple sont des objets qui combattent tous les soins que l'on peut prendre pour leur instruction." Complaint of François Le Bossu, Bulletin, etc., xxxiv. 401. Douen, La Révocation de l'Édit de Nantes à Paris, i. 583. This work has an interesting chapter on the destruction of the great Protestant place of worship at Charenton.

are blunted by the long practice of deceit. In attempting to blind the eyes of the outside world to the fact that the abundant crop of conversions in France was the fruit of compulsion not of rational conviction, the shrewd men that drew up the document had overreached themselves and jeoparded all the advantages of the Recall. If they did not see it, others saw it. In Poitou, for example, the Huguenots, perceiving that the article in question could have but one honest meaning, sent in petitions to the intendant from all sides, complaining that, in spite of the edict, they were still vexed by troops quartered upon them. Many that had succumbed to previous violence ceased going to mass. The Protestant nobles of upper Poitou, in fact, set themselves about despatching a deputation to Paris to inform the king of the breach of his law. This, of course, would never do. The sieur de Minières, who was a leader in the movement, " a seditious gentleman," in court parlance, was promptly arrested and hurried off to prison at Angoulême. It was very convenient at such times to have at hand a goodly supply of *lettres de cachet*, and the intendant gave to the officer who made the arrest an order signed by the king with a blank space which he could fill according to his pleasure.[1] Still the intendant Conversions was at first disposed to be much annoyed. Conver- delayed. sions were delayed. Obstinate Protestants vexed the righteous souls of new converts with reproaches on the score of lack of courage. There was nothing left to choose but a resort to extreme measures. Braving the dishonor of the situation, Foucault was compelled to suggest to the court that it might remove the prevalent false impressions, by charging the intendants to make inquest to discover the persons who were disseminating views contrary to the spirit of the edict and to the king's intentions, and to proceed against them as disturbers of the public peace![2] In a letter to his father, Foucault repeated the statement of the " great disorder " caused by the last clause of the edict. And his father, writing in reply, declared it to be a " contretemps " and a blundering phrase that might produce much embarrassment, unless remedied by an interpretative declaration

---

[1] " Suivant l'ordre du roi que je lui ai remis en blanc." Mémoires de Foucault, 137.   [2] Ibid., 138.

—that is, by one of those not uncommon afterthoughts in the way of legislation which disingenuously assert that the monarch meant the reverse of what he said. " The literal sense of the last article," frankly confessed the elder man, " seems directly opposed to the continuance of conversions ; and all this for lack of explanation or through too great haste ; for absolutely the more one examines this last clause, the more it will be found to be contrary to the intentions of the king." [1] It was an awkward plight for a Very Christian monarch, but Louis did not falter.

" The king," wrote Louvois to the intendant, " having been informed that, since the Revocation of the Edict of Nantes, the Protestants who have not been converted believe that, in virtue of the last clause of the Revocation, they cannot be pressed to change their religion, his Majesty desires that greater severity be used to oblige them to be instructed, and that both gentlemen and *roturiers* be constrained by the quartering of troops upon them." As to the gentry, the instructions of the monarch and his equally honorable minister were that " they should all be given to understand that they would never have either peace or quiet at home until they had shown the marks of a sincere conversion." [2] If any one had the audacity to hand in a petition, he must be treated as his insolence deserved.[3]

Louis interprets the article.

I have said that Foucault was not alone in his embarrassment. The Duke of Noailles, commandant of the king's forces in Languedoc, and (whatever his kindly, but much too partial, biographer may try to prove to the contrary) [4] a general who gave himself with pleasure to the work of conversion, was even more puzzled and vexed. In some alarm, he wrote to the Marquis of Châteauneuf, the king's secretary that, as we have seen, drew up

---

[1] Mémoires de Foucault, 143–145.

[2] Louvois to Foucault, November 6, 1685. Mémoires de Foucault, 145, and text in Appendix, 522, 523.

[3] " Il est bien à propos que vous fassiez punir avec beaucoup de sévérité les religionnaires de votre département qui, sous prétexte du dernier article de l'édit, qui revoque celui de Nantes, ont l'insolence de vous apporter des requêtes." Louvois to Foucault, November 20, 1685. Ibid., 521.

[4] It has been remarked as a peculiarity of the Mémoires de Noailles that the Abbé Millot, in drawing them up for the family, was forced to eulogize the duke's conduct, and yet, in order not to be untruthful, was compelled to state facts which not infrequently contradict his laudatory assertions.

the edict, to know whether the clause against troubling the Protestants was intended to prevent quartering troops upon them—"the thing," said he, "that troubles them most;" also, whether the prayers which a Protestant might hold in his own house, with his family and servants, were to be construed as one of the prohibited religious services. If not, the house of every individual Protestant would become a "temple." It may appear strange to us, but it was really the most natural thing in the world for Noailles and others to conclude that the revocatory edict was an amelioration of the condition of the Protestants! That he so thought is clear from a memoir which he despatched to the king himself after writing to the minister. He regarded the new law as likely to be not less injurious in its effects to those Huguenots that had not abjured, than to those that had. The former, seeing the liberty now accorded to them, were changing their minds, and, whereas they were previously on the point of yielding to the king's determination, now preferred to retain their old faith, even if they could have no public worship. On the other hand, the Huguenots that had been induced to abjure by the quartering of soldiers, and by the intimation made to them of the king's will, their sole purpose being to acquaint themselves with the truths which they were to believe—these, overwhelmed with grief and remorse, now appeared to regret their former condition. In future, they would prove to be so many relapséd persons *at heart*. They would not go to church, or, if constrained to go to church, would use the sacraments only to profane them. Certainly Protestant fathers would not rear their children in the sentiments of the Roman Catholic church. "They will find themselves," said Noailles, "obliged to profess a religion which they will detest, and deprived of the exercise of the religion which they would desire to cling to—a thing that tends to a form of irreligion that is worse than heresy." To this eminently just prophecy of the future of France, the duke added a frank and an unanswerable estimate of the ethics of the edict itself: "It is certain that the last clause of the edict, which forbids the molestation of the Protestants, is going to produce great disorder by arresting the conversions, or else, *by obliging the*

The edict supposed by some to be an amelioration of the condition of the Protestants.

"The king forfeits his word given in the most solemn edict he could make."

*king to forfeit the word which he has just given in the most solemn
edict he could make.*" [1]

It is not strange, therefore, that in a conference held at the
house of the attorney-general, less than a month after the publication of the Recall, to devise a method of converting
the Protestants of the capital without introducing
dragoons into Paris, the very first suggestion made

The Parisian
Huguenots
disabused.

was that the king should remove the confidence with which
the twelfth article inspired them, by issuing a Declaration, ostensibly to explain, in reality to annul, the objectionable paragraph.[2] What conclusion was tacitly reached, appears from the
fact that, within three days, the attorney-general received instructions from a secretary of state to inform the most obstinate among the Huguenots without hesitation (*sans difficulté*)
that "they must not expect to remain in quiet possession of
their property so long as they professed their religion, and that
their abode in Paris would not be an asylum to them." [3]   It
was quite in keeping with this that soon Louis approved a
proposal to compel these "most obstinate" Huguenots to close
their shops and to receive some archers quartered upon them
in their homes ; [4] that the sieur Gobelin, one of the number,
apparently a man of unusual obstinacy, was arrested by a *lettre
de cachet* and sent to the Bastile.[5]   Presently it was told as a
great secret that his Majesty had made up his mind to announce
within a fortnight to the recalcitrants that he gave them only
a month to decide what they would do. If they persevered
they were then to be banished to such places in the provinces
as it might be his pleasure to indicate.[6]

Meanwhile the intendants did not wait for the tardy explanations and directions of a bungling court, but addressed themselves with hearty good-will to the work committed to them.

---

[1] Noailles to Châteauneuf, October 24, 1685, and the Mémoire pour le Roi,
enclosed in a despatch to Louvois, October 27. In Mémoires politiques et
militaires du Duc de Noailles (Edition Michaud et Poujoulat), 23.

[2] November 20, 1685. Depping, Corresp. administrative, iv. 382.

[3] The Marquis de Seignelay to the procureur général of Parliament, November
23, 1685. Ibid., iv. 364.

[4] The same to the same, December 11, 1685. Ibid., iv. 366.

[5] The same to the same, December 19, 1685. Ibid., ubi supra.

[6] The same to the same, December 23, 1685. Ibid., ubi supra.

In every case, perhaps, one of their first acts was to summon all the Protestant nobles and to try to bring them to conver-

The intend-
ants assem-
ble the
Protestant
nobles and
summon
them to ab-
jure. sion in a body. The intendant, as the "king's man," made the address, the character of which varied somewhat in different places, according to the ability and attainments of the orator; but all the addresses had a single type. Their burden was a plea for instant submission to the will of the monarch. "See in what terms Louis has expressed his vehement desire to see his entire

Their ad-
dresses. kingdom united in one communion. If he says that he would give an arm for the conversion of his subjects, will not the conversion of those here assembled be more grateful to him than all the victories of these past fifteen years? Be moved to gratitude by this demonstration of the truly paternal love of the great son of Saint Louis. It is an illusion arising from blind prejudice, to attempt to distinguish between the claims of conscience and the claims of obedience to the king. The two duties are inseparable, and his Majesty is acting solely in the interest of religion. The king, as protector of religion and eldest son of the church, is bound to suppress heresy, and your religion has become heresy since the Revocation. It was only tolerated, not approved, in France, and the Edict of Nantes, rather extorted than granted, was only provisional, and subject to repeal. You should not complain of the means employed by the king. If recourse has been had to troops for the purpose of stimulating conversions, the troops were used only against such as refused to be instructed in the true sentiments of the Roman church. In fact, the king was constrained to employ them as the only adequate means of overcoming the prejudice arising from birth and from long familiarity with a religion that is convenient, independent, and flattering to the senses. Are you not afraid that by your obstinacy you may irritate a pious and powerful prince, who is entitled to regard his absolute power as a means given to him by the Almighty to establish in his realm the reign of the true religion, a prince who understands far better how to secure obedience than do the princes in whose states the *inquisition* is established, and who, desiring only what is just, is in a position to defy resistance to whatever he undertakes?"

Such arguments, if arguments they might be called, did the intendants everywhere urge. Such arguments did the ingenious and unscrupulous Foucault hold forth to the Protestant nobles of upper Poitou, assembled at Poitiers, together with hints of rewards to be given, and the announcement of a bulletin just received from Languedoc, to the effect that one hundred and sixty thousand Protestants, including all the nobility and fifteen ministers, had abjured their errors. Warning the assembled Huguenots not to suffer themselves to be deceived by an erroneous interpretation of a clause in the revocatory edict that had been inserted through the king's kind regard for the safety of the Protestants and *for the advantage of commerce*,[1] the intendant expatiated upon the glory of a prudent conversion upon the spot and upon the dangers of a perversity that would exasperate the powers of heaven and earth alike. Did any one still harbor lingering doubts, let him betake himself to the Bishop of Poitiers for enlightenment.[2]

The treacherous promise given for the benefit of trade.

With uncommon candor Foucault, who prides himself not a little on the neatness of his speeches, admits in his " Memoirs " that his address, delivered in the audience chamber of the presidial court of Poitiers, produced few conversions. Nothing daunted by this, he resorted to more forcible measures. Upon some of the nobles, disregarding their hereditary claim to exemption, he laid arbitrary and extraordinary taxes. To the houses of others he sent whole companies of dragoons. When they sent in complaints to Versailles, Louvois confirmed or aggravated their burdens. He instructed the intendant to make known the king's intention that the dragoons quartered on the Protestants of lower Poitou should remain there until these were converted, and that, *instead of the good order hitherto observed, the dragoons should be permitted to commit the greatest amount of disorder*

The dragoons to commit the greatest possible disorder.

---

[1] " Pour le bien du commerce." I have no doubt that in this Foucault is right. Among other marks of haste, this article, thrown in, at the last moment, with a special view to forestall, if possible, the alarm of foreign and native merchants, is not the least interesting.

[2] The whole address deserves a perusal. Mémoires de Nicolas Joseph Foucault, 139–143.

possible, in order to punish these nobles for their lack of obedience.[1]

Obedience to the king's commands! This was the key-note of the entire crusade. "*The king wills it! The king wills it!*" was the cry of the dragoon everywhere, as he burst, sword in "The king hand, into the house of defenceless and unresisting wills it!" Huguenots, and demanded the instant conversion of the terrified men and women and children. "*Le Roi le veut!*" It was an unconscious and profane parody upon the "*Deus vult!*" that had served as the war-cry of Peter the Hermit and of the hosts which, listening to his exhortations, poured forth from western Europe for the recovery of Holy Land from the defiling hands of the Moslem. It was that deliberate substitution of the good pleasure of a mortal prince in matters of religion for the will of the ever-living God, against which Claude was so soon, in his *Plaintes*, to enter a solemn protest. As military men, the officers and soldiers knew no other rule of conduct than obedience to Louis the Fourteenth. As the monarch's slavish followers, the intendants of "police, justice, and finances," cared for nothing else. In an enterprise purporting to be based upon an ardent zeal for religion, both officers and in-Irreligion of tendants displayed almost ostentatiously their utter the convert- irreligiousness. "You are going to send me to per-ing intend- ants. dition, my lord," said André Bernon, of La Rochelle, to the intendant of that city, "since it is impossible for me to believe the teachings of the religion which you wish me to embrace." "Much care I," replied the savage Arnoul, "much care I whether you go to perdition or not, provided you obey!"[2]

In the extremity of the pains and the terror to which they were subjected, men were brought to consent to sign a paper certifying that, in obedience to the king's commands, the Huguenots whose names were appended consented to be instructed or even to be converted. Many documents of the kind have

---

[1] Louvois to Foucault, November 17, 1685 ; Mémoires de Foucault, 521. See, also, ibid., 147.

[2] "Je me soucie bien que vous vous damniez ou non, pourvu que vous obéissiez." It is Tesseraud, in his contemporary Histoire des Réformés de la Rochelle, that mentions this incident. See Haag, La France Protestante (2d ed.), ii. 391.

come down to us, evidently approved by the negligent clergy.
A "collective and official abjuration" at Isle en Arvert, in
Saintonge, was drawn up by the curate of the parish
at the very time that Louis the Fourteenth was issuing
the Revocation. It simply states that the undersigned
have made the profession of faith above given, and abjured the
heresy of L'huter [Luther] and Calvin, whatever that may
mean ; and four or five of the "new converts," as they successively wrote their signatures, appended to them the significant words : "*in order to obey the will of the king.*" [1]   Respecting his own action, Dumont de Bostaquet, a gentleman of Normandy, tells us that his courage gave out when he heard the command given, in the presence of the Marquis of Beaupré and M.
de Tierceville, to quarter twenty-five dragoons upon him.   "The
fear of seeing so many women and girls exposed to the insolence
of the cavalryman to whom everything was permitted, forced me
to sign an engagement before these two men, as ugly as devils
and as full of malice and cruelty, to whom I promised, in obeying
the expressed will of the king, to embrace the Catholic religion
before Christmas." [2]   A promise for future delivery passed current as readily in the case of conversions as in that of any other
commodity.

Leaving out of consideration the sacrilege committed by those
who insisted upon these sudden and profane conversions at the
dictate of a mortal and fallible monarch, there was a large element of absurdity.   This was brought out distinctly by Monsieur de Fourques, a Reformed gentleman of Montpellier.   One
day this person presented himself at the episcopal
palace, and asked to see the bishop.   The latter, being occupied with company, sent word that the visitor
must call again another day.   But the Huguenot returned answer that he was there on the part of the king and for a matter
that brooked no delay.   Thereupon the prelate admitted him at
once, firmly believing that the gentleman brought him some
command of his Majesty.   "I am come here," said De Fourques,

Conversions in obedience to the king.

Monsieur de Fourques's pleasantry.

---

[1] Bulletin, etc., ix. 72.   It is noteworthy that in two cases the words in question, though still legible, have been carefully erased, as if the priest afterward
became ashamed of the revelation of violence which they make.

[2] Mémoires inédits de Dumont de Bostaquet (Paris, 1864), page 107.

in an earnest tone, not devoid of irony, "to tell you from the king that you are to receive my abjuration. It might perhaps have been better that I should have informed myself of your creed before embracing it, but the king is pleased to exempt me from this duty." The bishop, who was not insensible to the Huguenot's raillery, and who preferred not to expose himself to the ridicule which a conversion of this kind would be sure to bring upon him, replied: "Since you yourself admit that you require instruction, there is no need of haste. You shall freely have all the time necessary that you may be thoroughly informed." "The king will not have it so," rejoined De Fourques. "What!" exclaimed the bishop, "do you want me to receive you into our communion at the very time that you affect ignorance of our belief? I am not allowed to do that." "Nevertheless, that is the king's will," persisted the gentleman, "and you know that in this, as in every other matter, you must obey him." Nor did De Fourques yield the point, whatever objections the prelate might raise. In the end, the reluctant bishop felt himself constrained to receive the abjuration of his insincere convert, without any further formality. "Doubtless," quietly remarks the writer of the memoir to which we owe a knowledge of the curious incident, "the gentleman was wrong in making sport upon so solemn an occasion as this; but it must be acknowledged that they were far more criminal that gave occasion for such pleasantry. For it is certain that the papal ecclesiastics when they wished to convince the Reformed of the necessity of their changing religion, chiefly made use of this great argument, *le roi le veut*, and regarded it as so weighty that they repeated it every moment."[1]

The mask was dropped altogether. The demand was instant conversion, or the dragoons to-morrow. No pretence now of religious conviction. The mandate has gone forth from Versailles to the commandant of each province. With military precision the order is transmitted by the commandant to his subordinates, by them to the consul of each petty township.

---

[1] "La Sortie de France pour cause de religion de Daniel Brousson et de sa famille," 40, 41. Of this unusually vivid narrative, first published in 1885, by M. N. Weiss, of the French Protestant Historical Society, I shall more than once have occasion to make use.

Conversion, or abjuration, which was one and the same thing, was a simple matter of direction, as purely mechanical as a drill. I have before me two of the bulletins thus successively issued. In neither is there a word or a suggestion of Almighty God or of duty to Him. The Duke of Noailles, at Montpellier, having received his instructions, forwards the order to Duchesnel at Le Vigan. He sends him a statement of the inhabited places in the district of Le Vigan, and bids him visit each one, even to the smallest hamlet. " Compel all the Protestants that Compulsory remain to abjure instantly (*dans ce moment*). In case abjuration. of non-compliance with the order tell them that they shall have troops quartered upon them to-morrow. Send the troops. See to it that every place be visited within a week, even to the last house." And Duchesnel, with a subaltern's bluntness, sends the command on to the consul of Bréau, as it was sent to the consul of every other village. "In accordance with the above order, you shall not fail to visit immediately all the houses of Bréau, and in case you still find there any persons, be they women, girls, or children, above the age of fourteen years, even servants, that have not made their abjuration, you shall give me advice of the fact to-day at evening, in order that I may quarter soldiers. And if, in the visitation of your district, which I shall make, house by house, to-morrow, there be found any one [omitted], I shall hold you to account as for a thing contrary to the king's service."[1]

The Dragonnades now in progress differed little in character from those instituted four years before in Poitou by Marillac. Progress of But what a single intendant had timidly ventured to do the Dragon- in a single province, and had been removed from office nades. for doing, was now done with the utmost effrontery by all the intendants in every part of France, and with the full concurrence of the government of Louis the Fourteenth. For the ministers of state had hardened themselves to defy the public sentiment of the world, and, with an audacity almost phenomenal, deliberately to falsify the king's recent assurance, so solemnly given, of full safety to all peaceable Protestants.

---

[1] Bulletin de la Soc. de l'hist. du Prot. fr., ix. 219, 220.

Even the rights of foreign princes were not respected. The city and principality of Orange, though belonging to another, were treated by Louis the Fourteenth precisely as if they had been his own. Not content with ordering the instant expulsion of the ten or twelve thousand wretched fugitives that had taken refuge in the principality, the king directed his troops to invade Orange and reduce the citizens to the acceptance of the Roman Catholic religion. This was done without delay. None of the horrors that accompanied the Dragonnades elsewhere were spared on this neutral ground. To private wrongs were added public outrages, the destruction of the Protestant churches, with the accompanying circumstances of the mutilation of the Bibles and psalm-books which the soldiers found therein, and the tearing down of the coat of arms of the Prince of Orange that adorned the bench set apart for the members of the parliament of the place. The future king of England never forgot the affront.[1] The agents in the work of converting men by dragooning them in their homes, made merry, as usual, at the expense of their victims, and congratulated one another on their wonderful success. " The minister Chambrun, the patriarch of the region," wrote Count Tessé to the minister of war, " is the only person that would not listen to reason ; for the president (M. de Lubières), who aspired to the honors of martyrdom, would have become a Mohammedan, and so would all the rest of Parliament, had I so desired." [2]

The principality of Orange is not spared.

Jean Claude, in his " Plaintes des Protestants cruellement opprimés dans le Royaume de France," has furnished us an extended and truthful survey of the various forms of torture which the Huguenot subjects of Louis the Fourteenth were forced to endure. Many of the sufferers, particularly those that ultimately made good their escape to foreign lands, but some also of those that continued to languish in prison or aboard the galleys, wrote graphic and thrilling accounts of their own experience and the experience of their immediate friends. The original manuscripts of some of these narratives still exist, bearing every mark

---

[1] Les Larmes de Jacques Pineton de Chambrun, chapters v. and vi. (pp. 90–115). Count A. de Pontbriant, Hist. de la principauté d'Orange, 240–245.

[2] Tessé to Louvois, apud Pontbriant, 243.

of authenticity and credibility. Many were published at the time in Holland, in England, and elsewhere, finding hosts of interested and sympathetic readers. Others still, not less striking and valuable, are from year to year making their way into print, having until now been reverently preserved, among the most precious of heirlooms, by descendants who reckon the persecutions endured for the faith by those stalwart men and women of the seventeenth century more honorable than the achievements or the services to royalty by which others secured high titles and wide possessions.

The very summary of Claude is too long for insertion in these pages; not to say that many of his statements have been anticipated. And if I should undertake to select from the particular relations, where should I begin and where end? To whose pathetic story should I give the preference? To convey a general conception of what now took place, not in one city or province, but from one end of France to the other, I know not that I can do better than to transfer to these pages the impressions of Dr. Gilbert Burnet, subsequently Bishop of Salisbury, and one of the most able, as he was certainly one of the most conscientious men of his time, who crossed the Channel shortly after the accession of James the Second, and was a witness of the events he describes.

Bishop Bur-
net's ac-
count.

The revocatory edict promised that the Protestants should not be disturbed, "while at the same time," writes Burnet, "not only the dragoons, but all the clergy and the bigots of France broke out into all the instances of rage and fury, against such as did not change upon being required in the king's name to be of his religion, for that was the style everywhere.

"Men and women of all ages who would not yield were not only stripped of all they had, but kept long from sleep, driven about from place to place and hunted out of their retirements. The women were carried into nunneries, in many of which they were almost starved, whipped, and barbarously treated. Some few of the bishops and of the secular clergy, to make the matter easier, drew formularies, importing that they were resolved to reunite themselves with the Catholic Church and that they renounced the errors of Luther and Calvin. People in such extremities are easy to put a stretched sense on any words that may give them present relief. So it was said, what harm was it to promise to be united to the Catholic church; and the renouncing those men's errors did not renounce their good and sound doctrine. But it was very visible with what intent those subscriptions or promises were asked of them; so their compliance in that matter was a plain equivocation. But, how weak and faulty soever they might be in this, it must be acknowledged here was one of the most violent persecutions that is to be found in history. In many respects it exceeded them all, both in the several inventions of cruelty and in its long continuance.

" I went over the greatest part of France while it was in its hottest rage, from Marseilles to Montpellier, and from thence to Lyons and so to Geneva. I saw and knew so many instances of their injustice and violence, that it exceeded even what could have been well imagined; for all men set their thoughts at work to invent new methods of cruelty. In all the towns through which I passed I heard the most dismal accounts of those things possible; but chiefly at Valence, where one De la Rapine seemed to exceed even the furies of the inquisitors. One in the streets could have known the new converts as they were passing by them, by a cloudy dejection that appeared in their looks and deportment. Such as endeavored to make their escape and were seized (for guards and secret agents were spread along the whole roads and frontier of France) were, if men, condemned to the galleys, and, if women, to monasteries. The fury that appeared on this occasion did spread itself with a sort of contagion. For the intendants and other officers that had been mild and gentle in the former parts of their life seemed now to have laid aside the compassion of Christians, the breeding of gentlemen, and the common impressions of humanity." [1]

Among the multitudes of men and women that succumbed to the force of persecution there were some even of those who had been pastors of the churches, with a greater number of elders. Such falls are always to be expected in times of severe trial. I do not know that they were more numerous on this occasion than would have been looked

Fall of ministers and elders.

---

for. Indeed, astonishment has been expressed, in view of the
great inducements held forth, at the relatively small number of
the ministers that apostatized.[1] The prospective loss of all material support, the dread of life-long exile, the solicitations of
friends and connections, the seductive offer of rewards and preferment, and, in a few cases, the actual resort to bodily violence, would seem to have been among the most powerful motives that influenced men more worldly minded and of a less
vital faith than the great majority of their brethren in the
ministry. I have found no reason for believing that the entire
number of Huguenot ministers at the period of the Revocation
exceeded, probably it did not quite reach, eight hundred. Of
these about one hundred seem to have abjured.[2] It is but just,
however, to state that in the case of one-quarter of the number,
the lapse was only for a brief period. Conspicuous among
these last was Jacques Pineton de Chambrun, who in
his "Larmes" has left us a detailed account of his
fall and rising again—a touching narrative that affects
the heart of the reader of our days not less deeply than it affected the hearts of his contemporaries. He had been transported in a litter, although racked with gout and suffering excruciating pain by reason of a fractured thigh, from Orange to
Pont Saint Esprit, and from Pont Saint Esprit to Valence. He
had resisted argument and seduction alike. His pitiless
captors were about to prolong and aggravate his torture by carrying him still farther to the grim prison of Pierre-Encise, at
Lyons, when, in an unguarded moment, overcome by the agony
entailed by an attempt to dress for the journey, he uttered the

Jacques Pineton de Chambrun.

---

[1] Paul de Félice, in his Mer : son Église réformée, 105.

[2] O. Douen, Les Premiers Pasteurs du Désert, ii. (App.) 395 et seq., gives a
list of twenty-six ministers who apostatized for a time, and of seventy-one whose
defection was permanent. Besides these there were seven who abjured a little
later, chiefly ministers who having gone into exile and met with disappointment,
returned to France and took advantage of the king's offers. Haag, La France
Protestante (2d edit.) under the word *Cheiron*, iv. 286, gives a shorter list that
does not lay claim to completeness. I do not find in any list the name of
Damigrand, mentioned as a convert to Roman Catholicism by the Mémoires de
Foucault, 127, and described as a man of eighty-five who preached with as much
vigor as at forty, and as being the minister who enjoyed the highest reputation
in Béarn both for eloquence and ability.

"accursed" words of submission, "*Eh bien! Je me réunirai!*" That was all, but it was enough. It sufficed to plunge him in the deep remorse of the confessor that has forfeited his crown, and to call forth the piteous lament of the "Larmes," ceasing not even when having escaped to the friendly territory of his lord, the Prince of Orange, he was able to apply for and be admitted, on confession of his fault, to reconciliation with the Reformed Church.[1]

Very different from Chambrun were Cheiron and Paulhan, pastors of Nismes. Just one month before the publication of the edict (on Sunday, the twenty-second of September),

Cheiron and Paulhan, at Nismes.
at the Dragonnade began in the city. It was the turn of Cheiron, a minister of umblemished character and not destitute of learning, to occupy the desk. The peroration of his sermon was bold and thrilling. "Before I come down from this pulpit for the last time," he said, "I declare that here I have proclaimed nothing else than the truth. I call to witness the Lord before whom I shall perhaps appear this very day; for death hangs over our heads. But, Oh sheep of Israel whom He has confided to me, what shall I say of you to the sovereign Shepherd of souls, if He ask me: ' What hast thou done with my flock?' Shall I answer Him: 'Lord, it has forsaken me?' Ah! swear that you will remain faithful to Jesus Christ." At the closing words, the whole audience rose as one man and cried out with one accord: "We swear it!" Yet only twelve days elapsed before the terrible Dragonnade had done its work, and Cheiron and his colleague

---

[1] There is a direct conflict between the statements of Chambrun, in hi Larmes, p. 162, and of the Bishop of Valence in his Mémoires (Paris, 1852), ii 121-123. The former asserts that he never went beyond making the exclama tion referred to, never ratified the promise, never signed any abjuration the bishop, on the contrary, affirms that the Huguenot and his wife for a yea conducted themselves as good Catholics, confessing themselves and partaking o the mass. Between the two, I have no hesitation in believing the statement o the minister, whose entire narrative impresses a candid reader as sincere an truthful. The Duke of Saint Simon characterizes Daniel de Cosnac as in triguing, unscrupulous, and extremely ambitious: "Nul homme si propre l'intrigue, ni qui eût le coup d'œil plus juste; du reste peu scrupuleux, extrêm ment ambitieux," etc. (Mémoires, v. 208, 209.) A perusal of the account Cosnac's career which he has himself left us fully corroborates the Duke's es mate of the prelate's character.

from being towers of defence, had themselves succumbed and
offered their people a flagrant example of apostasy.[1] This was
nearly a fortnight before Louis signed the Revocation, and the
mercenary appeal made by Cheiron and Paulhan, or in their
name, reached the monarch in time to induce him to order the
insertion in his edict of those articles which, as we have seen,
guaranteed to converted ministers, together with some valuable
exemptions, an income larger than that which they had hitherto
enjoyed, together with an easy admission to the practice of the
law.[2] Cheiron became one of the consuls of Nismes.

Not the least remarkable feature in the singular drama of the
Revocation was the almost universal applause that it elicited.

I am not astonished, indeed, that the recall met with approval
at the hands of such men as Marillac, long since removed from
office in consequence of his criminal exploits in Poitou, but lately reinstated in the royal favor and appointed intendant of Rouen. Needless to say, he
regarded the proscription of the Protestant religion
(which he had not expected so soon) with its accompanying
Dragonnade as a complete vindication of the methods which he
had pursued and whereby he had earned the contempt and
execration of all Christendom. " It gave me great joy," he
said, " to receive that glorious edict suppressing the Edict of
Nantes, and to see that I had not been so much mistaken as
men thought in the choice of the means for effecting so great
an achievement, and that, in fine, I well understood the adherents of the so-called Reformed religion." [3] The extravagant

*The Revoca-
tion applaud-
ed generally
throughout
France.*

---

[1] Benoist, v. 815, 816. Haag, La France Protestante, iv. 285. Bishop Fléchier
to the Marquis of Châteauneuf, June 4, 1699 (Œuvres de Fléchier, x. 58).

[2] Louvois wrote to Basville. Intendant of Languedoc, Fontainebleau, October
15, 1685: " Sur le Mémoire qui vous a été présenté par les sieurs Chelat et
Paulhan, le roi a trouvé bon de faire insérer dans la déclaration qui doit être
publiée au premier jour pour abolir l'exercice de la R. P. R. dans tout le
royaume, faire raser tous les temples et faire chasser tous les ministres du
royaume ; que ceux qui se voudront convertir jouiront leur vie durant et, après
leur mort, leurs veuves, tant qu'elles demeureront en viduité, de l'exemption
des tailles et du logement des gens de guerre, qu'elle [qu'ils] auront des pensions
d'un tiers plus fort que n'étoient celles qu'elles [qu'ils] avoient des consistoires,"
etc. Bulletin, etc., xiii. 233.

[3] Marillac, intendant à Rouen, au contrôleur général.   October 26, 1685.
Corresp. des Contr. gén., i. 56.

praise given by better men than Marillac is more surprising. With one accord, the wits of the court and the literary men and women who basked in the sunshine of Louis the Fourteenth's favor, extolled to the skies, as a signal act of the most admirable piety a deed that had not cost the licentious monarch a single hour of self-denial, a moment of personal anxiety, a drop, I will not say of blood, but even of honest sweat.

Madeleine de Scudéry had long enjoyed the reputation of being one of the brightest lights of contemporaneous literature. Madeleine de Scudéry. She was the tenth muse, the "illustrious Sappho" of the age. Now a woman of seventy-eight, she lauded Louis without stint, both in prose and in verse. In a stanza of eight lines intended to fall under his eye, at the time the "good work" of harrying the Protestants was in full progress, she elaborated the thought that hitherto she had been able with no trembling hand to sing the glory of Louis's exploits and virtues, but now "a hundred peoples restored to the King of the universe" was a theme beyond her feeble powers. Earth must keep silence; for such praise a heavenly voice and the concert of angels alone were adequate.[1] In less stilted phrase she wrote to a correspondent: "The king is doing marvels against the Huguenots. It is a Christian and royal work. The authority he uses to bring them back into union with the church will be salutary to them in the end, and, at worst, to their children, who will be brought up in the purity of the faith. This will draw down upon him many blessings from heaven." And she added, possibly from a recollection of his none too edifying private life in the past: "He is living in a very Christian manner." [2]

The opinion of the caustic Bussy Rabutin might indeed be ruled out in any matter in which morals and religion were concerned; Count Bussy Rabutin. inasmuch as his "Amours des Gaules" had secured him a year's residence in the Bastile and long years of exile upon his Burgundian estates, as a defamer of the fair dames of the court. Looking at the Revocation from a political point of view, Bussy Rabutin exclaimed of the Hugue-

---

[1] The lines are given in the Bulletin, etc., xiii. 231, and again, xxvii. 384.

[2] Madeleine de Scudéry to Bussy Rabutin, Paris, September 28, 1685. Lettres du Comte de Bussy Rabutin, iv. 530.

nots, that one hundred years of war, costing the lives of three
hundred thousand men, had multiplied their numbers to two
million souls; but by twenty years of the withdrawal of favors,
of exclusion from public charges, in a word, of subtraction of
those things that went to nourish them, the king had almost
eradicated heresy from his domains, *without any resort to violence.* Should he continue to be successful in his plan, it would
prove to be the case that many of the battles and many of the
provinces he had won would be of less honor and advantage
than the overthrow of their religion.[1] And Bussy Rabutin's
cousin, the elegant Madame de Sévigné, usually as keen of apprehension as lively and delicate in the expression of her
thoughts, reflected the common sentiments of the brilliant coterie of which she was herself the most brilliant
member, when she wrote : "You have doubtless seen the edict
by which the king revokes the Edict of Nantes. Nothing is
so beautiful as all that it contains, and never has any king
done, none will ever do, anything more memorable."[2] And La
Bruyère, and La Fontaine, Madame Deshoulières, Quinault, and
Rancé, and scores of others of less note joined in the chorus of
praise. Every harangue delivered about this time in the
French Academy (that child of the Protestant Conrart) sounded
some notes of triumph in honor of the great king that had destroyed heresy, from the harangues of La Fontaine and Thomas
Corneille, in 1684 and 1685, to those of Dacier and Fleury, in
1695 and 1696.[3] Almost alone, Arnault from his exile at
Brussels, expressed a moderated satisfaction that there were no

(margin note: Madame de Sévigné.)

[1] Bussy Rabutin to Madeleine de Scudéry, November 18, 1685. Lettres du
Comte de Bussy Rabutin, iv. 532.

[2] Madame de Sévigné to Bussy Rabutin, Livry, October 28, 1685 (Lettres de
Madame de Sévigné, ed. by M. Monmerqué, Paris, 1862, vii. 470). To this
Bussy Rabutin replied : "J'admire la conduite du Roi pour ruiner les huguenots : les guerres qu'on leur a faites autrefois, et les Saints-Barthélemy ont mul-
tiplié et donné vigueur à cette secte. Sa Majesté l'a sapée petit à petit, et l'édit
qu'il vient de donner, *soutenu* des dragons et des Bourdaloues, a été le coup de
grâce." Ibid., vii. 474. In a letter to President de Moulceau, Paris, November
24, 1685, Madame de Sévigné returns to the subject: "En un mot, tout est
missionnaire présentement : chacun croit avoir une mission, et surtout les magistrats et les gouverneurs, soutenus de quelques dragons : c'est la plus grande et
la plus belle chose qui ait été imaginée et exécutée." Ibid., vii. 407.

[3] See Michel, Louvois et les Protestants, 311, 312.

public rejoicings over the recall of the edict and the conversion of so many heretics, not that he thought the means employed unjust, but because they were a little violent!"[1]

But what shall be said of the utterances of the bishops and archbishops of France, what of their active participation in the savage work of constraining the consciences of Protestants by means of severities rarely paralleled, while they professed none but the most kindly sentiments and disclaimed any methods but those of a gospel of peace?

On the thirtieth of October, eight days after the publication of the edict which he so much desired, died Michael de Le Tellier, Chancellor of France.[2] It was he who, when he affixed his signature to the fatal document, piously repeated the words of the aged Simeon and exclaimed: *Nunc dimittis servum tuum Domine, secundum verbum tuum in pace: quia viderunt oculi mei salutare tuum*—"Lord, now lettest thou thy servant depart in peace, according to thy word: for mine eyes have seen thy salvation."[3] The oration which was delivered at his obsequies, on the twenty-fifth of January, 1686, in the church of Saint Gervais, in the presence of all the men notable for rank and dignity in France, may well be taken as an expression, so far as that work to which the chancellor had given so much of his dying thoughts and words was concerned, as the united voice of the episcopate of the kingdom.

Death of Chancellor Le Tellier.

Funeral oration by Bossuet.

The orator was Jacques Bénigne Bossuet, Bishop of Meaux, the most eloquent preacher of the Roman Catholic Church. He said: "Let us not fail to publish this miracle of our days; let us transmit the recital to future ages. Take your sacred pens, ye that compose the

---

[1] "Car comme on y a employé des voies un peu violentes, quoique je ne le: croie pas injustes, il est mieux de n'en pas triompher." Letter to M. du Vaucel, December 28, 1685. In Michel, 311.

[2] Journal de Dangeau (i. 241), under date of Fontainebleau, Tuesday, Octobei 30: "M. le Chancelier mourut à Paris sur les trois heures, entre les bras de M. de Louvois, qui lui ôta d'abord la clef des sceaux qu'il avoit pendue au col."

[3] Bossuet, who does not give these words, paraphrases them. "Et il dit, ei scellant la révocation du fameux Édit de Nantes, qu'après ce triomphe de la fo et un si beau monument de la piété du roi, il ne se souciait plus de finir se jours. C'est le dernière parole qu'il ait prononcée dans la fonction de sa charge parole digne de couronner un si glorieux ministère." Oraison funèbre, u) infra, p. 175.

annals of the church. . . . Hasten to place Louis with Constantine and Theodosius. . . . Our fathers never saw, as we have seen, an inveterate heresy fall in an instant; the flocks that had gone astray, return in crowds, and our churches too contracted to receive them; their false shepherds forsake them without even waiting for the command, and happy to have their banishment to allege as an excuse; everything calm in the midst of so great a movement: the world entire astonished to see in so novel an event the most assured mark, as well as the finest use, of authority, and the merits of the prince more distinctly recognized and more highly revered than his authority itself. Touched by so many marvels, let us pour out our hearts in contemplating the piety of Louis. Let us raise to heaven our acclamations, and say to this new Constantine, this new Theodosius, this new Marcian, this new Charlemagne what the six hundred and thirty Fathers said of old at the Council of Chalcedon : ' You have confirmed the faith ; you have exterminated the heretics ; this is the worthy achievement of your reign, it is its true characteristic. In consequence of you, Heresy no longer exists. God alone was able to accomplish this wonder. King of Heaven, preserve the king of the earth! This is the prayer of the churches ; this is the prayer of the bishops.' " [1]

Without an exception, so far as I know, the bishops of France applauded and assisted in the enterprise of Louis the Fourteenth, which they had been for years, collectively, and, to some extent, individually, suggesting, encouraging, promoting. This was not strange. It was strange that they denied their part in it, denied that any violence had been resorted to, denied when there even seemed to be nothing to be gained by denial, denied when those to whom they made their denial knew that they spoke falsely. This, I am sorry to say, was conspicuously the case with the great orator and controversialist to whom I have just referred, Bishop Bossuet.

In addressing the " New Converts " of his diocese, in a pastoral intended for circulation far and wide, and like his other

---

[1] Oraison funèbre de Michel Le Tellier, Chancelier de France. Œuvres de Bossuet (Ed. of Paris, 1821), viii. 173–175.

and more imposing writings, possibly, for preservation for all time, the Bishop of Meaux asserted boldly that those to whom

Bossuet as a persecutor. he spoke had come into the bosom of the church freely and without the slightest constraint. "No one of you has suffered violence, either in his person or in his goods. . . . Far from having suffered torments, you have not even heard them spoken of. I hear the other bishops say the same thing. But as for you, my brethren, I tell you nothing that you do not say as well as I do. You returned to us peaceably. You know it. When I preached the Holy Word, the Holy Spirit made you feel that I was your pastor."[1]

I confess that I am inclined to condone the bitter remarks of Pierre Jurieu, who, in his first Pastoral Letter, after quoting this passage and similar utterances of Maimbourg, Varillas, and Brueys, exclaims, in the excess of his indignant scorn : "These gentlemen have foreheads of brass and can blush at nothing. . . . All France has seen it, all Europe is witness to it, and they dare affirm the contrary to what your eyes have seen. Do you think that these gentlemen dare not lie about the ages past, when they speak to you of tradition and of things said and done a thousand or twelve hundred years agone ? "[2]

There is nothing covered, that shall not be revealed ; neither hid, that shall not be known. The facts that conclusively disprove Bossuet's assertions have come out gradually and remorselessly. In some of the acts of violence done in his diocese the participation of the bishop was not at first known with certainty ; and the conscientious Benoist, while narrating them, studiously refrains from connecting Bossuet's name with them. The proof in a number of cases came out soon after, in the narratives which the sufferers or their friends, having reached a place of safety, gave to the world. It has fallen to the lot of fortunate searchers of our own times to discover, in the official

---

[1] Lettre pastorale aux nouveau convertis de son diocèse (March 24, 1686). Œuvres de Bossuet (Ed. of Versailles, 1817, xxv. 6).

[2] I quote the faithful contemporary version, entitled : "The Pastoral Letters of the incomparable Jurieu directed to the Protestants of France groaning under the Babylonish tyranny, translated ; wherein the sophistical arguments and unexpressible cruelties made use of by the Papists for the making of converts are laid open and exposed to just abhorrence." London, 1689. Page 13.

records of the government of Louis the Fourteenth that are still extant, other and still more authentic proofs of the prelate's complicity.

It was not difficult to demonstrate the falsity of Bossuet's statements in respect to the peaceable state of the region of which Meaux is the chief city. On the fourteenth of December, 1685, the minister of war informed Bossuet that the intendant, M. de Mesnard, had been instructed to confer with him as to " what was to be done for the conversions," and Louvois busied himself on Christmas writing to Mesnard a letter in which he told him that " the means of reaching the conversion of the people of the Pretended Reformed Religion of the bishopric of Meaux is to retain there the four companies of the dragoons of the queen and lodge them in their houses." [1] This course was pursued. "We are in confusion. Pray for us," said a Protes-

Treatment of the Prot- estants of his diocese.

tant letter from that unhappy place, about two months subsequently to the Revocation. "The dragoons are at Meaux, after having caused Claye to change religion. Nothing stands before them. Behold the pitiable state whereunto our sins have brought us." Another, a fortnight later, describes the same persecution as continuing. "In the confusion wherein we are, what shall I say to you? I am not able to speak to you but with tears of blood. The dragoons have made all to change by force in the districts of Meaux and Soissons." [2]

The reign of constraint and terror for the Protestants of the diocese of Meaux was not of a day or a month, but was protracted through many a year. Not until his death, in 1704, did Bossuet cease to take a leading part in suggestion, in guidance, in execution. He superintended the religious instruction of the New Converts, old and young, and wrote catechisms for the purpose. This was well. It would have been better, however,

---

[1] See note of F. Puaux to his edition of Claude's Plaintes (Paris, 1885), page 48.

[2] Letters from Meaux, December 15, 1685, and January 3, 1686, in Jurieu's eighth pastoral letter, page 179. "I do profess," comments Jurieu, "that reading the pastoral letter of M. de Meaux, I was tempted to believe that the Reformed of his diocese had all fallen only under the *fear* of evil ; for I was not able to imagine that any one should write falsely concerning a matter of fact whereof there are thirty or forty thousand witnesses."

had he seen to it that the New Converts were instructed in what
they were to believe, before they were forced to say that they
believed it. His more objectionable activity was in other directions. Ever in communication with the government, he solicits
and obtains orders for the imprisonment of Huguenots who
stoutly cling to their faith. Now it is a father and son, that are
not released until they succumb. Now the victims are a man
and his wife, at Fublaines, so stubborn as to have earned the
designation of " bad Catholics." Now it is Mesdemoiselles de
Neuville whom he induces the king to confine in the house of
the Nouvelles Catholiques at Paris, having drawn attention to
the fact that the orphans have a brother in England in the service of William of Orange. Now it is Mesdemoiselles de Cha-
lendos and Nolliers who, by his instrumentality, are consigned
to the tender mercies of the nuns of the same institution.
Keeping a close watch upon the movements of the former members of Protestant churches, Bossuet, from time to time, appears
in the light of an informer. " Sir," writes the minister to Mesnard, Intendant of the Generality of Paris, " the Bishop of
Meaux having written to me that there is some commotion
among the New Catholics of his diocese, who are selling their
furniture and seem to be preparing to leave the kingdom, letting
it even be understood that they are taking their children away
with them, I reported it to the king, who commanded me to
notify you, that you may examine whether the rumor has any
foundation, and may give such orders as you may deem necessary in the circumstances." In view of such acts of deliberate
cruelty as are revealed in the touching story of the persecution
of the two little Protestant girls, Marie and Madeleine Mirat, it
seems almost idle to speak of the bishop's other misdeeds, such
as his solicitation of the demolition of the Protestant churches of
Nanteuil and Morcerf for the erection of the hospitals of Meaux,
or even his eagerness to have the property of a Protestant ab-
sentee, as yet uncondemned, confiscated for the purpose of de-
fraying the expenses incurred in the instruction of the " New
Catholics." For all these things, which are matters of history, the reader must look elsewhere.[1] I have said enough to

[1] See my paper on Bossuet as a Persecutor, in the Methodist Quarterly
Review, for January, 1866, and the great number of details given in a series o

show what reliance can be placed upon the following assertions of Cardinal de Bausset, the biographer of Bossuet: "With the same sincerity we think that Bossuet has just claims to the esteem and the gratitude of Protestants. He combated their doctrines, he deplored their errors, he alleviated their sufferings, he protested against the laws that oppressed them, he never persecuted a single one of them, he was the stay, the consolation, and the benefactor of all those that invoked his name, his genius, and his virtues."[1] "He never asked this prince [Louis the Fourteenth] for an act of rigor against a single Protestant, and he obtained from him benefits for all the Protestants who invoked his credit and interest. We have had under our eyes all the papers of Bossuet, and all those of his secretary, and we have always found Bossuet unwavering in the opinion that one ought never to use anything save benefits and the means of instruction and gentleness for the reunion of the Protestants. There is no indication that shows that Bossuet took part in what immediately preceded or followed the Revocation."[2] Or those other words of the Abbé Guettée: "It must be said to the glory of Bossuet that, while approving in principle the revocation of the Edict of Nantes, not only was he not an advocate of cruelty, but he was not an advocate of certain acts of violence which other bishops regarded as necessary."[3] On the other hand, the celebrated Jesuit *convertisseur*, Père de la Rue, writing to Bossuet, fifteen or sixteen years later, seems even to make the Bishop of Meaux the prime author of the entire movement, when, in view of the evil effects of a diver-

The assertions of Bausset and Guettée.

---

articles on Bossuet et la Révocation de l'Édit de Nantes, in the Bulletin de la Société de l'histoire du Protestantisme français, iv., 113, 213, ix. 62. Besides which the reprints of the curious little book of a former canon of Sainte Geneviève, entitled Les motifs de la Conversion de Pierre Frotté (1690), ibid., xiii. 97–112, and of the contemporary account of the Mirat children, entitled Relation de la constance admirable de deux petites filles (1686), ibid., x. 50–66, may be read with interest.

[1] Histoire de J. B. Bossuet, évêque de Meaux, composée sur les manuscrits originaux. Par M. L. Fr. De Bausset, ancien évêque d'Alais (Versailles, 1814), iv. 142.

[2] Bausset, ubi supra, iv. 141.

[3] Abbé Guettée, L'Abbé Le Dieu. Mémoires et Journal sur la vie et les ouvrages de Bossuet (Paris, 1856), i., Introd., cxx.

sity of conduct on the part of different prelates in respect to the new converts, he says : "In God's name, who gave you, my lord, the strength to begin this holy revolution, use all the light and influence you possess to see with your own eyes the end and completion of your work."[1]

The story of the manner in which the news was received at Rome of the actual recall of the Edict of Nantes, and of the abrogation of all the privileges accorded to the Protestants of France, is an interesting chapter in the chronicles of the times.

How the intelligence of the Revocation was received at Rome.
It could scarcely be doubtful that the intelligence would be greeted with unfeigned satisfaction. The successor of the pontiff that openly applauded the assassination of Admiral Coligny and the Massacre of Saint Bartholomew's Day, could not be expected to do less than congratulate Louis the Fourteenth upon his royal piety in consummating the work to the performance of which the bishops and other clergy of the Roman Catholic church in France had for many years been ceaselessly urging the monarch. Yet it so happened, by the strange contrariety of fortune, that Louis and the clergy of his kingdom had, from various causes, incurred at this very period the severe animadversion of the Roman pontiff; and the dispute, threatening almost to become a schism,

The quarrel between Louis and the popes.
was by no means healed. In fact, the quarrel was destined to outlast not only the pontificate of Innocent the Eleventh, the reigning pope, but the pontificate of his successor, Alexander the Eighth, and to come to an end under Innocent the Twelfth. It does not belong here to detail the course of Louis the Fourteenth, a prince as arbitrary in his dealings with the church of Rome as in his treatment of the Huguenots, and as indignant that the pope should resist his imperious will as that one of the nobles of his own court should display an independent spirit. Suffice it to say, that, by his arbitrary confiscation of church property, by his oppression of the monastic orders, and by burdening church livings with military pensions, he had shown that a Roman Catholic sovereign might, under the guise of friendship, make himself scarcely less

---

[1] Letter of C. de la Rue, Nismes, January 17, 1701, in Œuvres de Bossuet (edit. de 1819), xlii. 683.

obnoxious to Rome than an open enemy; that he had undertaken to extend to provinces in which it had never been in
force, the right which his predecessors claimed of enjoying the
revenues of vacant bishoprics and of appointing clergymen to
livings dependent thereupon; and that he had wounded Rome
at the most sensitive point by exercising a close supervision of
the moneys annually remitted to the eternal city.[1] Above all,
the king had, in the convocation of the clergy, in 1682, secured
the adoption of the famous four articles which constitute the
shortest and most distinct enunciation of the Gallican liberties,
and of which Bossuet was the author—the independence of
kings and princes, in temporal matters, of all ecclesiastical
power; the superiority of councils over the pope; the invio-
lability of the customs and maxims received by the kingdom
and church of France, and the doctrine that even the pope's
judgment may be corrected, in case the consent of the church
agree not with it.[2] There was more to come; but this was
what Louis the Fourteenth and his clergy had done before
the Revocation.

It was natural that Innocent should not be quite as exuberant in his commendation of Louis's action as he might have
been in other circumstances. In fact, the pontiff was,
or pretended to be, opposed to a work undertaken
without his participation and executed with great
rigor, giving out, the Venetian Venier tells us, that it was inappropriate to make missionaries of armed men, and that this
method was not the best, inasmuch as Christ did not resort
to it for the conversion of the world. Besides which, the time
seemed inopportune for gaining over heretics when the controversies with the Holy See were at their highest.[3] Quite in
keeping with this view is the representation of the Duke of
Saint Simon : "This assault upon the Huguenots drew from him
not the slightest approval. He always persisted in attributing

Coolness of Innocent XI.

---

[1] I follow closely Ranke, History of the Popes in the Sixteenth and Seventeenth Centuries, book viii., p. 375.

[2] Adopted at Paris, March 19, 1682. Abbé Claude Fleury, Discours sur les
libertés de l'Église gallicane, reprinted in Leber, Collection de pièces rélatives
à l'histoire de France, iii. 209, 210.

[3] Venier, Relazione di Francia, 1689. In Ranke, History of the Popes, 376.

it to motives of policy, and regarded it as a measure to destroy a party that had agitated France so long and so deeply."[1] Shortly before the publication of the revocatory edict, and when the flagrant zeal of the king for religion was showing itself in the Dragonnades, the Venetian ambassador to France informed his government: "The whole court exclaims—and Monsieur de Croissy held the same language to me—that the pope alone is insensible to this beneficent work. The king himself," he adds, "has expressed his astonishment—maybe his grief—that the pontiff has not sent him any thanks or praised him for the very great service he has rendered to the church." And, even after the edict was issued, the pope was in no hurry to congratulate the monarch, while his nuncio at Paris grumbled much at the kind of conversion which satisfied the French ecclesiastics, but which, he hinted, would be likely to leave some seeds of heresy in the hearts of the new converts, or give them grounds for putting forward pretensions hereafter. He instanced the conduct of the Bishop of Grenoble, who seemed to have given the converts hopes that the communion under both forms might be tolerated, and the laxity of the Archbishop of Lyons, who permitted them to abjure "out of obedience to the king," and so to give a plausible ground for the assertion that they had been constrained by violence. To add to the discontent felt at the French court, it was rumored that the most perverse of the unconverted Huguenots had been allowed to find a safe refuge in the papal city of Avignon and the Comtat Venaissin.[2]

At length Pope Innocent the Eleventh was ashamed to in-

---

[1] Mémoires du Duc de Saint Simon, xxiv. 183.

[2] The Revocation of the Edict of Nantes illustrated from State Papers in the Archives of Venice. By Sir Henry Austen Layard, President of the Huguenot Society of London. Proceedings of the society, ii. 117–153. See, particularly, pp. 126, 128, 129. I fear Mr. Layard is correct in saying: "However much His Holiness may have rejoiced at the persecution of the Huguenots, it appears that he would have preferred that they should have been left unconverted, rather than that they should be instructed in the Roman Catholic faith by those who were, in his eyes, tainted with heresy." According to the advices of the Harlem Gazette, the commandant of the royal troops at Orange sent word to the papal legate that he would feel compelled to enter Avignon and the other towns of the Comtât, in case an asylum were afforded to the Reformed. Thereupon placard were posted enjoining the latter to leave the states of the pope. Despatch from Paris, November 23d, in Bulletin, etc., xxix. 266, 267.

dulge in farther delay, and, on the first day of December, some
six weeks after the Revocation, the nuncio sought and obtained
The belated a public audience in order to present to Louis an apos-
papal brief, tolic brief expressive of the pontiff's feelings. The
December 1,
1685. king, we are assured, showed himself well pleased, but
the French ministers did not conceal from the diplomatic corps
that more than a brief was required to remove the many existing misunderstandings ; nay, that, in their judgment, the king's
merit deserved a more conspicuous reward than a mere letter
of the kind.[1]

Yet the brief was to all appearance as cordial and complimentary as could well have been desired. Among all the
abundant marks of his congenital piety, Louis's excellent zeal,
worthy of a Very Christian king, was declared to be singularly
resplendent, a zeal that had moved him to abrogate all the
declarations favorable to the heretics of his kingdom, and, by the
issue of most wise decrees, to provide for the spread of the orthodox faith. " We have esteemed it our duty," said the pontiff, " to commend abundantly by the bright and enduring testimony of these letters, the illustrious religion of your soul, and
earnestly to congratulate you upon that height of immortal
praises, by which, in this notable deed, you have increased the
splendor of so many other actions most gloriously achieved by
you. Assuredly, the Church will record in her festive calendar
so great a monument of your devotion to her, and will celebrate
your name with undying praise. But, chiefly you may justly
expect an abundant recompense from the Divine Goodness for
so excellent an undertaking, and be persuaded that we shall
never cease for that end to offer continual prayers to the same
Goodness." The usual apostolic benediction was appended.[2]

Later, but only after receiving hints that his brief was con-

---

[1] Layard, ubi supra, ii. 133.

[2] See the original Latin text of the papal brief of November 13, 1685, together
with a French version, in Pilatte, Édits, Déclarations et Arrests (Paris, 1885),
Appendice, 605-7. An Italian translation is given by Casimiro Freschot, Ori-
gine, progressi e ruina del Calvinismo in Francia (Parma, 1693), 352. The document constitutes, as the author himself observes, the most appropriate ending
he could desire for his history—a work which from beginning to end is nothing
else than a truculent plea for the extermination of heresy. Freschot gives the
date as on the Ides (the 13th) of November, which seems to be correct.

sidered much too insignificant an acknowledgment of Louis's resplendent services to the Catholic church,[1] the pontiff held a solemn consistory, and gave public expression to the joy which he felt at the occurrence of so auspicious an event in French history as the suppression of the Huguenot religion. The Te Deum was sung, and for three days the whole city was illuminated.[2] Subsequently, a pompous celebration was made in the church of Trinità de' Monti under the aupices of a French prelate, the Cardinal d'Estrées. There was the usual mass, said by the Archbishop of Trebizond, there were the usual chants, sung by the best voices in Rome, there was a laudatory oration delivered in Latin by a Jesuit preacher, a grand banquet at the Propaganda, and at night a brilliant illumination of the gardens on the Pincian hill. Most remarkable was an allegorical representation above the church façade, Louis himself, in the guise of a French Hercules, enthroned under the shadow of a gigantic palm-tree, with the hydra of Heresy at his feet, its seven heads cut off, while Religion with one hand held a laurel wreath over the head of the hero, and with the other a similar wreath over the head of France seated by his side. The French Hercules and France together sustained the Keys of Saint Peter. Their act symbolized the implicit loyalty of Louis and his kingdom to the Roman pontiff with whom the king was engaged in an open quarrel.[3] The pontiff could scarcely bring himself to acknowledge at the hands of so contumacious a son of the church even such favors as the revocatory edict. The same unwillingness has also been re-

Celebration at the church of Trinità de' Monti.

---

[1] Louis wrote to the Cardinal of Estrées, February 15, 1686, that "the heretics could not have a greater pleasure, than to see the pope keep silence in an affair that gives them so much mortification." Douen, La Révocation de l'Édit de Nantes, à Paris, i. 56.

[2] "On mande de Rome," writes Dangeau in his Journal, June 12, 1686 (i. 349), "que le pape a fait faire de grandes réjouissances pour la conversion des hérétiques de France. Il a tenu un consistoire exprès, où il a donné de grandes louanges au roi, et a fait tenir une chapelle où l'on a chanté le *Te Deum*, ce qui a été suivi d'illuminations dans toute la ville pendant trois jours; le duc d'Estrées et le cardinal d'Estrées ont donné ensuite des fêtes magnifiques."

[3] A rare contemporary relation in French and Italian, published without designation of place or date, is summarized by M. Frank Puaux, in the Bulletin de la Soc. de l'hist. du Prot. fr., xxix. (1880), 518 et seq.

garded as the cause of a supposed failure of the papal court to
commemorate the act of Louis the Fourteenth with medals, such
as were customary on other signal occasions, but of which the
careful search of the curious revealed no trace. "The papal
court, always so eager to coin medals on the occasion of events
auspicious for the church," it has been said, "did not judge fit
to issue a single one relative to the ecclesiastical exploits of
Louis the Fourteenth and his counsellors."[1] A fortunate discovery, however, which I made some years since, enables me to
remove this common impression, and to bring to notice an issue
of the pontifical mint long overlooked and forgotten.
This large medallion bore upon the one side the familiar features of the French monarch, with the inscription LVD.MAGN.FRAN.ET.NAV.REX.PAT.PATR.REST.PIET
—"Louis the Great, king of France and Navarre, Father of
his Country, Restorer of Piety." On the reverse, the crowned
monarch standing upon the steps of the altar, extends to France
in the guise of the kneeling figure of a suppliant, the sceptre of
his mercy, while around run the words, SACR.ROMANA.RESTITVTA
—"The Roman Religion restored."[2]

A recently recovered medal in honor of the Revocation.

Almost alone in the Roman Catholic world, the eccentric
Queen Christina of Sweden strongly condemned the new method

---

[1] Numismatique antiprotestante des Papes et des Rois de France, a valuable monograph by the late Jules Chavannes, ibid., viii. (1859), 487.

[2] The story of the recovery of this medal may not be uninteresting to the
reader. In 1853, at a book stall on the Piazza Navona, in the city of Rome, I
secured, for the sake of an article upon another subject, which struck my eye, a
volume of the *Giornale de' Letterati per tutto l'anno MDCLXXXVIII*, published
at Parma "with license of the Superiors." In this antique periodical, one of
the earliest of literary reviews, I was surprised subsequently to come across an
article of six pages (pp. 23–28), in the form of a letter from Rome, January 1,
1688, "Sopra un medaglione nuovamente coniato in lode di S. M. Christianis-
sima," and accompanied by a well executed plate giving both sides of the medal
described. Ten years later, having read the statements of M. Jules Chavannes
to which I have referred in the text, I wrote to the Bulletin of the French
Protestant Historical Society a pretty full description of my find, which was
printed in the number for April, 1863 (xii. 114–116). With these indications,
my friend and correspondent, M. Edmond Hugues, set on foot a search in the
numismatical collections of the National Library of France, which was rewarded
by the discovery of a copy—possibly the very copy sent from Rome to the *grand
monarque* himself. M. Hugues has inserted an admirable reproduction of it by
heliogravure in his magnificent work, Les Synodes du Desert, vol. i.

of conversion by means of armed men in lieu of the ministers of a gospel of peace, and had the courage to say so. " I
should not wish to have set to my account," said she,
Queen Christina of Sweden expresses her disapproval. " all the sacrileges which these Catholics commit, forced
by missionaries who treat too cavalierly our holy mys-
teries. Soldiers are strange apostles. I believe them
better suited for killing, violating, and robbing, than for persuading." [1] When, to her surprise, her first letter found its way into
print, she wrote, from the city of Rome, a second not less strong
in its denunciation. " I pray with all my heart," she said, " that
this false joy and triumph of the church may not some day cost
her tears and sorrows. In the meantime, it must be known for
the honor of Rome that here all those that are men of merit and
understanding and are animated by true zeal, do no more lick
up the spittle of the French court in this case than I do." [2]

---

[1] Letter of Queen Christina to Chevalier de Terlon, Rome, February 2, 1686.
Nouvelles de la Republique des Lettres, for May, 1686 (Œuvres de Bayle, i. 556).
Also, in F. Puaux, Histoire de l'Établissement des Protestants français en Suède,
183, etc.

[2] Jurieu publishes Christina's second letter, Rome, May 18, 1686, in his own
second Pastoral Letter.

CHAPTER XII

FIRST-FRUITS OF THE REVOCATION—THE GREAT EMIGRATION

THE recognized existence of Huguenots in France ceases at
the publication of the law recalling the Edict of Nantes.
Louis the Fourteenth had willed that there should be no more
adherents of the Reformed religion in his dominions, and the
law, regarding the king's will as supreme and of ultimate authority, not only refused to accord them any of the rights of
men, but denied the very fact that they lived and breathed.
The signature LOUIS affixed to the Edict of Fontainebleau was
credited with having had the magical effect of transmuting all
the Huguenots of the realm into "New Converts," or "New
Catholics," as they were indifferently called; and, for one hundred and two years, the former dissidents from the established church, even though the pretence that they
had become reunited to the Roman Catholic church
was in many cases too flimsy to deserve a moment's
consideration, were officially known by no other designation.
It was only by accident that, through the force of ancient habit,
some one occasionally spoke of them as "Huguenots," or, as
"Religionnaires," that is, as members of the "Pretended Reformed Religion." For the first few years, the clergy, and that
large part of the population which seemed to have given itself up
to the clergy's inspiration, appeared to entertain the serious belief that the conversion of the "Calvinists" of France had either
been accomplished, or would be fully accomplished before long.
If not the parents, at least the children would be gained over.
If the former, constrained to profess a religion that was not of
their choice, bade fair to prove little better than hypocrites,
their sons and daughters, instructed from infancy in the tenets
of the church and familiar with its rites and practices, would
certainly be believers quite as sincere as the majority of those

*The Hugue-
nots are re-
puted New
Catholics
and New
Converts.*

that surrounded them. In the prevailing spirit of servility that characterized not only the governors of provinces, the governors of cities, and, above all, the intendants, but nearly every man of standing in the community, the mere knowledge that the monarch's heart was set upon the conversion of the heretics to Mother Holy Church, was enough to kindle the zeal of all to copy his example and earn his approval. Not more truly did the slavish troops of the oriental despot act as if they were persuaded that the eye of their master was ever upon them, than did the courtiers of Louis, discarding all considerations drawn from equity or honor, strive to merit his smile and to secure the favors which he dispensed in lieu of justice. Thus it was that persecution was bold and rampant, betraying no more fear of failure than sensitiveness of conscience. Thus, too, it was that men enjoying the highest reputation for integrity felt no compunctions; or, at least, betrayed no shame, when they endeavored to effect conversions by an appeal to ignoble motives. A single instance in illustration may suffice. The plates of the chronological tables of the distinguished Jean Rou, a work of conspicuous merit and the result of years of study, were unjustly seized and detained by the government, at clerical instigation, on the pretence that they contained matters unfriendly to religion. The Duke of Montausier, a nobleman worthy in the main of the respect and affection of which he was the object, having striven in vain to refute the calumny and secure for the poor and persecuted author the restoration of his property, reported to Rou the failure of his efforts, and added: "But God, who does all things for the best, and who makes use of every means to promote His glory, may He not have offered you this means to bring you back to the pale of the church? I pray Him with my whole heart that He may be pleased to enlighten you, and I conjure you, Sir, to be well persuaded that no one can have more esteem and consideration for you than have I." To which the exile aptly replied: "The loss of my tables, I do not hide it from you, my lord, is a loss that I feel deeply. . . . The wrong herein done is a crying injustice, astonishment at which will cease only through familiarity with the examples of which our age is full. But, happily, I had long since

Marginal notes: The zeal for making converts pervades all ranks of society.   Jean Rou and the Duke of Montausier.

prepared myself for it ; and, moreover I have other Tables much more precious than these to preserve. They are the Tables of the Law, my lord, and I have at least this consolation, that I cannot be robbed of the latter as of the former ; because they are graven on my heart by the very finger of God, whereas the others are only a work of man's hand on copper. I should but too openly betray my trust in respect to this divine Law, were I, from a cowardly regard for my interests, to abandon a communion that follows that law closely, turning neither to the right hand nor to the left, and embrace another communion burdened by a chaos of human traditions which, far from fulfilling it, destroy it altogether." [1]

But if Roman Catholics of every station in life seemed to have conspired to make a united effort, that once for all, should sweep the Huguenots from off the face of the earth, by converting them willingly or unwillingly into members of the church which Louis had decreed should alone exist in France, the Huguenots themselves were equally resolute in their purpose to adhere to the religion of their fathers. That numbers succumbed for the moment to the pitiless Dragonnades, is undeniable. But they succumbed only as the honest wayfarer beset by brigands yields to superior force and makes promises extorted from him at the point of the sword or with the dagger at his throat. The king whom they had served with almost idolatrous devotion from their earliest days, having transformed himself into a pitiless tyrant, resolved to wrest from them their religious convictions, a treasure more precious than any temporal possession, they pretended to acquiesce in his will only that they might find time and opportunity to transport themselves and their families, with such portions of their property as they might be able to carry away, to some land less sunny and less attractive in their eyes, it may be, than the land of their birth, but offering to them the inestimable privilege of religious liberty. Again and again a current of emigration had poured forth from the kingdom, on the occasion of successive intolerant edicts. After the publication of the law of 1681, authorizing the children

The great emigration.

---

[1] Mémoires inédits et opuscules de Jean Rou, publiés par Francis Waddington (Paris, 1857), i. 210–215.

of seven years of age to exercise the right of choosing their religious creed, the stream had swollen to a magnitude never before seen.   But now that all worship was proscribed, the stream
became a mighty river.

The moment predicted by Pierre du Bosc, seventeen years
before, had arrived.   The blow struck at the Edict of Nantes
produced exactly the effect which he so graphically portrayed in
the audience with the king.[1]   It was now no ordinary movement
among the Huguenots, but that *"débandade universelle"* of
which he spoke—a general and confused flight of men, women
and children, who took little account of prudence or worldly comfort, and were intent only upon getting beyond the borders of
land where the fondest hopes were disappointed, where the
most solemn engagements into which a monarch could enter
were perfidiously broken.

Human ingenuity was taxed to its utmost to devise means of
escaping the vigilant agents of the government.   There were
comparatively few obstacles to be encountered in traversing the
country until the neighborhood of the frontiers was reached
but there difficulties thickened and perils multiplied.   The Huguenots of the entire western part of France, from the Flemish
borders to the remotest corner of the Bay of Biscay
Flight from
the seaboard. turned their eyes to the Ocean, as offering them the
most practicable route for flight.   But the shores were narrowly
watched by coast guards.   There was not a port into which a ship
could enter, not a roadstead off which a vessel could lie to receive the fugitives under cover of night, that was not watched
with unceasing attention by officers assigned to such service.
Shipmasters were forbidden under the severest penalties to con-
nive at the escape of a Huguenot.   Large rewards were offered to
tempt the cupidity of informers.   No boat or fishing smack could
put to sea before its cabins, and even its hold, were rigidly
searched for absconding Protestants.   Woe to the captain with
whom any such persons were found !   Yet, in spite of vigilance
great numbers were continually making their way out.   Thrifty
mariners, willing to incur extraordinary dangers in order to
make extraordinary gains, conveyed across the Channel whole

---

[1] Supra, vol. i., page 459.

loads of Huguenots, whom they took on board, at dead of night, on some sequestered part of the French coast, and whom they landed safe and sound at Plymouth or in some other hospitable port. Others carried a smaller number whom, should the vessel chance to be visited by officers from one of the many cruisers patrolling the narrow sea, they were able to hide under bales of merchandise and loose articles of freight. Men and women, and even young children, voluntarily submitted to severe hardships and strange imprisonments, in order that they might gain a land

Huguenot children in empty wine-casks. of freedom. It was no rare thing for a child to be placed in an empty wine-cask and shipped to one of the Channel Islands or to England. A similar expedient was tried by the intrepid Susanne Collet, who of her own accord got into a cask which she directed to be carted over the northern frontier into Germany. She was indeed detected and brought back to Metz, but only to make another and more fortunate attempt to escape, having first filed away the iron bars of her convent prison and let herself down to the ground.[1] On the seaboard the plan was generally crowned with success. The family tradition, for example, that Henry, William, and Mary Portal, young children made orphans in the Dragonnades, were taken on board a merchantman and concealed in empty hogsheads placed among other hogsheads full of wine, rests, it is true, on no documentary proof, but is not improbable, because quite in keeping with what is known to have happened to others.[2]

Besides dangers from the vigilance of royal officers, there were natural perils to be encountered. The boats to which the Huguenots were compelled to trust themselves and those whom they held most dear, were often small and frail craft, and in tempestuous weather could not bear up against the gales with which they were but ill adapted to cope. If they did not go to the bottom, they landed their passengers weak and exhausted in consequence of long exposure to rain and cold. Stories were

---

[1] Journal inédit d'un fidèle de Metz.   Bulletin de la Société de l'histoire du Protestantisme français, xi. 290.

[2] Les Descendants des Albigeois et des Huguenots, ou Mémoires de la Famille de Portal (by F. de Portal).   Paris, 1860.   Page 410.

told, moreover, of crimes almost too black for belief, committed against the unfortunate Huguenots. Boatmen were accused of Treacherous purposely drowning the unsuspecting fugitives that shipmasters. committed themselves to their care, in order to secure the property which the latter had saved from their shattered fortunes. Nor were all the rumors false. Foucault tells us that, while intendant of Caen, he tried, found guilty, and executed by breaking them on the wheel, Goupil, a shipmaster, and Tilloc, a simple sailor, who were charged with having caused the death of many persons. They confessed that they had drowned five Huguenots, besides a burgher of Caen, in two trips alone, and explained the method they pursued. Seeking a convenient place between the two islands of Saint Marcouf, where the sea at low tide leaves the sands uncovered, they would anchor their boats here, and, under pretence that they saw French vessels approaching, would induce their passengers to descend into the depth of the hold. Then, when the tide began to rise, they closed the hatches, and opened an aperture in the side of the hold through which the sea soon poured in, filling the entire cavity, and rising a foot above the deck. The imprisoned Huguenots, unable to escape, were drowned like rats caught in a trap.[1]

Of the multifarious devices resorted to by the fugitive Huguenots to elude detection in their escape into Switzerland, Germany, and the Low Countries, the diligent historian of the Edict of Nantes has given us an entertaining account which I shall not transcribe.[2] Suffice it to say, that the most novel

---

[1] Mémoires de Foucault (under date of March 13, 1697), p. 320. Philippe Legendre refers to the same incident in his contemporary Histoire de la Persécution faite à Rouen sur la fin du dernier siècle (Rotterdam, 1704), 81, where he also states that grave suspicions were current that other Huguenot fugitives, of whom nothing had been heard, were put out of the way in the same fashion. "On n'a jamais eu de nouvelles non plus du Sʳ. Simon le Plâtrier Orfevre et de la Dame Marie Vereul sa femme : ou ils sont peris sur la Mer avec leur fille aisnée qui étoit avec eux : ou le Maître du Vaisseau dans lequel ils s'étoient embarqués leur aura coupé la gorge et se sera retiré dans quelque Isle du nouveau monde. Ce ne seroit pas le seul qui auroit fait de semblables coups : puis qu'on a execute a Caën un scelerat qui avoit noyé plusieurs de nos Frères reçus dans son bord en divers tems pour les passer en Angleterre."

[2] Especially as it is accessible on the pages of the History of the Huguenot Emigration to America, i. 251 et seq.

disguises were adopted and the most plausible tales were concocted to throw the most wary off their guard. The wealthy
and educated lowered themselves to the plane of the ignorant
boor, and passed unsuspected before the very eyes of the king's
sentinels, so perfectly had they counterfeited the appearance of
rude rustics. They drove cattle and sheep, they carried bundles, they trudged afoot in attendance upon the guides whom
they had paid well for their dangerous undertaking and who
rode on horseback in the guise of their masters. Delicate
women, accustomed to luxury and ease, assumed the garb of
menials, bedaubed or stained their skin to simulate the marks
of long and arduous toil, lest their faces and hands should betray them, and passed the frontiers unheeded, so well did they
play their part. It mattered as little to them, when once
they had reached the land of safety, that for a few hours they
had tried their strength almost beyond the power of endurance
to maintain the appearance of robust peasants, as that they
had masked as the obedient wives or daughters of their conductors, or taken the humiliating attitude of beggars and asked
alms and a morsel of bread from door to door. The noble
lady, spoken of by Benoist, who, for many successive days,
rubbed her face with nettles in order to give it the blotched and
pimpled appearance called for by the description contained in
a passport which she had bought of a Swiss servant, certainly
deserves special record, as the originator of a novel but not less
admirable self-immolation. I do not know that she had any
imitators.[1]

To the inhabitants of the capital and its vicinity the easiest
and most natural path of escape led to the north. The Flemish border was only about one hundred miles distant
from Paris, and could not be so closely guarded but
that great numbers reached it. There were several
roads known to the experienced, by which the fugitives could
be conducted to Holland without following the highways or
traversing the cities. Parties customarily left Paris
about midnight on a market-day, because on a market-day the gates were opened more readily than on other days.

Flight over
the northern
frontier.

From Paris.

---

[1] Benoist, v. 953, etc.

Before dawn the travellers found themselves near to Senlis, which they were wont to leave on their left hand. The next stage of their journey might be to Saint Quentin. Here, in a house that served as their rendezvous, they remained until a convenient season arrived for their guides to conduct them over the last and most dangerous part of the way. The exigencies of the times had developed a new and adventurous industry. There suddenly sprang up a class of men who for the sake of gain were not afraid to incur the pains denounced by the royal ordinance against all that in any manner should assist the Huguenots in their flight. Nor was their activity diminished when from a fine of three thousand livres, for the first offence, and corporal punishment in case of a second offence, the penalty was successively raised to life-long service in the galleys, and to death itself.[1] There were towns and villages that were very nests of guides. Such was Bohain, in Picardy. By advices that came to the Marquis of Seignelay, the place was said to be full of men that did nothing else than conduct fugitives to the Low Countries. Brought thither from Paris by one set of guides, the Huguenots rested there as long as they pleased, and were transferred to another set that were to see them over the frontier. For the most part the guides went two or three together. They made the Huguenots dress as peasants and peasant women, each driving a donkey before him. One of the guides went ahead, and as long as no one interfered, the other followed somewhat in advance of the company under his charge. If any body of men was encountered by the leader, the second guide, at the first disquieting sight or sound retraced his steps and led the Huguenots some other way. When this was judged impracticable, the whole company took the chances of pushing through. If those that stopped them were soldiers, the guides bought their complaisance with money. There was more difficulty in dealing with a body of peasants, for of these all were rarely of one mind; whereas the guards, being changed every week, were easily bribed. On the whole, as the journey was made chiefly

Bohain a nest of guides.

---

[1] By the laws of November 5, 1685, of May 7, 1686, and October 12, 1687. In Édits, Déclarations et Arrests, 248, 286, and 300.

by night, and as those nights were chosen by preference when there was no moon or there was a heavy fall of rain, the probability was that the fugitives would escape detection.[1]

It cannot truthfully be said that the French Government was altogether blind to the damage which the Huguenot emigra-
The government's fear well grounded.
tion was inflicting upon the trade and industries of the realm ; but its perplexity was great. The publication of the confidential communications that passed between the ministers and the intendants sets the difficulties encountered in a new and clearer light. France was threatened at one and the same moment with the export of a great part of its moneyed capital, with the loss of a considerable proportion of its most energetic workers, and with the transfer to other lands of its most important manufactures. But the problem which the ablest statesmen were unable to solve was, how to stop the outflow without abandoning the coercive measures to which Louis the Fourteenth had committed himself. Bezons, intendant of Bordeaux, confessed that he knew not how to treat the Protestants, now dignified with the name
Losses of Bordeaux.
of New Converts, in that great commercial mart. A year after the Revocation they were not less anxious to emigrate than they had been at first. He could not afford to relax his watchful observation of their actions, for they constituted the greater part of the chief merchants of the city, and, as in the way of trade they had all their property outside of the kingdom, the moment they departed all their money was lost to France. It was impossible to use much severity with them ; for some had left after having confessed and communed in the Roman Catholic churches. In point of fact, they were worse, he maintained, than in the beginning, when the suddenness of the blow they received in the Revocation, as it were, stunned

---

[1] I follow chiefly a secret report made to the lieutenant general of police in 1685 (MS. among the Papiers de La Reynie, in the National Library), and a letter of the Marquis de Seignelay to Chauvelin, November 5, 1686, respecting Bohain, both of which are printed in Depping, Correspondance administrative sous le règne de Louis XIV. (Collection de Documents inédits), iv. 398, 399. The third part of the fourth volume of this important government publication is devoted to " The Protestants: preludes and consequences of the Revocation of the Edict of Nantes."

them.[1] Three months scarcely passed before the same official reported that the search of vessels at the mouth of the Gironde had again become necessary, to prevent the flight of the New Converts; for six hundred persons from Mornac, Royan, and the vicinity had recently absconded, a part of a family going and a part being left behind. For eighteen months they had had troopers quartered upon them, and the great sufferings in consequence were surely reason enough for their action. While the intendant advocated milder treatment, he does not seem to have had much faith in the success of his own remedies, for he insisted on the necessity of having the rivers patrolled by frigates.[2] The process of depletion steadily advanced and nothing could stop it. The intendant, when consulted some time later, as to the propriety of the expulsion of the Portuguese Jews, and, subsequently, when informed that the king was thinking of sending away all English merchants of Bordeaux that were not Roman Catholics, protested energetically against so suicidal a policy. He declared that the former proposal could not be thought of in view of the losses entailed upon commerce by the continual flight of the New Converts.[3]

The evil fruits of economic blunders do not show themselves less surely, that they do not ripen in a day. When, at the close of fifteen years from the Recall of the Edict of Nantes, we are favored with a survey of France in the reports

The results after fifteen years.

of experts from different parts of the kingdom, we find them unanimous in their unfavorable review of the situation, and not less unanimous in ascribing the deplorable decadence in great measure to its true cause in the loss of a most industrious and valuable element of the population. Here is what two or three of them said : " The greater part of our manufacturing establishments have been transported by the Protestant refugees to foreign lands," remarks Mesnager, deputy of Rouen, in his paper upon the state of trade in general, handed in to the Council in December, 1700; "so that we now

---

[1] M. de Bezons to the controller general, December 16, 1686. Corresp. des Contrôleurs Généraux avec les Intendants, i. 91.

[2] The same to the same, March, 1687. Ibid., i. 97.

[3] Letters of Bezons, May 13, 1688, and July 1, 1689. Ibid., i. 149, 187.

receive from abroad more than we send thither. We have ceased exporting a great number of the products of our manu-
Reports from factures and the fruits of our lands which we were accus-
Rouen, tomed to export." He asserted that for the last fifteen years—the exact period that had elapsed since the Revocation —the imports had exceeded the exports, and he argued that, if France year by year sent abroad ten million francs less than she received, she became ten million francs the poorer.[1] Anis-
from Lyons, son, deputy from Lyons made a prominent cause of the little progress, or, rather, of the decline of French trade, to be "the flight of the Protestants, who have carried off much money, good heads capable of carrying on commerce, and good arms, in the large number of workmen they took with them ; persons who, by reason of their trades, have found a settlement among foreigners at the expense of their own country, a settlement accompanied with exemptions and privi-leges.[2] And the deputy of Nantes, in the course of a very ex-
and from haustive survey of the whole subject, remarked : "If
Nantes. foreigners get along without our wines, brandies, and salt, they also do without our linens, our papers and our lute-string. They have established manufactures of these goods in their own lands by means of the [French] Protestants."[3]

Emigration was encouraged by letters from those who had been so happy as to reach a land of liberty, and who desired in
Emigration turn to stimulate others to follow their example.
stimulated There came especially pastoral letters written by
by pastoral
letters. members of that worthy band of ministers sum-marily expelled from their parishes and from their native coun-try by Louis the Fourteenth. They wrote for the double pur-pose of urging to constancy such of their former flocks as were unable to leave France, and of exhorting such as could flee to abandon everything, if need be, for the purpose of securing the inestimable boon of complete religious freedom. The govern-ment knew and deplored the influence thus exerted by Pierre

---

[1] Mémoire de M. Mesnager, député de Rouen, remis au Conseil, le 3 Dé-cembre 1700. Ibid., ii. 477.

[2] Mémoire d'Anisson, député de Lyon (March 4, 1701). Ibid., ii. 479.

[3] Mémoire de Des Cosaux du Hallay, député de Nantes (March 4, 1701). Ibid., ii. 489.

Jurieu and others, but was at a loss to find means of counteracting it. One, and perhaps more than one officious intendant suggested that the mails be searched and that letters addressed to the so-called New Converts be seized; but Louis would not hear of this, because of the "infinite damage" it would do to trade. He was determined not to have "the sacred deposit of the post-office violated on any pretext whatsoever." [1] Which virtuous resolution of his majesty did not hinder him, some years later, from ordering the postmasters to intercept letters directed to a Genevese named Dupré sojourning at Paris, who was suspected of being a Protestant minister, or else a spy, and send them to M. d'Argenson, by whom they were to be examined for the purpose of seeing who the fellow was and what he was about.[2]

Louis refuses to allow the mails to be tampered with.

Unable to prevent pastoral letters from reaching their destination, the government endeavored to counteract their effect by spreading false or distorted statements respecting the reception of the refugees in the countries to which they fled, and where, it was averred, they were reduced to straits, being unable to obtain necessary subsistence, or being treated with cold disdain by those who should have received them as brethren suffering for a common faith. As the agents of the government abroad were not above attempting to prejudice the Protestants of other countries by representing the refugees to be restless persons who had fled from France, not from any necessity, but solely with a view to bettering their fortunes; so they are said not only to have sent home carefully prepared statements of foreign inhospitality, but to have bribed unprincipled men to return to the Protestants that still remained in France and recount a doleful tale of the harsh treatment which they themselves pretended to have experienced.[3]

Stories of foreign inhospitality.

Providence had opened to the fugitive from persecution in France, three doors of escape, which, could they but be reached, led to a safe retreat. They lay toward the east, the north, and the northwest. At every other point of the compass the way

---

[1] Louvois to Foucault, April 27, 1686. Mémoires de Foucault, 527.

[2] Pontchartrain to the Marquis de Torcy, November 1, 1702. Depping, Correspondance administrative, iv. 491.

[3] Benoist, v. 830.

was closed. A direct flight across the ocean to America was practically impossible for any considerable number of refugees. The lofty and rugged Pyrenees were less repellent than the land of the Inquisition lying beyond. The Mediterranean Sea might have invited the Huguenots to trust themselves to its waters, had there been any land of freedom on the other shore ; but there was none. Willingly would the Protestants have threaded the passes and confronted the dangers of the Cottian Alps, were it not that the passes brought the traveller into the dominions of the Duke of Savoy, a prince scarcely less hostile than Louis the Fourteenth, a prince who, in the very year succeeding the Revocation, carried fire and sword into the peaceful valleys of his loyal Waldensian subjects.

Countries hospitable to the refugees.

Happily there remained Switzerland, the Netherlands, and England—all three not only themselves hospitable, but permitting a passage to other and equally inviting regions at a greater distance. Not one of the three proved itself, at this emergency, inferior to its past reputation.

The Swiss Reformed cantons had not waited for the actual recall of the Edict to give practical expression to their sympathy for their suffering brethren in France. From 1683, and annually for many a year, they made collections for the relief of the victims of royal and popular oppression. Zurich, Basle, and Schaffhausen vied in liberality with the Pays de Vaud and with Berne itself ; nor did the petty vengeance which the French Government undertook to vent upon the Swiss merchants trading in the French dominions check the flow of the generous stream.[1] But now not merely money was required, but, most of all, an asylum from the violence of the tyrant. Right generously did the citizens honor the draft upon their hospitality. The little republic of Geneva was conspicuous, as it had always been, since the dawn of the Reformation, for disinterested devotion to the Protestant cause; although its smallness and its exposed position compelled it to measures of prudence. Just before the actual Revocation, almost the entire

Swiss sympathy.

---

[1] Mœrikofer, Hist. des Réfugiés de la Réforme en Suisse (Paris, 1879), 182 et seq.

Protestant population of the Pays de Gex, whose previous tribulations have already occupied us, fled to Geneva, driven by
intolerable persecution. Enraged at the friendly reception accorded the fugitives, Louis the Fourteenth
instructed Dupré, his resident at Geneva, to notify
the magistrates, that, unless they instantly sent back the refugees to their former homes and expelled every Protestant minister that had taken up his abode in Geneva within the past three
years, he would make them repent of having given him such
just grounds of complaint. But, although the magistrates went
through the form of publishing by sound of trumpet an order to
receive no more refugees from Gex, and to dismiss those that
were already in Geneva, to the number of about two thousand,
they made no real effort to stop the stream. Well pleased with
the apparent obedience of the city to his summons, the French
envoy immediately wrote announcing the pleasing intelligence
to Louis the Fourteenth. The next day he came full of fury to
the magistrates and exclaimed : " Gentlemen, what behavior is
this! In the afternoon you publicly drive forth the refugees, and
during the night you open the city gates and receive them anew
into your homes! I shall at once inform the king my sovereign."
And, on learning the incident, Louis the Fourteenth gave this
instruction to his agent: "Tell these gentlemen of Geneva that
they will speedily repent of having displeased me. I am going
to take the most righteous measures to let them know my resentment."[1] Soon the entire Protestant population of Gex, constituting fully two-thirds of the whole population of the district,
deserted, a great part remaining on Genevese soil. When the
king complained of this, he was informed, in all seriousness,
that Geneva had always been wont to get its serving-men and
serving-women from Gex, and that the burghers would really
not know how to provide themselves elsewhere.[2]

I must leave it to Mœrikofer and others that have written on
the theme, to recite the honorable list of the men of worth and

Side note: Geneva a re-
fuge for the
Pays de Gex.

---

[1] Gaberel, Les Suisses romands et les réfugiés de l'édit de Nantes (read before
the Académie des Sciences morales et politiques, 1860), 17.

[2] Mœrikofer, 191. See C. Weiss, Histoire des Réfugiés protestants de France,
ii. 196, 197.

distinction given by the emigration to Geneva. Yet the greater part of the refugees pushed on. The city was too small to contain them. Well has a modern historian exclaimed that little Geneva gave an example greater than can be found elsewhere in the history of human fraternity, when, at an enormous cost of money and persevering effort, a town of sixteen thousand souls, for nearly ten years, received, lodged, and fed four thousand fugitives.[1] Protestant Switzerland, with all its good will, was burdened by the number of Protestants thrown upon its hands. For, from first to last, it is estimated that sixty thousand refugees resided, for a longer or shorter period, in that part of the country in which the French tongue is spoken. Twenty-two thousand of these had need of pecuniary assistance.[2] German Switzerland was scarcely behind French Switzerland in self-sacrifice, and Berne rivalled or surpassed Geneva in intrepidity. To the complaints of Tambonneau, the French ambassador, that the asylum given to the Huguenots was in contravention of ancient compacts between the king and the Swiss cantons, Berne boldly replied that those compacts had reference not to fugitives for conscience's sake but to criminals, and took steps to secure that, in case any of the Swiss Protestant cities were attacked, the rest should pledge their lives, their property, and their honor in its protection.[3] In full harmony, cantons which, like Schaffhausen, lay on the road which the Huguenots must take on their way northward, manfully bore the extraordinary burden laid upon them of helping the new comers forward on their journey, while the Protestants of St. Gall, Appenzell, and the Grisons, traversed by few of the exiles, contributed of their resources to the maintenance of these unfortunates.[4]

Berne, and other cantons.

Upon Frankfort on the Main a goodly part of the stream pouring out of Switzerland converged, only to be directed from Frankfort to many another state of the empire. More than one hundred thousand refugees, mostly Huguenots, doubtless, but including a certain number of Waldenses from the valleys of Piedmont, passed through this

Frankfort and central Germany.

---

[1] Michelet, apud Bulletin, etc., ix. 142.   [2] Mœrikofer, 199.
[3] Ibid., 200, 201.   [4] Ibid., 224 et seq.

city during the first score of years after the Revocation, and thirty thousand more during the twenty years next following.[1] Some went, as we shall see, to Brandenburg, drawn by the extraordinary attractions offered by the Great Elector; others to Würtemberg and Baden, to Hesse-Cassel and elsewhere. Most unfortunate were those whom the Elector Palatine, Roman Catholic though he was, suffered to settle in the Palatinate, shortly before the proximity of that unfortunate region to the dominions of the French king made it a prey to the cruel devastation ordered by Louvois and approved by Louis the Fourteenth. The dispersion of that once flourishing Huguenot settlement scattered the survivors far and wide through Germany, Holland, and England.[2]

The Palatinate.

I shall not say that Frederick William, Margrave of Brandenburg, was the most ardent and enthusiastic friend of the Huguenots abroad; but he was certainly the most prompt of contemporaneous princes in offering them an asylum and extending to them the offer of large and generous privileges, with the view of leading them to direct their footsteps toward his dominions. In return for this hospitality, they and their descendants became no mean factor in rearing the fabric of the prosperity of the House of Hohenzollern. It was the same humane prince, commonly known in history as the Great Elector, who, as we have seen, remonstrated with Louis the Fourteenth, nineteen years earlier, when that monarch entered upon the course of systematic persecution which had now culminated in the Revocation.[3] With even more expedition than he had used in endeavoring to turn Louis aside from a policy which he foresaw must result in the unhappiness of many thousands of his own fellow believers and in great injury to the realm of his ally, Frederick William now hastened to throw his dominions open to the unfortunate victims of the blind bigotry of Louis the Fourteenth. On the twenty-second of October, the edict of recall was published in Paris and throughout France. On the twenty-ninth of October, Old Style, or the eighth of November,

The Great Elector promptly invites the Huguenots to his dominions.

---

[1] Poole, Huguenots of the Dispersion, 126.
[2] Ibid., 129, 130.   [3] See above, vol. i., page 450.

New Style,[1] the Great Elector gave to the world his famous
Edict of Potsdam, inviting the persecuted French Protestants to
his states. On the twenty-third of November, there went forth
throughout the region of Magdeburg and Halberstadt the call to
a general collection for the relief of the destitute French refugees.[2]

Scarcely could offers more extraordinary or more tempting
be made to an industrious but unfortunate people than those

The Edict of
Potsdam,
October 29,
1685.
extended by the Potsdam edict. Huguenots that had
made their way to the Netherlands were to apply to
the elector's envoy, or to his commissioner at Amsterdam, for subsistence and for the means of transportation to the
city of Hamburg, where a second commissioner would see to
their further journey to any part of Frederick William's dominions which they might elect. Refugees from the eastern or
southern parts of France, finding it more convenient to rendezvous at Frankfort on the Main, or at Cologne, would in like
manner be helped on their way by commissioners awaiting
them at these points. Once arrived in the elector's states, the
Huguenots were to be treated with all kindness, and to be provided with everything needful for their settlement. They were
to pay no duties on the property they brought with them. In
case there were any ruined and vacant houses in the towns or
villages which they might wish to inhabit, the refugees were allowed to take possession of them, the elector promising not
only to provide them at his own expense with wood, brick,
stone, lime, and other material necessary for the repair of their
homes, but agreeing to satisfy the former proprietors. Such
settlers were to be free of all imposts and from the quartering
of troops for the space of six years. If they built upon vacant
lands, the elector encouraged them by an offer of the needful
materials and of exemption from taxation for the space of ten
years. If they were unable to build at once, he instructed the
magistrates to provide them houses, and engaged to pay the rent
for four years ; on the condition that the refugees should pledge

---

[1] See Sander, ubi infra, 290.
[2] Henri Tollin, Geschichte der französischen Colonie von Magdeburg (Halle,
1889), vol. iii., part 2d, p. ii.

themselves to build, at the expiration of that time, on such sites as might be assigned to them. This was but a sample of the hospitable provision made. In every place where the Huguenots settled, they were to be received into the body of burgesses and into the trade guilds, and in every way treated as the elector's natural subjects were treated. Not only were such refugees as were disposed to establish the manufactures of cloths, hats, and other goods to receive "all the privileges and franchises which they could desire," but they were promised all the money needful to secure the success of their undertaking. Those that were simple peasants would be allotted lands to cultivate and would receive such help at the beginning as had been afforded to the considerable number of Swiss families to whom a home had previously been granted by Frederick William. The new comers were to be allowed to choose, in each town, a referee to whose decision were to be referred all differences arising among members of their own community. They were to have in each town a minister and a place of worship provided at the elector's expense, with religious services such as they were accustomed to, in the French language. Their nobles were placed on the same footing as the nobles of the country, and were assured the same rights and privileges. The sole qualification was that the aspirants to the elector's favors must be exiles from France for the sake of the Reformed religion. Persons professing the Romish religion could claim no part in them.[1]

The elector's appeal to his subjects to respond generously to "a Christian collection from house to house" was conceived in a spirit of loving tenderness for "an important part of the The call for Christian church suffering in France great want and a collection in behalf of persecution," "inasmuch as the Evangelical Christians the refugees. are forced by all conceivable means and violent proceedings to the denial of their faith and to an acceptance of papal statutes." And the pious were begged to contribute, in

[1] The Potsdam Edict is printed with the French and German in parallel columns by Tollin, ubi supra, iii., pt. 2, pp. 1-14 ; the German text is given by Sander, Die Hugenotten und das Edikt von Nantes (Breslau, 1885) 290-295 ; the French text by Charles Weiss, Histoire des Réfugiés Protestants de France, ii. 405-410.

particular, so that in case, at some future time, they or their descendants should be visited with similar misery and persecutions, they might meet with sympathy at the hands of their fellow Christians.[1]

Thus it was that a great and liberal prince, as wise as benevolent, undertook to provide a refuge for the persecuted of his brethren in the faith, while repairing the ravages of the Thirty Years' War and the calamitous hostilities that are said to have destroyed fully a third of the population of Germany. Even to unfortunate Magdeburg, victim of Tilly's unparalleled atrocity, prosperous days were to return with the growth of the peaceful industries introduced by the French Huguenots; and the wealth arising from its manufactures of stuffs and lace, exalting it soon to be a rival of the city of Leipsic itself,[2] would have made it forget, if anything could have given it the power to forget, the terrible tenth of May, 1631,[3] and the half century of misery that followed. Before long there were in Magdeburg no more "houses ruined, empty or abandoned by their owners, which the landlords were unable to put into good repair." [4]

Material advantages gained by Magdeburg.

No wonder that while Spanheim, the elector's envoy at the court of Versailles, published to the utmost the gracious decree of his master, the clergy of France tried to cover their vexation and to thwart Frederick William's beneficent scheme, by spreading discouraging doubts regarding the ability of the great Protestant prince to succor his unfortunate brethren in the faith. "There has appeared an edict of the Elector of Brandenburg by which he invites all our Protestants to come to his states," wrote the Père Léonard in his diary. "He promises them great advantages; but this prince has it in his power merely to promise much and to keep none

Discouraging reports spread by the Roman Catholic clergy.

---

[1] Tollin, ubi supra, iii., part 2, pp. ii., iii.

[2] Poole, 151.

[3] I am informed that upon the wall of the house of the commandant of the captured city, whom Tilly ordered to be beheaded, may still be read the words, "Remember the tenth of May, 1631."

[4] "Verfallene, wüste und ruinirte Häuser vorhanden, der Proprietarii nicht des Vermögens wären dieselbe aufzurichten, und in guten erbaulichen Stand zu setzen." Edict of Potsdam.

of his engagements. The fact is that he is unable to fulfil them." [1] But the great elector did fulfil his engagement, despite the calumnies of the enemies of Protestantism, despite what was a more serious matter—the lukewarmness, the suspicion, the positive scorn with which many at least of his Lutheran subjects were pleased to receive the refugees on their first arrival, as aliens in race and in speech, as outlandish in complexion and in dress, as of doubtful soundness in the Christian faith. Indeed, when the free-will offering for which he called, brought forth a miserable pittance, Frederick William followed it up with a compulsory contribution of from eight groschen to a thaler for every inhabitant. Even so the voluntary gifts of the electoral house are said to have exceeded the entire sum raised by its subjects.[2]

It might naturally have been expected that Sweden would range itself with Brandenburg as a hospitable refuge for the Huguenot exiles, and that Charles the Eleventh, occupying the throne once held by the magnanimous Gustavus Adolphus, would rival the Great Elector himself in the cordiality of the welcome extended to the French Protestants. Unfortunately Sweden forms an exception to the Protestant states of the period, and Charles to their sovereigns. He had indeed his own reasons for being indignant at the arrogance of Louis the Fourteenth, and was not slow to resent either the French monarch's insolent violation of the law of nations or the complacent acquiescence of Louis in the honors paid to him by flatterers to the disadvantage of his neighbors. He could protest with vigor and could sharply rebuke Louis for suffering his Resident at Hamburg to kidnap the child of a Protestant lady by force in a

---

[1] Journal du P. Léonard, under date of January 6, 1686. MS. Nat. Libr., apud Relation de la Cour de France en 1690, par Ezéchiel Spanheim (Paris, 1882), p. xxi, note.

[2] Fifteen thousand as against fourteen thousand thalers, according to Tollin (ubi supra, page iii), who somewhat enthusiastically exclaims: "Der Glaube der Hohenzollern is die Religion der Barmherzigkeit." I need scarcely say that the impression we derive from the picture drawn by Tollin of the aversion felt by the old burghers of Magdeburg for the manners and the language of the Huguenot fugitives (pages iv.-vi.), differs widely from the impression gained from Weiss, in his Histoire des Réfugiés protestants de France, from Poole and from others.

city outside of the French dominions. And when his attention
was drawn to a statue reared on the Place des Victoires at Paris,
as much to the disparagement of other rulers, as to the exaltation
of Louis—the "immortal" (*Viro immortali*), as he was styled
in the inscription upon the base—he showed a due amount
of displeasure. The Swedish ambassador at Paris was instructed to inform the French court that his master regarded it
as a wanton insult that the sculptor had been permitted to carve
a representation of Charles, true to life, upon one of the bas-
reliefs, in a posture unbecoming his dignity, with the crown not
upon his head but in his hand, almost as though he held it of
Louis's gift.[1] But if the Swedish monarch interceded, through
his ambassador, in behalf of the Protestants of Alsace, and if,
showing some compassion for the sufferings of the Huguenots,
Charles even ordered a general collection to be made at Stockholm for their relief, and offered inducements for Huguenot
manufacturers to remove to Sweden,[2] he would not grant them
what was a necessary condition to their coming—unrestricted
freedom of public worship. The French Protestants were
amazed and confounded by the intelligence that they were expected to exchange their creed and forms for those of the
Lutheran church, and that, in particular, every child born to
the refugees must be baptized by a Lutheran minister. The
very report of the declaration made to this effect by the king of
Sweden, it was confidently affirmed by Claude Brousson, would
be likely to prevent a great number of his French brethren in
the faith from attempting to escape from France in obedience to
the dictate of their conscience. It was no secret that the unfortunate course of Charles the Eleventh was owing to views
which he held in common with many, if not with most, of
the clergy of Sweden, who, far from recognizing the claims of
a common Protestantism, viewed the Reformed with undisguised
aversion, and were scarcely more tolerant of the Calvinists than
of the members of the Roman Catholic church.[3] The French

---

[1] Puaux, Hist. de l'établissement des Protestants français en Suède, 54–57.

[2] Ibid., 59, 61.

[3] See Puaux, ubi supra, 62, et seq., for the views propounded by Bishop Olaus
Laurelius and by Nicholas Bergius, pastor of the French *Lutheran* church which
the king took it into his head to establish at Stockholm.

emigration to Sweden, in consequence of this state of things, never became considerable. The report circulated in France that the King of Sweden had assumed so uncharitable an attitude toward the Huguenots, if it did not indeed, as Brousson feared, deter many from braving the dangers of an attempt to escape, at least induced them to turn their steps in some other direction than Sweden.[1]

A very different welcome was extended to them by the Queen of Denmark, who not content with relieving the necessities of all that threw themselves upon her tender compassions, provided generously for their spiritual interests by fostering the establishment of a large and flourishing church and providing it with pastors of marked ability.[2]

The refugees were welcome in the Netherlands, to which great numbers succeeded in making their way. All classes of the population in the republic were stirred with indigna-

Indignation in the Netherlands. tion at the accounts of cruelties perpetrated upon unoffending professors of the same faith that was held by the majority of the Dutch. Public reprobation was not diminished when Louis persisted in declining to accede to the request of the States General, that Dutch subjects who had been naturalized in France should be permitted to leave the kingdom. To the argument of the Dutch, that, when their countrymen sought and obtained naturalization, the French Protestants were in the possession of full religious liberty, and that his majesty had given a distinct pledge that the naturalized citizens should enjoy all the rights conferred by the edicts of pacification upon his own native-born subjects, Louis only replied by saying that as the former Hollanders now owed allegiance to him and to him alone as their sovereign, so they must be content to be treated as all the other inhabitants of the same faith in his kingdom were treated.[3] There came tales of peculiar atrocity,

---

[1] "Que le bruit même que peut faire en France la Déclaration du Roi de Suède empêchera peut-être un grand nombre de nos frères de sortir du Royaume pour satisfaire au devoir de leur conscience." Claude Brousson to De Mirmand, Lausanne, April 13, 1688. In Nègre, Vie de Brousson, pièces just., 160.

[2] Benoist, v. 959.

[3] Resolution of the States General of September 27, 1685, in Count d'Avaux's letter of October 5, 1685, and Louis XIV.'s letters of October 4 and 18. Négoci-

the effect of which could not be parried even by impudent deni-
als. Staremburg, envoy of the States at Paris, reported that
dragoons had been lodged in the house of the Dutch consul at
Nantes, contrary to the law of nations, and that these savage
guests had placed their host naked over a blazing fire and nearly
roasted him to death before he would consent to be "converted."[1] Such stories as that young girls had been subjected
to the like excruciating torture, their feet having been held over
the flames to secure their abjuration, transformed those who at
first were incredulous into firm believers of the French outrages.[2] The partisans of the Prince of Orange were foremost in
denunciation. Now it was seen that Louis the Fourteenth had
done no wise thing in expelling Jean Claude so summarily from
Charenton and from France. The Prince of Orange commissioned him to draw up a narrative of the persecution
to which the Huguenots were subjected; and, within
a few months, Claude brought out a work to which I
have had more than once occasion to refer—"The
Complaints of the Protestants cruelly oppressed in the kingdom
of France"—no tame recital, but a scathing indictment of the
crime of Louis and his ministry. In alarm Count d'Avaux appended a copy of the pamphlet to a letter that he wrote to his
master (on the eighteenth of April, 1686). Upon the pamphlet
he made this comment: "This is not a printed document con-
fining itself like the rest to religious matters or to exaggerated
accounts of what is done in France. This one goes farther: it
is, properly speaking, a manifesto for the commencement of a
religious war as soon as the Calvinists are in a condition to
wage one. The last four pages contain protests, in proper

William of Orange and Jean Claude's "Complaints."

---

ations du Comte d'Avaux, v. 85, 86, 93. The letter of October 18 was accompanied with a copy of the Edict of Revocation, soon to be published, and
contains these remarkable words : " It will meet with so much the less difficulty
in the execution, as there will be few persons so stubborn as to be willing still
to remain in error."

[1] Nég. du Comte d'Avaux, v. 105, 106. The consul begged the dragoons, his
tormentors, to kill him ; they replied that they were not permitted to do so,
but that they had received orders to do him all the injury he could endure
without dying. It was generally believed that he had since died of the severe
treatment received. Ibid., v. 109, 110.

[2] Ibid., ubi supra.

form, that can have no other end than this. There are many other very insolent passages in this work tending solely to ex-

A Protestant cite all Protestant princes against the king; as may be
manifesto. seen starting from the one hundred and fortieth page and especially from the one hundred and fifty-fifth, where the statement is made that after the Revocation of the Edict of Nantes, men ought not to trust either the word of France or the treaties of truce which she has made. To conclude, it remarks on the one hundred and fifty-fifth page: 'It is to be hoped that Protestant Princes and States will hence draw their just conclusions.'" All this is done, the ambassador further remarks, for the purpose of favoring the designs of the Prince of Orange against the King of England, and it will not be his fault if the latter be not involved in the most prejudicial of all wars —a religious war.[1]

This was thirty months before William of Orange landed at Torbay.

Meanwhile, not only the stanch Huguenots who stood out against all persecution, but their weaker brethren, who had suc-

Emigration cumbed for the moment and bore the deceptive appel-
to Holland. lation of New Converts, continued to stream into Holland, bringing great sums of money both in bills of exchange and in specie.[2] They could not be stopped. Much less could those merchants be stopped that were natives of Holland and had not renounced their birthright. A passport being demanded for one Vincent, heretofore a paper manufacturer, the ambassador was forced to write: "It is certain that this Vincent, who is in Paris at this moment, is a Hollander, and that he has not been naturalized; but it is even more certain that his departure will cause considerable damage; for with his brother, who is at Amsterdam, he has been giving employment to more than five hundred workmen near Angoulême." Many of these had, at the time Count d'Avaux wrote, already reached Holland, and the manufacture of paper was about to be commenced on Dutch soil.[3]

---

[1] Négociations du Comte d'Avaux (April 18, 1686), v. 130, 131.
[2] Ibid., under date of November 29, 1685, v. 97.
[3] Ibid., ubi supra.

But the loss sustained by France in its industries transferred to Holland was in reality trifling in comparison with the damage entailed by the emigration of the men and women that were the very bone and sinew of France.   When, in his touching history of the fortunes of his former church at Rouen, Philip Legendre tells us that, with his colleagues, he had had the consolation of seeing about two-thirds of his flock reach in safety a place of shelter from persecution, he records a fact even more significant of the moral and intellectual, than of the material decadence of the region that was deserted of such citizens.   Less to be pitied than their brethren who had been unable to follow their example, the fugitives for the most part prospered in the places of their dispersion.   Already when Legendre wrote there were to be seen "fine and flourishing families at Amsterdam, at Leyden, at the Hague, at Berlin, at London, Dublin, Rotterdam and elsewhere even to the utmost depth of the Indies, that had no reason to repent that they forsook their native land to follow the torch of the Gospel."[1]

I have already intimated that England offered to the Huguenots of the western seaboard an inviting place of refuge at the time of the Revocation.   It had, indeed, at intervals been a temporary home to many of their ancestors, from the time of Francis the First and Henry the Eighth, and throughout the period of the wars of the League.   Until now, however, the refugees had not crossed the Channel with the intention of protracting their stay beyond the term of violent persecution—a brief space, it was hoped.   If the faithful of Dieppe, for example, took to their vessels and transported their pastors and their church organization to the little port of Rye, in Kent, when the tide of proscription ran high under Henry of Valois, they promptly returned to their homes and resumed their "temples" in Dieppe the moment that more tolerant counsels prevailed in France.   At London and elsewhere Huguenot and Walloon churches of a more permanent character had indeed arisen ; but their number was small as compared with those that were now to be required for the accommodation

Emigration to England.

---

[1] Histoire de la persécution faite à l'église de Rouen sur la fin du dernier siècle (Rotterdam, 1704), 83.

of the great crowds of French Protestants that sought the hospitable shores of England. For many a town and city of France sustained a loss of population, through the emigration to the northern shore of the Channel, which was felt keenly for many a year, and of which the traces have scarcely been effaced until our own times. The official inquiries, whose results are to be found in the manuscripts of the national library at Paris, disclose both the extent of the depopulation of the western coasts, and the country which profited most by the loss sustained by France through the suicidal policy of Louis the Fourteenth. From La Rochelle, from the Isle de Ré and the Isle d'Oleron, from La Tremblade, from the Port des Barques, indeed from all the towns and villages of Aunis and the coasts of Saintonge, the current of Huguenot emigration set in with a steady stream toward England. It was probably much the same as during the exodus of the preceding four years which began with the law of 1681 regarding the Huguenot children ; of every score of fugitives seventeen fled to England or Ireland, the rest mostly to Holland, a very few to Boston or the Carolinas.[1]

Exodus from the Pays d'Aunis and La Rochelle.

James the Second had been on the throne of England for a little over eight months when the edict of revocation was signed. He was an avowed Roman Catholic and an ally of Louis the Fourteenth. He had no sympathy with refugees whose chief, if not their sole, claim upon the inhabitants of Great Britain was that they had suffered the loss of country, friends and worldly possessions solely because of their unwillingness to accept the Roman Catholic religion, to which their natural sovereign had attempted to urge them by the offer of favor and rewards, and to drive them by

Aversion of James II. for the Huguenots.

---

[1] There is extant a paper headed " Liste des familles de la religion prétendue réformée qui sont sorties du pays d'Aulnix, Isles et costes de Xaintonge pour aller dans lesdits pays estrangers depuis l'année 1681 jusques à la fin de May 1685," drawn up by the orders of the Intendant Arnoul. The list comprehends 867 fugitives. I find on examination that the place of refuge of 823 of the number is given. Of these just 700 seem to be put down as having reached England. I note as interesting the fact that the number of fugitives diminished from 310 in 1681, to 243 in 1682, and 98 in 1683 ; then rising in 1684 to 117, and to 99 for the first five months of the year of the Revocation. The MS. is in the Archives Nationales, TT. No. 259.

the most extreme of severities. James had, indeed, for many
months been listening with undisguised avidity to the accounts
that came from France of the success attending the
converting zeal of Louis. No sooner did the French
ambassador receive despatches from home, than James
would take him apart to inquire what news they contained on the subject that was so near to his heart. His zeal
for the advancement of the Roman Catholic religion in England was visibly augmented by the encouraging tidings.[1] Unable, however, to defy the common sentiment of his subjects,
who saw in the Huguenots not only brethren in the faith, but
stanch confessors who had risked all things in attestation of
that faith, the king of England could not do less than extend
a welcome to the new comers upon their arrival, and provide,
not indeed from his own pocket, but from the pockets of his
people, for the relief of their destitution. The Brief
which he signed at Westminster on the fifth of March,
1686, taking the refugees under his protection, and
ordering a general collection to be made throughout
his kingdom of England, principality of Wales and
town of Berwick on Tweed, is both a token of the charitable
urgency of the *people* of England and a proof of the lukewarmness of their *king*. The circumstance that the Huguenots are
fugitives for religion's sake nowhere appears from the document. It is the greatest prerogative and most desirable advantage of kings, says the preamble, to be able to give marks
of clemency and beneficence, in the exercise of which they
most nearly resemble the God of heaven from whom alone
they derive their authority. A great number of French Protestants—many of them persons of birth and quality, heretofore
living in abundance—having taken refuge in the king's dominions and being reduced to extreme want, while others, skilled
in various useful trades and manufactures, are, through want
of the means of life, quite unable to follow those pursuits, his
majesty believes himself bound by the laws of Christian love
and the common bonds of humanity, to take their deplorable

His delight at the conver- sions effected by Louis XIV.

He is com- pelled to issue a Brief ordering a collection for the fugitives.

---

[1] Barrillon to Louis XIV., Windsor, October 11, 1685, in Schickler, Les
Églises du Refuge en Angleterre, ii. 357.

condition under his royal care, tenderness, and compassion. To this end, he declares that he receives into his gracious protection all such of their number as will live in an entire conformity with and wise submission to his government as established *as well in state as in church*, and condescends to grant them permission to ask and receive the charitable gifts of his subjects. The greater part of the Brief is taken up with the details of the mode in which these gifts are to be gathered. The ministers, vicars, and curates are particularly enjoined to communicate to their flocks with zeal the contents of the royal missive, and to persuade, exhort, and urge them to contribute willingly and cheerfully for the succor of these distressed Christians. But it is noteworthy that they are required to *confine themselves to presenting such motives and persuasions as are contained in the present letters patent.* Evidently James would tolerate no appeals to the claims of a common Protestantism, no harrowing rehearsal of the sufferings undergone in their native land by the subjects of the great king of France, no word of condemnation of the inhuman Dragonnades, no reflection, however distant, upon the honor of a perjured king, his ally. The Protestants of England must know only that they had with them a crowd of needy persons whose necessities the monarch was graciously pleased to allow them to relieve![1]

No appeal to Protestant sympathy.

Let it not be supposed, however, that even so cold and unsympathetic a paper as the brief was obtained without the very greatest difficulty. The king was all French. Barrillon, the French ambassador, styled by John Evelyn, who had met him,

---

[1] I do not know where the English text of the Brief can be read. Mr. Poole merely refers to the issue of such a paper, but gives the date as March 29th (Huguenots of the Dispersion, 79). See, also, Agnew, i. 59. I have been so fortunate, however, as to secure a translation of the Brief, printed in French and German in parallel columns, with the title, "Ihrer Königlichen Majestät in Engeland Edict Die Reception der aus Franckreich dahin-geflüchteten Reformirten, und die zu Ihrem Unterhalt angeordnete Collecten betreffend. Gedruckt im Jahr 1686." This rare pamphlet of sixteen pages was evidently printed for circulation among the Huguenots that had reached Germany. I furnished a copy for republication in the Bulletin of the Société de l'histoire du Protestantisme français on the bi-centenary of the original issue, March, 1886, vol. xxxv. 124-130.

"a learned and crafty advocate,"[1] exerted upon his Majesty an almost unlimited influence. Had it been possible to keep back or deny events that were occurring at the very gates of England, this would certainly have been done. But *Opposition of the French ambassador.* when English shipmasters came in daily with reports that such a persecution was raging across the Channel "as hardly any age has seen the like, even among the pagans," and when they stated that their own vessels had been "insolently visited" and fugitives taken therefrom, though a favored few "escaped in barrels," the case was desperate even for hardened liars.[2] Yet the press said nothing. "One thing was much taken notice of," wrote Evelyn in November, "that the Gazettes which were still constantly printed twice a week, informing us what was done all over Europe, never spake of this wonderful proceeding in France, nor was any relation of it published by any, save what private letters and the persecuted fugitives brought. Whence this silence, I list not to conjecture; but it appeareth very extraordinary in a Protestant country that we should know nothing of what Protestants suffer, whilst great collections were made for them in foreign places, more hospitable and Christian in appearance."[3]

When public sentiment could no longer be resisted, and not till then, was the Brief for a collection issued. "It had long been expected and at last with difficulty procured to be published, the interest of the French ambassador obstructing it." So says John Evelyn, under date of the twenty-fifth of April, when he states that it was read in the church.[4] The delay had not prevented that virtuous prelate, Thomas Ken, Bishop of Bath and Wells, from preaching a most excellent and pathetic discourse, some six weeks before, in which he exhorted his hearers "to constancy in the Protestant religion, detestation of the unheard-of cruelties of the French, and stirring up to a liberal contribution."[5]

Barrillon avenged himself for the mortification to which the Brief subjected him, and still more for the general and generous

---

[1] Diary of John Evelyn, ii. 257.   [2] Ibid., ii. 255, 259.
[3] Ibid., ii. 254.   [4] Ibid., ii. 263.
[5] Ibid., ii. 261.

response of the people to the Brief, by moving James to decided measures against the book of Jean Claude—which had recently been received in England and had instantly been translated— that scathing indictment under which his proud master, while pretending a lofty disdain, winced as under no other lines written by mortal man. More sensible, however, than his envoy at the English court, Louis the Fourteenth had promptly written to him: "I do not wish you to use any diligence to have publicly burned, as you propose, the French book said to be written by the minister Claude, or to prevent its translation into English. For books of this kind ordinarily lose influence by little notice being taken of them, and are sought for only in consequence of the efforts made to suppress them."[1] When the letter reached Barrillon it was already too late. The hot-headed ambassador had found in James the Second a ready listener to his complaint, and the king promptly ordered that both original and translation should have a common fate. His council were not of the same mind. When Lord Sunderland read Barrillon's request, there was a promise of a warm debate. The Lord Chancellor himself, the infamous Jeffreys, was the first to express his surprise at the proposal. It would be right, he said, to make inquisition for the printer of the English translation; but it was a thing unheard of to burn a book written in French, printed in a foreign land and containing nothing to the injury of the state. James did not let him finish what he had to say. " I have made up my mind in the matter," he broke in. " Even dogs defend one another if one of their number be attacked. I think that kings should do likewise. Besides I have particular reasons that oblige me not to suffer such a libel against the king of France."[2]

" This day," writes Evelyn, " was burnt in the old Exchange by the common hangman, a translation of a book written by the famous Monsieur Claude, relating only matters of fact concerning the horrid massacres and barbarous proceedings of

---

[1] Louis XIV. to Barrillon, May 17, 1686. Monograph by F. Puaux, " Les Plaintes des Protestants brulées par le bourreau à Londres." Bulletin de la Soc. de l'hist. du Prot. fr., xxxv. 463.

[2] Barrillon to Louis XIV., May 13, 1686. Ibid., xxxv. 464-466. See also Macaulay, History of England, ii. 81.

the French king against his Protestant subjects, without any refutation of any facts therein ; so mighty a power and ascend-

Claude's book burnt in London by the common hangman.

ant here had the French ambassador, who was doubt-less in great indignation at the pious and truly gener-ous charity of all the nation for the relief of those miserable sufferers who came over for shelter." [1] The pretext used was that Claude's book contained " expressions scandalous," as the ambassador said, " to his Majesty the King of France." [2]

Yet, despite Barrillon's opposition and the subserviency of James the Second, the Huguenots who came to England had little reason to regret the course they had taken.   Evelyn might, indeed, bewail the fact that, " though multitudes of all degree sought for shelter and welcome as distressed Christians, they found least encouragement, by a fatality of the times we were fallen into, and the uncharitable indifference of such as should

Liberality of the people.

have embraced them," and might pray that this inhos-pitality should not be laid to the charge of the English people.[3]   It still remained the fact that the people responded to the appeal contained in the king's Brief with a liberality that knew no bounds but those of their pecuniary ability.   The new collections supplemented the balance remaining from a similar contribution made five years earlier for the relief of French Protestant refugees.   " The fund thus created," says the historian of the Huguenot Emigration to America, " eventually reached the sum of a quarter of a million pounds sterling.   It was known as the Royal Bounty.   But never was there a greater misnomer. For neither of the kings under whose auspices it originated— Charles the Second and James the Second—had any sympathy with the movement, or compassion for the persons to be helped. The fund was the English People's Bounty; the magnificent testimonial of a nation's hospitality." [4]

It was said that fifty thousand Huguenots—but the number

---

[1] Evelyn, under date of May 5, 1686, ii. 264.

[2] Autobiography of Sir John Bramston (Camden Society Publ.), 228, who makes the date May 8 (Old Style).

[3] Evelyn, ii. 253.

[4] Charles W. Baird, History of the Huguenot Emigration to America, ii. 155.

is altogether uncertain—found a home in Great Britain,[1] where their descendants have long been recognized as among the most respected and most prosperous of the inhabitants of the kingdom.

A portion of the refugees made England only a temporary stopping-place, and ultimately pushed on to the colonies of North America. Here they were rejoined by no inconsiderable number of their fellow believers who had either voluntarily emigrated to the French West Indies before the Revocation, or had been deported since that time, and now made good their escape to a land of religious liberty. But the story of their adventures, deeply interesting as it is, does not fall within the scope of the present work, and, moreover, has already been well told.[2]

Emigration to America.

The question naturally presents itself here. At what number of souls must we estimate the loss of France through the emigration of the Huguenots, immediately preceding the Revocation of the Edict of Nantes, or in consequence of it? The answer to this inquiry is the more difficult because of the circumstance that the exodus extended over a long series of years, and because the proportion of the Huguenots that fled from the different provinces of the kingdom varied much, being doubtless dependent in a great measure upon the facilities afforded by the geographical situation of the regions inhabited by those who desired to escape from the dominions of Louis the Fourteenth. Where the natural obstacles were easily overcome, the emigration was most general and took place most rapidly. Almost the entire Protestant population of the Pays de Gex passed over to Geneva, as we have seen, and from Geneva made its way to other portions of Switzerland and to Germany. It was much after the same fashion at points upon the northern border from which, though not without the endurance of hardships, it was possible to attain a friendly shelter. A few months before the formal recall of the Edict of Nantes, the Huguenots of Sedan fled by hundreds before the barbarous

The number of the refugees.

---

[1] Mr. Poole estimates the number that settled in England, with Ireland and America, at probably 80,000. Huguenots of the Dispersion, 169.

[2] See Dr. Charles W. Baird's volumes just referred to, especially, i. 201-237 the chapter on The Antilles.

persecution, taking shelter in the wild woods of the Ardennes on their way to a more perfect place of security. But especially on the shores of the British Channel and on those of the ocean were the districts peopled by the Protestants depleted of a great part, if not the greater part, of their Huguenot inhabitants. In some cases we have definite figures to note the extent of the flight. The historian of the parliament of Normandy, who is usually both accurate and well-informed, affirms that one hundred and eighty-four thousand Protestants forsook that maritime province alone, leaving over twenty-six thousand houses vacant; and that Rouen, the capital, lost a quarter of its population, which diminished, in the course of a few years, from eighty to sixty thousand souls. Foreign trade wellnigh ceased, and the manufactures not only of Rouen itself, but of such thriving towns as Caen, Elbeuf, Louviers, Saint Lô, Alençon, and Bayeux languished, because the master workmen had emigrated and their skilled operatives had followed them in great crowds.[1]

If the loss of Normandy was so great, what must the loss have been for the whole of France? One of the most judicious and careful of contemporary investigators, M. N. Weiss, supposing the Huguenot population of France, at the epoch of the Revocation, to have numbered a million and a half souls, believes himself justified in the estimate that of these more than a half, or, at the very least, between five and six hundred thousand made their way to foreign lands.[2] Nor would such an estimate as one-half, large though it is, seem exaggerated as respects certain parts of France. For the twenty-two " elections " into which " generality " of Paris was divided, we have an official census made by the order of the Duke of Burgundy in 1697. From this we learn that of nineteen hundred and thirty-three Huguenot families formerly resident, twelve hundred and two had left France, and only seven hundred and thirty-one remained.[3] It was therefore with regard to the Protestants of Paris much as

---

[1] Floquet, Histoire du Parlement de Normandie. vi. 183, 184.

[2] N. Weiss, Introduction to La Sortie de France pour cause de religion de Daniel Brousson et de sa famille (Paris, 1885), pages vi. and vii.

[3] Mémoires des intendants sur l'état des généralités dressés pour l'instruction du duc de Bourgogne (Doc. inédits sur l'hist. de France), vol. i., on the generality of Paris, 151–154. " Du nombre des huguenots sortis et restés."

it was with regard to their brethren of Rouen, where, as we have seen, nearly if not quite two-thirds of the church of which Philip Legendre was one of the pastors, took refuge in the Netherlands and elsewhere.[1]

I shall not undertake a minute calculation, based upon the known losses of a considerable number of different towns, districts, and provinces. This has been done by Charles Weiss in his history of the French refugees.[2] From the particular figures for which I must refer the reader to his pages, it would seem that if we suppose the total number of fugitives to have been about four hundred thousand souls, we shall not be far out of the way.

It may indeed be that the true figures were considerably in excess of this number. Certainly, if there went one hundred and eighty-four thousand from Normandy alone, the contingent from Guyenne, from Languedoc, from Dauphiny and from all the rest of France must have much exceeded two hundred thousand more. Of the vast multitude perhaps one-third found their way to Switzerland and through Switzerland to Germany; another almost equal number settled in the Netherlands; while the remainder were scattered through the rest of Europe—one hundred thousand in Great Britain, Ireland, and the English colonies in America, with a smaller number in northern Europe and elsewhere.[3]

The countries whither they went were enriched by the arts and trades which the French refugees introduced, still more by the examples of industry, probity, and sincere piety which they

---

[1] See above, page 92.

[2] Histoire des Réfugiés protestants de France, i. 104–116.

[3] Reginald Lane Poole (Huguenots of the Dispersion, 168, 169), whose conclusions seem to me to be fair and dispassionate, in the desire to be clearly within the bounds of moderation, reduces the total to between 300,000 and 350,000. He assigns nearly 100,000 exiles to Holland, 80,000 to England, Ireland, and America, 25,000 to Switzerland, and 75,000 to Germany, including Brandenburg; but very properly observes in respect to this last number: "We might increase the figure by an inference from the local divisions of the emigrants. Erman and Reclam notice the almost exclusive direction of the Huguenots of Languedoc, Provence, and Dauphiné, to Switzerland and Germany: Mémoires, i. 239. And on any showing the [Protestant] religion was more powerful in the south and east than in the other quarters of France."

exhibited in their own persons. Hospitably entertained, as men and women that had suffered dangers, hardships, exile, in not a few cases the loss of all things in attestation of their faith, they amply repaid the hosts that befriended them by becoming citizens whose integrity was as conspicuous as their patriotism. For the most part, they left France confidently expecting that amends would soon be made for the wrong that had been done them, when once the persecutor should awake to the enormity of his crime. As months and years passed by and nothing occurred to their advantage, they did not abandon their delusive dream. "There is reason to hope," they said, "that the successor of Louis the Fourteenth will repair the breaches made in the Edict of Nantes, if Louis the Fourteenth does not himself repair them. Nothing but false glory and a blind zeal stand in the way."[1] But when this anticipation was dimmed by the lapse of time, they accepted the situation ordered by Providence, and identified their interests with the countries that adopted them as children when they were cast out and disinherited by the land of their nativity. "I fear greatly," wrote an eloquent pen at the close of a final appeal for justice, "I fear greatly that we may be talking to men that are deaf. So much the worse for them. As for ourselves, our determination was taken from the moment of our departure, and the land of refuge is not so hard to be endured by us, but that we shall be able to end our days there in quiet. It may be that our children will be still more happy therein, and that in this new country they will forget the fatherland that persecuted them. The latter will then perceive, but too late, the loss it has sustained."[2]

A certain number of men and women confined in the prisons and convents of France earned, by the firmness with which they rejected every attempt at proselytism, the reputation of being obstinately attached to the Protestant religion, and were therefore summarily thrust out of the kingdom as persons whom it was both troublesome and dangerous to detain any longer, lest they should by their words or example affect others in a

---

[1] Réponse à l'Avis aux Réfugiez (Rotterdam, 1709), 442.
[2] Ibid., 449. This work is ascribed to De Larrey, a writer of no mean merit.

similar way.[1] With the exception of these "stubborn heretics,"
it was only to a very few persons that Louis the Fourteenth
saw fit to accord the liberty of expatriation. This
liberty has generally been regarded as an inalienable
right. Louis granted it as a special favor. The old

Marquis of Ruvigny and his son, because of their services as diplomatists; Marshal Schomberg, for the victories he
had won for the French crown; Madame Hervart, in return for
the acknowledged worth and integrity of her late husband, the
controller general of finances, were of the number. Even here
the petty tyranny of the monarch clearly displayed itself.

Admiral Du Quesne, who had given to the French
flag a distinction upon the seas such as it had never
before attained, was denied the poor boon of going to
end his days in a land of religious liberty. The king, judging
the magnanimous Huguenot hero by the standard of himself or
of his favorite courtiers, feared lest Du Quesne might reveal to
strangers the secrets of the navy of France, and would only
permit him to remain, undisturbed by reason of his faith, in
the country he had served so well. Personal solicitations of
German allies of the king induced him to allow the Princess
of Taranto, daughter of the Landgrave of Hesse and widow of
Henry of La Trémouille, to return to her native land. The
Duke of Zell had influence enough to secure a similar permission for his brother-in-law, the Marquis d'Olbreuse, and his
wife, ancestors of Queen Victoria, of England. Where he could
not altogether refuse, Louis accompanied the concession with
conditions that took away, or were intended to take away, a
good part of its value. Esther Hervart, daughter of the
controller general of finances, was compelled to leave behind
some of her children, to be brought up in the Roman Catholic

---

[1] For example, Louis XIV. wrote to De Creil, Intendant of Orleans, February
27, 1688, that he was quite unable to tolerate any longer people "so obstinate
in their bad religion" as those of whom the latter had sent him a list, and
therefore directed them to be taken to the nearest point of the frontier and
dismissed from the kingdom. But, said he, they must not be allowed to carry
off their furniture or effects of any kind, for these effects he desired to have
seized. He wrote to the same effect, March 2, to De Mesnars, Intendant of
Paris, and, March 3, to Bossuet, Intendant of Soissons. Correspondance administrative sous le règne de Louis XIV., iv. 414. This was sheer robbery.

religion. Marshal Schomberg was suffered to take up his abode only in the kingdom of Portugal, where the Inquisition reigned. He watched his opportunity to escape to Protestant Germany, and after being welcomed by the Elector of Brandenburg, was reluctantly permitted by that great and enlightened prince to exchange his service for the service of William of Orange at a time critical for the fortunes of the Reformation and of constitutional liberty. The younger Henry of Ruvigny, created Earl of Galway by William the Third, and Marshal Schomberg incurred the special indignation and detestation of Louis and his court. The death of Schomberg, victorious at the Battle of the Boyne, almost reconciled Versailles to the defeat of its allies; and Madame de Sévigné's joy at his fall was only less exuberant than it might otherwise have been, because the first accounts of the engagement had falsely made, not Schomberg, but the Prince of Orange himself, to have lost his life in the great Protestant victory.[1]

Ruvigny and Schomberg.

If Schomberg was the most distinguished of the officers whom the cruel persecutions of Louis the Fourteenth drove into the service of his enemies, he was far from being the only one. Schomberg was allowed to expatriate himself; those who rejoined him on foreign soil came without the king's license. When Marshal Vauban, in 1689, sent to Louvois his celebrated paper advocating the recall of the Huguenots, he estimated, in enumerating the losses entailed by the Revocation, that the edict of October, 1685, had augmented the fleets of the enemies of France by eight or nine thousand of the best sailors of the kingdom, and their armies by five or six hundred officers and ten or twelve thousand soldiers far better trained in war than their own, as had been only too clearly seen on subsequent occasions when they were employed against the French troops.[2] Not to speak of the refugee,

Huguenot officers in the service of foreign states.

---

[1] See the chapter on "Les Protestants autorisés à sortir de France," in Douen, La Révocation de l'Édit de Nantes à Paris, ii. 414–427.

[2] "Pour le Rappel des Huguenots." This document is marked on the margin: "Fait et envoyé à feu M. de Louvois au mois d'Oct. 1689." Louvois died in 1691. After Louvois's death the marshal again handed in his mémoire, with additions, in 1692. See the text in Bulletin de la Soc. de l'hist. du Prot. fr., xxxviii. (1889) 194–209, with the remarks of M. Charles Read.

officers in the Prince of Orange's regiments of infantry, we have the names of fifty-four French Protestants that served in the two regiments of dragoons, the "reds" and the "blues."[1] Attached to a single petition presented to their High Mightinesses the States General, on the fourteenth of July, 1688, may still be read the names of one hundred and seventy-one persons lately holding commissions in the army and navy of the king of France, who "had forsaken their property and their places, in order to retain their holy religion and to offer up their lives and fortunes in the service of this (Dutch) State." They were fresh arrivals, having come since their brethren whom the hospitable Netherlands had seen fit to admit to their service. Some had been in Holland a year, others eight or ten months, but had used up their slender resources and were destitute of all things. "Most of the last comers in fact," said they, "are confessors that have escaped from the prisons, and are absolutely unable to subsist, unless your High Mightinesses have the goodness to relieve our extreme need by treating us with the same charity that you exhibited to the other officers who arrived before us for the same reason; of which there shall be everlasting remembrance."[2]

A petition to the States General of the Netherlands.

It has been well said that it would be hard to overstate the importance of the French contingent in the Prince of Orange's little army of fifteen thousand men, a contingent of which both officers and privates had been trained in that best contemporary school of the military art, the ceaseless warfare provoked by Louis's ambition.[3] At the same time, many Huguenot officers took refuge in Brandenburg, and, from that period until the present, the fugitives from religious persecution in France have been well represented in the Prussian army. It was remarked, a few years since, that of the distinguished staff officers of the German army that invaded France in 1870, a considerable number—some said not less than eighty—were

A revenge of history.

---

[1] Dumont de Bostaquet, who was one of the captains, not only makes the statement in his Mémoires, p. 195, but gives the list: "Noms des officiers qui ont passé en Angleterre," etc. Ibid., 341, 342.

[2] Requête adressée aux États Généraux des Pays-Bas, 14 juillet, 1688. Bulletin de la Soc. de l'hist. du Prot. fr., xxxvi. (1887) 197-203.

[3] R. L. Poole, The Huguenots of the Dispersion, 103.

descendants from Protestant families that fled from France for religion's sake at the Revocation of the Edict of Nantes.[1]

There were results of the fatal decree of Louis the Fourteenth which the distant future alone could reveal. Contemporaries could make a shrewd guess respecting them, but had no certain knowledge. The nearer effects, however, were patent even to men of that generation. The Duke of Saint Simon was a boy of ten years when Louis signed the edict at Fontainebleau. He lived to see and to record what he saw of the mischievous fruits of the recall in a well-known passage, which I shall quote because it is perhaps the most fearless and out-spoken condemnation uttered in that age by a Roman Catholic and a courtier :

"The Revocation of the Edict of Nantes, without the slightest pretext or the least necessity, as well as the various declarations, or rather proscriptions, that followed, were the fruits of that horrible plot which depopulated a fourth part of the kingdom, ruined its trade, enfeebled it in every quarter, gave it over for so long a time to open and avowed pillage at the hands of the dragoons, and authorized those torments and sufferings by means of which they actually compassed the death of so many thousands of innocent persons of both sexes—a plot that brought ruin on so great a body of people, that tore asunder countless families, arraying relatives against relatives, for the purpose of getting possession of their goods, whereupon they left them to die of hunger—a plot that caused our manufactures to pass over to foreigners, made foreign states flourish and overflow with wealth at the expense of our own, and enabled them to build new cities—that presented to the nations the spectacle of so vast a multitude of people that had committed no crime, proscribed, naked, wandering fugitives, seeking an asylum afar from their country—that consigned the noble, the wealthy, the aged, those highly esteemed, in many cases, for their piety, their learning, their virtue, those accustomed to a life of ease, frail, delicate, to hard labor in the galleys, under the overseer's lash, and for no reason save their religion—a plot that, to crown all other horrors, filled every province of the kingdom with perjury and sacrilege ; inasmuch as while the land rang with the

---

[1] The statement is attributed to Jules Simon, for a time premier of France.

cries of these unhappy victims of error, so many others sacrificed their consciences for their property and their ease, purchasing both by means of feigned abjurations; abjurations from
which they were dragged, without a moment's interval, to adore
what they did not believe in, and to receive what was really the
divine body of the Most Holy One, while they still remained
convinced that they were eating nothing but bread, bread indeed which they were bound to abhor.   Such was the general
abomination begotten of flattery and cruelty.   Between torture
and abjuration, between abjuration and the Communion, there
was often not an interval of twenty-four hours, and their tort-
urers were their conductors and their witnesses.   Those who
subsequently seemed to have made the change with greater
deliberation, were not slow in giving the lie to their pretended
conversions, by the tenor of their lives or by flight." [1]

---

[1] Mémoires du Duc de Saint Simon (Paris, 1853), **xxiv.** 181, 182. This passage
has been given by my brother in his Huguenot Emigration to America, i. 259-
261. I have followed his translation for the most part.

CHAPTER XIII

THE EFFORT TO MAKE FRANCE ALL CATHOLIC

If, leaving the consideration of the great exodus of Huguenots from France consequent upon the Revocation, we revert
once more to the condition of the country from which the refugees made good their escape, we shall find the minds of the
monarch and his obsequious ministers, for the remaining years
of the century, to have been singularly absorbed by an attempt
to solve two problems. The first of these was, How to make
good the truth of the king's position in the edict of recall, by
compelling all his subjects to embrace the religion which he
prescribed. The second and equally important problem was,
How to compel the New Converts to remain converted.

I need not dwell at further length upon the story of the
Dragonnades, much as the repeated perusal of the detailed accounts of individual experiences at the hands of brutal soldiers
and not less brutal officers, perpetrating the most extreme violence to person and property, may make one realize that the
effort to describe such outrages in general terms must necessarily fail to convey even an approximate notion of their horror.
For the situation of defenceless men and of tender and shrink-
ing women and children when a horde of unprincipled and
rapacious troopers are let loose upon them and are quartered in
their houses, not so much with the distinct understanding, as
with the express commission, to do to them and to their property almost every conceivable form of damage, is a situation too
atrocious for words. It baffles description. The imagination
of the reader must supply the inadequacy of words to do it even
approximate justice.

But with regard to the extent to which the Dragonnades prevailed throughout France, one additional remark must be made:
there seems to have been no part of the country peopled

by Protestants in any considerable numbers that was a stranger to the demoniac device to secure religious uniformity. It
Paris not exempted from the Dragonnades. would, indeed, have been a strange thing if, amid the
general harrying of Huguenots, those of the capital
had been exempted. Yet this is what has been commonly reported and what Voltaire distinctly asserts. "Paris,"
he says, "was not exposed to these vexations ; the outcries
Voltaire's mistake. would have made themselves heard by the throne from
too close at hand. Men were quite willing to make
unfortunates, but they were pained by hearing the clamors of
those unfortunates."[1] Nor does the usually accurate Henri
Martin hesitate to say the same thing, and to give satisfactory
reasons for the indulgence extended to the Huguenots of the
capital. "Louvois dared not show such sights to the society of
Versailles and Paris; the king could not have endured them."[2]
Yet Jean Claude, in his *Plaintes*, than whom no one was better
qualified to speak, had expressly informed us that Paris was not
treated with more consideration than the rest of the realm.[3]
The office which elsewhere the intendant of the province performed, was discharged by a secretary of state, and Seignelay
himself was not ashamed to gather in his own house, by sum-
The Hugue-not mer-chants and secretary Seignelay. mons, a crowd of the most notable Huguenot merchants of the capital, before whom was laid a paper
containing a profession of the Roman Catholic faith
and a rejection of all the heresies and erroneous opinions condemned by Rome. When the merchants demurred and
declined to subscribe, the doors were closed and the Huguenots
were bluntly informed that they would not be permitted to
leave the room until they had signed the document.[4] It was a

---

[1] " Paris ne fut point exposé à ces vexations ; les cris se seraient fait entendre
au trône de trop près. On veut bien faire des malheureux, mais on souffre d'entendre leurs clameurs." Siècle de Louis XIV., c. xxxvi. Œuvres complètes de
Voltaire (Paris, 1832), xxvii. 108.

[2] Histoire de France (Paris, 1850), xvi. 67. How far he is mistaken in his
assertion that there were no striking acts of violence, and that the last article of
the revocatory edict was pretty nearly observed in Paris and its vicinity, will be
seen below.

[3] " 'Paris,' dis-je, 'n'a pas été plus ménagé que le reste du Royaume.' "
Plaintes (ed. Puaux) 99.

[4] This was on the 14th of December, 1685. Claude refers briefly to the mat-

contemptible trick, which, despite the long weeks spent in con-
certing it, met only with mediocre success. If, out of some
three hundred merchants whom Seignelay had endeavored to
get together, sixty-three were induced under threats of duress
to place their names at the bottom of the mongrel paper laid
before them, purporting to be a promise to abjure and a profession of faith at one and the same time, it was plain that not
even this small number believed the engagement to be binding
upon their consciences. Few, if any, were prompt in fulfilling
a forced and distasteful promise. Some were arrested as they
were making their way abroad. Others were successful. Of
this number were the banker Moïse Cousin, Testard, Bouxin,
who found a shelter in England, with all his family excepting one
daughter, and Vernezobre, who reaching Brandenburg founded
a manufactory of ribbons in that hospitable land. It was at
the house of the banker Haran, who seems to have succumbed
on this occasion, that secret Protestant meetings were held,
twelve years later, in Louis the Fourteenth's very capital.[1]

In the provinces the intendant's labors with the notables were
accompanied or immediately followed by the appearance of the
dragoons; in Paris, his Majesty's natural reluctance to bring
these in any sooner than might be necessary, led him first to
authorize the employment in their stead of such police officers
as the city could itself afford. One week after the meeting in
the mansion of Seignelay, that minister was already directing
Harlay to quarter upon the houses of the Protestants of Paris
Archers used
at first in-
stead of
dragoons. — he still deigned to style them "those of the Pretended Reformed religion " — "the sergeants of the
Châtelet, the archers of the prévôt de l'Ile, of the *lieutenant criminel de robe courte* and of the watch." He bade him
place in each house just as many of these as he might deem
best. "I think," he added, "that we must at one stroke make
a great movement throughout Paris, and give the burgesses of
the Religion to understand that, while waiting for the troops,

---

ter (ubi supra, 101), and Douen, in the chapter of his great work on the Revocation at Paris entitled "La journée du 14 décembre 1685," ii. 155-186, has discussed in an interesting manner the preparations made for the meeting and the
paltry results.

[1] O. Douen, La Révocation de l'Édit de Nantes à Paris (Paris, 1894), ii. 178.

his Majesty will make use of these archers, and try by this means to derive the same advantage that is derived in the provinces from the use of the troops."[1] What the meaning of this language was, it would be hard to say, unless it meant that the violent treatment of the Huguenots by the archers enjoying the greatest license should prove as effectual as that practised by the dragoons of Foucauld and Marillac and Saint Ruth. Scarcely had twenty-four hours more passed, when, the king being apparently annoyed that from the lists submitted to him it appeared that only one-quarter of the Parisian Protestants had hitherto been induced to abjure,[2] Seignelay requested the lieutenant of police to act with greater harshness than heretofore against those that remained, in order that when his majesty should adopt the resolution to expel them from Paris, this should apply to only a small number."[3] In point of fact, however, while such of the wealthy Parisian Protestants as had country seats seem to have been compelled to go thither that they might more conveniently be "dragooned" there,[4] as in a less conspicuous place, before many weeks the troops were brought into Paris itself, the king being determined to make short work of the recalcitrants.[5] This was the first week of the new year, and the dragonnade lasted until about the middle of February, being doubtless characterized, both within the city and in its environs, by the same compulsory watches, by the same obscenities, by the same insults to women, in short, by the same means of conversion that were practised elsewhere.[6] Not but that there was a chance for the display of that exquisite politeness upon which the elegant Frenchman of the age of Louis the Fourteenth prided himself. As when, in a letter that

---

[1] " Sa Majesté ne voulant point se résoudre à faire venir des troupes à Paris, ni à se servir des soldats du régiment des gardes pour mettre chez ceux de la R. P. R., elle m'a ordonné ce matin de vous dire qu'elle croyait qu'on pourrait faire le même effet par les sergents du Châtelet," etc. Seignelay to Harlay, December 21, 1685, MSS. Nat. Lib., in Douen, ubi supra, ii. 197.

[2] Only 1,230, as against 3,823 that had not abjured.

[3] Letter of Seignelay, December 22, 1685, ibid., ii. 198.

[4] Douen, ubi supra, ii. 198, 199.

[5] Extracts from the Gazette de Hollande, dated Paris, January 8, 1686, in Bulletin de la Soc. de l'hist. du Prot. fr., xxix (1880) 402.

[6] Douen, ubi supra, ii. 202.

has come down to us, Monsieur D'Artaignan in command of the king's ministers of destruction, implored the rich banker Sam-
Politeness of uel Bernard to spare him the necessity of fulfilling his
D'Artaignan. commission to lay waste a fine residence in the environs. "I am very sorry, Sir," he wrote, "to be obliged to place troops in your house of Chennevières. I beg you at once to forestall the consequences by making yourself an apostolic Roman Catholic, without which I have orders to permit my soldiers to live there at free quarters; and when nothing remains, the house will run a great risk. I am in despair, Sir, to be intrusted with such a commission, and, above all, that this should fall on a person like you. Permit me, therefore, to beg you to seek the remedy; for there is none other than that you send me the abjuration of yourself and of all your family. . . and believe me Sir, your humble and very obedient servant, Artaignan." [1]

The Dragonnades, however, whether in the capital or elsewhere throughout France, might perhaps be esteemed the most
Treatment of tolerable of the inflictions to which the Huguenots
"obstinate" were subjected. For those that stood firm under this
Huguenots. form of persecution, for those who, in the phraseology of the day, stubbornly refused to comply with the king's commands, imprisonment was reserved. It was reserved for those also who, having professedly abjured, showed themselves only imperfectly converted, refused to attend mass or went there with great irregularity, in short, made no secret of the insincerity of the profession to which they had been forced. Protestant parents whom it was not deemed convenient to arrest, saw themselves compelled to resign their children. A letter of

---

[1] Bulletin de la Soc. de l'hist. du Prot. fr., v. 50, 51; Douen, ubi supra, ii. 205. It so happened that the great financier, destined to continue to the end of his days a warm friend of the Protestants, had been compelled to abjure fully a fortnight before this letter was written, but the elegant major of the guards did not know the fact until Chennevières had been pretty thoroughly ransacked and plundered. For the great quantity of wine sold or drunk, for the furniture stolen or broken, for the linen purloined, and for a variety of injury to furniture and place stated in curious detail, the banker petitioned the monarch for redress, and being so important a personage in a court that needed all the pecuniary accommodation it could get, he readily obtained it. The memorandum to the amount of 10,016 livres damages is given by Douen, ii. 207.

the king directed to the intendant of Paris (on the second of May, 1686), bade him notify all such that they must send their children to the parish schools there to be catechized, it being his Majesty's intention, in case of non-compliance, to have the boys placed in colleges, the girls in the convents, where they were to be kept at the expense of their parents.[1]

The reader of our times, familiar only with the structures which a more humane and enlightened age has erected for the The prisons. detention of criminals, can form little conception of the sombre and repulsive buildings in which, two centuries ago, it was not deemed strange nor unjust to incarcerate those unfortunates upon whom society had laid its hand. But the foulness of the dungeons which these prisons contained and concealed from public view, subterranean, dark even at noonday, reeking with filth of every description—pestilential abysses whose air bred disease and death—this and much more I cannot describe in these pages. It must be learned in those narratives that have fortunately come down to us in considerable numbers written by the sufferers themselves, or in the indignant, but scarcely exaggerated, diatribes of Michelet.[2]

For the most part the " obstinate " Huguenot women were consigned either to the so-called " Houses of the New Catholics " Houses of the or to the convents. In the case of those women who "Nouvelles Catholiques" had been arrested while making an ineffectual attempt and convents. to fly from the kingdom, the judicial sentence that committed them contained the provision, that their hair should be shaved, and that they should be immured for the remainder of their days in such places as the judge saw fit, their goods being confiscated for his Majesty's advantage.[3] To be intrusted to the care of the nuns, women devoted, by their voluntary act, to a life of religion and charity, might seem, apart from the loss of personal freedom, likely to entail little annoy-

---

[1] Lettre du Roy écrite à Monsieur l'intendant de la généralité de Paris (M. de Mesnars) du 2 mai 1686. Édits, Déclarations et Arrests, 285.

[2] In his " Louis XIV. et la Révocation." See also Douen who, in his " Révocation de l'Édit de Nantes à Paris " has made use of Michelet and has added much from original sources.

[3] " Confisquez à nôtre profit." Declaration of May 7, 1686. Édits, Déclarations et Arrests, 286.

ance and hardship.   The facts prove the contrary, and place it
beyond a doubt that, for pitiless and unrelenting persecution, the convents fell little short of even the public prisons, if
indeed they did not surpass them.   Claude Brousson, the future martyr, did not express himself too strongly, when, in his
" First Letter to the Roman Catholics, containing very humble
remonstrances respecting the great ills which the Protestants
are made to suffer in the States where the Roman Catholic religion is dominant," he says : " The women and girls who are
pious are shut up in convents, in which, for the most part, ignorant and furious nuns regard it as a merit to torment them incessantly." [1] If any one incline to regard with suspicion the
statement of the Huguenot, gentle and fair though he always
was, the testimony of Madame de Maintenon cannot be rejected for prejudice, who in the earliest of her extant letters, to
which I have made reference on a preceding page, described to
her aunt the " life worse than death " which she led in the house
of the Ursulines of the faubourg Saint Jacques, while the nuns
were striving to convert her to their religion.   The " so-called
house of God " had become a very " hell," by reason of " the
ill-treatment, the harshness, and the cruel actions of the women
who had been constituted the guardians of her body ; " her soul,
she said, they could not reach.[2]   With such testimony before
us, and the reproof which Bossuet, Bishop of Meaux, was
obliged to administer to the nuns of La Ferté sous Jouarre, in
his own diocese, who used to gag the little Protestant girls intrusted to their care,[3] we should be unreasonably sceptical, did
we refuse to credit the stories that come to us from purely Huguenot sources.[4]

---

[1] Brousson's Lettres aux catholiques romains were published " Au Désert,"
1687. The book having become very scarce, some extracts, including the first
letter entire, have been reprinted in the Bulletin de la Soc. de l'hist. du Prot.
fr., xxxiv. (1884) 428 et seq.

[2] Françoise d'Aubigné to Madame de Villette, Paris, October 12, (1649) ; Geffroy : Lettres de Madame de Maintenon, i. 4. See above, p. 16.

[3] Bossuet to Madame de Tanqueux, the lady superior, November 3, 1687, in
Œuvres de Bossuet (Versailles, 1818), xxxix. 654.

[4] E. g., the indecent flogging in the presence of the major of the regiment of
Vivonne and of the city judge, to which the superiors of the house of the " Nouvelles Converties " or the " Sœurs de la Propagation " of Uzès, subjected eight

It was the lot of Blanche Gamond, who has left us an auto-biography of rare truth to nature and pathos, to be transferred from the dungeons of Grenoble, where she had made a steadfast profession of her faith, to the Hospital General of Valence. The governor of the institution was Herapine, better known as La Rapine, an intimate friend of Cosnac, the bishop of the place, with whose fiery zeal for the destruction of Protestantism in France his fervid addresses in the assemblies of the clergy and before the king have made us acquainted. Less cultivated than the prelate, La Rapine was equally ardent and far more practical in his methods. Of the women that were so luckless as to fall into his clutches, none escaped the marks of his mad fury, before which few failed to succumb. He had but one object : to bring his prisoners to abjure ; but a single means of persuasion : corporal chastisement. When, on the evening of her arrival, Blanche declined to go to the chapel to attend La Rapine's prayers, three or four of the women in waiting dragged her before sister Marie, under whose direction, with many a blow and kick, she was forced, crying and resisting, into the hallowed precincts. " Beggar, dog of a Huguenot, you will not go to church ! " said the nun. This was but a hint of what was still to come. The next day Blanche and her companions were brought into the presence of the terrible governor himself and warned of what they might expect. " You are stubborn, rebels against the king and against God ; but you will have to change, or you will die under the blows. I shall bring you over, cursed race of vipers, by means of floggings. For I know my business by rote. I am fifty-six years old. I shall make you obey, knaves, better than any other man in the kingdom. The hospital is not made for you ; but you are here to obey the orders of the hospital, and this is the command of my lord the Bishop of Valence. You shall be the filth and the offscouring of the hospital. You shall sweep from morning till night, and, if you fail, you shall have a hundred blows with

Marginal notes: The Hospital General of Valence. — Herapine or La Rapine. — His address to the Huguenot women.

---

or ten young girls between sixteen and twenty-three years of age, who did not seem to them sufficiently well converted. Benoist, Hist. de l'Édit de Nantes, v. 893, whose account does not differ essentially from that given in the Pele document, Bulletin de la Soc. de l'hist. du Prot. fr., xi. 389.

a stick. After that I shall see that you are thrust into a dungeon where I shall make you die of hunger. But in order that you may linger the more, you will have a little bread and water, and it is impossible that you should be able to stand the blows you shall receive. In the end you will be dead in thirty or forty days at most ; we know it, for we have tried the experiment. After all that, you will be cast into the common sewer ; the king will be rid of a bad subject. There will be a dead dog, wretched in this life, damned in the next. You may count upon it, dogs, beggars ; that is your portion." La Rapine's acts were as brutal as his words. It was through no fault of his that his sinister prophecy failed of complete fulfilment. The girls of the hospital were his faithful executioners, at whose hands Blanche Gamond received such scourgings as I hesitate to describe. She endured them with the patience of a martyr, rejoicing that by her pain she might be made conformable to the sufferings of the Lord Jesus Christ.[1]

Treatment of Blanche Gamond.

Blanche was but one of the many victims upon whom La Rapine vented a fury that seemed to know no bounds. Yet even the monster was amazed at the fortitude displayed by some of the women of rank and gentle birth whom the Parliament of Dauphiny turned over to him to " convert." " Mademoiselle," he said to one—a De la Farelle—" I am astonished that you should be able to endure so many hardships." " I suffer nothing, it is nothing ; Jesus Christ suffered much more for me," she stoutly replied. None the less did the pitiless jailer labor on at his congenial task, devising new and strange methods, now taking a cane into his own hands and beating the defenceless ladies upon the back, upon the arms, upon the face, until they could neither put one foot before the other, nor carry their hands to their mouth, nor move an arm ; and presently varying the wretchedness of their lot by plunging them, several times a day,

---

[1] Le Récit des persécutions que Blanche Gamond, de Saint-Paul-Trois-Châteaux, en Dauphiné, agée d'environ 21 ans, a enduré pour la querelle de l'Évangile, ayant dans icelles surmonté touttes tentations par la grâce et providence de Dieu. First printed from MS. in the Bulletin de la Soc. de l'hist. du Prot. fr., xvi. (1867), with an introduction by the late Théodore Claparède, 366–416, 431–464, and 481–521.

in a pit of mud and fetid water, from which he drew them out only when they had lost consciousness.[1]

There were other conventual houses and prisons that rivalled, if they could not surpass, the infamy and horror in which was held the Hospital General of Valence. The most noted was the Tour de Constance, at Aigues Mortes.

About a score of miles south of the flourishing city of Nismes stretches a low and uninviting tract of land, broken up by extensive pools and marshes, and intersected by sluggish streams and canals. Another such desolate region, another such insalubrious neighborhood it would be hard to find in France.

Aigues Mortes. Aigues Mortes, the only inhabited place above the rank of a hamlet, scarcely deserves the name of a town ; for its population is but four thousand persons, whose sole dependence for a livelihood is upon fishing and the preparation of salt on the adjacent flat and pestilential meadows. The soil occupied is evidently alluvial matter brought down, ages since, from the sides of the Swiss Alps or the nearer vine-clad hills of the Côte d'Or ; for the edge of the delta of the Rhône extended, at one time, to this point. But the capricious river, having long since diverted its stream into other channels, now seeks the Mediterranean much to the east of Aigues Mortes. The name of the town distinctly points to the change that has taken place ; and Aigues Mortes, or *eaux mortes* (*aquæ mortuæ*), is no inappropriate designation of a spot from which the waters have retired, save as they remain in the form of stagnant lagoons, taking with them the very life of the community.

Yet Aigues Mortes boasts an ancient origin and a curious history. It was on the seashore, some three miles distant, that lay the fleet of Louis the Ninth, or Saint Louis, in the year 1248, when that prince undertook to execute a vow made during his illness, and to lead another crusade for the recovery of the Holy Land from the infidel. Modern investigation has disproved the notion, once generally held, that the walls of Aigues Mortes were even then washed by the waves of the sea ; but it was at

---

[1] A contemporary account entitled Cruautés exercées à Valence par La Rapine, gardien de l'hôpital, in Bulletin de la Soc. de l'hist. du Prot. franç., xi. (1862) 387.

the foot of those walls that the adventurous monarch, embarking in a small boat, made his way without difficulty through the narrow channel, since neglected and now choked with rubbish, to his principal vessel. The massive fortifications that greet the traveller's eye—a great rectangle provided with fifteen towers, some square, others round—were built, or completed, by Louis's eldest son, known in history as Philip the Bold. He thus carried into effect his father's purpose to make of the only convenient port which he possessed on the southern edge of his kingdom a well protected haven. By far the most striking portion of the work is a great circular structure standing out at one of the angles, and by comparison dwarfing all the rest. Constructed by Louis the Ninth himself, it has, perhaps from the date of its erection, borne the name, strangely appropriate to its destination, of *La Tour de Constance.*[1]

During the last quarter of the seventeenth century and throughout the greater part of the eighteenth, this historic pile, sombre and forbidding, served as the prison to which, in preference to all others in the southern part of France, were consigned such of the Huguenots as it was desired to immure with little hope of ultimate release, with no hope of escape by flight. Nearly ninety feet in height and sixty-six in diameter, its sides are fully eighteen thick. The interior consists of two great circular and vaulted chambers, placed the one over the other. The only light that straggles into the lower enters through a few high and narrow loop-holes and from a round aperture in the ceiling, the only direct communication between the chambers. The upper, in like manner, has a corresponding opening toward the terrace above, through which the rain pours in inclement weather.[2] More famous after it became, early in the eighteenth century, the sole abode

The Tour de Constance.

---

[1] See the interesting account of Aigues Mortes, its environs and its history, in Frossard, ubi infra, ii. 207-221.

[2] E. Hugues has an excellent heliogravure of the Tour de Constance in the third volume of Les Synodes du Désert, which Mr. Tylor has reproduced in his book, The Camisards. E. B. D. Frossard, in his Tableau pittoresque, scientifique et moral de Nismes et de ses environs, à vingt lieues à la ronde (Nismes, 1834-1838), has pen and ink sketches of the fortifications of Aigues Mortes, and an interior view of the lower chamber of the tower. I have followed the figures which he gives of the dimensions (ii. 215).

of Huguenot women imprisoned for their faith, I shall have more particular reason to refer to the Tour de Constance in connection with the fortunes of the churches of the Desert. Meantime, it was no less dreaded than the Bastile of Paris. An escape from its walls seemed impossible but by a miracle; and Abraham Mazel, who has left on record the story of his flight with sixteen companions, very naturally ascribes the plan to supernatural inspiration. "The wall was thick," he says. "We were on the second story a hundred feet above the ground. I had no tools. There were thirty-three other prisoners with me in the same room. All these men were to be gained over and found faithful, or we might be accused by some one of them. We must have ropes to let ourselves down. When we were down, there were high walls to scale, sentinels to avoid, great marshes full of water to traverse; and, after all that, we knew not where to get bread nor where to find shelter. But with God's help I surmounted all these obstacles after seven or eight months of work. Sixteen of my companions followed me; courage failed the other seventeen." [1]

The unsuccessful attempt to flee from the kingdom, which in the case of Huguenot women, was punished by condemnation to incarceration in the convents for life, had for its penalty, in the case of Huguenot men, with equal uniformity, life-long service in the royal galleys. What these galleys were, and what the service of a galley slave imported, are questions that require a few words of explanation, in view of the entire change which warfare upon such seas as the Mediterranean has undergone.

Service in the galleys.

The galley had come down from antiquity, and had, as yet, lost little of its former importance as an effective and formidable engine of war. Upon the more quiet waters of an inland sea, and even on the coasts of the ocean during the fair season, a vessel rapidly propelled by a multitude of oars had a signal advantage over a ship wholly dependent on variable winds. While the latter might be becalmed on a glassy sea, unable either to advance or retreat, powerless even to veer so as to re-

---

[1] Théâtre des Cévennes (ed. of A. Bost), 85. The incident occurred July 27, 1705. Sagnier, La Tour de Constance et ses prisonnières, 12.

ceive the shock of the enemy's attack with the least damage, the former was alert and agile, instantly obeying the word of command. The galley's onset was resistless when dashing upon the broadside of the enemy's ship. When once its deadly fire had been delivered, the galley drew off as promptly as it had approached. Vessels of a far superior size were not secure against attack. A bevy of galleys would not infrequently gather about some great hulk of a ship, as a great number of dogs about a more powerful animal left to contend alone against their separate and distracting assaults. Then, by their united efforts, the marines upon the different galleys would clear the decks of the common enemy, or, coming to close quarters, would grapple with and board the vessel, swarming over its bulwarks and speedily overpowering resistance.

The motion of the galley had all the precision and almost the speed of the steamship of the present day. Each galley was furnished with three hundred slaves for rowers, their hands upon the oars, their bodies securely chained to their places, which they left neither by day nor by night, seeming to be a part of the vessel to which they stood in lieu of machinery. At a signal from the officer in charge, the entire mechanism was set in motion; at another signal it instantly ceased to move.[1]

The king's purpose was to have a large fleet of galleys always in commission.[2] Consequently, he must at all times have a cor-

---

[1] Marteilhe, of whom I shall soon have occasion to speak, appends to his Mémoires a "description of an armed galley and its construction." The galley was generally one hundred and fifty feet long and forty feet broad. It was provided with fifty benches, twenty-five on either side of the *coursier*, or passage-way that ran from the prow to the stern of the boat. Each seat was ten feet long and six rowers were chained to it. Each oar was fifty feet long, about thirteen feet being within the *aposti*, or beam, that formed the rim of the galley. This being the thicker end, weighed as much as the remaining thirty-seven feet. As it was too stout to be grasped, there were wooden handles (*anses* or *manilles*) nailed to the oar for each of the six rowers to hold. Mémoires d'un Protestant condamné aux Galères de France pour cause de Religion (Paris ed. of 1865), 435.

[2] Bion in the preface to his Account of the Torments which the French Protestants Endure Aboard the Galleys (London, 1712), states that there were in his time twenty-four galleys at Marseilles and six upon the ocean. According to Bonnemère (p. 99), Colbert, at an earlier date, wanted the king to have a force of one hundred galleys. This would have required thirty thousand galley slaves.

respondingly large force to man them. But how could the oars-
men be obtained? It would have been idle to call for volunteers
How the gal- to enlist in a service unsurpassed for hardship and se-
ley slaves   verity. No sane man would elect a branch of the ser-
were re-
cruited.   vice in which any inattention to orders, any flagging of
exertion, any murmur even was instantly punished with the pitiless lash laid by the " comite," or overseer, upon the bare shoulders and back of the rower. Captives taken in war against the
Turk furnished a certain number of candidates for the rower's
bench ; but the source was inadequate and variable. The main
supply must of necessity be derived from the ranks of the men
imprisoned for some breach of the laws of the realm.[1] Legislation had therefore been artfully contrived to meet the king's
exigencies. Condemnation to the galleys was made the legal,
but disproportionate, penalty for a great variety of offences, not
a few of these offences being of the most trivial character.
There were judges that gloried in sending men to the galleys
for the simple crime of being vagabonds. Arnoul, intendant of
the galleys at Marseilles, boasts, in an extant letter, that he has
condemned to the galleys five men that happen to have fallen
into his hands, respecting whom he knows nothing except that
the people of a certain district have told him that these vagrants
do nothing else than hang around the village " perhaps, for I do
not know anything concerning the matter," he says, " watching
for an opportunity to steal." [2]

    In view of the severity of the penal laws, the supply of gal-
ley slaves might have been expected to be amply sufficient to
meet the demand. It would have been sufficient, we are told,

---

[1] Bion conveniently divides the galley slaves into five classes : First, Turks,
captives bought with money, strong in body, and the least unfortunate of the
crew, not being chained but wearing only a ring on the foot as a badge of slavery,
permitted when in port to trade and often accumulating and sending to their
families considerable sums of money. Second, " Faux-sauniers," or persons convicted of some violation of the unjust and vexatious regulations respecting the
sale of salt. Third, Deserters. Fourth, Highwaymen and other felons. Fifth,
Protestants. Ubi supra, 17, et seq. A Turk generally sat at the head of each
rower's bench, and, on account of his superior strength, pulled at the end of the
oar. The fact of his greater liberty made it possible for him to discharge the
kind offices for the Huguenot galley slaves which I shall refer to farther on.
[2] Bonnemère, Les Dragonnades. Histoire des Camisards, 99.

had not the officers of the crown, in their anxiety to spare themselves all possible trouble and expense, been culpably negligent
in the prosecution and punishment of criminals.[1] To remedy
this crying "abuse,"[2] Louis the Fourteenth did not cease to exhort the judges of his courts to sentence to the galleys
as many as possible of the culprits brought to the bar,
commuting the death penalty as often as possible into
the more profitable penalty of serving the king on the rower's
bench. Intendants and others were not slow in discovering
what intelligence would be most gratifying for his Majesty to
hear, and made the most of their opportunities. " I have a fine
convict," wrote Chevalier de Gout from Orange, " whom I have
had condemned by the parliament here. I shall send him to
Toulon, and if I succeed in catching in addition two Huguenots
who acted insolently at the time of the procession on Corpus
Christi day, I shall send them to keep company with him." At
another time Colbert himself wrote : " It is a piece of good news
for his Majesty that there are thirty good men for the galleys
(*forçats*) in the *conciergerie* of Rennes."[3]

Anxiety of Louis XIV. to obtain rowers.

It was, doubtless, in part with a view to the advantage of obtaining additions to the ranks of his rowers, that Louis the
Fourteenth made the galleys the penalty for so many offences
of a religious character, and that he encouraged, if he did not
positively enjoin, the practice of sending to the galleys for life,

---

[1] Jean Marteilhe was found innocent of the crime of seeking to leave the
kingdom, and was on the point of being set at liberty. A letter was received
from the Marquis de la Vrillière containing the king's order to condemn him to
the galleys. The judges complied with the order and in their sentence falsely
declared him " attainted and convicted." Mémoires, 103, 104.

[2] This is not the most singular application of the word *abuse* in the legislation
of Louis XIV. About the year 1694, the tailors began to make *buttons* out of the
same material as the coats on which these were sewed. Heretofore the buttons had
been mostly of *silk*, and there had been a great consumption of this substance,
giving employment to many persons, especially in Languedoc. To check this
novelty, *this abuse*, as he termed it, Louis XIV. issued a Declaration, September
25, 1694, fining the tailor who should put a button of the same material upon a
coat five hundred livres, to be equally divided between the informer, the hospitals and his majesty ; and the wearer of the garment three hundred livres, of
which half was to go to the hospitals and the other half to the king. Isambert,
Anciennes lois françaises, xx. 227.

[3] Bonnemère, 104, 105. This refers to the years 1661–1666, in particular.

mere lads of fifteen or sixteen, or even, apparently, of barely twelve years of age, for so innocent an action as accompanying their parents to a Huguenot place of worship.[1]

If anything more were needed to exhibit clearly the spirit of utter and shameless injustice that permeated the entire administration of the government of France, under the monarch who wished to be regarded as the embodiment of every high and godlike virtue, it might be found in the fact that Louis the

Fourteenth systematically detained in the galleys

Galley slaves rarely discharged. every able-bodied man that was so unfortunate as to be sent there. In this particular form of despotism, the vaunted reign of the "great monarch" enjoys a pre-eminence attained probably by no other tyrannical ruler. The galley slave might be condemned to serve for the term of five years, for the term of ten years, or for life. It made no difference. He received no discharge. No notice was taken of the expiration of his sentence, and, as a rule, his service ended only with his life. This statement is no calumny of an enemy, but is vouched for by a high officer of the government. "The king," writes Dangeau, on the twenty-fifth of November, 1697, "has resolved to remove from his galleys many of those that have served out their time; although the custom was long since established of leaving in the galleys alike those that were sentenced for their entire lives and those that were sentenced for a certain number of years." And he gives a last touch to the

picture of Louis's baseness, when he adds: "All the

A few deported to America. invalids will also be withdrawn, and it has been resolved to send the whole of these wretches to people our islands in America."[2] In other words, men guiltless in the sight of the law, since they had atoned for their sins by suffering the full measure of their sentences, were to be deported to

---

[1] Admiral Baudin, of the French navy, in 1852, transmitted to the French Protestant Historical Society, then just formed, some leaves of a register of the galleys of Marseilles belonging to the early years of the eighteenth century. They are published in the first number of the society's Bulletin, pp. 52–58. Among other things, he discovered a memorandum of the condemnation of a child "pour avoir, étant agé de plus de douze ans, accompagné son père et sa mère au prêche."

[2] Journal du Marquis de Dangeau (Paris, 1854), vi. 233.

a distant land, the horrors of a residence in which, added to the terrors of the dangers to be encountered in reaching that land, caused exile thither to be commonly regarded as worse than death!

And Dangeau's statements are borne out by those of one who had been for years a Roman Catholic chaplain on board of a galley—John Bion, whom the sight of the constancy of Protestant martyrs led finally to embrace the faith for which they suffered. Referring to men sent to the galleys for a violation of the royal ordinances respecting the purchase of salt, he says: "These, indeed, are condemned only for a time, perhaps five, six, or eight years, but the misfortune is that having served out their time, if they outlive it, they are still unjustly detained; for penance or masses avail nothing in this purgatory, indulgences are here excluded, especially if the man be unfortunately strong and robust, let his sentence be what it may." Bion, however, did not know, as we know, that this outrage was committed with the full approval of the king, and he blames Louis only for not seeing that his orders are better executed.[1] So uniform, in point of fact, was the violation of equity and common decency by the continued detention of galley slaves whose terms had expired, that the same Arnoul to whom reference has already been made, seems to have felt compelled to excuse himself for having made an apparent exception in behalf of a favored few of the number. If he had granted them their freedom, it was only because they had given him each a Turk to serve in their place; or, in the case that they were men of good family two Turks apiece.[2]

No wonder that men whose term had expired and who yet were not discharged, men that had been detained twice or even three times as long as they had been sentenced to serve in the galleys,[3] grew desperate, and in their frenzy inflicted wounds

---

[1] J. Bion, Account of the Torments which the French Protestants Endure Aboard the Galleys, 21.

[2] Bonnemère, 101.

[3] "Les plus pressantes [plaintes] sont de ceux qui ont doublé et triplé le temps porté par leurs condemnations, et ont de la peyne à prendre patience. Si le roy jugeoit à propos de donner tous les ans la liberté à quelques uns des plus anciens, en ayant communiqué avec Mr. Arnoul, il croit que cela produiroit un

upon themselves that would incapacitate them for farther service and might secure them release.[1]

To such a life of aggravated slavery and life-long hardship the most excellent of the Huguenots, because the most true to their conscientious convictions, were remorselessly condemned for the sole crime of endeavoring to exchange their native France for some foreign land in which, it might be in poverty and obscurity, they would enjoy the precious boon of freedom to worship God. No exception was made in favor of the highest rank, or the most advanced age. David de Caumont, Baron of Montbeton, sprung from a branch of the same family that had produced the Duke of la Force, companion in arms of Henry of Navarre, was a man of over seventy years when discovered in the hold of a vessel in which he was about to sail from Bordeaux to the hospitable shores of England. None the less was he sentenced to a punishment which only the most criminal could deserve, and only the youngest and most robust seemed likely to survive. Attached with others to the chain, on foot and almost crushed by the weight he had to carry, the aged nobleman, who had sat in the States of Languedoc, was led, as though he had been the vilest of malefactors and the basest of knaves, from Bordeaux to Montpellier, from Montpellier to Marseilles.[2] If, however, it had been the object to humiliate the prisoner and to dishearten his fellow believers, the attempt utterly failed of its purpose. The verses in which Montbeton celebrated his " chain " excited courage as well as compassion wherever they found their way ; and his sufferings unmistakably tended rather to the furtherance than to the repression of the cause he rep-

Baron Montbeton sent to the galleys.

---

bon effet." The Bishop of Marseilles to Colbert, January 31, 1673, Depping, Correspondance Administrative, ii. 938, 939. The bishop had been administering confirmation to the miserable galley slaves, but there were yet eight or nine hundred asking for it, he says.

[1] Arnoul, who gives us the fact, suggests the policy of occasionally releasing a few " under this pretext," that is, because their time had expired, in order, as he whimsically expresses himself, " to heal their wounded fantasy." Letter to Colbert, October 2, 1666. Ib., ii. 912.

[2] Haag, La France Protestante (2d ed.), iii. 899. Bulletin de la Soc. de l'hist. du Prot. fr., xxxiv. 464, etc.

resented.[1] It was not to the credit of a civilized government
to have riveted upon the neck of so distinguished a nobleman,
a confessor of such unblemished character, an iron collar
which, when he was tardily released, it required almost as
many blows of the hammer to remove as the wearer had lived
years.[2]

Undoubtedly the most vivid impression of the experiences
of a Huguenot galley-slave is obtained from the narrative of a
less distinguished, but not less gifted, sufferer, Jean
The suffer- Marteilhe [3]—a work of such conspicuous interest and
ings of Jean
Marteilhe. merit as to have found a translator in the person of
Oliver Goldsmith,[4] and of such permanent value as to be styled
by the most picturesque of recent French historians, " a book
of the first rank for the charming naturalness of the narrative
and the angelic gentleness [of its spirit], written as it were
between earth and heaven." [5]   Arrested on the borders of
Flanders, Marteilhe served first for many years in the galley
L'Heureuse, at Dunkirk, and on the shores of the British
Channel, and later at Marseilles, on the very galley, La Grande
Réale, to which Montbeton had been consigned about a score
of years before.   Of the painful journey from the shores of the
ocean to those of the Mediterranean the horror cannot well be
conceived.   There were about four hundred men in all, or two
hundred couples, in the chain-gang.   Twenty-two of these men
were Huguenots.   A chain about a yard in length joined the iron

---

[1] See his verses and his correspondence with that intrepid fellow sufferer for
the Huguenot faith, Jean Mascarene, or Mascarenc, in the Appendix of Charles
W. Baird's Huguenot Emigration to America, ii. 375-377.

[2] " Nous fûmes conduits à Marseille dans la galère La Grande Réalle, où je ne
fus pas lontems. Mais pour ôter le clou de mon collier, on donna soixante et
dix coups de marteau, le collier faillit m'étrangler, et il ne s'en fallu peu qu'on
ne me cassât la teste." Inedited MS. in the Walloon Library of Leyden,
printed in the Bulletin de la Soc. de l'hist. du Prot. fr., xxxiv. (1885) 469.

[3] Mémoires d'un Protestant condamné aux Galères de France pour cause de
religion, écrits par lui même. Originally published at Rotterdam, 1757. I
have used the Paris reprint of 1865.

[4] The translation was published in London, 1758, with the title Memoirs
of a Protestant condemned to the Galleys of France for his Religion. Goldsmith concealed his name under the pseudonym *James Willington*.

[5] J. Michelet, Louis XIV. et la Révocation de l'Édit de Nantes (Paris, 1860),
334.

collars of each couple, with a large ring in the middle, through which passed the links of the ponderous *grande chaine* which kept the whole gang together. The weight which each man bore was about one hundred and fifty pounds.[1] The rapacity of the escort aggravated the hardship incident to the march. At Charenton, and twice subsequently, in freezing weather, all the prisoners were compelled to strip themselves, to march across the court-yard in which they were confined, and for two hours to remain stark naked while their clothes were searched, ostensibly for the purpose of seizing anything that might enable them to file away the chain. Afterward came blows, when the victims were too stiff to move, and they were dragged back to their places by the chain attached to their necks, like beasts ready for the shambles. It was no wonder that on this and the succeeding day eighteen men died of exposure and ill-usage.[2] Among these there were no Huguenots, for the one hundred crowns which the kindness of their fellow believers had enabled them to place in the hands of the keepers had at least spared them the blows and the rough handling. In truth, the tenderness and sympathy with which from time to time they were treated by their weaker brethren, " New Converts " of the places through which they passed, constituted a redeeming feature in the tale of their hard experience. " Courage, dear confessors of the truth," they would say, " endure with constancy for so excellent a cause ; meanwhile we shall not cease to pray to God to grant you His grace to sustain you in your severe trials." Among those that came to visit them were even persons of distinction.[3] Those that could reach them embraced them. More miserable than the chained prisoners, these victims of their own lack of resolution listened with envy to the singing of the familiar psalms, and were filled

Horrors of the chain-gang.

---

[1] According to the estimate of the captain of their guards. Marteilhe, Mémoires d'un Protestant condamné aux Galères de France, 331.

[2] Ibid., 333-35. The captain received twenty crowns for every galley-slave that he delivered alive in Marseilles, and nothing for those that died by the way. As it would have cost him forty crowns to carry in a cart any one that was ill, it was to his pecuniary advantage to rid himself of all the infirm This he did, killing them by hard blows, and leaving to the village curates the task of giving them the rites of Christian burial! Ibid., 337, 338.

[3] Ibid., 330.

with grief and remorse at their own pusillanimity. "The conduct of these New Converts shows very clearly that the Roman
Church, instead of converting, only makes veritable hypocrites,"
was the galley-slave's soliloquy.[1] But no sympathy of fellow
believers could mitigate the discomforts of the Huguenots,
when, as at Rouen, they were thrust with the other
convicts into a foul hole, or, as at the *Tournelle* of Paris,
were chained by the neck to huge beams, in a half-re-
clining posture, unable either to stand, or to sit, or to lie at full
length.   More fortunate than many, Marteilhe was detained
here but three days and nights.   What must have been the tortures of men from all parts of the kingdom kept in this prison,
and in this very cellar, for three, or even six months, until the
" great chain" should be ready to start for Marseilles?[2]

The prisons of Rouen and Paris.

Yet, after all the hardships of the chain gang,[3] came the protracted sufferings endured in the galley itself, where the rower
was chained to his bench, where at any moment of the
day a brutal captain, such as the chevalier de Langeron
Maulevrier, might from mere wantonness issue to the overseer
such an order as, *Va rafraichir le dos des huguenots d'une salade
de coups de corde,* [4] and at any minute of the night arouse them
from the sleep into which they had fallen from sheer exhaustion,
for the purpose of showing a visitor how promptly he could at
a word and a blow, set the whole equipage in motion; where,
for the most trifling of offences and on the most groundless of
suspicions, a man might suffer the horrible bastinado, held prone

Brutality of the officers.

---

[1] Marteilhe, Mémoires d'un Protestant condemné aux Galères de France, 302.

[2] Ibid., 316, 318. "We lie, fifty-three of us, in a place which is not above
thirty feet in length and nine in breadth. There lies on the right side of me a
sick peasant with his head to my feet and my feet to his head. . . . There
is scarce one amongst us who doth not envy the condition of several dogs and
horses." The Sufferings and Martyrdom of Louis de Marolles (London, 1712),
52, 53. This eminent man had been Counsellor of the king and held a high
position at Saint Menehoult.

[3] In the case of Marteilhe, however, the longer term of his service had preceded his transfer from Dunkirk to Marseilles. I do not know whether his
journey was exceptional (it was indeed in the dead of winter), but he candidly
admits that it entailed more positive suffering than the whole of the twelve
preceding years of imprisonment and service in the galleys. Mémoires, 340.

[4] Ibid., 130, 131. There were on each galley three *comites*, or boatswains.
Bion, 12.

by four fellow slaves on the great cannon on the prow—the *coursier*—and lashed upon the bare back by a Turk, the latter urged on by a savage overseer, and himself beaten should he for an instant from compassion spare the victim.[1]

The sublime audacity that ventures, in our times, and occasionally upon the very ground once drenched with the blood of

The missionaries try to persuade the Huguenots that they are not suffering for religion's sake.

the martyrs for their faith, to assert that the Roman Catholic church has never persecuted, seems at first sight to be unparalleled for effrontery. What shall be said, however, of ecclesiastics who, during the atrocities consequent upon the Revocation of the Edict of Nantes, undertook to persuade the very victims, then at hard labor in the galleys, that it was all a delusion that they were there through the agency of the Roman Catholic church; or, indeed, that they were, as they imagined, suffering at all for religion's sake? Yet this was precisely what Père Garcin, superior of the missionaries of Marseilles, attempted in his conversations with Jean Marteilhe. The latter thus describes his interview with the priest.

"'Do you know,' he asked me, 'what persecution is? 'Alas, sir,' said I, 'my state and that of my suffering brethren has made me know it sufficiently well.' 'Nonsense,' said he, 'there is where you are mistaken; you take punishment for persecution, and I am going to convince you of it.' 'How

---

[1] The victim's sufferings were intensified by washing his wounds afterwards with vinegar and salt, ostensibly to restore sensitiveness and prevent mortification. Marteilhe, Mémoires d'un Protestant condamné aux Galères de France, 123, 124. Bion, 50, 51. It is but justice to note that both Marteilhe and Bion have only words of praise for the Turks—at least, for the Turks of Asia and Europe, especially those from Bosnia, the borders of Hungary and Transylvania, and Constantinople, captured by the imperial troops and sold in Italy to serve as galley slaves. Charitable to an extreme, they showed the utmost kindness to the Huguenots, whom they called "their brethren in God." A Turk eagerly undertook the office of receiving and distributing the alms sent to them by their brethren of the French churches in the Netherlands, although he well knew the danger he incurred of being bastinadoed to death to compel him to reveal the name of the banker from whom he obtained the money. Not only did he faithfully discharge his duty, but stubbornly refused all remuneration, which, he said, would have robbed him of all his merit in the sight of God and provoked God's displeasure. When this excellent Moslem was killed in battle, ten or a dozen of the same faith solicited the privilege of the succession, as though it had been to a lucrative office. Marteilhe, 254-256.

comes it,' he asked me, 'that you are in the galleys, and what
was the ground of your sentence ? ' I replied that, finding that
I was persecuted in my native land, I determined to
leave the kingdom, in order to profess my religion
freely; and that I was arrested on the borders, and,
condemned for this to the galleys. 'Is not that just what I
told you a moment ago, that you do not know what persecution
is ? I teach you, then, what it is, when I tell you that persecution, for the sake of religion, is when one maltreats you in
order to compel you to renounce the religion you profess.
Now, religion has nothing to do with your case, and here is the
proof. The king has forbidden all his subjects to leave the
kingdom without his permission. You undertook to leave ;
you are punished for having violated the king's orders. This
is a matter that relates to the management of the government,
not to the church, nor to religion.' He next addressed one of
our brethren there present, and asked him also why he was in
the galleys. 'For having prayed to God, sir, in a meeting,' the
brother replied. 'Another violation of the king's orders,' resumed Father Garcin. 'The king,' said he, 'has forbidden
coming together to pray to God in any other place than the
parish and other churches of the kingdom.' Another of our
brethren told him that, being ill, the curate came to his bedside
to receive his declaration as to whether he wished to live and
die in the Reformed or in the Catholic religion ; that, having
recovered from his sickness, he was arrested and condemned to
the galleys. 'Still another violation of the king's orders,' said
Father Garcin. 'His Majesty will have all his subjects live
and die in the Romish religion. You have declared that you
will not do so. That is contravening the king's orders. So,
gentlemen, all of you that are here have violated the king's
commands. The Church has nothing to do with it. She was
not present at your trial ; she did not preside over it. In a
word, the whole took place outside of her and of her cognizance."

It would have been impossible to induce the priest to admit
the sophistry of his argument; nevertheless Marteilhe exposed
it with singular shrewdness. Pretending to be satisfied with
the explanation given, he asked whether, while waiting to be

Jean Mar-
teilhe and
Father Gar-
cin.

further instructed on some difficult points he might not be
delivered from the galleys before making his abjuration. "Assuredly not," was the reply; "you will never be released before
abjuring with all the customary forms." "And if I do thus
abjure, may I hope to go forth soon?" "In a fortnight thereafter, on the word of a priest," rejoined Father Garcin; "for
you see that the king promises release in such a case." Whereupon Marteilhe, throwing aside his assumed air of docility,
called the attention of the now discomfited controversialist to
the fact that by two simple questions he had shown that it was
religion and religion alone that held him and his brethren in
the galleys.[1]

Father Garcin, of Marseilles, was only one of the many
champions of the ecclesiastical order who impudently affirmed,
even in the presence of the victims of the persecution now raging throughout France, the innocence of the church to which
they belonged, and threw the entire responsibility upon the
king. Daniel de Cosnac, Bishop of Valence, than whom there
was no prelate of the realm that had more distinctly encouraged, or applauded with more adulatory words, the work of
Louis the Fourteenth—Daniel de Cosnac, the instigator and
abettor of La Rapine in his hideous efforts at converting Protestant women like Blanche Gamond in the Hospital General,
Daniel de Cosnac repeatedly maintained the same thing in
Bishop Cos- conversation with Jacques Pineton de Chambrun, the
nac and   captive pastor of Orange. And this he did, although he
Pineton de
Chambrun. knew that his auditor was fully aware that the assertions were false. "Men believe," said he, "that the bishops are
the cause of the manner in which the work of reunion is undertaken at the present day. Assuredly this is a mistake. We
have duly expressed our opinions on this point; but it is the
king's will, which nobody can oppose." And Chambrun tells

---

[1] Now and then the admission was made in official documents, quite naturally
and as if by accident, that the Huguenots were suffering not for insubordination
but for their religious convictions. All three of the lists of prisoners confined
in the castle of Alais, for whose support the intendant of Languedoc, Lamoignon de Basville, made provision in September and October, 1690, are headed
" Roolle des prisonniers *pour la religion*," etc. Bulletin de la Soc. de l'hist. du
Prot. fr., xxxvii. (1888) 301, etc.

us that when from the bed on which he lay a helpless cripple he heard the prelate talk after this fashion, he used to raise his eyes to heaven in amazement that a bishop was capable of speaking so falsely. "He spoke as if he detested violence, and yet no sooner had he left the house, than I learned that he had mounted a horse and was gone, at the head of the dragoons, to torment those that had not abjured, or that refused to go to mass."[1] So had the bloody Cardinal of Lorraine sworn to the Duke of Würtemberg, in the name of God his Creator, and pledging the salvation of his soul, that he was guilty of the death of no man condemned for religion's sake. So had that prince of the church called the Almighty to witness his asseveration, that there was no man that hated extreme measures more than he did; although it was well known that those extreme measures were "altogether by his occasion."[2]

In the galleys was developed a high type of Christian character. The Protestant galley-slave could scarcely be less than a man of sterling integrity and of uncommon devotion to principle. It was because of adherence to a proscribed and unpopular religion that he was in the galleys at all. The thoughtless, the weak and wavering, the lukewarm did not take the path that led in this direction; or, if by any chance they had taken it, the vexations and privations to which they were subjected, the separation from home and friends, the poverty of their lot, the ignominy of association with the vilest of criminals—everything, in short, conspired to induce them to choose the shortest road out of their deplorable condition. That road lay through abjuration—an act, to a man holding lightly by his convictions, the most venial of sins. A promise, the signing of a paper containing a profession that might be made with the lips and repudiated by the heart—that was all. In a fortnight, as Father Garcin promised, on the faith of a priest, the bondage would be over. Not only so, but possibly a pecuniary reward might be secured.[3]

Integrity of the Protestant galley-slaves.

---

[1] Les Larmes de Jacques Pineton de Chambrun (Reprint of Paris, 1854), 180.

[2] See Rise of the Huguenots, ii. 16, 17.

[3] Everywhere the clergy held the key that could at any moment unlock Huguenot prisons. A single illustration out of a multitude of examples must suffice. On the 5th of June, 1695, Pontchartrain wrote to the Archbishop of

Hypocrites do not thrive in such a school of suffering. Commendation and occasional praise from distant admirers do not compensate for present and constant annoyance. The demand is for men who have appropriated the belief of the Apostle, and who esteem it a rare and crowning favor accorded to them by Christ, to be permitted not only to believe in him, but to suffer for his sake. Yet it is worthy of notice that the pious galley-slaves themselves were far from resting secure in the belief that their position necessarily shielded them from spiritual peril. On the contrary, they believed it to conduce to their advantage, and to their pleasure, to stimulate one another and to exercise a mutual watchfulness. We read with tenderness, and almost with wonder, the regulations which the more active and zealous of their number drew up, pledging themselves to the faithful oversight of their peculiarly constituted community—a community destitute of ministers of religion, without regularly constituted church, without place of common worship, living ever in the eye of a harsh and implacable enemy. As when the officers of a well disciplined company having been all shot down in battle, some firm and resolute man steps from the ranks and assumes command, so "in the sad condition to which they see themselves reduced by a just judgment of God who has thought fit to place them in the crucible of affliction to purify them of their defilement," these confessors recognize their obligation "to serve as pastors, the one to the other," and engage "to watch carefully over their entire suffering body, reproving and correcting the vicious, encouraging and strengthening the weak and wavering, consoling those that are sick or are objects of extraordinary persecution, and cutting off the cowardly and scandalous." The discipline which they lay down could scarcely have been more strict. Temporizers who,

Their regulations for the community.

Paris : " The mother of the young lady Batelier having presented to the king the accompanying petition asking for her daughter's release, I have been unwilling to report upon it to the king without learning your opinion on the contents. This woman was placed in a convent at your request, because it was alleged that she performed no religious act. Her mother has appended a certificate stating that she has frequented the sacraments. You will judge whether she ought to be detained any longer." MSS. Nat. Archives, printed in Douen, Révocation de l'Édit de Nantes à Paris, ii. 592.

from hope of release or for any other cause, failed to make an
open profession of their holy religion, not less than the drunk-
ard, the profane, and the breaker of the weekly day of rest, were
to be "absolutely cut off from their association." But, if the
discipline was strict, it must be remembered that it was not a
rule which the Protestant galley-slaves imposed upon others,
but which they voluntarily accepted for themselves. Yet for
the feeble, for those who, for example, while not disguising
their Protestant faith, yet, through fear of horrible punishment,
removed their caps when the mass was celebrated upon the
galley, though they did not kneel in adoration of the host, they
showed a tender consideration, and, while exhorting them to
prefer the fear of God to the fear of men, bore with them as
brethren, until the work of the Lord should be perfected in
them.[1]

"The chief thing," said these noble heroes for their faith, "is
that we should all live in such a manner as to give no scandal
to any person, and that no one may be obliged to censure and
reprove us. . . . Let us remember that time is nothing,
and eternity is our all, and that we ought chiefly to aspire to
the eternal and glorious liberty of the sons of God. We shall
always be free enough in the midst of our slavery, when we are
loosed from the bonds of the sin that so easily besets us and
know how to rule ourselves and our own passions."[2]

It would indeed seem that all the virtues had forsaken the
walks and marts of men that believed themselves to be free, and
had taken refuge in the community of the galley-slaves![3]
Their words were brave, but their deeds were braver than their
words; for whilst they could die, they could not be constrained

---

[1] "Règlements faits sur les galères de France par les confesseurs qui souffrent
pour la vérité de l'Évangile." This interesting document is contained in a long
letter sent, under date of "Marseilles, on the galleys of France, February 25,
1699, and the fourteenth year of our sufferings," to the churches of Geneva and
the Protestant Cantons of Switzerland. The letter is signed by thirteen Protestant galley-slaves. Printed in the Bulletin de la Soc. de l'hist. du Prot. fr.,
xvii. (1868) 20–29, 65–73.

[2] Ibid., ubi supra, xvii. 67, 69.

[3] "Oh! noble cité que celle des galères! Il semblait que toute vertu s'y fût
réfugiée! Obscur ailleurs, là Dieu était visible." J. Michelet, Louis XIV. et la
Révocation de l'Édit de Nantes, 331.

to do what their conscience condemned. The extracts from the letters that kept the foreign Protestant world advised of what occurred from month to month on the galleys, are a very panorama of exalted virtue triumphant over suffering and temptation. Jean l'Hostalet was one of the many who were mercilessly scourged on the galley Guerrière for declining to give the idolatrous salute to the host.[1] Upon two successive days he received the terrible bastinado. On the first day, some seventy blows were inflicted; on the second, forty-five more blows, struck with the coarsest cord. So heavy were they that it seemed to L'Hostalet that he was smitten with a thick bar; so fast did they fall that he had scarce time between the blows to finish the words "My God!" He nearly died. A third infliction would infallibly have proved fatal, and he was told that he should have to endure it. The "comite," the almoner, and others came continually to him, as he lay covered with wounds and bruises. In vain they told him that he was a stubborn fellow, that the raising of his cap was only a trifle, that he was going to be his own murderer. Sent to the hospital, he proved a troublesome patient and was sent back to the galley long before he was fully cured. "Blessed be God for ever!" he wrote to a friend. "I should not be out of the hospital yet had it not been that a man named David Trinque died there, professing the Protestant religion, which he had previously abjured. I was sore beset : the missionary and the doctor threatened me with the bastinado, because they accuse me of having spoken to him (Trinque), and I say that it was a stroke from heaven, that it was God himself that spoke to him." [2]

Jean l'Hostalet.

---

[1] Every lawyer knew that to punish for declining to perform an act of Roman Catholic worship a man who had been sent to the galleys as a penalty for refusing to change his religion, was in point of fact a violation of an established principle of French jurisprudence prohibiting a double punishment for one and the same fault—*Non bis punitur in idem.* But, as Bion well observes, " in France, properly speaking, there is no law, where the king's commands are absolute and peremptory." The Sufferings of the Protestants in the French Galleys, 44, 45.

[2] Journal des Galères. Extrait de lettres écrites par les fidèles confesseurs de Marseille, 1696-1708. Bulletin de la Soc. de l'hist. du Prot. fr., xviii. (1869) 369. The incident referred to in the text belongs to October, 1700.

It was not the only time that the sight of the holy patience with which the galley-slaves endured their manifold afflictions, Influence of as witnesses of a good confession, seemed to those that
the pious beheld them a very voice or blow from heaven. One
galley-
slaves. of their own number could without vain boasting assert : " We can bless God and say that there are among us Lots who live in Sodom without partaking of its impurity. In the place that is the most abandoned and infamous of all places, by reason of the vices and impiety that reign there, there are men that live a life as different in morals and in conversation as in religion, in such wise that our superiors and our greatest enemies cannot themselves help making our defence." [1] The number of Roman Catholics, galley-slaves, that were converted to
Conversion Protestantism by this means was not small.[2] There
to Protes-
tantism in were more important converts than galley-slaves. Jean
the galleys. Bion, a priest and chaplain of the galley La Superbe
deserves special mention. He had for some time been half
Bion, chap- convinced that the Protestant was the better faith.
lain of the He had felt horror when informed by the " comite " that
galley La
Superbe. certain Protestant galley-slaves had failed to kneel when he elevated the host, and that the captain's attention must be drawn to the fact, in order that they might receive the bastinado. He begged the " comite " to wait a week, and used the interval in endeavoring to persuade the Huguenots to yield. He sent them food, to bribe them ; he threatened them with what they were sure to suffer, should they persist ; he brought Scripture to bear on their resolution, by reminding them that Saint Paul declares that he who resists the higher power resists God. It was all in vain. " I could not but admire," he writes, " both the modesty of their answers and the greatness of their courage. *The king,* say they, *is indeed master of our bodies, but not of our consciences.*" The next Sunday, out of twenty Huguenots only two kneeled at the elevation of the host. The other eighteen received, stretched out on the *coursier,* and held by four Turks, the full punishment with which they had been menaced. Bion visited them after-

---

[1] Letter of Jean Musseton, Marseilles, April, 1696. Bulletin de la Soc. de l'hist. du Prot. fr., xviii. 40.

[2] Relation touchant la conversion et les souffrances de Jean Fayan, 1700-1712. Ibid., xvii. 338–342. Fayan had been sent to the galleys for desertion.

ward and could not, he tells us, refrain from tears. "They quickly perceived it, and though scarce able to speak, by reason of pain and weakness, they thanked me for the compassion I expressed and the kindness I had always shown them. I went with the purpose of administering some comfort to them, but I was glad to find them less moved than I was myself. It was wonderful to see with what true Christian patience and constancy they bore their torments, in the extremity of their pain never expressing anything like rage, but calling upon Almighty God and imploring His assistance. I visited them day by day; and as often as I did visit them my conscience upbraided me for persisting so long in a religion whose capital errors I had long since perceived, and, above all, a religion that inspired so much cruelty—a temper directly opposite to the spirit of Christianity. At last, their wounds, like so many mouths preaching to me, made me sensible of my error, and experimentally taught me the excellency of the Protestant religion." [1]

Foreign Protestants did well to honor such stanch witnesses for their common faith. A number of captives having been, through the intercession of Queen Anne, released and suffered to go abroad, their brethren of the consistory at Amsterdam were both kind and wise, when, in an address full of tender feeling, they urged them to give token of their faith by edifying the church by a life above reproach, that should correspond to the constant profession of confessors of the truth, which God had given them the grace to sustain upon the galleys. [2]

Despite prison and convent and condemnation to the galleys, the emigration from the dominions of the king of France did not cease. Even the threat of transportation to America proved of no avail; although so terrible a sound, we are told, had the word "slavery," especially slavery in a foreign land beyond the sea and among unknown savages, that many yielded who had held out against every other menace. And yet it was known that of those that had

Terrors of deportation to America.

---

[1] An Account of the Torments which the French Protestants endure aboard the Galleys. By John Bion, sometime priest and curate of the parish of Ursy in the province of Burgundy, and chaplain to the Superbe Galley in the French service (London, 1712), 51.

[2] Marteilhe, Mémoires, 416, 417.

not been drowned on the way to the French Antilles a goodly number, if not indeed the greater part, succeeded in making good their escape to Jamaica and other possessions of the British crown.[1] Now the prisons, the convents, the galleys, the colonies being full to overflowing, Louvois was induced reluctantly to yield to the suggestion that possibly the very prohibition to emigrate led to the attempt. The French, it was said, always desire the impossible. Let the passages but be left open for a while, and no one will of his own accord leave the kingdom. The experiment was accordingly tried, but for a very brief period. It proved an entire failure ; the Huguenots poured forth with still greater alacrity, when they found that they could journey to a land of religious freedom. The gates had once more to be closed and barred.[2]

The experiment of opening the passages.

Meanwhile, such artifices were freely employed as might seem likely to further the work of conversion and lend to a violent proceeding some show of an appeal to reason and intelligent persuasion. To two things the Huguenots had been accustomed from their earliest days—religious books, especially the Holy Scriptures, in their own tongue, and preaching in exposition of the doctrines of the Scriptures. Some attempt was made to meet both of these demands on the part of the so-called "new converts." Fénelon early saw the lack of the books and wrote to Secretary Seignelay : "We ought to have a very great abundance of books, especially of New Testaments, and of translations of the mass with explanations ; for nothing is accomplished unless the heretical books are taken away, and it drives men to despair to take them away unless we give as fast as we take away."[3] And returning to the same theme, a few days later, he wrote : "If we take away their books without giving them others, they will say that the ministers rightly told them that we were not willing to let them read the Bible, through fear that they would see the condemnation of our superstitions and idolatries. They will be in despair. In fine, sir, if to these helps are always

Providing the "new converts" with religious books.

---

[1] Benoist, v. 978.

[2] Ibid., v. 979.

[3] Fénelon to the Marquis of Seignelay, La Tremblade, February 26, 1686. Lettres de Fénelon, in the Appendix of Douen, Intolérance de Fénelon, 290.

joined the vigilance of the guards to prevent them from running away, and the rigorous execution of the penalties pro-

Fénelon's opinion. nounced against those that run away, there will remain nothing more to do but to secure to the people as much comfort in dwelling in the kingdom as they incur peril in undertaking to go out of it. That is, sir, what you have begun, and what I pray God that you may be able to accomplish according to the full extent of your zeal." [1]

The books that were thus to be judiciously used as an adjunct to the convents, the prisons, and the galleys, were of various kinds. There were, apparently, several versions of the Sacred Scriptures employed. The most remarkable was an

The falsified New Testament of Bordeaux. edition printed at Bordeaux in 1686, with more zeal than discretion, wherein some rather extraordinary measures were adopted to convince the "New Converts" that they had all along been deceived by the wiles of the French reformers that had translated the Scriptures from the Greek original. Not content with the results at which the Roman Catholic theologians of Louvain had arrived, they substituted for the renderings of the latter, as often as convenient, some direct reference to doctrines challenged by Protestants. If Saint Paul wrote to the Corinthians of a certain person that his work would be burned and he would suffer loss, but that he himself would be saved, yet so as by fire, these ingenious editors made the addition of the two words "of purgatory." And if the Louvain translators of their own church found the meaning of a phrase in the second verse of the thirteenth chapter of the Acts of the Apostles to be "*Eux donc servant le Seigneur en leur ministère*" ("As they ministered to the Lord"), the Archbishop of Bordeaux thought that he had made a capital point against Sacramentarians and others by improving it as follows: "*Comme ils offraient au Seigneur le Sacrifice de la Messe*" ("As they were offering to the Lord the sacrifice of the mass"). After which it is not surprising that the *sacrament*

---

[1] Fénelon to the Marquis of Seignelay, La Tremblade, March 8, 1686. Lettres de Fénelon, in the Appendix of Douen, Intolérance de Fénelon, 294–295. Cardinal de Bousset, as unfaithful as an editor as he was inexact as a biographer, has in part omitted, in part unwarrantably altered, this troublesome passage.

of marriage, *pilgrimages*, the *Roman* faith, and *venial* sins, made their appearance under the hands of an unscrupulous falsifier.[1]

The effort of the forger, who while making such bold changes had not hesitated to retain the words "translated from Latin into French by the Theologians of Louvain," was too audacious. So much indignation was expressed that the entire edition is said to have been destroyed with the exception of eight copies.[2] One of these is in the Library of Geneva, and, by the book-binder's blunder, contains a tell-tale leaf which shows how the publisher, acting doubtless under the archbishop's orders, endeavored to retreat from a position that made the church the laughing-stock of all intelligent men.[3] Other editions, especially that of Bishop Godeau, were circulated instead. Louis the Fourteenth had become the patron of the work, though under strange stipulations. "You may have the New Testament and the Psalms of M. Godeau's French translation printed for distribution to the new converts," Louvois wrote to the intendant of Poitiers, "on the condition that you take all the copies for the king and then have the type broken up."[4] Evidently the old Catholics were not expected to read the Bible in any version.

The circulation of Roman Catholic translations of the Scriptures and of works explanatory of the ceremonial of the church

---

[1] See Benoist, v. 944, 945.

[2] Bulletin de la Soc. de l'hist. du Prot. fr., xi. 417.

[3] In the attempt to restore the rendering of the passage in Acts xiii. 2, given by the theologians of Louvain, the publisher at Bordeaux contented himself with reprinting a single leaf. The binder was directed to cancel the original leaf, retaining only so much of the inner margin as was needed to paste thereupon the substituted leaf. But, in at least one copy, he accidentally mistook the leaf that should have been cut out. As the result, in the copy now in the Library of Geneva (catalogued Bb 813), in its original binding, there are two successive leaves, numbered alike, while the leaf that should follow is missing. The two leaves differ only in the rendering of the passage above referred to. I owe these details to the kindness of my correspondent, M. Th. A. Dufour, Director of the Library, in a letter dated December 13, 1894. M. A. Bohin, of Bellocq, Basses Pyrenées, who drew attention to the volume, a few years since, in the Protestant Béarnais, from a less careful examination came to the conclusion that the falsified page was substituted for the more correct original.

[4] "A condition d'en prendre tous les exemplaires pour le roi et de faire rompré ensuite les planches." Louvois to Foucault, October 28, 1685. Mémoires de Foucault, 518.

effected little or nothing. The employment of preachers was scarcely more useful.

If ignorant priests gathered into the churches congregations of New Converts, to instruct them in the doctrines that were to be believed, they were not by any means sure of a respectful hearing from men and women to whom their voices were as hateful as the doctrines they inculcated were repulsive. A whole assembly of Huguenots forced to come to listen to a Roman Catholic preacher at La Rochelle surprised him in a most disagreeable manner, when he was about to begin his sermon, by breaking out with one accord in singing the metrical version of the twenty-fourth psalm, which they all knew by heart, and thus giving him the clearest evidence that they were fully determined, whatever they might be forced to seem to be, to be Huguenots at heart.[1]

The New Converts of La Rochelle sing Huguenot psalms.

Of the attitude of the clergy in relation to the work of conversion and the difficulties they encountered through the determination of the Protestants to retain their old faith and to bring up their children in that faith, the correspondence of the prelates themselves gives perhaps the clearest view. De Maupeou, appointed bishop of Castres, wrote to the controller general that he was still assiduously applying himself to the observation of the conduct of the new converts, which he confessed was "not very regular." In this assertion he was certainly keeping within bounds, since these refractory sheep of his fold had of late been coming together stealthily for divine worship. A handkerchief or a key would seem to have been the token left at the houses of the faithful to signify the time and place of the meeting. In fact, one such unlawful gathering had recently been surprised on Easter Day, at the very hour of the services in the established church ; the worshippers being taken in the very act of "preaching and singing the psalms of Marot." True, the whole number present was but ten persons, seven women and three men, and the preachers were a simple baker and a shoemaker; but the lady at whose house apparently they met was of some prominence,

Perplexity of the clergy.

---

[1] News-letter in the Gazette of Haarlem, under date of La Rochelle, October 29, 1685. In Bulletin de la Soc. de l'hist. du Prot. fr., xxix. 264.

since she was a sister of De Bonrepaux, formerly an intendant of the navy and at present an ambassador of the king, and of D'Usson, a *maréchal de camp*. The prelate was not without hope, however, that Basville, whose zeal was well known, would make such an example of these lawbreakers as to disabuse the Calvinists of the false impression under which they were laboring, that the royal intendants had received instructions to shut their eyes and let the Protestants do pretty much as they pleased. All this comes, said the bishop, of not compelling them, as "at the beginning of the conversion," to attend the public services. Religion is acquired by habit. In the time of the Albigenses, he adds, his mind reverting to the history of the very region from which he wrote, they were obliged to observe this practice very strictly. "Now, however," he ruefully observes, "our churches are entirely deserted. The schools alone continue to exist, and this through the unremitting attention we give to them. I do not fail myself to visit the schools in the city twice a week, and those in the country every two months. But these people are so wayward, that the parents every night do all in their power to make their children forget whatever the latter have learned during the day. One of them, the other day, seeing that his son was attending mass on feastdays and Sunday, and not being able to prevent him, took away his son's shoes and restored them to him only when the hour for mass was past. Never in my life have I seen people more wayward and more ill-intentioned. There is nothing so discouraging as to labor in such a work, where one meets with such slight success, for, upon my word, we know not how to treat them."[1]

A wayward flock.

The manifest insincerity of the conversion which so many of the Protestants had been forced by the dragoons to profess, continued to be a source of constant annoyance and perplexity to the king's civil and military officers. Some of their efforts to solve the difficult problem were sufficiently absurd. At one time, the Marshal d'Estrées conceived the brilliant idea of making the Protestants who had

New converts forced to promise to be instructed.

---

[1] This very interesting and instructive letter, dated March 27, 1693, is published in Boislisle, Correspondance des Contrôleurs généraux des finances avec les Intendants de province (Paris, 1874), i. 315, 316.

abjured in Poitou sign a promise to be instructed. But Louis himself saw at once to what ridicule he would expose himself by permitting such a course to be pursued. It would be a palpable and irrefragable proof that the abjurations thus far made were the result not of religious conviction but of compulsion. M. de Pontchartrain received instructions to order this signing to stop instantly. The thing might be good in itself, but it would lead to too important consequences. It was a species of new abjuration. If it extended to the whole kingdom, any "New Converts" that contrived to avoid signing the new promise would regard themselves as absolved from the obligation of their former engagements, because extorted by force, and would feel free to live just as they pleased.[1]

The intendants, such especially as desired above all things to curry favor with their royal master, did not relax their efforts to "convert," and to make it appear that those efforts were crowned with complete success. In their representations they were seconded by prelates and missionaries. No assertions were too bold for them to make, for little fear was entertained lest a ray of truth might ultimately penetrate even the close seclusion of the monarch, and bring to the light their fabric of lies. The correspondence of Le Gendre at Montauban with the controller general at Paris may serve in illustration. This intriguing official, sent to the city which had always been a citadel of the Reformed faith, started upon his course determined to outdo all rivals in zeal for the spread of "the king's religion;" and the easy assurance with which he recounts his pretended exploits, as if they had to do with anything rather than with the conscientious convictions of a large number of the king's subjects, lends interest to his letters.

"You did not take me for a missionary," he wrote to Chamillart, "when you sent me to this region; nevertheless I am preaching like a devil. My chest is somewhat the worse for

---

[1] Pontchartrain to Marshal d'Estrées, October 20, 1699. Depping, Correspondance administrative (Collection de Documents inedits), iv. 474. It is characteristic of the way in which matters were managed under Louis XIV., that with the command to discontinue the exaction of the promise in question, it was intimated that no one must know the order which the marshal had received, and that he might use any pretext he pleased for his change of tactics.

it, but religion goes better in consequence.   Not a day passes but I lead five or six new converts to mass.   There were forty of them that went there last Sunday.   There must have been fully twenty this morning, though it was the day of the Virgin, which as you know is not held in veneration among those gentlemen."   The intendant asserted

<small>Intendant Le Gendre preaches " like a devil,"</small>

that he was hoping for wonders with Chamillart's help, but he added that, without that help, neither the bishop nor he could do anything.   His plan of action comprised three points—gentleness toward reasonable men who were disposed to be converted and toward *merchants ;* the expenditure of money upon such as interest alone deterred at present from renouncing their heresy ; and the judicious resort to exemplary severity in dealing with the refractory.   It is hard to say which of the last two methods of conversion Le Gendre considered the more promising.   Seven or eight thousand livres from the controller general's liberal hand would draw in more Huguenots than the finest sermons that could be preached.   The king would derive great satisfaction from seeing his bounty usefully employed for the advancement of true

<small>but finds great virtue in the use of money and *lettres de cachet.*</small>

religion and the entire destruction of heresy in Montauban, which was regarded as the centre of " Huguenotism."   On the other hand, there was such great virtue in the *lettres de cachet,* that the intendant earnestly asked that his Majesty would be pleased to let him have a dozen of them, *with the space for the name left in blank,* promising to make use of them only in an extremity.[1]   Nor was the actual resort to this fearful instrument of tyranny very probable, since, as Le Gendre himself suggested, when renewing his request, a few days later, the mere sight of the *lettre de cachet,* with the ominous void which the intendant's pen could so easily fill, struck terror into the hearts of those who might the next moment be the victims.[2]

A year passed without any visible diminution in the intendant's zeal or in his confidence.   Meantime the " poor priests "

---

[1] Le Gendre to Chamillart, February 2, 1700, Correspondance des Contrôleurs généraux avec les Intendants, ii. 23.

[2] " Dont la seule inspection fera trembler ceux qui en seront menacés." Le Gendre to Châteauneuf, Secretary of State, February 24, 1700, ibid., ii. 28.

who devoted themselves to the work of instruction derived their
support from one part of the income of the property of the ref-

Glowing ac-
counts given
by the inten-
dant and the
Jesuit mis-
sionary. ugee Protestants, while another part went to reward
the work of other persons toiling for the same end.[1]
Le Gendre was jubilant. " The new converts," he exclaimed, " are continuing to do marvels in Montauban
and throughout the whole generality. There is not one of them
that fails to go to mass. More than two hundred partook of the
sacraments at Easter with edification, and more than three hundred in the rest of the generality. Here is the fruit of one year's
labors ! What may we not expect after from such happy beginnings ? . . . It is wonderful to see the churches that
were empty a year ago now crowded with people. It seems that
God grants a special blessing to the city of Montauban where
Heresy triumphed for so many years." [2]

The intendant's glowing accounts were fully sustained by the
representations of De la Rue, Jesuit missionary extraordinary
in Languedoc. The latter had labored seven months with Le
Gendre at Montauban, and, when on the point of undertaking a
similar work in the Cévennes Mountains, he wrote to court and
extolled the results of the complete harmony of action of Le
Gendre, the Bishop of Montauban and Basville. Would to
God that such good understanding existed between all the prelates and intendants of the realm. But the new converts are
told that the king does not want them to go to church ; the
work has dragged along for years and will never be accomplished ;
" and six hundred thousand souls without a religion will form
within the kingdom a people equally inimical to the church and
to the state." Not so at Montauban, where the victory of the
Roman Catholic Church has been effected by the gentlest of
methods. " Neither banishment, nor imprisonment, nor violence
has been required to bring the new converts to discharge the
external duties of religion." [3]

---

[1] Le Gendre to Chamillart, January 16, 1701, Correspondance des Contrôleurs
généraux avec les Intendants, ii. 66.

[2] Le Gendre to Chamillart, April 13, 1701, ibid., ii. 72.

[3] " Il n'a fallu ni exils, ni emprisonments, ni violence, pour les engager aux
devoirs extérieurs de la religion." Report of Père de la Rue to Chamillart giving an account of his mission, September 21, 1700, ibid., ii. 56.

It would, at the first sight, seem absurd to question the accuracy of such positive statements, and the most vehement denial of their truth emanating from a Protestant source might with some show of reason be rejected as inspired by blind party spirit.

Fortunately the contradiction comes not from an enemy but from a member of the established church—from the priest Olivier, an ecclesiastic living and officiating in Montauban itself —who attested the truth of what he said by affirming that he had just celebrated the most august Sacrament in order to pray Heaven to grant that the government might profit by the information he was about to send.[1]

"The opinion you entertain," says this candid witness, "based upon the reports made to you by M. Le Gendre and Sieur Daliès, that there now exists only a single religion at Montauban, compels me to write to inform you, with truth and for the glory of God, *that there have been no genuine conversions here*, and that the two men whom I have named have only had in view to pay court to his majesty, by persuading him of the utility and the fruitfulness of their efforts. . . . We are experiencing the consequences of their altogether human views, and we see with grief that there is in the new converts *more aversion to the Catholic religion than there had ever before appeared to us to exist.* We know of a certainty that all the exercises of the Protestant religion are celebrated in this city, that there are secret meetings, that the Lord's Supper is administered, and, in a word, that private houses have become temples of the former error. *This is what the imprisonments, the fines, the frequent insults, and the continual threats which Mr. Le Gendre has made use of have produced!* Gentleness and instruction would have won more hearts than has violence."[2]

Contradiction by a brother ecclesiastic.

It is not often that a forgotten letter, rescued from its obscurity in the state archives, has more directly given the lie to magnificent boasts.

---

[1] "Ce que j'ai l'honneur de vous dire est pour l'intérêt de Jésus-Christ, que je viens d'offrir à son Père dans le saint sacrifice de la messe, pour le prier qu'il vous fasse profiter des sincères avis que je vous donne."

[2] Le sieur Olivier, prêtre à Montauban, au Contrôleur général, 28 Juin, 1704, Correspondance des Contrôleurs généraux avec les Intendants, ii. 189.

If there is no doubt that with the vast majority of the Huguenots who were claimed by the clergy as new converts, there was no real change of sentiment, there is as little doubt that these "new converts" intended to return to an open profession of their faith at the first good opportunity, or, at latest, at the approach of death. Such in point of fact was the course which many adopted; and those who in health had exhibited, as they themselves were the first to recognize, a lamentable weakness, gathered up the courage to avow their convictions when the hour came at which considerations of a temporal character recede from view in proportion as the issues of eternity assume an importance hitherto but partially apprehended. It would seem to require less courage to declare that one desires to die in the doctrines of the Reformed religion, when a few hours more will place the spirit beyond the reach of annoyance and constraint, than to avow an intention to live in the profession of that religion with the prospect of many years in which one's resolution will have full occasion to be put to the test. It was no rare case therefore for a man or a woman who had signed a promise to abjure, and, possibly, had even been constrained to attend the mass, to feel upon the death-bed a poignant remorse for past cowardice and display a firmness of resolve which no solicitations of friends and no menaces of troublesome curates and monks could shake. In their impotence to discover other means of remedying what, to use the favorite phraseology of the legislator of the time of Louis the Fourteenth, threatened to become so formidable an "abuse," the government, at priestly suggestion, determined to influence the mind of the dying by a consideration of the fate awaiting him should he recover, and his lifeless remains, in case he should die.

How to prevent "new converts" from relapsing.

Of all the penalties meted out for religion's sake, that was unquestionably the most abhorrent to every sentiment of humanity which was inflicted upon the mortal remains of such of the "new converts" as had refused, in their last hours, the sacraments of the established church. Nor is the legislation and practice in regard to the corpses of these persons the least curious chapter in the history of persecution in modern times.

A law of Louis the Fourteenth, issued on the twenty-ninth c

April, 1686, or about six months after the publication of the
revocatory edict, recognized and deplored the fact that some,
at least, of those who had previously abjured Protestantism retracted their words in the extremity of
illness, and died in their error. Their conduct rendered it necessary to take steps to check so flagrant

Penalties
for refusing
the sacra-
ments *in
extremis.*

a crime. In the case of those persons who might ultimately
recover after rejecting the offices of the clergy, the king declared
it to be his pleasure that the men be sent to the galleys, that
the women be imprisoned, that both be subjected to the *amende
honorable*, and that the property of both be confiscated. As to
those that died, his Majesty decreed that proceedings be instituted against their dead bodies, or their "memory," as provided by the criminal code then in force, and that the corpses
be dragged on a hurdle and thrown into the common sewer.
The property of the deceased was to be confiscated.[1]

Such was the barbarous law which was to restrain or punish
the candor of the dying by the foreknowledge of the poverty
and disgrace that must befall the survivors—a fresh attempt to
prolong hypocritical professions, extorted by violence, to the
very last breath of life.

The curates were the instruments of terror, as they were also
the chief informers. I cannot better illustrate the fact than by
telling the touching story of a poor old Breton woman, Esther
Verger, of Paimbœuf, at the mouth of the Loire. The pathos
of the last scene will not be lessened, and the truthfulness of
the account of the distress of the victim will be established, by
allowing the curate of Paimbœuf to describe the incident in his
own words.

"On the twenty-third of January, 1687, the seneschal of
Nantes informed me that a woman recently converted, of the
number of those women whom he had captured in a vessel pur-
posing to leave the kingdom, was far advanced in age and very
ill. Thereupon I went several times to the houses where she
was. . . . I asked her whether she had not reflected on the
word that I had heretofore spoken to her; to which she did
not reply, but merely shook her head. Seeing this, I asked her

---

[1] Édits, Déclarations et Arrests, 282-284.

if she did not purpose to persevere in the good resolve which she had had of living as a Catholic in making her abjuration. To which she answered that she had truly been compelled to abjure by force, and that what she had done was only in order to escape more easily the higher powers. Thereupon I told her that she ought to rectify so bad an intention, and that she must not hope for salvation dying separated from the Roman, Catholic and Apostolic church, that being the only church in which there was salvation and in whose sacraments our Lord Jesus Christ had enclosed his precious blood that washes us of our sins. Wherefore I conjured her, by her soul's salvation, to prepare herself to receive them by becoming reconciled to that holy church, or at least to tell me if she had any difficulty, to the end that I might enlighten and help her in the matter of her salvation. She replied to this by a shake of the head, without vouchsafing to utter a single word. Then I entreated and urged her to reply to me whether she did not again abjure her error, and whether she would not receive the means of her salvation which the church presented to her by my ministry. To this she replied several times, '*No ! No ! No !*' Nevertheless I continued to address to her the most moving and pressing words which it pleased God to suggest to me, and I repeated the same request. To which she replied again, '*No ! No ! No !*' Then I frankly told her that she could not flatter herself with the prospect of a long life, inasmuch as her illness was mortal, and she could not outlast the night, as far as I could conjecture, and that she should not risk so precious a thing as her soul's salvation by her stubbornness. To this she refused to make further reply. In about two hours, that is, at ten o'clock in the evening, she fell into the death-struggle, during which several persons conjuring her to think of her salvation and to heed what I had said, she addressed to them injurious words. Her agony lasted until midnight, during which time she exhibited no sign of conversion, but, on the contrary, gave marks of obstinacy and perseverance in her malicious error until her death. When she had died, care was taken to wrap her in a winding-sheet and to entomb her in a sand-hill which is near Paimbœuf on the banks of the river. Of this I took as witnesses Messrs. De la Reauderie-Ozon, Guil-

laucheau, Laquin, and Josias. *Signed,* Louis Dudoyer, priest
vicar at Paimbœuf, the twenty-seventh of January, 1687."

Thus far the curate's own account.[1] His activity did not,
however, end here. The officers of Paimbœuf, probably from
motives of pity, declined to institute proceedings against the
corpse. The records show that the priest's compassion for
poor Esther Verger, so effusively displayed before she expired,
was less potent after her decease and did not prevent him from
lodging a complaint with the king's attorney at Nantes. The
latter demanded of the court in his majesty's name "that the
body of the deceased be disinterred from the place where it had
been buried by the public executioner, be dragged through the
streets of Paimbœuf, and be cast into the sewer, all persons being forbidden in any wise to give it burial, on pain of confiscation of their property."[2] It was so ordered and done.

For many years the history of France abounds in records,
full and circumstantial, of ghastly suits, in which an inanimate
body, scarcely cold in death, having been formally in-
dicted, was tried, condemned, and punished according
to the tenor of the law. For the speechless defend-
ant a curator, or guardian, was appointed to appear and to plead
at the bar of justice. Witnesses were summoned and examined
—curates and vicars who testified to the "conversion" of the
deceased and to his subsequent refusal to confess or commune,
and nurses and attendants who endeavored to break the force of
such testimony by alleging tokens more or less significant of a
disposition, at the eleventh hour, to submit to the authority of
the Roman Catholic church, or, as was most frequently the case,
were forced reluctantly to admit that the deceased died an
avowed Protestant. There were the accustomed appeals to a
superior court. Occasionally a conflict of jurisdiction arose
between the judges of different towns, and the suit must abide
the settlement of the rival claims by the royal intendant.
Meanwhile, the case was of a kind that did not brook the law's
delays. Between the desire to obey the king's ordinance to the

The trial of the dead bodies of Huguenots.

---

[1] The original is in the judicial records of Nantes. It is printed in Vaurigaud,
Histoire des Églises Réformées de Bretagne, iii. 121, 122.

[2] Ibid., ubi supra.

letter and to drag the remains of the dead Huguenot upon the
hurdle through the populous streets, and the impossibility of
executing the sentence of the law upon a mass of corruption
spreading infection far and near, the officers of the king's justice
were at their wits' end. In one place, during the heat of summer, a Norman judge seems actually to have ordered the remains of a Protestant to be salted down, just as the carcass of
a sheep or a bullock might have been, in order that,
the body being locked up in prison, the children of
the deceased might be prevented from stealing them
away for burial.[1] The body of a young girl, Judith

Corpses salted or embalmed to be produced in court,

Piat, of Châtillon-sur-Loing, Admiral Coligny's home in the
previous century, was graciously permitted to be embalmed, in
answer to the petition of her sister Louise, who sought to withdraw the lifeless remains from the care of the guards, who, as
she said, "have committed and continually do commit notable
acts of insult to the body." [2] This privilege was granted, however, only upon condition that Louise should produce the
remains whenever called for, and we have the judge's memorandum that, apparently for future verification, he had "affixed
to the forehead of the corpse the seal of his jurisdiction." [3] In the
end, the case went against the brave Huguenot girl, and the
king's attorney, Bouvier de la Mothe, brother of the famous
Madame Guyon, whose name it seems strange to meet in the
course of such proceedings, made a motion that the body of
Judith Piat " be brought a prisoner to the royal prisons " of Mon-
targis. It was impossible to execute the order. The court was
compelled perforce itself to remove to Châtillon, and even there
it was with extreme difficulty that the formality of verifying the
sealed corpse could be observed.[4]

---

[1] " Et de faire transférer le dict cadavre aux prisons de la dicte, pour esvitter
à l'enlevement que ses enfans en pouroient faire pour l'entérer, et de faire saller
le dict cadavre pour esvitter à la corruption et putréfaction d'iceluy, et pour le
conserver jusques à la perfection de son procez." Documents in S. Beaujour,
Hist. de l'Égl. Réf. de Caen, 471 (Caen, 1877)). This cause began June 26th,
and was not finally decided until October 31, 1686.

[2] " Les huissiers commis à la garde du corps ont comis et comettent continuellement oprobres sensibles à l'endroit du corps."

[3] " Et à l'instant avons marqué ledit cadavre, sur le front, du scel de nostre
jurisdiction."

[4] Bulletin de la Société de l'hist. du Prot. fr., xxvi. (1877), 319.

The trial was only inferior in barbarity to the execution of the atrocious sentence. Brought from out of the prison, the body was placed upon a rough hurdle or crate tied to the end of a cart. Men and women, young and old, rich and poor, were thus dragged about the streets of the city or town, exposed to the hooting and jeering of the low populace. There was no distinction of rank and station, as there was no respect for age or sex. In many cases, if not in all cases, the corpse was stripped of its clothing. The widow Petineau, of Gien, was disinterred six weeks after burial and thus exhibited to the public gaze, a loathsome sight.[1] Paul Chenevix, about eighty years old, and for fifty-three of these years a judge of the parliament of Metz—or, as a contemporary of Metz expresses it, who had sat fifty-three years on the *fleurs de lis*—the ablest and most venerable of judges, and a man universally respected for learning and probity—was dragged about the streets of Metz stark naked.[2] A little later, the mortal remains of the widow of Pierre Hémery, sixty-six years old, were treated with the same indignity on a market day in the streets of Thorigny.[3] For all the destination was the same. It was to the *voirie*, or public sewer, where the carcasses of animals were thrown to rot, and where, in at least one recorded case, the human bodies were in part consumed by roving dogs. Here they might still be pelted with stones or otherwise insulted. In the end some friend contrived to steal them away and give them the burial which the state denied. Four hundred Huguenots of Metz came boldly to claim the body of Paul Chenevix, and on the margin of the *voirie* sang with a loud voice

Marginal notes: and dragged naked on a hurdle to the public sewer. — Paul Chenevix, a judge of the Parliament of Metz. — Buried by bold Huguenots.

---

[1] Bulletin, etc., xl. (1891), 38, 39.

[2] The parliament of Metz, we are told, had some horror at seeing the oldest member of its company treated thus, and suspended the execution of the sentence, but word came from Versailles ordering it to proceed. "Ce vénérable corps," writes one who was probably an witness, "fut dépouillé tout nud, sans la moindre couverture, même sur les parties. On le traîna avec la dernière ignominie. Le bourreau étoit armé. Le peuple jeta, à ce spectacle, des cries perçants vers le ciel." Journal inédit d'un fidèle de Metz, Bulletin, etc., xi. (1862), 283. The official minute of the execution may be read in Haag, La France Protestante (s. v. Chenevix), iv. 297.

[3] S. Beaujour, Hist. de l'Égl. Réf. de Caen, 470.

those words of the seventy-ninth psalm of Clement Marot, in the use of which the Huguenots of the sixteenth century had mourned the butchery at Vassy and many another deed of blood:

> Les gens entrez sont en ton heritage . . .
> Ils ont baillé les corps
> Des tes serviteurs morts
> Aux corbeaux pour les paistre.
> La chaire des bien-vivans
> Aux animaux suivans
> Bois et plaine champestre.[1]

It must in fairness be remarked that Louis the Fourteenth was soon disappointed, possibly both ashamed and disgusted, at the operation of his inhuman law against the corpses of Huguenots. This, of course, it would have been beneath the dignity of the king, as that dignity was then understood, to acknowledge in a manly fashion. All that his ministers would, therefore, admit in their secret instructions to the intendants, was that his majesty's edict had not had all the good effects that had been looked for, and he authorized a certain moderation in carrying the law out. If some Huguenot that had been converted was known when upon his death-bed to have declared openly and ostentatiously (*avec éclat*) his purpose to die in the Protestant religion, and if his relations mentioned the fact ostentatiously as something of which they could boast, the law must be rigorously executed. Otherwise, if the dying man's utterance arose from simple obstinacy and met with the disapproval of his relatives, it would be well to pass the matter over without notice. The king would have the ecclesiastics to understand that they should abstain from so freely calling in the judges as witnesses;

---

[1] Besides the Journal inédit d'un fidèle de Metz above quoted, see the sketch by Oth. Cuvier, "Paul de Chenevix, Conseiller au Parlement de Metz," Bulletin, etc., iii. 566–575. The cases of this barbarous infliction of indignities upon the dead to which I have referred all belong to 1686 or 1699. Other examples, also belonging to these years, at Proisy, in Vermandois, and at Mas d'Azil, in Foix, are given in the Bulletin, etc., ix. 73, xxvii. 16, and xxxii. 554. To 1686 seems to belong the case of the wife of Jaquot de Caussade, of Saint Antonin, who refused extreme unction, and whose body was disinterred and dragged on a hurdle by the executioner accompanied by six soldiers. Bulletin, etc., xlii. (1893), 205.

in order that it might not be found necessary to execute the law to its full extent.[1]

In fact, so odious became the practice of dragging the nude corpses of respectable and even venerated persons on hurdles through the public streets, that prudent intendants, such as Bezons of Bordeaux, confessed that, as matters stood, he did not now dare even to entertain a suit for the confiscation of the property of a new convert that died persisting in his profession of a preference for his old faith and rejecting the sacraments, for fear of being compelled to afford the people a sight which, he euphemistically states, experience had taught us "produces no good effect."[2] It took five or six years more for the government at Versailles to become so fully convinced of this as to instruct the judicial officers to prevent any more unedifying scenes of the kind ; and a month more for the same conclusion to be reached respecting the amende honorable in the case of the new converts who recovered. However, so strongly influenced was his Majesty by the puerile fear of seeming to admit that he had made a mistake, that he bade the judges pass the customary sentence, but see to it that they did not execute it. The order was to be kept a most profound secret.[3]

Dragging on the hurdle and the amende honorable found unedifying.

---

[1] Seignelay to De Creil, Intendant, February 3, 1687. Depping, Correspondance administrative, iv. 401. See, also, a despatch of Count Pontchartrain, of March 12, 1691, to the same effect, ibid., iv. 425.

[2] "Au lieu que l'on n'ose le faire présentement, parce que l'on a connu par experience que l'exemple de tirer un corps sur une claye ne produit aucun bon effet." Bazons to the controller general, July 21, 1693. Corr. des Contrôleurs généraux, i. 329.

[3] Pontchartrain conveys the last directions to the first president of the Parliament of Paris in his letter of Versailles, October 26, 1699, which refers to the issue of similar directions, respecting the dragging of the dead on hurdles, in the preceding month of August. Depping, Correspondance administrative, iv. 495.

CHAPTER XIV

THE EARLY CONVENTICLES AFTER THE REVOCATION

THE strange and unforeseen vicissitudes that befell the Huguenots in the latter part of the seventeenth century placed them in a situation presenting certain marked points of resemblance to the condition of their fathers in the early part of the sixteenth century, at the dawn of the Reformation. A storm of unprecedented violence had descended upon the land, and every institution of the Protestant religion had been swept from its surface. The edifices in which worship had been held were gone—either demolished to the very foundations, or appropriated by an inimical faith. That was a comparatively insignificant loss; material structures can easily be replaced by the same self-sacrifice that originally reared them. It was a much more serious thing that churches of living men and women had been dispersed, that many of their members had succumbed to fear, that some had apostatized. Without a recognized existence, without organization, deprived of religious guides and teachers, what could a mass of laymen do, in the presence of the active and vigilant opposition of the strongest government of Europe, informed and instigated by a clergy that seemed to be everywhere present and to learn promptly whatever occurred?

Yet, if the impression prevailed that the prostration of Protestantism was too complete that it should ever raise its head again, it was only because men did not sufficiently count upon the strength and vitality of moral forces. Violence, in suppressing the outward forms of the Reformed religion, failed conspicuously and ignominiously to eradicate the attachment of the heart to the doctrines, usages, and worship of the Reformed religion. Robbed of their sanctuaries and of the services of their ministers, there was nothing left for the Huguenots to do,

there was nothing, in fact, more natural for them to do, than to
fall back upon methods long since discontinued. In lieu of the
church, there again arose the conventicle; and this very
speedily. Barely two months after the Revocation of the Edict
of Nantes, Cardinal Le Camus, writing from Grenoble to a fellow bishop, gives us a picture of renascent Protestantism which
may serve as well for many other parts of France as for Dauphiny. "The women," he remarks, "have shown themselves
much more attached to their religion than the men. Their
psalms, the notes of their Bibles, and the books of their ministers strengthen them [the Protestants] in their views, and we
see no way of taking these books away from them. We have

Cardinal Camus on renascent Protestantism (1685). been promised books [of our own], but none have
been sent us to substitute in the place of theirs. They
hold small secret meetings, at which they read some
chapter from their Bibles and their prayers. After
that, the most able of their number makes an address. In a
word, they do just what they did at the birth of heresy. They
have an insuperable aversion to service in an unknown tongue
and to our ceremonies. I have sent out missionaries. They
cannot abide monks. The rest have accomplished very little,
and I have been obliged to go in every direction to calm their
minds and to soothe them. But as one cannot be everywhere
present, what one fancies done is undone within three days. I
have noticed that by offering them prayers in French, readings
from the epistles and gospels, and expositions of these readings, we attract them to the church; and that by talking much
concerning the conversion of the heart and the other prepara-
tives necessary to penitence and communion, concerning the
corruption and frailty of man, the power of grace, and the effi-
cacy and application of the merits of Jesus Christ, we open the
way to give them a relish for the other truths of religion. The
communion under both forms is the height of their desires; but
nothing can be done in that matter without the help of Rome." [1]

Such conventicles as those to which the cardinal refers be-

---

[1] See the very interesting letter of Cardinal Le Camus to the Bishop of Luçon,
Grenoble, December 16, 1685, first published, I believe, by Father Ingold,
priest of the Oratory, in 1885, and reprinted, in part, in the Bulletin de la Soc.
de l'hist. du Prot. fr., xxxvi. (1887), 273.

gan almost immediately to be held in every part of France; if, indeed, they were not rather held even before the signing of the revocatory edict. The number of worshippers was greater or smaller according to circumstances; but all that attended took their lives in their hands. The Edict of Revoca-

A royal law of July 1, 1686, makes death the penalty for attendance on the conventicle.

tion made the act a crime of the first magnitude, punishable by "confiscation of body and goods," an expression which might have been understood to signify imprisonment for life, but which a subsequent Declaration of the first of July, 1686, distinctly interpreted as meaning death.[1]

Nor was the law intended to become a dead letter. As early as in February of that year, the list of those brave men and women who, during the greater part of a century, are to suffer death for the simple offence of worshipping Almighty God in gatherings unauthorized by the king, begins with the name of François Teissier, *viguier*, or royal judge, of the village of Dur-

François Teissier, the first martyr of the conventicles.

fort, in the Cévennes Mountains. Tessier had attended a secret conventicle, held about midnight, in a lonely country house lying near Monoblet, St. Felix and Durfort, to which the faithful came from places as distant as Anduze, on the one hand, and St. Hippolyte du Fort, on the other. It was a simple religious meeting. Prayers were offered, psalms were sung. Brought before the intendant, Lamoignon de Basville, Tessier did not deny that he had disobeyed the king, but asserted the superior claim of allegiance to God. Under the circumstances his fate was sealed. "Blessed be God," he quietly said to those who signified to him that, by the sentence of the presidial court of Nismes, he was to be hung that very day, "I shall die as did my Master. My body is at your disposal, gentlemen; but my soul belongs to God." Aiguisier, a missionary stationed at La Salle, labored to convert him to the Roman Catholic religion, and betrayed greater emotion than the prisoner. The more urgent Aiguisier became, the more fervently did Tessier exclaim, raising his eyes heavenward:

---

[1] "Voulons pareillement et entendons que tous ceux de nos Sujets qui seront surpris faisant dans nôtre Royaume et Terres de nôtre obéissance, des assemblées ou quelque exercice de Religion autre que la Catholique, Apostolique et Romaine, soient punis de mort." In Édits, Déclarations et Arrests, 293.

"My God! suffer me not to yield to temptation." The priest's evident earnestness and sincerity of purpose, and the copious tears he shed, touched the victim's heart, and led him
His forti-
tude and his at last to utter a prediction. "Sir," said he, "God be-
prophecy.
holds your charity and your zeal; you will not be without your reward, you will die in our religion." "Yes," jocularly remarked a nobleman who was present, "you will do what Saint Stephen did, you will convert Saint Paul." The missionary, however, was in no mood to jest, and, as he informs us, scarcely thinking what he said, replied : "Ah, well, sir, pray God that he may convert me!" The words bore fruit. Not many months later, the priest, convinced less by the words that he heard than by the example that he beheld, fulfilled the dying man's prophecy. He made his way to Berne and there obtained admission to a church of which he had not dreamed that he would ever seek to become a member. Meantime, on the present occasion he redoubled his efforts to gain over the Protestant. When Tessier exclaimed, at the sound of the preparation of the gallows : "Courage, my friend, they are making ready a ladder for me to mount to the skies," Aiguisier responded by the assurance that, on the contrary, Tessier was about to be precipitated to the lowest depths of hell. The compassionate executioner wept as he bound the prisoner. To the assembled crowd Tessier cried out: "I die a Protestant" ("*Je meurs de la Religion*"). Aiguisier tried in vain to drown his voice; then, following him up two rounds of the ladder, implored him to have a thought of his soul's salvation and to renounce heresy, if he desired to enter paradise. When the missionary paused to recover his breath, Tessier for the last time addressed the people and told them that he had indeed been present at the assemblies of the faithful. It was the only crime that he had committed. He died of the religion and for the religion. His last words were loud and distinct. It was appropriate for the first martyr of the conventicles of the Desert that he should die with the lines of a cherished psalm of Theodore Beza upon his lips—the fifth verse of the thirty-first psalm : [1]

---

[1] Histoire du martyre du sieur F. Tessier, viguier de Durfort, dans les Cé-

> "Mon âme en tes mains je viens rendre :
> Car tu m'as racheté,
> O Dieu de vérité."

The early days of the Reformation in the sixteenth century can boast no more simple and touching story of martyrdom than this. But although it converted the missionary that witnessed it, the report of such courage and constancy, if it reached the ears of Louvois and his master, only infuriated them the more against fanatics so stubborn as to question the king's right to exalt obedience to himself above obedience to the divine commands.

Between the sanguinary minister of war and the intendant of the province, often no less sanguinary, there was an ignoble

Orders to fall upon the gathered Huguenots.

emulation as to which of the two should execute with the greater severity the king's purpose of putting an absolute end to the troublesome assemblies of Protestants, meetings which were no sooner apparently suppressed in one spot than they were again reported to have been held in another. "If it happen again to be possible to fall upon such gatherings," Louvois wrote to Foucault in Poitou, "let orders be given to the dragoons to kill the greatest part of the Protestants that can be overtaken, without sparing the women, to the end that this may intimidate them and prevent others from falling into a similar fault." [1] Again and again he gave out that

vennes. Berlin, 1702. This very rare account, written by the former missionary Philippe Aiguisier, is reprinted in the Bulletin de la Soc. de l'hist. du Prot. fr., v. (1857), 214–224, and in the Petite Bibliothèque du Protestantisme français. The preface and the concluding remarks are by Tessier's son. On Aiguisier himself, see an article by Jules Chavannes, in the same Bulletin, x. (1861), 396–399, and s. v. in Haag, La France protestante, i. 55–57. It is not surprising that in the title of a poem, an adaptation of Racine's Esther, which he prepared for recitation by the pupils of the college of Vevay, of which he became principal, Aiguisier styled himself "*the proselyte of Providence.*"

[1] Louvois to Foucault, Versailles, March 1, 1688. Mémoires de Foucault, 539. In other letters there was always the same bloodthirsty command. "The king's intention is ever that the attempt be made to fall with troops upon all the meetings that may take place, and if, after having killed a very large number, you take a few prisoners, that their trial be carefully instituted," etc. Louvois, March 17, 1689. Bulletin de la Soc. de l'hist. du Prot. fr., xxxiii. 242. And the Count de Broglie, lieutenant general of the king in Languedoc, rightly apprehended the royal pleasure when, in 1690, he announced : "It must be understood to be his Majesty's intention that no meeting be tolerated, either in the

the king would have no distinction made in favor of the weaker
sex, and in the letter from which I have just quoted, perhaps
thinking that so ignominious a punishment would have more
effect than the infliction of death itself, he directed that some
at least of the women arrested should be publicly flogged.[1]
Foucault passed, perhaps with justice, for the most violent of
intendants.   I have on a previous page given Chancellor
d'Aguesseau's verdict on "this distinction that did him little
honor."   Louvois himself had more than once to moderate the
intendant's fury in words that must have stung a nature very
sensitive on the point of self-esteem.   But Louvois in turn gave
Foucault an opportunity to retaliate, when, having instructed
the intendant to level with the ground the abodes of all the Huguenots that might have been present at a conventicle, the latter
called the attention of the minister to the circumstance that the
royal law of July, 1686, enjoined the penalty of death, but said
nothing of razing houses, and remarked that "judges are not
permitted to add penalties to those imposed by the laws."   "M.
de Louvois does not scruple to place himself above these laws,"
the intendant quietly observes in his Memoirs.[2]   Having such a
minister and such a subordinate to deal with, even if the one
might object to the other's order in some minor respect, it fared
ill enough with the district within whose bounds a Protestant
meeting was known to have been held.   It was represented by
them both to be the particular wish of the ruler who claimed to
New Dragon- be the father of his people, that the unfortunate com-
nades.   munity should have one or two companies of dragoons
quartered upon it for a whole month, with full license to live in
the most wasteful manner.   The king's object, said Louvois, is
to make that kind of people learn that they must not merely
abstain from attending the forbidden assemblies, but either prevent any of their number from going, or else denounce and arrest the guilty.[3]

---

open country or in houses, and that as soon as an officer shall receive notice of
one, he must charge the meeting in question and kill (faire main basse), without
any distinction of sex."   Bulletin de la Soc. de l'hist. du Prot. fr., xxxi. 179.

[1] Mémoires de Foucault, ubi supra.
[2] Ibid., 175.
[3] Ibid., 539.

But how to prevent men and women from going where their religious instincts led them ? How to induce them to denounce and arrest others for an act which commended itself to their own moral sense ? These were difficult problems, and intolerance is prone to attempt the solution of difficult problems of the kind in the most puerile and absurd of fashions. In the lack of anything better, a promising method of putting an end to the forbidden religious conventicles was found in gathering together the members of strongly Protestant communities, and inducing them to make professions which every one knew belied the real sentiments of their hearts, and extorting their signature to promises which every one possessed of a grain of sense must know they had no purpose to fulfil. At Nismes, at Sauve, at Anduze, at Ribaute, at Saint Jean du Gard, and probably at many another place in the strongly Protestant regions of the south, this course was pursued. Time has spared some specimens of the results of the so-called deliberations. Apparently the meetings were all held in the month of November, 1686, and it is almost needless to say that the conclusions were arrived at unanimously. The very language of these various documents is often identical. The new converts promise to live and die in the faith of the Roman Catholic Church to which they now have the happiness of being reunited. They engage to regard as sworn enemies of religion and of state all who shall fail to do their duty in respect to attendance on the mass, preaching, catechising, instruction, or other Catholic exercises. They will endeavor to discover such persons and hand them over to justice. They either ask for the appointment, or themselves make selection of certain persons to act as special " inspectors " over the entire community, for the purpose of detecting and denouncing these " violators of divine and human ordinances." They agree to place "spies " on all the highways of the parishes to prevent men from going to unlawful conventicles. In some cases they appoint a feast to be held for all time on the anniversary of the general abjuration, in order to celebrate by high mass and otherwise the singular goodness of Louis the Great in interesting himself for their eternal salvation. They beg the intercession of their superiors with the intendant and the

Promises extorted from Protestant communities.

commandant, or with his Majesty himself, " that he may have compassion on this parish." The last words betray the condition of a community that has suffered and is suffering.[1]

The secret of this strange similarity of insincere profession on the part of Protestants lately forcibly " converted " to Roman Catholicism, is found in a sentence or two of the Memoirs of the Duke of Noailles. " In regions that seemed habitable only by bears, the chief communities of the Cévennes entered into engagements, each man for all and all for each, to prevent conventicles and other contraventions of the king's orders, to give up the guilty and to raze their houses. But these deliberations were adopted under the eyes of an officer expressly sent with his detachment of troops. Men ought long since to have distrusted every forced promise that wounds the conscience." [2]

Contemporary writings abound in accounts of the fearful exactness with which were executed the commands of Louvois, to massacre as many as possible of the attendants upon the forbidden meetings of the Protestants. He that loves to read of horrors may have his appetite gratified and sated in the pages of the *Mercure historique et politique*, published monthly at the Hague, with authentic information from the neighboring kingdom, or in the still more detailed narratives, derived from every part of France, which Pierre Jurieu incorporated in his *Pastoral Letters*. But there is a dreary sameness in the chronicles of bloody persecution, and, while the historian is not permitted to pass over unnoticed events constituting an essential and peculiar feature of the period, neither is he compelled in fairness to give to his recital the character, much less the fulness, of the professed martyrology. In place, therefore, of attempting to chronicle in detail a great succession of massacres effected year after year, I may let a single para-

Various massacres.

---

[1] Borrel, Histoire de l' Église réformée de Nîmes, 324, gives the substance of the paper adopted at Nismes, and some of the signatures. J. P. Hugues inserts in his Histoire de l'Église réformée d'Anduze, 667–69, the text of the document extorted from the Protestant city whose fortunes he has so well illustrated. The Bulletin of the French Protestant Historical Society has also published the full text of similar documents adopted at Ribaute (xxx. 24–27), at Saint Jean du Gard (xxxi. 372–75), and at Sauve (xxxi. 499–504).

[2] Abbé Millot, Mémoires du Duc de Noailles (Edition Michaud et Poujoulat), 25, 26.

graph, taken from the fourth of Jurieu's pastoral letters, serve
as a sufficient account of the barbarous treatment which the
Huguenot worshippers suffered for more than two generations
of men.   The events occurred in and near the Cévennes during
the summer of 1686.

" The thirtieth of June there was a meeting of about two
thousand persons on the road from La Calmette to Barutel. The
dragoons from Nismes came and captured thirty or forty prisoners, whom they led to the tower of La Vinetière, attached to the
walls of Nismes below the *arènes* (the old Roman amphitheatre).
The next Thursday there were two more meetings, the one at
Saint Césaire, a village half a league from Nismes, and the other
at the iron cross, only a quarter of a league distant from the same
city.   Several others were held in the same district, and everywhere there were massacre, bloodshed, persons hung on the
spot, and a great number of prisoners.   But the greatest massacre was that near Uzès on the road toward Bagnols.   On the
seventh of July there were there fully twelve hundred persons.
The dragoons from Uzès learned it, and running to the place
found the faithful at their devotions. They surrounded them on
all sides.   Our friends did nothing else than raise their hands
and faces toward heaven, throwing themselves on their knees to
receive death in this attitude.   The dragoons fired upon these
unarmed people : their shots were so effective that, besides the
wounded, the ground was covered with the dead.   An eye-witness who visited the place three weeks later found thirty bodies
of women half decayed.   In addition to this the dragoons
strangled a number of persons with the halters of their horses
They took three hundred women whom they stabbed with their
bayonets in their sides and breasts.   They cut off the clothes of
some to the hip, stripped others naked, and returned to Uzès
with the spoil and with the prisoners." [1]

As François Tessier was the first martyr of the conventicles
so Fulcran Rey, a young candidate for the ministry, is entitled
to rank as the first of the preachers who, after the Revocation
expiated by a triumphant death the pretended crime of proclaim

---

[1] Pastoral Letter of October 15, 1686. The publication of these letters was b
gun September 1, 1686, and they were published twice a month.

ing the gospel in these assemblies to multitudes famishing for the word of God. He was a native of Nismes, had studied in the Académie of Geneva,[1] but had been prevented from seeking ordination at one of the synods of the Reformed churches of France, by the abolition of those ecclesiastical bodies and the recall of the Edict of Nantes by the king. But a rare devotion to the work to which he had consecrated his life, made him refuse to leave the kingdom and prefer the perils of a ministry in the interest of his fallen fellow Protestants to security in a foreign land. That ministry was very brief. He had been preaching only a few weeks in the Cévennes when he was betrayed to the government by a pretended friend and placed under arrest. His deportment was firm and courageous. The seductive offers made to him were not only rejected but spurned. "Mr. Rey," said the intendant Basville, who seemed to be touched by what the young man said, "you still have time to save yourself." "Yes, my lord," he replied, "and it is that time I want to use for my salvation." "Mr. Rey, you must change, and you shall have life." "Yes, lord, I must change, but it is to go from this life of wretchedness to the kingdom of heaven, where a blessed life awaits me, which I shall soon have and possess." "No longer think," he added later, "of terrifying me by means of death. If I had apprehended it, I should not be here." "Where did you preach?" the intendant asked him. "Wherever I found the faithful gathered." "But the king forbids it." "The King of kings has ordered me to do it, and it is right to obey God rather than men." Far from being cast down by the prospect of the gallows, he greeted the sight with strange and unconcealed delight, and left to all succeeding ministers that were called upon to attest their faith in a like manner the resplendent example of a Christian victor. He declared, and we have no reason to doubt the truth of his declaration, that when stretched upon the rack he scarcely felt any pain at all, and that he believed that those who were charged with interrogating him suffered more than he. The pious words

Execution of Fulcran Rey, at Beaucaire, July, 1686.

---

[1] The signature "Fulcrandus Rey Nemausensis" appears on the matriculation book of the Académie, under date of May 21, 1678. Le Livre du Recteur (Genève, 1860), 171.

of this young man, of only twenty-four years of age, lingered long in the memory of men, and served to edify the down-trodden communities not only of the Cévennes but of all Protestant France. He was executed at Beaucaire, on the seventh of July, 1686.[1] The authorities had feared to put him to death in a Protestant city like Nismes. He was to be followed, within less than a century, by eighty-seven other preachers of the gospel—ministers or candidates for the ministry—a noble band of heroic men, who died, one and all, for the same cause and with the same triumphant fortitude. France can boast no names more worthy of being held in everlasting remembrance.[2]

Three courses lay open to the Huguenot pastors of France at the Revocation—either to submit to the king's order and go into Exile of the exile, or to accept the king's offers and apostatize, or ministers. to defy the king's threats, and, remaining in France, endeavor to thwart his plans of converting their flocks to the Roman Catholic religion.[3] We have seen that the great majority chose the first course. Of nearly eight hundred ministers, perhaps two hundred had been driven into banishment in the years preceding the Revocation. Of the other six hundred, five hundred now followed, or attempted to follow them, being expelled from France, for the most part, with extraordinary and uncalled-for harshness. For if the Protestant religion had, up to this moment, enjoyed at least a legal toleration, secured by edicts solemnly enacted, endorsed by successive monarchs as perpetual and irrevocable, and repeatedly recognized as of binding force even by the reigning sovereign, was it too much to expect, in all equity, that, should his Majesty change his mind and determine to repeal the laws for the protection of Protestantism, he would guarantee to the ministers of that religion an unimpeded exit from the realm, with their wives, their children, and their goods?

---

[1] The fullest account is contained in a contemporary letter : ''Lettre d'un ami à un Protestant réfugié sur le sujet de la personne et de la mort du sieur Fulcran Rey, proposant.'' Printed in the Bulletin de la Soc. de l'hist. du Prot. français, x. 122-136. Jurieu and Benoist refer to Rey more briefly. Daniel Benoit gives a good sketch in his Église sous la Croix (Toulouse, 1882), 1-35.

[2] See the long list in Douen, Les Premiers Pasteurs du Désert, ii., App., 399-402.

[3] O. Douen, Les Premiers Pasteurs du Désert, i. 80, etc.

Instead of this, they were, in many cases, the victims of a malice as petty as it was contemptible. They found difficulties on every hand. They were refused permission to take with them their children that were above seven years of age. They were fortunate if they were allowed to carry out any considerable part of their meagre substance. They must have passports, and these were grudgingly furnished. Such provincial pastors as were in Paris at the moment of the recall of the edict were refused facilities for reaching the frontiers with promptness. It appeared as though the government were anxious to make it impossible for them to avail themselves of the fortnight's grace, so that the king might have the satisfaction of sending them to row in the galleys. The three pastors of the church of Montpellier vainly sought to obtain the necessary papers for leaving France from La Reynie, head of the police of Paris. They fared no better at Versailles, where the Marquis of Châteauneuf, after keeping them several days waiting, informed them that the king bade them go back to their province to get their passports. The distance from the capital to Montpellier is not much short of five hundred miles. It was impossible for them to get there before the expiration of the fourteen days. On their arrival, the intendant, Basville, incarcerated them for several days in the citadel, and came near sending them to the galleys. At last he placed them in the hands of a guide, to whom they paid a round price to take them to a place of security.[1]

I have already adverted to the deplorable fact that probably not less than one hundred pastors succumbed, at least for a time, to fear and apostatized.[2]

The number of the ministers that took the third course, and undertook to brave the terrible fate awaiting any Protestant preacher that remained in France longer than two weeks, was small. We know the names of five,[3] including Fulcran Rey. How many more there were, it is, in the very nature of the case, difficult to say. For the most

Obstacles maliciously placed in their way.

A few undertake to remain in France.

---

[1] Douen, ubi supra, i. 84.

[2] Supra, c. xi. p. 50.

[3] The other four were Jean Lefèvre, of Sedan; Sebastian Balicourt, of Metz; David Martin of Lacaune, and Gardien Givry. Douen, ubi supra, i. 86.

FRANCE

Military Divisions established by the
Political Assembly of La Rochelle (1621)
and
The Huguenot Cities of Refuge under
the Edict of Nantes (1598-1622)

(After Anquez)

⋈ Hostage Cities proper
○ "Places de Mariage"
🏰 Royal Free Cities
△ "Places particulieres" held by Huguenot nobles
All Huguenot cities, by whatever tenure held,
are underscored.

part, the Protestant ministers who stanchly maintained their religious creed saw before them no alternative but exile, and so far submitted as to leave France.

Before long the propriety of their conduct was called in question. Bossuet, in his funeral oration in honor of Chancellor Le Tellier, had the effrontery to cast in the teeth of the pastors whom the king, obedient to the behests of the established church, had expelled from the kingdom, the reproach of having deserted those whom they had been set to instruct and guard. As unscrupulous respecting the truth as when he affirmed that the Protestants of his own diocese had not been subjected to the slightest persecution, he pretended that the Protestant ministers throughout the kingdom left of their own free will. For it was no falsehood of ordinary magnitude for him to describe them, in the hearing of those who knew the full facts, as false shepherds, forsaking their flocks without even waiting for the order, and happy to allege to them their banishment as an excuse.[1] Others less eloquent and famous repeated the calumny. There soon appeared at Amsterdam what purported to be an appeal of the Protestant captives in France addressed to their pastors who had taken refuge in England, Holland, Germany, Switzerland, and elsewhere.[2] After beginning with the expression of warm thanks for the pastoral letters which the ministers had written them with the view of consoling them in their affliction, the writers quickly changed their voice to one of bitter censure. They asked them, as cowardly shepherds that had abandoned their flocks, how they would be able to give an account to the sovereign Judge of heaven and earth who had entrusted these flocks to their keeping. They reminded them that Jesus Christ has said that the good shepherd lays down his life for the sheep. They met the allegation that our Lord himself directed his disciples, when persecuted in one place to flee to another, by replying that one may indeed yield to the force of the torrent, and stand aside a little, so to speak, to avoid its fury, but that the

Bossuet accuses the ministers of cowardice.

A pretended appeal to them to return.

---

[1] See supra, page 56.

[2] Lettre des réformez captifs en France aux ministres réfugiez en Angleterre, en Hollande, en Allemagne et en Suisse et autres lieux. Du 29 mars 1686. It is printed in the Bulletin de la Soc. de l'hist. du Prot. fr., xii. (1863), 300-305.

true pastors of the Gospel ought never to go so far from their sheep as not always to be ready and in a position to succor those that need them, even at the cost of their lives. For this they cited the examples of the apostles and of the early fathers. They conjured them to return, and try to save the residue of the house of Israel. It was not, indeed, a time to cry aloud; but it was a time to dwell concealed in the wilderness, in the clefts of the rocks, and in the woods, after the example of the first Christians and of the blessed fathers in the days of the Reformation. If God should call them to a martyr's death, at least they would earn the joy of having courageously sacrificed their lives to retain in France that ark of the covenant "which," said the writers, "you have unhappily abandoned to the fury of the Philistines, and which we shall endeavor to retain in its place and preserve, should it cost us our lives, as it has already cost the lives of some of our brethren, whose blood not only cries before God for vengeance, but accuses you of your want of firmness and zeal in the sight of men and of angels."

In reply to the reiterated and urgent calls of the refugee ministers to leave all, and, despite every obstacle, make their way to a land of religious freedom, the writers, in the name of the Protestants still remaining in France, decline the invitation. "We are persuaded that if God had intended to remove His candlestick outside of this kingdom, He would have opened the door and have facilitated the egress of an infinite number of good souls that have remained. Do not therefore believe, dear fathers, that we shall take the advice which you have given us to follow you in your flight. We shall not take it. Our churches have been torn down, our pastors have abandoned us, our property has been taken away, as also the liberty of many of us: what matters it? The woods and forests, the grottoes and caverns serve us for churches. God's holy word, which we have in our hands, is a lamp to our feet and a light to our path. God even gives to the most simple of us the tongue of the learned to expound his word. In place of the goods of which we have been robbed, we already possess the pearl of great price which no one can take from us. We are in no doubt respecting the charity exercised by our brethren toward you, and we readily believe that you derive great satisfaction from being able to frequent, publicly and without fear, the exercises of piety, and to sing aloud the praises of God; but this contentment is a trifle in comparison with the holy joy which we experience when at night, by the light of a thousand heavenly lamps, and while all nature seems buried in thick darkness, we find ourselves in some wood, holding converse about the word of God, singing His divine songs, and hearing the echoes on every side repeat after us the praises of the Lord.   Our joy is so great that it seems to us that the angels take part in our divine concerts, and it may be that it is not all a fancy, as men have tried to make us believe." [1]

Much more there was to the same effect, with a final entreaty, in the name of God who had honored them with the sacred ministry, no longer to dishonor that sacred charge by a shameful withdrawal, and to have compassion on so many weak souls, tottering on the brink of a precipice, whom a helping hand might rescue from their perilous situation.

Was the letter, as it purported to be, the work of a French Protestant sincerely distressed by what he honestly regarded as the cowardly desertion of ministers, each one of whom, no longer interesting himself in the flock committed to his charge, went so far as to style himself "heretofore" pastor of such or such a church?   Or, was it the production of an enemy, intended to discredit the Protestant refugee pastors and counteract the potent influence of their ardent pastorals upon the unfortunate "new converts?"   The future historian, Élie Benoist, who replied to it in a strong and carefully prepared vindication of the conduct of himself and of his fellow pastors,[2] took the latter view; and a recent writer does

Benoist vindicates their course.

---

[1] "Notre joye est sy grande, qu'il nous semble que les anges se mêlent à nos divins concerts, ouye les anges, et ce n'est peut-être pas tout une chymère, comme on a voulu faire accroire."

[2] Under the title Histoire et apologie de la retraite des pasteurs à cause de la persécution de France (Frankfort, 1687).   See Haag, La France Protestante, ii. 272.   I am not sure, however, that Benoist did not subsequently change his opinion.   In the last volume of his great history of the Edict of Nantes, which was published eight years later (Delft, 1695), he refers (v. 942) to the letter that occasioned his apology and to the apology itself in these words: "De la bouche de ces ennemis l'accusation passa dans celle de quelques Reformez; dont quelques-uns même firent courir quelques lettres au desavantage des Ministres. Cela fit prendre à quelqu'un d'eux la résolution d'écrire leur apologie."

not hesitate to pronounce the letter a piece of raillery of the most odious sort, in which the hangman taunts his victim.[1] Certainly the general harshness that characterizes the whole letter, and the suspicious uniformity with which the word "Father" is applied to Protestant ministers, seem to betray a Roman Catholic hand in the composition. However, it is immaterial to our purpose to decide the truth or falsity of the conjecture: all that really concerns us to notice is that, whether as a taunt of an enemy or as a friendly remonstrance, the reproach was laid at the door of the ministers of too ready a compliance with the king's command to leave the realm.

I shall not undertake to rehearse the arguments alleged in refutation by Benoist and others. Much less is my intention to attempt the solution of a moral problem of no little difficulty, in which the answer must necessarily depend upon a variety of considerations which a person far removed from the scene can scarcely weigh with accuracy. This much is certain: that the pastors of France in the first consternation produced by the recall of the Edict of Nantes deemed it little short of a physical impossibility to subsist in their native land, and regarded the attempt to remain for the purpose of strengthening the weak and raising up the fallen among their fellow believers as sheer madness. It would have been useless to try to reach people who, for the moment, at least, were too much terrified to risk the danger of drawing down upon themselves the pains incurred by harboring the proscribed pastor, and without a shelter the most devoted of pastors could not but fail to effect anything.[2]

Some short space of time is required to overcome the first bewildering effects of such a blow as befell the Huguenots. The moment of recovery had arrived even before the publication of Benoist's monumental history, for he thus briefly alludes to it: "Meantime, as there still dwelt in France many families that, having come to themselves after the first violence of the dragoons, sighed for the consolations which they had lost

---

[1] O. Douen, Les Premiers Pasteurs du Désert, i. 137.

[2] Fulcran Rey found that he could do nothing at Montauban and Milhau. At Saint Affrique, where he had relatives, he could get no one to take him in. At Pont de Camarès no one would listen to him. See the contemporary letter referred to above, Bulletin de la Soc. de l'hist. du Prot. fr., x. 124.

and manifested a great desire again to see some ministers, there
were a number [of the latter] who re-entered France from different quarters, and who went to labor for the relief of these
burdened consciences."[1]

This return of pastors to France seems to have been to no
inconsiderable extent the consequence of the views propounded
by Pierre Jurieu in his celebrated work on " the Fulfilment of the Prophecies ; or, the Approaching Deliverance of the Church." [2]   In this work the author

Effect of
Jurieu's
" Fulfilment
of Proph-
ecy."

proved, according to the lengthy statement of the title-
page, that Popery is the reign of Antichrist, and that this reign
is not far from its fall ; that this fall will begin shortly ; that
persecution may cease in three years and a half ; that after that
will begin the destruction of Antichrist ; that this will continue
into the approaching century, and that finally the reign of Jesus
Christ will come on the earth.   According to this view, the two
witnesses of Revelation slain by the Beast, whose dead bodies
were to lie unburied three days and a half, until the Spirit
should enter them, were the Holy Scriptures and the preachers
of the Gospel.   It was not difficult to identify the year 1685,
which saw in France the Revocation of the Edict of Nantes,
and in Great Britain the accession of the Roman Catholic
James the Second, with the date of the triumph of Antichrist.
If so, his overthrow must coincide with the period of the years
1688 and 1689.   This persuasion, however fanciful the grounds
on which it was based, exercised no small influence in forwarding the success of the designs of William of Orange in the invasion of England.   It seems also to have impressed upon the
mind of more than one pastor who had made good his escape
to a foreign land of safety, that he ought to return to his native
France and have a share in the accomplishment of the predictions of Holy Writ.[3]   Be this as it may, there is no doubt that
the movement in question took larger dimensions just about
this time.   It speaks well for the sincere piety and self-devo-
tion of those same ministers, upon whom their retirement

---

[1] Histoire de l'Édit de Nantes, v. 943.

[2] L'Accomplissement des Prophéties, ou la Délivrance prochaine de l'Église,
etc.   Rotterdam, 1686.

[3] See O. Douen, ubi supra, i. 156 et seq.

from France, when proscribed by the revocatory edict, had
brought unmerited censure, that during the remaining twelve
or thirteen years of the seventeenth century, not less
than about fifty returned to labor for the recovery
of the persecuted French Protestants.[1] For no one
knew better than they did, the appalling dangers which they
were about to confront, and to which a large proportion were
destined to fall victims. More fortunate than were the contemporaries of the events, we are now able to read, on the one hand,
the records of the preparations for their desperate mission,
made with the utmost secrecy by these heroic men, and, on the
other, the instructions of ministers of state and heads of police
to watch for them, the reports of spies that dogged their steps,
the denunciations of informers who wormed their way into the
confidence of the men whom they intended to betray, and the
very orders issued from Paris or Versailles that consigned
them to an imprisonment worse than death. For it is a source
of satisfaction that, if much of the evidence of the crimes
committed by the members of the government of Louis the
Fourteenth was purposely destroyed, not a little has escaped
through accident or negligence.

Return of Protestant Pastors to France.

Some of these daring pastors were not only very active but
remarkably successful, in the brief space of time allotted to
them, and in face of stupendous difficulties. De Malzac, who, after serving some three years as extraordinary pastor at Rotterdam, re-entered France about the
beginning of 1690, was among those that escaped the clutches
of the police for the longest time. His missionary activity
extended over somewhat more than two years. Half a year he
spent in Paris, where he held a great number of private meetings. The next six months were consumed in traversing a
great part of the central and southern provinces of France.
For a full year he was again in the capital. The Protestants
heard him gladly, and began to recover from their depression.
When arrested and examined by the civil authorities, he estimated at not less than twenty thousand the adherents of his
own religion whom he had exhorted, and at between two and

De Malzac.

---

[1] O. Douen, ubi supra, i. 159.

three hundred the Roman Catholics who, convinced of the errors of their faith, had abjured it in his presence and had been admitted to the Protestant communion.[1]

From 1688 to 1690, three different ministers—Cottin, Masson, and La Gacherie—came, the one after another, to visit their brethren in Normandy. One of them wrote that the fruit of their toil surpassed all expectation. They were everywhere welcomed, even by those who stood in the greatest dread of renewed persecution. Everywhere those that had been compelled by violence to abjure Protestantism gave signal evidence of regret for their weakness, and repaired their fault, so far as possible, by setting their names to a declaration of adhesion to their original belief. At Rouen, in particular, "everybody had been converted." Many were received into the peace of the church in the presence of a handful of the faithful. Doubtless the ceremony had no external grandeur; but, simple as it was, like all other services of a religion placed under the ban of the law, it was invested with a rare pathos. There might be not more than twelve or fifteen present—a greater number could not be brought together because of the malevolence of those who watched all the actions of the "new converts"—yet the joy was "inexpressible" with which the minister was received. Gradually there came to be meetings of about three hundred Huguenots. Two such gatherings were held on the morning and evening of Pentecost, or Whitsunday, 1688—one of the three or four festivals at which the Huguenots had always observed the celebration of the Lord's Supper.[2]

(marginal note: Cottin, Masson, and La Gacherie.)

---

[1] See page 319 of the sketch of De Malzac in Douen, Les Premiers Pasteurs du Désert (i. 296–339). The article contains a rough draft of a sermon on the text "Whosoever will come after me, let him deny himself and take up his cross and follow me" (Mark viii. 34)—one of twenty-two sermons of De Malzac which are preserved among the MSS. of the French National Library.

[2] Francis Waddington, Le Protestantisme en Normandie depuis la Révocation de l'Édit de Nantes jusqu'à la fin du dix-huitième siècle (Paris, 1862), 21–23. Mr. Waddington gives, from A. Court's manuscript history of the Reformed Churches of France, now in the Library of Geneva, the full text of the declaration, which was signed by a great many persons in Paris, Normandy, and elsewhere. Douen gives a copy of the same. Les Premiers Pasteurs du Désert, i. 178.

Sooner or later all these venturesome ministers, with rare exceptions, dropped out of sight. In some cases they were never again heard of by their friends; in others, only after the lapse of a great number of years. Arrested by the government after a patient and assiduous waiting, they were not publicly tried, nor executed, nor sent to the galleys. The most profound secrecy was affected by their captors. In December, 1689, the Walloon church of Ardembourg granted to its pastor, Pierre de Salve, a furlough, "that he might go and terminate some important matters"—the established formula in such a case—allowing him to supply his place with a competent minister. The next month De Salve was arrested in Paris and placed in the dungeon at Vincennes. Five years after, his family did not know his fate. Ten years passed and the Synod of Zutphen did not know whether he was dead or alive. Twenty years from his incarceration his brother expressed a hope that peace might soon be concluded and De Salve might be liberated. The release came at last; but it was the merciful hand of death that set the weary prisoner free.[1]

Long before that time, Legendre had written, in his history of the persecution of the church of Rouen, respecting the disappearance of another pastor, Cardel: " It will soon be fifteen years since he has been in so deplorable a state, without being heard of, any more than Messrs. Mathurin, Malzac, and De Salve—three other pastors who successively left the United Provinces for the same object, and shared the same fate. The ignorance in which all their friends are as to what may have happened to them during so long a detention is a certain mark of their immovable steadfastness. For, had they shown the slightest feebleness, it would not have failed to be published." [2]

The fact was that Louis the Fourteenth took a childish delight in shrouding the fate of the returning ministers that fell into his hands in the most profound mystery. They were consigned to the most distant and lonely fortresses of the kingdom, with every precaution taken that as few as possible should know who they were and whither

Disappearance of the captured preachers.

Sent to the Iles Sainte Marguerite.

---

[1] Douen, ubi supra, i. 265, 266.

[2] Histoire de la Persécution faite à l'Église de Rouen sur la fin du dernier siècle. Rotterdam, 1704 (Fac-simile reprint of Rouen, 1874), 94, 95.

they went. "I have charged the Sieur Auzillon," the Marquis of Seignelay wrote to the governor of the Bastile, "with an order to take the minister Cardel and conduct him to the place which will be indicated to him. The king orders me to tell you so to manage that no one may know what has become of him; and to this end his Majesty wills that you have him placed in Auzillon's hands at ten o'clock at night, when he will come to get him." To the governor of the Iles Sainte Marguerite[1] the king himself wrote the same day: "Monsieur de Saint Mars, I send to the Iles Sainte Marguerite the man named Cardel, a former minister of the pretended Reformed religion, to be kept there for his entire life. And I write you this letter to tell you that my intention is, that you receive him, that you have him placed in the most secure place possible, and that he be carefully guarded and hold no communication with any person, whoever he may be, by word of mouth or in writing, under any pretext whatsoever;" a command which the minister of state accompanied with a note of his own: "I add to the king's letter that his Majesty will not have the man who is to be placed in your care known by anybody, whoever he be, and that you keep the matter secret in such wise that it may come to nobody's knowledge who this man is." Two months later, Cardel having apparently become ill, the Marquis of Louvois wrote from Marly to Saint Mars: "If the last prisoner placed in your hands should have extreme need of bleeding, you may have him bled in your presence, taking all the precautions necessary to prevent the surgeon from knowing who he is."[2]

The reader will, I doubt not, have been reminded by the singular precautions here taken—and the same precautions were taken for each of the pastors subsequently sent to join Cardel in captivity—of the strange story of the Man of the Iron Mask.

---

[1] The fort known by this name is situated on one of the two Lérins islands, about a league from the mainland, opposite the town of Cannes, on the Mediterranean.

[2] The first three notes are of April 18, 1689; the last note of June 24, 1689. Douen, Les Premiers Pasteurs du Désert, i. 187-189. Some additional orders of the same kind are given, ibid, i. 262-64, and in the Bulletin de la Soc. de l'hist. du Prot. fr., iv. 121 et seq.

This famous personage, respecting whom a hundred theories have been fruitlessly started, but who remains a riddle as inscru-

Fellow pris-
oners of the
Man of the
Iron Mask. table as ever, is also said to have been for twelve years (1686–1698) an inmate of the dungeons of the Îles Sainte Marguerite, where he too was closely guarded by Monsieur de Saint Mars. It was by Saint Mars himself that, at the king's command, he was conducted to the Bastile, where he died on the nineteenth of November, 1703. I offer no new solution of the historical enigma that has baffled every attempt to explain it. A contemporary though he was with the Huguenot pastors, incarcerated in the same lonely prison on the shores of the Mediterranean, and intrusted to the vigilant care of the same nobleman as jailer, the fanciful notion that he might actually have been one of their number[1] is disproved by the still more extraordinary measures adopted, it is said, to conceal his identity, and by the circumstance that when he died he was buried as a Roman Catholic, in consecrated ground, in the cemetery of Saint Paul.

When I referred above to the conversion of a very considerable number of Roman Catholics to the Reformed faith in con-

Conversion
of many
Roman
Catholics. nection with the perilous ministry of Malzac, it was far from my intention to represent this as a solitary phenomenon. On the contrary, it would seem from the secret advices received by the government from its spies, that the same thing occurred as a characteristic of the activity of the other workers. Gardien Givry, who in his peregrinations also went by the pseudonym of Duchêne, was particularly favored

Gardien
Givry's
work. in this regard. A special interest attaches to this preacher, at the time of which I speak a man in middle life. Born in Vervins in 1647, he studied in the Académie of Geneva, and was admitted to the sacred ministry. Seven years before the Revocation he was deposed from his office for an act of immorality by which he had disgraced it. When, full of repentance, he sought, a year before the Revocation, to be restored, there was no longer a synod in France

---

[1] " *L'Homme au masque de fer*, serait-ce donc tout simplement un de ces pauvres ministres de la R. P. R., traités en prisonniers d'État, et au sujet desquels au prescrivait le secret le plus absolu ? " Bulletin de la Soc. de l'hist. du Prot. fr., iv. 120.

capable of removing the censure; but the office was performed at Lausanne, in Switzerland, by a body composed of seven refugee French pastors and of a few elders of churches. He asked and obtained permission to preach and administer the sacraments, with the express condition that he should find the field of his labors in the regions where the Reformed religion was proscribed—or, in the significant phrase that appears in the documents of his trial, when, at a subsequent time, he was arrested, that he should " preach under the Cross." [1] It was thus that he threw himself into the work with a peculiar zeal, eager, as more than once he tells us, to efface by the good which he might accomplish, even at the risk of his life, the scandal of his past course. [2]

Givry's first efforts, in the midst of the consternation of the Dragonnades preceding the formal recall of the Edict of Nantes, were abortive, and he shortly left the country. It was quite otherwise when, a few years later, in fulfilment of his vow, he re-entered France from the north. He had feared coldness and apathy at the hands of the Protestants who knew his history, because of his personal unworthiness of his high office. Instead of this, even the Protestants of Vervins and its vicinity embraced him with a thousand marks of friendship and esteem, and blessed God who had sent him, for having inspired him with the necessary zeal and courage for so great an enterprise. [3] Where a few timid Huguenots, to the number of fifty or sixty, had already begun to meet secretly on Sundays to read God's

---

[1] " Mais il ne fut rétabli qu'à condition de prêcher sous la croix, ce qui veut dire parmi ceux de la R. P. R., à condition de prêcher dans les lieux où l'exercice de la R. est défendu, et pour cela il retourna à Montpellier, où le temple avait déjà été abattu." Interrogatory of May 24, 1692, apud Douen, Derniers Pasteurs, i. 357.

[2] His own words are touching : " Je bénis de toute mon âme sa bonne et sage Providence, qui m'avait conduit si heureusement parmi tant de hazards, et qui m'avait ramené en ma patrie après tant d'années pour y réparer les désordres de ma vie passée, par tous les bons offices que je pourrais lui rendre au péril de ma vie. Rien ne me toucha plus que la gloire de mon Dieu et l'édification de son Église, et je compris par ces premiers soins de la bonté de Dieu, qu'il m'appelait à consoler une partie de ses enfants affligés, quelque indigne que je me fusse rendu de le servir dans la glorieuse charge de ministre de l'Évangile." Autobiography, ibid., i. 364, 365.

[3] Ibid., i. 366.

Word, there gathered to hear him more persons than the place
of worship could contain. He had been told a hundred times,
in England and Holland, that nothing could yet be done in
France. Instead of this, he discovered a rich harvest awaiting
the reaper. He found meetings of four or five hundred persons.
Men came from every direction and followed him wherever he
went, " to pick up some crumbs of the bread of life, and to try
to refresh themselves with a few drops of that water springing up
into everlasting life which long since had ceased to flow in the
desolated region." [1] Most of all was he rejoiced to receive a
deputation from seven villages not far from Saint Quentin.
The delegates represented places inhabited exclusively by Roman Catholics, who had never seen a preacher nor heard a Huguenot sermon, but who professed an incredible ardor to see
and hear one that might communicate to them the truth, in
place of the falsehood and superstition with which they had
been surfeited. When, a few days later, he visited
them, there was assembled in that curious natural depression known as "La Boîte à Cailloux," [2] a respectful audience of five hundred persons, representing one hundred
families, who, to the light of bonfires and torches, hung upon
his lips, from nine o'clock in the evening until an hour after
midnight, as he set forth the truth for which they had been waiting. The same scene was repeated when he revisited them a
week later. [3] The eagerness of his hearers seemed to Givry little
less than a miracle from heaven. Cautious as he was not to admit any persons to the communion of the Reformed churches
until they had had time to acquire a more perfect knowledge of
Protestant doctrine, and to prove the sincerity and persistence

The converts at " La Boîte à Cailloux."

---

[1] Autobiography, apud Les Premiers Pasteurs du Désert, i. 368.

[2] M. Douen has given a long description of the spot and its neighborhood,
ubi supra, i. 349–356.

[3] Ibid., i. 369–370. Rossier, Histoire des Protestants de Picardie (Paris, 1861),
267, 268. Besides his sketch of Gardien Givry in Les Premiers Pasteurs du
Désert, i. 349–401, M. Douen read a valuable paper on the same subject before
the French Protestant Historical Society in 1860 (Bulletin, ix. 174–192), and
referred to Givry's missionary activity in his long treatise, La Réforme en
Picardie, published in the same learned periodical in 1859, and subsequently
in a separate work with the title Essai historique sur les Églises Réformées du
Département de l'Aisne (Paris, 1860).

of their purpose, he had no reason to deplore their inconstancy. It is of interest, as an indication that great religious movements, if rapid, yet may be enduring, to notice that each of the seven villages which, up to Givry's time, had contained only Roman Catholics, is said at present to boast a Protestant place of worship.[1] Needless to say, Louis the Fourteenth, when informed of these and other conversions to Protestantism, felt sincere annoyance that, while he was flattering himself with the prospect of speedily putting down "heresy" in France by compelling its adherents to enter the established church, a goodly number of persons that had been members of that church from their birth were actually embracing "heresy." However, he knew no more manly way of meeting the difficulty than is indicated in a letter which one of his secretaries wrote to the bishops whose dioceses were concerned, under date of the fourteenth of October, 1692. "As his Majesty has ascertained that these perversions can be prevented and the New Catholics be sincerely reunited, if the bishops apply themselves to learn the persons that conduct the Protestants to the places where the services have been held, and to gain them over by his Majesty's recompenses and benefits, he has ordered me to instruct the intendant to confer with you as to what is to be done, and to write to you that you can do nothing more pleasing to him than to prevent these perversions."[2]

It is proper here to notice certain phenomena recorded in documents of the period under consideration which, although not without a parallel elsewhere, are none the less remark-able and interesting. I refer to the reported "songs and voices which were heard in several places in the air," and to the predictions of the so-called "little prophets of the Cévennes."

Reported wonders.

Times of great mental strain and excitement, especially if long continued and intense, are wont to breed a kind of exaltation or enthusiasm that takes less account of the ordinary im-

---

[1] Bulletin de la Soc. de l'hist. du Prot. fr., xviii. (1869) 245. Some of these churches appear to be among the most flourishing of the region ; Hargicourt, for instance. See H. Perrenoud, Étude historique sur les Progrès du Protestantisme en France (Paris, 1889), 218.

[2] Rossier, ubi supra, 269.

pressions made upon the senses than of such as the observer receives, or fancies that he receives, in modes as strange and unusual as the circumstances in which he finds himself placed are extraordinary and outside of the range of familiar experience. The Huguenots remaining in France in the last years of the seventeenth century underwent the most startling change of fortunes. They were robbed by their king of the privilege of professing a religion which, whatever that king had been led by misrepresentation to believe to the contrary, they ardently loved. Their public worship in the use of the holy Scriptures, the familiar forms of Calvin's liturgy, and the no less familiar psalms of Clément Marot and Theodore Beza, was silenced. Their spiritual leaders were in exile. Their " temples," or sacred edifices, from one end of France to the other, had been razed to the ground : the ruins stared them in the face and daily reminded them of the happier hours of the past, as often as they walked through the town or suburb. Regret was rendered more poignant in the case of many by the pangs of wounded conscience. Men and women could not forgive themselves who in a moment of weakness, but not infrequently under a pressure of persecution which it is difficult for us to estimate, had made an insincere profession of another religion. To such no word of exhortation to repentance or of comfort came from living man or woman, save possibly from some layman in a secret and proscribed conventicle. Books of devotion, and particularly the Bible, were all that remained; and of the Bible those portions seemed most appropriate to their condition, and were most eagerly read, that treat of the mysterious realm of prophecy and under figurative terms hold forth promises of the future overthrow of the wicked and the ultimate triumph of the cause of the oppressed.

Under these circumstances it is not strange, perhaps, that many of the Huguenots were in a frame of mind that disposed them both to imagine that they themselves heard supernatural voices in the air, and to lend a ready belief to those who af-
The "voices in the air." firmed, with every indication of honesty and full conviction, that they had heard them. Thus it is that, from the journal of one of the members of the former church of Metz, we learn that on the twenty-third of December, 1685, " a

number of persons went to the ramparts of the fortifications and spent the greater part of the night listening to the singing of psalms that were sung in the air—a thing that is certified by many persons, including the Romish soldiers who were on guard near the demolished 'temple,' who frequently heard voices in the air, of an admirable melody, as they said. They were forbidden by their officers from publishing it in the town." [1]

One of the most entertaining of the " Pastoral Letters " of the famous Pierre Jurieu, whom his adversaries honored with the title of " the Goliath of the Protestants," and who was himself a firm believer of this modern miracle, is devoted to the theme. [2] Its strange statements are not only given in detail, but are attested by certificates signed by reputable persons, who profess either themselves to have heard the voices, or to have received the direct testimony of friends that had heard them. Some had heard them in the Cévennes ; one had heard them as he passed by the church of Vassy, in Champagne ; the greater number testified to what had occurred at Orthez, a considerable town in Béarn, after Protestant worship was proscribed in the Huguenot " temple." It was generally about eight or nine o'clock in the evening that the voices were heard at Orthez, sing-

At Orthez.

ing most melodiously what the auditors recognized distinctly as the psalms. Rarely could the words be caught ; but once the first verse of the forty-second psalm, " As the hart panteth after the water-brooks," was distinguished, and at another time a part of the one hundred and thirty-eighth, " I will worship toward Thy holy temple." Magendie, formerly pastor of Orthez, testified that Mademoiselle de Casenaue had told persons worthy of credit that she and a multitude of others, one evening about eleven o'clock, were " ravished with that pleasant melody which they heard in the air," and returned home " with this great consolation to have heard these psalms sung in the air which they could no more sing in their church which had been interdicted for some months past ; " and they added " that it seemed to them that they heard them sing after the same manner which they used to sing in their church, and

---

[1] Journal inédit d'un fidèle de l'ancienne église de Metz. Bulletin de la Société de l'hist. du Prot. franç., xi. 174.

[2] It is dated December 1, 1686.

that, after the singing had ceased, there was a voice which spake, but after a manner inarticulate and confused, so that they could not distinguish what was said." "This gentlewoman is very well worthy of credit," noted Magendie.[1]

What the pastor had only learned from others, Bergerit and Jean de la Bordette and Mademoiselle Deformalagues affirmed over their signs manual that they heard with their own ears, in the months of September and October, 1685. The last named had listened, in company with a great number, "which had ran together from all parts to hear this heavenly voice," "a melody so ravishing that I never heard anything like it," "a charming music which represented to me a great number of voices that agreed exceedingly well." In fact, in her enthusiasm, she ran to call a Roman Catholic physician of her acquaintance, who on his arrival also heard, but observed : "Alas! I observe here a crafty wile of the devil. He causes these voices in the air to keep the world in error and hinder this poor people from converting [being converted] and embracing the Catholic faith." Whereupon the Huguenot aptly inquired whether he had ever heard that the devil sang the praises of God.[2]

Nor was this all. We are assured that "an infinite number of persons of Orthez do say that they have heard the singing of psalms, which they call the singing of angels, and that they exhorted each other on the day to be present in the night in certain places of the city to satisfy this holy curiosity; which was the reason that the magistrates of Orthez published an ordinance whereby they forbade all persons from going out of their houses or assembling themselves by night for hearing these voices which filled this poor afflicted people with joy and extraordinary consolation." Thus states Magendie; while Pierre Mauperg, of Orthez, adds : "I have heard a proclamation published to all sorts of persons, at the sound of the trumpet, by the crier of the city, called Monleres, containing that none were to go out at night to hear the singing of psalms, under the penalty of imprisonment."[3]

An ordinance forbidding men from going to hear them.

---

[1] Certificate of Magendie, dated Amsterdam, November 23, 1686.

[2] Certificate of Mlle. Deformalagues, dated September 4, 1686.

[3] Certificate of Pierre Mauperg, aged twenty-three years, dated November 22, 1686.

Finally, anticipating the demand of the sceptical for the production of the ordinances of the Parliament of Pau and of the
magistrates of Orthez containing the prohibition in question,
Jurieu observes that it was not at all probable that those who
desired to obliterate the knowledge of so extraordinary an event
and so disadvantageous to them, would consign the ordinance
to paper, much less print it. He appeals to the direct testimony
of one respectable witness who declared that he heard the proclamation, and to the fact that two thousand citizens held it to
be authentic. And he adds, in words that seem almost to an-
ticipate the results of modern invention in our own times : " If
this be not sufficient to convince those that doubt, they may
tarry, if they please, till men have found the secret of collecting
the impressions that words make upon the air and rendering
them visible, and then they will be made to see all things in
their original." [1]

More important than the delusion respecting the " voices and
songs in the air," because less easy of explanation by rational
conjecture and at once more permanent and far more intimately
affecting the interests of Protestantism in its approaching efforts to rise into newness of life, was the appearance in the
southeastern part of France of a number of persons, former
adherents of the Reformed faith, who claimed the possession of
The Cévenol an extraordinary gift of prophecy from heaven. The
Prophets. origin of the movement is obscure and uncertain.
While we have for its later developments the sympathetic accounts of friends, or of fair-minded opponents, for its beginnings
we are wholly dependent upon two hostile sources : the distorted
narrative of Brueys, who from a minister of the Reformed Church
had become a Roman Catholic priest and a virulent enemy of
the religion of his youth and of all that remained faithful to it,
and the scarcely less inimical writings of Fléchier, Bishop of
Nismes. The latter, a contemporary and living not far from
the scene, believes it probable that the impulse of the pro-

---

[1] I quote from the quaint translation published in London in 1689, under the
title of "The Pastoral Letters of the incomparable Jurieu, directed to the Protestants in France groaning under the Babylonish Tyranny, 160." The certificates or depositions which I have drawn upon are all contained in the seventh
letter, 143–165.

phetic movement came from Geneva, as the result of concerted action, and that the date was about the fifteenth of January, 1689.   According to Fléchier, a glass-founder of Dieu-le-Fit, in Dauphiny, one sieur Du Serre, was its first apostle.   The manufacture of glass was, as is well known, a privileged trade wherein a man of family could engage without forfeiting his claim to nobility.[1]   As a *gentilhomme verrier*, Du Serre exerted a considerable influence in the region. He is represented as an unprincipled impostor, who, returning after a sojourn on the banks of Lake Leman, brought with him the gift of prophecy, which he pretended to impart first to his wife and the members of his large family, and afterward to a great number of boys and girls.   These he systematically trained, in his school of enthusiasm, to fall as though suddenly affected by some uncontrollable force, and, while lying supine in a species of trance, to excite the popular wonder to the highest pitch by giving utterance to more or less incoherent rhapsodies composed of certain formulas of preaching, some Gospel exhortations, and frequent invectives against the papal church and its ceremonies.   His example was emulated by the widow of a counsellor of the parliament of Grenoble, Madame du Bays, who undertook to fashion a few of the novel preachers; while a young girl, Isabeau Vincent, a wool-carder's daughter, better known from her striking appearance as *La Belle Isabeau*, and Gabriel Astier, of Clieu, became ardent votaries of the sect. If Du Serre was a cheat, his followers, at least, were sincere. Inciting the peasantry to a rising against the royal tyranny, in league, as they said, with a corrupt church, they did not shun an encounter with the troops sent against them, but encouraged one another to believe that no weapon could injure them, as they bared their bosoms to hostile missiles, and raised a wild and meaningless cry of *Tartara !*   Many of the fanatics were slain; the fair Isabeau was captured and, we are told, was led, when in prison, to recognize the falsity of her hopes and her dreams; Astier escaped for the moment, only to be subsequently detected at Montpellier in disguise, and to expiate his

Fléchier's story of their origin.

---

[1] "Le métier de verrier ne dérogeait pas à la noblesse."   Dict. de l'Académie.

offence against king and church by an excruciating death upon the wheel.

Such is the sum of the information that comes to us from a suspicious source, together with many circumstantial details, which go less to prove the truth of the narrative than to illustrate the prejudice and the levity of the clerical narrators. For the scorn with which the prelate and academician tells the strange story of a popular delusion and its uncouth displays is equalled only by the relish with which he dwells upon every suggestion of possible immorality on the part of the humble actors in the novel drama.[1]

In the paucity of certain information that has come down to us, I hesitate to express a decided opinion respecting the relative amount of truth and of misrepresentation that exists in the statements of Fléchier and the chronicler who closely follows him at most points.

Its improbability.

The cautious reader, in view of the improbability of a considerable portion of the account of the origin of the prophetic movement in the south of France, will doubtless incline to ascribe most of the grosser and more grotesque features to the fondness of the bishop to draw upon his fund of caricature in portraying a movement that was confined to the humblest ranks of society. Certain it is that in tracing the origin of the Cévenol spirit of prophecy to Geneva, Fléchier commits a palpable and inexcusable blunder. The pastors and professors of that conservative city were from the start vehemently opposed to the demonstration ; and they never afterwards swerved from their antagonism.

---

[1] The curious will read with interest Bishop Fléchier's " Récit fidèle de ce qui s'est passé dans les assemblées des fanatiques du Vivarais avec l'histoire de leurs prophètes et prophétesses, au commencement de l'année 1689. A. M. le duc de Montausier " (Œuvres, ix. 441–480). Also several other minor treatises : " Mémoire touchant la bergère de Crest et deux autres filles du diocèse de Castres, mises au rang des nouvelles prophétesses," " Mémoire sur les visions de la fille du diocèse de Castres," etc. (Ibid., ix. 480–496). See, also, Brueys, Histoire du fanatisme de nostre temps (Paris, 1692) passim. The frontispiece represents Du Serre instructing two groups of boys and girls in the art of falling to the earth and prophesying. After the Camisard War, Brueys incorporated this volume in his larger work describing that conflict, for which he retained the same title (Utrecht, 1737, in three volumes).

In the suppression of the prophetic movement in Dauphiny and Vivarais, the royal commanders resorted to the most Attempts at vigorous measures. The troops were ordered to fire suppression. remorselessly upon unarmed gatherings of men, women, and children, who believing themselves proof against injury from the enemies of God, suffered the foe to approach without fear or attempt at flight. The chronicler narrates in cold blood and without regret how on various such occasions hundreds of innocents were left dead upon the ground, while others were wounded and still others taken prisoners. And he thus comments upon what he believed to be the sudden close of the delusion : " Thus ended the fanaticism of the province of Vivarais. Never was revolt more prompt, more violent, more dangerous; never revolt appeased with more diligence, wisdom, and activity. In less than a fortnight twenty thousand persons had made an uprising, in less than half that time everything was tranquil and all possibility of future commotion was precluded." [1]

Predictions of the kind are proverbially dangerous. The prophetic movement, so far from being suppressed, was to extend from Dauphiny and Vivarais to the Cévennes, The movement and there and elsewhere to strike so deep a root as spreads. scarcely to be eradicated within the compass of a quarter of a century. Its close connection with the Camisard War will occupy us in the sequel. Meantime it is in place to remark some of its leading characteristics.

Respecting the physical manifestations, there is little discrepancy between the accounts of friend and foe. The persons Singular affected were men and women, the old and the young. phenoména. Very many were children, boys and girls of nine or ten years of age. They were sprung from the people—their enemies said, from the dregs of the people—ignorant and uncultured ; for the most part unable to read or write, and speaking in every-day life the *patois* of the province with which alone they were conversant. Such persons would suddenly fall backward, and, while extended at full length on the ground, undergo strange and apparently involuntary contortions ; their

---

[1] Brueys, ubi supra, 176.

chests would seem to heave, their stomachs to inflate. On coming gradually out of this condition, they appeared instantly to regain the power of speech. Beginning often in a voice interrupted by sobs, they soon poured forth a torrent of words— cries for mercy, calls to repentance, exhortations to the bystanders to cease frequenting the mass, denunciations of the church of Rome, prophecies of coming judgment. From the mouths of those that were little more than babes came texts of Scripture, and discourses in good and intelligible French, such as they never used in their conscious hours. When the trance ceased, they declared that they remembered nothing of what had occurred, or of what they had said. In rare cases they retained a general and vague impression, but nothing more. There was no appearance of deceit or collusion, and no indication that in uttering their predictions respecting coming events they had any thought of prudence, or doubt as to the truth of what they foretold. Brueys, their most inveterate opponent, is not less positive on this point than are the witnesses who are most favorable to them. "These poor madmen," he says,

Conceded honesty of the prophets. "believed that they were indeed inspired by the Holy Ghost. They prophesied without any (ulterior) design, without evil intent, and with so little reserve, that they always boldly marked the day, the place and the persons of whom they spoke in their predictions."[1] A Protestant, M. Caladon, of Aulas, whose words are so much the more interesting as his account bears the impress of unusual impartiality, expresses himself in very similar terms. "I have seen a great number of these inspired persons," he remarks, "of every age and of both sexes. They were all people without malice, in whom I perceived nothing that I could suspect of being of their invention. They made very beautiful exhortations, speaking French during the revelation, some better, some worse. It should be remarked that it is as hard for the peasants of those regions to discourse in French as it would be

---

[1] "Au lieu que ces pauvres insensez croyoient être effectivement inspirez du Saint Esprit; prophétisoient sans dessein, sans malice, et avec si peu de retenue, qu'ils marquoient toujours hardiment le jour, le lieu, et les personnes dont ils parloient dans leurs prédictions." Histoire du fanatisme de nostre temps (Ed. of 1692), 146. Utrecht ed. of 1737, i. 165.

for a Frenchman who had just landed in England to speak English." [1]

The "prophets" themselves declared that they were consciously moved by the Holy Spirit. Élie Marion and others of the number have left on record detailed statements of the feelings which they experienced, beginning with the occasions when they first received the divine "gift." These interesting narratives may profitably be compared with the accounts of the phenomena attending the great revivals of the eighteenth century, to which they bear not a little resemblance. A profound sense of personal unworthiness and of humiliation because of the magnitude of sins committed, was ordinarily a prominent feature of the initial stage ; but the sins that formed the chief object of repentance were rather external than intimate, rather connected with a cowardly conformity to the worship and practices of the church of Rome than the deeper emotions and feelings of the heart. The widespread apostasy from the faith by a hypocritical adhesion to the mass furnishes the keynote of the religious experience of the time. A determination to brave every danger by a complete renunciation of the corruptions of the papacy is the most conspicuous factor in the consequent repentance and purpose to lead a new life.

Claims of the prophets to inspiration.

The immediate effect of the rise of prophecy was a quickening of religious life. The dormant masses were startled from their torpor by the rumor and by the sight of a strange and incomprehensible movement. The prophets were directed by the Spirit, so they said, to call together the dispersed Protestants in some sequestered spot ; and these came, wondering and disturbed in mind, at the appointed time. From every hamlet of the neighborhood men and women, boys and girls, even little children, flocked to the rendezvous, leaving their cottages, threading their way through the forests, climbing

A quickening of religious life.

---

[1] "Ils faisaient de fort belles exhortations, parlant français pendant la révélation. Il y avait du plus et du moins. On doit remarquer qu'il n'est pas moins difficile à des paysans de ces quartiers-là de faire un discours en français, qu'à un Français qui ne ferait que d'arriver en Angleterre, de parler anglais." Déposition de M. Caladon, d'Aulas, dans les Hautes-Cévennes, datée de Dublin, le 19 mars 1707. Théâtre sacré des Cévennes (Ed. of A. Bost, Melun, 1847), 44.

the rocks, and hurrying that they might be in season. When
the crowds were assembled, the prophet after having experi-
Religious worship conducted by prophets. enced the customary agitation, began the worship by
repeating the prayer with which for generations the
Huguenots had been wont to begin the services of
the Lord's Day ; then led his auditors to join with him in singing some one of the old psalms of Marot or Beza, with which,
from long association, they were so familiar. An address would
follow, in which the prophet spoke as the mouthpiece of the great
Being by whose spirit he proclaimed himself inspired, and cries
of " Mercy ! " with denunciations of the priests, of the Romish
church, of the mass, vied with exhortations to repentance and
predictions of the approaching end of all things.[1]

Such, according to an enemy, was the procedure in these wild
and extravagant assemblies, nor is the representation probably
far from the truth. Irregular in their very constitution, and
presided over by men of little or no education, indeed, but animated by a fervid zeal and under the influence of strong emotions, they assumed a type strangely at variance with the usages
of so staid and orderly a body as the old Reformed churches,
whose destruction Louis the Fourteenth had decreed at the
Revocation of the Edict of Nantes. In the entire destitution
of an ordained ministry, the prophets believed themselves to
have been raised up by an extraordinary call, laymen though
they were, to fill the gap and perform many of the functions of
They exercise the functions of pastors. the former pastors. Brother La Valette, who had already made proof of his gifts as a preacher, received
from heaven, as he thought, a secret order to administer the sacrament of the Lord's Supper, and Brother Élie
Marion, all unworthy as he felt himself to be, was directed by
the Spirit to take part in the same sacred act as his assistant.
" We had a great number of communicants," writes one of the
two that officiated. " It was an admirable thing to see all these
poor Christians hungering and thirsting for the heavenly food,
who came to the holy table with a devout countenance, their
faces wet with mingled tears of contrition and joy."[2] What-

---

[1] Brueys (Ed. of 1692), 130, 131, 135.
[2] Déposition d'Élie Marion. Théâtre Sacré des Cévennes, 61.

ever the abuses to which the prophetic movement gave rise—
and that they proved great cannot be concealed—thus much may
certainly be asserted with safety : they kept alive the flickering
flame of Protestantism in the region of the Cévennes, at a time
when it seemed about to be quenched.[1]

Of all the pastors who, at the eminent peril of their lives,
undertook to revisit France and awaken the piety of their brethren, but one—François Vivens—seems to have been so deeply
moved by the sight of the intolerable persecution they endured,
as to entertain a serious design of calling in the intervention of
the Protestant Powers, with the view of putting an end to the
reign of tyrannical oppression.   It is true, indeed, that a Protestant (who was possibly Pierre Jurieu) writing in Holland, proclaimed in a book entitled "Soupirs de la France esclave qui
respire après la liberté," of which the first number appeared on the tenth of August, 1689,[2] some truths to
which the French world had long been a stranger,
boldly taking the ground that the nation that has
made a king, retains the right to rid itself of him, whenever
he transcends the legitimate bounds of his authority.   He reminded his readers that the memory of Louis the Eleventh had
been blackened and that he passed for a cruel prince because he
had caused the death of four thousand of his subjects ; whereas Louis the Fourteenth had sent ten times as many to the
grave.   It was a view of royalty and of its limitations that recalled the weighty words with which, more than a hundred years
earlier, on the morrow of the Massacre of Saint Bartholomew's
Day, François Hotman propounded, in his "Franco Gallia,"
the superior authority of the nation, as contrasted with the
claims of a single individual, the ruler.   One could almost hear
in it the ring of the sentiment of the great jurist of the sixteenth

*Jurieu re-
vives the
political
views of
François
Hotman.*

---

[1] " Les effets de ces dons célestes ont été de rappeler à la communion des
fidèles un grand nombre de faibles que la violence des persécutions avait fait suc-
comber, les mettre en état, à l'avenir, de sceller la vérité de l'Evangile par diverses sortes de souffrances et par diverses sortes de martyres, porter à la sanc-
tification ceux qui ont été rendus participants de ces grâces, convertir à la foi
plusieurs de ceux qu'on appelle vulgairement catholiques romains, et enfin,
d'affaiblir le bras du grand oppresseur et du grand ennemi de l'Église."   Théâtre Sacré des Cévennes, 23.

[2] See Douen, Les Premiers Pasteurs du Désert, ii. 82, 83.

century, that not only is the glorious right of the people to hold
its public assemblies sacred and a part of the common law of
nations, but the king who by wicked arts shall undertake to
crush it, violates that which is the heritage of all mankind, is an
alien from human society, and as such must henceforth be regarded, not as a king, but as a tyrant.[1]

But, as I have said, of the pastors that preached in France
after the Revocation, François Vivens alone advocated foreign

Vivens advocates foreign intervention. intervention. He was a young schoolmaster whom
his uncontrollable zeal led to preach in his native Cé-
vennes when the dragoons had overrun them and had
forced the inhabitants by thousands to make an outward profession of the Roman Catholic religion. He began his ministry nearly two years before the recall of the Edict of Nantes.
His success was brilliant. Basville having fully determined to
put an end to the great gatherings of Protestants, whom he
might massacre by the soldiers he sent against them, but whom
he could not thus prevent from coming together to worship the
God of their fathers, bethought him of a shrewd device to effect
his purpose. The intendant entered into negotiations with the
young preacher, and promised to give him a safe-conduct out of
the kingdom with as many as might wish to follow him, upon
condition that he should pledge his word not to return. Vivens

Double dealing of the court. fell into the snare, and handed in a list of three hundred Huguenots. Instead of fulfilling his engagement
honorably, Basville permitted only seventy to go.
These he sent in two companies, not directly to Switzerland or
Germany, but where they would be most likely to come to grief
—forty-eight to Spain, the land of the Inquisition, and twenty-
two, after imprisonment and hardship intended to break down

---

[1] As the "Franco Gallia" is a somewhat difficult book to consult, I am sure that
my readers will not be sorry to have me reproduce from my own copy this
noble passage in the original: "Quæ cum ita se habeant, cum, inquam, gentium ac nationum omnium commune hoc institutum semper fuerit, quæ quidem
regio ac non tyrannico imperio uterentur, perspicuum est, non modo præclaram
illam communis concilii habendi libertatem partem esse juris gentium, verume-
tiam Reges qui malis artibus illam sacrosanctam libertatem opprimunt, quasi
juris gentium violatores, et humani societatis expertes jam non pro Regibus, sed
pro tyrannis habendos esse." Franc. Hotomani jurisconsulti Francogallia.
[Genevæ] 1573, page 86.

their religious constancy, to the shores of Italy, whence they were left to make their way as best they could to the Protestant lands beyond the Alps. The remaining two hundred and thirty Huguenots, of whose names the intendant was now possessed, became the prey to his perfidy. The villages in which they lived received orders to arrest and give them over for trial, on penalty of themselves having troops quartered on them at discretion. The consequence was that the unfortunate victims of Vivens's mistaken confidence in a treacherous magistrate were hunted like wild beasts through the woods and dells of the Cévennes. Such as fell into the hands of the troops were sent to the galleys or deported to the French possessions in America.[1]

This flagrant breach of good faith absolved Vivens, both in his own eyes and in the eyes of all reasonable men, from his engagement not to re-enter France. It also deepened in a strong, vehement, and impressionable nature a sense of the outrage to which the so-called new converts, his brethren in the faith, were subjected. In 1689, that is, some eighteen months after his departure, Vivens was again in the south; no longer a simple preacher, but an advocate of armed co-operation with those who, whether within or without the kingdom, were in favor of setting bounds to the despotism of Louis the Fourteenth. The plans suggested by the Marquis of Miremont, Armand de Bourbon Malauze—last representative of a Huguenot branch of the royal family descended from Charles the Bastard of Bourbon, that had deserved well of the Protestant cause in the times of Henry of Navarre—had as yet borne no fruit.[2] But Vivens, fired by the wonderful success attending Henry Arnaud and the Waldenses of Piedmont in their "Glorious Return" to their valleys amid the Alps, effected this very year (August and September, 1689[3]), laid plans of his own. The

Vivens's return, 1689.

---

[1] Douen, ubi supra, ii. 21–32.

[2] See Haag, La France Protestante, ii. 1081–84; Douen, Les Premiers Pasteurs du Désert, ii. 91 et seq.

[3] Henri Arnaud was not only a devoted pastor and an intrepid captain, but he was also a forcible writer. This modern Xenophon has left us a narrative of his wonderful march which has been much admired, but has been less frequently read than it deserves. It is accessible to English readers in the translation by Hugh Dyke Ackland, The Glorious Recovery by the Vaudois of their Valleys,

time for passive and uncomplaining submission had passed; and if the explosion was delayed that came a dozen years later in the revolt of the Camisards, the minds of a few men had begun to turn in the direction of resistance. The "Manifesto of the Inhabitants of the Cévennes," a pamphlet of the period, distinctly affirmed: "We shall make just reprisals against the persecutors, in virtue of the law of retaliation, ordained by the Word of God and practised by all the nations of the world." [1] Accordingly, when the number of ministers judicially murdered amounted to almost a score, and a still greater number of conventicles had been fired upon and dispersed, with incidents of barbarity almost too horrible for belief, certainly too horrible for recital, the indignant Cévenols gave some significant indications of the gathering storm, by attacking and slaying a few of the more officious and cowardly of their persecutors, priests who had instigated the troops to carnage, or renegades that had acted as spies in the service of those that sought their blood. [2]

It was under such circumstances that Vivens, burning with indignation at the calamity of his people, drew up the plan of a military campaign that has come down to us in the pages of Brueys, future historian of the Camisard War. The His letter to the Duke of Schomberg. document containing it was a letter addressed to Duke Charles of Schomberg, son of the marshal, who had been sent by William the Third of England to the relief of the Duke of Savoy, the latter having come over to the side of the coalition against Louis the Fourteenth. The missive was dated "from the Desert," on the eighth of March, 1691. It showed Schomberg how the success of his projected invasion of southern France might be facilitated through the timely seizure of the Cévennes mountains by a small auxiliary force detached from the main army. It revealed the insignificance of the royal militia by which the impatient Cévenols were kept in terror and

---

from the original by Henri Arnaud (London, 1827). The bulletin published by the Société d'Histoire Vaudoise on the bicentenary of the event (Turin, 1889) contains not only a detailed itinerary, but an excellent map of the route taken by Arnaud and his band from Prangins on the Lake of Geneva over the Alps to Bobbio in their native valleys.

[1] Apud Douen, see Premiers Pasteurs du Désert, ii. 110.

[2] Ibid., ii. 110–112.

subjection. It even pointed out the exact path which the troops might take from the sea-coast, near Aigues Mortes, in order to reach the very heart of the region whose inhabitants they wished to raise in arms, in the neighborhood of Saumane and La Salle.[1] The project, like so many other projects of co-operation between the Huguenots and a relieving army, came to naught. When Duke Schomberg actually set foot in Dauphiny, he did, indeed, publish a proclamation calculated to rally to his standard all true patriots, and, especially, all fearless Huguenots. His Britannic Majesty — such was its substance — in causing his troops to enter France, has no other aim than to restore the nobility and gentry to their ancient splendor, the parliaments to their pristine authority, and the people to their just privileges, the established clergy being also protected. "The kings of England being warrantors of the Edict of Nantes by the Peace of Montpellier and several other treaties, the king my master," said Schomberg, "deems himself obliged to maintain this guarantee, and to cause the Edict to be re-established."[2] It was from Embrun, and on the twenty-ninth of August, 1692, that this manifesto was sent out; but the French preacher, whose vigor might have secured successful co-operation, had

---

[1] Brueys, Histoire du Fanatisme (Utrecht, 1737), i. 252-57. The historian states that he copied the paper from the original, which fell into the hands of the French government on the frontier, at the gates of Geneva, and was forwarded by the French Resident to Basville, at Montpellier. It is reproduced by Léopold Nègre, Vie et Ministère de Claude Brousson, 161-163 ; by Corbière, Histoire de l'Église Réformée de Montpellier, 545-547; and by Douen, ubi supra, ii. 116-118. His enemies accused Claude Brousson of being the author of the letter. It was one of the charges when he was put on trial and executed at Montpellier. He himself admitted frankly that the intercepted copy was in his handwriting, but he asserted, and his words bear the entire impress of truth, that Vivens drew it up and that he merely transcribed it. His own statement in the letter which he wrote to the king just before his death, is that he " se laissa enfin aller aux semonces du dit Vivens et à celles de M. de Schomberg, et qu'il écrivit de sa propre main au dit sieur de Schomberg un billet que le dit Vivens avait déjà tracé, et par lequel il lui marquait le moyen par lequel il pouvait envoyer quelques troupes dans les Cévennes ; lequel billet fut intercepté et n'eut point d'effet." Corbière, ubi supra, 314, gives the entire letter.

[2] The text of the proclamation is given in Agnew, Protestant Exiles from France, iii. (Index volume) 140, 141. It was written for Schomberg, says Agnew, by his chaplain, the refugee Jean Du Bourdieu.

been dead a full half year, and had left no one capable of taking his place.[1]

The price set upon Vivens's head had lately been raised from two thousand to five thousand livres, and rare activity was put forth to hunt down the dauntless Huguenot. At length, being discovered in a cave in which he had taken refuge, he was killed by one of his pursuers, after a short but determined defence, on the twenty-fifth of February, 1692. It was Jourdan, a renegade, that fired the fatal shot. Cavalier and his Camisards remembered the fact, some years later, when the man fell into their hands.[2] They that take the sword shall, no doubt, fulfil our Lord's prediction, and perish with the sword; but so far as the proscribed pastors of France were concerned, it may well be doubted whether their lot was less enviable than that of those who, like Claude Brousson, rejected the resort to arms.

Vivens is hunted down and shot, February, 1692.

With the mention of this illustrious victim, unquestionably the ablest, as he was the most influential, of those who preached to the early conventicles of the Huguenots, up to the close of the seventeenth century, I shall close the survey.

Claude Brousson, the intrepid lawyer of Toulouse, the fearless advocate of the oppressed churches, when to oppose the unrighteous chicanery of courts seeking to close and demolish the "temples" of the Huguenots, was to incur not only the rancor of a clergy that never forgot, but the displeasure of a king and his counsellors who saw nothing but rebellion in any attempt to resist the schemes they had formed to overthrow the Reformed religion—Claude Brousson, in this phase of his activity, is already familiar to the reader. In a previous chapter we saw that in his house the secret meeting was held which drew up the famous "Project" of 1683. It was he that planned that simultaneous demonstration of worship on the ruins of the demolished "temples" that was to prove even to an incredulous monarch that the Huguenots, so far from being indifferent to their faith, were ready to expose themselves to the most appalling danger to prove their attachment to it. Had the Marquis of Ruvigny and other prominent

Claude Brousson.

---

[1] Douen, ubi supra, ii. 119, 124.   [2] Infra, chapter xv.

men been equally wise and equally zealous, the result might have been different.

Compelled to flee for his life, Claude Brousson did not, as an exile, renounce his interest in the welfare of his brethren. By driving him out, the tyrant had lost far more than he had gained. Henceforth it became the one object of Brousson's life to forward all measures that might thwart the nefarious designs of Louis the Fourteenth. By his voice and by his untiring pen, he labored to obtain for the refugees in foreign lands the most tolerable conditions. By voice and pen he comforted and exhorted to patience and resolute adherence to their faith those who had not been so fortunate as to make good their escape from the house of bondage. Brousson's first aim was to give to the rulers and people of Christian states a just conception of the persecutions to which the Huguenots were subjected even before the formal Revocation, and to justify the effort, unsuccessful as it had proved, by which they had demonstrated their attachment to the religion of their fathers. In this plea there were passages of rare force, because of their rare moderation and dignity. Never, perhaps, were the sufferings of the Huguenots, as members of the body politic, better summed up than in these few sentences which trace their disabilities from the first·moment of existence to the last: "Our adversaries arm themselves with rigor against us before we are born, and deprive us of the persons that help us at birth. When we are come into the world, they persecute us from the cradle; they compel us to live in obscurity, amid alarms, suffering, and wretchedness. When we are ready to leave the world, and to go and seek in heaven the rest which we have been unable to find on earth, it seems that they are vexed that we should escape their animosity, and they come and torment us in the midst of our last agony. When we are dead, they pursue our bodies to the tomb. They rob us of the places where the bodies of our fathers rest, and where ours should rest also. They do not suffer all our relations and all our friends to honor our burial by their presence, and they frequently exercise their rage upon our corpses, which would be objects of pity for the most barbarous peoples." [1]

---

[1] État des Réformés en France, i. 137, apud Douen, ubi supra, ii. 144.

With impartial hand Claude Brousson directed his letters, on the one side, to the Roman Catholic clergy of France, endeav-

He calls on the exiled ministers to return. oring to convince them of the innocence of those whose persecution they had instigated, and, on the other, to the French Reformed pastors who had taken refuge in Protestant states, setting forth the desolation of the churches and holding them in no slight degree responsible for that desolation. The pastor had not the right possessed by the simple member of the churches, and might not flee before persecution. " It is true," he said, " that men have forbidden you to preach, but God commands you. It is God who has ordered you to proclaim his gospel; He alone has the right to impose silence upon you. . . . To-day the storm is not so furious, and you may daily learn that God is raising up other pastors to bring back the sheep that have gone astray, that the sheep hear their voice and that they follow them. Do not say that, before going to a distance from them, you warned them of their danger and gave them your counsels. If they were counsels and exhortations to obedience, you did well to address them, but that does not dispense you for the future from the exercise of your ministry. Were there but one sheep remaining that had gone astray, you ought to leave the others, and go and seek out that one. If long since you had taken the trouble to make your people and the enemy know that you were quite ready to prefer your duty to your life, it may be that your people would have had more firmness and your enemies would not have driven you to extremities. If thereafter you had escaped the search of the persecutors; had you at first made your hiding-place in the woods, in the caverns and clefts of the rocks; had you then gone from place to place, had you exposed your lives in order to continue to instruct and reassure the persons whom the first onset of the enemy had affrighted, and had you suffered martyrdom with constancy when Providence called you thereto, as other faithful men have done who have exercised your sacred offices in your absence ; it may be that these examples of constancy, zeal, and piety would have revived the courage of your flocks and stopped the fury of your enemies. When God permits pastors to be put to death for the Gospel, they preach more loudly and more effectually in the grave than they did in their lifetime, and, meanwhile, God does not fail to raise up other laborers for His harvest."[1]

These were brave words, said some of the pastors in foreign lands that chafed under the rebuke, but they would have sounded better in the mouth of one that had followed his own prescriptions and jeoparded his own life by exposing himself to the penalties incurred by virtue of the act of preaching the gospel to the persecuted Protestants in France. Now Claude Brousson was not a minister but a lawyer, and had not at first felt himself called upon to discharge duties for which he had had no training. Yet the covert reproach which he had drawn upon himself, of inviting others to dangers from the place of safety which he occupied, led him not only to anxious thought but to prompt action. Three times did he visit France and assume the duties which he had recommended to others.

His first mission to France, 1689-1693. When he entered upon his first mission, of more than four years (1689-1693), he had not been ordained to the ministry, and his authority to administer the holy sacraments was derived, so far as men were concerned, from the expressed desire of the faithful. It was not until his return to Switzerland that his ministry was recognized and confirmed by the laying on of hands, at Lausanne (on the twenty-fourth of March, 1694)[2] and again a second time, a few months later (on the tenth of August), by a more orderly consecration by the synod of the Walloon churches meeting at Tergoes.[3] As for himself, Brousson was far more anxious that the gospel should be preached than solicitous that those who preached it should have been regularly set apart for the work. "The reformers," he said, "whom God raised up in an extraordinary manner in France, at Geneva, in Switzerland, in Holland and elsewhere had not received the laying on of the hands of men; but the hand of the Lord was on them, and that is good laying on of hands."[4]

---

[1] Lettres aux Réfugiés de France, apud Léopold Nègre, Vie et Ministère de Claude Brousson (Paris, 1878), 44-46.

[2] Douen, ubi supra, ii. 228, 229.

[3] Ibid., ubi supra, ii. 232, 233.

[4] " Mais la main du Seigneur étoit sur eux, et c'est là la bonne imposition des mains." Lettre d'un serviteur de Dieu à l'Église de Dieu qui est sous la croix.

Other preachers shrouded their entry into France in the utmost secrecy, vainly hoping thus to escape observation; Brousson, while taking all reasonable precaution to avoid arrest, was at no pains to prevent the government from learning his advent. Yet, while many of them were soon cut short in their course, and, within a few weeks or months, expiated the crime of preaching the gospel by a death upon the gallows, Brousson enjoyed a comparatively long ministry, although hunted for, denounced, the object of special hatred and special efforts because of his exceptional boldness and success. It was not chiefly because Basville held him, though unjustly, responsible for the "project" of Vivens that he moved heaven and earth to effect his ruin. Brousson had, indeed, for a moment been drawn into the scheme of active resistance, and the copy of Vivens's paper which fell into the intendant's hands was made by Brousson: it was the solitary instance in which he departed from the principles which he practised all his life.[1] The true reason was rather to be found in the fact that barely had Claude Brousson set foot in the Cévennes before he addressed the haughty intendant, whose word was law from the Rhone to the foot of the Pyrenees, a paper very different in tone from the humble petitions to which he was accustomed. Far from cringing in the dust, far from suing for favor, far from pleading for mercy, Brousson laid down authoritatively the principles of eternal right. Here was a man that did not mince his words, a man that had no fear of man, a man that branded crime and boldly predicted the consequences of crime, a man that not only did not admit that the Reformation was dead in France, but suggested that, inasmuch as the repeal of the Edicts of Pacification, whose observance had been solemnly sworn, had already inflicted so great damage upon the state and still continued to injure it and produce division among the king's subjects, at a time when the kingdom was surrounded by enemies, it would be reasonable to give heed to better counsels than those that

Basville's efforts to secure him.

His intrepidity.

Archives of Montpellier. Printed among the documents given by Léopold Nègre, Vie et Ministère de Claude Brousson, 177-191. See page 183.

[1] Douen, ii. 189.

now prevailed. Here was a man who could tell Basville of his
mistake in supposing that the men who were preaching in the
Cévennes were emissaries of foreign powers, and assure him
that they had come of their own zeal, and in obedience to the
dictates of conscience, to labor for the recovery of their brethren
and for the re-establishment of the true service of God. If but
a few of the exiled pastors had returned, it was only, he informed him, because they hoped soon to do so with greater
safety. Please God, they would all re-enter France, sooner or
later. As to the future, Brousson did not dissemble his confident expectation. "Men are greatly moved," said he, "at
sight of the assemblies, and recourse is had to the most violent
remedies to prevent them. But one may venture to say, my
lord, and the event will justify the assertion, that either the
state must perish or liberty of conscience must be re-established therein. The danger has never been fully recognized of
forcing two million persons to abjure a religion which they are
persuaded is the only one that is in conformity with the word
of God and in the profession of which one can be saved." As
to the fate of Protestantism, he foresaw that, were the persecution now raging to last a hundred years, the stream of the
king's subjects seeking relief for their conscience in a land of
religious liberty would still continue to flow, while those that
remained at home would expose themselves daily in order to
render to God the worship prescribed in His word. Executions
and massacres would stop them no more than they had stopped
their fathers in the last century, or the primitive Christians.
Nay, Claude Brousson went still farther, and hinted not ob-
scurely that persecution might breed revolt and war. "It is
always strange, men will say, that subjects should take up arms
against their prince; but they take them up only in defence of
their lives, when they see that preparations are made to massacre them. The patience of the most moderate changes into
fury, when it is driven to extremities. The most peaceable
grow weary at length of being preyed upon without a reason,
of being treated as slaves, and of being butchered like beasts.
Permit me, if you please, my lord, to represent to your grace
that there is no man so ignorant and stupid as not to know
that it is not just so to treat a people that has signalized its

loyalty to its king on important occasions, and that now desires
to render to its God what is His due, as it renders to its king
what is due to him; above all when the right it possesses to
render to God the worship due to Him is fortified by perpetual
and irrevocable Edicts, very just in themselves, absolutely
necessary for the quiet and prosperity of the state, founded on
treaties of pacification, signed by both parties, rendered sacred
by divers solemn oaths, and, in fine, several times confirmed by
his Majesty." [1]

These and other magnanimous sentiments did the writer
utter, signing himself " BROUSSON, *Minister of the Gospel*," and
dating his letter " from the Cévennes, this first day of October,
1689." Is it any wonder that when this intrepid man had
labored long, returning to France for a second, and even for a
third time, preaching incessantly, holding, as a general thing,
three conventicles a week, each lasting three or four hours, not
to speak of prayers with the families that sheltered him; when
he had seemed to be everywhere, exhorting, comforting, encouraging the Protestants, and yet escaped as by a miracle
every snare and trap laid for him, is it any wonder, I say, that
Basville could not conceal his vexation, or that at one time he
wrote : " It is certain that this man does infinite damage," [2]
and at another : " This man torments me more than ever " ? [3]

When the danger of apprehension became extreme, Brousson
retired from France in 1693, returning the next year and again
retiring in 1696 ; for the pastorate of the chief Walloon church
at the Hague to which he was called, and where he officiated a
short time, could not long detain him from his chosen work in
France.[4]

Meantime, on the thirtieth of September, 1697, the desperate
struggle between Louis the Fourteenth and the confederated

---

[1] The text of this admirable letter, now in the Archives of Montpellier, and
bearing the indorsement of Lamoignon de Basville himself, is printed in full
among the documents given by Léopold Nègre, Vie et Ministère de Claude
Brousson, 164-169.

[2] Lamoignon de Basville à Monsieur de Nismes (Bishop Fléchier), Montpellier, May 3, 1698.   Bulletin de la Société de l'hist. du Prot. fr., **xv.** 133.

[3] Letter to the same, July 22, 1696, apud Douen, ii. 268.

[4] Ibid., ubi supra, ii. 245, etc.

powers of Europe was suspended by the conclusion of the
Treaty of Ryswick. The Huguenots had for years founded
The peace sanguine expectations upon the assurances of states-
of Ryswick, men and friends that, in the settlement of the quarrel,
September
30, 1697. their interests should not be forgotten. Much was
looked for from King William the Third of England and from
the son of the Great Elector. The former, in particular, had
been lavish of promises. In 1691, when, James the Second
having been compelled to cross the sea, after the disastrous
campaign in Ireland, and again take refuge with Louis the
Fourteenth, William was warmly congratulated by the refugee
ministers, he replied to their solicitations in behalf of the Huguenots by saying: "I hope that the Providence that has
guided me until now will give me the grace to work for the re-
establishment of the church for which I shall always sacrifice
what I hold dearest in the world."[1] Just so he had previously expressed himself in answer to Jurieu, who wrote to him
on his accession to the British throne. "Be assured," said he,
"that I shall neglect nothing in my power to protect and advance the Protestant religion. God will, I hope, give me the
means to the end that I may sacrifice the rest of my life to the
advancement of His glory."[2]

The greater part of the refugees desired as the height of
their ambition the re-establishment of the Edict of Nantes in
its entirety. Élie Benoist, the historian, alone demanded more,
and called for liberty of conscience, not by grant or favor, but
as "belonging to man by natural and divine right."[3] It was
such a claim as might have been advanced a century later in
the great French Revolution. Fresh from the study of the
history of the great charter granted to the Huguenots by Henry
the Fourth, Benoist maintained that all the vexations to which
they had been subjected for the last forty years had flowed

---

[1] Mémoire sur les arcs de triomphe élevés le 3 fév. 1691, et sur la députation
de l'Église de Savoie et des ministres réfugiés. Court MSS., apud F. Puaux
fils, "Négociations des Réfugiés au traité de Ryswick." Bulletin, etc., xvi. 259.

[2] Puaux, ubi supra.

[3] "Il faut la présupposer appartenant à l'homme, de droit naturel et divin."
Mémoire sur le sujet du rétablissement des Églises de France. Apud Puaux,
ubi supra, xvi. 263.

from the interpretations based upon the possible ambiguities of the Edict of Nantes.[1]

But, while it is very certain that under no circumstances would Louis the Fourteenth, at this time, have accepted peace on the condition of renewing the Edict, much less of making still larger concessions to the Protestants, it is equally certain that the Protestant princes who had profited so materially by the industries of the French refugees had no intention to forego these advantages by insisting on the readmission of the refugees into the French realm on the only terms upon which they would have returned. As to the Huguenots who had settled on the states of the Elector of Brandenburg, he regarded them as having renounced forever their allegiance to the crown of France, and they did not hesitate to call themselves " his very humble subjects." [2]

Thus it was that the plenipotentiaries of the allied powers, instead of making the redress of the wrongs of the Huguenots a necessary condition of peace, confined themselves to handing to the French ambassador, for form's sake, after the peace was fully determined upon, a paper which we are told Louis the Fourteenth read with great irritation, asserting that he did not meddle with what took place in his neighbors' dominions, but which, possibly, he might with greater reason have treated with contempt. For in the " Memoir in favor of the French Refugees " which the Earl of Pembroke presented in the name of his colleagues, it was made a principal motive to influence Louis the Fourteenth, that, should the evils endured by the Huguenots continue after the re-establishment of peace, these might be attributed to an aversion of his Very Christian Majesty to the Protestants in general, a thing which would greatly afflict the Powers belonging to that religion, who hoped to live henceforth in amity and good intelligence with his Very Chris-

---

[1] " Il n'est pas un qui fasse réflexion que toutes les vexations qu'on a faites aux Réformés depuis quarante ans, n'ont été que des conséquences tirées de l'Édit à causes des ambiguïtés dont les articles sont susceptibles." Puaux, ubi supra, xvi. 264.

[2] The very title of one of their petitions shows this : " Requête présentée à Sa Sérénité Électorale de Brandebourg par *ses très-humbles sujets* les réformés de France réfugiés dans *ses États.*" Puaux, ubi supra, xvi. 308.

tian' Majesty. The feeble plea which the ambassadors made for the release of captives in prisons and elsewhere was offset by an implication as false as it was absurd, to the effect that the allied powers were desirous of facilitating the return of the refugees to their native land.[1]

So far from ameliorating the condition of the Protestants yet remaining in France, the conclusion of the peace only aggravated it tenfold. The war had compelled Louis to turn his attention and direct his troops against the foreign foe; he had liberty now to employ his soldiers in crushing his unfortunate subjects of the Reformed faith. It would seem that he thirsted for blood. Sixty days had scarcely elapsed before a law was published, to which I shall have occasion later to advert, pronouncing the sentence of death upon any French Protestant that should go to the principality of Orange (just restored to the prince to whom it belonged), either to worship, or to contract marriage, or to attend upon the administration of baptism![2] What the sufferings were which the troops inflicted, a vast army coming back to practise upon French soil the outrages which they had been accustomed to perpetrate in the Palatinate and elsewhere, Claude Brousson saw and has left on record. A few days before the conclusion of the peace, that veteran missionary had again returned to the scene of his former activity, which was now to become the scene of his death. And what he witnessed there was a persecution but little less severe than it had been when the Dragonnades first burst upon the land. Every time the Protestants failed to go to mass, or to send their children to the Romish instructions, they were condemned to exorbitant fines, a single infliction generally surpassing three or four times the amount of the capitation tax. These fines were exacted by quartering troops upon the families, each soldier being en-

The conclusion of the peace aggravates the persecution.

---

[1] Mémoire de la part des Alliés de la Religion Protestante en faveur des réfugiés français, presenté au médiateur [le Baron de Lillieroot], par son Excellence Monsieur le Comte de Pembroocke, ambassadeur d'Angleterre, le 9/19 Septembre 1697. Text in Douen, Premiers Pasteurs du Désert, ii. 291, 292. See also M. Douen's remarks.

[2] Declaration of Versailles, November 23, 1697. Édits, Déclarations et Arrests, 363–365.

titled to fifteen sous a day, besides his food. The number of soldiers was doubled day by day, if there were enough at hand. The old story of the Dragonnades was repeated, the furniture was broken, or carried off and sold, the priests being the purchasers at a low price; the wine was poured out in the cellar; the heads of families were imprisoned; the girls carried off to convents. If the passages had been open, the emigration would have been immense, possibly surpassing the emigration of thirteen years ago. The Protestants were abandoned to the fury of the clergy, which directed the persecution in conjunction with the royal intendants. Much more there was to the same effect; but I spare the reader the recital.[1]

None the more, however, did the indefatigable Claude Brousson intermit either his ministry to the Protestants or his wonderful literary activity. For it was in the midst of the continual attempts to seize him that he wrote a series of appeals to the tyrant upon the throne, in one of which he plainly told him of the foreordained failure of his plans to eradicate Protestantism in France. "'If we cannot have the fathers,' we are still told, 'we shall have the children.' But must the fathers be driven into impiety that their families may be secured? Are those God's methods? Moreover, we see, throughout the entire realm, that the children have still more aversion than their fathers for the Romish communion, and that recourse must be had to new acts of violence to force them to enter it, or to pretend to enter it." [2]

Brousson's appeals to the king.

But Claude Brousson's remarkable course was drawing to its close. Closely pursued, his steps dogged by spies and traitors, to whom the price long since set upon the Huguenot's head, and recently increased to the unusual sum of "six hundred louis d'or of fourteen francs each," was a powerful incentive, the proscribed preacher had left the east, and had sought to accomplish something for the good cause by holding meetings in Toulouse itself, in Foix and still closer to the foot of the Pyrenees. It was at Oloron, in Béarn, that he

The price set upon his head increased.

---

[1] See the particulars, taken from Brousson's correspondence, in Douen, Premiers Pasteurs, ii. 299–301.

[2] Douen, ubi supra, ii. 309.

at last fell into the clutches of the government; but his activity had so long been associated with Lower Languedoc, and Basville *His capture* had so long made it his concern to pursue the dreaded missionary, that the intendant of Béarn manifested no reluctance to comply with Basville's repeated messages and send him to Montpellier for trial. That trial was brief. Not *and trial.* for a moment did Brousson's manly composure or his Christian fortitude desert him. There were three heads of accusation against him: First, that he had held conventicles contrary to the king's orders. Second, that he had taken part in the Toulouse meeting, in 1683, which planned the renewal of Protestant services on the spots where those services had been interdicted. Third, that he had written the letter intercepted at the gates of Geneva, wherein the route was pointed out to Schomberg by which a foreign auxiliary force might penetrate to the Cévennes. There is no question that Claude Brousson cheerfully admitted all the charges excepting the last, and that with regard to the first he took the high ground that obedience to God is more imperative than obedience to a man, even to a king. Necessity was laid upon him to preach. As to the second charge, he maintained that the king's Protestant subjects were bound to make known to the king their attachment to their faith, even must they patiently suffer *False state-* and lay down their lives. Respecting the third charge *ments of the historian* Brueys tells a strange and dramatic story. Suddenly *Brueys.* confronted with the tell-tale letter to Schomberg, of the existence of which in Basville's possession he was until this moment entirely ignorant, the Huguenot, who had hitherto been firm in his protestations of innocence, was disconcerted and grew pale, then after a few moments recovered himself, denied that the letter was in his handwriting, and in a trembling voice asserted that he had not formed this project. In reply to whom Basville contented himself with the remark that, in this at least, Brousson did not imitate the Apostles, who never lied; and informed his prisoner that he had documents in his possession that proved that he did not tell the truth which he had promised to tell with hand uplifted to God. If we may believe the writer, the papers discovered upon Brousson's person when he was arrested were compared with the letter in question, and the writing corresponded so precisely that Brousson was himself compelled to admit that he had forsworn himself.[1] The account of the incident being spread abroad that very day, brought astonishment to the Protestants of Montpellier, who learned that their pretended martyr, in the attempt to save his life, had uselessly added perjury to the greatest of all his crimes.[2]

Such is the story which Brueys gave to the world, and which still passes current among Roman Catholic historians for undoubted truth. And yet it is a tissue of falsehood.

Happily the official records of Claude Brousson's trial have come down to us and we can read the very minutes of his examinations both at Pau, before Pinon, Intendant of Navarre and Béarn, and at Montpellier, before Lamoignon de Basville, Intendant of Languedoc. All the papers in the case are extant, most of them in the archives of Montpellier, from the official report of the arrest and the long and precise inventory of every letter, book, and paper found in Brousson's possession, down to the final sentence. From these it appears that Brousson never denied that the letter to Schomberg was in his handwriting. Both at Pau and Montpellier, when interrogated upon the point, he simply threw himself back upon the recent treaty of Ryswick. By virtue of that treaty all previous acts of war were covered as by an impenetrable veil. " This defence," as M. Corbière well observes, to whose investigations and lucid exposition we owe the first full and truthful view of the matter, "was already an avowal ; but the interrogatories are more explicit. That of Pau says positively that the document of which it gives the beginning and the end was placed under his eyes, and that he agreed, without the slightest hesitation, that it was in his writing (minute of the third session)." [3] When this point was reached in the interrogatory at Montpellier, in place of a simple reply, the official documents show that Brousson asked for paper and ink, and, having been allowed time to write, drew up a long letter to

Corrected by the extant records.

---

[1] Brueys, Histoire du Fanatisme, i. 278, 279.　　　[2] Ibid., i. 280.

[3] Corbière, Histoire de l'Église Réformée de Montpellier (Montpellier, 1861), 309.

the king in justification of his entire course. In words, which
I have already quoted,[1] he explicitly admitted that, although
the composition of the letter was Vivens's, the writing was his
own. He did not conceal the fact that, great as had been the
provocation to which the persecuted and proscribed Protestants
of France had been subjected, he regretted the solitary instance
of his life in which he had departed from the line of passive
submission which he had otherwise always practised and advocated. Indeed, for this he asked pardon of the king. But
his firm position was taken upon the results of the Treaty of
Ryswick, and "he claimed, with deep humility, the justice and
protection of his Majesty, begging him very humbly to be
pleased to secure to him the enjoyment of the general and
mutual pardon conceded by that peace, as those enjoyed it elsewhere who might have engaged therein on his Majesty's side."[2]

Thus much for this matter. Brousson's letter was never forwarded to its destination. It would have done no good had it
been. Louis never forgave a personal offence.

Throughout his trial Claude Brousson maintained the dignity
of a good man brought into undeserved misfortune, and the
courage of a Christian martyr. He was frank in
everything that pertained to himself and his movements. He had preached the gospel in all places in
which he had been able to gather hearers. He would not say a
word to inculpate others. He had sworn to tell the truth, and
to declare everything that he could reveal without wounding the
honor and duty of a pastor, in relation to his ministry. He
would give no names of persons at whose houses meetings were
held, nor state who were present. The application of torture—
both the "*question ordinaire*" and the "*question extraordinaire*"
—did not wrest from him a single secret that he considered
sacred. He was sentenced to be bound to the wheel and broken
alive. It was no feeling of compassion, which the intendant
would have deemed a weakness, but, as he himself tells us, a

*Brousson's
composure
and dignity.*

---

[1] Supra, page 194.—So also when questioned by torture, he said, "Qu'il n'y a
eu que Vivens qui le composa et qu'il l'écrivit." Procès verbal de la Question
(November 4, 1698), in Léopold Nègre, 215.

[2] Letter of Brousson to the king (November 2, 1698), in Léopold Nègre, Vie et
Ministère de Claude Brousson, 204–214 ; Corbière, ubi supra, 310–319, etc.

desire " to have done with the show as speedily as possible,"
that led Basville to order the prisoner to be strangled first.[1] I
shall not describe at length his execution, for which a
scaffold had been erected on the Esplanade of Montpellier, in sight of the citadel. Ten thousand persons
viewed it, and soldiers were on hand to prevent any
commotion or attempted rescue. They were not needed; the
crowds wept, but confined themselves to admiring the sufferer's
courageous bearing. At the door of his prison, he began to sing
the thirty-fourth psalm of Theodore Beza,

*He is execut-
ed at Mont-
pellier, No-
vember 4,
1698.*

Jamais ne cesserai
De magnifier le Seigneur ;

but the guard that walked at his side requested him, in the intendant's name, to stop ; and soon a band of twenty drummers
began to make so great a din that his voice could not be heard.
The priest who had accompanied him, and had in vain begged
him to embrace the Roman Catholic faith, is reported to have
observed in all good faith that Brousson died a true Christian;[2]
the hangman, that he had executed more than two hundred condemned men, but that none had ever made him tremble as Monsieur Brousson.[3] It matters little whether the reports were true.
The veteran lawyer, preacher, publicist, who had freely offered up
so large a part of his life and of his toils, who had exposed himself to countless hardships and dangers in order to promote the
spiritual interests of his oppressed fellow Protestants, did not
cast discredit by the manner of his death upon a course than
which none more honorable, few more powerful for good, could
be found in the Huguenot annals. The bloodthirsty Basville
openly exulted in his work, and encouraged himself with the
thought that the man whom for years he had pursued with all
the rancor of personal enmity was at length put out of the way.
" Devout women," he jocularly wrote to Bishop Fléchier, " will

---

[1] " J'ai fait ajouter à l'arrêt qu'il serait étranglé, afin de finir promptement le
spectacle." Basville to Bishop Fléchier, Montpellier, November 4, 1698. Bulletin de la Soc. de l'hist. du Prot. fr., xv. 135.

[2] Relation venue de Montpellier, datée du mois de novembre 1698, apud L.
Nègre, 218–225.

[3] De Félice, History of the Protestants of France (Amer. trans.), 425.

weep for Brousson, but it is sure, sir, that he will do no more harm." [1] Upon which words the sentiment already quoted from Brousson's own pen [2] may serve as a sufficient commentary : " When God permits pastors to be put to death for the Gospel, they preach more loudly and more effectually in the grave than they did in their lifetime, and, meanwhile, God does not fail to raise up other laborers for His harvest."

With the exception of Roman, the young candidate for the ministry, who, after a series of thrilling adventures and hair-breadth escapes, retired to spend the rest of his days in Germany and Holland, the year after Brousson's death, [6] Claude Brousson was the last of the corps of French pastors that returned to France to assume labor under the most perilous circumstances in behalf of the Protestants remaining in France. Many of them, like Brousson, laid down their lives in the work, others even now were languishing in hopeless confinement in the dungeons of the Îles Sainte Marguerite, or in some other obscure prison. Yet their toils and sufferings had not been in vain. They had preserved the flame of piety from extinction, and God was still to raise up those " other laborers " for His harvest, not, indeed, from abroad, but reared on French soil itself, to found the Churches of the Desert.

Meanwhile, before that consummation was reached, southern France was to pass through a period of commotion and bloodshed, resulting from the very violence of persecution, in the so-called War of the Camisards.

Reference has been made in these pages to the application of torture. The forms employed had varied considerably at different periods, and underwent some change during the period with which alone we have to do in this history. No account is to be taken, of course, of the strange and repulsive punishments inflicted, with the view of aggravating and protracting the pains of death ; for it must be remembered that, both in theory and in practice, torture was regarded not as a punishment for crime, but simply as a means for ascertaining the guilt or the innocence of accused persons.

The modes of torture in vogue in France.

---

[1] " Les dévotes pleureront Brousson, mais il est seur, Monsieur, qu'il ne fera plus de mal." Letter of November 5, 1698. Bulletin, etc., xv. 136.

[2] Supra, page 197.

[3] See the account in Douen, Les Premiers Pasteurs du Désert, ii. 380 et seq.

Torture was divided, according to its severity, into two kinds, known respectively as the *question ordinaire* and the *question extraordinaire*. In both a change was effected by a decree of the Parliament of Paris, January 18, 1697 (Isambert, Recueil des anciennes lois françaises, xx. 281). Previously to that date, in the *question ordinaire*, the victim having had his hands The "estra-　strongly bound together back to back behind him, with a piece of pade."　iron between them, was drawn up by a rope attached thereto to the distance of a foot from the floor. Under this form of torture a weight of one hundred and eighty pounds was attached to the right foot. In the *question extraordinaire*, the wrench was augmented by increasing the weight to two hundred and fifty pounds, and the man was raised as high as the ceiling of the room would permit. Thus suspended he was thrice permitted to fall suddenly to within a yard of the floor, a process that almost always resulted in a temporary loss of consciousness, and rarely failed to cripple him for life. The modification introduced by the parliamentary order of January 18, 1697, is described with painstaking and almost revolting minuteness in a document entitled " Mémoire instructif concernant la manière en laquelle se donne la question, par extension ou par brodequins." (Text in Isambert, xx. 281–283 note.) The victim, if a man, clad in a shirt alone. or if a woman, with a skirt in addition, Torture by　was tied by four ropes attached one to each wrist and ankle. The " extension."　two head ropes passed through rings in the side wall set a little over two feet apart and fully three feet above the floor ; the other two ropes ran through rings firmly fixed in the floor at a distance of at least twelve feet from that wall. The ropes were tightened to the utmost by main force, after which a trestle or table, of the prescribed height of two feet, was placed beneath the victim and was forced along as near as possible to the rings for the feet. Next, while an assistant held the victim's head a little down and kept his mouth open by the insertion of a horn, the executioner slowly poured into it the contents of four successive jars of water, each with a capacity of a little more than two quarts. Between each jar, the sufferer was solemnly adjured by the judge to confess the truth. This was " torture by extension " in its milder form. If it was thought fit to resort to the *question extraordinaire*, the same process was repeated, with four more jars of water, but, instead of a frame two feet in height, one of three feet and four inches was substituted to give still more terrible effects by being, as before. slipped along as far as possible toward the lower rings. It must be noted, however, that torture by extension was not ordered until a medical examination had furnished proof that there was no internal rupture, and that the victim would not be likely to die under the operation. The "brode-　Otherwise, the implement facetiously styled the " brodequins "—or quins " or　the " boot "—was employed. The feet, each encased between two " boot."　boards, were closely bound together by ropes tightened to the utmost ; after which the executioner with his mallet forcibly drove eight wooden wedges between the two central boards. Previous to the insertion of each successive wedge, the judge was directed to summon the accused to disclose the whole truth. If, as usually happened, the latter swooned, he was to be revived by a draught of wine. Whether the " brodequins " were more merciful than the torture by extension is perhaps an open question.

BOOK FIFTH

THE CAMISARDS (1702–1710)

BOOK FIFTY

BOOK FIFTH

THE CAMISARDS (1702–1710)

CHAPTER XV

THE UPRISING OF THE CAMISARDS

For nearly seventeen years the history of the enforcement of
the revocatory edict, and of the succession of declarations and
orders in council intended to carry that iniquitous measure into
complete effect, had been, on the part of the Huguenots, a record of almost undeviating submission to the
abuse of legitimate authority. They did indeed repudiate as
unsound the maxim that the sovereign may prescribe the religion of his subjects. In the closing paragraphs of his immortal complaint against the cruel oppression to which his
fellow believers were subjected in France, the eloquent Jean
Claude uttered, as we have seen, a protest that might well have
entered even the closed ears of tyrants, against the acceptance
of a principle which not only ignored the common rights of
humanity, but infringed the cherished prerogative of the Almighty. But the persecuted Protestants made no armed opposition to injustice exercised in the name of the king. In
strange contrast to the course adopted by their ancestors in
the sixteenth century, and even in the early part of the seventeenth, the Huguenots of the reign of Louis the Fourteenth,
while assured of the righteousness of their cause, and conscious
that they possessed the sympathy of no inconsiderable part of
the inhabitants of neighboring countries, made no appeal to the

arbitrament of the sword. Those who could do so fled from the kingdom in great numbers, carrying with them as much of their movable property as they were able, but leaving behind them the larger part of their worldly possessions. The great majority, lacking the ability or the disposition to expatriate themselves, and believing, in many cases, that the suppression of the Protestant religion would be only temporary, and that the glorious charter given by Henry the Fourth could not fail shortly to be re-enacted, bore the brunt of their present misfortunes with a courage bred of their hopes of future deliverance. Of no serious breach of the peace, occasioned by a resistance to the royal agents, is there an example until nearly a score of years had passed from the fatal month of October, 1685. Then, as if to prove to the world how futile was the attempt to extirpate by force a firmly rooted religious belief, there occurred, in a remote part of France, a singular uprising, of which I must now give an account.

The scene of conflict was laid in the eastern part of the extensive province of Languedoc, and chiefly in that mountainous region which divides the longer rivers, flowing westward toward the Bay of Biscay, from the streams that empty by shorter courses into the River Rhone or pour directly into the Mediterranean Sea. The bleak sides of the Cévennes, inhabited by a hardy race, inured to toil and privation, and retaining more love of independence than almost any other part of the kingdom, were themselves well adapted to be the field of a desultory warfare, in which success is wont to depend quite as much upon a thorough knowledge of the intricate paths and mountain passes as upon the preponderance of numbers. They had, three-quarters of a century earlier, supplied the Duke of Rohan with his best troops for service in an unequal struggle with the armies of Louis the Thirteenth ; and neither luxury nor idleness had crept in to render the present inhabitants inferior in courage and endurance to their ancestors. Throughout the region Protestantism had, for four or five generations, been more firmly grounded than in almost any other part of the kingdom, and Nismes, the chief city of the southern portion, was not less devoted to the doctrines of the Reformation than was Montauban or La Rochelle. There was many a parish in the Cévennes,

The Céven-
nes.

as also in the neighboring province of Vivarais, on the one side, and the region of Castres, on the other, where there were absolutely none but Protestants, and where the intendant Basville, much against his will, was compelled to take the mayors and consuls from the ranks of the adherents of a hated religion.[1] The six episcopal dioceses which covered this territory contained a population of about two-thirds of a million of souls, and of this, even so late as 1698, when all the public religious exercises of Protestantism had for thirteen years been utterly proscribed, a full quarter were still Protestants. Yet the adherents of the Reformed faith were somewhat unequally distributed. In the diocese of Mende they constituted only one-eighth of the population, in the diocese of Viviers but one-seventh, and in that of Uzès less than one-fourth. On the other hand, they embraced fully one-third of the inhabitants of the diocese of Montpellier, and boasted of having a clear majority of the population of the diocese of Alais. In the diocese of Nismes they were scarcely less numerous.[2]

Protestant population.

The Camisard war was a revulsion against the systematic persecution which for years had made the life of the large body of dissidents from the established church an almost intolerable

---

[1] Between the three districts there were more than three hundred such parishes. "Dans tous les lieux un peu considérables, je tascheray de ne mettre que des anciens catholiques ; mais il y a en Vivarois, dans les Cévennes et dans l'évesché de Castres, plus de 300 paroisses où il n'y a que de nouveaux convertis." Basville to the controller general, December 28, 1692. Corresp. des Contrôleurs Généraux, i. 308.

[2] The "Mémoires pour servir à l'hist. du Languedoc" by Basville, apud Court, i. 126-131, give the exact figures, which some readers may be curious to see : Mende, 128,302 Roman Catholics, 18,689 Protestants; Alais, 30,390 Roman Catholics, 41,766 Protestants ; Viviers, 198,336 Roman Catholics, 33,198 Protestants ; Uzès, 78,502 Roman Catholics, 23,112 Protestants ; Nismes, 40,720 Roman Catholics, 39,664 Protestants; Montpellier, 20,674 Roman Catholics, 10,348 Protestants. The total population was, therefore, 663,701 souls, of which 166,777 were of the Reformed faith.—As the two dioceses of Nismes and Alais contained 120,000 Protestants in 1677, and only 82,050 "Nouveaux Convertis" in 1698. it is calculated that 37,950 of the Protestant, that is of the most industrious and prosperous, citizens had been killed or expelled. The figures are suggestive of the immense loss sustained by France, in a merely material and economic point of view, through the repeal of the Edict of Nantes. See a memoir drawn up toward the close of the eighteenth century, in the Bulletin de la Société de l'histoire du Prot. franç., xxix. 190.

burden. In the glow of the apparent success attending the
Dragonnades, Basville, intendant of Languedoc, felt quite sure
that his province, and especially this portion of it, was permanently recovered to the faith. Writing almost the very day
that Louis the Fourteenth signed the revocatory edict at
Fontainebleau, he said to the controller general : "I believe
that I can now inform you of the conversion of all Languedoc.
At least the Cévennes are entirely converted. There is not a
place of any size which I have not visited, in company with
the Duke of Noailles, and everybody was converted at his
coming. Moreover, there is not a parish that has not been well
cleaned out. . . . This is a great work, but, in truth, we
must not regard it as wholly consummated. Much care is still
demanded. The matter in hand is to gain the hearts, and to
make this great number of converts understand that they have
done well in adopting this course, which they have taken only
in blind obedience to the king's orders. They have appeared to me
to be strongly disposed to receive instruction and to desire it
ardently ; but everything is wanting here—bishops, priests,
curates, churches. The churches of the Cévennes are not larger
than a very small chamber ; they are very ugly, and very dark and
destitute of everything. In the places which contain five or
six thousand converts, there were, a month ago, only seven or
eight families and a wretched priest, a perpetual vicar with a
living of two hundred livres, ignorant and often dissolute." [1]

Sixteeen years later, the intendant, if equally determined, was
less sanguine and a trifle disgusted with his task. His letters
still breathed slaughter. Thus to a prelate he wrote : "The
prophet, sir, whom you questioned, will soon be despatched. I
sent to Sommières to arrest him, and I have appointed a commissioner to try him. An example must be made at Uchaud to
keep all the region in check. M. de Broglie has sent a detachment of thirty men. It is a mutinous parish which must be
humbled and punished. I have more than three hundred fanatics in the prisons. That is a fine refreshment after the [pro-
vincial] states and the passage of the Queen of Spain. This

---

[1] Basville to the controller general, October 15 and 19, 1685. Correspondance
des Contrôleurs Généraux, i. 55.

morning I condemned to death four preachers from Vivarais and a woman who pretended to shed tears of blood in the assemblies. She used indeed to besmear her face with blood, and it was a sight capable of moving all Vivarais. I also condemned a celebrated woman preacher to be flogged and branded with the fleur de lis. *Malis ingravescentibus*, says the law, *pœnœ exacerbandœ*. We shall see what the effect of the remedy will be. I shall show no favor to the preachers. It is a sad and annoying employment when one has been at it for seventeen years." [1]

The author of this letter is the same Lamoignon de Basville of whom a modern biographer has written that he was accused of rigor in his treatment of the Protestants after the Revocation and in the Cévennes, but that the charge has not been proved.[2] His correspondent, bishop of one of the dioceses which formed the theatre of the coming war, demands our particular notice at this time; for, as he has fortunately left us ample writings of the most authentic character, we may learn from them the spirit that animated the clergy in their dealings with the Huguenots of the southeastern part of France. He is the prelate upon whose account of the Cévenol Prophets I have drawn in a preceding chapter.

Esprit Fléchier, Bishop of Nismes, was no ordinary man whom the accident of wealth or noble birth had insured high ecclesiastical preferment. A scholar of merit, a graceful writer, and a polished orator, he rivalled his colleague of Meaux in the esteem of the learned and the admiration of the king. As a court preacher, he was not inferior to Bossuet for the studied elegance of his periods. What he lacked in native force was made good, in some measure, by the judicious appreciation and practice of the rules of art. His funeral oration delivered over the remains of Turenne, in particular, won him applause in an age in which, of all arts, the art of panegyric was the most highly prized. Louis the Fourteenth, when conferring upon him the bishopric of Lavaur, his first episcopal see, apologized for the tardy recognition of Fléchier's

Esprit Fléchier, Bishop of Nismes.

---

[1] Basville to the Bishop of Nismes, Montpellier, November 4, 1701. Bulletin de la Soc. de l'hist. du Prot. fr., xvi. 136, 137.

[2] Feller, Biographie Universelle, s. v. Lamoignon.

abilities by ascribing the delay to his own unwillingness to lose the pleasure of hearing Fléchier's sermons at Versailles. This was in the very year of the Revocation. Two years later the fortunate ecclesiastic was transferred to Nismes. We may still read in his collected works his "humble and pious remonstrance to the king" with the view of refusing the new bishopric, a field of labor which he declared to be, in comparison with that which he had held, vast in extent and difficult to govern.[1]

In what a spirit and with what purposes did this highly educated prelate, this eminent member of the French Academy, enter upon the discharge of his responsible functions, in a diocese one-half of whose members were avowedly adherents of another faith? How did he deport himself toward the Protestants during his long episcopate of twenty-three years?

Certainly, the words of gentleness were upon his lips, and, could we permit ourselves to judge by these alone, we should of necessity acquit him of every charge of harshness. "Violence and oppression are not the paths which the church has marked out for us, and which Jesus Christ made use of to gain souls and to establish his faith. We know that religion is a matter of persuasion and not of command; that the heart must be gained through the heart, and that nothing leads to the truth so naturally as charity."[2] Thus he wrote to a Protestant, three years before his elevation to the episcopate. In the same strain he continued to write to the end of his days. But, strangely mingled with these kindly expressions, we find everywhere a hearty approval of the application of a little salutary rigor. As time passed, and as the hollowness of the profession of Catholicity to which the new converts had been driven by the Dragonnades became more and more evident,

He approves resort to salutary rigor.

---

[1] Dated August 27, 1687. Œuvres complètes de Fléchier, x. (lettres), 16–18. In justice to the prelate, it should be said that his complaint respecting the extent of his new diocese was well grounded. The diocese of Alais was not set off from that of Nismes until seven years later (1694), and, at first, the jurisdiction of Fléchier stretched far up the Cévennes Mountains, and embraced more than 80,000 Protestants. See his Discours à l'assemblée générale du clergé de France, au sujet de l'érection de l'évêché d'Alais, Œuvres complètes, ix. 82–84, and Court, Histoire des Troubles des Cévennes, i. 127.

[2] Fléchier to Vigier, St. Germain en Laye, December 14, 1682. Œuvres, x. 5, 6.

the necessity made itself increasingly felt of using unremitting pressure to conserve even the little that had been gained from the body of unwilling Protestants. Having in a moment of weakness yielded to superior force and signed a brief promise to be converted, having once or twice attended mass, those whom the court was pleased to call the new converts, as a general thing, claimed that they had done all that could be reasonably expected of them. They neither attended church nor sent their children to be instructed in the doctrines of a hated religion. The bishop would fain believe that what remained of Calvinism was no longer a religion, but a party that sustained itself, as best it could, by the concerted action of parents, themselves accustomed to live without exercises of worship, and teaching their children the solitary maxim, that it was better to do without a religion than to embrace the Roman Catholic. In the eight or ten years of liberty in which they had lived since their formal conversion, despite all that had been written or uttered from the pulpit to persuade them, the bishop would have it that not a solitary proselyte had been gained.[1] "In order, then, not to lose all the fruit of the past and all the hopes of the future, they must be urged, by a firm and uniform conduct, to make a public profession of the Roman Catholic religion." And he concluded with St. Augustine that to incite our brethren to seek their salvation is to love them. We must not look to see whether they are pushed, but in what direction they are pushed; for the righteousness, the charity, and the usefulness of the end abundantly justify the slight severity of the means employed. Not that Fléchier would have the bishops and other ecclesiastics meddle with the punishment of the disobedient; albeit St. Gregory and divers councils have given to the clergy the authority to do so. Their ministry is a ministry of peace. Yet it

---

[1] "Depuis huit ou dix ans qu'on les a laissé dans leur liberté, quoi qu'on ait écrit et qu'on ait prêché, en a-t-on vu revenir quelqu'un ?"—As the years referred to must be those reaching from 1688 or 1690 to 1698, the bishop evidently means by liberty only a slight relaxation of the stringent measures employed toward the Protestants when once their nominal change of belief had been gained. Those who know that the new converts felt the harrow at this time but little less than before or after, will, perhaps, hold that a special glossary is needed to understand the meaning of Fléchier and kindred writers.

is the prerogative of princes to protect the church. The king can and ought to compel the new converts to attend church, to listen to instruction, to witness the mass. The bishop's argument, more fully developed in a later part of the document before me, is not undeserving of notice. St. Paul, he says, in his Epistle to the Galatians, declares that every man that is circumcised is bound to keep the whole law. The new converts have by baptism and abjuration become subjects and children of the Roman Catholic Church, and are therefore bound to observe its laws. Therefore, according to the apostle's teaching, they may and ought to be constrained to do so. It is useless to say that they have changed their minds; a rebellious subject or a disobedient child cannot relieve himself of his obligations. Fear is entertained lest we may make hypocrites. St. Augustine had the like fear, but he overcame it. Our intention is to make real Catholics; if they deceive us, and their religion is a hollow pretence, it is not for us to act as judges. The office of judge belongs to God. The king has deemed it his duty to compass, by all sorts of methods, the salvation of his subjects, by " compelling them to come in," in accordance with the gospel prescription. It is not less proper that, after their abjuration, they should be obliged to fulfil the promise which they have made to God. It is not enough for us to educate the children in the Roman Catholic religion; for the lessons learned at home will efface those learned at church. Such, says the bishop, are the reasons that make me wish that the king should declare it to be his will that the new converts be present at instruction, at mass, and at the other exercises of the Roman Catholic religion (participation of the communion being excepted). And the disobedient should be punished, by a fine or otherwise; for, when once the king has made known his will, it is neither just nor honorable that it be neglected with impunity. How will the new converts believe, unless they hear? How will they hear, unless they be preached to? How will they be preached to, unless they assemble together? Where shall they assemble, if not in the churches? Nor is there any objection to their witnessing the sacred mysteries, since they are neither infidels nor simple catechumens—they professedly know Christ and have been baptized in his name. Nor are they avowed heretics, at least they ought not to be regarded as such. They have submitted to the church by a solemn engagement; that is, by a public act accompanied by an affirmation and an oath. And there appears no retraction, at least no public one. The evidence of their abjuration entered upon our public records is still at hand for us. We have a right to regard them as our brethren, even should their conversion be only a feigned one.[1]

In December, 1698, a royal Declaration was published intended to secure "the instruction of those who have re-entered the Catholic Church and that of their children."[2] It is plain from the bishop's correspondence with the secretary of state, the Marquis of Châteauneuf, that its provisions would have pleased him better had they contained a little more severity, and a little less of that royal kindness which, nevertheless, after the fashion of the accomplished courtier, he did not fail to laud. Unable to stem a resistless tide, he gave up as hopeless the attempt to convert thoroughly the men and women who, finding themselves no longer pressed to go to mass, deserted the churches in a body, leaving the sacred edifices pretty much to the Old Catholics. On the other hand, he devoted himself with renewed energy to the attempt to obtain control of the Protestant children. At this point, he tells us, the parents fought him with desperate determination. They would permit their offspring to go neither to church nor to "instruction." They resorted to every available pretext. They pretended that they needed their children's help at home. They took refuge in the article of the royal declaration itself which limited the age for instruction, and made it compulsory only for boys and girls under fourteen years old. The imposition of fines upon recalcitrant parents, we are informed, sometimes effected the purpose intended; yet even then constant watchfulness was needed to

---

[1] See the long and instructive paper entitled Lettre en forme de Mémoire à Monseigneur l'Archevêque de Paris concernant les nouveaux convertis, Œuvres complètes de Fléchier, v. 258–277. The document bears no date, but the expression, "Chargé, dans mon seul diocèse, de quarante mille nouveaux convertis, avec lesquels je converse *depuis onze ans*," shows that it must have been written in 1698.

[2] Declaration of December 13, 1698, in Édits, Déclarations et Arrests concernans la R. P. R., 371–379.

prevent the children from soon absenting themselves. As for
the girls, the bishop found that the most effectual means was to
tear them from home and place them for some months in a convent. "There is nothing," he said, "which badly converted"
—that is, Protestant—" parents are more afraid of, both because
of their reluctance, however rich they are, to pay the sum for
their board at such institutions, and because of the acquaintance with and inclination for the Catholic religion which, by
this channel, enter their families." His only regret was that
there were not similar establishments for boys. For he was
forced to confess that recent occurrences showed only too
clearly the care taken by Huguenot parents to "pervert" their
children and render futile all the labors of priest and teacher
alike. A boy of fourteen or fifteen and a girl of about the same
age, having within a short time fallen dangerously ill, were
visited by their respective curates, and were solicited to receive
the sacraments of the Roman Catholic Church. Neither of the
children would consent. Both boldly declared their intention
to die in the Reformed faith. This, too, though they doubtless
knew the penalties which the barbarous law of April, 1686, pronounced upon them should they chance to recover—upon their
inanimate bodies, should their illness prove fatal. What was
most aggravating was the fact that both children had attended
the schools and had frequently answered the catechetical questions put to them. Had the children lived in the age of pagan
persecution, and showed the same contempt for the iniquitous
legislation of a Decius, the good bishop would doubtless have
had no hesitation in assigning them a conspicuous place among
Christian confessors. As it was, their audacity filled him with
amazement, and he remarked: "Unless parents be made responsible for their children, and be punished in such circumstances, they will become yet bolder in estranging them from all
the practices of the church." [1]

With ecclesiastics possessed of such a spirit, and with a royal
intendant so ready as Basville to carry the suggestions of the

---

[1] See the whole of the very interesting report of Fléchier to the Marquis
Châteauneuf, "on the state of religion and the disposition of the new converts
of his diocese," Nismes, June 4, 1699, Œuvres complètes, x. 56–62.

ecclesiastics into practice, the lot of the Huguenots of the province of Languedoc, and especially of its eastern portion, had
long been an unenviable one. Apprehension dwelt in
The Hugue-
nots of Lan-
guedoc. the heart of every man. Had the new converts been
content to be what Fléchier maintained that they
were—men without religion—they might possibly have contrived to expose their persons and their estates to less danger.
But to be deprived of the exercise of the only worship into
which they could heartily enter was precisely the thing to
which they could never bring themselves to submit. Consequently, not being permitted to assemble openly, they assembled
by stealth. The authorities, if they learned of the gathering in
time, sent troops to fall upon the inoffensive men and women
engaged in prayer to Almighty God, and butchered as many of
them as possible. The house or hamlet that was believed to
have harbored the meeting was razed to the ground; the men
that had attended were sentenced to the galleys, the women to
imprisonment. If a village contained many Protestants who
neglected to frequent mass, it was likely to receive the unwelcome garrison of one or two companies of soldiers, who either
exacted a sum of money of the delinquents, or were billeted
upon them, with full license from their superior officers to live
in the most wasteful and riotous manner.[1] For any venturesome preacher that fell into their hands the magistrates reserved
Fate of the
preachers. the worst treatment. In this there was nothing
strange. He certainly knew well enough that, by the
king's decrees, his life was forfeited to the state. But what
shall be said of the penalty which was visited, as we have seen,[2]
upon a simple woman, who, inspired by a prophetic frenzy,
deemed herself commissioned of heaven to exhort her neighbors
to repentance, and pointed to the tears of blood which she occasionally shed as proofs of her divine commission? A milder

---

[1] In December, 1696, the village of Pont de Montvert had two companies of
soldiers quartered upon it for this reason. Mémoires de Pierre Pons, published
in the Bulletin de la Société de l'histoire du Protestantisme français, xxxii.
(1883), 218. In January, 1698, the same punishment was again meted out to it,
because it was learned that a religious assembly of four thousand persons had
been held at a spot known as Le Mas de Moncur, not far distant. Ibid., 221.

[2] See Basville's letter, quoted above, page 219.

judge would have endeavored to destroy the effects of the strange phenomenon by unveiling the deception or by referring it to a physical cause, and would, at worst, have sent the woman to prison or to the madhouse; Basville knew no other way to deal with it than by consigning the Huguenot prophetess to the gallows.[1]

By such frequent and successive acts of cruelty the minds of the Cévenols were wrought up to a state of excitement bordering upon insane desperation. The constraint, which to the elegant prelate, in his episcopal palace at Nismes, seemed to fall

Desperation of the Protestants.

so far short of the "compulsion" authorized by his interpretation of our Lord's parable of the Great Supper as to constitute an objectionable "liberty" enjoyed by the new converts to abstain from the practice of the duties of members of the Roman Catholic Church, was to new converts themselves the most galling form of tyranny, confronting them at every turn in their daily walk. It was the more intolerable because the acts of outrage of which they complained were directly instigated, where they were not actually perpetrated by those very men from whose lips the words of love and gentleness, of charity and forbearance were most frequently heard, and who, at the very moment they were directing the terrible artillery at the disposal of the established church against the persons whom they styled heretics, never failed to represent that church and themselves as the victims of unprovoked persecution at the hands of their enemies.

For here it should again be noted that while the intendants and other royal officers were for the most part the instruments, Roman Catholic clergymen were the authors of nearly every par-

---

[1] Louvreleuil, Le Fanatisme renouvelé, ou Histoire des sacriléges, des incendies, des meurtres, et des autres attentats que les Calvinistes revoltez ont commis dans les Sevenes, et des châtimens qu'on en a faits (Avignon, 1704), i. 12. Brueys, Histoire du Fanatisme de notre tems (Utrecht, 1737), i. 290-291.—Notwithstanding the passion that appears on his title-page, Louvreleuil, who was a priest of the Christian Doctrine and had been curate at St. Germain de Calberte, is a fairer and more trustworthy authority than Brueys, who could never forget that he had once been himself a Huguenot and a minister. It is characteristic of the two men that here Brueys, as if ashamed to tell the full truth, merely informs us that the woman was "punished" for her imposture, while Louvreleuil candidly admits that she was "executed." See, also, La Baume, 36.

ticular act of cruelty. That the clergy had paved the way for the Revocation by its persistent efforts, kept up throughout the entire seventeenth century, to secure the withdrawal of one after another of the privileges conceded to the Protestants by the Edict of Nantes, has already been seen. Scarcely a single assembly of its representatives had failed to remonstrate against the liberty allowed to the Huguenots, or to petition the crown that Hatred of the priests. this liberty should be abridged. But even this fact does not altogether account for the intense hatred with which the Protestant laity of the South viewed the Roman Catholic priesthood. Although the Revocation was now an accomplished fact, the curates of the towns and villages would not leave the unfortunate Protestants alone. Had they been content to act as the pastors of their own flocks, the Huguenots, who recognized in them few of the lineaments of the true spiritual shepherd, would have borne them no special ill will, or, at all events, would not have disturbed them in their ecclesiastical functions. But, unfortunately, to be a priest was to be a spy ever on the watch to detect and bring to grief those who failed Harshness of the meddlesome ecclesiastics. to discharge the duties of sincere children of the established church. Having forced such Protestants as had not fled the kingdom to profess Roman Catholicism, the ecclesiastics now sought to force them to be constant in the profession. The harshness of their conduct toward the Protestants is admitted even by so zealous a Roman Catholic as the historian La Baume, himself a judge of the royal court at Nismes. "It is true," he says, "and this is a fact that ought not to be concealed, that there were many ecclesiastics, among those that were charged with the general instructions given to the new converts, who abused the kind of authority intrusted to them. They treated them with so little charity, and sometimes with so much rigor, that they furnished them one of the pretexts of which they laid hold to make an uprising."[1] The hand of the priests was in every act of oppression, even though,

---

[1] Relation historique de la révolte des fanatiques ou des Camisards, par M. Charles Joseph de La Baume, conseiller au Présidial de Nîmes, pp. 27, 28. This work was known and used in manuscript by Antoine Court, and was printed for the first time in 1874, under the editorship of the Abbé Goiffon, archivist of the diocese of Nismes.

from motives of prudence and a decorous regard for the claim of the church to be the author of peace and the enemy of suffering and bloodshed, they often concealed the fact. Their contemporaries knew it. Even had the fact escaped their notice, the governmental archives, with their multitude of priestly denunciations, now for the first time brought to the light of day, would amply establish it. To be irreverent at mass or to abstain from going thither at all, much more to turn into ridicule any of those who frequented the ceremonies of the church, was quite enough to call forth a secret missive from a priestly hand, suggesting to the intendant or his agents that for such an one a term of residence in some citadel or other prison would not be amiss.[1] Information from this source received immediate attention. In many cases, however, the priest did not shrink from becoming himself the open persecutor.

Of the most obnoxious type of meddlesome and tyrannical clergymen, François de Langlade du Chayla, prior of Laval, and archpriest of the diocese of Mende, was certainly a notable example. In his youth he had labored as a missionary to the heathen in the distant regions of Siam. For the past seventeen years he had found more congenial occupation in the Cévennes Mountains in striving to procure the conversion of the Protestants. What were his methods in his first field of work we are not informed. But in the discharge of his functions as Inspector of Missions, a position to which M. de Basville called him in the very year of the Revocation, he displayed untiring zeal and a boundless fertility in expedients.[2]

The Abbé du Chayla.

---

[1] The correspondence of Basville, at Montpellier, contains a great number of these curious documents, to which, for the most part, the prudent writers were careful not to append their names, lest they should fall into the wrong hands. Here is a sentence, however, from one which is both dated and signed : " Monseigneur, J'ay appris depuis quelques jours les mauvais discours que tient le sieur Trinquelaigue, père, dont le nom ne vous est pas inconnu ; non content d'estre fort mauvais catholique, il se met sur le pied de tourner en ridicule ceux qui font leur devoir, il rôde continuellement dans plusieurs communautez, où il nous fait beaucoup de mal ; c'est un homme qui mourra tel qu'il a vescu ; cependant je crois que quelque citadelle luy feroit du bien ; je luy attribue mesme une bonne partie de l'obstination qui règne à Lussan." Abbé Poncet de la Rivière to Basville, Uzès, May 25, 1701. G. Frosterus, Les Insurgés Protestants sous Louis XIV. (Paris, 1868), 43.

[2] " La subtillité à trouver les expédients dans toutes les difficultez," is one of

When tidings were brought him of an unauthorized meeting of Huguenots for worship not far from his abode, it was he who, without losing an instant, set off for Mende, to arrange for bringing troops to live at free quarters upon the wretched inhabitants of the place that had been guilty of tolerating the assembly. It was he that obtained the necessary order from the intendant. It was he that went to Florac to see that the soldiers were promptly despatched. It was he, too, that came at their head to ascertain, if possible, the names of those who had taken part in the meeting, with the view of sending them to Montpellier for condemnation to the galleys or the gibbet.[1] Not that, in the case of persons against whom he entertained no special animosity, he was inaccessible to offers of money made for the purpose of effecting the release of insignificant captives. Twenty *pistoles* in hand paid by the father of Élie Marion purchased from the abbé the freedom of the future "prophet" when the youth had been arrested for attending secret conventicles in the neighborhood of Barre des Cévennes.[2] Frequently he took the law into his own hands, and, with an ingenuity that would have done no discredit to a mediæval inquisitor, applied himself to extracting the proofs of crime from the unwilling confessions made by his victims under torture.

A modern inquisitor.

---

the particulars in the long list of admirable qualities which the curé of St. Germain de Calberte tells us he set forth in his funeral oration over Du Chayla's remains. Louvreleuil, i. 42.—Court places his coming to the Cévennes two years later, in 1687. More candid than Louvreleuil, La Baume admits the severity of the abbé, who, he tells us, since his return from Siam, had applied himself without respite to the attempt to make good Catholics out of the new converts of the Cévennes, "but with too much rigor and harshness toward those who did not do their duty. Charitable, whenever the toleration of the assemblies, which have been the source of the troubles, was not in question, he worked with constant effort to prevent and to discover them. This drew upon him the hatred of the new converts, who accused him of being interested and taking advantage of the authority that had been intrusted to him, to enrich himself." Relation historique de la révolte des fanatiques, 28, 29. The assertion of Abbé Valette, prior of Bernis, that Du Chayla was "always indulgent for the new converts," may therefore without any uncharitableness be set down as a deliberate falsehood. Histoire des troubles des Cévennes, MS. i. 277, in a note of Abbé Goiffon to his edition of La Baume, p. 28.

[1] Mémoires de Pierre Pons, ubi supra, 221, 222.

[2] Déposition de Marion, Londres, Janvier 1707. Théâtre Sacré des Cévennes Ed. of 1847), 56.

The cellar of his house became a veritable prison. Those who were so unfortunate as to be confined in it were subjected to the most excruciating torments. From one he would pluck out with pincers the hairs of his beard or his eyebrows, to compel him to denounce his brethren. Another was forced to hold glowing coals in his grasp until the flesh was burned to the bone. The hands of another were wrapped in cotton dipped in oil, to which the flame was then applied. His most exquisite contrivance for inflicting pain was the *ceps*, a species of stocks, wherein he made his captives fast by the hands and by the feet, and held them in so distressing a position that they could neither sit nor stand without extreme suffering. Many had been the victims that tasted the horrors of the protracted ordeal; some bore the marks of it to the day of their death. As if this were not enough, there were well-accredited accounts of punishments inflicted by the abbé in his outbursts of passion almost too ferocious to be believed, certainly too horrible and inhuman to be narrated here.[1] The title which one of his warm admirers confers upon him of *the scourge of the wicked*[2] may be taken to indicate sufficiently the character and life of the untiring persecutor, who would neither rest nor allow those who opposed him to rest. The more temperate among the Roman Catholics themselves, when they heard of the expeditions which he made hither and thither in quest of prey, laying aside his priestly character to become the guide, the commander of troops, the very executioner of a law of Draconian severity, blamed him and the ecclesiastics that resembled him for their excesses, and expressed their sympathy with those who were so cruelly maltreated.[3] The abbé's intimate friends, among whom was the

---

[1] The authority of Antoine Court, a dispassionate man, who was familiar with the scene of the events he describes, and who, if not himself a witness, enjoyed remarkable opportunities of reaching the truth in conversing with those who could testify from their own personal knowledge, must be accepted as conclusive. See Histoire des troubles des Cévennes, i. 25-30.

[2] "Le fléau des méchans." Brueys, i. 303. "Scourges" more or less resembling Chayla seemed to have abounded in France. Of Bégon, curate of Mer, not far from Blois, the friendly "Répertoire de l'ancien État civil" of that place says : "He was the scourge of the Calvinists in the parish, of almost all of whom he effected the conquest *with the help of the secular arm, which he had at his command*" (à sa discrétion). P. de Félice, Mer, son Église Réf., 125.

[3] The admission which so prejudiced a writer as Brueys makes (i. 293, 294)

curate that has left us the earliest and one of the best accounts of the events soon to be narrated, foresaw the danger of a popular uprising against his extreme measures, and warned Du Chayla, but in vain, to have greater care of his personal safety.[1] The explosion, long repressed, took place in the summer of the year 1702.

The chief functions of a missionary in the Cévennes are summed up by Basville in the maintenance of religious worship in the region—a duty which he admits the curates to be incapable of discharging—and watchfulness to transmit intelligence as to current movements.[2] The vigilance exercised by Abbé du Chayla over the Huguenots of the Cévennes was rewarded by a valuable capture. One Massip, an adventurous mountaineer, who had more than once successfully acted as guide for fugitives seeking a place of safety beyond the Alps, was arrested just as he had started with a fresh detachment of Protestants whom he had engaged to lead to Geneva. Among them were three boys, and as many girls, from the village of Moissac. The latter, for greater safety and ease in travelling, had disguised themselves in men's clothes. Massip and his company were soon lodged in the prison cellar of the abbé, and were allowed to test for themselves the merits of the redoubtable *ceps*. Delighted at his good fortune, the inspector of missions hastily sent for a deputy judge of Basville, and prepared to inflict ex-

---

in the following sentence is well worthy of notice : " Ceux-ci, qui pendant la paix avoient souffert, sans se plaindre, les sollicitations charitables de ceux qui travailloient à les rendre bons Catholiques, commencèrent à crier et à murmurer hautement contre les moyens dont les Ecclésiastiques se servoient pour les obliger d'aller à la Messe, et d'envoyer leurs enfans aux Catechismes; et ces cris et ces murmures firent tant de bruit, et furent si bien colorez, que quelques Catholiques mêmes s'y laissèrent surprendre, et crurent, qu' effectivement on avoit traité les Religionnaires avec trop de severité."—In reading the literature of the reign of Louis XIV., a fair-minded man often stands in doubt whether he ought rather to be indignant at the audacity, or to be amused with the puerile simplicity of the self-contradictory statements customarily indulged in by the apologists of persecution. If the means employed to make good Catholics of them were only "charitable solicitations," how could the Protestants ever have been tempted to complain; and what misrepresentations could ever have induced tender-hearted Roman Catholics to view those means as too severe ?

[1] Louvreleuil, i. 30.

[2] Basville to the controller general, September 12, 1693.　Corr. des contr. gén., i. 334.

emplary punishment. In vain did the relatives of his victims
come and implore his clemency. He was proof even against
the offer of a large sum of money, and brutally informed the
petitioners that the guide would swing upon the gallows, while
the rest would, according to their sex, be consigned either to
the galleys or to prison.

On Sunday, the twenty-third of July, a Huguenot gathering
for divine worship was held on a retired spot on the Montagne
du Bougés, within two or three leagues of the Pont
de Montvert.[1] Here their friends, half-crazed with
apprehension respecting the fate impending over the
captives, came and implored aid. The appeal did not fall upon
dull ears. A few bold spirits agreed to meet on the ensuing
day. At the appointed time some forty or fifty men, all of
them active and dauntless Cévenols, were assembled at the entrance of the forest covering the highest part of the mountain,
known in the dialect of the country by the name of *Alte Fage*,
from the beech-trees of which it was composed.[2] Enthusiasm
was kindled by the exhortations of prophets. Pierre Esprit—
otherwise known as Séguier—Salomon Couderc, and Abraham
Mazel, who had heretofore passed for " inspired persons,"
claimed to have been favored with distinct revelations from the
Almighty, and predicted success in the worthy enterprise upon
which the braves were embarked. The arms carried by the
men were of various kinds. A very few had guns or pistols ;
others had swords. Some had found old halberds. A number
had been able to provide themselves with nothing better than
scythes or reaping-hooks. Before starting they joined in a
prayer for the divine guidance. Then, throwing forward a vanguard of eight of their number, they set out for Pont de Montvert. Close to one of the three bridges that span the river
Tarn, here as yet an insignificant stream, stood the house toward which they directed their steps. Formerly the property

The affair of Pont de Montvert.

---

[1] The scene of this religious assembly was within the bounds of the parish of
St. Maurice de Ventalon, and a few miles east of the spot that became the rendezvous of Laporte's band on the morrow.

[2] Hard by the spot stands the village or hamlet of Grizac, noted as having
been the birthplace of Pope Urban V., and as having in his honor been exempted
by King John from all royal taxation. Joanne, Les Cévennes, 190.

of a Protestant gentleman, it had, since his murder for his religion's sake, passed by way of royal gift into the hands of the Abbé du Chayla. Here the inspector of missions was now residing; his captives were in the dungeon below-stairs.

It was about nine o'clock in the evening when the Huguenots entered the little town. As they did so, with the instinct of former days, they raised the clear notes of one of the good old psalms of Marot and Beza, such as had been sung on many a field when men were marshalled under Admiral Coligny or Henry of Navarre, such as were soon to be heard in the humbler contests of the Cévennes. They wisely selected [1] that poetical version of the sixty-eighth psalm, by Beza, which by common consent is entitled to rank as the national hymn of French Protestantism, the very Marseillaise of the Huguenots,[2] every line of which thrilled their hearts as a call to arms and an assurance of victory:

Attack on the house of Abbé du Chayla.

> Que Dieu se monstre seulement,
> Et on verra soudainement
> Abandonner la place
> Le camp des ennemis espars,
> Et ses haineux de toutes pars,
> Fuir devant sa face.

A few minutes more, and the Huguenots were at the abbé's door, noisily demanding admission and the liberation of the prisoners. At the first sound of the forbidden psalm, the ecclesiastic had conjectured that some of the new converts were on their way to a meeting for worship, and had begun to take measures for their arrest. Undeceived by the tumult in the street, he ordered some soldiers that were with him to fire upon the crowd. One man of Séguier's company fell dead

---

[1] Memoirs of the Wars of the Cévennes, by Colonel Cavalier, 2d ed. (London, 1727), 35, 36.

[2] O. Douen, Clément Marot et le Psautier huguenot, i. 10. The well-chosen action of the music of this psalm is compared by M. Douen to the progress of a storm ; the first strains representing the suppressed and muffled grumbling of the approaching tempest. In the middle, the sharp and prolonged notes recall the crash of the elements, bursting forth clap upon clap ; while the finale is not without analogy to the rolling away of the thunder that loses itself in the distance. Ibid., i. 657. The tune was an old Alsatian air, adapted by Bourgeois.

upon the ground. Infuriated at this, the rest speedily broke
down the doors, and rushed within. Their steps were first
directed to the gloomy chambers where their fellow believers
were languishing, and where some of their own number had not
long since made trial of the abbé's tender mercies. The pitiable
condition in which Massip and his companions were discovered,
unable, even after their release from the *ceps*, to stand without
support, determined the course of events. The abbé had, from
the moment the doors were burst in, betaken himself to flight,
and now that the assailants sought him with cries that augured
ill for his life, his voice was heard again calling on his friends
to fire upon the intruders. When a second Huguenot was
wounded, the word was given by his comrades to set the house
on fire and drive the enemy from his hiding-place. The flames
spread rapidly. Du Chayla was compelled to consult safety by
lowering himself from one of the windows looking out upon the
neighboring garden. In his descent he fell, fracturing his
thigh, but yet had strength, with the help of a faithful servant,
to drag himself to the encompassing hedge. He, would, perhaps
have escaped, had not the glare of the burning house revealed
him to the eyes of his enemies. They rushed forward with the
cry, "Come, let us throttle this persecutor of the children of
God!"

And now a wild and weird scene arose. Pressing around
their prisoner, the motley crowd, with swords and scythes still
in hand, began to reproach him with each individual act of
cruelty committed during the past seventeen years. At the
same time they bade him prepare at once for a death
which could not possibly come up to the measure of
his ill desert. It is unnecessary to decide whether,
as his friends averred, he met his fate with heroic fortitude, or,
as is asserted by his enemies, in a spirit of abject fear. Friendly
and hostile eyes often see very different things in the same
phenomena. The abbé's response to those that denounced his
sufferings in another world did not necessarily indicate undue
trepidation. "Ha, my friends! If I have damned myself, do you
wish to do the same by yourselves?" But certainly the historians who would exalt the abbé to the rank of a martyr for his
faith make too large a draft upon our credulity when they ask

Death of the Abbé Du Chayla.

us to believe that his captors offered him his life on condition
that he renounce his religion and become their minister!
Louvreleuil, indeed, undertakes to give us the very words of the
Huguenots' offer and the abbé's refusal. Interposing between
Du Chayla and the men who thirsted for his blood, the prophet
Esprit Séguier exclaimed : " God wills not the sinner's death,
but that he turn and live. Let us grant him his life, if he
will consent to follow us (*s'il est en estat de nous suivre*), and to
discharge among us the functions of a minister of Almighty
God." "Rather would I die a thousand times," the archpriest
replied. " Well, then, thou shalt die," was Esprit's rejoinder.
" Thy sin be upon thee ! " [1]

But, however well suited for such a charge Louvreleuil and
Brueys may have esteemed him, it may well be asked what
were the Abbé du Chayla's qualifications for the sacred office
in the eyes of men that knew him only as a merciless persecutor
whose hands were red with the blood of their brethren.

And now Du Chayla was put to death, not by one blow, but
by the blows of all the Huguenots present. As each delivered
his thrust, he addressed the victim with such words as these:
" This is for your violent treatment of my father or my mother ! "
" This, for the outrage you did my brother or my sister ! "
" This, for having secured such an one's condemnation to the
galleys ! " "This, for having ruined such a family ! " "This,
for having caused such a man or woman to be put to death ! "
Never, perhaps, has a criminal met with a death at which each
separate sin has arisen so distinctly to confront him, and each

---

[1] Le fanatisme renouvelé, i. 36, 37. Brueys, as usual, does little more than
embellish Louvreleuil's simpler narrative. Histoire du fanatisme, i. 300. We
must acquit Louvreleuil, who is, for the most part, an honest, although a very
partial historian, of the charge of inventing this myth. M. de Broglie, in his
first despatch to court, written from Montpellier, July 28, 1702, or four days
after the occurrence of what he somewhat euphemistically styles " a disagreeable
adventure which had just befallen the Abbé du Chayla," relates that the captors
proposed to the unfortunate priest that he should go and sing psalms with them
and change his religion ; to which he replied that he preferred to die. " Ils
le prirent et lui proposèrent d'aler chanter des pseaumes avec eux et de changer
de religion. Il leur répondit qu'il aimoit mieux mourir." MS. in archives
historiques du Min. de la Guerre, printed en J. P. Hugues, Histoire de l'Église
d'Anduze, 667–669.

victim has become, through a personal representative, the Nemesis of the oppressor's misdeeds. A single human body was almost too small to receive all the expiatory wounds. On the corpse were counted fifty-two. There were twenty-four, any one of which alone would have been mortal.[1]

Whether Séguier and his band had originally contemplated anything beyond the release of the prisoners confined in Du Chayla's dungeon is doubtful. On at least two or three previous occasions the priest fell into Protestant hands and might easily have been put to death, had his enemies chosen to imbrue their hands in his blood.[2] The sight of the deplorable condition of his most recent victims, and the shots that killed one and wounded another of their own number seem to have determined the assailants of his house at Pont de Montvert to put the sanguinary ecclesiastic out of the way. However this may be, the death of the Abbé Du Chayla marks the beginning of a conflict of no mean historical importance, in which, although the malcontents sprang from the humblest class of the population, and never amounted to more than a mere handful of men, their reduction required the efforts of three marshals of France, successively sent to direct the movements of corps of troops numbering at times many thousand men.

The signal of a Protestant uprising.

The success of their first undertaking prompted the com-

---

[1] For the death of the Abbé du Chayla, our principal authorities are Louvreleuil, who was, as has been stated, curate of the parish of Saint Germain de Calberte, about ten miles distant from Pont de Montvert, and an intimate friend of the victim ; De la Baume, a counsellor in the presidial court of Nismes ; Brueys, whose account has little independent value ; Abraham Mazel, one of the Huguenot band, who in his deposition (Théâtre sacré des Cévennes, 78, 79) describes the events briefly. Antoine Court, besides having before him the works of the writers just mentioned, enjoyed, as I have said, unsurpassed opportunities for learning the truth on the spot and from the men who, like Mazel, had been actors in the tragedy. He had, for instance, several conversations with the guide Massip, and obtained from him full particulars of the incidents of his own capture, imprisonment, and subsequent liberation, as well as of the abbé's tragic end. I make little account of the Memoirs of Cavalier and of the anonymous Histoire des Camisards (2 vols., London, 1754), the latter an utterly untrustworthy book. There are readable accounts in many modern works, such as Alby, Bonnemère, etc.

[2] Court, i. 43.

panions of Séguier to hold together, with a view to other and more important enterprises. A realization of the wide-spread commotion which the fate of so notable an ecclesiastic as the inspector of missions would surely create dictated a 'speedy retreat into the wild mountain forests, where none but men well acquainted with the country could follow them. Their track was marked with blood. The first victim was the priest of the neighboring village of Frugères, known to have been a friend and assistant of Du Chayla in his persecution of the Protestants. On his person was found a letter to the abbé, in which he gave the names of a score of his parishioners whom it would be well to arrest. For other acts of violence there was less occasion; and the malcontents disgraced themselves by needless cruelty. Before a week had elapsed, learning of the magnitude of the preparations made for their capture, and knowing the importance of securing a supply of arms,

Capture of the castle of La Devèze. they invested the castle of La Devèze, the nearest place from which they might hope to obtain them. Unfortunately, the gentleman to whom the place belonged not only refused their summons to deliver up his ammunition, but rang the tocsin to alarm the neighborhood, and fired a few shots at the assailants, killing Couderc, one of their number. The malcontents thereupon burst into the castle, and pitilessly slew the entire family, from the aged grandmother of eighty years to the fair young girl who in vain begged for her life on her knees before her murderers. This done, they burned the castle to the ground. It was a horrible butchery, denounced alike by friend and foe; and, by common consent, the disaster which, two days later, befell three of those who took a leading part in its commission, was regarded as a just retribution of Heaven.[1]

---

[1] Louvreleuil, i. 47 ; Brueys, i. 308, 309. The former gives additional pathos to the story, when he relates that the murderers, among other spoil which they divided among themselves, carried off the sum of five thousand livres which they discovered in a chest, the destined dower of the young girl whose throat they had just cut. Antoine Court (Histoire des troubles, i. 50–51) learned from Rampon, one of the chiefs that survived, that the accusation was false, and was informed by him that no harm would have been done to any one had not the guns been refused, and had not M. de la Devèze ordered the firing. "But what an apology is this," he well exclaims, "for so detestable an action!" Cavalier blunders as usual in his statement of the case, but nevertheless remarks : "All

Meanwhile the news of the insurrection spread far and wide. The curates of the region, fearful of their lives, fled to the walls of Alais and to other places of refuge. The churches were deserted. The Roman Catholics trembled, while of the Protestants those that did not join in the revolt secretly gave it what aid and comfort they could.[1] M. de Broglie, commanding the royal troops in Languedoc, and M. de Basville, the intendant, hastened to the scene of action, the former with what forces he could muster, the latter taking measures, with characteristic promptness, to institute at Florac, not far from the original source of the outbreak, a judicial chamber to pass without delay upon such culprits as might be apprehended. To discover the enemy, however, was no easy matter. M. de Broglie, pushing on to Pont de Montvert, and thence up the steep rocks and through the dense woods of the surrounding hills, found to his cost that the Cévenols always eluded his grasp, for, learning his advance from the peasants who secretly favored their cause, the insurgents easily disappeared by paths with which they alone were conversant. Broglie's lieutenant, Poul by name, a man of wonderful endurance and intrepidity, was more fortunate.

Repulse at Font Morte. Scarcely had he reached the post to which he was assigned, at Barre des Cévennes, when he heard that the mountaineers, on their retreat from the scene of their late adventures, were in his immediate vicinity. Without delay he pressed forward with a small detachment, and fell unexpectedly upon them on the little plain of Font Morte, later to be the scene of two other engagements. The insurgents were thrown into disorder and fled precipitately to the covert of the woods, which on two sides sloped rapidly down to the adjoining valleys. Their loss in killed and wounded was very small, but there were three prisoners whose capture delighted the hearts of the pursuers. The most important was Esprit Séguier himself, the prophet, and, up to this time, the leader of the malcontents. Thus, by a singular fatality, the Cévenol chief was taken within a mile or two of his birthplace, the hamlet of Magestavols, the

---

the Protestants of that neighborhood disapproved mightily of the burning of that castle." Memoirs, p. 37.

[1] Brueys, i. 310.

roofs of whose cabins could be distinctly seen embowered in the beech forest.[1] So valuable a prize must not be left out of Capture and execution of Esprit Séguier. his triumphant enemy's sight. Poul, as he rode back with the rough mountaineer at his side, could not refrain from taunting him with allusions to the sorry plight into which the fortunes of war had brought him. "Well, wretch," said he, "now that I hold thee, after the crimes thou has perpetrated, how dost thou expect to be treated?" "As I should have treated thee, had I taken thee," was Séguier's prompt and undaunted reply.[2] And now the chamber of justice which Basville assembled at Florac had an opportunity to display its zeal in the suppression of the revolt. It was well improved. The prisoners were expeditiously tried and as expeditiously sentenced to death. Yet in the mode and place of their execution a careful discrimination was made. Esprit Séguier, who made no attempt to deny that his was the first thrust under which the Abbé du Chayla succumbed, was condemned to be burned alive at Pont de Montvert, the scene of the priest's death. Pierre Nouvel was ordered to be broken on the wheel at La Devèze, the ruins of whose castle had scarcely ceased to smoke. His companion, Moïse Bonnet, was adjudged the milder death upon the gallows at St. André de Lancize, where a priest had been killed and a church and a rectory had been consumed by fire. The other less noted rebels were to be hung at various other points in the Cévennes. Thus Basville's court started out well in its course, and bade fair to emulate the The bloody assizes of Florac. example of that other "chambre ardente," in the early days of Protestantism in France, which enjoyed the unenviable reputation of uniformly sending to their death whatever "Lutherans" were brought to its bar.[3] The sole difference was that whereas the "estrapade" was the favorite instrument with the Parisian judges of the sixteenth century,

---

[1] See the description of Font Morte by N. Lamarche, in the Bulletin de la Société de l'histoire du Protestantisme français, xxxvi. (1887), 565.

[2] Brueys, Histoire du fanatisme, i. 318; Histoire des Camisards, i. 132; Court, Histoire des troubles des Cévennes, i. 53; Louvreleuil, Le fanatisme renouvelé, i. 50-52.

[3] The resemblance is noted by Court, Histoire des troubles des Cévennes, i. 55, 56.

the wheel and the gallows were preferred by the court that sat at Florac, in the eighteenth. As to the first victim of this tribunal, his demeanor at the stake did not disgrace the calm self-control with which he had deported himself since his apprehension. Neither when his hand—the hand that struck Du Chayla—was cut off at the wrist, nor during the last agony in the flames, did he change countenance. For the most part he maintained a dignified silence where speech would have been wasted. He closed his ears to the exhortations of a Capuchin monk whose religion he abominated as idolatrous. He refused to beg the pardon of the king or his judges, against whom he denied that he had committed any crime, and would ask forgiveness of his sins of God alone. In view of this, a contemporary chronicler declares that, as he had lived an impious man, so he died a reprobate.[1] A more charitable writer, on the other hand, finds in the Cévenol prophet's deportment all the marks of a Christian hero from whom not even the heat and violence of the flames can extract a single complaint, a single sigh.[2]

The government was, indeed, resolved to stamp out the fire that had broken forth so unexpectedly, even to the most insignificant sparks which the wind might fan into a flame. At five of the most important points in the Cévennes corps of fusileers were posted—at Pont de Montvert, at Collet, at Ayres, at Barre, at Le Pompidou—ready, at a moment's notice, to hasten to any place where the malcontents should be reported as showing themselves. Whatever suspicious person was discovered was hurried to the bloodthirsty court at Florac, of the number of whose victims little is known or ever will be known; so quietly and relentlessly did it pursue its way. But contrary to all the expectations of Basville and Broglie, and of the court at Versailles, the very measures taken to repress only irritated. Far from being terrified into submission, the Protestant mountain-

---

[1] "Le faux prophete n'avoua rien dans la question qu'on luy donna, il ferma les oreilles de son cœur aux remonstrances du Capucin qui l'accompagna au supplice, et ne voulut demander pardon ni au Roy ni à la Justice, mais à Dieu seul. En un mot, il avoit vécu en impie et il mourut en réprouvé." Louvreleuil, i. 51, 52.

[2] The anonymous Histoire des Camisards (London, 1754), 132.

eers saw in the inhuman executions which the judges ordered,
and in the illegal violence of the soldiers, only new incentives
to desperate exertions.　For every Huguenot hung,
The Cévenols
retaliate. burned, or broken on the wheel, some Romanists must
be hung on a hastily erected gallows, or shot forthwith.　In the
expressive words of a writer unsurpassed by any of his contemporaries for virulent hostility to the new movement, "these
madmen took the crazy notion into their heads that they had a
right to retaliate upon all the Catholics that fell into their
hands."[1]　The admission of the partisan historian reveals the
true origin and nature of the Camisard revolt.　A fortuitous
occurrence, the sudden and unpremeditated attack of a small
party of Protestants upon the house in which some of their
friends and relatives of the same faith were unjustly detained,
involving the death of the ecclesiastic who was their jailer, was
the spark that fell upon combustible material that had long
been accumulating.　The conflagration that ensued,
An unpre-
meditated although the natural consequence of the existing state
uprising. of affairs, was an unforeseen result, and was in no wise
due to any plan of insurrection, whether formed within or without the kingdom.　Its rapid spread was due as much to the ill-
considered measures adopted to extinguish it, as to the fact that
the fuel for it to feed upon lay ready for its advent.　Men who
might have hesitated to throw in their lot in a perilous enterprise, had the choice been offered them of leading a quiet
life, ceased to deliberate when the dangers of submission were
scarcely inferior to the dangers of armed resistance.　If die
they must, the Protestants of the Cévennes preferred to die in a
struggle for religious freedom.　Whatever attempts were subsequently made outside of France, but unfortunately too late and
in too feeble and clumsy a manner to be of use to the combatants, it is beyond reasonable doubt that the Camisards began

---

[1] "L'on avoit cru que les exécutions terribles qu'on venoit de faire des plus
scelerats, auroient fait perdre aux autres l'envie de les imiter, mais on avoit à
faire à des fols, sur qui les exemples ne faisoient rien, et que les gibets, les
roues, ni les buchers ne pouvoient rendre sages.　On apprit même par la suite,
qu'on avoit par-là irrité le mal, au lieu de le guerir, parce que ces furieux
s'allèrent follement mettre en tête, qu'ils étoient en droit d'user de represailles
sur tous les Catholiques qui tomboient entre leurs mains."　Brueys, i. 328.

their war, and prosecuted it for the whole period of two years
that elapsed before it degenerated into a mere struggle of a few
scattered chiefs for existence, without the suggestion and without the material support of sympathizers in foreign lands.
That singular person, the Abbé de La Bourlie, otherwise known
as the Marquis de Guiscard, respecting whose schemes at a
later time I shall have occasion again to speak, does indeed advance a claim to have instigated the earliest outbreak. He
would have us believe that, in the furtherance of his projects
for the recovery of the political freedom of France, it was he
that planned "to cause to fall upon the Cévennes the first
sparks of the fire which he intended to kindle throughout the
kingdom, in order to melt, as it were, and consume the chains
of his wretched countrymen;" that, accordingly, his emissaries
were sent in 1701 and 1702 to urge the Cévenols to extreme
measures against the most violent of their persecutors; and that
thus in particular he occasioned the murder of the Abbé du
Chayla and Monsieur de Saint Cosme.[1]   But the unsupported
authority of La Bourlie cannot be regarded as of much account,
in view of the fact that Antoine Court knew of no such foreign
instigation at this stage;[2] and Frosterus, who is most charitable
in his suppositions, concedes that any influence the abbé may
have put forth must have been of secondary importance and
have reached but a small number of persons.[3]   La Bourlie is
best known to readers of English history for the mad attempt
he made, when under examination before the council on a
charge of plotting to assassinate Queen Anne, to murder Robert
Harley, Earl of Oxford.

Much as the opponents of the Camisards have endeavored to
represent their movement as an unpatriotic struggle that took
advantage of the embarrassments of France abroad, to
distract the attention and weaken the efforts of the
royal government by erecting a standard of revolt at home,
there was absolutely no connection between the foreign relations of the kingdom and the actions of the insurgents.   If the

No foreign
instigation.

---

[1] Mémoires du Marquis de Guiscard, reprinted in Cimber et Danjou, Archives
curieuses, seconde série, xi. 207, etc.

[2] Histoire des Troubles des Cévennes, ii. 50, etc.

[3] Les Insurgés protestants sous Louis XIV., 56, 57.

affair of Pont de Montvert happened to succeed by only twenty-two days the formal declaration of hostilities by Louis the Fourteenth on entering upon the War of the Spanish Succession,[1] the circumstance may be referred to the category of fortuitous coincidences, and no connection between the two can be established save on the delusive maxim of *post hoc, ergo propter hoc*. Only the most prejudiced or the most credulous of writers could see in the rupture of the Peace of Ryswick the cause of a passionate outburst of the indignation of a handful of Cévenol peasants against the persecutor of their brethren, than which no local commotion ever seemed, at the first, less likely to assume the proportions of a wide-spread struggle for the recovery of lost religious privileges.[2]

So far from disbanding after the reverse at Font Morte and the consequent executions, the malcontents only increased in number and spirit, for, in place of the wild enthusiasm of a prophet, they gained the leadership of a chieftain of marked military abilities. Laporte, who by the votes of his companions was elevated to the position that had been held for a few days by Esprit Séguier, with the consent rather than by the choice of the insurgents, properly ranks as the first real head of the Camisards. A man of some military experience, gained in the king's service, it was he who, when the Protestants, discouraged by the reverse that they had just met with, were deliberating as to the place to which they should betake themselves for safety, whether within the bounds of the

Laporte, leader of the insurgents.

---

[1] " Pour faire voir que les Rebelles agissoient de concert avec nos ennemis, et n'attendoient que de nous voir aux prises avec eux, pour arborer l'Etendart de la revolte, je dois faire remarquer ici, que la France avoit declaré la guerre le second du mois de Juillet de l'an 1702, et que ce fut précisément vingt-deux jours après, que ce soulevement arriva ; comme si le choc des Armées, qui alloit commencer au dehors de ce Royaume, eût été le signal des troubles qu'ils vouloient exciter au dedans." Brueys, i. 304, 305.

[2] It is only in order to enhance the contrast with the subsequent commotion that Brueys depicts the calm reigning among the Protestants of the Cévennes, under the peace of 1697, as so profound : " Tout y paroissoit tranquille. Les Religionnaires sembloient être revenus de leurs égaremens et rentrez dans leur devoir : on n'y parloit plus d'Assemblées contre les ordres du Roi ; les Pasteurs instruisoient librement leurs troupeaux : et si les Nouveaux Catholiques ne profitoient pas comme ils devoient de leurs exhortations, du moins ils écoutoient sans aigreur." Histoire du Fanatisme, i. 286, 287.

province or outside of France, succeeded in persuading them, by a speech full of earnestness akin to native eloquence, to assume the offensive.[1] Among his earliest acts was the preparation of a challenge which he sent to Poul. The letter was dated " from the Camp of the Lord in the Desert of the Cévennes ; " and Laporte signed it as " Colonel of the Regiment of the Children of God who are seeking for Liberty of Conscience."[2] The very audacity displayed by the appeal to arms gave courage to his followers.

It was not long before to the first band of armed insurgents a second was added, under the leadership of a nephew of Laporte, bearing the same name, but better known henceforth as Roland.

Roland.   He was at this period about thirty years of age, a man of middle stature, slight, active in his movements, with a fresh and ruddy complexion somewhat marred by traces of small-pox, with large eyes in which glowed the fire of a resolute character. He was soldierly in bearing, and seemed born to command, but he was somewhat cold and taciturn in his intercourse with men. Born in the little hamlet of Mas Soubeyran,[3] not far from Mialet, at one of the southern gateways of the Cévennes, he was equally at home upon the mountains and in the plain that skirted their southern side. He brought to the popular movement not only a greater familiarity with military tactics and organization than any one else, but a mind more capacious of great designs and possessed of greater tenacity of purpose. Above all rivals Roland deserves to be regarded as the most representative figure in the new Protestant war.

---

[1] A summary of his address is given by Court, i. 57–59.

[2] Louvreleuil, i. 52.

[3] The house in which Roland was born, and which was his home until his death, is still to be seen. In 1880, a successful effort was made to purchase it from the last surviving representative of the Laporte family, himself a Protestant. The quaint and humble cottage is now the property of the Société de l'Histoire du Protestantisme français. With its interesting associations and a few relics of the Camisard hero—a Bible which he read, a halberd which he used, and a singular excavation popularly supposed to have served as a place of concealment for him when hard pressed by the enemy—the " Maison de Roland," as it is still termed, promises to go down to posterity a suggestive memorial of a thrilling episode of French history. See the communications of M. Jules Bonnet to the Bulletin of the French Protestant Historical Society for May and June, 1880.

About the same time a third band was formed under the leadership of Henry Castanet, destined to play a conspicuous part in the events of the next two years. His parentage was obscure, and his occupation had been that of a simple forester on the slopes of the range of Mont Aigoual.[1] Hardy and severe as the wild heights which had been his haunts, he had something bordering upon fierceness in his mien and in his mental characteristics. A writer by no means friendly to the cause which Castanet espoused draws an uncomplimentary portrait of the young mountaineer. "He was of about the height and the shape of a small bear, an animal of which, moreover, he had all the ferocity. But as he had in his childhood been taught to read and write, and as he had passed his life in the solitude of the woods, he had tried to make up intellectually for what nature had denied him in body, by applying himself, in his retreat, to the study of controversy, and even to the composition of sermons. These he delivered in the religious meetings with so much earnestness that he passed among the fanatics for the greatest of their preachers."[2]

Such were the first leaders of the exasperated mountaineers of Languedoc. In view of the terror which their exploits speedily spread in every direction, it is not surprising that the heated imagination of the oppressors, until now exercising their cruelty with little or no resistance, conjured up the spectre of former days of blood, and declared that not even the union of Octavius, Mark Antony, and Lepidus made a greater sensation throughout Italy than did this new triumvirate of arrant scoundrels in the rocky region of the Cévennes.[3]

---

[1] His birthplace was the hamlet of Massevaque (in the parish of Fraissinet de Fourques) close to the lofty Col de Perjurat, the narrow tongue of land, scarcely half a mile in breadth, which like a veritable isthmus extends across from Mont Aigoual and connects to its sister heights that singular plateau, the Causse Méjan, which otherwise would, as it were, be a detached island in the midst of the Cévennes. For here alone is there a break in the deep chasm at the base of the high and precipitous cliffs of the Causse, in which the Tarn and its tributaries flow. Louvreleuil, i. 53. See Joanne, Les Cévennes, 180.

[2] Brueys, i. 332, 333.

[3] "Il est certain que le fameux triumvirat de l'ancienne Rome ne fit pas autrefois plus de bruit dans l'Italie, que ces trois insignes scélérats en firent alors dans les Cevennes." Ibid., ubi supra.

Meanwhile, events in the more level country of the neighborhood of Nismes had prepared the way for the success of Roland
in his attempt to recruit a formidable company among the
Protestants of the plains, and thus to distract the attention of
the government from the operations of Laporte. Here, too, intolerable injury on the part of the stronger had bred desperation and violence in the weaker party, and the bloody reprisals
of the authorities had only tended the more rapidly to swell the
numbers and weight of the malcontents. A Protestant nobleman of some prominence, M. de Saint Cosme, abjured
his faith at the time of the Revocation of the Edict of
Nantes, and had received a substantial reward from
Louis the Fourteenth, in the shape of an annual pension of two
thousand livres. So liberal a recognition of the value of his
conversion, at a time when persons gained from the dregs of
the Protestant population were regarded as entitled on the
average only to a single paltry payment of a few livres, seems to
have incited Saint Cosme to earn yet greater recompenses by
signal exhibitions of proselyting zeal. The man that had once
held the office of elder in the Reformed Church, accepted the
office of inspector of the New Converts of his district, and, at
the head of the troops placed under his command, fell upon one
religious meeting after another, butchering his former brethren
and sisters in the faith without hesitation, and, apparently,
without remorse.[1] Even the barbarous massacres perpetrated
upon the assemblies of Protestants at the village of Saint Cosme,
at Candiac, at Garrigues de Vauvert, might, however, have
failed to arouse the patient Huguenots to violent measures, had
not the author of these atrocities ventured upon the ill-advised
measure of undertaking to disarm the entire population of the
lowlands from Aimargues to Saint Gilles. Men accustomed to
support themselves and their families chiefly, if not solely, by
hunting and fishing, were driven to extreme resolutions, when
they saw penury or famine staring them in the face. Six youths,
more impulsive than the rest, undertook to rid the country of

M. de Saint
Cosme
killed.

---

[1] The Abbé de la Bourlie does not hesitate to style Saint Cosme " un de leurs
plus cruels persécuteurs, quoique nouveau catholique." Mémoires du Marquis
de Guiscard (Archives curieuses seconde série, tome xi.), 212.

the oppressor, and lay in wait for him upon the main road between Vauvert and Coudognan. In default of weapons of their own, they killed Saint Cosme with the very arms he wore about his person.[1] In this case, too, the guidance of heaven is said to have been sought and was believed to have been secured by the insurgents. " My brethren," exclaimed Bousanquet, who was reputed a prophet, "there comes our enemy. Let us inquire of the Lord whether it be His pleasure that the man shall be slain by us." Thereupon the band knelt in prayer, the prophet was violently convulsed, fell backward upon the ground, and remained quiet for a few moments. Then rising to his feet, "The Spirit has just declared to me," he said, "that Monsieur de Saint-Cosme must be put to death."[2] So bold an act, committed against his agent, within less than ten miles from Nismes, and almost before his very eyes, inflamed the anger of the intendant to a still greater heat. The insult could be washed out only by Huguenot blood, and among the victims of Basville's rage little distinction was made between the innocent and the guilty. The only result was to drive many of those who had hitherto taken no part in the movement, but who now saw their friends and kinsmen involved in the common ruin, to adopt such resolutions as despair is wont to suggest. The bands of malcontents were swollen suddenly to portentous dimensions, while those Protestants that did not forsake their ordinary pursuits of trade or agriculture were driven by the sight of the savage cruelty perpetrated upon their fellow believers into so cordial a sympathy with the bold followers of Laporte and Roland that they stood ready to reveal to them every movement, every project of the enemy that reached their ears. Nor was this true of the inhabitants of the mountains alone. The environs of Nismes, with the lowlands stretching to the shores of the Mediterranean, gave the government little cordial support; while in that rich valley which lies to the west of Nismes, popularly known as *La Vaunage,* almost the whole body of the inhabitants seemed to be in secret league with the new champions of an oppressed religious creed. When

La Vaunage, or Little Canaan.

---

[1] Louvreleuil, 59-62 ; Brueys, i. 341-345 ; Court, i. 60-62.

[2] Brueys, ubi supra.

the Edict of Nantes still remained in force, La Vaunage—the "val," or "vau," of Nages, now an insignificant hamlet of scarcely more than five hundred souls, but in the Middle Ages the most important place in the valley—could boast, it is said, some thirty organized Huguenot churches and as many temples or places of worship. So deep had the doctrines of the Reformation struck their roots, so fully had they taken possession of the soil, that the favored region was familiarly styled by the Huguenots *La petite Canaan*—Little Canaan. La Vaunage was scarcely less Protestant at the time of which I write.[1]

And now began a reign of terror for the priests and for those dependent upon them. The manses which they had made haste to abandon, were ruthlessly destroyed. The churches fared no better. It would be a tedious and unprofitable task to rehearse the numerous ecclesiastical edifices, of which Louvreleuil and Brueys are at the pains to give the list, consigned by the insurgents to the devouring flames. Respecting a policy which at the first glance would appear to be inspired by a spirit not only of sacrilege but of pure vandalism, one or two observations should be made, by way not of justification, but of needful explanation. The first is, that as the buildings used for religious worship were, throughout the Cévennes, uniformly constructed of stone, the conflagration was of necessity pretty much confined to the shrines and to those objects which, in the minds of the Protestants, were inseparably associated with a service regarded by them as idolatrous and therefore offensive to the Divine Majesty. "When I have spoken of churches as burned," says the curate Louvreleuil, "I have not meant the buildings themselves,[2] as these are all arched, but I have intended to speak of the tabernacles, the wooden altars, the chancel rails, the benches, the paintings, the pulpits for preaching, the covers of the baptismal fonts, the furniture of the vestry-rooms, the confessionals, and generally of everything that was found of a combustible nature."[3] The other is, that the edifices in question might have escaped even

Destruction of churches and rectories.

---

[1] Brueys, i. 335, 336.—At the present day it is still described as "région peuplée presque exclusivement de protestants." P. Joanne, Les Cévennes, 204.

[2] "Les corps des églises."

[3] Le fanatisme renouvelé, i. 200.

the iconoclastic zeal of the insurgents, had they not been employed by the priestly party, with singular uniformity, as arsenals in which to store the weapons and ammunition designed for use in the repression or subjugation of those who would have none of their religion, and as strongholds whence to fire upon all assailants.[1] "This is the reason," aptly remarks the author of the "Memoirs of Jean Cavalier," "why the priests complained so much : we had burned a great many churches. But who are the most guilty—those who make the houses of prayer dens of thieves, or those who demolish them when they are such? Those who turn into citadels the churches they look upon as sacred, or those, who esteeming them idolatrous, burn them? Let any impartial man judge, and chiefly let him consider that we never meddled with any church wherein there was no garrison, nor took anything out of it."[2]

And here, if it be insisted that the religious teachers of the Protestants ought to have enjoined upon them to exercise self-control, and should have urged them not to disgrace a cause righteous in itself by acts of lawless violence, the very criticism brings into bold relief the fatuity of the course adopted by the crown at the instigation of the clergy of the established church. The religious teachers that enjoyed the esteem and confidence of the Huguenots, and that would have inculcated the practice of moderation, had been banished from France, on pain of death if they returned. The sister churches of Switzerland and Germany might express in distinct tones their disapprobation, and imitate in this the example of John Calvin, who, a century and a half earlier, in a letter addressed to the Protestant church of Sauve, a small town in the heart of this very region, expostulated in vehement terms with the perpetrators of what he denominated the "mad exploit" of burning images and overturning a cross.[3] But

Marginal note: Lack of religious teachers to restrain iconoclastic excesses.

---

[1] Court, i. 80.

[2] Memoirs of the Wars of the Cevennes under Col. Cavallier [Cavalier] in Defence of the Protestants Persecuted in that Country (London, 1727), page 49.

[3] The letter of Calvin to the church of Sauve, July, 1561, may be read in the original in Bonnet, Lettres françaises de Jean Calvin, ii. 415–418, or in the American translation (Philadelphia, 1858), iv. 205–207. The minister of the place, who had been a leader in the acts of vandalism and persisted in justify-

there was not now, as there had been then, a body of intelligent and regularly educated and ordained ministers of the gospel to receive and profit by their friendly admonitions; there were no synods and other ecclesiastical courts to enforce by censure and, if need be, excommunication or deposition, the observance of the dictates of Christian sobriety and good order. Prophets and preachers, who had rather taken upon themselves than received from others the authority to act as public teachers of religion, could exercise no such corrective and restraining power. The clergy of the established church had themselves to thank for the loss of the guarantees for the safety of their own persons and of their ecclesiastical edifices, which they once possessed in the conservative organization of the Reformed churches.

The general destruction of church buildings and manses was an incident of the war scarcely more annoying to the provincial Protestant authorities than was the marked increase in the number conventicles. ber of the meetings of the Protestants for the celebration of their proscribed worship, and the great concourse of people on such occasions. Care was taken by the Huguenots, however, to select the most unexpected times and places for the assemblies, with a view to the possibility of a surprise by royal troops, with the disastrous consequences of such a surprise. On one occasion they resorted to an ingenious plan, the success of which fully realized their sanguine expectations.

A single Reformed "temple," or church, was the exception to the general ruin of the Protestant places of worship, consequent The "tem- upon the efforts of the clergy in the previous century. ple " of Col- It stood in the village of Le Collet de Dèze, whose pict- let de Dèze. uresque site, far up in the Cévennes, on a peninsula bounded on three sides by the Gardon, here for a while a sluggish stream, delights the eye of the traveller who leaves the beaten roads to thread the more secluded paths of the mountains. In fact this venerable but unpretending, edifice has

---

ing his course, was deposed from the sacred office by a provincial synod meeting at Sommières. Calvin briefly gives his conception of the proper functions of a minister of the gospel when he expresses great astonishment, "qu'il y ait en une telle témérité en *celuy qui devoit modérer les aultres et les tenir en bride.*" For the attitude of the Reformed churches on this subject, see The Rise of the Huguenots, i. 487 ; ii. 43.

come down to our own times, and is said to be the only structure of its kind in the whole region that spans two eventful
centuries in the fortunes of Protestantism—the first, a century
of persecution during which the voice of the preacher of God's
word was not heard within it save perhaps on one single occasion; the second, an age of toleration gradually expanding into
complete religious liberty, when its walls have again resounded
with the tones of divine worship and praise.[1]

The Huguenot edifice had thus far been spared only because
the Marquise de Portes, a person of position and influence in
the region, had intimated her purpose to convert it into a hospital.[2] The Cévenols longed once more to have the privilege
of worshipping in a place hallowed by many memories of more
prosperous days. Unfortunately, Le Collet de Dèze was one
of the five important points where Broglie and Basville had, as
we have seen,[3] thought fit to post a company of fusileers. However, Huguenot ingenuity proved equal to the emergency. The
meeting was duly appointed for the evening of the eighth of
September. That very day the captain of the troops, Monsieur
de Cabrières, received a letter giving him the information that the Protestants intended to assemble in the
evening for worship in the territory which he had been appointed
to guard, but designating a distant spot as the place of meeting. The ruse effected its purpose. At the very hour Cabrières
and his men were awaiting elsewhere the advent of worshippers
who never came, the Cévenol Protestants were pouring unmolested into their "temple." Their service continued several
hours. It was not until after midnight that the congregation
retired well satisfied with the rare opportunity they had enjoyed.[4] Not so with curate Louvreleuil, at Saint Germain de
Calberte, who, having but lately come back to his parish with

A successful ruse.

---

[1] My authority is Paul Joanne, Les Cévennes (Paris, 1888), who states (p. 192):
"Le Collet possède le seul temple protestant qui n'ait pas été détruit dans les
Cévennes lors de la révocation de l'Édit de Nantes."

[2] "Il fut au Colet de Dèze avec son monde, où il prêcha et fanatisa dans le
temple; c'est le seul qu'on eût conservé pour en faire un hôpital." De la
Baume, Relation historique, 54.

[3] Supra, page 240.

[4] Louvreleuil, i. 66 ; Brueys, i. 356.

the assurance that he would be safe in resuming his pastoral functions, was awakened from sleep with the unwelcome intelligence that the Huguenots had gathered a few hours before at a place scarcely two leagues distant.

It was not too late for pursuit, and the good Roman Catholics of Saint Germain, with the aid of an officer, the same Poul that had taken Esprit Séguier at Font Morte, and some soldiers that happened to reach the village upon another errand, were so expeditious as to overtake some of the departing Protestants near a spot known as Champ Domergues. The Protestants, with Laporte at their head, posted themselves upon a slight eminence. They used the brief respite, while their enemies prepared to dislodge them, in singing a few lines of one of their favorite psalms. Then, not waiting to be attacked, they themselves ran down and fell upon the Roman Catholics. The numbers were unequal : the little band of sixty Huguenots was greatly outnumbered, for there were three of the enemy to every man in their own ranks. Yet they did not shun a conflict which they might have avoided with the same ease as that with which they subsequently retired. Against combatants consisting in part of trained troops and led by an officer of experience, the raw recruits fighting by the side of Laporte, himself a novice in the art of war, acquitted themselves without discredit to their valor. Curate Louvreleuil claims for his parishioners and their associates no superiority, save that, whereas the heretics generally missed their aim, the Roman Catholics killed or wounded a man for every shot they fired. And the partisan Brueys, though rarely having a word of praise for his antagonists, admits that Laporte stood the first charge of the enemy with great steadiness; being careful to add, "so true is it that folly gives men prowess." In the end, the Huguenots, who had somewhat recklessly exposed themselves, while their opponents prudently obeyed their leader's direction by crouching on the ground or by protecting their bodies behind trees, withdrew to the heights, whither Captain Poul did not think it advisable to follow them.[1]

It was the first engagement worthy of the name. What loss

Conflict at Champ Domergues.

---

[1] Louvreleuil, i. 68, 69; Brueys, i. 357–360; Court, i. 74–76.

the insurgents experienced is uncertain ;[1] but confessedly the affair had no effect in making them less eager to continue the strife. On the contrary, immediately after its occurrence Laporte's band broke up into three portions, each of which took a different path and inflicted no small damage upon the district traversed. Roman Catholic churches were burned, manses and other ecclesiastical property were not spared, and ill fared such of the curates as fell in their way. There were a thousand grievances treasured up in the memory of the sufferers, however completely they had faded from the remembrance of the priestly authors. The curate of Saint Germain de Calberte tells us that he discovered a plot to compass his death and the death of his vicar, of which one of the principal causes was that he and his vicar required of the New Converts intending to marry, an unreasonable term of probation, in order to test the sincerity of their profession of Roman Catholicism.[2] As the law permitted no one but a clergyman of the established church to perform the nuptial ceremony, the tyranny which the parish priest had it in his power to exercise was peculiarly vexatious.

It must be confessed that the position of such of the priests as had not fled to a place of refuge, or, having fled, had returned to their fields of labor, upon an assurance of adequate protection, was not altogether enviable. They knew not upon whom to rely. The very sentinels sympathized with the enemy. The curate of Saint Germain mournfully informs us that the two men that were placed on guard by

Protestant sentinels on guard.

---

[1] The bad faith of Brueys seems clear. Louvreleuil speaks of some fifteen Protestants as killed or wounded ; Brueys, though for the most part copying Louvreleuil slavishly, doubles the Protestant loss. The curate of Saint Germain is honest enough to admit that Laporte and his men took the initiative in the combat ; Brueys reluctantly gives them courage enough, when they thought the enemy was alarmed at seeing them, to stand their ground and receive the attack. It does not add to our confidence in Brueys, as an accurate historian, to find that, after despatching the " prophet " Salomon (Couderc) in this fight, he is forced to bring him to life in order to kill him once more in 1706 ; this time by the executioner's hand. Histoire du fanatisme (edition of Utrecht, 1737), iii. 505–517. Court. i. 76, using the older edition of 1709–1713, discovers an intermediate resurrection, or, at least, an intermediate death, which has, it would seem, been judiciously eliminated from the impression before me.

[2] Louvreleuil, i. 79.

night, the one in front of his house and the other behind it, did not hesitate to steal away about ten o'clock, or so soon as they believed him to be asleep; while those that stood on guard at the entrance of the borough behaved even worse. They relieved the tedium of their ungrateful occupation by singing the Huguenot psalms, so as to intimate distinctly enough to any of the malcontents who might come that way that they were their brethren and would offer no resistance.[1]

And now it became necessary to find, or to invent, some suitable designation for the Huguenots that had taken up arms, in contradistinction from their brethren who remained at home. The insurgents, it is true, needed to coin no new word for their own use. They styled themselves simply, *Les Enfants de Dieu*—"The Children of God"—and their quarters, wherever these might be, *Le Camp de l'Éternel* —"The Lord's Camp." Nor are the Roman Catholic historians, who give us the earliest connected account of the exploits of the insurgents, ever at a loss for terms by which to characterize them. "Fanatics," "Rebels," "Madmen," and "Scoundrels" are some of the milder names of their copious vocabulary.[2] The common people, desiring some more specific nickname, soon began to call them *Houssards*—"Hussars"—because of their dash and daring, or because of the terror which their appearance inspired; or *Barbets*, an appellation long since given to the neighboring Waldenses of the Valley of the Durance, as well as to the more distant Waldenses of the Alps, with whom they were supposed to have some connection.[3] Before the close of the year

Designations of the insurgents.

---

[1] "Celles qu'on mettoit aux avenues du Bourg chantoient de tems en tems des Pseaumes rimés pour faire entendre aux Fanatiques, s'ils s'approchoient, qu'ils étoient leurs Confrères, hors d'état de s'opposer à eux." Louvreleuil, i. 78.

[2] *Canaille, bandits, maudite troupe, brigands, impies, misérables, malfaiteurs d'habitude, hommes de sang, pendards,* and the like, figure among the playful variations employed. See Louvreleuil and Brueys, passim.

[3] Court, i. 77.—"They gave us," say the Memoirs of Cavalier, "the name of Barbets, intending thereby to father that nickname upon us, as they had since the Reformation on the Vaudois. For the word *barbe* doth originally, and in the language of Piedmont, signify 'uncle.' It was by way of respect chiefly given to their pastors; but the Italians, to shew their hatred and contempt of them, formed out of this word 'barbe,' the name of *barbet,* and gave it to an ugly and shaggy kind of dogs. They named the Vaudois *Barbets,* as being the barbes' disciples, and, in process of time, the Papists of other countries have called all

1702,[1] however, the new designation of *Camisards* was fixed
upon, which ultimately drove out the preceding names. Re-
The Cami- specting the origin of the word the utmost uncertainty
sards. prevails ; neither those who applied it to their enemies,
nor those to whom it was applied, being able to throw much
light upon the matter. Those singular explanations which
would lead us back to a Greek or Hebrew origin may well be
consigned to oblivion, or, at least, reserved for the special de-
lectation of those who value an etymology only the more because
it is unnatural or impossible. It is more than likely that the
word has a close connection with the word *camisade*, applied, as
is well known, to the nocturnal expeditions in which the participants were wont to wear a shirt—*camise*—over their armor, in
order to be easily recognized in the darkness by their comrades,
and which took place at such hours that the enemy, being surprised, would issue but half clad to repulse an attack. A more
interesting, but less trustworthy, interpretation traces the word
Camisard to the same article of apparel, it is true, but makes it
originally an allusion to an incident said to have been of frequent occurrence at a later time in the war, when the insurgents,
begrimed and weather-stained from long exposure, did not
scruple, upon entering some town or village, to appropriate to
their own use such new or freshly washed linen as they laid
hands upon, leaving their own soiled and tattered garments in
exchange. The word Camisard, according to this explanation,
would simply resolve itself into an equivalent for the plainer
designation of " voleur de chemise." [2]

Reformed, of what nation soever, Barbets." The author appears to be in doubt
whether or not the name was applied originally to the Camisards in consequence
of a rumor that in a certain fight there were seen in their ranks foreigners,
" soldiers with long whiskers that seemed very frightful."

[1] Court finds the name Camisard in a manuscript journal as early as in December, 1702, and in the public prints of January 6, 1703, or fully two months earlier
than the date assigned for its first appearance in the Memoirs of Cavalier (page
157). Louvreleuil speaks for the first time of " les Rebelles, appellez vulgairement Camizards," in connection with an event that occurred January 12, 1703.
Le fanatisme renouvelé, i. 109.

[2] Court, i. 149. The Memoirs of Cavalier quaintly remark (page 158) that of
the inhabitants of Ganges who suffered from the Camisard exchange " some
were sorry and some were glad ; but there were amongst them some jocose men

As winter approached, the uprising became more general and assumed startling proportions. The golden days of Prot-
Spread of the revolt. estantism seemed to be about to return. Nothing was heard of, says Louvreleuil, save strange and unparalleled enterprises. The religious meetings multiplied everywhere. At these men renewed their profession of the pretended Reformation. Little children were brought to be baptized. Betrothed persons were married. The Lord's Supper was celebrated. Men were forbidden to go to mass, to mount guard, to pay tithes to the priests. The farmers of church livings were ordered to pay over to the leaders of the insurgents all they owed for the past, in order to provide for the support of their soldiers. Now the crosses erected along the public roads were thrown down. Anon threatening letters were despatched to those who refused to take the side of the revolt. Presently convoys were carried off, or men were sent to search country houses in quest of arms, or contributions were levied upon sequestered hamlets. Churches and priests' houses furnished fresh fuel for the all-devouring flames. From the open country the families of those who sided with the government fled to Alais, to Mende, to Florac, to any place, in short, which offered some hope of safety. In their consternation at the gathering storm the States of Languedoc, then in session, authorized an additional force to be set on foot consisting of thirty-two companies of foot and four companies of dragoons.[1]

In such a warfare as that in which the Camisards were enengaged there was abundant room for the employment of spies and traitors, and Laporte fell into the toils. Sur-
Surprise and death of Laporte. prised by the indefatigable Captain Poul, at Montlezon (on the twenty-second of October), he lost his life after a brave resistance. Eight of his companions shared the same fate. The heads of the slain Camisards were cut off and sent in baskets to M. de Basville, at Montpellier, for the double purpose of delighting the intendant, and of serving as trophies to attest Poul's success, which his enemies at-

---

who, hearing their neighbors curse and swear, told them they were happy we had not taken away their skins instead of their shirts."

[1] Louvreleuil, i. 83–85.

tempted to discredit. It is even asserted by a Protestant writer that, to make the greater impression, Poul did not hesitate to decapitate the corpses of three of his own followers who had fallen in the engagement. Their heads went to swell to a round dozen the number of heads exposed to the public execration on the bridge of Anduze and at Saint Hippolyte.[1]

Meantime, the number of distinct bands of insurgents had been increased, shortly before Laporte's death, by a fourth company, gathered by a leader destined to make himself more famous than any of his predecessors or associates.

Jean Cavalier. Jean Cavalier was a mere boy of twenty years of age.[2] He looked even younger. His origin could scarcely have been more humble, his personal appearance more insignificant. He was slight and short of stature, of a ruddy complexion, with bright blue eyes and flowing hair. One would have been slow to pick this stripling out of a crowd to be a commander of men. Yet a closer inspection was sure to show that the first view had done him injustice; for he had a robust and agile form and his glance was quick, intelligent, and keen. When it came to military action he was prompt in detecting the purpose of his opponent, not less prompt in discovering the weak point of the enemy's position, while his brain was fertile in devices for thwarting all hostile movements. He seemed born for daring adventure.[3]

Cavalier's first occupation when a boy had been that of a *pitot*, or shepherd's attendant. Later he was apprenticed to a

---

[1] Louvreleuil, i. 86, 87; Court, i. 88.

[2] He was born November 28, 1681, and baptized in the Protestant church of Cardet, Sunday, December 7th following, as the baptismal record still extant sets forth. Haag, La France protestante, 2me édition, iii. 926.

[3] Brueys gives a portrait which is evidently as flattering as the writer believed himself permitted to draw of a heretic and a leader of rebels. Cavalier was short of stature, robust, indefatigable, daring, and tolerably well proportioned *in comparison with the other chiefs, who were all ill-looking*. Fanaticism, which led him to encounter fearlessly the greatest perils, stood him instead of valor ; and, because his intellect was *a little less affected* by prophetic revelations than the intellects of the rest, he passed among them for a sensible and judicious man. He spoke and wrote *a little less coarsely* than his associates, and acted *with a little more discretion* in all his undertakings. This gave him great reputation, etc. Histoire du fanatisme, ii. 61, 62.

baker in the town of Anduze.[1] Born of Protestant parents, four
years before the Revocation of the Edict of Nantes, he had
His previ-   been baptized by a pastor of the Reformed Church,
ous history. and was studiously, but secretly instructed in the
doctrines of the Reformation. His mother resolutely clung to
her ancestral faith, even when her husband, a weaker character,
conformed to the established church, and insisted on sending
his children to the schools which had been instituted for the
purpose of acquainting the children of Protestants with the
tenets of the Roman Catholic Church. So far as mere knowledge went, this object was fully attained. The lad and his
brothers became thoroughly acquainted with the catechism, and
could answer every question to the satisfaction of their priestly
instructors, who deemed them promising members of their flock.
So exemplary a pupil, indeed, did Cavalier appear that when,
at the age of about thirteen, he was confirmed and admitted to
his first communion, the Bishop of Alais, delighted with the
good accounts that were given of him, called him aside and
held before him the prospect of being sent shortly to study the
languages in one of the houses of the Jesuits. If Cavalier's
mother had previously been careful to counteract the religious
teachings to which her son was subjected, by leading him to
read the Holy Scriptures and such books of devotion and controversy as she had succeeded in concealing from the domicil-
iary visits of the clergy, she now redoubled her efforts. It was
about this period of his life that, for the first time, Cavalier
had the opportunity of attending one of the proscribed assemblies of the Desert, and of hearing a minister—it was the celebrated Claude Brousson—whose words made an indelible impression upon him. A few years later, Jean Cavalier was
forced to escape from the kingdom, to avoid the dangers that
began to thicken about him.[2] Under the care of a guide ex-

---

[1] The certificate has been found which Duplans, the master-baker, gave to
Antoine Cavalier, expressing satisfaction with the boy's conduct as an apprentice. It is dated at Anduze, April 11, 1701. J. P. Hugues, Histoire de l'Église
d'Anduze, 722.

[2] The particular occasion of his flight would seem to have been the circumstance that the curé of Arvieu instituted legal proceedings against him, both on
civil and on criminal charges at the same time. The grounds of both suits were

perienced in such matters, a company of a dozen young men who desired to leave a land of persecution, successfully made their way from the Cévennes to Geneva. It was a hazardous undertaking and required eight days for its accomplishment; but the guide knew how to personate a recruiting officer of the king, and his followers passed easily for a body of fresh soldiers destined to replenish the depleted ranks of the royal army. Not many months elapsed before news from home recalled Cavalier to France. His parents had been arrested and thrown into prison because of their son's flight. Cavalier returned to Ribaute, only, however, to find that, meantime, his parents had been released upon their making a promise to attend mass and conform to the established church. By his earnest remonstrances he succeeded in inspiring them with a more courageous spirit. It had been the young man's first intention, after securing this object, to return once more to the shores of Lake Leman. The exciting events that now occurred gave a new turn to his life. The "Memoirs" that go under his name claim for him the honor of having been one of the ardent company whom the prophet Esprit Séguier addressed and exhorted, not without effect, to make the perilous attempt to rescue from cruel imprisonment the unfortunate victims of the malice of the Abbé du Chayla; while admitting that because of his youth and of his want of familiarity with the neighborhood of Pont de Montvert, Cavalier was not allowed to be one of the party of rescue.[1] Antoine Court, on the contrary, denies the statements, and maintains, upon the testimony of all the insurgents of the time with whom he had conversed, including such as had been present upon the particular occasion referred to, that Cavalier was not there.[2] Be this as it may, there is no doubt that, shortly after, Jean Cavalier set on foot an

---

religious. De La Baume, Relation historique, 62. Haag, La France protestante, iii. 926. The corrections and additions to this excellent article are by the late Charles Sagnier, a careful and indefatigable investigator of the history of this region.

[1] Memoirs of the Wars of the Cévennes, 35.

[2] Histoire des troubles des Cévennes, i. 85: "Ce qui est contredit non seulement par ceux que j'ai vus qui assistèrent à cette assemblée, mais par tous les mécontens d'alors, auprès de qui j'ai pu m'en informer."

enterprise of his own, in the lower district, adjoining his birthplace, and that in its execution neither his youth nor his
He gathers   inexperience in military affairs proved any impedi-
a band.   ment.   He gathered by night eighteen or twenty young
men (not one of them over twenty-four years old, in a barn between Anduze and Alais, and urged them to emulate, in behalf
of their own kindred languishing in confinement, the example
set them by the resolute Protestants of the Higher Cévennes.
"We are indeed cowards," he exclaimed, "if we do not join
with them in endeavoring to deliver our relations and friends
out of prison, and to free ourselves from the persecution we are
groaning under.   Our religion ought to be dearer to us than
our lives."[1]   The immediate object sought was to create a diversion of Broglie's troops ; the first obstacle to be overcome
was the entire want of arms.   This difficulty was removed by
address and without bloodshed.   The house of the priest of
Saint Martin contained an abundant supply of the guns and
swords, which, when the Protestants of his parish had been
disarmed by the king's command, he could not avoid receiving
and storing in his manse.   The ecclesiastic, in truth, had nothing of the persecutor in his nature, and was a man of a jovial
disposition, more addicted to making merry with his parishioners than of annoying those of them who happened to differ
from him in their religious sentiments.   When, then, a band of
men, partly disguised and speaking a loud and unintelligible
jargon, to give the impression that they were foreigners from
England, Holland, or Germany, made their appearance at his
door, and, having gained admittance, politely asked him for the
articles of which they were in need, assuring him that he should
receive no injury at their hands, the good-natured priest not
only complied with their request but treated them, as they
themselves admitted, with signal courtesy.   It fared very differently with one Jourdan, once a Protestant, but turned papist
and persecutor, who years before had killed the preacher Vivens,
as narrated in a previous chapter.   When discovered in his
house at Bagart, which Cavalier's troop next ransacked, and
asked respecting this and other murders laid to his charge,

---

[1] Memoirs of Cavalier, 56.

Jourdan replied : "I did it by the king's order, and am very sorry for it." "And we too are very sorry," said his unwelcome visitors, "to see ourselves obliged to put you to death, but thereby our enemies will see that we can make use of reprisals."[1]

About the same time with Cavalier, two other chiefs gathered new bands whose exploits in the Higher Cévennes soon made them formidable to their opponents—Joany and Couderc, the lat-

Other leaders—Joany and Couderc.

ter one of the many unfortunates who had experienced the cruelty of the Abbé du Chayla and never forgot the ingenious instrument of torture in whose jaws they had been held. Couderc seemed to thirst only for vengeance upon the oppressors of his fellow-Protestants. His resentment was said, probably with truth, to amount to sheer ferocity. Woe to the priest that fell into his hands ! Deaf to all appeals addressed to his feelings of clemency, neither prayers nor intercessions availed to move him from his purpose.[2]

Far from shunning danger, Cavalier seemed determined to fly into the very jaws of death. He directed his course toward Nismes, and at Aigues Vives, less than twelve miles from Bishop Fléchier's episcopal palace, held an assembly for divine worship upon the ruins of the old church of the Protestants. Here,

A conventicle on the ruins of a "temple."

uniting the functions of preacher to those of secular leader, he addressed a fervid discourse to the great crowd of Huguenots that streamed to the spot from all the neighboring villages of the Vaunage. He was greeted with loud acclamations by those who thought they recognized in this stripling the chosen deliverer of the children of God, the new Gideon before whom the hosts of the uncircumcised were fated to melt away and flee in wild confusion.[3]

---

[1] Memoirs of Cavalier, 57–60.

[2] Court, i. 91.—Couderc was imprisoned a month before the affair of Pont de Montvert, being reserved until Basville's pleasure respecting him should be learned. Meantime his mother succeeded in supplying him with a saw, which he dexterously employed in sundering the formidable gyves that held him. He was fortunate enough to make good his escape. Louvreleuil, i. 92. Brueys (ii. 14, 15) describes him as the most cruel man the Cévennes Mountains ever produced. He was a little man, he tells us, about thirty years of age, whose physiognomy corresponded perfectly well with the wicked actions he committed during his life. His birthplace was the hamlet of Mazel Rolade, near Saint Germain de Calberte. He assumed the name of *Lafleur.*

[3] Court, i. 93.

If the first flavor of the forbidden fruit of religious worship according to their ancestral rites was sweet to the Protestants of Vaunage, who had been so long famishing for it, the aftertaste was certainly bitter enough. Basville had just been invested, by an order of the royal council at Versailles, with almost absolute power of life and death. The document conferred upon him authority to take " cognizance of all crimes connected with the uprising, with power to establish such judges as he might deem proper, to try the cases of the accused and to judge them in last resort." [1] The intendant used his new commission to wreak signal vengeance upon the unhappy village in which Cavalier had preached. He assembled all the inhabitants of Aigues Vives within the parish church, and there selecting sixteen of their number to bear the penalty of all, he gave, with the assistance of the presidial judge, a verdict based rather upon suspicion or caprice than upon certain knowledge. Four persons were sentenced to be hung. An almond-tree hard by the door of the church served as the gallows. A dozen were sent to row as galley-slaves; the consul of the village was of the number. Others were publicly flogged by the hangman, a few houses were razed to the ground, and a fine of one thousand livres was imposed upon the place.[2]

The vengeance wreaked upon Aigues Vives.

Nothing could have happened more opportune for the insurgents than this act of severity in which the innocent were evidently confounded with the guilty. Cavalier's ranks were rapidly filled with new recruits, fleeing not because of what they had done or were preparing to do, but in consequence of the misdeeds falsely ascribed to them by some enemy acting as a secret informer. Before long the young captain had followers enough to march hither and thither, to the beat of the drum, disarming the Roman Catholics, and observing the forms of open warfare. Four men joined him of greater experience than he had himself—Espérandieu, Rastalet, Ravanel, and Catinat—but when, at the urgent recommendation of the first of these, it was resolved that the time had arrived for the formal election of a leader, by a plurality of votes the choice of the Camisards fell

---

[1] La Baume, Relation historique, 61.
[2] Louvreleuil, i. 100 ; Court, i. 94 ; Brueys, ii. 22 ; La Baume, 62.

not upon any one of them but upon Cavalier; so strong a hold had the beardless boy taken upon the confidence and affection Election of of those who had associated themselves with him. Cavalier. And Cavalier, though displaying some reluctance to assume the responsibility of command, in the end accepted it. He stipulated, however, that he should be obeyed implicitly and should enjoy the right to put any of his band to death without waiting to call a council of war. The "Memoirs" that pass under his name assert that he never exercised the right, and that he made it his constant rule to conclude no important affair without first obtaining the advice of six of his chief officers.[1]

The events of the next few weeks amply justified the choice of a leader. Everywhere fortune smiled on Cavalier's undertakings. Captains Bimar and Montarnaud, with three companies of burgess militia, hearing that the Camisards were in the wood of Vacquières, between Alais and Uzès, had the temerity His success. to go and attack them, but paid the forfeit with their lives. The insurgents had posted themselves advantageously about a narrow ravine. Ravanel awaited them at the farther end. Scarcely had the unfortunate gentlemen approached him when they beheld Cavalier and his followers running down upon them from the copse on either side. The soldiers finding themselves enveloped on all hands were thrown into disastrous confusion and fled, pursued for a full league by the insurgents whom they had come to seek. Two-thirds of the soldiers are said to have perished in the woods, while Cavalier's loss was only four men. In the old Huguenot fashion he gathered his band upon the field and rendered thanks to the God of battles, through whose favor the victory had been won and a considerable store of arms, clothing, and money, much needed at this juncture, had fallen into his hands. Another captain with a company of militia fared no better at Cendras. Bonnefoux, who commanded a body of fusileers quartered in Calvisson, and who came out hoping to overwhelm a religious meeting which Cavalier was holding in the neighborhood of the

---

[1] Memoirs of the Wars of the Cévennes under Colonel Cavalier, 78, 79. It will be noticed that I conform to the ordinary spelling of the name; although the chieftain himself always wrote it *Cavallier*.

village of Saint Cosme, was only more fortunate in that by precipitate flight and on foot he gained the friendly shelter of the
castle of Caveirac and saved his life. The uniforms that fell
into Cavalier's hands, either stripped from the corpses of the
slain or taken from the prisoners, stood him in good stead, as
they enabled him to execute more than one daring enterprise.

The castle of Servas, situated east of Alais, interfered greatly
with the Camisards' movements, and the soldiers of its garrison
had rendered themselves specially obnoxious by acts
of cruelty. Cavalier resolved to take the castle by a
ruse and to put its defenders to the sword. Dressing
thirty of his men in the royal uniform, he himself marched at their
head in the garb of an officer. He had taken the precaution
to bind six others of his band, whom he led ostensibly as prisoners. On reaching Les Plans, the nearest village to the castle,
he halted, and sending for the consul informed him that he was
the nephew of Count de Broglie, and that he had just met and
defeated the Protestant insurgents, of whom he had taken a
half a dozen men alive. The hour was too late for him to pursue his journey, and the village too open to attack from the
neighboring rebels, irritated at their recent loss. He ordered
the consul, therefore, forthwith to precede him to the castle and
request the officer in command to allow him to place his prisoners for the night in the safe shelter of the dungeons of the keep.
There they would remain until he might find means to deliver
them into the hands of his uncle, who would immediately sentence them to be broken upon the wheel. So well did the Camisard play his part that both consul and officer were thoroughly
deceived. The former ran with alacrity to carry the message,
the latter was so delighted to do the king service that he came
in person to meet Cavalier, and not only received his prisoners
within the castle, but insisted that their captor should himself
take refreshments and a bed with him. Broglie's pretended
nephew, yielding to the officer's entreaties, left his soldiers
drawn up outside, not without strict orders to maintain exemplary discipline, and himself entered to partake of the proffered
hospitality. While supper was being made ready, his host courteously invited Cavalier to take a walk upon the walls and to
inspect the advantages of a fortress which he boasted was im-

The castle of Servas taken by a ruse.

pregnable. He called upon him to admire the depth of the fosse and the solidity of the walls. "You must know," said he, "that the Duke of Rohan laid siege to this castle, but after twelve days he was forced to raise it, and certainly I shall keep the *Barbets* out of it." A little later they sat down to take their evening meal. Meanwhile, upon one pretext or another, many of the disguised insurgents had slipped into the castle. As soon as he felt sure that a sufficient number of his supporters were at hand, Cavalier gave the signal that had been agreed upon; the insurgents fell upon the surprised garrison, upon the guards at the gate, upon the commanding officer himself. Resistance was vain. The soldiers were easily overborne and despatched. Not one seems to have escaped. The treacherous work was expeditiously and effectually performed. The castle itself was consigned to the flames, that it might not again be garrisoned by royal troops. Happily we are not called upon to vindicate the honor or the humanity of the Camisard leader who could butcher in cold blood those who had so kindly entertained him, even to the officer with whom he had eaten salt. History will be slow to accept as sufficient justification for so signal a breach of faith the plea that the massacre was in revenge for the many cruelties perpetrated by the garrison, and, in particular, for the murder of several Protestants of the neighborhood.[1]

Before the close of the year Cavalier and his band had the opportunity to prove that they were not inferior to their enemies in courage upon the field. Not without a touch of bravado, the young chieftain appointed a religious assembly to be held early on the morning of Sunday, the twenty-fourth of

Christmas festivities at Saint Christol interrupted.

December, at Saint Christol, not over two or three miles from the city of Alais. Indignant at the presumption of the Protestants who ventured to celebrate their Christmas festivities so close to a fortified place, the capital of the Cévennes, the commandant sallied out at the head of a band of fifty mounted officers, impatient to distinguish themselves and display the superiority of their valor

---

[1] The story is told at length in Cavalier's Memoirs, 85–88, and by Court, Histoire des troubles des Cévennes, i. 109–112.

over that of the rabble whom they were called upon to put down. He was followed by the garrison of Alais and some six hundred of the burgess militia. At the news of his approach Cavalier dismissed the religious meeting, but resolved to make a firm stand, taking advantage of an embankment that offered a sort of natural breastwork. The enemy made the attack, but its first discharge did little or no damage. The fire which the malcontents returned was well directed and deadly. Some of the riders were killed outright, others had their horses shot under them. In a word, the surprise and terror was so great in the ranks of the assailants that they turned and fled precipitately in the direction from which they had come. The fugitive officers threw the infantry into disorder, and despite the frantic efforts of their commander to stay them, the flight became a rout. Cavalier and his handful of men pursued the enemy until the latter gained the friendly shelter of a neighboring castle. It looked at one time as if they would enter the gates of Alais itself at the heels of the fugitives. As it was, the Camisards, less than fourscore all told, returned at their leisure to render thanks to God upon the scene of the engagement, and to possess themselves of the clothing, the weapons, and the ammunition which had opportunely fallen into their hands.[1]

Their recent successes emboldened the malcontents. They resolved to attempt the surprise of the little town of Sauve.

Camisard attempt foiled at Sauve by a woman's shrewdness.
For this purpose Roland and Cavalier united their forces. A ruse much like that employed so successfully at the castle of Servas was resorted to. Detaching fifty of their united forces, under command of two officers, they sent them in advance, with drums beating, to the gates of Sauve ; they themselves followed at a more leisurely pace. Questioned by the sentry as to who they were,

---

[1] La Baume, Relation historique, 77. According to Cavalier's Memoirs, the Protestants found a mule-load of rope which the governor of Alais had sent for use in binding and hanging the rebels, but wisely refrained from meddling with it. "However," the writer adds, "we stayed an hour in the field of battle, to render our hearty thanks to Almighty God who had fought ours, and to carry two loads of ammunition and a good quantity of arms which the enemy had thrown from them to lighten their flight." Memoirs of the Wars of the Cévennes, 75-78. See also Court, i. 112-114.

and what was their errand, the two officers boldly asserted that they were in the king's service, and that with a company of burgess militia they were in quest of the enemy. Admitted to the town, the false captains made bold to ask to see M. de Vibrac, who was lord of the place, and the latter not only gave them audience but requested them to sit down with M. de Sauve, his son, and with his daughter-in-law, and partake of the meal about to be served. Thus far the deception had been perfect: the very boldness of the Camisards' approach disarmed suspicion, and the white ribbons which the mountaineers had taken care to pin upon their hats gave them the appearance of country recruits of the king's forces. There was one thing, however, which the Camisards had forgotten: it was impossible for rustics to counterfeit the manners and conversation of officers in his Majesty's service sprung from the ranks of the nobility. A woman's keen intuition first penetrated the disguise, and her quick tact found the best way of escape from an unpleasant predicament. Controlling the fear into which she was thrown by discovering who her dangerous guests were, Madame de Sauve waited till a loud wrangle in the castle-yard arose between the pretended soldiers and the servants, or, as others say, till a larger force of men, in reality the main body of the Camisards, was seen approaching the walls of the place. Then appealing to the gallantry of her guests, she begged them to exert themselves in her behalf. No sooner, however, had they descended the great stairs as if to fulfil her request than, with her own hand, she closed the great iron door and rendered impossible the return of the unwelcome visitors. Meanwhile the latter, hastening with their followers, as though to meet the enemy, opened the gates to the band without the walls, and Sauve was for a time at their mercy. The terrified inhabitants, however, who expected nothing less than to be put to the edge of the sword, suffered little injury. The Camisards had no designs save upon their arms and their provisions, and any articles of lead or pewter which could be melted up into musket-balls. Unhappily an affair that might otherwise have been bloodless was stained by the butchery of a Capuchin monk, shot in his attempt to escape, and of three ecclesiastics, accused, it is said, of wrongs done to Protestants. These last were more deliberately put to death, and probably with less excuse. The parish church was given over to the flames.[1]

Never had the malcontents been more active or enterprising than in the early months of the year 1703. The revolt assumed larger dimensions. No longer did the bands of Roland and Cavalier, of Joany and Castanet content themselves with skulking in the woods and mountains, in whose inaccessible passes they found a safe refuge and to which they retreated on approach of the enemy. They came boldly to measure their strength with the king's troops in the very neighborhood of the cities, and openly defied superior detachments of trained soldiers. The anxiety of the court to quell the insurrection displayed itself in the despatch of new and more experienced captains, among whom Julien and Parate were particularly noted, the former soon to obtain unenviable notoriety.

Increasing boldness of the insurgents.

Meanwhile Poul, hitherto the most successful of the officers of the king, upon whose skill great hopes had been founded, had lost his life in an engagement of more than ordinary importance five or six miles south of Nismes. The scene was a slight elevation, known in the dialect of Languedoc as *Lou cros de Val de Bane*.[2] The Camisard band that took part was that of Cavalier, temporarily under the command of his lieutenant, the fierce Ravanel. At the sight of the superior force of dragoons led out against them by General de Broglie himself, the Protestants did not quail. They knelt upon the ground and setting up one of their familiar psalms, while holding their weapons

---

[1] The accounts of Louvreleuil La Baume, and Brueys, on the one hand, and of Cavalier and Court, on the other, are irreconcilable at some points. According to the first three named, Roland himself was the officer whose rustic ways and speech betrayed to Madame de Sauve the imposition that had been practised upon her husband. Louvreleuil, i. 115, etc.; La Baume, 97, 98; Brueys, ii. 37–43. Cavalier, in his Memoirs, 80–82, and Court, i. 115-119, represent the two principal chiefs of the Camisards to have remained outside with the main body of the troops. Their united bands amounted to two hundred and thirty men. The anonymous Histoire des Camisards (London, 1754), i. 278, carries his justification of the Cévenol warriors to an absurd extreme, when he denies that a single drop of blood was shed at Sauve. Antoine Court, pre-eminently a fair historian, confirms the story of the murder of the priests, basing his statements on the testimony of eye-witnesses whom he met at Sauve and questioned.

[2] Aigaliers describes the place as upon the " Garrigue de Nismes."

ready for use, they waited until the enemy were near enough, and then discharged a murderous fire upon the vanguard, led by Poul. It was a mere lad from Milhaud that shot the royal champion with his gun; or, as some reported, like an-

Death of Poul.

other David, he smote Poul with a stone upon the temple, then ran up and having despatched him possessed himself both of his sword and of his horse. The terror that seized the troops was carried by fugitives to Nismes, and Cavalier, who happened at that very moment to be in the city in the disguise of a merchant, assumed to enable him to purchase the gunpowder of which his store had run low, has left us an amusing account of the consternation felt by the citizens for the safety of their homes.[1] In other combats the Camisards inflicted even more injury upon their opponents. They, too, had their share of disasters, and an attempt made by Cavalier to cross the Ardèche and penetrate into Vivarais, with the view of widening the theatre of war, proved abortive and ended in two engagements at Vagnas, on successive days (the tenth and eleventh of February), in which, though at first successful, the Camisard leader lost not only a good number of his brave men, but a trusty friend and officer, Espérandieu, whom he could ill spare.[2] Less than a month later (on the seventh of March, 1703) the united bands of Roland and Cavalier, the latter commanded during Cavalier's illness by his lieutenants Catinat and Ravanel, were skilfully surrounded by Parate at Pompignan, near Saint Hippolyte, and were dispersed with a loss of two

---

[1] Cavalier, 95–99 ; Brueys. ii. 35–37 ; Louvreleuil, i. 110–113 ; La Baume, 79–81 ; Court, i. 157–159; Rossel d'Aigaliers, 22, 23.

[2] Anyone who should undertake to reconcile the conflicting accounts of the numbers of slain and wounded in the different engagements of the Camisard war, would soon renounce the attempt in sheer despair. So far as a judgment is possible, La Baume and Louvreleuil are honest, though excessive, in their estimate of Camisard losses ; but Brueys's perverse exaggeration is so constant as almost to preclude a charitable interpretation. In the present instance, Cavalier (p. 146) admits a loss of fifty or sixty men in the two engagements. Louvreleuil (i. 123) and La Baume (p. 94) agree in making the number of Camisards slain in the second conflict alone amount to one hundred and fifty men. Brueys (ii. 69), not satisfied with killing over three hundred on the spot, will have it that almost as many more perished in their flight. See Court, i. 178, 179; Cavalier, 133–146.

hundred men.[1] Yet, for the most part, the Cévenol bands roamed, almost at will, over the territory that formed the scene of their exploits, and everywhere left in their track the marks of their hatred of the clergy and of those that took the clergy's part. In the two months of December and January it was reckoned that forty churches were given up to the flames.[2] It would be more difficult to compute the number of castles and smaller houses that were destroyed, and of human beings immolated on the altar of revenge. To have betrayed, or to be suspected of having betrayed the plans of the Camisards, to have maltreated the Protestants in any way, to have taken up arms to oppose the bands of malcontents—these were accounted ample justification for bloody reprisals.[3]

Unfortunate was the whole of a region, in which the inhabitants of Protestant villages, on the mere suspicion of complicity with the revolt, were imprisoned or transported, while the Roman Catholics, whose zeal for the triumph of the royal arms had led them to indulge too openly in demonstrations of hostility to the insurgents, became the mark at which were aimed the retaliatory measures of the Camisards. But most unfortunate were those parts whose population was mixed, and which, consequently, suffered at the hands of both parties. Vicissitudes of Genolhac. Such was the case with the canton of Genolhac, far up in the ravines on the eastern side of Mont Lozère, now pierced by the tunnels of the ever-encroaching railway, but, at the time of which I write, a region retired and difficult of access. Its vicissitudes, tossed, as it were, to and fro like a shuttlecock between the two parties, are not unworthy of record. The New Converts had shown how little they cared for the Roman Catholic Church, by holding a Protestant conventicle at which they sang the old psalms and joined in the prayers of Calvin's liturgy. In punishment for this offence, a company of burgess militia was quartered upon the Protestants. The distress of the poor villagers being reported to the Camisard leader Joany, he took advantage of the absence of Julien from the neighborhood, to make himself master of Genolhac and expel the unwelcome guests. Not long after, a

---

[1] Court, i. 227, 228.   [2] Ibid., i. 172.   [3] Ibid., ubi supra.

new body of royal troops having been introduced, Joany came a second time, and, meeting with armed resistance, this time not only dispossessed the enemy, but killed almost the whole number. His stay was not long. A royalist captain made his appearance, with a force of several hundred men, and speedily overpowered the Camisard band, which had the temerity to oppose him. The Protestant inhabitants, who had taken no part in the affair, became the victims of the vicissitudes of war. One hundred of them were butchered in their homes. Barely had four days passed when, for a third time, Joany returned to the wretched district, to wreak a sanguinary revenge upon the Roman Catholics, who were said to have joined with the soldiers in attacking and plundering the houses of their neighbors of the Reformed faith. If the atrocities which are ascribed to Joany and to his followers, and are recorded in full detail by Louvreleuil and La Baume, were actually committed—and I see no reason to doubt that their statements are essentially correct—Joany certainly deserves the reputation he gained of being the most pitiless of all those who took up arms against the royal troops in the Cévennes Mountains. The innocent perished at his hands with the guilty. Neither age nor sex was spared. Helpless infancy appealed in vain to the compassion of a leader and of followers whose hearts seemed to have been turned to stone. The terrors of death were rendered doubly frightful by the new and strange devices of cruelty by which the infliction was accompanied.[1]

The cup of the misfortunes of the luckless place was not even now full to the brim. Hearing of Joany's inroad a royal officer, M. de Marsilly, hastened to Genolhac, and, if we may credit the friendly assertions of the local chroniclers, with a far inferior force defeated and dispersed the Camisard band, driving the fugitives into the recesses of the Cévennes, whither he was powerless to pursue them. Into the particulars of the atrocities that ensued, these cautious writers are too prudent to enter with the minuteness of description which they regard as appropriate in the recital of the misdeeds of rebels. But when they agree that the Roman Catholic captain commanded his troops to lay violent

---

[1] See Louvreleuil, i. 114, 124–127, and La Baume, 104, 105.

hands upon the hundred wretched New Converts of either sex who had not succeeded in escaping with the rest, and abandoned the village to plunder, we can easily read beneath the laconic statement a story of blood not less revolting than that of which they have been at the pains to set forth the full horrors.[1]

The fact was, that in the murderous work of war the one party vied with the other in barbarity, each justifying itself by the plea of a just retaliation. And if the zest of the butchery was increased by the added spice of surprise, the perpetrators gained a grim satisfaction. Thus it was when Joany made his entry into the village of Le Pradel. Riding proudly at the head of seven hundred men, well mounted and dressed in a red military cloak, wearing a handsome wig, and with a hat profusely adorned with gold lace upon his head, Joany could easily be mistaken for a royal officer going in quest of the insurgents. No wonder that the villagers flocked to meet him, and officiously made proffer of their services to help him in discovering the retreats of the Protestant miscreants with whose plunder they were eager to enrich themselves. Great was their astonishment when their welcome was answered by a volley of musketry that laid twenty of their number in the dust, while the Camisards, turning about, rode away without the loss of a single man.[2]

Outside of France the Camisards endeavored to enlist the sympathy of the Protestant nations in their behalf. A paper printed about this time in Holland, in the guise of a manifesto of the insurgents, sought to justify their movement in the eyes of the world by a survey of the oppression to which the French Protestants had for long years been subjected. Its author boldly proclaimed the policy adopted by the Camisards. " Our resolution and intrepidity," he said, " have until now disconcerted our enemies. We shall not be appalled by their great number. We shall pursue them everywhere, but without harming those that do not wish us evil. Yet we shall make use of just reprisal against the persecutors, by virtue

Joany at Le Pradel.

A Camisard manifesto.

---

[1] Louvreleuil, i. 127–128 ; La Baume, 107. Compare Court, i. 182, who makes Julien the leader of the royal troops.

[2] La Baume, 162 ; Louvreleuil, i. 172 ; Court, i. 233, 234.

of the law of retaliation ordained by God's Word and practised by all the nations of the world. We shall never lay down our arms until we be able to make a public profession of our religion, procuring the revival of the edicts and declarations which authorized its free exercise." [1]

An amusing incident needs here to be mentioned. In order to account for the wonderful activity of the Camisards, their enemies busied themselves in the circulation of startling stories respecting the fierce zeal of men whom they charged with being possessed of an insatiable thirst for the blood of honest and inoffensive Roman Catholics. In attestation of this, they pointed to certain outlandish coins or medals that were said to have made their appearance in various provinces of the kingdom, containing covert exhortations addressed to the Huguenot youth to butcher the adherents of the other church. On the one side, these sufficiently commonplace bits of metal bore the representation of a prostrate dragon pierced by an arrow; upon the other, there were two crossed pikes. There were two short inscriptions—on the face, the capital letters C. R. S., on the reverse, J. O. V. R. S. M. To both was given a truculent interpretation. The former was held to stand for " *Christiani Romanos Sacrificate* "—" Christians, sacrifice the Romanists! " The latter was as conclusively read " *Juvenes Offerte Veræ Religioni Sacrificium Magnum*,"—" Young men, offer up a great sacrifice in honor of the true religion! " The medals were said to have been struck in the Netherlands, and, with their blood-curdling injunctions, were accepted and proclaimed as being a further proof of Camisard, or Protestant, malignity; although, as Louvreleuil naïvely states, this additional proof was not needed to acquaint the world with the nefarious designs which these impious men had formed, and which they tried to execute through numerous enterprises. [2] The curious

Pretended Camisard medals.

---

[1] Antoine Court has incorporated the text of a great part of this document in his Histoire des troubles des Cévennes, i. 208–220.

[2] Le fanatisme renouvelé, i. 193 ; La Baume, 96. Brueys, who never does anything by halves, is good enough not only to mention the appearance of such a coin or medal as he describes in several provinces of France, but to give us a plate purporting to represent it, and to assert that one of the coins was found on the persons of the greater part of the fanatics that were taken prisoners or killed (Histoire du fanatisme, ii. 122).

reader will be pleased to learn that the piece of metal which
was supposed to serve as a token by means of which the Camisards could recognize their friends,[1] and to which so sinister an
import was ascribed, was in reality nothing but an innocent prod-
uct of a Swedish mint. The three capitals of the one inscription stood simply for *Carolus, Rex Sueciæ*, "Charles, King of
Sweden," while the abbreviation of the other side indicated the
amount for which the coin passed current. The crossed pikes,
or rather darts, with the superimposed crown, were the arms of
the province of Dalecarlia, or Dalarne. The dragon pierced by
an arrow was none other than the symbolical lion of the Goths.[2]

There was, however, no need of medals, true or supposi-
tious, to attract the attention of Protestants outside of the king-

dom to the struggle going on in the South of France,
Foreign Protestants remonstrate at the policy of retaliation. and to elicit from them a hearty disclaimer of the violent course of some of the Camisard leaders. An un-
friendly hand has preserved for us the text of a protest,
couched in the form of a pastoral letter, which is said to have
been drawn up by a Protestant synod, held in a city beyond the
confines of the kingdom, and circulated far and wide among
those whose action it was intended to influence. The origin of
the protest is involved in doubt, and the purpose of the historian to whom we are indebted for its preservation is evidently to
prejudice the cause of the Camisards. None the less, however,
does the document bear considerable internal evidence of authenticity. It may be regarded as a fair expression of the sentiments of the great majority of unprejudiced men of the Reformed faith. If it unduly emphasizes the doctrine of passive
obedience, and if its criterion of duty accords better with the
theories in vogue two centuries ago than with the views preva-

---

[1] "Medaille(s) des fanatiques dans les Sevennes et qui leur servoient à se faire
reconnoître entr'eux." Heading of the plate in Brueys.

[2] I find in Elias Brenner, Thesaurus Nummorum Sveo-Gothicorum Vetustus
(Holmiæ, 1731), several coins, all belonging to the reign of Charles XI. (1675–
1697), which bear a general resemblance to the pretended Camisard medal. One
of these, on page 237, may have been the identical type. It is described as follows: "Clypeus coronatus, leonem ferens Gothicorum additis literis C. R. S. et
anno 1673. Insignia Dalarensia, cum valore 1 ör. S. M., *i.e.*, *Sölfwer-Mynt*."
The Sveriges Historia, by Oskar Montelius and others (Stockholm, 1881), also
gives, iv. 423, a very exact reproduction of a similar piece bearing the date 1669.

lent in our own liberty loving age, its tone is nevertheless frank, manly, and uncompromising.[1]

Meantime, it is not inappropriate at this stage of the Camisard revolt to take a view of the internal condition of the movement. Happily, in the attempt to reproduce the leading traits, we have the help of the accounts not only of those who were witnesses but also of some who took an active part.

The moral and religious condition of the Camisards is best understood in connection with the continued prevalence of the prophetic enthusiasm which, it has been seen, arose about the time of the Revocation of the Edict of Nantes, and as a direct consequence of the state of mingled expectation, grief, and remorse that followed the forcible suppression of all public worship and the almost universal destruction of the churches. Personal and family piety was still sustained and strengthened by the prayers and exhortations of men, and, occasionally, of women, claiming direct revelation from heaven and the inspiration of the Holy Ghost. However rude and uncouth their language, however fanciful their reported visions, however forced and inept their interpretations of the meaning of what they alleged that they had seen, the prophets of the Cévennes enjoyed a reputation for honesty of purpose, and exerted an influence upon the conduct of affairs that can scarcely be exaggerated. It is not an extravagant statement of Durand Fage in the *Théâtre sacré des Cévennes*, that every step taken either by the common band, or by the individual Cami-

Continuance of prophetic enthusiasm.

---

[1] The pastoral letter occupies a number of pages at the close of Louvreleuil's first volume, 203–218. It is addressed " Aux.fidèles des Sevenes." If, as I assume, the document is genuine, it would seem to have been written by a leading pastor in the name of his colleagues and by their authority. This is evidenced by the occasional interchange of the singular with the plural number, as where the composer says: "En verité, mes très chers frères, quand j'examine tout ce qui se passe parmi vous, il me semble que c'est l'accomplissement de la prophétie," etc. (page 217). Some expressions may be thought too full of denunciation to have been penned by a Protestant, but are quite in keeping with the declamatory pulpit oratory of the times; *e.g.*, " Que vous êtes éloignez de la conduite de Jesus-Christ, malheureux incendiaires, cruels meurtriers, hommes sanguinaires, femmes et filles aveuglées par le demon d'orgueil, et par la langue de malice ! Que vous sçavez mal de quel esprit vous devez être animez, vous qui portés contre les regles de la charité l'épée et le flambeau chez vos ennemis, et même chez des personnes qui ne vous ont fait aucun mal ! "

sard, was believed to be dictated by the Divine Spirit.[1] The af-
firmations of the most obscure believer, of the youngest child,
were received with implicit faith, their directions were

*The proph-
ets implicitly*
obeyed.

executed with unreflecting obedience.   Incidents so
strange as to be almost incredible, yet too well authen-
ticated to be rejected as fabulous, corroborated the general confidence in the reality of a direct and miraculous guidance.
Prophets made it their practice to go through the crowded assemblies of the Protestants, before the celebration of the Holy
Supper, and, on their own authority, to bid this or that person
to depart from the ranks of the faithful, alleging that his unworthiness to partake of the sacred emblems had been made
known to them by secret monitions from heaven.   In these
cases the selection of the person to be excluded may have been
guided to some extent by the previous knowledge of the
prophet, and the propriety of his action may not have been
susceptible of positive proof.   But in the discovery of intended
treachery, the same prophets, although not uniformly successful, made such happy guesses as to amaze both partisans and
opponents, and to close the mouth of such as might be disposed
to cavil.   More than once the eagle eye of a prophet lighted upon
a false brother, possibly with the price of his contemplated
crime in his pocket at the time, and singled him out in a crowd
where he seemed to be securely hidden.   What might have been
mere surmise at the first was speedily turned into certainty,
when the culprit, convicted by his own conscience, and persuaded of the futility of denial, came forward and acknowledged
his guilty secret.

A considerable number of the prophets were also preachers,
and undertook to guide the public devotions of the people.

Unlearned
preachers.

Among them all there was not one that had been regularly inducted into the sacred office.   In the absolute
dearth of religious guides trained by long study and set apart,
with solemn rites and with the approval of their colleagues, to
discharge their important functions, the churches, harried by

---

[1] "Tout ce que nous faisions, soit pour le général, soit pour notre conduite
particulière, c'étoit toujours par ordre de l'Esprit." Théâtre sacré des Cévennes
(Réimpression de A. Bost), 122.

persecution, not only robbed of their spiritual homes erected by their own exertions and at the expenditure of their own means, but disorganized and distracted, fell back, in their hour of helplessness and despair of usual remedies, upon the reserved rights of the Christian church, and especially upon the prerogative of self-preservation. The experiment was the last resort in a desperate case, and the event justified the venture.

The religious meetings conducted by such preachers may not have been characterized by a close observance of ecclesiastical usage, but they were full of a religious zeal that was undoubt-
Divine wor- edly sincere. Men and women do not expose them-
ship.   selves to extreme peril of life and property in order to participate in a worship for which they have no heart. For death or the loss of liberty and all things stared in the face every one that accepted the invitation, secretly conveyed to him, to be present at the conventicle to be held in the cavern, in the woods, or on the moor.[1] The surprise of such conventicles by a detachment of soldiers was a matter of common occurrence. The worshipper might at any moment be shot dead while engaged in prayer or in praise, with the words of the petition or the psalm still fresh upon his lips. If he escaped this danger, it might be that he was spared only to be condemned to serve in the galleys for life, or, if the worshipper was a woman, only to wear out an existence that was worse than death, immured in some convent of pitiless nuns or in the frightful prison of Aigues Mortes. It may therefore be assumed as beyond dispute, that the more formal meetings on the Lord's day, to which the armed bands of the Camisards took pains to invite, as often as possible, all the Protestants that were within reach, were not lacking in spirit or devotion. The preacher might be the captain of the band. Cavalier was the most distinguished preacher in the band which had elected him to be its chief; Roland, Salomon, Couderc, and Castanet officiated in the same capacity each in his own troop, while the names of Moïse, of Saint Paul, and of others were well known. The services were simple. Some chapters of the Holy Scriptures were read, a psalm or several

---

[1] "We had sometimes upwards of two thousand people in our congregations." Memoirs of Cavalier, 120.

psalms were sung, according as the distance from the posts of
the enemy made discovery more or less probable and dangerous,
The services. and the prayers of the Liturgy of Calvin, supplemented by special supplications dictated by the exigencies
of the times, were offered up to heaven.[1] There was, in addition
to this, a sermon, either the address of the preacher composed
with the view of meeting the special wants of the hour, or some
more orderly production, the discourse of a minister of the old
Reformed church laboriously committed to memory. Not infrequently the less regular utterances or trances of prophets interrupted the progress of the meeting, which, on important occasions, closed with the administration of the Lord's Supper.

We have it upon the faith of the memoirs of the most celebrated of the Camisard chiefs, that the daily life of his followers
Manners and morals. bore the practical impress of the religion which they
professed, and in the name of which they had taken up
arms. And certainly men who, in addition to their worship on
Sundays and on extraordinary occasions, were wont to observe
prayers three times on every week-day, might reasonably be
expected to evidence in some degree the sincerity of their purpose. " To the end that all things might be done in order and
with decency amongst us," says Cavalier, " we chose elders,
who for the most part had formerly served as such in our
churches. Our overseers took special care of the poor and sick,
and supplied them with all necessities. No quarrels, enmity,
calumny, or thievery was heard among us. All our goods were
in common. We had one heart and mind. All swearing, curs-
ing, and obscene words were quite banished out of our society.

---

[1] " We ordinarily made use of the French Common Prayer Book, and did also
form a prayer fitted to our present circumstances and occasions, which our ministers added to the others." Memoirs of Cavalier, 121. Elsewhere the same
work says : " As the number of our ministers increased, they ordered their affairs among themselves so that they officiated by turns. They constantly read
the Liturgy used since the Reformation in all the French churches, they
preached twice every Sunday and prayed in the evening. When we were
obliged upon a march to delay our duty, the first thing we did (tho' we arrived
ever so late in any place) was to go to prayers. We always sung psalms with
loud voices ; our ministers used to christen children, to administer four times
in the year the Holy Communion, and to marry those who had a mind to it."
Ibid., 119, 120.

Happy time! had it lasted for ever."[1] The impartial historian, Antoine Court, admirably situated as he was to judge of the truthfulness of this representation, declares his belief in its substantial accuracy; yet the writer whom I have just quoted, in his last sentence, himself implies that the strict discipline of the Camisards was evanescent. It is of the very nature of war to lead to demoralization. It fared with the admirable regulations of the Camisards much as with the excellent discipline initiated by Gaspard de Coligny at the beginning of the first civil war. The admiral had no great faith in the permanence of his own creation, and barely gave the goodness of his Huguenot soldiers a term of two months to change into malice.[2] It is probable that the golden age of Camisard warfare was not much more enduring.

In a warfare such as that in which the Cévenols were engaged, the two most difficult problems confronting the insurgents are apt to be, how to procure the necessaries of life, and how to secure the arms and ammunition indispensable to the continuance of the struggle. Both problems were satisfactorily solved under very adverse circumstances. It is true that the Camisards possessed the great advantage that they lived in a region whose population was for the greater part of the same religious belief as that which they professed, and almost openly favored their undertaking. So far as the peasantry of this part of Lower Languedoc could supply their necessities, there was little danger that the champions of Protestantism and of religious liberty would want. For the men and women that remained at home not only parted gladly

Provisions and ammunition.

---

[1] Memoirs of Cavalier, 121.

[2] "C'est voirement une belle chose moyennant qu'elle dure," said the great admiral to François de la Noue and to Charles de Téligny, his future son-in-law; "mais je crains que ces gens icy ne jettent toute leur bonté à la fois, et que d'icy à deux mois il ne leur sera demeuré que la malice." Mémoires de la Noue, chap. vi., p. 599. Coligny's quotation of the old proverb, "De jeune hermite, vieux diable," was not less apposite in one case than in the other. See Rise of the Huguenots, ii. 66, 67. On the corrupting tendencies of war, men otherwise most diverse come to a substantial accord. The curate Claude Haton thought much as did Coligny and La Noue: "C'est grand pitié que de la guerre : je croy que si les sainctz de Paradis y alloient, en peu de temps ilz deviendroient diables." Mémoires, ii. 843.

with a portion of the means of their daily subsistence which
they could ill spare, but exposed their lives with heroic fortitude
to the dangers entailed by detection in the act of lending help
to their brethren upon the mountains, or even by the suspicion
of having assisted them. It was with the Protestant peasants
as it was with the Camisards captured in battle, from whom
neither the rack nor the prospect of death on gibbet or wheel,
could wring a single word respecting the route taken by their
brethren or the place where their stores could be found.[1] Yet,
notwithstanding the assistance of the sympathizing peasants, the
difficulty of the situation was appalling in a district now overrun with soldiers under the command of experienced officers.
Even so, however, by the application of order and system, it is
said that an abundance of bread and of the other simple ali-
ments required by the sturdy mountaineer was rarely wanting.
The Camisard leaders providently laid up in the depth of the
forests, and in recesses and caves with which they
alone were familiar, such stores of provisions as they
were so fortunate as to obtain, either by the voluntary contributions of their fellow Protestants, or by their levies upon the
houses of the priests and of their other enemies. The discovery
of these secret accumulations by the royalists, at a subsequent
stage in the war, was the most deadly blow that the cause of the
insurgents received. Meanwhile a constant source of anxiety to
the leaders was the continual struggle to keep their followers
well shod and provided with the implements and necessaries of
war. Ingenuity was taxed to its utmost, in particular, to obtain a sufficient supply of gunpowder. In default of the usual
appliances, a part of the necessary quantity was slowly and
laboriously manufactured with no better help than the rude
mortar and pestle. Merchants were tempted by the offer of a
great profit to risk the dangerous attempt to import it into
Languedoc from the neighboring Comtat Venaissin. But, most
singular of all, the royal soldiers were themselves tampered with
and induced to sell to the enemy, whom they had been sent to
fight, the substance without which all their valor would have
been fruitless. There was less trouble in obtaining lead to

Secret stores.

---

[1] Brueys, i. 346.

mould into bullets. The Camisards did not scruple to employ for this purpose the covering of the roofs of the Roman Catholic churches. When this supply ran low, they employed in place of lead the metal of the pewter vessels that fell into their hands. The only objection to the substitution was that the wounds inflicted with balls made of pewter were more dangerous and were reputed incurable; a circumstance that gave rise to the common rumor that the Camisards resorted to the use of poisoned missiles.[1]

---

[1] I have drawn largely in the account given on the preceding pages upon the Memoirs of Cavalier, book ii., 115, etc., and especially upon Court, i. 131-148.

CHAPTER XVI

THE WAR OF THE CÉVENNES

THE unflinching courage with which the Camisards held out against the forces sent to crush them, at length drew the particular attention of the court of Versailles to an uprising originally viewed with contempt as certain to be quelled with little difficulty. A large force of regular troops were ordered to proceed to Lower Languedoc; and inasmuch as the recent losses, and especially the defeat of the Roman Catholics at Val de Bane, were currently ascribed to the incompetence of their leader, the Count de Broglie was removed from the command of military operations in this province. His place was supplied by an officer of higher rank whose services on other fields had just been rewarded with the baton of a marshal of France. Nicolas Auguste de la Baume, Marquis of Montrevel, was a man of narrow views and of scanty literary ability, whose extant letters exhibit none of the directness and vigor that so often characterize the productions of men more given to the use of the sword than of the pen. Handsome in person, and possessed of a dash that rendered him a favorite with the other sex, he carried into the society of women the same presumption that he exhibited as a soldier. Because of the signal successes that had attended his campaigns on the northern and eastern frontiers, and had attracted to him the notice and favor of his sovereign, he looked for a short and easy triumph over such insignificant foes as the rebels of the Cévennes, and soon revealed a purpose to make compensation for his temporary exile from the attractions of the court of Versailles by free indulgence in such pleasures as Languedoc could afford. It now became evident that the new marshal knew no other means of accomplishing the destruction of the Camisard party than the use of fire and sword, and that his

Removal of the Count de Broglie.

Appointment of Marshal Montrevel.

policy would differ from that of his predecessor in no other respect than the more rigid application of a pitiless system of repression.[1]

And here it is in place to inquire more particularly into the character of the measures adopted by the royal government for the suppression of the revolt. If a Joany and some of the other leaders of the insurgents, rude and uncultured men sprung from the people and smarting under the memory of recent injuries, waged a warfare so cruel as to elicit from the Protestants of other lands strong expressions of disapproval and earnest protests, how was the contest carried on by the agents of a king who prided himself on being the most enlightened and powerful monarch of Christendom, agents who were themselves officers of high rank, of respectable education, and of supposed intelligence? What, also, was the attitude of the clergy of the established church in whose interest the conflict was carried on?

That the Camisards, when taken in battle, should be remorselessly put to death, was little. The chances of war were equal, and it was quite as likely that the king's soldiers would fall into the hands of the Camisards as the reverse. But it was necessary to prevent the insurgents from finding a retreat and subsistence. To meet this end, Marshal Montrevel published severe ordinances. One of these emanated from the king and pronounced the penalty of death without form of legal process upon all persons taken with arms in their hands, and ordered the confiscation of their property and the destruction of their houses. It went further, and enjoined that the parents and relatives of the insurgents should give them no harbor or food under pain of being tried by such officers as the Intendant Basville might select, and of being

Severe ordinances of the government.

---

[1] Montrevel reached Nismes February 15, 1703, and was welcomed with equal joy by the Intendant Basville and the Bishop Fléchier. The three were in full accord respecting the necessity of suppressing the revolt by inexorable severity. See the letter of Fléchier of April 25, 1703, in which the prelate expresses his ardent prayer that God will bless the new marshal's arms, and, as will be seen further on, has only words of approval for the massacre which, soon after his arrival, affixed an indelible blot of barbarity upon the marshal's name. Œuvres complètes de Fléchier, x. 116–122. See, as to Montrevel's character, the excellent monograph of the late Charles Dardier, Le Maréchal de Montrevel, page 8; and Court, i. 187, 188.

condemned to the punishment incurred by rebels. The same fate was reserved for any persons, natives or strangers, who might be arrested within the province of Languedoc away from their homes, unprovided with certificates from the proper royal officers or with passports from his Majesty's ambassadors in foreign parts.[1] Another ordinance was from the hand of the marshal himself, and undertook to make the Protestant inhabitants of parishes collectively responsible for all acts of hostility to the established church committed within their bounds, by placing the priests, monks, laymen, and edifices of the Roman Catholics under their special protection. Should but a single "accident" of the kind referred to occur, should but a single soldier of the king be killed, on the very morrow the entire parish or village was to be consigned to fire and utter destruction.[2]

The savage decree of Marshal Montrevel met with scant favor even among those who were ready to approve almost any measure that promised to reduce the enemy's strength; nevertheless it was too mild a measure to satisfy fully the truculent spirit of the doughty general. He gravely proposed to go further and compel each town or village inhabited by Protestants to place in his hands hostages of the Reformed faith, with the understanding that for every Roman Catholic that might be killed there should be two of the other religion hanged. Happily not only the court to which he had written, but even the Intendant Basville, a man not often troubled by scruples of humanity, rejected this new proposal as too violent.[3] Meanwhile, the marshal made full use of the powers with which he was clothed, and proved that his ordinance of the twenty-fourth of February was no empty threat. The inhabitants of places suspected of furnishing the

Montrevel's extreme proposals.

---

[1] See the royal declaration of Versailles, February 23, 1703, in Brueys, ii. 107–110; and in Court, i. 194; summary in La Baume, 130.

[2] Text in Court, i. 196, 197; see Brueys, ii. 162. The document is dated at Quissac, February 24, 1703.

[3] Brueys, ii. 163; La Baume, 131, 132, makes the proposal even more sanguinary: three or four Camisards were to swing upon the gallows for every Roman Catholic that might be killed, and for every conflagration of a church or manse. According to him, it was the court of Versailles that refused consent.

rebels with provisions were commanded to bring all their grain
into the nearest of the neighboring towns and cities—some to
Alais, others to Anduze, others to Florac. When the village
of Mialet refused or neglected to obey the injunction, the inhabitants incurred a terrible fate.[1] M. de Julien, the

Julien's
treachery at
Mialet.

marshal's lieutenant, whom Montrevel despatched to
the unhappy place was an equal of his master in
cruelty, a superior in cunning. It is his own narrative that I
shall follow. Taking with him from Anduze, scarcely more
than a league distant, four hundred and fifty troops of the
regiment of Hainault, the wily officer quieted the fears of the
villagers whom his unexpected arrival had greatly disturbed, by
assuring them that he came neither to plunder nor to burn. He
merely intended to learn who of their number were disaffected,
and this he would easily ascertain when he had discovered who
had forsaken their homes. As to the absentees, unless they
returned by the next day, he would be compelled to burn their
houses. Meanwhile, the better to lull his hosts into security,
he issued strict orders that the soldiers, whom he distributed
in every dwelling, should observe exemplary discipline and demand only the bare necessaries of life. The plan was so completely successful that when, the next morning, the population
in mass was placed under arrest, Julien congratulated himself
that he was able to report to his superior that of the inhabitants of the whole parish, with its seven dependent hamlets,
whom he found at home upon his arrival, not ten had effected
their escape. It was a sorry procession of two hundred and
ten men, two hundred and eighty women, and over one hundred
and eighty children of fourteen years and under, whom their
grim escort brought into Anduze, victims of Julien's bad faith
and of their own credulity.[2] Their homes destroyed and their
entire property given over to plunder, they had but so much
left them as the garments they wore about their persons. Two
or three days later, many men, women, and children, were

---

[1] Louvreleuil, i. 164, 165.

[2] Despatch of M. de Julien, Brigadier-general, to the Marshal of Montrevel,
from Saint Jean du Gard, March 29, 1703, Arch. du Ministère de la Guerre,
apud J. P. Hugues, Histoire de l'Église réformée d'Anduze (Paris, 1864), 728–
730.

snatched in like manner from the little village of Saumane, farther up the rocky course of the Gardon d'Anduze. Their offence
Deportation was that they had suffered Roland and Castanet, with
of the in-
habitants of their troops, to take rest and refreshment in the village
Saumane. for several days, and had not notified the authorities
of the province. The Camisard leaders received timely notice,
and decamped at midnight. Julien did not reach the spot
before daybreak. But, if he came late, he did his work thoroughly. The best of the spoil of the industrious peasants was
carried off on the backs of the mules with which he had provided himself; the rest, together with the dwellings of the people, became a prey of the flames.[1] As for the wretched owners,
in company with the exiles from Mialet, they were shortly
taken by Basville's orders to the province of Roussillon, on
the Spanish frontier, there to languish as prisoners in the
damp dungeons of Salces.[2] It was the first deportation of the
inhabitants of the Cévennes. Not long after, twenty-two villages of the diocese of Nismes suffered the same fate, varied in
some instances apparently by exile over the seas to America.
No punishment had hitherto been discovered better calculated
to produce consternation in the hearts of the Protestants of
the region.[5]

For all the misery entailed by these and other harsh measures taken against the Camisards, Marshal Montrevel was
directly responsible. The question whether in their execution
he was doing violence to a heart merciful by nature, or was
gratifying a cruel and bloodthirsty disposition, can best be answered after the narration of an event that occurred on Palm

---

[1] Louvreleuil, ubi supra.

[2] The insignificant village of Salces is situated on the landlocked bay, or
lagoon, known as the Étang de Leucate, ten or twelve miles north of Perpignan.
See Brueys, ii. 147, according to whom it would seem that only the men were
deported.

[3] Louvreleuil, i. 181. If, as this writer states, the voyage, whether to Roussillon or to America, was made "sur de vieilles tartanes," there was good reason for the "silence de desespoir et de consternation" into which the New
Converts of Languedoc were cast. Little coasting vessels, carrying but a single
lateen-sail, and old at that, were not well adapted to buffet with the winds and
waves of the Mediterranean when angry, not to speak of the dreaded Atlantic
Ocean. A voyage to Guadeloupe in such a craft, if actually intended or made,
had a sinister meaning, suspiciously akin to a *noyade*.

Sunday, which this year fell on the first day of the month of April.

A little before noon on this eventful Lord's Day, a company of Huguenots assembled, as they had assembled on several The mill of the Agau at Nismes. previous occasions, in a mill standing on the bank of the little channel of the Agau which runs through the city of Nismes, and not more than twenty paces outside of a gate of the city known as *la Porte des Carmes*.[1] All comers of the Reformed faith were welcome, for though the mill belonged to the Marquis de Calvière, his tenant, Mercier by name, was a devoted Protestant, or, as his enemies designated him, " one of the most ill-intentioned of the New Converts." The preacher was the miller's brother-in-law, one Jean Frèze, a man some thirty-seven years of age. The audience was composed chiefly of married women and young girls, with but few men ; the husbands and brothers may have been serving with Roland or Cavalier. The worshippers had come in one by one and had escaped particular notice at the time. It was a purely devotional meeting of people who, in the present famine for the preaching of the word of God, embraced every opportunity and were willing to incur any risk or danger to satisfy their longing again to hear one of their beloved preachers, whether he read the time-hallowed prayers of Geneva or expounded the doctrines held by the fathers of the Reformed church. About this there is no dispute, even on the part of the most ardent apologists for the marshal. " It was not a gathering of armed men who designed undertaking some military expedition," says the most envenomed of those who have A peaceful meeting of Huguenot worshippers. described the Camisard war, " it was only one of those unlawful assemblies which a blind religious zeal had convoked contrary to the king's orders, for the purpose of preaching in spite of his prohibition." [2] An hour or two of undisturbed worship had passed — the prayers had been

---

[1] La Baume, 165. As this was at or near the present *Place des Carmes* (Charles Dardier, ubi infra, 9), the mill cannot have been many hundred feet from the spot where now stands the " Grand Temple " of the Protestants. See the plans of the city in E. Frossard, Tableau pittoresque, scientifique et moral de Nismes et de ses environs, and elsewhere.

[2] Brueys, ii. 128.

offered and the psalms had been sung, through want of caution, with too loud a voice, when the news reached Marshal Montrevel, whose lodging was hard by, that a Huguenot conventicle was at that very moment in progress in his neighborhood and barely a stone's throw from the city walls. Inflamed with anger, he rose from his meal and hastened to the spot, accompanied by a detachment of royal troops. It is needless to pause and discuss the accuracy of the account of his apologist, who at this point depicts for us a supposed conflict in the general's breast between feelings of compassion, such as no one else, I believe, has ever credited him with, and a profound sense of duty to the king's service.[1] If such a mental struggle took place, the issue was decisive and big with disaster for the Protestant worshippers. A cordon was drawn around the

A merciless massacre. building that none might escape. Then the dragoons were ordered to break down the door, to rush in, sword in hand, and put to death all upon whom they might come. The command was obeyed with alacrity and executed with promptness. The sole entrance was held and none could escape. Some, indeed, say that from an upper window overlooking the water five or six persons precipitated themselves into the rivulet or canal, but that they were overtaken in an adjoining garden and put out of the way. The marshal was impatient to be done with the work. Besides, in the various stories of the building, some secret nook might be overlooked, and thus a few of the late worshippers might avoid their doom.[2] The woodwork of the mill was dry and inflammable. Montrevel ordered the building to be set on fire.

Thus far there is little discrepancy between the various accounts. On other points there is doubt. It is said that the Huguenots imprisoned in the burning mill, to the number of

<hr />

[1] "M. le Maréchal fut un quart d'heure à se déterminer sur le parti qu'il devoit prendre. D'un côté, ces malheureux," etc.

[2] "Les soldats entrèrent donc avec fureur, tirèrent sur ces pauvres gens, qui se cachoient dans plusieurs endroits de ce lieu, qui étoit assez spacieux et où il y avoit plusieurs étages; mais le maréchal, pour ne perdre point de tems, et pour que personne ne pût échapper, fit mettre le feu, qui prit avec violence dans ce moulin à huile. Ce fut alors qu'on vit un spectacle bien affreux," etc. Mémoires de Rossel d'Aigaliers, 23.

eighty or more, appealed in vain to the pity of the merciless soldiers, who with their weapons drove back into the raging conflagration all that attempted to force their way out. One person, and one alone, was spared for the moment. The marshal's own valet was touched by the beauty and distress of a young Huguenot girl, or was not proof against the temptation of the ring, or the purse, which she offered him, and undertook to rescue her from the flames. His tender-heartedness, or his greed, was of no avail to the maiden, while it came near proving his own ruin. The marshal ordered her to be at once despatched by his troopers, and it was with great difficulty that the intercessions of the compassionate ladies of Nismes rescued the valet from the gallows already erected for his execution. As it was, the marshal dismissed him from his service and bade him never again show his face.[1]

It is a pitiful illustration of the power of party prejudice and religious intolerance to pervert the moral sense, that the very authors who are loudest in their denunciations of the inhumanity of Joany, not only fail to stigmatize the action of Marshal Montrevel according to its desert, but actually applaud it as a wholesome and necessary exercise of authority. "Rebellions," observes the presidial judge La Baume, " call for a pitiless physician who treats them at the start with fire and sword; for otherwise the cure is not merely slow, but sometimes impossible." [2] To such writers the unpardonable offence was the audacity of the sectaries, who ventured to hold their services at the very gates of Nismes, and at the time when so august a personage as a marshal of France was there.[3] In the eyes of Esprit Fléchier, writing

The butchery approved by the Roman Catholics and their bishop.

---

[1] The accounts of this incident of the Camisard war are numerous. The reader may consult Louvreleuil, i. 170, 171; Brueys, ii. 128, 129; Rossel d'Aigaliers, 23, 24 ; La Baume, 164-166 ; Court, i. 237-245 ; Charles Dardier, ubi infra ; A. Borrel, Histoire de l'Église réformée de Nimes, 355-359 ; and Abbé Valette, prior of Bernis, in his Histoire des prophètes des Cévennes, a manuscript preserved in the library of the city of Nismes, from which M. Charles Sagnier has printed the very vivid story of the massacre in Bulletin de la Soc. de l'hist. du Prot. fr., xxvii. 544-548.—In a note at the close of this chapter I shall consider the doubts recently raised by M. Rouvière as to the magnitude of the massacre.

[2] Relation historique de la révolte des fanatiques ou des Camisards, 166.

[3] "Le jour, le lieu, l'heure et la présence de M. le maréchal, qui étoit alors à

from his episcopal palace, three weeks after the occurrence, it was their presumption in singing their psalms and holding their preaching service in their rude mill at the same hour at which, with his attendant clergy, he was engaged in singing vespers under the roof of the sumptuous cathedral.[1] Although he admits that it is painful for a bishop to see the destruction of those whom he claims as belonging to his flock, he regards the execution as necessary for example's sake. Consequently no words of condemnation fall at this time from the lips of a prelate who never tires of adverting to the inhumanities of the Camisards, which, he declares, fill men with horror.[2]

As respects the marshal himself, a voluptuary in whom the proverbial union of savage cruelty and lust in the same character was realized even more fully than is common, it is more than doubtful whether he ever experienced any compunctions for the authorship of a butchery that had sent so many innocent persons to the grave.[3] Indeed it would be amusing, if the subject were less painful, to institute a comparison between the complacency with which he regarded his own action and the severity of the verdict he passed upon minor faults of the men with whom he was contending. Only three days after he had made a holocaust of human beings whose only crime was that they had worshipped the Almighty Father in a manner upon which Louis the Fourteenth had set the seal of his disapproval,

Nimes, rendoient cette entreprise d'autant plus criminelle, qu'on ne pouvoit douter que c'étoit principalement pour lui faire voir le peu de cas qu'on faisoit de son autorité et des ordres de la Cour, puisqu'on avoit l'audace de les violer en sa présence." Brueys, ii. 128.

[1] Letter of April 25, 1703. Œuvres complètes de Fléchier, x. 120. The prelate does not give us the vivid account, for which we have to turn to the pages of Brueys, of the great excitement that arose in the cathedral, when the noise of the storming of the mill on the Agau led to the belief that the dreaded Camisards had burst into the city. The future Bishop of Castres, then a simple canon of Nismes, mounted the pulpit, at the suggestion of Fléchier, who was not himself well enough to preach, and made, we are told, a very eloquent harangue on the text, " Why are ye fearful, O ye of little faith ? "

[2] " Des inhumanités qui font horreur." Ibid., x. 118.

[3] " Je ne sais," says the Baron d'Aigaliers, " s'il craignit que les dames pourroient lui savoir mauvais gré de cette action, mais il est certain qu'il fit de son mieux pour gagner leur bienveillance par quantité de fêtes et de parties de plaisir, dans lesquelles il faisoit quelquefois d'assez mauvaises chansons le verre à la main." Mémoires de Rossel d'Aigaliers, 24.

Montrevel described the simple burning of a few edifices of wood and stone in words such as these : "The church of Esperon, with the house of the curate and four or five others of the place, has been burned by these horrible monsters. I am very much annoyed that they continue to practise their cruelties. I hope, if it please God, shortly to be able to repress their insolence and punish them as they deserve." [1]

It is almost needless to say that the court of Versailles approved the conduct of Marshal Montrevel, pronouncing the Complacence slain to have been justly punished.[2] Of all crimes the of the court. most heinous and unpardonable in the eyes of Louis the Fourteenth and his ministers was an attempt to serve one's Maker with any rites but such as were well-pleasing to the king.

And equal-handed Justice, not content to close her eyes and take no notice of the horrible violation of all laws, human and divine, perpetrated by the commander of the royal troops in Languedoc, must needs applaud his action by affixing the stigma of dishonor to the names and memory of his victims, now passed beyond the reach of human pains and penalties. The flames were so far merciful to the corpses of a few of the Protestants at the mill, as not to burn them beyond the power of recognition. Against these remains legal proceedings were Legal pro- promptly instituted before the "presidial" judges of ceedings against the Nismes. In order that none of the forms of law deceased. might be neglected, a solicitor practising before the court was appointed to guard their interests ; witnesses were summoned and heard, the testimony was compared and

---

[1] Letter of Marshal Montrevel to M. de Largentière, governor of Le Vigan, April 4, 1703. Of this hitherto inedited document M. Charles Dardier gives an extract in his pamphlet, Le maréchal de Montrevel, Nismes, 1889, p. 10, together with the entire text of several other letters of no small interest.

[2] At least so La Baume apologetically asserts : " On ne peut rien imaginer de si affreux qu'une exécution si terrible, qui remplit tout le monde de crainte et d'horreur. Mais comme cette assemblée si elle avoit demeuré impunie, auroit pu avoir des suites fâcheuses, et produire de grands maux, et que, dans la situation où étoient les affaires, ce châtiment, quelque sévère qu'il fût, étoit nécessaire, la Cour approuva la conduite de M. le Maréchal, et les nouveaux convertis de Nismes en furent si épouvantés qu'ils n'osèrent plus faire d'assemblées nombreuses et donnèrent même, quelque mal intentionnés qu'ils fussent, des apparences de soumission et d'obéissance aux ordres du Roi." Relation historique de la révolte des fanatiques, 166.

weighed; the arguments of the king's attorney and of the counsel for the accused were duly made; and after a trial that
dragged its slow length for over two months, a conclusion was
reached on the sixteenth of June. The sentence was that all
the accused "were duly convicted of having been present, with
many others unknown, at an unlawful and seditious meeting,
held, on Palm Sunday, in the mill of the sieur de Calvière,
situated opposite the Porte des Carmes of this city, where
they were killed by order of Seigneur the Marshal of Montrevel;" as reparation for which, the court "orders that their
memory shall remain extinguished, condemned, and suppressed
for ever, their goods acquired by and forfeited to the king,
with deduction of the costs and expenses of the trial."[1]

Such was the verdict passed by the judges of Nismes upon
the corpses of about a score of persons—mostly women—taken
not from the dregs of society, as the historian of Nismes has
maintained, nor indeed from the nobles and higher gentry, but
from the industrious and useful artisans of the place, with but
one or two persons of a superior station—for the most part the
wives or daughters of millers or masons or bakers or weavers
and the like. Their names, consigned by contemporary judges
to oblivion or ignominy, are carefully cherished by a succeeding
generation, and, instead of being rejected as infamous will be
held in long and affectionate remembrance by History which
duly weighs the honorable actions and the misdeeds of the past.

If the reduction of the Camisards was within the power of
the most powerful monarch of Europe, his advisers were resolved to accomplish it. The forces now accumulated in Lower
Languedoc were kept perpetually in motion, to strike now here,
now there, in the disaffected region; and the bloody revenge
taken upon such villages as were merely suspected of rendering
assistance to the insurgents in the field, was only less frightful

---

[1] The original sentence, dated Saturday, June 16, 1703, is among the MSS. of
the Archives de la cour d'appel de Nimes, 25ᵐᵉ div., Sentences criminelles,
liasse 9. It has been published by the late Charles Sagnier in the Bulletin de la
Société de l'hist. du Prot. franç., xxvii. (1878), 554–556. It is interesting to notice
that among the judges signing it is La Baume, author of the Relation historique de la révolte des fanatiques, to which I have had occasion frequently to
refer.

than the menace of deportation, now fast becoming an actual fact, and dooming entire communities as well to loss of country and of life, as to forfeiture of all the accumulated fruits of years, or even generations, of industry. Scarcely less terrible, however, to the Protestants in their homes were the ravages of the irregular bands of Roman Catholic peasants gathered together more for the sake of plunder than of supporting the cause of imperilled religion. The government, otherwise so jealous of its authority and resolute to permit no assemblages of armed men, first winked at an irregularity which it afterward formally approved, and at length, when license had run riot, was compelled to restrict and attempt to render amenable to the laws of civilized life. The church lent its sanction to the practice of this extraordinary warfare, and openly encouraged the classes most likely to engage in it to persevere in their laudable pursuit.

Irregular troops.

Those that banded together for the defence of the Roman Catholic religion and its ministers adopted, as a badge by which to recognize one another, a small white cross, which they attached to the flap of their hats that was turned back. This practice led them to assume the appellation of *Cadets de la Croix*. At an early stage in the conflict they were called *Florentins*, from the village of Saint Florent, whose inhabitants earned the distinction of giving a designation to the whole body by outdoing the rest in daring and cruelty. Later, the peasants surnamed them *Camisards blancs*, or "White Camisards," when the terror which they spread among the inoffensive communities had made them not less an object of terror than the Protestant insurgents, whom now, for clearness' sake they spoke of as the "Black Camisards" —*Camisards noirs*. It mattered little, however, by what name they might be called; they were soon actively engaged in a work of destruction which offered a rich harvest of plunder. Before long these bands of marauders began to plunder and kill indifferently friends and enemies, a course which, with consistency, they continued to pursue so long as the existence of war gave them a plausible excuse for taking the field. The government was obliged to make the attempt to moderate their zeal, by strictly forbidding them from acting save under the guidance

"Cadets de la Croix," "Florentins," or "Camisards blancs."

of leaders with whom it undertook to furnish them ; but the
prohibition met with indifferent success.[1] Scarcely distinguish-
able from these lawless bands were the select companies which
certain enterprising spirits were authorized to enlist among the
men most suitable for daring enterprises and to furnish with
regular pay on the same scale as the old troops. That body,
which made itself most formidable and inflicted the most serious
injury upon the insurgents, was composed of two hundred bold
and indefatigable youths whom La Sagiote, better known as
"The Hermit," had picked out, and at whose head he sallied
forth. By birth a gentleman of Dauphiny, he long
served as a captain in the king's armies, but had, some
time since, renounced the world, and, under the name of Friar
François Gabriel, had taken up his solitary abode in a desert
place near Sommières. His religious contemplations were
rudely interrupted by a band of Camisards, who plundered his
scanty possessions and burned his retreat over his head. The
exploit cost them dear. The sight of arms revived La Sagiote's
martial spirit. His losses created within him an insatiable
thirst for revenge. It was no difficult matter to obtain a dis-
pensation from the vow he had taken to practise an austere seclusion ; for Bishop Fléchier of Nismes, his superior, fell in
fully with his project, and heartily commended him to Marshal
Montrevel. The latter recognized in the hermit, now become
warrior again, a valuable ally. Nor were general and prelate
mistaken. Despite his sixty years, the new partisan leader,
with the corps which he organized and trained with a true
soldier's skill, pursued the insurgents day and night with untiring energy, and made himself so redoubtable by his savage on-
sets that Cavalier is said to have sent word to the officer in
command at Nismes that, unless an end were put to the hostile
operations of The Hermit, he would feel himself obliged to give

*"The Her-
mit."*

---

[1] When Brueys (ii. 240) affirms that Montrevel's order, "arrêta un peu leur
violence, et fit cesser les plaintes de plusieurs nouveaux Convertis, qui, quoiqu'
innocens, étoient exposez à leur fureur, comme les plus coupables," he but half
states the truth. A year later, when Marshal Villars, having been sent to replace
Montrevel, reached Pont Saint Esprit on his way down the Rhone, his ears
were at once greeted with complaints of fresh outrages perpetrated by the "Cadets de la Croix." Mémoires de Rossel d'Aigaliers, 36.

no quarter to such of the Roman Catholics as fell into his hands.[1]

The picture drawn by Baron Rossel d'Aigaliers, a moderate writer, who describes what he has seen, is a faithful representation of the excesses of the irregular troops of the province. "In order to try our patience to the utmost, the bishops of Alais and Uzès secretly armed Catholics, to whom they gave their blessing and the name of 'Cadets de la Croix.' These troops, under these two illustrious chiefs, and by their order, carried off all the flocks of the Protestants, killed the shepherds, and at the gate of the cities butchered such of our religion as had the imprudence to sally forth; after which they showed themselves on our public places, relating their exploits, and, under the protection of their good prelates, they were assured of impunity for their crimes. Our complaints were our sole resource against this new disaster. So numerous were those complaints, made even by the Papists, against the crimes of these new crusaders or brigands, that M. de Basville could not avoid arresting a few, who were kept a while in prison, after which the touching and pathetic prayers made by the bishops in behalf of these zealous defenders of the Roman church extricated them from their trouble. It was not so with the Camisards. As soon as they were captured they were put to death by the most cruel forms of execution. Men have been burned alive on the bare suspicion of having been among them, many of them on false testimony."[2] Nor was the support given by the episcopate to the "Cadets de la Croix" a Huguenot calumny. Bishop Fléchier, of Nismes, in a letter written immediately after his return from the meeting of the provincial estates of Languedoc, at which loud murmurs had been heard against the conduct of the Cadets de la Croix, and especially of the terrible "Hermit," exclaims "We must encourage Friar Gabriel," adding the significant words: "Men endeavor to decry him, but we have well sustained him."[3]

Bishop Fléchier supports him in the states of Languedoc.

---

[1] Brueys, ii. 239-245 ; La Baume, 170, 171; Louvreleuil, ii. 184-187; Court, i. 266-268 ; Rossel d'Aigaliers, 25.

[2] Mémoires de Rossel d'Aigaliers, 25, 26.

[3] " Je vois dans une partie des troupes si peu de zèle pour le service de Dieu et du roi, que je n'attends pas de grands succès des expéditions qu'on médite,

Meanwhile a higher dignitary than the three bishops within whose dioceses the Camisard conflict chiefly raged, lent the authority of his name and influence to the suppression of the insurrection. Pope Clement the Eleventh, having been informed by the French ambassador at Rome that "the heretics in the Cévennes, the cursed race of ancient Albigenses, had lately taken up arms against church and king," fulminated a solemn bull against them, on the first of May, 1703. "In order to put a stop to the contagion of so furious a plague, which we thought to have been already destroyed by the piety of Louis the Great," wrote the pontiff, " we think it fit to follow the laudable example of our predecessors in the like cases. To this end and for the purpose of engaging and encouraging God's elect to exterminate that cursed race of wicked men who in all ages have been an abhorrence both to God and to Cæsar, and relying upon the power of binding and loosing granted by our Saviour to the chief of the apostles, we grant and freely give plenary forgiveness of all sins whatsoever, to all who will enlist in this holy warfare, if it should so happen that they be killed in the fight."

A papal bull against the Camisards.

In transmitting a copy of this charitable document to each of the vicars in his diocese, to be posted on every church door, the Bishop of Alais took good care to inform the faithful that, "as Louis the Great has resolved, according to the wholesome advice of the holy Pontiff and the bishops of his realm, not to leave a single heretic alive in all his dominion, thereby the Majesty of Almighty God, the honor of the Catholic Church, and the prince's royal dignity shall be kept inviolate." [1]

It does not appear that the discharge of the pontifical artillery, and the institution of the new crusade, exercised any appreciable influence upon the contest. If we may credit Cav-

---

si le ciel n'éclaire et n'échauffe nos guerriers. Il faut donner courage à Fr. Gabriel. On tâche de le décrier lui et sa troupe, nous l'avons bien soutenu. Je ne sais quelle est sa destinée, mais je voudrois bien qu'il fit quelque coup d'éclat." Letter of February 9, 1704, Œuvres complètes de Fléchier, x. 143. The principal burden of this letter is the blindness and inaction of those who ought to put a stop to the fury of the Camisards.

[1] Cavalier, Memoirs of the War of the Cévennes, 218–221. See Court, i. 219, etc.

alier's assertion, the Camisards were more afraid of a musket-ball from the king's soldiers than of the thunderbolt hurled from the Vatican. The vicars took good care not to affix the papal bull to the doors of any of the churches in places which the Camisards were wont to visit.[1]

The particulars of the military operations which occupied the spring and summer of the year 1703 would neither be very clear to one unfamiliar with the mountains which were their principal scene, nor be very essential to an understanding of the general result. If the Camisard arms won no decisive advantages over the forces brought against them, neither was the spirit of the insurgents broken either by occasional reverses or by the inhuman treatment meted out to such of their numbers as were so unfortunate as to fall into the hands of the Roman Catholics. A surprise, indeed, which the latter inflicted upon the followers of Cavalier, now grown to a formidable band, seemed, humanly speaking, to threaten them with entire destruction or dispersion. The event proved very different. That brilliant leader, stung to the quick by the news of the outrage cruelly perpetrated by Marshal Montrevel upon the unoffending worshippers in the mill upon the Agau, resolved to take signal revenge upon such Roman Catholics as sided with the persecutors of his brethren. Places that had distinguished themselves for hostility to the adherents of the Reformed faith fared worst, being singled out for exemplary punishment. Of this number was Montlezan, where all the inhabitants that were captured outside of the village church, whither the majority of the citizens had betaken themselves for refuge, and whence it was impossible to dislodge them, were put to the sword. Of this number was also La Salle, above Alais,[2] where the blunder committed a few weeks before at Le

---

[1] Cavalier, ubi supra, 221.

[2] "C'est un village à une ou deux lieues au dessus d'Alais, proche de Branoux." Mémoires de Jacques Bonbonnoux, 17; Court, i. 255–257. This place must, therefore, not be confounded with the much more important town, inhabited in great part by Protestants, situated five or six miles west of Anduze. The Memoirs of Cavalier, 197–199, contain a graphic account of this event, which agrees substantially with that given by Bonbonnoux. I strongly suspect that the story related of Joany at Pradel is a misapprehension, and that Louvreleuil and La Baume have erroneously ascribed to Joany an incident which in reality occurred to Cavalier. Le Pradel, being near Portes, according to La

Pradel was repeated, and the villagers welcomed for friends of the priests Cavalier and his men, disguised as troops of the king, only to be undeceived when it was too late, and to pay the penalty for former acts of hostility with their lives. But one night at Collet de Dèze the Camisards were surprised by the attack of a new and active officer, the Brigadier de Planques. If they escaped serious loss, this was due to the promptness with which they fled and took refuge in the neighboring mountains, to which their enemies would not or could not pursue them.[1] The Camisards were less fortunate a little later, when Cavalier left the highlands and approached the towns of Alais and Anduze. On the morning of Sunday, the twenty-ninth of April, when it was scarcely dawn, the Camisards met at an appointed spot,[2] to celebrate divine worship. In the course of the day not less than three sermons were preached in the audience of a great throng of Protestants who had come from far and near to be present and take part. That night, the religious rites being over, the followers of Cavalier betook themselves to a lonely

Cavalier's disaster at La Tour de Belot. farm-house, known in the region as La Tour de Belot, situated midway between Alais and Anduze, expecting there to receive the provisions which the well-affected peasants of the vicinity had promised to bring, and hoping to enjoy much-needed rest. But in supposing that their arrival had escaped the knowledge of the vigilant enemy, they committed a fatal mistake. A spy had kept De Planques informed of all their movements. Scarcely, therefore, had the wearied Protestants fallen into a deep sleep, before they found themselves surrounded on all sides by the troops, so advantageously posted as to preclude the possibility of escape, while the stealth of their approach had effectually cut off those who were outside

---

Baume, can scarcely be more than four miles north of the La Salle, or Les Salles, referred to by Bonbonnoux. See V. Monin, Atlas national des départements de France, f. Gard.

[1] Louvreleuil, i. 174, 175 ; Mémoires de Jacques Bonbonnoux, 17–19. As the Roman Catholic author speaks of but three or four Camisards as killed at Collet de Dèze, and the Protestant, who took part in the fray, narrows down the misfortune of his associates to the loss of their drums and horses, it would seem that the chief gain of De Planques was in the moral effect produced by the dispersion of the Camisards.

[2] A retired glen known as *Malle Bouisse.*

of the building from joining or rendering effective assistance to those who had shut themselves within it. A desperate struggle ensued; but in the darkness it was well nigh impossible to distinguish friend from foe, and the discharges of firearms from windows and doors were as likely to cost the lives of the Camisards who were attempting relief as of the royalists who were storming the place. In the end Cavalier and the portion of his band that were without were compelled to disperse, leaving the unfortunate occupants of the Tour de Belot to their fate. Among these a very few succeeded in breaking through the lines of the enemy and escaping. Of those that were found within by the royalists not one was spared. An unfriendly but generous chronicler does them the justice to admit that they made as vigorous a defence as could have been expected from good troops in a bad position,[1] and a comrade assures us that they fought until their powder and lead had altogether given out.[2] The besieging party succeeded in throwing in hand-grenades and set fire to portions of the building. Unable to extinguish the flames, the brave Camisards sold their lives dear, retreating from room to room, and meeting their pursuers with desperate courage, until they fell overwhelmed by superior numbers.[3] As usual, it is difficult, among the conflicting accounts, to ascertain the losses on either side; for, unfortunately, it too often happens that the zeal or the ignorance of partial writers leads them to exaggerate the number of the enemy slain or wounded in the same proportion in which they diminish the figures that represent their own casualties. The claim made in Cavalier's name by the writer of his memoirs, that the Camisards killed twelve hundred of their opponents and themselves lost by death only two hundred men, is scarcely more absurd than the statements of the Roman Catholic chroniclers who estimate the Camisards killed at four or five hundred, and will admit the death of but a handful of officers and men upon their own

---

[1] "Une deffense aussi vigoureuse qu'on l'auroit pu attendre de bonnes troupes mal placées." La Baume, 169.

[2] Bonbonnoux, 23.

[3] "Ils se défendirent en desesperez de chambre en chambre," says Brueys, ii. 150.

side.[1] The struggle lasted many hours, beginning about mid-night and scarcely closing by eight o'clock in the morning.

It was hoped that this severe blow, involving a loss of men and of arms which the Camisard leaders, with their relatively far inferior numbers and poor equipment, could but ill afford, would end the war. Instead of this, it only gave the Camisards new resolution and an increase of forces. In a few days, with the fresh recruits that came from beyond the Gardon, they were more numerous than ever.[2]

In the higher Cévennes, Castanet met with little resistance, and having about this time celebrated his nuptials with a young girl of the region, was magnanimous enough, in honor of the auspicious event, to spare the lives of twenty-five prisoners whom he had just taken, upon the simple condition that they would not henceforth do any harm to the inhabitants of the little village of Massavaque, his own birthplace.[3] Of such clemency there were but few examples. The royalists, in particular, reserved their prisoners taken on the field only for a more horrible doom. Julien, a hard-hearted officer, to whom was committed the work of devastation to which our attention will shortly be turned, was not so cruel as some of his associates, when he summarily put out of the way those that fell into his hands. "Inasmuch," he wrote to Chamillart, the minister of war, "as during our marches, at the slightest alarm, we should have been embarrassed to keep our prisoners, I took pains to have them shot as fast as they were brought to me. The king is saved the expense of trial and exe-

Castanet's marriage and clemency.

---

[1] Compare Louvreleuil, i. 178–181; Brueys, ii. 146–153; La Baume, 169, on the one side, with the Memoirs of Cavalier, 207–209, on the other. Court, i. 263, displays a commendable spirit of moderation, and Bonbonnoux, who alone took part in the engagement, wisely refrains from any attempt at an arithmetical computation. It is characteristic of the religious character of this writer, who, after the suppression of the Camisard war, spent the rest of his life as one of the devoted pastors of the Desert, exposed to dangers scarcely inferior to those encountered during his military career, that he regarded the defeat of the insurgents at La Tour de Belot as a direct visitation from heaven, to punish them for unnecessarily putting to death three armed peasants whom they found at table in a cottage, as they were returning from a day of such spiritual privileges as they had enjoyed at Malle Bouisse.

[2] La Baume, 169.

[3] Brueys, ii. 158, 159.

cution, as well as the corruption of inferior judges, who often, from motives of interest acquit the guilty. They are dangerous serpents, whose heads it is well to crush as soon as possible."[1]

Four Protestants captured about the same time were accused of unpardonable offences; two of having given refreshments to the Camisards—these were condemned to the galleys—the other two, but falsely, of having taken part in the slaughter of the inhabitants of Fraissinet de Fourques, a village on the northwestern slope of the Cévennes. Of the latter, one by the name of Jacques Pontier was ordered to be broken upon the wheel. The story of his last hours, for which we are indebted to the curate of Saint Germain de Calberte, is worthy of record as exhibiting the fact that, even amid the horrors of an internecine war, the old religious spirit still survived, and that the martyrs of the eighteenth century were not altogether unworthy of being ranked beside their brethren of the age of Henry the Second and his sons.

"One of these men," writes Louvreleuil, "died obstinate in the fatal prejudices of his heretical birth and education. When

Louvre-
leuil's ac-
count of the
end of a
Camisard
martyr.

I approached him, immediately after his sentence had been read to him, he thrust me back, and said: 'Get you behind me, sir, you are a Satan to me! Begone!' I answered him, 'My very dear brother, I come in God's name, at the prompting of love, to console you in your affliction and to give you help in view of the horror of a violent death.' He replied: 'I have no need of you. It is not in men that I must put my trust in my calamity, but in God alone.' Then, raising his eyes toward heaven he cried: 'It is to Thee alone, Thou Saviour of the world, that I have recourse. Look upon me in pity in this day of tribulation. Thou hast not bidden me address myself to any minister; but Thou hast said to me and to Thy faithful children, "Come unto me all ye that labor and are heavy laden, and I will give you rest." Extend to me, therefore, at this hour, gentle Christ, Son of David, Thy greatest mercy!' As soon as he had ended these first exclama-

---

[1] Julien to Chamillart, February, 1703. MSS. Archives of French War Depart., printed in Bonnemère, 218, and Charles Dardier, Le Maréchal de Montrevel, 9.

tions I tried to speak. Immediately he interrupted me by
repeating an entire psalm, which he uttered, his eyes fixed on
high, with a stoic gravity. After having listened to him for
about an hour, without having succeeded in getting him to
listen to me, I made as though I would take my leave, and
said : 'My very dear brother, since I am useless to you for your
soul's salvation, I offer you my care for the assistance of your
family, which is going to be deprived of your property by confiscation, and I promise you to do for it all that you may wish.'
He was touched with emotion, and replied, 'You know that
Our Lord has said, "Inasmuch as ye have done it unto one of
the least of these My brethren, ye have done it unto Me." I
shall believe that you will keep your promise. Write, therefore,
if you please, a line or two on a half-sheet of stamped paper.'
I did as he requested me, and set down in this memorandum
that he gave his blessing to his wife and children and committed them to God's keeping, and that he begged certain persons whom he named, to hand to them or to me what he had
lent them without taking a receipt and on their word, to some
in the form of money, to others in the form of commodities.
Afterward he made a gift to the poor of some bushels of wheat
which one of his friends owed him, and then signed this little
will as best he could with his hands bound.

"The judge, to whom I showed it, permitted me to keep it
and to secure its execution. But it was impossible for him to
compel the man to admit the facts for which he had condemned
him, and for me to persuade him that he would be shut out
from paradise if he died outside of the Catholic church. He
persisted until death in his obstinacy, despite all the remonstrances that were made to him by the father who taught theology in our seminary at Mende, when he accompanied him to
the place of execution. And thus it was that, failing in one
essential point, he failed in everything, and ruined himself dis-
astrously in his vain ideas and his false hope. So true is it
that Heresy is a blindness that prevents those who die in it
from discerning the cause of their death and the punishment
which it makes them suffer."[1]

---

[1] Le fanatisme renouvelé, i. 186-189. Court, i. 273, furnishes us with the
name of the Camisard.

It must not be supposed, however, that the fortitude and piety with which Pontier met death in its most terrible form were rare. On the contrary, they were the rule rather than the exception. The civil and military authorities, reinforced by the ecclesiastics of the established church, were as powerless to shake the firmness of individuals as they were to break the courage of the Camisards in the field. The latter were willing to expose themselves to any peril in order to secure for their brethren the right to worship God according to the dictates of their consciences ; the former were equally ready to lay down life in the same sacred cause. To this fact their enemies continually give testimony, which is none the less valuable to us that they customarily stigmatize the sufferers, however innocent, as villains and murderers, represent their courage to be audacity, their piety a delusion, their resolution stubbornness, their heroic endurance a pertinacity inspired of the devil. A judge who, as a member of the presidial court of Nismes, had extraordinary opportunities for clear observation, deplores the utter failure of the measures adopted by Marshal Montrevel and Intendant Basville.

Fortitude of the sufferers.

" Gentleness and negotiation were employed to no purpose in bringing them back. They rejected with insolence the amnesty that was offered. Their defeats and the great number of executions made, instead of intimidating them, redoubled their rage and audacity. Many were shot by the troops, and a very great number perished by different kinds of torments at Montpellier, at Mende, at Alais, and, above all, at Nismes. But, as we have already said, those frightful spectacles made no impression. On the contrary, the New Converts looked upon the condemned as martyrs. The steadfastness which these displayed when dying confirmed them in their former religion, and, if one may say so, the examples given to the public produced an altogether contrary effect from that which had been expected. Almost all died as they had lived. To prove this, we have already reported the death of Jean Vedel ; we shall add, at this point, that of Pierre Caussi, of Boissières. He was condemned, at Nismes, to make the *amende honorable*, to have his hand cut off at the wrist, and then to be broken upon the wheel while still alive. The scoundrel spat in the face of the curate who

Judge de la Baume's testimony.

undertook to exhort him . . . and died crying that he suffered with pleasure for having defended the glory of the Almighty and the worship of the true religion. This was the
ordinary language of those that were put to death." [1]

If the Camisard martyrs sometimes rejected the advice of
their ghostly attendants with a little more determination than
would at first sight seem to be called for in the circumstances, it must not be forgotten that they regarded
them not as the ministers of a gospel of peace but as
the sole authors of the reigning war and confusion, and the prime
instigators or abettors of the present horrible persecution. Taking advantage of the privilege which their sacerdotal office conferred, these ecclesiastics of a hostile creed, not content with en-
trapping their victims and securing their condemnation to a cruel
and ignominious death, persisted in forcing their hateful presence and offices upon unwilling eyes and ears, and beset and
worried men about to die, robbing them even of the comfort of
a few moments of undisturbed meditation and prayer to God
in view of their fast approaching end. Nor was this all. The
single priest or monk that was called to wait upon the condemned in the mistaken mission of trying to wring from his
feebleness some expression that might be construed as an
acceptance of the faith of the Roman Catholic Church, was
accompanied often, if not in most cases, by a number of other
ecclesiastics, whom curiosity had attracted to the place of
execution, apparently to gloat over every pain of the sufferer.
The fact rests upon no partial evidence; the abuse called
forth about this time the notice and reprobation of Bishop
Fléchier in a pastoral letter addressed to the priests of his
diocese, who, having fled from their parishes through fear of the
armed bands of the Camisards, had congregated in the walled
cities and enjoyed abundant leisure to devote to the contempla-
tion of the punishment of such heretics as fell into the hands of
the intendant and his military allies. "We have learned with
some grief," says the prelate, "that many among you, contrary to
the rules of gentleness and ecclesiastical propriety, go to be

Ecclesiastics frequent the executions.

---

[1] Relation historique de la révolte des fanatiques ou des Camisards, par Charles
Joseph de la Baume, 159.

present at the frequent executions which are being made of the murderers who persecute us. We have designated spiritual consolers for them; and those that are not set apart to be the ministers of their salvation have no right even to go so far as the foot of the scaffold, to become the spectators of their torments. The church, so circumspect and so charitable, cannot approve these exhibitions of a mournful and unbecoming curiosity.[1] She is wont to pray for her persecutors, far from taking interest in seeing them punished. . . . Gentleness and humility are the portion of Christians, and chiefly of priests; it looks as if a man has not quite forgiven an enemy whom he wishes to see expiring on the wheel, and however innocent may be the intention, the action is not a good example. What an occupation for an ecclesiastic, to be the witness of the impatient actions of a man that is suffering, and perhaps of the impenitence of a dying man, and to carry to the altar where he offers the propitiatory sacrifice a mind full of these bloody images."[2]

Nor was it simple priests alone that exhibited the "indecent curiosity" which the Bishop of Nismes reproved. Some of his own colleagues certainly laid themselves open to the same animadversion in connection with a Protestant nobleman whose misfortunes must here be recorded.

François de Pelet, better known by his territorial title as Baron of Salgas, sprang from one of the most ancient families The Baron of Salgas. in the kingdom. Of a commanding stature, sprightly and intelligent, possessed of several important estates, and enjoying an income which for the time and region was regarded as ample, he was now, in his fifty-sixth year,[3] despite the fact of his Protestant birth, a person of great local distinction and influence. Proud of his descent, it was his boast that his ancestors for many generations had testified to their loyalty

---

[1] "Ces tristes et indécentes curiosités."

[2] Pastoral letter of September 6, 1703, "to all priors, curates, priests, and other ecclesiastics of his diocese, concerning the persecution of the fanatics," Œuvres complètes de Fléchier, v. 148.

[3] "La première [raison] est que je suis sur ma fin, courant dans la soixante-neuvième année, et treize ans de mon esclavage, qui m'en ont mis vingt sur le corps." Baron de Salgas to Mlle. de Saint Véran, June 10, 1715, Bulletin de la Société de l'histoire du Protestantisme français, xxix. (1880) 185.

to the kings of France, several of them having died on the battlefield, as had also, in more recent times, two of his own brothers. He had himself formerly served in the armies of Louis the Fourteenth, and had enjoyed the friendship not only of the Marshal of Noailles and M. de Broglie, but of the intendant, Lamoignon de Basville. Although a decided Protestant at heart, none of the New Converts of Languedoc had practised greater caution or displayed more worldly wisdom. A timid Huguenot. He had studiously avoided the prohibited religious assemblies, and when his wife, more ardent and uncompromising in her religious attitude, secretly escaped to Geneva, for the purpose of enjoying liberty to worship God without restraint, he not only remained behind with their six children, but made a show of endeavoring to pursue and bring her back. The Abbé du Chayla, indeed, had frequently dropped the remark to intimate friends, such as the curate of Saint Germain de Calberte, that the Baron of Salgas was a very dangerous man in the matter of religion, as his deeds would show in the sequel. But if, as the curate subsequently maintained, the Protestant nobleman was one of the most zealous partisans of fanaticism in the diocese of Mende, it must be confessed that he had taken good care to cloak his religious fervor with an exterior of the greatest coldness.[1] His prudence, however, did not save him. Two circumstances precipitated his ruin. The Camisard chieftain Castanet, whose birthplace was not far distant, and whose haunts were in this quarter of the Cévennes, impatient that a Protestant nobleman should so ostentatiously hold aloof from the exercises of his religion, one day presented himself unannounced at the castle gates. He was mounted and led a band of eighty men, armed with guns, pistols, and swords, and marching at the beat

Castanet compels him to attend a Protestant service.

---

[1] It is only just to say that the interesting correspondence of the baron, published for the first time in the Bulletin de la Soc. de l'hist. du Prot. franç., contains abundant evidence of the sincere regret he subsequently felt for his lack of courage. Thus in the letter from which I have already quoted, he observes respecting his life: "Eh! mon Dieu, combien la mienne a-t-elle esté bizarre, ayant donné le printemps, l'esté, l'automne de ma vie au monde, au grand scandale de mes prochains, et n'ayant réservé au bon Dieu que l'hiver, s'il faut ainsy dire, qui est proprement l'égout et la lie de mes années." Ibid., ubi supra.

of the drum. It was a Sunday afternoon, the eleventh of February, about two o'clock, and the baron was in his own room, engaged in private devotions. On being asked what was the reason of this unexpected visit, the Camisard for all reply exclaimed: "Not satisfied with absenting yourself from the religious assemblies of the Protestants, you prevent your household from attending. Now you must go, or else we shall burn you out this very hour." Remonstrance proved unavailing. Castanet would not listen to the baron's timid suggestion that compliance with the demand would involve him in ruin. "One never risks anything by serving God," was Castanet's uncompromising rejoinder. Resistance was out of the question. There were but two muskets; had there been more, there was no garrison to use them. One gate had already been broken down. The iron gate was about to be burst from its hinges, and the Camisards were resolutely bringing brands to execute their threat. Salgas concluded to yield to so pressing an invitation, and he accompanied his rough visitors. Forty men preceded him, the other forty brought up the rear. Between the two detachments, the baron was conducted unharmed a mile or two farther up the Tarnon, where, at the village of Vebron, part of which belonged to his own fiefs, a company of Protestants had convened for religious worship. Prayers were offered, psalms were sung, the Scriptures were read, and a sermon was delivered. When all was over, the baron was permitted to go whither he would; but tarried for two good hours with the worshippers, endeavoring, as he asserted, to provide that his castle should not share the fate of neighboring castles, five or six of which Castanet had burned within the week. It may well be questioned whether the adventure was quite to the taste of the Protestant nobleman. It was destined to entail disastrous consequences.[1] Meanwhile, upon his return home, he at once despatched a messenger to the intendant Basville to acquaint him with the violence that had been done to him. His excuses were at the time apparently taken in good

---

[1] See Copie des mémoires des malheurs du sieur de Salgas, tirée de l'original qui est escrit de sa propre main, MS. Collection Court, printed in Bulletin, etc. **xxix**. (1880) 73-79.

part, nor did Marshal Montrevel, to whom Salgas subsequently presented himself, at the assembly of nobles called at Nismes, disclose any hostile intentions. But when, a few weeks later, the marshal sent him an order to come again to Nismes, and, on the ground that it was too dangerous for him to traverse the Cévennes without an escort, the baron neglected to obey the command, a prompt punishment was meted out. Arrested in his castle by a detachment of seven or eight hundred soldiers, he was taken first to Saint Hippolyte, and thence to Alais. Against so cautious a man it was difficult to obtain certain proofs of complicity with the Camisards. None the less did the intendant institute a trial with judges drawn from the presidial court of Nismes, and scour the region for witnesses that might testify to some overt act. The baron himself was called up for examination before Basville not less than eighteen times, and was stretched upon the rack for the purpose of extracting from him some admission of guilt. But neither form of torture elicited anything to satisfy the desires of his accusers. The united testimony of the twenty-eight witnesses of the crown, to use his own expressive words, did not establish against him so much as would have secured a schoolboy a flogging.[1] His condemnation, however, was a foregone conclusion;[2] and, a victim to the suspicions of the government, he was sentenced to serve in the king's galleys for the term of his natural life. The destruction of his residence at Salgas was ordered; another castle at Rousses, not far distant, as the scene of a Protestant religious meeting, was to be razed to the ground. All his property of every description was declared to be forfeited to the state. It is said that the personal influence of Basville saved Salgas from a worse fate, and that Marshal Montrevel openly grumbled at the leniency of the court.[3] As it

Salgas is arrested and put to the torture.

Salgas sent to the galleys.

---

[1] Mémoire, ubi supra, xxix. 78.

[2] "To send a gentleman of quality to the galleys, to confiscate his property —this makes a sensation and checks others. Thus my fate was instantly sealed." Mémoire, ubi supra, xxix. 79.

[3] The supposition that Salgas owed his life to the generosity of Basville, and that the penalty of the galleys was preferable to death, arouses the indignation of Rossel d'Aigaliers, who thus apostrophizes the nobles of France, and in par-

was, the sentence is itself a convincing refutation of the un-supported allegation of the local chroniclers that the baron had been a prime mover in the butchery of the inhabitants of Fraissinet de Fourques. Had that been true, no intercession of Basville could have saved him from the halter, nor would the intendant have had any desire to interfere in his behalf.[1]

The condemnation of so distinguished a personage, a man of mature age, to an ignominious punishment, generally reserved for the worst of criminals, created a deep and wide-spread sensation. The grief experienced by the better part of the community did not affect the prelates of Lower Languedoc. The bishops of Montpellier and Lodève, happening to visit the royal galley to which the baron was attached, as it lay in the harbor of Cette, had the ignoble curiosity to see the nobleman plying the oar in servile degradation, and requested the captain to procure them this gratification. The latter readily gave his consent. Though the vessel lay at anchor, heading to the shore, and could not move, at the given signal the galley-slaves took their places and handled their ponderous implements. Three times had they bent to their laborious task, when the *comite*, or overseer, who had taken notice of the difficulty with which the baron followed the actions of his comrades, impatiently exclaimed "Enough!" and put an end to a shameful exhibition.[2]

gnoble curiosity of the bishops.

---

cular a brother of the baron then serving in Prussia : " O! noblesse françoise, otre cœur seroit bien changé et bien avili, si un pareil traitement pouvoit us sembler plus doux que la mort ! O ! brave Racoule, aurois-tu remercié le ige qui a usé d'une telle clémence à l'égard de ton frère? O Dieu! dans quel épris et dans quelle ignominie sommes-nous tombés ! "

[1] On the Baron de Salgas, see Louvreleuil, i. 185, 186, ii. 11–14 ; Brueys, ii. 50, 169–171 ; La Baume, 203, 204 ; Rossel d'Aigaliers, 26 ; Court, i. 304–314.

[2] Court, i. 315, 316. See a slightly different account in a letter of Beausobre Court, Berlin, May 28, 1737, in Bulletin, etc., xxix. 237. Baron de Salgas as kept in the galleys for nearly fourteen years, and was at last released in '16, in response to the urgent appeal which the Princess of Wales, subsequently ieen of England, made by letter to the Duchess of Orleans, mother of the egent. Upon obtaining his freedom, he went to Geneva, where his wife was, it he survived his imprisonment less than a year. Antoine Court states that, ing too old to row, Salgas was, after a while, relieved of this duty, and uvreleuil, that the baron was at first allowed the unusual privilege of wearing ockings and of having a small cushion to sit or lie upon ; a mark of extraordi-

It is a circumstance not unworthy of notice that the same person who when a freeman gave to others a very unedifying example of a time-serving policy and laid up for himself an abundant store of painful memories of cowardice, became among the galley-slaves a conspicuous illustration of courage and devotion to religious convictions.

Salgas becomes an intrepid confessor.

Nothing short of the violent wrench to which he was subjected could have wrought so complete a transformation. The genuineness of the change is demonstrated by the additional calamities in which it involved him. Not only did the new zeal of the Baron de Salgas to confirm his fellow prisoners in their Protestant faith and to thwart the efforts made to convert them to the king's religion, draw down upon him harsher treatment than his captors were disposed to give to a man of his rank, but it delayed his release far beyond the term at which the majority of his companions were liberated. All doubt on this point is set at rest by the testimony of his jailers themselves. For eleven years had Salgas been confined to his ship, never setting foot upon dry land nor moving from the galley to which he had at first been consigned, when, in deference to the request of the master of the galleys, orders were issued for the baron's removal to a separate room in the convict hospital. The sole purpose was declared to be to deprive him of the means of communication with the rest of the Protestants, and to free him from the troubles which he had brought upon himself and which were quite likely to keep him confined alone in the galleys when all other persons of much less consideration should have been set at liberty. "His misfortunes," writes

---

nary consideration which the writer will have it was taken away because of the discovery of additional guilt which ought to have secured for him the punishment of being broken upon thew heel ! Le fanatisme renouvelé, ii. 13, 14.   A contemporary fragment found in the large manuscript collection of historical material accumulated by Court tells the story of his sufferings tersely.   "Ce monsieur a souffert avec beaucoup de patience la question ordinaire et extraordinaire.   Il a fait 13 mois de compagnie avec deux chaînes pendant 5 mois, qui pesoit plus de 80 livres, et qui l'avoient ulcéré les jambes jusqu'au os.   On le fit voguer avec les robes de la chiourme tierselot, pour servir de spectacle à messieurs les évêques de Monpélier et de Lodève qui le voulurent voir couché sur une planche petite et courte, aiant les genoux au menton, sans estre despouillé pendant les 13 mois.   Je vous dis ceci par son ordre."   Bulletin, etc., xxix. 188

Arnoux to Marquis Châteauneuf, who had taken the trouble to write in Salgas's favor, "come from nothing else than his mad determination to be always the preacher, the protector, and the support of the fraternity even in his chains. So that you will easily judge, from what I have the honor to show you, that it is only his own fault that he does not enjoy the same freedom as formerly, and that he would, perhaps, even long since have obtained complete liberty but for this obstacle."[1] It was this, doubtless, that prevented the name of Salgas from being included in the list of the one hundred and thirty-six Protestants set free after the treaty of Utrecht, in 1713, at the intercession of Queen Anne.[2] Nearly a year passed after his closer incarceration when the baron was again transferred by night to a still more inaccessible cell. Here he saw no one save the guard that came, three times a day, to bring him food or a candle. He was not even permitted to write to his family without submitting his letter to the royal commissioner, for fear that he should write to Protestants.[3] For greater precaution against surreptitious correspondence, one half of the only window of his cell had been walled up and the remainder covered with an iron plate, pierced by a thousand holes, through which a coarse needle could scarcely pass. Nor was he long left in doubt respecting the reason of these extraordinary precautions. The commissioner before whom he was taken, "a perfectly civil man," informed him. "You are accused," he said, "of confirming the Protestants, of preaching to them, and of supplying them with money—a fault," he added, "which is worthy of you, but is contrary to the views of the court."[4]

The Camisard struggle had lasted a full year. The small body of troops in Lower Languedoc at the time of the death of the Abbé du Chayla had been reinforced by soldiers drawn from many quarters. Miquelets, accustomed in Roussillon to scale the rugged sides of the Pyrenees, had for months been serving side by side with battalions of marines from Toulon, and with entire regiments or chosen com-

Varying success in the struggle.

---

[1] Letter of March 24, 1714. Bulletin, etc., xxix. (1880) 128.

[2] Ibid., xxix. 129.

[3] " De peur, disent-ils, que je n'escripve aux gens de la religion."

[4] Salgas to Mlle. de Saint Véran, February 4, 1715; Ibid. xxix. 182, 183.

panies drawn from corps inferior to none in the service—the regiment of Hainault, the dragoons of Firmacon, the fusileers of Provence, and others whose names figure in the list given by contemporary writers.[1] These soldiers, in the aggregate far outnumbering the Cévenol insurgents, had met with varying success. On several occasions, encountering the despised mountaineers with superior forces, they were shamefully beaten. Often the victory remained with them, and the followers of Cavalier or Roland were forced to consult safety by flight into the recesses of the woods and mountains. But nothing ever seemed to produce a lasting impression. The Camisards had an incalculable advantage over their enemies in their better knowledge of the entire country, and were strong in the affection of the inhabitants of all the mountain villages and hamlets, who, with few exceptions, gladly furnished them provisions and shelter, despite the prohibitions issued by Montrevel and Basville, and who exposed their own lives with reckless daring to give them tidings of the enemy's movements. Mouths from which not even the application of torture upon the rack proved sufficient to extort information unfavorable to the cause of the Camisards, were unsealed to communicate to the insurgent leader anything that might facilitate his movements. To this was it owing that an air of secrecy and surprise invested all the actions of the Camisard bands. If worsted in combat and pursued by the enemy, they suddenly vanished from sight, leaving no more trace of the direction they had taken than if the earth had opened and swallowed them up. With equal mystery they reappeared when least expected, possibly at some distant point, to fall with resistless force upon some detached troop of soldiers resting in the confidence of assured safety, or to visit pitiless retribution upon a village whose Roman Catholic inhabitants had, under the influence, and at the suggestion of an ecclesiastic, perpetrated inhuman excesses upon their Protestant neighbors. Against brave mountaineers, ably led and apparently endowed, like some favored hero of the Arabian Nights, with

---

[1] See La Baume, Relation historique de la révolte des fanatiques, 245–47, for a complete list of the troops, together with the names of the commanding officers.

the magical power of rendering themselves visible or invisible at will, the best of regular troops were unable to cope save at great odds. Exemplary punishment had been meted out to individual communities found guilty, or even merely suspected of giving the Camisards aid and comfort. But the remedy was partial and ineffectual. What could be done when an entire mountainous region, from one end to the other, was full of refuges to which the insurgents could readily betake themselves, and from which they could as readily sally forth to fall upon the troops of their oppressors?

The Marshal of Montrevel, whose soul revolted at no deed of cruelty, had long since made his proposal to the court. It aimed at nothing less than the total devastation of the higher Cévennes. Indeed, there is, as will shortly be seen, good reason to believe that it even contemplated the wholesale slaughter of the inhabitants. The court of Versailles had long withheld its consent from so drastic a measure. But now, in the early part of the autumn of the second year of the war, Louis the Fourteenth yielded to the urgency of the members of his council and reluctantly permitted the marshal to carry his scheme into execution.[1] Desperate diseases, it was held, justify recourse to extreme remedies. It was noted as a mark of the monarch's goodness that he stipulated that, in the removal of so large a body of people, care should be taken to provide it with the means of subsistence and of transportation, especially in the case of the children, the women, and the aged. Could a ruler with any claim to the possession of the most ordinary instincts of humanity have been expected to insist upon less than this?

A proclamation of Marshal Montrevel bore to the Cévenols the first tidings of approaching calamity. It was the carefully studied result of the deliberations of a council of war. The

The king consents to Marshal Montrevel's project.

---

[1] "La chose étoit trop importante," says Brueys, ii. 221, "pour être exécutée sans en informer la Cour. M. le Maréchal et M. de Basville en écrivirent aux ministres. Le Roi eut d'abord quelque peine à y consentir ; mais il se rendit enfin aux pressantes raisons de son Conseil. Cependant, par un effet de sa bonté, il voulut que dans la transmigration de tant de peuple, on prît soin de sa subsistance et de son transport, principalement des enfans, des femmes et des vieillards."

preamble was abrupt and startling. His Majesty was resolved
to put it out of the power of certain places to furnish the rebels
with provisions or assist them with recruits. Consequently, he
had determined to make them desolate without any to dwell
therein. Yet, anxious to provide for the subsistence of their
present inhabitants, he was pleased to order that instructions
be granted to them for their guidance. These instructions the
marshal proceeded to convey to the unfortunates. All the inhabitants must repair without delay to certain designated
spots, bringing with them their furniture, their cattle, and all
their portable effects. Having reached the rendezvous, they
were to await further orders. If they failed to comply with the
command, their goods would be seized and confiscated by the
troops employed to destroy their houses. The better to insure
obedience, all other communities were forbidden to receive the
dispossessed villagers, on pain of having their own homes razed
to the ground, of losing their own property, and of being treated
as rebels against the commands of his Majesty. Ten places
of safety were next appointed, in as many paragraphs containing each the list of the parishes and villages whose inhabitants
were to have a common refuge. Not a village, not a hamlet,
not a farm within the specified limits was to be excepted, and
three days from the date of the service of the present proclamation to the local magistrates, was the brief term allowed for the
removal.[1]

The tidings brought consternation to the Cévenols, who saw
their own homes and the homes of their ancestors for many a
generation consigned by a single stroke of the pen to utter destruction. What other and greater horrors were in reserve for
them, they knew not. It was clear that they were to be robbed
of the chief fruits of their industry and toil, and of every
cherished possession, save such trifling articles as they might
be able to carry with them in their hurried flight, and the cattle
which they were graciously permitted to drive before them.
But for what purpose were they to be congregated at a few
points, unless for a universal massacre, a faint copy of the

---

[1] The text of the proclamation dated Alais, September 14, 1703, is in Louvreleuil, Le Fanatisme renouvelé, ii. 68–71.

Parisian Matins of which they had heard from their fathers, or for a scarcely less dreaded deportation in mass, of which the experiment had recently been made in the case of a few villages?

In their bewilderment the wretched mountaineers adopted different courses. Some saw no choice but to proceed to the appointed places, even though they knew not but that they were going as sheep to the slaughter. All the bravest and most resolute of the young men now determined to take a step respecting which they had hesitated hitherto; they promptly joined the Camisards in the field, thus swelling the numbers of the followers of Roland and Cavalier. A large proportion, wavering between hope and fear, unable to tear themselves from the spots where they had passed their entire lives, and cherishing a secret persuasion that the marshal's proclamation would prove to be an empty menace that would never be carried into effect, lingered about their former homes, wasting precious hours and days in irresolution.

Upon the other side, there was neither indecision nor sluggishness. The agents to be employed in the barbarous work The plan of had been carefully instructed both as to what they were operations. to do, and how they were to do it. A district which may be roughly described as reaching from the Montagne de la Lozère, on the northeast, to Mont Aigoual, on the southwest, was to be given over to destruction so thorough and complete, that save at five points [1] (where villages were to be spared that were inhabited by Roman Catholics and were intended to watch over the desolated region), not a vestige of the works of men's hands was to be left. The tract measured twenty-five or thirty miles in length and a little more than half as much in breadth. It occupied the territory now comprised in the southeastern part of the Department of Lozère, but included a small portion of the contiguous Department of Gard. The Roman Catholic parishes into which it was divided, belonged almost exclusively to the diocese of the Bishop of Mende. To Julien was com-

---

[1] These were Saint Étienne de Valfrancesque, Saint Germain de Calberte, Barre, Pont de Montvert, and the town of Florac. La Baume, Relation historique de la révolte des fanatiques, 199.

mitted the task of destroying two hundred and thirty-four villages and hamlets, and he was to begin on the north at Fraissinet de Lozère. The Marquis of Canillac received the command
to visit a like ruin upon the parishes farther to the south and
west, in the vicinity of Mounts Aigoual and Espérou. Marshal
Montrevel had reserved for himself the congenial work of dealing
with the villages lying between the fields of operations of the
other two. He was, in fact, directing his course to Saint Julien
d'Arpaon, intending there to make a beginning, when events to
which I shall hereafter refer caused him to hasten to the lowlands, and, soon after, to despatch orders to the Marquis of
Canillac to follow his example. For the restless Camisards under their adventurous leaders, not to be idle while their mountain haunts were in the possession of the enemy, had descended
into the plains, with greatly increased forces, and were carrying
terror even to the gates of Nismes. Meanwhile, the appearance
of two hostile men-of-war off the coast aroused new fears of a
foreign invasion instigated by sympathizers with the Camisard
cause. Thus it was that upon Julien alone devolved the entire
work. Nor did that merciless soldier prove incompetent to
perform the laborious task. For three months, from
autumn to winter, through fair weather and foul, from
early morning to nightfall, in rain and in snow, with a
perseverance and an industry worthy of a better cause, the soldiers from Hainault and the troops drawn from the neighboring
province of Gévaudan, toiled with spade and mattock, with pick-
axe and crowbar, sapping the walls of human habitations, tearing down doors and windows, overturning ovens and chimneys,
destroying the carefully constructed arched roofs, removing
everything that might furnish a shelter to man or beast. If by
chance the house of an " ancient Catholic " should be met with,
in a region where the inhabitants were almost to a man of the
Reformed faith, the orders were to spare it for the time, until
the king's pleasure might be learned. Otherwise, nothing escaped. The accurate map of the Cévennes that had recently
been printed in Paris, based upon a careful survey of the ground,
was studied with minute attention, that no hamlet, however insignificant might be passed over. While a part of the soldiers
were thus occupied, their comrades watched over them, arms at

The task committed to Julien.

hand, ready to repel the attacks of straggling Cévenols, infuriated at the loss of home and property, but impotent to prevent it. Even thus, however, the task seemed to grow as the workers advanced; for half their time was wasted in endeavors to find the hut or cabin to which no distinct road led, hidden in some recess of the hills or in the depth of the forest. It might have required not three months but a year or more, had not the permission been asked and obtained to employ fire to complete the work of destruction.[1] Louvreleuil, curate of Saint Germain de Calberte, who, in describing the operations of Julien, betrays as much zeal for the thorough destruction of the temporal possessions of the new converts, as he ever exhibited for the salvation of their souls, descants with feeling upon the extent of his single parish. It had a circumference, he tells us, of nine leagues, and comprised one hundred and eleven hamlets containing two hundred and seventy-five families, of which only nine were Catholic. The church, situated in the middle of the parish, was a league and a half distant from the two extremities. "In a general visit which I made to discover all the parishioners," he writes, "marking their names and surnames from the aged down to young children, and going from house to house, I spent seventeen days in the month of September, although I started early in the morning, returned only at nightfall, and rode on horseback. It is true that there were seventeen hamlets which could be reached only on foot, because of the danger of the paths, which were impracticable in many places. The parish of Saint Étienne de Valfrancesque was still more extensive and more populous by a third. There were fewer royal roads, and consequently it was much more difficult

Curate Louvreleuil's parish.

---

[1] " Ces contre-tems furent cause que cette entreprise importante alla très-lentement, et que Monsieur de Julien, qui en étoit le conducteur, representa fortement à la Cour et à Mr. de Montrevel, combien il étoit difficile et penible de faire ces demolitions par main d'homme, et la necessité qu'il y avoit de se servir du feu au lieu des instrumens de fer qu'on employoit, pour éviter les inconvenients qu'il prevoyoit, et finir dans deux ou trois mois l'ouvrage d'une année entière. Ses lettres furent lues avec attention, et le Roy, qui avoit defendu precisement de brûler, permit l'usage des flammes pour avancer cette triste besogne." Louvreleuil, ii. 112. La Baume virtually says the same thing. Relation historique de la révolte des fanatiques, 199.

to go about in it. The other parishes were about in the same
condition, in proportion to their circuit." [1]

It may strike the thoughtful reader as somewhat incongruous
that a shepherd of souls should discourse with so much apparent satisfaction respecting the dispersion and ruin of
his unhappy flock, only deploring the hardships encountered in effecting it, and he may be pardoned if
possibly a suspicion enter his mind that the solicitude
which the pastor previously exhibited to bring his errant sheep
into the ecclesiastical fold was due rather to regard for the value
of the fleece than to anxiety for the safety of his charge. It is
scarcely less startling to find a bishop of literary culture express in well-turned phrases his entire acquiescence in a policy
that made of a part of a neighboring diocese a desolate wilderness. Again it is Fléchier, of Nismes, who has for Marshal
Montrevel and his barbarous work no words but those of encouragement and approval, and reserves his condemnation
solely for the audacity and impiety of the outrageous Camisards
that dared retaliate. "The plan you are executing," the bishop
wrote, "is a severe one, and will doubtless be useful. It cuts
down to the very root of the evil. It destroys the refuges of
the seditious, and confines them within limits in which it will
be more easy to hold and to discover them. But, although
we were quite prepared to expect that, during the expedition
you are making in the mountains, the rebels would fall upon us
in the plain, and commit some ravages in our neighborhood, yet
we could not have imagined that they would perpetrate so many
acts of cruelty, and come and burn, under our very eyes, the
churches, the villages, and the best estates of our open country." [2]
The prelate, it will be seen, does not measure impartially the
enormities of royalist generals and Camisard leaders. A
writer who can say of brave men that ferocity stands them in
stead of courage, and that they do not fear death because they

The execu-
tion approv-
ed by Curate
Louvreleuil
and Bishop
Fléchier.

---

[1] Le fanatisme renouvelé, ii. 110, 111.

[2] Letter of October 1, 1703, Œuvres complètes de Fléchier, x. 122, 123. Here
the name of the prelate's correspondent is not stated. Antoine Court, ii. 41,
gives it as Marshal Montrevel. I am not sure that the communication was not
addressed to M. de Julien.

know that they deserve it,[1] can scarcely be expected to weigh
the deeds or misdeeds of friends and foes in the impartial balance of justice.

I have spoken of the apprehensions of the Cévenols that
their mountains were destined to witness a general slaughter of
the wretched inhabitants. Their fears do not seem to
have been altogether unjustified in the circumstances;
and certainly the wording of a paragraph in the instructions given by Marshal Montrevel warrants the inference
that something of the kind had been deliberately proposed to
Louis the Fourteenth. For, while directing his officers, should
they find any inhabitants in the places that were to be burned,
to read and explain to them the ordinance forbidding their return to their dwellings, he added the significant sentence : "But
no harm shall be done to them ; the king having refused to hear
of any shedding of blood."[2] The suspicion which Antoine Court
expressed over a century ago seems now to be converted into a
certainty; for it will shortly be seen that proposals similar to
those which Louis the Fourteenth is believed to have rejected
at this time were made a few months later, by Marshal Montrevel himself, whose insatiable thirst for the butchery of the
Protestants caused even the sanguinary Lamoignon de Basville
to recoil in horror, as from the prospect of a repetition of the
infamous crime of Catharine de' Medici. Be this as it may, it
fared ill with those whom love of home or any other reason led
to revisit the haunts from which they had been driven ; they
were remorselessly put to death by the soldiers into whose hands
they fell. Such was the fate of a young man who, having a
property worth four thousand livres at the village of Fraissinet
de Lozère, conceived the imprudent idea of going to see in what
condition his house had been left by the troops, and was captured and summarily despatched without form of process, by
way of punishment for his disobedience.[3]

In the matter of their possessions, Protestant noblemen of

*Was a gener-
al massacre
proposed?*

---

[1] Letter of April 25, 1703, Œuvres de Fléchier, x. 121.

[2] " Mais on ne leur faira point de mal ; le Roy n'ayant pas voulu entendre
parler d'effusion de sang." Instructions signed by Marshal Montrevel, in Louvreleuil, ii. 98.

[3] Louvreleuil, ii. 117.

unchallenged loyalty were treated no better than their more humble neighbors. In reply to the intercession of the Marquis of Ganges, who prayed that the castle of Moissac, belonging to a gentleman connected with him by marriage, might be exempted from the general conflagration, Marshal Montrevel stoutly replied: "I have severe orders from the Court; it is the king's pleasure that the country of the Higher Cévennes shall be uninhabited and uninhabitable, as an everlasting mark of the revolt of the people of that district."[1]

At length, the weary, half-fed army of desolation concluded its inglorious campaign. On the fourteenth of December Julien reported to Montrevel the completion of the task upon which he had entered upon the twenty-ninth of September. Statistics convey but a faint notion of such calamities as had befallen the Cévennes. The result could be summed up thus: Thirty-one or thirty-two parishes were ravaged, and four hundred and sixty-six villages or hamlets were utterly destroyed which previously had contained a population of nearly twenty thousand souls.[2] It was a sorry exhibit. Well might the king's officers complain that in such service there was no glory to be gained. Was it likely to compass the object in view? Julien himself doubted it. "My expedition is finished," he wrote to Chamillart, the secretary of war, "but I do not yet foresee that all these disorders and troubles are nearly ended. I really fear, my lord, that the great chastisement which I have just inflicted upon a vast and extended region, may rather make a noise and a sensation in the world, than allay the revolt and bring advantage to the king's service. With all my heart, however, I wish that I may be mistaken."[3]

Julien was not mistaken. The barbarous devastation of an entire region, which, if not rich, had yet enjoyed a certain amount of prosperity, and where men ved contentedly upon the fruits of the earth and the increase of their thousands of flocks of sheep, produced no lasting effects. The restless mind of Marshal Montrevel had another and yet harsher scheme to propose.

The results.

---

[1] November, 1703. Louvreleuil, ii. 147.

[2] La Baume, p. 201, says 19,500. Court, ii. 37, 38, gives his reasons for be lieving the number to be greater.

[3] Julien to Chamillart, December 14, 1703, Louvreleuil, ii. 172.

Not the Higher Cévennes alone, with their comparatively sparse population, but the whole of that part of Lower Languedoc, among whose population the insurgents found secret sympathy and encouragement, must be so treated as to make it impossible for the Camisards to obtain shelter or subsistence within its bounds. Marogier, of Vauvert, who was broken upon the wheel, had declared in his last moments that the Protestants were all enlisted in the movement, from the age of fifteen upward, and that there was not a town, not a village, not a hamlet or farmhouse that did not supply the rebels with food. To remedy

Montrevel advocates more stringent measures. this evil, the marshal prescribed heroic treatment. He would transfer all the inhabitants of the little places, the hamlets and the farmhouses, to the towns and large villages, which should not only be fortified with walls, but be garrisoned by troops to secure them against the enterprises of the Camisards. All the provisions would be carried in thither, and those who went out to work in the fields would be permitted to take with them only the exact quantity of food they required for their subsistence. Happily even Lamoignon de Basville saw at a glance the folly of this suicidal plan, and refused to support it. The full execution of the scheme might, indeed, he thought, starve out the Camisards in the course of a few months, but would be more than likely to entail the ruin of the province. Most of the arable lands would be left untilled, and the flocks of sheep, which constituted one of the chief sources of the prosperity of Lower Languedoc, would perish. When the question about which the marshal and the intendant disagreed was referred to the court of Versailles, the desperate course advocated by Montrevel was rejected. This incident and some other differences of opinion, we are told, led to an estrangement between the two great agents in the work of repression.[1]

Yet, after all, the government knew no more effectual means of repression than the forcible removal of entire villages, of which,

Abbé Poncet's paper. as we have seen, a first experiment had been tried at Mialet. This plan was recommended as the panacea for all the woes of Lower Languedoc by Abbé Poncet, vicar

---

[1] La Baume is an unimpeachable authority. See Relation historique de la révolte des fanatiques, 215, 216. I have closely followed his statement.

general of the Bishop of Uzès. Starting from the premiss that all the Protestants of the province were responsible for the excesses of the Camisards, inasmuch as the honest men among them, men who had a natural horror of bloodshed and incendiarism, were induced by "the vain hope of obtaining liberty of conscience," to acquiesce in the conduct of those that were in arms, Poncet proceeded to discuss the various expedients that had been proposed, and touched upon the proposal to put to the edge of the sword the New Converts of the villages and hamlets in which Old Catholics had been butchered. But he stigmatized this course, albeit in precise agreement with the advice given by the Cardinal of Tournon to Francis the First in the early days of the spread of heresy, as inconsistent with the precepts of true religion, which distinguishes between the innocent and the guilty, and as impolitic, in view of the desperate courage with which it would arm the rebels. The abbé recommended instead a general removal, first, of the relatives of the insurgents, who ought to be transported beyond the seas ; next, of a few of the chief men of each locality who were likely to corrupt others and who might advantageously be sent to some Roman Catholic region far distant from the province, and, thirdly, of all the young men of questionable loyalty and capable of being induced to join the rebel bands. Whither the last should be taken, the abbé did not suggest. In all cases, however, the abandoned villages might be repeopled by the introduction of Old Catholics brought from other provinces. Thus would the understanding which the Camisards maintained with the entire Protestant population be effectually destroyed.[1]

Meanwhile, if Julien affected to despise the courage of "Messieurs the fanatical generals," because, as he alleged, they had not dared to take advantage of more than one hundred and

---

[1] Antoine Court has quoted the Abbé Poncet's paper in connection with the events of the spring of 1703 (see Histoire des troubles des Cévennes, i. 247-251). But the writer uses language which can only apply to a date about six months later, or to November, 1703, when he says : "Ceux qui font les massacres sans distinction d'âge ny de sexe, ny de condition, et les incendies des églises depuis quinze à seize mois sont assurement très criminels." The fifteen or sixteen months must certainly be counted from the latter part of July, 1702. See Avis de Mr. l'Abbé Poncet sur le moyen d'éteindre la révolte, in Louvreleuil, ii. 180-184.

fifty places in the Cévennes where they might easily have attacked him and caused great damage to his army without exposing their own men to any loss,[1] those worthies had amply vindicated their reputation from his aspersions by the terrible execution they had done where their blows could be most effective. Scarcely had the work of devastation begun in the mountains, when the flames were set to churches and rectories, to windmills, and even to whole villages in the plains. Within a month Bishop Fléchier, glad to have his person safe inside of the walls of Nismes, was writing to a friend: "Our province is ruined beyond recovery. The rebels are masters of the open country. We lay waste their mountains, they lay waste our plain. There remain scarcely any churches in our dioceses, and, as our lands can neither be sown nor cultivated, they yield us no income. The body of Catholics that had been forming in the villages since the wars of the Duke of Rohan is almost wholly destroyed, and the king no longer has there any loyal servants."[2] The two foreign vessels that had been seen in the offing and had spread fear of a projected landing of English or Dutch troops upon the French coast, it is true, effected nothing for the Camisard cause. If any action had been intended, it failed through lack of concert. But Roland and Cavalier were never more alert and daring. Two letters purporting to be written by the former have come down to us. They may be genuine. They are addressed to particular villages. In one Roland informs the inhabitants of Saint Germain of the speedy coming of "the children of God," led by his brother Cavalier and himself, acting under inspiration of God's holy Spirit, to set fire "to the Babylon, to the Seminary, and other buildings," warns them that no fortifications will be able to withstand them, and challenges the enemy to meet them for battle on the Champ Domergue. In the second he styles himself "Count Roland, general of the Protestant troops of France gathered in the Cévennes in Languedoc," and orders the dwellers in Saint André de Valborgne to forbid the priests from saying mass or preaching, and to expel them from the place, on pain of

Camisard retaliation.

---

[1] Julien to Chamillart, December 14, 1703, Louvreleuil, ii. 172.

[2] Letter of October 23, 1703, Œuvres complètes de Fléchier, x. 128.

being burned alive together with their church and their houses.[1] About the same time Cavalier addressed to the king himself a long and respectful plea for his brethren, full of passages of the Sacred Scriptures to prove the justice of their struggle to secure liberty of conscience. He dwelt at length upon the harsh treatment received from bishops and priests that had driven them to take up arms, and pledged his word that they would lay their arms down as soon as his Majesty should grant them religious freedom and the release of their prisoners. He assured him that the king had no more loyal subjects than they, nor subjects who would more cheerfully pour out the last drop of their blood for his service. But he warned him that if their just requests were denied (inasmuch as we must obey God rather than man) the insurgents would defend themselves to the last extremity. He subscribed himself CAVALIER, chief of the troops sent by God."[2]

The most daring enterprise of the Camisards was the attack made by Cavalier, early in October, upon the suburbs of Sommières, a small but well fortified town on the river Vidourle. Of the consternation that ensued, Bishop Fléchier, in a letter written to the nuns of his diocese, has left a graphic description.[3] The prelate makes no mention of the cruelty with which the garrison had treated the Protestant villages of the neighborhood, and which the insurgent chief gives as the cause of his coming to Sommières.[4]

Cavalier's attack upon Sommières.

To describe the ravages of the Camisard bands in the fertile lowlands, and among the villages bordering upon the Vaunage and elsewhere, would be tedious and unprofitable. In the midst of the destruction of ecclesiastical property and of the houses and possessions of those who had distinguished themselves for

---

[1] Louvreleuil, Le fanatisme renouvelé, ii. 87, 88.

[2] The letter was dated "In the Desert," September 14, 1703. Summary in La Baume, 196.

[3] Œuvres complètes de Fléchier, v. 156-189. See La Baume, 222-224; Cavalier, 177, 178 ; Louvreleuil, ii. 119, etc. ; Brueys, ii. 228, 229 ; Court, ii. 73-76.

[4] Cavalier, ubi supra.—La Baume describes Sommières as "a little town of which two-thirds of the inhabitants were New Converts." It is noteworthy that of the present population, which is set down as 4,010 souls, the Protestants number at least 1,700. H. Perrenot, Etude historique sur les progrès du Protestantisme en France au point de vue statistique (Paris, 1889), 238.

hostility to the Protestants, the memoirs of Cavalier assert that the leader maintained a high degree of discipline among his soldiers, especially in the matter of murder and robbery. And they instance the case of a Camisard soldier, who, having met a trader on the road from Alais to Uzès, made bold to compel him to exchange his handsome clothes for the worn and possibly tattered suit of the former. When the theft came to the ears of Cavalier, he at once condemned his follower to be put to death ; and though the sentence was subsequently remitted at the earnest solicitation of the compassionate trader, he was not pardoned until he had first been forced to run the gauntlet of the troop. " My enemies as well as my friends," says Cavalier, " did me always the justice to say that never was discipline better observed than mine ; and truly it was what always maintained us and preserved us good friends."[1] Making some allowance for exaggeration, we may accept the assertion of the Camisard chief as virtually true. The insurgents were no robbers or murderers intent either upon private gain or upon private revenge. They slew without mercy, as they plundered without remorse ; but their blows were directed against the persons and the property of those whom they esteemed the enemies and the oppressors of the children of God. Such a thing as appropriating the spoil for their own individual use would have been to repeat the sin of Achan, and would have drawn down a punishment scarcely less severe than that visited upon Achan. Hence it is that in the multitude of instances of cruelty with which the unfriendly pages of the contemporary Roman Catholic chroniclers abound —some in all probability false, many distorted and exaggerated by partisan prejudice, but many others unquestionably true— there is an absolute dearth of examples of avarice profiting by the misfortunes of enemies, as there is a noteworthy absence of accusations of offences against the honor of the sex which is always most exposed to the insults of a lustful soldiery. We may shudder at the sight of combatants fresh from scenes of carnage engaging with apparent earnestness and reverence in the worship of a God of love and mercy, as we are startled to

The good discipline he maintained.

---

[1] Memoirs of the Wars of the Cévennes, 232, 233.

find the solemn chant of the psalms of Marot and Beza the ac-
companiment and incentive to the bloody execution, but we are
forced to look to their religious ideas, sincerely held, for the
reconciliation of the strange incongruity. In this view of the
matter it is interesting to read that, according to the inimical
judge of Nismes, Cavalier reproved with uncommon severity the
sin of taking the name of God in vain. To one who excused
himself for not coming until he had been twice sent for to bring
his arms, by assuring Cavalier with an oath that he did not receive the first summons, the chieftain indignantly said : " You
swear by the name of the Almighty ! If you were not one of
our brethren I should have you shot ; and if it ever happen to
you again to be found swearing, I shall inflict so severe a punishment that you will serve as an example to all those who profane the name of the Lord." [1]   It was quite in keeping with this
incident that in the same town of Vauvert, where this occurred,
Cavalier assembled the inhabitants for divine worship, that he
uttered in their hearing a long prayer, supplicating Almighty
God for the king and begging Him to prevent Louis from following the evil counsel which he received ; and that he exhorted
his brethren to sacrifice their lives, if need be, for the re-establishment of their churches, assuring them that the omnipotent
arm, which had always helped them, would still be outstretched
for their defence, and would render them invincible. [2]

It would have been strange had not the leaders, men of obscure origin, who by their boldness and their military ability
Roman Cath-   had made themselves feared, and, to a certain extent,
olic accounts   respected, even by officers high in rank in the ser-
of the Cami-
sard leaders.   vice of the king, been betrayed into some extravagant methods of displaying their importance. But the stories
that have come down on this point reach us through channels
so untrustworthy, wherever anything to the disadvantage of the
Camisards can be alleged, as to merit no credence unless corrob-

---

[1] La Baume, 228.

[2] Ibid., ubi supra. The same writer pays an unconscious tribute to Camisard
honesty when he relates that at the bridge of Codognan the insurgents stopped
the royal courier and took from him two bundles of letters from Paris. but
touched neither his other letters nor the twenty crowns which he had with him.
Relation historique de la révolte des fanatiques, 227.

orated by more impartial testimony. Thus when Louvreleuil
states that Roland, as commander general of the Camisards,
boasted of being master of a part of the province, assumed imperious airs, and affected to be addressed by all that spoke to him
as *Monseigneur*, or that Cavalier, having fallen in love with a fair
young damsel of the village of Ners, announced his intention
of marrying her in a great gathering of the Protestants, clothing
her in gorgeous apparel, and conferring upon her the pompous
title of "Duchess of the Cévennes," he is probably as far astray
from the truth as when he asserts, without proof, that the
former, from the absolute control he exercised over their predatory expeditions, had so enriched himself as to be the most af-
fluent of the rebels.[1] Yet had Roland and Cavalier exhibited
even greater elation than that of which they are accused, it
would perhaps have been nothing unnatural in view of the picture of the state of one of the most flourishing provinces of the
French monarchy, drawn by Louvreleuil, about the expiration of
a year and a half of strenuous efforts on the part of the government to suppress the Camisard uprising. "These two insolent
bandits," says the curate of Saint Germain de Calberte, "had
made themselves so formidable, the one from Montpellier to
Nismes, and the other from Nismes to Alais, that the couriers
from Paris did not dare to proceed upon the former of these
roads without an escort, and that the ordinary carriers, fearing
the perils of the second road, substituted for themselves a Camisard of their acquaintance, who hid official letters, now in a bag
of chestnuts, now in a bag of charcoal or of wheat laid on the

---

[1] "C'étoit à luy [Roland] principalement qu'on s'addressoit pour recevoir
l'ordre des expeditions qu'il y avoit à faire. C'étoit luy qui donnoit les charges;
c'étoit luy qui partageoit le pillage. Enfin c'étoit luy qui étoit devenu le plus
riche de tous les Revoltez pour avoir eu une disposition despothique de toutes
leurs rapines." Le fanatisme renouvelé, ii. 164, 165. Antoine Court has conclusively proved the falsity of these assertions, and has shown that the only title
either Cavalier or Roland affected was the simple designation of "Frère"—
"Brother." And if Cavalier had ever dreamed of a title of nobility for his
future bride, it would certainly not have been drawn from the *Cévennes*, which
were Roland's district, but from *Languedoc*, which Louvreleuil himself tells us
Cavalier frequented. Histoire des troubles des Cévennes, ii. 128. Equally un-
true is it that either leader assumed any control over the movements of the other.
Each was supreme among his own retainers.

back of an ass, which was driven on certain days to Anduze and on others to Nismes. The towns that found themselves destitute of salt were obliged to ask the commanders of the king's troops; and the Catholic peasants were reduced to the necessity of dying from hunger or risking their lives in going to obtain in the cities their scanty provisions." [1]

War is at its best a barbarous pursuit, drawing in its train a host of domestic and personal hardships; and the evils wrought by the well-ordered plans of the conscientious general are augmented a thousandfold by the unauthorized acts of the guerilla or the camp-follower intent only upon gain. Among the most *The story of the murder of Madame de Miraman.* touching incidents of the Camisard war was the murder of Madame de Miraman at the hands of some brutal men of Cavalier's band. The story of the capture and assassination of this young lady, not perhaps in itself more pathetic than the end of many another unfortunate victim, has come down to us in the simple and touching narrative of the humble attendant who shared her perils and barely escaped participation in her fate. [2] The wife of a man of rank, the daughter of the Baron of Meyrargues, and a relative of the Marquis of Castries, she had left Uzès on her way home to Saint Ambroix in a chaise. The driver and lackey, together with a chambermaid and nurse, were her sole escort. She had been urged to secure a guard of soldiers, since the road that she was to take was said to be frequented by a body of Camisards; but she had resolutely declined. She had nothing to fear, she said. On a previous occasion she had fallen in with the insurgents, and they had treated her with respect and suffered her to go on her way unharmed. It was not so now. At a distance of a musket-shot from the village of Vendras the carriage was stopped by three armed ruffians. They first bound the driver and lackey; then dragged the lady out, and bound her and her attendant

---

[1] Le fanatisme renouvelé, ii. 165, 166. This was under the date of December, 1703. About two months later, the price of one thousand crowns was set upon the head of Cavalier dead or alive—a very moderate sum under all the circumstances. Ib., ii. 221.

[2] Louvreleuil's account is the best; he incorporates in it a good part of the servant's narrative. Le fanatisme renouvelé, ii. 149-159. See also Brueys, ii. 230-233; La Baume, 237-239; Cavalier, 229-231, and especially Court, ii. 101, etc.

women. To her entreaties to spare her life, the answer came :
" You have nothing to fear for yourself; but the Holy Spirit
has inspired us to put these two men to death." In vain she
offered her purse, with its contents of fifty louis d'or, and her
costly jewels. Her captors were inflexible, but consented not to
slay the men in her presence. Led off some distance from the
highway, she was allowed to sit down upon the greensward,
and here it was that she met her end. Four others joined the
members of the band into whose power she had fallen. These
were as deaf to her entreaties and her proffers of gold and precious stones as had been the first, and thirsted for the lady's
blood. " I mean to kill every Catholic," said one, " and you all
this very hour." And when she had received at the hands of
the new comers the blows that were soon to prove mortal, the
poor woman—she was but twenty years of age—gasped out, in
the hearing of her faithful domestic, who, though herself
wounded, survived her injuries and ultimately crept to a place
of safety : " Leave me not, Susan, until I shall have breathed
my last. I die for my religion, and I hope the good God will
have pity on me. Tell my husband that I intrust to him our
little girl." When, three days later, she was found by the parties that had been sent out to scour the country in consequence
of the tidings brought by the escaped servant, her body was so
lifelike in appearance that she could scarcely be taken for one
dead. Her gown, her gloved hands, her well-shod feet, her head-
dress, the diamond pendants in her ears—nothing had been
touched. The chroniclers tells us of the pompous funeral held
in her honor, of the mortuary hangings embroidered with the
arms of her husband and with her own, of the troops of poor
pensioners upon her bounty, now robbed of their chief benefac-
tress, who walked in the procession carrying tall tapers, and followed the noblemen and gentlemen that bore the pall, of the
goodly number of priests that each said masses for her soul's repose and afterward sang the solemn office for the dead in the presence of the assembled crowds. They justly dwell upon the barbarity of the crime and the cry of execration that went up from
every one that heard of it. They might also have been candid
enough to record the fact that Protestants vied with Roman Catholics in their condemnation of the act, and that Cavalier, far from

justifying or condoning so foul a deed, perpetrated by men pretending to belong to his party, embraced the earliest opportunity to arrest and try the authors. Of the four, three were sentenced to death by the council of war and were executed on the spot. The fourth is said to have escaped, but whether by proving to the satisfaction of his judges that he was guiltless, or by seizing an opportune moment to abscond, is uncertain.[1] At any rate, the Camisard leader placed the seal of his unqualified disavowal upon the crime, and proved that, however much of excess and cruelty may have been committed in the name of the insurgents, the charge of the causeless murder of the innocent could not justly be laid at the door of the true guides of the movement.

It would have been well for humanity, not to say religion, had the leaders upon the opposite side shown any similar or adequate purpose to put an end to atrocities far more numerous, atrocities not less abominable by reason of the fact that the victims were for the most part obscure persons about whose deplorable fate neither rank and wealth, nor youth and beauty, threw an interest such as invested the end of Madame de Miraman.

The life of a Camisard chief was never lacking in romantic adventure. Twice within the compass of a fortnight, Cavalier and his band risked being surrounded and cut to pieces while in their favorite haunts in the strongly Protestant Vaunage. On the first occasion, at the village of Nages itself, which gives name to the district, the Camisards receiving but a brief warning of their danger, had barely time to draw off to a slight elevation, whence they dashed down with such irresistible fury upon their confident assailants that they drove them in flight quite into the plain of Calvisson. Here the intrepidity of the Protestant wives and daughters had a chance to display itself. Some thirty women, who had come to bring provisions to their brethren in arms, happened to be with Cavalier's band, and were forced to retreat with the braves to the neighboring height; with the braves they also fell upon the enemy. Inspired by a martial valor not a whit inferior to that

Adventurous warfare.

---

[1] The Memoirs of Cavalier (p. 231) assert the former, but Antoine Court had it on the testimony of eye-witnesses of the execution, that the latter was the case. Histoire des troubles des Cévennes, ii. 106.

of the men, they were foremost in the pursuit of the discomfited dragoons. Most of all did a young girl of seventeen years of age, Lucrèce Guignon, distinguish herself by prodigies of courage. With wild shouts of "The sword of the Lord and of Gideon," she stimulated the men to action, and, snatching their sabres from the relaxed grasp of the fallen cavaliers, she and her companions despatched the wounded but resisting, and bounded off in pursuit of the fleeing. It was not the only time in the course of the war when the sturdy women of the Cévennes or of the plains did effective service, and more than once prophetesses, like her who was known as *La Grande Marie*, left their bodies on the battle-field covered with honorable wounds. Cavalier had his full share of adventure. Returning from a brief reconnoissance before the engagement, he found himself cut off from his band by three of the enemy who had stealthily crept up a ravine. "You are Cavalier," exclaimed the nearest man advancing; "I know you. Surrender, for you cannot escape, and you shall have good quarter." "I shall do nothing of the kind," replied the unterrified Camisard, who, raising his gun, first shot his exulting assailant dead; then drawing his two pistols, successively slew the others, and opened the way for himself to rejoin his followers.[1]

At Vergèze, ten days later, Cavalier was in equal, if not in greater peril. Having entered this Protestant village in quest of provisions, with a band of barely eighty horsemen, he assembled the inhabitants for worship; and after the conclusion of the services was trying the case of a village mason who, contrary to the warning he had received, had helped the enemy in building a wall about the place. At this moment news came to him that he was surrounded on all sides by the dragoons of the Count of Fimarcon,[2] anxious to avenge themselves for their

---

[1] Court, who had before him the impartial and manifestly truthful diary of a Roman Catholic writing at Calvisson, corrects in his accounts of the affair of Nages (which occurred November 13, 1703) the gross misstatements and exaggerations of Brueys and La Baume, on the one side, and the errors of the anonymous author of the Histoire des Camisards and the Memoirs of Cavalier, on the other. See Histoire des troubles des Cévennes, ii. 91-95; Louvreleuil, ii. 143-145; Brueys, ii. 238; La Baume, 235; Cavalier, 183-187.

[2] Jacques de Cassagnet, Marquis de Fimarcon. Abbé Goiffon, Note to La Baume, 235.

recent disgraceful repulse. Now again the Cévenol chief's indomitable bravery stood him in good stead. Not waiting to be attacked by the overwhelming force that threatened him, he became himself the assailant, and throwing his little band with irresistible impetuosity upon the cavalry that formed the vanguard of the enemy, drove it back upon the infantry, which was following more leisurely. Then, making use of his advantage, he drew off rapidly, but in safety, to an olive-grove hard by, where the count feared to attack him, believing that the main body of the Camisard foot lay concealed within or behind it.[1]

And thus the year 1703 closed, leaving the insurrection no less formidable than it had been a twelvemonth before. It is true that the Higher Cévennes, which had afforded the malcontents so friendly a retreat, had been laid waste, the thriving villages and hamlets utterly destroyed, and the whole region rendered incapable of supplying from its stores the food and ammunition of which the Camisards often stood in urgent need. But the bands that had been driven out of the mountains had signally avenged themselves in the plains of Lower Languedoc, whose miserable condition, suffering at the hands of Camisards and Cadets de la Croix alike, was humorously, but not inaptly, likened to the plight of the unfortunate graybeard of the fable from whose head the younger wife plucked every white hair, while the elder pulled out every black one, and who between the two became in the end totally bald.[2]

And still the war went on. Of foreign intervention in behalf of the Protestants of Southern France there was as yet no sign. A few months earlier it had appeared probable that the allies, now at war with Louis the Fourteenth, might make a serious attempt to create a diversion from the German and Belgian frontier, by promoting an invasion of the Mediterranean provinces.[3] The sudden de-

Hopes of foreign intervention disappointed.

---

[1] Court, ii. 95, 101 ; La Baume, 237 ; Louvreleuil, ii. 160.

[2] Brueys, ii. 263.

[3] A French Protestant officer serving in the Prussian army with the rank of major, submitted to Queen Anne a plan for a descent upon the French coast at Cette, for which a force of not less than seven or eight thousand men would be needful, sufficient to maintain itself in the *plain*. A smaller body of troops, it is said, if compelled to take to the Cévennes, would perish of famine

fection of the Duke of Savoy, Victor Amadeus the Second, who, abandoning the French, made common cause with Germany, by signing the treaty of Turin with the emperor, on the twenty-fifth of October, 1703, raised new hopes in the breasts of the oppressed subjects of Louis ; but these hopes had as yet received no fulfilment, and were destined to disappointment. The adventurous duke, far from being able to make an inroad into Provence, was himself driven out of his ancestral possessions, before entering upon the course of prosperity that might ultimately have led him to the realization of his ambitious designs and to the acquisition of the regal dignity. Meanwhile the efforts of sympathizing friends in England and Holland came to nothing. In September, two suspicious persons had been arrested by the vigilant care of the government, the one at Montbrison, in Forêt, the other at Pont Saint Esprit. Both were Frenchmen by birth, but held commissions in the Dutch service, Peytau as captain, Jonquet as lieutenant. Taken to Alais and examined by the intendant Basville, they disclosed the fact that they had been instructed by the friends of the Camisards in Holland to obtain exact information respecting the condition of the insurgents, to promise them help in money and arms, to discover how far they might favor a descent upon the coast of Languedoc, and to promote the revolt in the neighboring districts of Vivarais and Dauphiny. At the same time, they were to urge the Camisards to desist from burning Roman Catholic churches and putting priests and others to death, and to base their movement simply upon their desire for the re-establishment of religious liberty, for places of worship, and for the diminution of oppressive taxation. The

---

after starving the poor mountaineers to death. In default of the requisite number of soldiers, it would be better to confine the help to money and arms alone. At the same time the writer recommends that a British fleet be sent to surprise Bordeaux, both as a diversion from the Cévennes and as a promising measure in itself. With Bordeaux in the possession of the queen's troops, it is "indubitable" that the entire provinces of Béarn, Languedoc, Poitou, and Saintonge, which are full of Protestants, not to speak of Guyenne itself, will rise in rebellion against the government of Louis XIV. The more than four hundred French officers who served England in the late war and are pensioners in Ireland would be of service in this enterprise. See Mémoire adressé à la reine Anne, etc., in Bulletin de la Soc. de l'hist. du Prot. franç., xxix. (1880) 307–316.

insurgents were to be pressed to refuse to accept any amnesty that might be offered to them. The life of Jonquet, who feebly consented to tell what he knew of the project, was spared in order that he might serve in the identification of the others who had entered France with similar designs. Peytau, from whom no admissions were wrung, save under the torture of the rack, was broken alive upon the wheel. Earnest remonstrances were made to the magistrates of Geneva against permitting Dutch officers to gather in their city with a view to entering the kingdom in the interest of the insurgents.[1]

A more vigorous attempt to widen the scene of the revolt toward the west of the Cévennes had also failed. Laurent Boeton, a Protestant of considerable power of organization, had set on foot a movement in Rouergue (the present department of Aveyron), and had promised Cavalier to act in conjunction with a small force of Camisards that was to be sent to him. Three of Cavalier's officers, men of some experience—Catinat, Dayre, and Pierrot—came with the Cévenols, and were conducted by Boeton to the mountainous range known as La Caune. Here they were to remain quiet for a few days, until at the appointed time a junction of forces should be effected. Boeton himself engaged to sally forth from the old town of Saint Affrique, whose brave defence by the Protestants against the Prince of Condé in the civil wars under Louis the Thirteenth, eighty years earlier, has been described in a previous chapter. But when, at the head of six hundred men, Boeton made his appearance on the spot previously agreed upon, he did not receive the expected support. On the very eve of the critical day, the Camisard leaders had been unable to restrain themselves, and entered, in higher Languedoc, upon a course of destruction similar to that in which they had been accustomed to indulge in the Cévennes. At the news of the ruin of churches by Huguenot hands, the province far and near arose; and, while the timid Bishop of Castres, fearful of what might occur, betook himself to some safer place of refuge, the nobles and burgess militia of Rouergue united and easily crushed the Camisards.[2]

Laurent Boeton in Rouergue.

---

[1] Brueys, ii. 208–213, who gives the fullest account; Louvreleuil, ii. 64, 65; La Baume, 194, 195. See also Court, ii. 61–66.

[2] "Le sieur Barbara, mon subdélégué à Castres, fut assez habile pour mettre

Catinat, whose destructive zeal caused the failure of the undertaking, made good his escape. Dayre was taken, and broken upon the wheel at Montpellier, displaying a firmness and contempt of suffering such as Camisards were wont to display, exciting the wonder of all beholders. Boeton, failing of the assistance upon which he had counted, retired into the mountains, seized the castle of Ferrières, and was able to secure from the respect, or the fear, of the enemy the most favorable of terms. He received amnesty for himself and for his followers.[1] He was destined later to engage in another and even less fortunate conspiracy, and to meet with a tragic death.

It is fitting that we should here turn aside from the immediate story of the Camisard uprising, to consider the experience of the Protestants of a neighboring city and district whose fortunes were somewhat intimately affected by the events recounted in the present chapter and in the chapter next preceding it.

The city and principality of Orange had been seized by Louis the Fourteenth in 1660, ostensibly for the purpose of keeping it in trust for its rightful owner. But the very Christian The fortunes of the principality of Orange. king, when he razed to their foundations the massive bastions reared by Prince Maurice, acted rather as absolute master than as a faithful administrator of the property

---

en vingt-quatre heures 8,000 hommes de milice sous les armes, qui tombèrent sur les attroupés, qui furent presque tous pris, tués ou pendus. Ce fut un service signalé qu'il rendit qui est resté sans récompense." Despatch of Basville to Chamillart, April 1, 1707, Bulletin de la Société de l'histoire du Prot. franç., xvi. (1867), 273.—Barbara will be remembered as the officer before whom Mascarene or Mascarenc was examined (C. W. Baird, The Huguenot Emigration to America, ii. 342, etc.). He is appropriately styled by D'Alquier de Montalivet "le grand inquisiteur du pays castrais." Bulletin de la Société, etc., xxiv. 46.

[1] Louvreleuil, ii. 92, 93 ; La Baume. 220, 221 ; Cavalier, 229 ; Court, ii. 43–46. The Abbé de la Bourlie, known as the Marquis of Guiscard, refers to the imprudent action of Catinat and his associates as one of the " unhappy mischances " that put it out of his power to execute his great projects (Mémoires du Marquis de Guiscard, dans lesquels est contenu le récit des entreprises qu'il a faites dans le roiaume de France, pour le recouvrement de la liberté de sa patrie, reprinted in Cimber et Danjou, Archives curieuses. 2de série, xi. 273–275). What those projects were, he states in great detail, even giving the text of manifestoes which he intended to issue but did not. There is little in his narrative which it would be safe to credit without corroboration from other sources. See the monograph of Jules Chavannes, " L'abbé de la Bourlie," in Bulletin de la Société de l'histoire du Prot. franç., xviii. (1869), 209, etc.

of another. By the terms of the Peace of Ryswick, on the twentieth of September, 1697, the principality was restored to the
Stadtholder William, now become King of England. The Protestants of Orange and of the three dependent towns of Courthezon, Jonquières, and Gigondas had more than once been
tried by the ordeal of fiery persecution. The horrors of the
sack of the city by Fabrizio Serbelloni, the cousin of Pius the
Fourth and papal general of Avignon, in 1562, during the
first civil war under Charles the Ninth, were remarked as exceptional even in an age well accustomed to the practice of inhumanity.[1] Less atrocious, yet scarcely less harrowing, were the
incidents of the extension of the Dragonnades to the principality in 1685. Such of the Protestants as had not at that time
found a refuge in foreign lands now breathed freely when, as I
have said, Orange once more came into the possession of its
rightful owner. The public exercises of the Reformed worship
were resumed. The four Protestant pastors, after a rigorous
imprisonment of twelve years and one month, were restored to
their jubilant flocks. These brave men had first been threatened
with death if they declined to apostatize. One of their number
was distinctly told by Count de Tessé that he should be hung on
the gallows the next day. Remaining constant, they were confined in the jails of Orange and then during long and dreary
years in the dreaded Pierre-Encise. There their pious fortitude
made them the object of the admiration of all honest men of
both faiths. Of this they had the proof when released. Their
brief stay at Lyons was almost a continual ovation. The royal
commandant not only invited them to dine with him and treated
them "magnificently," but apologized to them for the treatment they had received. At Orange hundreds of their parishioners awaited them on the banks of the Rhone, and escorted
them into the city with the discharge of musketry and loud
cries of "Long life to the king and to our dear pastors!"[2] At

---

[1] See Rise of the Huguenots, ii. 48, 49.

[2] "Les Larmes de Jacques Pineton de Chambrun (Ed. of 1854), 104, 105.
The letter of the four pastors—Gondrand, Aunet, Chion, and Petit, names worthy of perpetual remembrance—written, after their return to Orange, to Pielat,
pastor of the Walloon church of Rotterdam (ibid., appendix, 260–264), affords
an interesting view of the welcome extended to them both by Protestants and
by Roman Catholics.

once great numbers of Huguenots, the new converts of the nearest provinces—Languedoc, Dauphiny, Provence, the Comtat Venaissin—men and women famishing for the preaching of the word of God, of which they had long been deprived, flocked to the temples of Orange. Great was the scandal of the clergy, great was the rage of Louis. Prompt measures were taken to put an end to the pious pilgrimage. Two " declarations " were issued from Versailles in quick succession. By the first of these, published scarcely two months after the cession of the principality, all Frenchmen that might have taken up their abode in Orange were warned to return, and all others were warned not to go there to live, on the pain of imprisonment and confiscation of property. To attend any Protestant worship, to be married or to send children to be baptized by Protestant ministers, or to be taught by them, was a crime to be punished with death.[1] The second law prescribed that, while new converts might freely go to Orange for purposes of trade, they must first provide themselves with a written permission from the royal governors or intendants of the province they left, and again from the officials of the nearest province to the principality, setting forth the precise object of their visit. For a neglect to observe this formality the men made themselves liable to be sent to the galleys for life, the women to five years' imprisonment and a fine of three thousand livres. The judges were expressly deprived of the power to moderate or remit the penalty.[2]

Savage laws against Protestants frequenting Orange for worship.

How far did these stringent measures check the current that had set in toward the Protestant places of worship in Orange? The extant records of the office of the intendant of Languedoc, at Montpellier, enable us to answer the question. During four months and a half alone, in the single year 1698, not less than one hundred and one men were condemned for this offence to the galleys for life, while thirty-three women were condemned

---

[1] Déclaration du Roy du 23 Novembre 1697 portant défenses à ses sujets de s'établir à Orange et d'y faire exercice de la R. P. R. Édits, Déclarations et Arrests (ed. Paris, 1885), 363–365.

[2] Déclaration du Roy du 13 Janvier 1698 sur ce qui doit être observé par les nouveaux convertis qui iront à Orange pour leur commerce. Ibid., 366–368.

to be immured in prison for five years and to pay the fine imposed.[1] The arrests were made, for the most part, by a special body of guards instituted for the sole purpose of watching the borders of the principality, and supported at the expense of the new converts.[2] It must be confessed that they did efficient service.

On the eighth of March, 1702, William of Orange died. At once the Prince of Conty asserted his claim to the principality of Orange. A few months later, he ceded his rights to Louis the Fourteenth, for valuable considerations; and the latter prepared to take possession, not in the name of another but in his own name. To this act he was incited not merely by the ordinary desire of extending his dominions, but by the persuasion that the existence of the independent principality so near at hand both encouraged the Protestants of Languedoc to cling to their ancient faith, and tended to protract the Camisard struggle. Not only did the adherents of the Reformed religion, throughout a wide district, continue to defy the monarch's commands and to resort from time to time, braving every difficulty and danger, to the Protestant temples in Orange; but they were accused, whether truthfully or not, of ministering aid and comfort underhand to the bands that held the field in the interest of religious liberty. It was matter of common notoriety that no inconsiderable part of the gunpowder, which the Camisards found it so difficult either to purchase from abroad or to manufacture for themselves, was obtained from smugglers that bought it in from Orange.[3] Most influential, however, was, doubtless, the motive supplied by the zeal felt by Louis to remove the blot of heresy from a point situated within his own domains, and to merit more fully the pæans sung in honor of the triumph which he had once before effected for the Roman Catholic faith in Orange.

The Count de Grignan, governor of Provence, was despatched with an army to take possession of the principality. On the

Death of William of Orange.

---

[1] Paper of P. Corbière, in the Bulletin de la Soc. de l'hist. du Prot. franç., xii. (1863), 233, 234.

[2] Ibid., ubi supra.

[3] Court, i. 145.

day of his arrival—the twenty-eighth of March, 1703—the Protestant " temples " were closed by order of the king, and all exercises of Protestant worship were forbidden on pain of death to the ministers that should conduct them. The fear entertained of a repetition of the barbarities of the Dragonnades happily proved to be unfounded. A proclamation, made at the sound of the trumpet, on the public squares of Orange and Courthezon, permitted all the Protestant inhabitants to dispose by sale of their lands and houses, as well as of such furniture as they could not take with them, and to follow their pastors into foreign lands.

The principality again occupied by the French.

Emigration of the Protestants.

Such clemency from a king who elsewhere in his dominions was relentlessly enforcing conformity to the established church and sending to the galleys any that were caught attempting to escape from the kingdom, can be explained only by the desire of the Prince of Conty to conciliate his new subjects in the principality of Neuchâtel, recently claimed by him, and by the intercession which he consequently made to Louis in behalf of the domain which he had just renounced. It is needless to relate the difficulties encountered by the Huguenots of Orange in their attempt to avail themselves of the permission received, or to detail the hardships endured in their escape from the kingdom. The women and children, who went first and took the more direct road to Switzerland, fared much worse than the rest, and scarcely anticipated, in point of time, the men, who remained longer to complete the arrangement of their affairs and were allowed to go no other way than by a circuitous route through the city of Nice and the duchy of Savoy. So far from refusing them a passage, the Duke of Savoy gave peremptory orders that these travellers should be treated with kindness. The Governor of Nice courteously entertained at his own table such Protestant members of the nobility or gentry as were of the company ; and the English consul distributed among the poor no inconsiderable sum of money. The

Hospitality of the Duke of Savoy and the Swiss.

hospitality of Geneva was as unstinted as it had been on so many occasions during the two preceding centuries. Private citizens vied with each other, in charitable rivalry, for the honor and expense of bringing to their own houses and tables the outcasts of Orange. The plain artisan or mechanic insisted upon having his share in the generous work.[1] The deputies of the four cantons of Zurich, Berne, Basle, and Schaffhausen, meeting in extraordinary session at Arau, took upon them the support of a part of the refugees until the coming spring. The King of Prussia, to whose pressing letters to the Duke of Savoy the exiles had been in great part indebted for their kind recep-

Generosity of Prussia and England. tion south of the Alps, and who had made a prompt remittance of money to assist the ministers driven out of Orange, distinguished himself by his subsequent exertions in behalf of these sufferers for their faith. The English people, never behindhand where the interests of continental Protestantism are concerned, made a noble response to the letters patent of Queen Anne (Westminster, the eleventh of November, 1703), enjoining a general collection throughout the churches of the realm in behalf of the exiles for conscience' sake.

The blow which Louis the Fourteeth had struck, nearly a score of years before, at the prosperity of France entire, he had now aimed with effect at a single community. As it is, for the most part, easier to measure results upon a small than upon an extended field of action, it may be worth while to take account of the material loss suffered by Orange and its dependent

Decadence of Orange. towns. The houses and lands were left, as well as much of such personal property as could not be readily removed; but the city lost a great part, probably the greater part, of its most industrious classes. Out of a population possibly numbering eight or nine thousand souls, three thousand or more emigrated. Among these a well-informed contemporary writer counted up by name fifteen hundred and forty with whose means and social standing he was acquainted. They included six hundred and ninety-three persons subsisting upon the revenues of their offices or upon the income of their property;[2] and eight hundred and forty-seven who supported themselves

---

[1] "Comme ou commença à les loger chez les magistrats, les ministres et les professeurs, le petit peuple, craignant d'être privé de cette consolation, en forma des plaintes et voulut avoir part à la générosité publique."

[2] Officers of the garrison, of the parliament, of the bureau of domains and finances; pastors and elders of the churches, women of quality, lawyers, physicians, notaries or their widows, burgesses, merchants, with their families.

by their trades.[1] He professed his ability to mention a number almost equal to this aggregate, composed of persons without property of any kind, men and women servants, peasants, orphans, invalids of all ages, as well as a number of refugees from neighboring provinces who had obtained the favor of being permitted to leave the kingdom. To these he would add a few persons that he had seen arrive since he completed his list, persons who had not been able to bring themselves to embrace the Roman Catholic religion, but of whom he knew neither the names nor the social standing.[2]

If the true wealth of a nation or of a community is best gauged by the number of its virtuous, intelligent, and laborious citizens, there can be little doubt that, in the expatriation of the Protestants, Orange incurred a disastrous loss, from which it is not astonishing that she has not even now fully recovered, after the expiration of nearly two centuries.

During the opening months of the year 1704 there seems to have reigned an ignoble rivalry between Cévenol and royalist in the infliction of causeless misery. The soldiers commanded by officers holding a regular commission from Louis the Fourteenth held the slightest disobedience a sufficient excuse for the massacre of inoffensive subjects, and made no discrimination of age or sex. The Count of Tournon, colonel of a regiment stationed in the higher Cévennes, repeatedly sent out detachments to traverse the burnt and depopulated region and see to it that none of the former Protestant inhabitants lurked in the houses of Roman Catholics which had been spared. On one of these occasions, forty of the miserable outcasts were discovered in the neighborhood of Saint Julien d'Arpaon. All succeeded in making good their escape, with the

Cruel excesses of the combatants.

---

[1] Tailors or seamstresses, hatters, shoemakers, silk and wool carders, laborers, bakers, weavers, masons, manufacturers of stockings, blacksmiths, tanners, coopers, lace-makers, etc.

[2] I have followed in my account of this interesting episode the monograph of M. Gaitte, "L'émigration des Protestants de la principauté d'Orange sous Louis XIV," in the Bulletin de la Société de l'histoire du Prot. franç., xix. 337-353. This valuable paper is chiefly based upon the very rare work of one of the pastors of Orange, Jean Convenent, who was subsequently settled as pastor in London: "Histoire abrégée des dernières révolutions arrivées dans la principauté d'Orange," London, 1704.

exception of a few old women whom age or infirmity prevented from following the example of the rest. " Our soldiers," quietly observes the clerical chronicler who relates the transaction, " killed them, and carried off several pots, caldrons, and other articles used in cooking." [1] With such examples before their eyes, the Cadets de la Croix entered upon an ever widening career of bloodshed and plunder. Not content with confounding unarmed Protestants and armed combatants, they were not always careful to distinguish between the adherents of the two opposed religious creeds, when there was a prospect of rich booty. So many quiet and blameless peasants of the Reformed faith were savagely butchered by two or three of the most notorious of the Roman Catholic freebooting companies, that Cavalier is said to have sent this short but pointed note of warning to the governor of the city of Nismes :

" Monseigneur, I write to your excellence to tell you that unless the Hermit, Florimond, and Lefèvre cease from killing our brethren, I shall use the arms of the Lord to exterminate the Catholics and shall go and burn your mills. I am your affectionate servant,   JEAN CAVALIER." [2]

Sometimes a fortunate capture was put to good use by the Camisards. When Castanet's wife, the pretended " Princess of the Cévennes," the *Mariette* over whose nuptials the chroniclers make merry, fell into the hands of the royal troops, the husband deemed himself happy in taking prisoner a lady of gentle blood belonging to the town of Valleraugue, and managed so well as to secure an exchange of the two.[3] And when in February, 1704, the sister of Lefèvre, one of the most unscrupulous of the captains of the burgess militia, or the Cadets de la Croix, was taken prisoner, Cavalier himself made bold to write to Lefèvre, and inform him that she would never be restored to him until the release had been effected of the prophetess known as *La Grande Marie*, then lying in the dungeons of Uzès.[4]

---

[1] Louvreleuil, ii. 195.
[2] La Baume, 249; Louvreleuil, ii. 200.
[3] Louvreleuil, ii. 146; Court, ii. 124.
[4] Letter of Cavalier dated " Au Désert, ce 10 février 1704," in Bulletin, etc.,

And thus it was that, by way of reprisal, the Camisards deemed themselves justified in exercising signal vengeance upon the Roman Catholics of Languedoc. Whoever will take the pains to peruse the chronicles of La Baume, Louvreleuil, and Brueys will find a sickening catalogue of their alleged misdeeds, given with minute particularity and with every trait calculated to enhance the feeling of abhorrence for the perpetrators—from the murder of the priest shot at the moment when he is quietly engaged in reading his breviary, to that of the shepherd whom they killed within a stone-throw of the city of Nismes. He must indeed be ill-read in these partial chroniclers who has not discovered that he must accept the accounts with much suspicion. If he be at a loss to determine the precise amount of truth that enters into their stories, he will at least infer, from the spirit of exaggeration that pervades their narratives of matters of such common notoriety as the issue of battles and the numbers slain on either side, that they or their informants have given quite as free a rein to their imagination in recording Camisard excesses. Most of all will he have reason to believe that they have taken the liberty to suppress those circumstances that might essentially modify, or possibly reverse, the judgment of history upon the events as they are stated. The Camisards have unfortunately left us no written contemporary apology, or connected register of events, containing documentary evidence that would serve to substantiate or refute the assertions of their antagonists. Were it otherwise, it is not improbable that it might appear that the ecclesiastic killed while at his private devotions was a less conspicuous fellow disciple with the Abbé du Chayla in the same school of persecution, or that the shepherd had added to his more innocent pursuits the functions of a spy upon the movements of the Cévenol bands. In the absence of the fuller knowledge that would be desirable, however, we are compelled to accept the accounts of the Roman Catholic narrators as presumably based upon fact, while making no little reservation of our faith in particular cases, not so

---

ix. (1860), 79. **M. J. P.** Hugues, to whom we are indebted for the discovery of this and two other curious letters of the Camisard leader, failed to recognize under the old spelling " Lefebure " the name of a redoubtable partisan officer who gained an unenviable notoriety by his pitiless warfare.

much because of a wilful purpose on their part to mislead, as because they wrote with a bias that dethrones Justice and places Prejudice in her seat.   For it may be affirmed with confidence that the very narratives of their enemies betray the fact that the occasional barbarities of the Camisards did not compare in atrocity with the systematic cruelty practised by the Camisards Blancs or the Cadets de la Croix, if not by the orders, yet with the connivance of the government.   Thus Louvreleuil tells us that these ardent defenders of the faith made it a practice to stop travellers upon the highways, and, in order to learn whether they were Roman Catholics, compelled them to say in Latin the Lord's Prayer, the Hail Mary, the Apostles' Creed, and the General Confession.   It was a perilous test; for those who could not repeat them were put to the edge of the sword.[1] The Cadets had the boldness to stop the noble Abbot of Saint Gilles upon the road and demand the surrender of one of his servants, who was a Protestant.   It was in vain that the indignant ecclesiastic replied that they ought not to put such an affront upon a man of his birth and station.   The Cadets were resolved to kill the new convert, and it was only by throwing his arms about the man and holding him tightly in his embrace that the abbot contrived to save his life.[2]   One band, the judge of the presidial court of Nismes informs us, ravaged all the property belonging to the Protestants between that city and Beaucaire, killing here a woman and two children, there an old man of eighty, at another place a young girl, a number of persons elsewhere, and carrying off the flocks and burning the houses and barns.   Another band did the same near Bagnols and Uzès "killing, burning, pillaging everywhere."[3]   So rich a field for plunder invited the covetous from outside of Languedoc, and for a short time the Roman Catholics of Provence crossed the Rhone to take part in the predatory work.[4]

---

[1] "Ils arrêtoient les voyageurs dans les grands chemins.   Pour connoître s'ils étoient catholiques, ils les contraignoient à dire en Latin *l'Oraison Dominicale, la Salutation Angélique, le Symbole de la Foy, et la Confession Générale.   Ceux qui ne sçavoient pas ces Prières publiques passoient par le fil de leurs épées.*" Le fanatisme renouvelé, iii. 3, 4.

[2] Ib., iii. 36, 37.   [3] La Baume, 263.

[4] "Il vint même des catholiques de Provence qui se joignirent à eux ; mais ces derniers se retirèrent peu de tems après." La Baume, ubi supra.

Instead of putting an end to these outrages by compelling the Cadets de la Croix to disband, the royal government roughly treated the Protestants of Nismes who came to pray for an abatement of the insults to which they were daily exposed. When Albenas and Restauran, at the head of a deputation of the chief men of the Reformed faith, proffered their help in putting down the insurrection, and asked permission to set on foot an armed band to go out and fight the Camisards, Marshal Montrevel very curtly denied their request, not concealing his want of confidence in their loyalty.[1] He declared that he was only surprised that the patience of the Roman Catholics had held out so long. Now that they had gotten the upper hand, he could not restrain them from action. The petitioners, he went on to tell them, had no need of arms; what they really wanted was a good will that should prompt them to go and find their brethren the Camisards and induce them to lay down their weapons. After that was done, all of them ought to come together, with the halter about their necks, suing for mercy. In that case, he would exert himself to obtain pardon for them, should they deserve it by their loyalty. But if they persisted in their evil ways, they would find that the candle would burn at both ends. There was no disaster for which they might not look.[2] It is true that at the same time the marshal issued a proclamation which strictly forbade any bands from taking the field save under captains appointed by him, and which ordered the restitution of all plundered property to its rightful owners.[3] But the document did not put an end to the evil; nor did the few and inadequate punishments inflicted.

The desultory warfare in the course of which the Camisards approached so near Anduze as to burn the mills that stood about it, and to threaten the surburbs of Nismes, was succeeded, on the fifteenth of March, by the most signal advantage won by the insurgents in the course of their contest.

Cavalier's success at Les Devois de Martignargues.

---

[1] Louvreleuil, iii. 7, gives the Protestant petition. He admits that the marshal answered them "fièrement." Ib., iii. 5.

[2] Louvreleuil, iii. 4, 5 ; La Baume, 264, 265.

[3] Ordonnance de Nicolas de la Baume Montrevel, Maréchal de France, etc., Nismes le onzième Mars 1704. Louvreleuil, iii. 8–12. See La Baume, 265, 266.

Learning that a large force of Camisards had assembled in the neighborhood of the village of Saint Chaptes, Marshal Montrevel, who had just reached Uzès, despatched a body of troops in quest of them. The soldiers consisted of five or six hundred picked men of the marines and of some dragoons of the regiment of Saint Sernin. They were under the command of La Jonquière. This self-confident officer ardently longed for an opportunity to distinguish himself by crushing the mountaineers,[1] and, in his assurance of victory, had dismissed, as unnecessary, an additional company of cavalry which the marshal had ordered to follow him in case La Jonquière desired to have it. The presumptuous leader wished to have all the glory of his approaching victory.

Not finding the Camisards at Saint Chaptes, La Jonquière passed on to Moussac. The enemy was leaving the place, on the one side, as he entered it from the other. Hence, after a night given to plunder and revelry, the Roman Catholic soldiers, laden with their booty, advanced northward over the tongue of land that stretches between the Gardon and the smaller stream of the Droude, through Bignon and Cruviers to Lascours. Here La Jonquière inquired of the inhabitants respecting the whereabouts of the Camisards, and having received the reply that they had not seen them, indulged his troops, by way of diversion, with the permission to shoot some of the villagers, among them a married woman and two young girls. They were *believed*, we are told, to be prophetesses. The fourth person, a man, was *suspected* of being a rebel.[2] It went hard in these times with any person, especially any Protestant, who could not prove his innocence. All the presumptions were reckoned against him. With fresh plunder and inflamed by new potations, the soldiers had not gone much farther when they came upon the enemy.

Cavalier was in command of the Camisards. He had carefully selected for the scene of the encounter a wild spot somewhat south of the hamlet of Martignargues, and therefore

---

[1] "M. de la Jonquière, qui souhaitoit cet emploi avec passion," says La Baume.

[2] "On y tua même une femme et deux filles qu'on crût être des prophetesses, avec un homme qu'on prit pour un des rebelles." Louvreleuil, iii. 18.

known by the inhabitants of the region in their dialect as *Les Devis*, or *Devois de Martignargues*.[1] His main force was drawn in line on rising ground, with a ravine in front. Beyond this and toward his left he had posted a small body of thirty horse, while on the right he had in like manner thrown forward a corps of sixty picked footmen. Both of these detachments were concealed from sight—the former by a thick undergrowth of bushes, the latter by their position, for every man had been ordered to lie at full length on the ground. The Camisard chief improved the time, while awaiting the enemy's appearance, by offering a prayer at the head of his troops, invoking the help of the God of battles, and then addressed his followers a few words of exhortation to a courageous struggle for the defence of liberty and religion.

La Jonquière had sufficient warning to advance cautiously. A more experienced, or more prudent, subaltern who rode forward to reconnoitre brought him back word that it was likely that Cavalier was holding in reserve some portion of his forces, and suggested that the Roman Catholics should follow similar tactics. La Jonquière, however, had attained the goal of his desires, in coming up with the rebels. He had feared that they would elude his pursuit. Therefore, having no thought but of engaging them as soon as possible, he plunged recklessly into the net spread for him. As he came in sight, the Camisards of the main body, whom alone he detected, were kneeling upon one knee, and held their muskets aimed. They had been ordered not to fire until the enemy should have sent his first volley. "Courage! my boys," exclaimed the royal officer, "here at last are those wretches of whom we have so long been in quest." Hurriedly advancing, he gave the word to fire. The shots of the marines did no execution, for the Camisards were out of range. La Jonquière, apparently believing that, on the contrary, he had slain or disabled many of the enemy, gave the command to charge with the bayonet. That moment the Camisards delivered a well-directed and deadly discharge. Then, not waiting to reckon the damage they had inflicted, they rushed forward,

---

[1] M. Charles Dardier explains the word *Devois* by "*Devia*, lieu écarté, désert."

crossing the brook at their feet, to encounter the reeling body
of the royal troops. Now it was that the Camisard cavalry revealed itself, and poured, through the thicket upon the left, a
destructive fire. Now it was that Cavalier's faithful lieutenant, Ravanel, and his men in ambush upon the other wing
rose suddenly to their feet and dashed upon the flank of the astonished soldiers, loudly singing those ancestral psalms of the
Huguenots, every verse of which sounded a knell of destruction
to the appalled hearers. A sudden terror seized the troops,
when they found themselves thus surrounded, and all turned
in headlong flight. Among the officers there were many that
displayed courage and strove to stop the disgraceful rout; but
neither threats nor entreaties availed. The dragoons were
conspicuous for their pusillanimity. The marines scarcely did
better. With loud cries of "We are lost!" and closely pursued
by the Camisards, who spared no one that fell into their hands,
the fugitives threw away their arms, and everything that could
impede their steps, even to the thick *justaucorps* with which
they were provided as with a means of defence. A few, but
only a few, made good their escape. Some dragoons swam across
the Gardon and reached Boucoiran. Fifty marines succeeded
in making their way in the opposite direction to Saint Césaire;
a hundred or more gained the woods near Uzès. It was told
with horror that one poor fugitive, entering the first door he
found open in the village of Saint Maurice, and throwing himself at the feet of the woman of the house, was pitilessly beaten
to death while craving mercy at her hands. In all it was said
that only four officers and one hundred and eighty men escaped, and these without arms of any kind and scarcely half-
clad. La Jonquière was of the number. Stopped in his flight
by a wall, he abandoned the handsome steed with which he
rode into battle, but was fortunate enough to find on the other
side a horse that had lost its rider. On this he reached Boucoiran. By his headstrong folly and lack of military skill he
had lost twenty-five officers, all of them men of good families,
and a number of soldiers variously estimated at between three
and six hundred men. Cavalier obtained this brilliant success
without the loss of a single man killed and with but a dozen
men wounded. His little army picked up upon the field not less

than four hundred muskets, and his followers supplied themselves with all the pistols, swords, and bayonets which they needed. Their leader secured a number of horses for his cavalry. The charger of La Jonquière fell to Cavalier's own share.[1]

The defeat of Martignargues is said to have caused, or hastened, the recall of the Marshal of Montrevel. Justly or unjustly, it was reckoned his blunder that he had sent against Cavalier a portion of the troops at his disposal, instead of going in person with an overwhelming force.[2] Certainly if the general, during the full year that he had conducted military operations against the Camisards, had succeeded so poorly that the latter might, at its conclusion, be said with truth to be stronger and more defiant than at its commencement, he had made for himself an uncommonly large number of enemies, among Roman Catholics as well as among Protestants. We have seen that his severity, amounting to a savage thirst for blood, aroused the indignant protests of sensible and humane men of both religions. Even the intendant of Languedoc, a man rarely credited with feeling, recoiled from the lengths of persecution to which the marshal was disposed to go, and Louis the Fourteenth could not bring himself to sanction so sanguinary a policy. It is not impossible that the monarch's weariness or disgust at being so frequently reminded of the only plan of which the marshal's mind was capacious enough to conceive, contributed to the celerity of Montrevel's overthrow. For even in his last letter to his Majesty, written on the eve of the engagement of Martignargues, he again called up the savage project which Basville stigmatized as perilously near another Saint Bartholomew's-Day massacre,[3] and ventured to censure the king's scruples as a weakness that had protracted the war against the

(side note) Recall of Marshal Montrevel.

---

[1] See the Memoirs of Cavalier, 223-225 ; La Baume, 272-277 ; Louvreleuil, iii. 17-22 ; Brueys, ii. 257-260 ; Rossel d'Aigaliers 34 ; Court, ii. 221-227.

[2] Brueys, ii. 257, 258.

[3] "Lorsque je lui demande par quel moyen il veut apaiser ce mouvement et mettre fin à tant de maux, il m'assure toujours qu'il est impossible de le voir finir avant la paix, ou il propose de si étranges extrémités, *qu'elles approchent fort de la Saint-Barthélemy.*" Confidential letter of Basville to the minister of war, April 1, 1704. MSS. Archives of minister of war, vol. 1796, fol. 103, printed in M. Charles Dardier's reply to M. Tallon, entitled Encore les Camisards (Geneva, 1890), 9, 10.

Camisards. Referring to the critical moment when the declaration by the Duke of Savoy of his purpose to espouse the side of the powers allied against France raised up a new war and called the troops in Languedoc in another direction, Montrevel allowed himself to say: "The fanatics were scattered, the inhabitants [of the Cévennes] were ruined, and it was easy to exterminate them in their flight by an illustrious example of the punishment of the unruly, if your Majesty had not preferred to resort to clemency. Your Majesty believed that the spirit of revolt had been stifled by the dispersion of the rebels. But these wretches, taking advantage of the new diversion excited for your arms, have assumed new strength, and their fury but too strongly confirms what I had the honor to show your Majesty respecting the conjuncture of this revolt, against the opinion of those who at first despised it."[1]

It was, however, not so much the marshal's brutal policy as his failure to accomplish the end for which he had been sent to Languedoc that compassed his downfall. This failure was due in no small degree to an inordinate love of pleasure that led him to neglect the pursuits of Mars for the worship of Venus. Complaints were openly made of the disastrous consequences of his gallantries, and the archives of the war department still testify to the number of anonymous letters which the ministry received, setting forth in terms more forcible than polite the miserable state of Languedoc. While the general was at home enjoying his ease, the inferior officers, it was said, took good care not to find the rebels, lest there being no more Camisards left to fight, they should be compelled to return to harder service in Flanders and Germany. Hence it was that the insurgents were suffered to come and burn houses, even at the very gates of places where there was an abundant supply of troops that declined to sally forth and meet them. Hence it was that, when forced to go in quest of the miscreants,

His gallan-tries and negligence.

---

[1] Marshal Montrevel to the king, Quissac, February 14, 1704, in Louvreleuil, iii. 12–15; and Court, ii. 228–230. There is an error in the place or in the date of March 14, assigned by Louvreleuil to this remarkable letter, since the marshal could not have been elsewhere than at Uzès, on the eve of the engagement at Martignargues, which occurred March 15, according to Court, and, apparently, March 14, according to La Baume's narrative.

the officers never took the direct road pointed out by their guides, but either went astray or came up too late to be of any service. They were even accused of sometimes purposely making a loud noise in order that the Camisards might give them a wide berth.[1] Meanwhile, Montrevel at Montpellier, at Alais, and wherever he went, was engaged, as though it were his most important duty in life, in making love to the ladies of the province. In his mad desire to please his principal mistress there was no end of his expenditures, all wrung from the inhabitants of an impoverished province. One hundred thousand livres had gone for one purpose, another hundred thousand for another. Houses were torn down and rebuilt at the public expense. The finest edifice in Montpellier, in which princes had formerly dwelt, was not sufficiently stately, but must be remodelled and beautified for the accommodation of its present fair occupant.[2] The very troops murmured at the ignoble uses to which they were put, and complained that when they should have been employed in the king's service they were escorting from place to place the favorite of the marshal.[3]

His profusion.

Evidently the province was well rid of so cruel, lustful, and extravagant a taskmaster. Meantime, however, fortune smiled upon the attempt which he made to render his exit from office somewhat more glorious than the previous twelvemonth of his command had been.

---

[1] "Lorsqu'ils vont en détachement ils ont tousiours quelque raison pour ne passer pas par le même chemin que les guides veulent, soit pour allonger soit pour éviter les Camisards ; ou ils font du bruit pour estre entendus de loin." Anonymous letter to Chamillart, August, 1703.

[2] Alais, as well as Montpellier, received marks of the marshal's profuse expenditure of money. The fine walk in front of the old castle, now used as a prison, from which an extensive view is obtained of the valley of the Gardon and the range of the Cévennes, still bears the name of *La promenade de la Maréchale,* because made while Marshal Montrevel commanded the troops sent against the Camisards. P. Joanne, Les Cévennes, 33. It is the same work that is referred to by Court, ii. 231, as "une belle terrasse à Alais."

[3] "Cant on veut dire quelque chose aux officiers : ' Que fetes vous au Sévenes ? ' —'Nous servons de macareau au maréchal, de dupe à l'intendant.' " Anonymous letter to Chamillart, from Montpellier, September 16, 1703. The three epistles, perhaps purposely misspelt, drawn from the archives of the ministry of war, which M. Charles Dardier has inserted in his monograph, Le maréchal de Montrevel (Nismes, 1889), are both interesting and important.

Cavalier's victory at Martignargues had considerably increased the numbers of his band, which now amounted to one thousand foot and two hundred horse. Disdaining secrecy, his men now marched to the sound of the drum and fife, and after partially successful assaults upon Boucoiran and Saint Géniés, made their appearance at Caveyrac, a few miles distant from Nismes. But in the midst of their fancied prosperity, a deadly blow was in preparation for them. A month had passed and the marshal's successor was already appointed and upon his way to assume control of the troops in Languedoc. Montrevel had withdrawn to Sommières, giving out that he was to start on the sixteenth of April for Montpellier, and proceed to Guyenne, where the king had ordered him to replace Marshal Rozel. In order further to increase the false security which the intelligence of his prospective departure had created in the mind of the Camisards, he sedulously spread a rumor that the troops garrisoned at Nismes were to march to meet the new commander who was descending the Rhone and might soon be expected at Pont Saint Esprit. Meanwhile he had in reality arranged that all the forces at hand should concentrate upon the

He surrounds and surprises Cavalier.

unfortunate Cavalier. The latter, far from suspecting his imminent danger, was meditating to take advantage of the departure of the leading general to make a new and formidable move in the Vaunage. The ruse was eminently successful. Montrevel, tardily aroused to the necessity of vindicating his military honor, did not commit his troops to subordinate officers, but took the field in person. Scarcely had he left Sommières before he abandoned the road to Montpellier, and wheeled suddenly in the opposite direction. Reaching Clarensac after a rapid march, he deployed his forces on the heights of Montpezat and Saint Cosme, and extended his lines eastward to Caveyrac and then southward, with the view of completely enveloping the enemy. His manœuvre was supported by Grandval, with soldiers from Lunel, on the south, and by Courten, on the east, with all the dragoons and Swiss that could be spared from the garrison of Nismes. Grandval starting promptly from Lunel and taking a more direct course, was the first to attack Cavalier, whom he found with his band in the considerable depression between the villages of Boissières, Saint Dionysy, and Nages. Although surprised by the dragoons, the Camisards went out boldly to meet them and forced them to fall back, pursuing them sharply until they reached the infantry that was following them at a considerable distance. Over these, too,'they hoped to have as easy a victory as they had had a month before over the marines at Martignargues. In this they were disappointed. The battalion of the Charolais regiment received their fire without being disconcerted, and, returning it, inflicted quite as much injury as they themselves had experienced. It was necessary for the Camisards to retreat, and this they did with little or no molestation until they reached the spot from which they had started. Meanwhile, guided by the sound of the discharges of fire-arms, the marshal had attained the top of the opposite heights, from which, looking down, he saw that the Camisards were so hemmed in on all sides that the road toward Nages furnished the only means of escape. This he at once despatched his entire force of infantry under command of Menon to seize. The movement was unseen by the Camisards below in the vale. When this was effected, Montrevel signalled Grandval to advance, while he himself fell upon the enemy sword in hand. The insurgents received both assaults with even more than their wonted courage. According to the admission of their opponents, they fought with the fury of madmen and nowhere showed any signs of weakness. But they were confronted with greatly superior numbers, and the royal troops were led by an experienced general, who, having thrown off his disgraceful sloth, was resolved to show that he had not altogether forgotten the bravery that once won him military distinction. Unable to resist the overwhelming weight of numbers, Cavalier tried the road to Nages, only to find it in the possession of a force which all his efforts proved powerless to dislodge. He turned to the heights above the place, hoping thence to find an easier escape in the direction of the woods that had often in the past furnished him a safe refuge. There too the enemy had anticipated him. Nothing remained for the Camisards but to break up into small companies and to seek, with the desperation that flies into the very jaws of death, to purchase the escape of a part of the braves at the expense of the lives of those that must fall by the way. This course was favored by the nature of the ground, full of hollows, intersected by ditches, and broken up by loosely built stone walls that rendered pursuit difficult. The struggle of man with man was long and severe. When ammunition gave out, the Camisards fought with stones. Cavalier narrowly escaped death, and owed his deliverance, if we may credit his memoirs, to the intrepidity of his youngest brother, a boy of scarcely ten years of age, who, mounted on a little horse of the breed raised on the marshes of the Île de la Camargue, and armed with weapons of a diminutive size adapted to his youth, shared the chieftain's flight as he had shared the perils of the engagement. Seeing the men disposed to press forward forgetful of their captain, who was far in the rear, the stripling stopped them pistol in hand at the crossing of a bridge over a small stream, and ordered them to stand along the brink to facilitate his brother's passage. Be this as it may, it was only after hard work and at the cost of one-third, if not of one-half, of his entire force that Cavalier extricated himself from the toils of the enemy and found a temporary refuge in the woods of Puéchredon. On the disastrous field of Nages he had lost, as he truthfully acknowledged, a greater number of men than in any previous contest.[1]

Marshal Montrevel returned to Sommières and the next day departed for Guyenne. "This is the way," he said, " that I take leave of my friends."

Disheartening as was the reverse sustained by Cavalier and his followers at Nages, it was scarcely as disastrous in its bearing upon the fortunes of the war as was a discovery, made

---

[1] La Baume (289, 290) contains one of the clearest accounts of the Camisard defeat. It is supplemented and made more vivid by Bonbonnoux (Mémoires, ed. Vielles, 29–32), who participated in the action, but gives a better notion of the character of the rout than of the engagement that preceded it. In reading Cavalier's Memoirs (252–257) one is, as usual, at a loss how much of the account to credit to the Camisard leader and how much to his blundering amanuensis. See Louvreleuil, iii. 56–61 ; Brueys, ii. 280–288 ; Court, ii. 236–242 ; Rossel d'Aigaliers, 35, 36. Brueys, rarely fair, and never generous, in his treatment of the Protestant champions or their followers, is compelled to admit that Cavalier managed his retreat after the rout in the Vaunage "with a good deal of firmness and prudence "—"avec assez de fermeté et de conduite." Histoire du fanatisme, ii. 317.

shortly after, of the stores and hospital of the Camisards in the neighborhood of Alais and Vezenobres. The Cévennes Mountains abound in natural caverns and in openings of various sizes, many of them the lairs of wild beasts and the habitations of men in prehistoric ages. Known only to the natives of the region, and easily escaping any but the most careful search, these recesses offered to the Protestants, especially after the devastation of the district burned by the troops of Julien, an inviting receptacle for the storage of ammunition and provisions. It was both easier to accumulate a hoard without attracting attention, and safer to draw upon it in case of necessity. One such cavern had come to light, a little earlier, far up in the recesses of the mountains near Cassagnas and Majestavols, close to the Plan de Font Morte where Esprit Séguier was captured. It proved to be an extensive opening in the bowels of the mountain. The soldiers sent thither from Barre des Cévennes found within a flock of a hundred sheep, twenty beeves, a great quantity of wheat, and two hand-mills for grinding it. Happily the Camisards had notice of the discovery of their secret receptacle, and, though powerless to prevent the plunder of the contents, gained the neighboring heights, from which they watched the progress of the raid.[1] But the cave in the woods of Euzet—a village as noted in the last century as it is at the present day for its mineral baths—was, both because of its situation in the lower plains and from the uses to which it was put, a far more important place. It had come to the knowledge of La Lande, commanding at Alais, that the insurgents possessed some hidden resort in the vicinity. An old woman had often been seen carrying broth into the woods. It was suspected that she was waiting upon sick or wounded Camisards. She acted with too much caution to permit her steps to be dogged, and when apprehended and brought before the general, she stoutly denied her guilt. As neither promises nor threats were sufficiently powerful to wring her secret from her, La Lande ordered her to be sent to the gallows. The sight of the instrument of death unsealed her tongue, and she not only revealed the situation of the Camisard

Capture of the hospitals and stores of the insurgents.

---

[1] Louvreleuil, iii. 23, 24 ; Brueys, ii. 266-268.

retreat, but herself consented to become a guide to the spot. The lives of thirty of her brethren were the price of her weakness ; for the hospital of the insurgents was discovered and its unfortunate inmates were butchered. In addition to other supplies which might have been replaced, there fell into the enemy's hands a great quantity of powder, as well as of charcoal and saltpetre to be used in the manufacture of powder. The loss of this was irremediable. Without medicines and appliances for the cure of the sick and wounded, and deprived of the ammunition so laboriously provided, it seemed a task well nigh hopeless to prosecute the war farther. Yet there were stout hearts whom even these difficulties did not cause to quail.[1]

Let it not be imagined, however, that the massacre of thirty sick or dying patients in a hospital—persons over whom the common law of nations has charitably thrown the mantle of its defence—was the only crime of the kind perpetrated by this savage commander. Fire and blood marked his excursions through plain and over mountain. As brutal in mind as he was repulsive in form, La Lande found in the Bishop of Alais a congenial companion, and both were equally hated by the gentry and the common people, for both seemed to be inspired by an inextinguishable hatred of the human race.[2] Having defeated, as he reported, the united bands of Roland and Joany with great slaughter, La Lande wreaked a merciless revenge upon every village or hamlet in the neighborhood which was suspected of having harbored the Camisards or given them food. At Brenoux, where Louvreleuil

La Lande's exploits.

---

[1] There are the usual discrepancies in matters of detail between the statements of Cavalier (258–260), Louvreleuil (iii. 70–71), Brueys (ii. 292), and La Baume (292, 293).

[2] Such is the portraiture of the general by Rossel d'Aigaliers (Mémoires, 38). who adds some ludicrous traits to the picture. La Lande, he informs us, was caressed by the ladies of Alais much for the same reason that compels the Indians to conciliate the favor of the devil by sacrifice. Nor will the comparison seem extravagant if it is true that an ordinary diversion of La Lande was to go from time to time and burn some country-seats of his best friends of the gentler sex, and to kill their tenants, upon the pretext that the Camisards had been there ; a day or two after which he would call upon the poor women and relate to them with an air of infinite unconcern these glorious exploits of war, to which they were constrained to listen with expressions of admiration by the fear lest otherwise a worse thing might happen to them.

asserts that the inhabitants admitted that the rebels had made a sojourn, of which they had failed to give him due notice, "he chastised their criminal silence by abandoning them to the Old Catholics of Saint Florent that were banded together, who killed more than two hundred persons, sparing none but the little children, and set fire to all the houses." More candid than the curate of Saint Germain de Calberte, the judge of Nismes, La Baume, confesses that *all* were put to the sword. There was no pretence of distinguishing between the innocent and the guilty, between men who may have given aid and comfort to the enemy, and weak women and prattling children whom their sex or age freed from any possible responsibility in the matter. And thus it was in " eight or nine other circumjacent places," whither La Lande despatched an inferior officer to carry out a similar scheme of rapine and destruction. "Followed by the Cadets de la Croix and by four thousand soldiers, including the militia, this commander," says Louvreleuil, " ravaged these villages successively with fire and sword, after having given them up to pillage. Quarter was given only to the women and the babes at the breast." (In reality, these were butchered with the rest.) "As to the men, they were all put to the edge of the sword. A very great booty was obtained ; for a prodigious quantity of cattle were carried off. One cannot imagine to what excesses the havoc made by these troops went. It will be sufficient to say that they poured out more than seven hundred hogsheads of wine, and that they left standing but five or six houses belonging to Old Catholics. Even these were demolished a short time after." [1]

M. F. Rouvière, of Nismes, has examined with great care the incident of the massacre of the Huguenot worshippers in the mill on the Agau, on the first of April, 1703, availing himself of the light thrown upon the occurrence both by the judicial documents published by M. Charles Sagnier, in 1878, to which I have referred above, and by some additional papers since discovered. See the article entitled " L'assemblée du moulin de l'Agau à Nismes," in the Bulletin de la Soc. de l'hist. du Prot. franç., xlii.

The massacre of the mill on the Agau.

---

[1] Louvreleuil, iii. 65, 66. Compare La Baume, 292, who informs us that Brenoux, Soustelle, and Saint Paul de la Coste were destroyed on the eighteenth of April, two days after the defeat of Nages.

(1893), 617–649. The papers in question were recently found in a damp cellar of the Palais de Justice of Nismes, in a heap of other papers mouldy and considered valueless. They contain the proceedings and, particularly, the attested declarations of the witnesses, upon which the decision of the court was based. They thus supplement the documents given to the public by Sagnier in vol. xxvii. of the same learned journal. From the circumstance that only twenty-one or twenty-two names of persons seen in the mill are mentioned by the witnesses, and that only these were condemned by the judgment of the presidial court of Nismes, M. Rouvière concludes that this number includes the sum total of the victims of the massacre. A calculation of the size of the mill leads him to the conclusion that, although the worshippers may have numbered considerably more at first, they could not have approached the figure of one hundred and fifty Protestants indicated by La Baume, the Abbé La Valette, Antoine Court, and Ménard, much less the three hundred and more of whom Brueys speaks. While I have read his discussion with interest, and while I have weighed carefully the force of the documents, I confess that they have failed to convince me that all the contemporary writers without an exception fell into so great an error. I grant that Louvreleuil, in his parish of Saint Germain de Calberte, thirty-five or forty miles distant, may have taken his facts and figures from hearsay, when he makes the dead amount to one hundred and fifty ; and I can readily set aside as worthless the estimate of an author so much given to exaggeration and so uncritical as Brueys. But would Bishop Fléchier, being present in Nismes at the time of the occurrence, be so ill informed as to double, and more than double, the number of the dead, and, in a letter written about three weeks after the event, speak of upward of fifty slain when there were only twenty-one, all told ? Most important, however, is the authority of La Baume. M. Rouvière, in quoting La Baume's statement from the "Relation historique de la Révolte des fanatiques ou des Camisards," refers to him as a member of the Académie of Nismes, but makes no allusion to the judicial position which he held. He could not be ignorant of the fact that Charles Joseph de La Baume, the author, was for many years one of the "conseillers" or judges of the presidial court of Nismes, and in fact the same judge that with others tried this very case, signing the decision with his ordinary signature De la Baulme, or Baume. Born in 1644, he had, in 1703, honorably discharged the office of judge for thirty-eight years. He died in 1715. In addition to a narrative of his travels in Italy, he wrote not less than three works bearing upon historical themes, besides his history of the Camisard troubles. Respecting this latter, his editor, the Abbé Goiffon, late archivist of the diocese of Nismes, writes, in the preface to the second edition (Nismes, 1874), that La Baume was in a position to inform himself better than others in regard to these troubles, "because he sat on the bench at the trial of most of those that were apprehended, and because it was from the proceedings themselves that he drew his narrations." In view of these facts, it appears to me clear that no man in France could have enjoyed better opportunities for ascertaining the exact truth respecting the events that occurred at the mill on the Agau at Nismes. Nor can I conceive that, if he learned from the judicial inquest that only twenty-one or twenty-two persons lost their lives, he could in any way have put the number down in his history at nearly four times that number. I cannot forbear quoting a few sentences from a letter recently written to me by the venerable Abbé Goiffon, which seems to me to present a correct view of the case : "I believe the account given by La Baume in preference to the accounts given by M. Rouvière, who, however, is generally accurate. M. de La Baume, the author of the manuscript that I edited on the Camisards, was the counsellor in the *présidial* who judged the cases of this period, and who was, consequently, at the very fountainhead of the most precious information. I am convinced that the number of the victims of the mill of the Agau surpassed that of the twenty-one whose trial was made after their death. The others must have been considered as persons that were drawn into the matter, and not as the abettors of the forbidden gathering. The figure given by Fléchier seems to me the most probable one. I have seen in my childhood the spot on which formerly stood the famous mill, and if we take into account that a part of those that attended could be outside, but within reach of the preacher's voice, the number of one hundred and fifty attendants does not appear exaggerated."

CHAPTER XVII

OVERTHROW OF THE CÉVENOLS

THE general selected by Louis the Fourteenth to succeed Montrevel in the command of the troops in Languedoc was a second marshal of France, who, in the wars against the empire, had won still greater distinction than his predecessor. Louis Hector, Duke of Villars, born at Moulins, in 1653, was a soldier in the very prime of life, and fresh from effective service rendered in the field of battle. He had twice been ambassador to the court of the emperor, and had exhibited diplomatic tact and dexterity. But it was chiefly in the conduct of military affairs that he achieved renown. In the war that ended with the Peace of Ryswick (1697) he attracted the king's notice by the ability with which he led the cavalry; and when, after the outbreak of the War of the Spanish Succession, he was intrusted with the supreme command over the army of the Rhine, he more than justified the confidence reposed in him. On the twentieth of September, 1703, he gained the decisive battle of Hochstedt, and would have opened the way into the very heart of Austria, could he have induced Louis's ally, the Elector of Bavaria, to consent to a march upon Vienna. In disgust at the loss of so excellent an opportunity, he begged to be recalled to France. He had been for some time at Versailles, when the monarch offered him the important but uninviting commission to reduce the Camisards of the south. "Wars more considerable to conduct," said the king to him, "would be more suitable for you; but you will render me a very important service if you succeed in arresting a revolt that may become very dangerous, especially at a juncture at which, while I am waging war against the whole of Europe, it is very embarrassing to have another in the very heart of the kingdom."

Appointment of Marshal Villars.

The king's flattering commission.

---

[1] Mémoires du maréchal de Villars (Michaud et Poujoulat Collection), 136.

So complimentary an invitation could not be declined. Loath as the marshal was to renounce, for the present, a return to scenes where he might confidently expect further laurels, he turned his steps southward to try his skill against the insurgents of the Cévennes and their plebeian leaders who had successfully resisted the efforts of two generals of no mean abilities. Ambitious, pliable, fully persuaded of his superiority, and not a little given to boastfulness, he was resolved to merit the future favors of the crown by the rapid success of his mission. Inasmuch as Broglie and Montrevel had signally failed in a course of unparalleled severity, Villars determined to begin by measures of affected gentleness.

A short time before the appointment of the duke, there had come to Paris a young nobleman who was destined to exercise Baron Rossel an important influence upon the solution of the Camid'Aigaliers. sard difficulties; although the question whether his exertions were for the ultimate advantage or injury of his fellow believers has been differently answered both by them and by the adherents of the established church. Happily he has left us authentic memoirs of his life and negotiations, constituting, in fact, from this point on, the only strictly contemporary records emanating from a Protestant hand whereby the more numerous and extended accounts of writers hostile to the Camisard cause can be corrected or refuted. These memoirs will enable us to form as intelligent a judgment as the best informed men of his own time could reach respecting the questions at issue; and it may be that our very distance in point of years shall secure to us the advantage of greater calmness and impartiality.

Jacob Rossel, Baron of Aigaliers, belonged to an ancient Protestant family of consideration, residing in Uzès, and possessing lands in the vicinity.[1] His father was a counsellor in the royal *cour des comptes* at Montpellier, who had left the kingdom for religion's sake. His mother had been confined in a convent,

---

[1] The insignificant village of Aigaliers, whose population of less than five hundred souls is probably smaller than it was two hundred years ago, is situated six or seven miles toward the northwest from Uzès. The ancient castle, now in ruins, occupies a commanding position on a lofty hill, from which there is an extensive view northward of the exterior of the great amphitheatre of the Serre du Bouquet and westward of the Cévennes Mountains.

and an uncle had long been kept in prison, charged with the crime of attending a number of Protestant meetings. In the general, but insincere submission to which the Protestants of Languedoc had been forced in the years immediately succeeding the Revocation, it is not improbable that the young nobleman succumbed to what appeared to be an irresistible pressure, and made a profession of the Roman Catholic faith. Be this as it may, at a later date he appears as a decided believer in the doctrines of the Reformation. For the purpose of enjoying liberty to profess those doctrines he went for a time into foreign parts, and only returned to France, shortly before the outbreak of the Camisard war, in order to facilitate the escape of his mother from the kingdom. When the mountaineers, infuriated by the intolerable cruelty exercised by the Abbé du Chayla and other ecclesiastics of the same type, flew to arms, the baron, although he had grievances of his own and felt deep compassion for the lot of his less fortunate brethren, remained quietly watching the course of events. During the whole of the struggle until now, he was so far removed from an active participation in the contest that he tells us that, at the time he resolved to exert himself to secure a speedy peace, he was not personally acquainted with a single Camisard.[1] At the same time he did not dissemble the fact that he was not at heart a Roman Catholic, though he professed to be a good servant of the king.

In holding aloof from the movement Rossel d'Aigaliers was but following the example of the entire body of the Protestant gentry of Languedoc. The reason of this strange reluctance to take part in the struggle must not be regarded as being altogether, or chiefly, the apathy or lack of courage of a privileged class. " Our condition," says Aigaliers, " being much more deplorable than I have been able to depict it, it is surprising enough that none of the gentry were led to take up arms.

---

[1] "D'ailleurs, je puis assurer avec vérité que je ne connoissois pas un seul Camisar, et il s'agissoit pourtant de les porter à se soumettre." Mémoires, 31.— The Mémoires de Rossel d'Aigaliers, although they have long been known in manuscript, were first printed, with an introduction by Professor Frosterus, of the University of Helsingfors, in the Bibliothèque universelle et Revue suisse, and also in a separate form, Lausanne, 1866. This publication has since become scarce, and I am indebted for my copy to the kindness of Professor Frosterus.

What prevented them was, in the first place, the aversion which in France education instils into the nobility to any uprising against their sovereign, and especially into those who have been so happy as to be born in our religion and to be acquainted with it. In the second place, having no other resource than to throw themselves in among the Camisards, they were deterred by those ' prophecies ' which appeared so strange to them ; inasmuch as it was confidently asserted that these prophecies caused the Camisards to commit a vast number of murders and acts of incendiarism. However, the situation was too critical to admit of our remaining neutral. It was easy for a young man to get himself out of harm's way, by going to a distance. Many young people did this. As for me, who loved my country, my relations, and those whom I regarded as my brethren in Jesus Christ, I mentally sought for some means of serving them, and I was resolved, in case I could find no other, to run the risk of dying with them." [1]

The young enthusiast gave to the subject, he tells us, a great deal of thought, not unaccompanied with prayer to the Sovereign Judge of the universe, and that he reached the conclusion that the war must be brought to its close by no one else than the Protestants of Languedoc, who, like himself, had taken no part in the struggle. This was the more necessary from the consideration that, should the Camisards be destroyed by means of the troops and the counsel of Basville, the peaceable members of the former Reformed churches would be treated with renewed severity and merited contempt, as cowards whom nothing had prevented from openly espousing the cause of the insurgents but their fear of extreme punishments and death.[2] What then did Aigaliers definitely propose to do ? In the first place, to petition the government to suspend the measures of persecution and repression, which, instead of making sincere Roman Catholics out of the professed New Converts, had, as exercised by intolerant priests, first driven a few to armed revolt and then, being continued, had swollen the stream of rebellion until it had reached its present formidable proportions. Next,

His scheme of pacification.

---

[1] Mémoires de Rossel d'Aigaliers, 29, 30.   [2] Ibid., 30.

to obtain permission for such a number of the Protestants of Languedoc as might be judged proper to take up arms and go out to meet the Camisards and convince them that, so far from being in sympathy with their rebellion, their fellow believers thoroughly disapproved of it, being resolved either to bring the insurgents back to their loyalty by their example, or to confront them on the field.   In either case, whether the Camisards submitted or resisted, the king and all France would bear witness to the integrity of the Protestants and the calumny of their enemies, the ecclesiastics. And the plan must commend itself to the court by the great advantages it would secure. Should the Camisards resist the importunity of their brethren in the faith, they would render themselves odious in the eyes of the entire Protestant world; while, if they fulfilled the sanguine hopes of the negotiator, influenced by the confidence that thus they might effect the release of captives languishing in prisons and galleys, the monarch would gain no inconsiderable accession to his forces. For then he would be able to use elsewhere against his foreign enemies the troops now serving against the Camisards, while the Camisards themselves might be employed under suitable officers for the same purpose, the exercise of their religion being conceded to them, and an end being put to the frightful slavery into which the Protestants had fallen in consequence of the suspicion and distrust in which they were held.

So great a service rendered to the crown, it was thought, would doubtless cause the cessation of the outrages to which the Huguenots of France had for twenty years been Confessedly a novel plan. subjected. The method employed in reaching this grand consummation was confessedly so novel as to startle many. The majority of the pagan world and of the persecuting members of the established church would condemn it; but it sufficed its advocate that it should obtain the approval of Christians.[1] Yet Aigalier's eyes were not blind to the dangers

---

[1] " J'avoue que ce moyen de se délivrer de ses ennemis n'est pas trop en usage ; que la plupart des païens et des papistes ne l'approuveront pas ; mais j'espère qu'il le sera des chrétiens, et c'est tout ce que je demande." Ibid., 33. Elsewhere (page 25), Aigaliers explains himself: " Par ce mot de papiste, on n'entend pas les catholiques gens de bien, mais seulement les persécuteurs et leurs satellites."

of the movement which he initiated. "Men will not fail to meet me with the assertion that we have baleful examples in France of the ingratitude with which alone our services have been requited. But do I know the time when God shall be pleased to touch the heart of our rulers and people? If divine Providence suggests to me a means of converting them, ought I not to make use of it, especially when it may serve to rescue us from a frightful abyss whence no other issue is visible?"

It cannot be denied that the scheme of the Protestant baron did credit to the kindliness of his heart, while it evidenced the piety and loyalty which formed the basis of his char-

An impracticable undertaking.

acter. But into what a condition did it propose to bring the Camisards, who alone in France were battling in behalf of a noble principle, battling to secure one of the inalienable rights of man? A condition, certainly not very dissimilar to that which they occupied two years before, when the intolerable practices of the Abbé du Chayla and a host of other ecclesiastics of like character drove them, as a last resource of oppressed innocence, to the desperate venture of grasping the sword and musket in vindication of the right to worship God according to the dictates of the individual conscience. Yet Aigaliers expected Louis the Fourteenth and his advisers to concede to the unarmed loyalty of the Protestants, now voluntarily laying aside their weapons of defence, a moral principle which that monarch had never been willing to recognize during the long years of vexatious and inhuman persecution leading to the formal Revocation of the great edict, and during the dreary years that succeeded the Revocation. Had not the Huguenots of the seventeenth century sufficiently attested their loyalty? Had they not incurred the risk of leading the world to condemn them of weakness and of inferiority to those other Huguenots, who, with Admiral Coligny and Henry of Navarre at their head, conditioned their submission to an earthly monarch by the proviso "if only the sovereign sway of God remain in its integrity." [1] Those heroes of a former age, at least,

---

[1] The phrase, it will be remembered, dates from the Confession of Faith of the French Churches formulated in 1559, and presented to King Francis II. at Amboise in 1560, which in its fortieth and last article declares the duty of full and willing obedience and submission to kings and magistrates, even should

speaking through Agrippa d'Aubigné as their mouthpiece, repudiated as guilty of little less than wilful murder the man who would recommend his fellow believers to place themselves without guarantees in the hands of their enemies, thus offering their throats to the knife of the butcher.[1] By all means, said they, let the nobler instincts of rulers and of peoples be invoked, but let the appeal be accompanied by the most virile assertion of the rights of man.

It required some ingenuity on the part of the Baron d'Aigaliers to obtain the necessary passport to visit Paris. In the capital he was received with some favor by persons to whom he unfolded his plan. Chamillart, secretary of war, introduced him to Marshal Villars, then under orders to take Marshal Montrevel's place, and the new commander of Languedoc bade him to precede him to Lyons and there await his arrival. Together they descended the Rhone. On the way Aigaliers had an opportunity to set forth his views at some length, endeavoring to forestall the misrepresentations of those who would certainly try to prove that gentle measures would be sure to fail, and that the Camisards could only be reduced by the extermination of the Protestants. Villars assured Aigaliers that he would always keep his two ears open, in order that he might hear both sides of the matter. There was soon good need of this. At Tournon, Julien, the hero of the devastation of the Cévennes, came on board, who ridiculed all ideas excepting the project of wholesale slaughter; while at Valence tidings came to the marshal of Cavalier's great loss at Nages. Julien denied that Aigaliers would be able to find even four Protestants, not to speak of the thousands upon whom the latter counted, that would consent to go out and fight the Camisards. Nothing would answer but the complete extirpation of the Protestants. If his counsels had been followed, there would not now, he said, be a single Camisard in the province. To compass this end, however, it would have been necessary not to stop with the one

Aigaliers visits the court,

and returns with Villars to Languedoc.

---

they be unbelievers—" moyennant que l'empire souverain de Dieu demeure en son entier." Recueil des choses mémorables (Petits mémoires de Condé), 1565, i. 69.

[1] The Huguenots and Henry of Navarre, i. 334.

hundred and four villages demolished in the Cévennes, but to destroy all the rest and kill all the peasants found in the open country. To which Aigaliers fearlessly rejoined that the famous desolation of the Cévennes, on which Julien dwelt, had only been the means of augmenting the forces of the Camisards, and that the measures which Julien now recommended would lead to a universal uprising.

When Nismes was reached, Aigaliers had an opportunity to begin his operations. The Protestants of the place, delighted to be permitted to come together without the risk of being fired upon and massacred, gladly drew up a petition which M. d'Alberas, at the head of seven or eight hundred of the citizens, came and presented to Marshal Villars, professing their unqualified loyalty and begging permission to go out and either bring the Camisards back to obedience, or fight them in token of their own fidelity. The paper was signed by many of the gentry and by almost all the lawyers and merchants. The marshal replied in a conciliatory speech. He thanked the petitioners for their offer, and promised them that, as he had no doubts respecting the sincerity of their protestations, he would, should their help be found necessary, make use of them with the same confidence with which he would employ the Old Catholics. He hoped, he said, to bring back the rebels by kindness, and would be very glad to have them spread the intelligence that he offered full pardon to all who, within eight days, might return to their homes bringing their arms with them.[1] Villars spoke in similar terms whithersoever he went on a short trip of observation upon which he now started, visiting successively Sommières, Sauve, Saint Hippolyte, Alais, and Uzès. But while Aigaliers everywhere found his fellow Protestants ready to enter into his plans, he had more difficulty in obtaining the marshal's definite consent. There were plenty of interested opponents. Basville, who accompanied Villars, and who entertained him in as sumptuous a manner as became so prosperous a host—" Basville for thirty years king and tyrant of the great province of Languedoc under the

Petition of the Protestants of Nismes.

Villars's conciliatory words.

Aigaliers's plan opposed by Basville

---

[1] Aigaliers, 36, 37 ; La Baume, 293, 294.

name of intendant—Languedoc's terror and horror"—to use
Saint Simon's expression,[1] was little disposed to further a
scheme whose success would only prove that all the cruelty
of his administration in the past had been worse than useless.

and by the bishops of Alais and Uzès. The bishops of Alais and Uzès seconded the representations of Basville. With the former we have some
acquaintance. It was the Bishop of Alais to whom
the Swiss colonel, Court, on one occasion said, with more
frankness of speech than the prelate was accustomed to : " You
and those like you are the cause of all the misfortunes of the
province, for you have driven men to desperation by your inordinate persecutions. "[2] Michel Poncet de la Rivière, the
Bishop of Uzès, who lodged Villars and his suite in his magnificent episcopal palace, richly furnished, and embellished with
beautiful gardens and with a park that is still admired, was not
less inimical to a policy of mildness and toleration.[3]

With such men of position dissuading Villars from making
what they represented to be a ridiculous venture, Aigaliers was
unlikely to obtain a trial of the merits of his plan; for Villars
could not bring himself to incur the risk of a loss of prestige,
should the effort, made without their concurrence, and indeed
against their advice, prove futile. In these circumstances the
Protestant baron shrewdly saw that his only hope of success

---

[1] "Basville, depuis trente ans roi et tyran de cette grande province sous le
nom d'intendant . . . il en était la terreur et l'horreur." Mémoires de
Saint Simon, xxix. 192.

[2] Aigaliers, 38.

[3] Of this voluptuous ecclesiastic the baron paints (p. 39) an uninviting picture.
"Passionately addicted to all forms of pleasure—music, women, and good living
—he always has with him good musicians, pretty girls for whom he cares, and
excellent wines which visibly augment his vivacity. He never leaves the table
without being extremely lively; and then, if he takes it into his head that any
one in his diocese is not so good a Christian as he himself is. he writes to
Monsieur de Basville to send him into exile. He has frequently attacked the
canons of his cathedral, who have always had him condemned to heavy fines, a
circumstance that must prove that the bishop is a very unjust man." Much,
however, as Poncet de la Rivière hated Baron d'Aigaliers, whose father and
mother had more than once suffered at his hands, he was at a loss how to act.
It would have been vain to tell Villars that Aigaliers was not a Roman Catholic ;
the marshal knew that perfectly well. and that it was precisely as a Protestant
that he expected to do good service to the king. (Ibid., 40.)

lay in enlisting the co-operation of the capital enemy both of
his family and his religion, the all-powerful intendant, a man
whom he had hitherto so studiously avoided that, during the present tour in Languedoc, he had almost
starved himself that he might not be indebted to him

Aigaliers gains over Basville.

for a morsel of bread or a glass of water. In the interview which
he now sought with Basville, so far from ignoring their mutual
antipathy, Aigaliers rather emphasized than passed lightly by a
feeling, due, he said, to the fact over which they had no control,
that they had been born in different religions. But his frankness and the tact with which he showed that, if nothing were
gained, certainly nothing could be lost by trying the experiment which he proposed, won over the redoubtable intendant,
and he being gained, Villars made no further objection. He
only expressed a desire to see, before leaving Uzès, the men
whom Aigaliers might gather to serve in the new warfare,
and the latter, though he had but a single night to issue his
invitations and collect his recruits, presented to the general
in the morning, not, as he had agreed, *fifty*, but *eighty*
men, all of them stalwart and of good family, some
even belonging to the gentry. We are told that when

His band of loyal Protes- tants.

the marshal and the intendant descended into the court-yard
of the episcopal palace to inspect the Protestants and to praise
their loyal zeal in the king's service, the Bishop of Uzès, viewing
the scene from above, nearly fell from his balcony in surprise
and chagrin at the strange scene. Aigaliers received a formal
commission to lead his company against the Camisards. His
men were furnished with muskets and bayonets, taken, greatly
to the disgust of the clerical party, from the hands of the burgess militia. Early on the morning of the fifth of May, 1704,
with the baron at their head, they sallied forth in quest of
Cavalier, whose ordinary haunts were in the region west and
north of Uzès. It was four or five days before they succeeded
in meeting him. Meanwhile an important series of events had
begun.[1]

---

[1] We are entirely dependent upon the narrative of Rossel d'Aigaliers in his
Memoirs. He inserts the short commission of Marshal Villars, dated Uzès,
May 4, 1704. Mémoires de Rossel d'Aigaliers, 40-43.

Seeing the marshal decided, despite their opposition, to make trial of gentleness in reducing the Camisards, the military com-

mander at Alais, and the bishop of that city, resolved that, at least, the credit of success, should there be any, must not fall to the share of the Protestant Aigaliers. While, therefore, the baron was in the field, seeking an opportunity to hold a conference with Cavalier, La Lande despatched an agent to the Camisard chief to propose an interview with him. This agent was none other than Lacombe, who having been Cavalier's master at the time the latter served as shepherd boy, only a few years since, had kept up occasional intercourse with him and was possessed of considerable influence over him. Lacombe's advances were well received. He came at an opportune moment. The Camisard had somewhat lost heart. The defeat at Nages, followed so closely by the discovery of the principal stores of the insurgents, plunged him in despondency respecting the future. ⸱ The region which he frequented was in great part devastated, the prisons were full of Protestants, the love of many had grown cold, the purses of all were exhausted, and the hopes of help from abroad had signally failed. Such at least was the dark picture, possibly too sombre, which Cavalier himself painted in later years, when defending his course against the aspersions of detractors.[1] It was true that the scattered fragments of the little army surrounded and dispersed by Montrevel were gradually reunited; that Cavalier had again begun to make himself formidable, and that in the Upper Cévennes the strength of Roland and the other leaders was yet intact. None the less was Cavalier ready, as never before, to listen to an invitation to treat for peace with the king. There was nothing base or cringing in his attitude. In fact the reply which he was at first disposed to make to La Lande's letter was so determined and haughty that Lacombe declined to take charge of it. But the insolence which it is said to have contained was probably nothing more than a pretty distinct demand for the restoration of religious liberty as a necessary condition of peace and the sole basis of negotiation. Lacombe persuaded him to draw up

---

[1] Memoirs of the Wars of the Cévennes, 259.

a more politic reply and to send a letter to the commandant of Alais consenting to the proposed meeting. The bearer was The intrep- the intrepid Abdias Morel, a lieutenant of Cavalier, id Catinat. who, from the circumstance that he had served in Italy under the great captain of Louis the Fourteenth that bore the name of Catinat, had himself been thus surnamed by his associates in arms. Riding boldly into the city of Alais, he presented himself at the castle and asked to be admitted to an audience with La Lande. The latter on seeing him asked his name. "I am Catinat," was the reply, "commandant of the cavalry of the Camisards." "What!" rejoined the general. "Are you not the man who massacred so many persons in the vicinity of Beaucaire?" "Yes, sir, it was I that did it, and that deemed it my duty to do it." "You are very bold to venture into my presence." "I am come," steadily answered Catinat, "in good faith, believing you to be an honorable man, and on the word given me by brother Cavalier, that no harm would come to me." "He is right," exclaimed La Lande, and having read Cavalier's letter, he informed Catinat that in two hours' time he would go to meet that chief accompanied by twenty dragoons and by a few officers. Being informed by Catinat that he doubted whether Cavalier would consent to come with so small a body-guard, he declared that Cavalier might bring what number he would, but that as for himself he would have no larger escort. He would trust Cavalier, since Cavalier trusted him.[1] That very day the interview took place at a The collo- bridge known as the Pont d'Avesnes, two or three quy at Pont miles from the gates of Alais.[2] It was two o'clock in d'Avesnes. the afternoon of Monday, the twelfth of May. The general and the Camisard chief vied with each other in the exhibition of mutual confidence. Cavalier left the greater part of his band at Méjannes, and advanced with sixty foot soldiers and eight horsemen. The foot soldiers were left at a certain distance from the bridge, the horsemen a little further on, and

---

[1] La Baume, 296 ; Louvreleuil, iii. 105–107 ; Brueys, ii. 312.

[2] The Memoirs of Cavalier are alone in saying that the interview was at Saint Hilaire, which, however, is in the same neighborhood, and not over a mile or two distant.

Cavalier came alone to meet La Lande. La Lande did about the same thing. The conference lasted two or three hours, and was courteous, almost cordial. The Camisard whose name had for nearly two years been a terror throughout Lower Languedoc, and upon whose head a price had been set, whether he were taken dead or alive, and the sanguinary commandant whose sword had, within a few weeks, been butchering innocent women and children at Brenoux and Soustelle, discussed the terms of peace with as studious a regard to courtesy as if they had been the representatives of equal powers, and not a royal general and an unforgiven rebel.

Unfortunately the details of the conference cannot be stated with certainty. It was the capital mistake of Cavalier that, upon his return to his partisans, he affected an air of mystery, and, presuming doubtless upon the absolute obedience which it was his boast that his soldiers willingly rendered him, refused to divulge any particulars of the demands which he had made. And if in later years he published to the world, in the memoirs to which I have had frequent occasion to advert, a narrative purporting to give an accurate statement of the facts, the mistakes and blunders of that work are known by the learned to be so numerous and fundamental in other particulars that we can repose little trust upon its assertions in the present instance. There can, however, be little doubt that the first demand put forward was, as the memoirs assert, for the restoration of complete liberty of religious profession and worship, as guaranteed by the edicts revoked by Louis the Fourteenth. The great object of the insurrection could scarcely have been ignored, or thrown into the background, by one who had long been doing valiant battle for the Protestant cause. It seems to be equally clear that, at the bare mention of this claim, La Lande expressed in the strongest terms his conviction that the king would never hear of a proposal to grant the exercise of any other religion in France than that which he himself professed, and therefore that, if this point were pressed, it would be as well to abandon all hope of agreement. Cavalier, young, unaccustomed to debate, a novice in negotiation, bewildered by the strangeness of the situation, unwilling, in the weakened condition of his forces, to dismiss off-hand the alluring prospect of a peaceful settlement of a protracted and difficult conflict, was induced so far to acquiesce in the view presented by the general, a man of age and experience, as reluctantly, but none the less decidedly, to forego insisting upon the only true and stable ground of pacification. We may well believe that the second demand was for a general release of all the French Protestants confined for religion's sake in prisons or galleys. Nor, perhaps, need we question the assertion that Cavalier stipulated next that in case his Majesty refused to grant to the Protestants full liberty of conscience, he should permit them freely to leave the kingdom. When La Lande asked the number for whom Cavalier asked this privilege, it is not at all unlikely that the ignorant youth, so lately a peasant, somewhat embittered by the indifference or cowardice that seemed to have kept the Huguenots of France at large from coming to the assistance of their brethren in Lower Languedoc, should have narrowed down the claim to ten thousand persons of both sexes and all ages, and that for these ten thousand persons he should have demanded the right to dispose of their lands and possession within three months. But it is not probable that La Lande encouraged Cavalier to believe that a permission, which could not be accorded to ten thousand, might be granted by the king to one-fifth of that number. Indeed the whole course of subsequent events leads to the conclusion that, before the long interview was over, Cavalier had virtually receded from this demand also, and confined himself to a stipulation in behalf of a still smaller number of his own followers.[1]

Cavalier's mistake.

Emerging from the obscurity investing the interview of the Pont d'Avesnes into the sunlight of authentic history, we find that, at the conclusion of the parley, La Lande had the curiosity to approach the Camisard troops and see with his own eyes the

---

[1] Cavalier's memoirs must be examined, pages 261–263, and compared with La Baume, 296–297, and Louvreleuil, iii. 107. Antoine Court's discussion of the evident falsehoods in Cavalier's account is judicious and convincing. Histoire des troubles des Cévennes, ii. 270–274. See also Fléchier's letter to M. de Calvisson, May 13, 1704, in Œuvres complètes, x. 150. Of Cavalier he writes : "Les raisonnemens du paysan sont assez grossiers et sauvages, quoiqu'il soit prédicateur, prophète et général d'armée ; mais il ne laisse pas d'avoir un bon gros sens qui va à ses fins."

men who so often, ill clad and indifferently armed, had prevailed over the disciplined soldiers of the king. As he rode up
to them he exclaimed, "La paix est faite!" "Peace
is concluded!" At the same time he threw them a
handful of gold pieces, with which to drink to the
king's health. Not a man of them would touch the
money. "Thanks!" cried out some of these sturdy men, "but
what we want is not money, but LIBERTY OF CONSCIENCE!"[1]

La Lande promised Cavalier to forward his demands to the
king. So much in earnest was the general that he rode all
night to carry them to Villars at Nismes. The latter sent them
by special messenger to Paris. Meanwhile, on the strength of
the partial agreement that had been reached,[2] Cavalier proceeded openly to the village of Vezenobres, where he billeted
the members of his troop upon the citizens, precisely as if they
had been regular soldiers of the king. And here, after taking
their evening meal, the Camisards with one accord betook themselves to the old Protestant "temple" of the
place, which had not shared in the common destruction of the Reformed places of worship throughout the kingdom,
and held a public religious service. The peasants of the place
came in to enjoy the unexpected privilege, listened to a sermon
by Moïse, who officiated as preacher, and joined in the rendering of praise and the singing of the psalms.[3] And yet neither
the followers of the Camisard leader nor the people of Vezeno-

---

[1] Cavalier, 263; La Baume, 297 ; Louvreleuil, iii. 108. The last named will
have it that it was Cavalier who *urged* the soldiers to take the money and to
drink the king's health. Aigaliers (p. 43) says : "Après des discours, il [La
Lande] voulut leur donner cinquante pistoles. Ces pistoles lui furent jetées au
nez, et il n'y eut que Cavalier qui voulut l'écouter, se croyant obligé à cela par
la parole qu'il lui avoit donnée." Aigaliers is not quite right ; for, although the
Camisards would have nothing to do with the gold, regarding it, according to
Bonbonnoux, as an "accursed thing," and not one of them being willing to be
an Achan in the camp of the children of God, it was finally gathered up and
handed to Cavalier, who distributed it by the hands of Lacombe among the poor
of Vezenobres. Mémoires de Bonbonnoux, 35, 36.

[2] When the Memoirs of Cavalier (page 263) make him and La Lande "part
without concluding anything," they contradict the known facts of the case as
directly as when they assert that on his return to his troop the Camisard gave
an account of the conference.

[3] Mémoires de Bonbonnoux, 36.

bres knew what had been concluded; for Cavalier had vouchsafed no explanation, and had simply said when he returned
from his interview with the royal general: "Men, if you have
any relations that are prisoners, let me know it, and I promise
to restore them to you very soon." [1]

The next day (the thirteenth of May) Cavalier met Rossel
d'Aigaliers by appointment at Saint Jean de Ceyrargues. The
two leaders embraced as cordially as if old friends and
not strangers. The fifty men raised by the baron with

Conference of Cavalier and Aiga-liers.

Villars's permission, and armed with the weapons of
the burgess militia for the purpose of either bringing back the
insurgents or fighting against them, openly fraternized with the
Camisard veterans; and, while Cavalier and Aigaliers conferred
together, began as by a common instinct to sing the psalms that
were equally dear to both. The same harmony characterized
the intercourse of their leaders. Cavalier and such of his supporters as were consulted, agreed with Aigaliers, that they
ought to make their submission to the king in order to secure
the best interests of their brethren through the cessation of the
present calamities. Aigaliers, on his part, pledged his word
that no harm should befall them, but that they would be permitted to follow their own inclinations as to leaving the kingdom or entering the King's service. "I believe this last to
be the best course, provided we be left free to worship God
according to the dictates of our conscience," said the baron;
"because I hope that by our faithful service his Majesty will
come to know that he was imposed upon when we were accused
of being bad subjects, and thereby we shall be able to obtain
the same liberty of conscience for the rest of the people. I see
no other way to change our deplorable condition. As for you,
you may contrive to maintain yourselves for some time in the
woods and upon the mountains; but it will be out of your
power to prevent the inhabitants of the cities and the fortified
places from perishing." On the other hand, Cavalier, while not
ignorant of the bad faith of the Roman Catholics in the matter

---

[1] " Quelles feurent leurs délibérations ? c'est ce que nous ne sumes jamais à
fond, Cavalier nous en faisant un mistère. Il nous dit seulement en nous ap-
prochant: ' Enfans, si vous avez des parents prisonniers, déclarez-le moi, et je
vous promet de vous les faire revenir bientôt.' " Mémoires de Bonbonnoux, 35.

of promises given to Protestants, professed his willingness to risk his life for the relief of his brethren and of the entire province. Yet he hoped, he said, that in committing himself to the clemency of the king, for whom he had never ceased to pray, no evil would betide him. All that were admitted to the conference agreed to submit with Cavalier, and Aigaliers pledged himself to share their fate, whether in serving within the kingdom or in expatriating himself.[1]

When Cavalier and Aigaliers parted, the latter was the bearer of a letter written by the Camisard chief to Marshal Villars. The memoirs of both of these personages record the fact, although unfortunately neither has given the text of the important communication. It is probable, however, that we have in a document inserted in his history by the curate of Saint Germain de Calberte, but out of its true place, the missing epistle.[2] The tone is so remarkable that it should be placed before the reader's eye.

"Monseigneur," it ran, "although I had the honor to write to you yesterday, I cannot refrain from again having recourse to your excellence, to beg you very humbly to grant me the favor of your protection, for myself and for my troop, who burn with an ardent zeal to repair the fault which we have committed in taking arms, not indeed against the king, as our enemies have been pleased to allege, but for the purpose of defending our lives against our persecutors, who have attacked them with such great animosity that we refused

Cavalier's submissive letter to Marshal Villars.

---

[1] The memoirs of Aigaliers (pages 43 and 44) and Cavalier (page 265) are here in substantial agreement. According to the latter, the Camisard leader was somewhat distrustful of the baron on account of his alleged apostasy to the Roman Catholic faith. Bonbonnoux gives no hint that any of Cavalier's officers were present at the interview, and indeed seems to imply that it was private from beginning to end. Certainly Bonbonnoux himself, though at the time somewhat more than a common soldier, was not admitted to it. Mémoires, 36.

[2] This is the opinion of Antoine Court (Histoire des troubles des Cévennes, ii. 279), who supports it by La Baume's statement: "He [Aigaliers] obliged him [Cavalier] to write a very respectful letter to Marshal Villars, wherein he informed him that he submitted himself unconditionally to whatever the king might be pleased to command. This was a clever stroke of M. d'Aigaliers in order that his services might not appear useless, but might secure him some reward." Relation historique de la révolte des fanatiques, 298.

to believe that it was by his majesty's order. We know that it is written in Saint Paul that subjects should be submissive to their sovereigns. If, despite these very sincere protestations, the king demand our blood, we shall be ready within a brief time to deliver our persons to his justice or his clemency. We shall esteem ourselves very happy, monseigneur, should his majesty, touched by our repentance, after the example of the great God of Mercy, of whom he is the living image upon the earth, show us the favor to pardon us and to receive us into his service. We hope that by our fidelity and zeal we shall acquire the honor of your protection, and that under an illustrious and beneficent general such as you are, we shall glory in shedding our blood for the interests of the king." With " profound respect " and with " perfect submission," the writer signed himself " Your very humble and very obedient servant, CAVALIER." [1]

This was indeed a very different kind of production from those letters in which the quondam shepherd boy of Ribaute had, not many months since, announced to the Governor of Nismes that he would burn the city's mills unless the savage captains of the Cadets de la Croix instantly put a stop to their murderous executions, or warned one of those captains himself that he would hold his sister, whom the Camisards had taken captive, as a hostage for the safety of the prophetess, la Grande Marie, lately fallen into the hands of the Roman Catholics. Not less remarkable than the contrast between the short, careless, and misspelt sentences of those letters and the neat and studiously rounded phrases of the present epistle is the contradiction between the frank and defiant spirit of independence which they breathe and the obsequiousness, going to the length of cringing servility, of which we have a specimen in this later paper. We are ready to pronounce it impossible that documents, so different in tone, emanated from the same brain and hand. Nor is this judgment altogether unwarranted. If the signature was that of Cavalier, the body of the letter to Marshal Villars was undoubtedly written or dictated by Rossel d'Aigaliers, who, in order to attain the worthy end which he hoped to compass, was quite willing to put into the mouth of the plain Cévenol chief the sentiments of un-

---

[1] Le fanatisme renouvelé, iii. 103–105.

reserved and unmanly loyalty to the crown which had been in vogue in higher social circles for a full century. The mere boy who yesterday, conscious of his inexperience and low birth, had failed duly to assert or maintain the just demands of his fellow Protestants in the presence of a military officer whose rank, long service, and authority awed him, to-day succumbed to the literary skill and persuasion of a gentleman of his own faith, in contrast with which his own attainments seemed in truth to be paltry. A really great man, of strong and inflexible character, would have been proof both against the glitter of rank and against the seductions of superior education. But Jean Cavalier was not really great.

We must, however, do him the justice to admit that, at a later time, he himself saw the errors he committed throughout this entire negotiation and candidly and correctly traced them to their origin. Referring to the next blunder in order he said : " A man of greater experience than I was [possessed of] would perhaps have acted with more caution on this critical occasion, and would probably have avoided to treat with the marshal personally, but would have appointed a deputy for that purpose ; but my youth and unexperience gave me confidence, and the rather because there were none about me much wiser than myself, or more practised in affairs of this nature, that I could confide in." [1]

It was in every way desirable for the purposes of the government that the young Camisard leader, who, in his two interviews with its agents, had shown that he scarcely possessed that stubborn resolution with which the insurgents were generally credited, should be encouraged in sentiments of unbounded submission to the king such as those which he had lately expressed. Were he but to recover himself, were he but once more to recall to mind that he had been intrusted with the standard of religious liberty, and that not the Protestants of the Cévennes alone, but the Protestants of the entire realm were watching his defence of it with anxious eyes, might he not, before it was too late, draw back from the chasm into which he was about to precipitate himself, involving in the same fate as many of his associates as he

---

[1] Memoirs of the Wars of the Cévennes, 266.

could influence ? To preclude a disappointment of their hopes, and to occupy some of the time that must elapse before the messenger sent to Versailles for instructions could return, Villars and the intendant welcomed the suggestion of Rossel d'Aigaliers that Cavalier should be invited to come and present himself to the marshal in person. La Lande alone, jealous of his rival in the negotiations, affected to despise the plan, and ridiculed the thought that Cavalier would consent to brave the dangers, real or imaginary, attending a visit to the city of Nismes. Yet, within two or three days, the skilful agent accomplished his purpose, and Aigaliers had brought Cavalier, attended by his young brother and a few of his officers, to an interview with the dreaded authorities of the province of Languedoc.[1]

Meanwhile, an event occurred in another part of the district which had nearly thwarted the baron's designs. This was a signal advantage gained by the united bands of Roland and Joany over a Roman Catholic detachment. The Count of Tournon, commanding at Florac, started from that place for the purpose of conferring with La Lande at Alais, on the very day upon which the latter met Cavalier at the Pont d'Avesnes. He had crossed the greater part of the Cévennes without meeting a Camisard, and at Saint Jean du Gard, having no fear of hostile interference, he sent back an escort of three hundred men of whom he had no further need. At the Plan de Font Morte, heretofore the scene of deadly encounter, the insurgents lay in wait for them. Joany and his band were posted in the woods on the north, Roland with his foot soldiers occupied the south, his cavalry were by themselves on the west. The enemy was allowed to pass the first corps unmolested, but when the *miquelets* from Roussillon, who led the van, perceiving some Cévenols in front, became involved in combat with them, the Camisards rose in every direction from their ambuscade, and poured destructive volleys upon the surprised and terrified troops. Surrounded on all sides and unable either to advance or to retreat, a mere handful of the latter succeeded in cutting their way through. The lieutenant colonel in command, with almost all of the officers and

Roland and Joany cut to pieces a hostile band.

---

[1] Aigaliers, 44, 45.

more than two hundred men, fell upon the battle-ground. Some of those who were taken prisoners, especially such as had incurred the particular enmity of the Camisards by acts of cruelty or otherwise, received barbarous treatment. The Camisards had but four men killed and five wounded.[1]

The success of his associates in the higher Cévennes, which at another time might have made Cavalier less anxious for an accommodation with the government, was in the present juncture only a subject of regret; and, fearful lest it might interrupt the progress of the negotiations, he sent to explain to the marshal that the affair had occurred simply because he had not had time to communicate to Roland the sort of armistice into which he had entered with La Lande.[2] For, elated by the marks of distinction that had been shown him, Cavalier had begun to conceive of his authority as paramount, and, while consulting neither the other leaders of the insurgents nor his own followers, he fancied that whatever he might decide for himself would obtain the unquestioning acquiescence of the rest. On this point he was destined before long to be painfully undeceived.

The interview between Cavalier and Marshal Villars took place on the sixteenth of May, in the garden of the monastery of the Recollet monks, just outside of the walls of Nismes.[3] The scene was novel and of dramatic interest. The Camisard chief, for whom in the official correspondence of the day, as well as in the writings of ecclesiastics and laymen attached to the established church, the most opprobrious epithets seemed too weak as an expression of contempt and detestation, was received with all the honors of war and with all the formalities usual in the case of a high dignitary. Hostages were given for his safety and

Interview between Cavalier and Marshal Villars at Nismes —May 16, 1704.

---

[1] See Louvreleuil, iii. 109–113; Brueys, ii. 319–322; La Baume, 298, 299; Court, ii. 283–286.

[2] La Baume, 300.

[3] "Trusting entirely in Providence, I resolved to go and confer with the Mareschal Villars, who appointed me to meet him in a garden belonging to a convent of the Franciscans opposite one of the gates of Nismes." Memoirs of the Wars of the Cévennes, 266. The Recollets are a reformed order of Franciscans.

kept at Saint Césaire under guard of Ravanel and the foot soldiers until his return—a captain of dragoons, a captain of infantry, and two other officers. He was preceded by M. de la Lande, a royal general and commandant at Alais, who had ridden out nearly to Caveyrac with thirty dragoons to meet him and to bring him to Nismes. Part of his own cavalry accompanied him to the heights above the city ; the rest went before him and cleared the way, or brought up the rear. The crowds that flocked to see him could not have been greater had he been the king himself.[1] Nearly the whole population of Nismes was there. It might be that, as Brueys asserts, the fools looked upon him with admiration, the sensible with horror; at any rate, by that hostile writer's own admission, neither class of men could understand how the little man, who had scarcely reached years of maturity, had been able to make himself absolute master of so many places and so great a population in the Cévennes.[2] Clothed in a close-fitting brown coat trimmed with gold lace and a jacket and breeches of scarlet, with a white plume in his hat, and riding between his faithful lieutenant, Catinat, and Daniel Billard, his favorite preacher, and closely followed by his young brother upon his little Camargue horse, even those of the spectators that were most disposed to ridicule his pretensions could scarcely deny that, despite his youth, he deported himself with surprising dignity.[3] At the convent door, finding the marshal's guard drawn up on one side, he drew up his own in a line on the other side. When he alighted and entered, the intendant and the marshal courteously advanced to meet him, but paused and exchanged glances of surprise when they saw before them a mere boy, as if doubting that it was the person whom they had been expecting. "He is a peasant of the lowest grade, who is not over twenty-two years of age and does not appear to be eighteen," Villars wrote a day after the interview ; "short of stature and with no imposing looks (qualities necessary for [controlling] the masses of the people), but with surprising firmness

---

[1] "Il n'y auroit pas eu un plus grand concours, si c'eût été le Roy." Louvreleuil, iii. 114.

[2] Histoire du fanatisme, ii. 324.

[3] La Baume (p. 302) speaks of his "air ferme et gracieux." See Louvreleuil, ubi supra.

and good sense. I will relate an instance of it. It is certain that, in order to hold his men in check, he often put some of their number to death, and I asked him yesterday: 'Is it possible that at your age, and not having been long in command, you had no difficulty in frequently ordering the death of some of your own followers?' 'No, sir,' he replied, 'when it appeared just.' 'But whom did you employ to inflict it?' 'The first man to whom I gave the order, and no one ever hesitated to follow my command.' I think, sir, that you will find this surprising. Moreover, he has a great deal of skill in arranging for the subsistence of his men, and he disposes of his troops for an action as well as could be done by intelligent officers. I shall be happy if I may deprive them of such a man." [1]

Recovering from his astonishment the marshal was the first to speak, welcoming the Camisard with some complimentary remark, which the latter answered as appropriately as he could. As if he did not recognize the intendant, Cavalier soon began to set forth to Villars the demands of the Protestants, but was interrupted by Basville, who angrily exclaimed: " The king is very merciful to condescend to treat with such a rebel as you." " This," retorted Cavalier, " is not the business about which I came. If you have nothing else to say, I might as well have staid away, and I shall withdraw." And he added: " You alone have forced us to take up arms by your tyranny and cruel procedures." But Villars was not willing to be cheated of the interview and of all it might accomplish, by reason of the intendant's passion, and he hastened to say that his majesty's intentions were to spare his subjects and to use easy methods to recall them to their duty. Turning to Cavalier he said: " Sir, it is with me that you are to treat." Basville, however, was still in an ill humor, and interposed the observation that Cavalier ought to esteem himself too happy that the king should be willing to grant him pardon, without pretending to insist upon any articles. " Sir," rejoined Cavalier, " I did not take up arms on my own account, and since my brethren and friends have reposed their confidence in me, I am bound to support and maintain their interests. The outrages perpetrated upon us

---

[1] Mémoires du maréchal de Villars, 139.

having driven us to the extreme measures that we have been forced to adopt, we are resolved either to obtain our just demands or to die with arms in our hands." Basville, still more provoked by these stout words, would have said something further, but Villars, "a polite fine gentleman," as the Camisard thought him, would not allow an altercation, and said, "Monsieur Cavalier, take no notice of what Monsieur Basville says. I told you it is with me you are to treat."

Thus far there is no reason to doubt the accuracy of the account which the memoirs that pass under Cavalier's name give us of an interview respecting which not one of the other three persons present has left any details. Unfortunately more suspicion attaches to the narrative from this point on. When Cavalier had stated his demands "by word of mouth," we are assured that Villars replied: "You insist upon liberty of conscience. The king is willing to grant it to you. You shall live as you think fit. He will also permit you to meet and to have service in your own way, but not to build churches. You ought to be satisfied with this, after having taken up arms against his majesty. And you are to receive this as a proof of his great clemency. If you refuse it, he will find other means to bring you back to your duty." More was added to the same effect. "Then he asked me," says Cavalier, "whether I was willing to serve the king, which would be more honorable than to quit my country. I answered that I would serve him with all my heart; provided my demands were granted, he should find his majesty had not a more faithful subject. He then desired that I would write them down, not having seen the paper I had given to the Baron d'Aigaliers. I promised to give them in the next day, as also, according to his desire, to forbear hostilities till he had sent and received an answer from court." [1]

Amid much that is manifestly false in this statement, it is not easy to ascertain positively what is true. It is more than probable that the demand for liberty of conscience, if made at all, was not insisted upon with any degree of resolution. At most it was a vague petition, wherein it was not certain whether

---

[1] Memoirs of the Wars of the Cévennes under Colonel Cavalier, 266-269.

the Protestants at large or the men that were in arms were to be the beneficiaries. And it may be asserted with still greater confidence that if ever the marshal undertook to pledge the king to give a favorable response on this point, he certainly did not go to the preposterous length of representing Louis the Fourteenth as disposed to grant the Protestants not only full liberty of conscience, but even permission to hold religious assemblies in which God should be worshipped, not as he dictated, but as their own preferences should dictate—everything in short but the right to build churches! I shall not do the good faith of Villars the injustice to believe that he could have attempted to impose upon Cavalier by so patent a falsehood, nor so underrate his perspicacity as to imagine that had Cavalier showed that he believed it, the marshal would have praised him as a man of good sense. What is true is probably that Villars accompanied the recommendation that Cavalier should enter the king's service with some vague assurance that his conscientious opinions and the opinions of the Camisards that followed his example would be respected. With this view the brief statement of Rossel d'Aigaliers is in perfect accord. To the assurances given him by Villars and Basville, the baron tells us that Cavalier replied that he had never waged war against his sovereign, but merely to protect his own life against the persecution of the priests, and that if he were to be left free in his religion, he would esteem himself very happy to exhibit his zeal for the king's service. No word here in behalf of the Protestants at large or even in behalf of the Protestants of Languedoc ; nothing but a plea for his personal religious liberty. No wonder, then, that Villars replied by assuring him that no attempt would be made to sound his heart to find out what sentiments he cherished, nor that Basville sneeringly remarked that he knew that Cavalier was a pious man, but he was not compelled to talk about religion.[1]

However, this may be, the young Camisard leader, at the close of a long conference, was dismissed with flattering atten-

---

[1] " M. le maréchal lui dit qu'on n'iroit pas pénétrer les sentiments qu'il avoit dans son cœur, et M. de Baville ajouta qu'il savoit que Cavalier avoit de la piété, mais qu'il n'étoit pas nécessaire qu'il parlât de religion." Mémoires de Rossel d'Aigaliers, 45.

tions. La Lande was seen to lean in a friendly manner on his shoulder, and Villars bade him good-by with the words "Adieu, Seigneur Cavalier."[1] Before leaving the garden, he held a levée, and talked freely with a number of persons who pressed about him, respecting the causes that had led to his taking up arms. Then, hat in hand, he passed through the immense crowd that had gathered about the convent of the Recollets, dined in a neighboring inn, and went to visit the gardener, Guy Billard, father of his favorite. Two Camisards, sabre in hand, cleared the way for him. Before he left Nismes, a number of ladies sought the honor of being presented to him, and it is not at all improbable that the scoffing remark of the Roman Catholic counsellor that they esteemed themselves blessed in being permitted to touch the hem of his garments, was true not only of them, but of many another inhabitant of the Protestant city of Nismes.[2] It was but little over a year since the innocent had been butchered and burned, an accursed holocaust, in the mill on the Agau, for the simple crime of meeting together for the worship of God according to the rites of the Reformed religion. And now the champion of that same religion, whose sword had slain many hundreds of its oppressors, was actually at the same city of Nismes, conferring with a marshal of France, telling the dreaded intendant of Languedoc to his face the true causes of the insurrection, crossing and recrossing the esplanade with his own troopers acting as lictors, treated not as a rebel but rather as an honorable foe whose valor had won him the highest consideration! Had not Villars and Basville and everybody in short dropped for the time the opprobrious epithet of *Camisards*, and begun to call them by the affectionate name they gave each other—"the Brethren"—*Les Frères?*[3]

Thus it was that to the sound of the psalms of Marot and Beza, with which the band rode away from Nismes, it reached

---

[1] La Baume, 301.

[2] Ibid., 302.

[3] "Il faut que je dise ici en passant que, pendant le tems que je restoi avec Cavalier, je fus fort édifié de la dévotion que témoignèrent *les Frères*. C'est ainsi que M. le maréchal, M. de Baville et tout le monde appeloient les Camisars dès qu'ils eurent convenu de se soumettre." Rossel d' Aigaliers, 45.

Saint Césaire and liberated the Roman Catholic hostages that
had been left there.

If the incidents of the interview were novel and interesting,
the occurrences at Calvisson a few days later were still more
startling and impressive. It had been agreed that,
pending the return of the messenger from court with
the announcement of the king's good pleasure respecting Cavalier and his band, these should take up their abode
in Calvisson, the principal place in the Vaunage and an ancient
marquisate, where they were to be supplied with provisions at
the public expense. Thither accordingly did the Camisard
leader conduct them, after sending an express to acquaint
Roland in the Cévennes with the negotiations upon which he
had entered with the government and the armistice that had
been agreed upon. If we may credit Cavalier's memoirs, Roland consented to the suspension of warfare, professed himself
ready to make his own submission, provided the terms proposed were granted and observed, but gave expression to his
doubts on the subject, and declared that it would be madness
to trust the bare promises of the court without some substantial
security. As for his part, Roland said that he would die sword
in hand, rather than expose himself and his men to the snares
of an uncertain peace.[1]

Meanwhile, Calvisson was making extraordinary preparations
to receive its strange and unexpected guests. Two or three
days in advance of their arrival, a regiment that had been
stationed there received orders from the marshal to evacuate
the town and come to Nismes. The consuls were instructed by
the quartermaster general of the army to provide comfortable
lodgings for Cavalier and his followers, according to the lists
that would be furnished to them. Wagons laden with grain,
flour, hay, and other provisions reached Calvisson, and were followed by herds of cattle and flocks of sheep. A number of
clerks belonging to the commissary's office came to superintend
the systematic distribution of rations. The preparations for the
reception of the Camisards were more careful and thorough
than were usually made for his majesty's own troops.

*The Cami-
sards at Cal-
visson.*

---

[1] Memoirs of the Wars of the Cévennes, 270.

Early on the appointed day (the nineteenth of May), Catinat made his appearance with a dozen of the horsemen. He was received at the gates by a body of eighty of the burgess militia, who had been forbidden on pain of severe punishment from uttering a single word that might offend the new comers. Cavalier himself arrived an hour before sunset. A great crowd came out to meet him. He was at the head of his cavalry, after which marched the whole body of his foot soldiers. There might be six hundred men in all, forty mounted and two hundred well armed with muskets. Their approach was heralded from afar, for all sang as they marched the good old Huguenot psalms. They continued to sing when, on entering the town, they were drawn up under arms in front of the principal church, then listened with reverence to a long and edifying prayer offered up to heaven by their general himself. From the first, Cavalier assumed the command of Calvisson, posting his own men at the gates, and sending out scouts on all the roads for at least two miles in every direction. His headquarters were in the best house in the place ; sentries guarded the street, and a body of thirty men occupied the hall. The soldiers were billeted with military system in the homes of the inhabitants. Scarcely had two hours been yielded to necessary rest and refreshment, when with one accord the Camisards and the peasants that had flocked to Calvisson betook themselves for worship to the spot where the Huguenot "temple" stood before the Revocation of the Edict of Nantes, and where even now, a score of years having passed since the ruthless destruction of the sacred edifice, its foundations were yet visible. In punishment of this very act—the attempt to worship God among the ruins of the churches torn down by the good pleasure of Louis the Fourteenth—many a religious assembly of the Reformed had been attacked and dispersed during the past quarter of a century ; now the prayers were undisturbed, the loud psalms resounded in the air, and the word of God was proclaimed with bold and joyful voice. For the enjoyment of so rare and highly prized a privilege the long hours of the night seemed all too short. One token there was of the change in the religious condition of France. No ordained pastor of the Reformed churches was there to conduct the

Prayers and psalm-singing on the ruins of the temple.

services in the orderly fashion laid down by national and provincial synods. There was none in Calvisson, none in Languedoc, scarcely one in the whole realm. We must pardon Castanet, and Moïse, and Pierre de Gallargues—yes, and even the prophetess that is said by one writer to have taken part—if, as best they could, they strove to satisfy the ravenous hunger of a people long famishing for the Word of God. It was three o'clock in the morning before the people were willing to disperse. All that night and in the early dawn, the news flew to the villages and hamlets of the Vaunage that the long-expected manna had fallen in their very neighborhood. An "innumerable multitude" was at once on foot, of all ages, of both sexes, of every condition. To satisfy them there must again be a service, a sermon, prayer, psalm-singing. In the afternoon the gathering of people was so vast that no open space in the town could contain it, and the open fields were sought for its devotions.

The third day the movement redoubled its fervor, as the numbers of the worshippers went on increasing. The whole region resounded with their voices. There being nothing to fear, says the curate of Saint Germain de Calberte, they came from Montpellier, from Lunel, from Sommières, from Nismes, from all the parishes that are about those cities. It was calculated that during the sojourn of the Camisards at Calvisson forty thousand persons flocked thither.[1] No wonder that with such an influx of Protestants, to whom by no stretch of the imagination could the designation of "New Catholics" be regarded as appropriate, the customary procession through the streets of the little borough upon the festival of Corpus Christi was prudently intermitted.[2] The fact was that the exercises of piety were attended by a continual stream of worshippers whose zeal never flagged and who, in their eagerness to participate with their brethren, thought every moment lost that was not spent in the spot outside of the town, where they gathered by day, or on the ruins of the "temple," where they met at night. It was scarcely an exaggeration to

The Protestants of the region flock to Calvisson.

---

[1] The estimate is that of La Baume (p. 305); Louvreleuil is content to make it fifteen thousand.

[2] Louvreleuil, iii. 118, 119.

say that of the twenty-four hours full twenty were daily devoted to God's worship.[1] In these numerous assemblies it would
be absurd to suppose that there was nothing to offend
a refined taste or the delicate sense of a decent and orderly conduct of public devotions. Of extravagance and
irregular enthusiasm there was a superabundance. Happily the
poor Protestants of Languedoc, whose spiritual wants had been
sorely neglected for nearly twenty years past, were not over-
nice in such matters, and readily accepted the evangelical truth
and the comfortable exhortations of religion, even if offered by
somewhat rude preachers and disfigured by unseemly physical
contortions, by wild prophetic utterances, and by strange appeals to the ordeal of fire in attestation of the truth of revelations said to come from heaven. As usual, the attention of the
Roman Catholic chroniclers is arrested by these manifestations,
to the exclusion of the grand and touching import of the singular phenomenon, which Rossel d'Aigaliers, a sympathetic eye-
witness of the scene, was able to apprehend. "One could not
but be moved with pity and with terror," he writes, "at the
sight of a people scarcely escaped from burning and butchery
that came to mingle its tears and groans and was altogether
famishing for the Word of God. You would have said that they
were men coming out of a besieged city where they
have endured long and cruel starvation, to whom, together with peace, food is offered. They begin by devouring it with their eyes, and, falling upon it, swallow it down
eagerly, making no distinction between meat, bread, and fruit.
In like manner, these unfortunate inhabitants of the Vaunage,
and of more distant places, when they saw the brethren holding
their meetings in the meadows at the gates of Calvisson,
gathered in crowds around the man or the woman that started a
psalm, and in this way four or five thousand persons, melting in
tears, sang and prayed prostrate for the entire day, with cries
and with a devotion that thrilled the heart and deeply affected
the soul. This was kept up in about the same manner for the

*and hold al-
most inces-
sant services.*

*"A famine
for the Word
of God."*

---

[1] "Les prédications, les prières, le chant des pseaumes et les révélations
alloient toujours leur train. Ils étoient au moins vingt heures du jour dans ces
différens exercices, qu'ils faisoient le jour à la campagne et la nuit sur les
masures du temple." La Baume, 308, 309.

whole night, and nothing could be heard but preaching, singing, praying, and prophesying."[1]

It would be difficult to express in words the anger and indignation aroused in the breasts of the priests and the bigots of their party at the unexpected turn which the Camisard conflict had taken. That an armistice had been entered into with the rebels was bad enough ; but that the exercises of the Protestant religion, so long proscribed, should be tolerated in the largest town of the Vaunage, and that all the inhabitants of the adjacent country who saw fit to go should be suffered to join in them, was an intolerable insult offered to the established church. What was this but a tacit admission of the utter failure of all the means sedulously employed for a good part of a generation of men? What but an open proclamation to the world that Protestantism, far from being dead, was intensely vital? What would the present age, what would future ages say, when it should be recorded that in the midst of a province such as Languedoc, where so great a number of troops were massed, a large body of insurgents, accused by their enemies of every form of crime, should not only be collected together by order of the government and allowed to worship God according to the dictates of their consciences, but actually be lodged and fed at the public expense, and be caressed and made the recipients of those marks of favor and good-will usually accorded only to the objects of singular affection.[2] There was no lack of men that grumbled at the "scandal" and would have been glad to induce Villars to put an end to it, even had he to attack the Camisards—a breach of faith to which, it must be noted to the credit of his good sense, the marshal would not give his consent. So impolitic a course would have ruined all hopes of reconciliation.[3] The wily general was

Indignation of the clergy.

---

[1] In fact, Wincierl, the marshal's quartermaster, unable to get any sleep, had to beg Cavalier to put an end to these nocturnal services. All that the people would consent to was to hold none near his house. Mémoires de Rossel d'Aigaliers, 48, 49.

[2] See Brueys, ii. 331, whose complimentary epithets I have omitted. Bishop Fléchier could scarcely maintain his equanimity, but, upon the whole, did not consider the price paid for the purpose of securing the peace of his diocese to be exorbitant. Letter of May 23, 1704, Œuvres complètes de Fléchier, x. 153.

[3] "On pouvoit les faire cesser," says Brueys (ii. 334), "en donnant ordre aux

less tolerant of the outcries of the priests whose impatience at the scenes enacted at Calvisson he remarked was somewhat absurd. "I do not know," said he, "how many letters I have received full of complaints, as if the prayers of the Camisards not only grated upon the ears but excoriated the entire body of the clergy. I should rejoice with all my heart to find out the names of the writers (who took good care not to sign them), so that I might give them the bastinado. For I regard it as a a very great piece of impudence for those who caused this disorder to complain and disapprove of the means employed to put an end to it." [1]

Such bright days for the Protestants of Languedoc could not last long. About a week after his arrival at Calvisson, Cava-

The pretended royal answer to Cavalier's demands. lier, according to the account he has left us in his memoirs, betook himself, in company with his favorite Billard, to the city of Nismes, for the purpose of hearing the answer that had been received from the court of Versailles. The reply consisted, we are told, of a brief memorandum, sometimes merely the word "*Granted*" or "*Refused,*" jotted down at the foot of each article of the demands. And what were these demands? In reply to this question the memoirs give the pretended text of what may well be styled a very extraordinary document, scarcely less incredible in its petitions than in the answers given to those petitions. There are eight articles, of which two are flatly denied by the king, two are granted unconditionally, four are granted with certain restrictions. The two requests that are directly refused are that no capitation tax should be paid by the province of Languedoc during the space of ten years, and that the four cities of Montpellier, Cette, Perpignan, and Aigues Mortes should be placed in the hands of the Protestants as "cautionary towns." The absurdity of the stipulation, on the part of a few armed Huguenots, that a broad province, the most extensive in France, and inhabited by a population the great majority of which was Ro-

---

troupes de charger ces imbeciles." It is to be hoped that he does injustice to Villars when he adds: "M. le maréchal *fut sur le point de le faire;* mais c'étoit remettre le feu dans la province, et disperser sans espoir de retour, des gens qu'on avoit déja heureusement assemblés."

[1] Mémoires de Rossel d'Aigaliers, 50.

man Catholic, should for a whole decennium be freed from taxation, at a time when the kingdom was staggering under its financial burdens, is only paralleled by the folly of asking for cities, which, unlike the places of security once held by the Huguenots in the days of Henry of Navarre and the Duke of Rohan, were inhabited by a population either hostile or profoundly indifferent to the success of the Camisards. In making the Protestants demand, and the king consent to the release from prison and from the galleys, within six weeks, of all persons apprehended for religion's sake since the Revocation of the Edict of Nantes, and the exemption of the inhabitants of the Cévennes whose houses had been burned from all imposts for the next seven years, the memoirs observe at least a semblance of probability. The same thing may said of the request that all persons that had left the kingdom on account of religion should have liberty to return and should be reinstated in their estates and privileges, which is marked as granted on condition that they take the oath of allegiance to the king. The article wherein Cavalier begs " that out of a body of two thousand of those who were actually with him, or such as shall be delivered out of the several prisons, he shall raise a regiment of dragoons to serve in Portugal, and that he shall receive his orders immediately from the king," accords so nearly with known facts that it might be accepted as genuine, were it not that it is accompanied by a reply that makes, without solicitation, the promise that, " provided the remainder lay down their arms, the king will permit them to live undisturbed in the exercise of their religion." An article calling for "the re-establishment of the parliament of Languedoc on its ancient footing," betrays the hand of a clumsy forger, who has failed even to make clear his meaning.

There remains to be considered the alleged demand, which is placed first on the list, apparently because regarded by Cavalier as of prime importance. It is in these words : "That his Majesty be pleased to grant us liberty of conscience in all this province ; and to hold religious assemblies in such country places as they [the Protestants] shall think convenient, and not in cities or walled towns." The recorded answer is : " Granted, provided they do not build churches." Unfortunately for the reputation of Cavalier as a

The alleged conditional grant of liberty of conscience.

disinterested and patriotic champion of the Protestant cause, and for the credit of the memoirs that pass under his name as a truthful record of actual events, the proof is overwhelming that no such concession on the part of the crown was ever dreamed of, and that, indeed, no demand of the sort was seriously offered. It will shortly be seen that, when Cavalier returned to his expectant troops, he made no pretence that the king had granted the liberty of conscience for which they had so long been battling; and that it was his failure to give them this assurance that led directly to their desertion of a leader whom hitherto they had obeyed with unquestioning submission. The evidence presented by a proclamation made by Marshal Villars on the twenty-ninth of May, or within two or three days of the date at which the supposed concession of the king must have been received, if received at all, is equally conclusive. The proclamation was published for the express purpose of disabusing those persons among whom false hopes had been raised of " a liberty for the exercise of the alleged Reformed Religion." Villars declared that no proposition looking to that liberty had ever been made, and that, if it had been made, it would have been rejected with all merited severity, as utterly opposed to the will of the king.[1] In order to prevent the mischief which so erroneous an impression might produce, the marshal made known that all unlawful assemblies under pretext of religion were expressly forbidden upon the penalties denounced in his Majesty's edicts and ordinances, which would be still more severely punished in future than they had been in the past. The troops under his command were ordered to fall upon any such assemblies as might be . discovered, and the New Converts of the province were warned of the loss of property, the ruin of families, and the devastation of the country which their disobedience would infallibly entail.[2]

The fact was that all that Cavalier received at Marshal Villars's hand was the information that the king was graciously willing

---

[1] " De fausses esperances de liberté pour l'exercice de la Religion Pretendue Reformée, dont il n'a jamais été fait aucune proposition, et que nous aurions rejetté avec toute la severité que nous devons, comme étant entierement contraires à la volonté du Roy."

[2] Text of the proclamation in Louvreleuil, iii. 130–133.

to pardon the crime which he and his followers had committed
in resisting the royal authorities, and to suffer such of them as
pleased so to do, to enter his service and fight against his enemies. This was the meagre gift which the former Camisard
leader was to bring back to Calvisson and to induce his own
followers, as well as the followers of such independent leaders
as Roland and Joany, to accept. For it is manifest that we
must dismiss the document inserted in the memoirs of Cavalier
as an apocryphal paper, composed long posterior to the events
with which it deals ; [1] a paper forged with the scarcely disguised
purpose of rescuing from merited reprobation the conduct of a
man whom his previous actions had invested with a certain air
of greatness, but whose littleness of soul was brought to the
light when the crisis arrived for instant choice between selfish
advantage and the pursuit of the general good.

The king having consented to employ the Camisards in his
armies, Villars despatched to Cavalier a commission to serve as
colonel, with authority to select all inferior officers, at
the same time giving him a yearly allowance of twelve
hundred livres for himself and the rank of captain for
his young brother. It was a large reward in the eyes of the lad
who but a few years ago had been shepherd boy and baker's
apprentice. In return Cavalier submitted to the marshal the
scheme of the regiment which he was to bring with him to Portugal, or wherever else the king should command him to go.
It comprised a little over seven hundred men, divided into sixteen companies. Cavalier had named the captain and lieutenant of each company. La Baume amiably suggests that they
were the men who had recommended themselves for this distinction by the enormity of their past crimes.[2]

But when Cavalier undertook to put the plan of Villars into
execution with his own followers, and to induce the other Cam-

*Cavalier re-
ceives a royal
commission.*

---

[1] So much later, indeed, that the writer gives it the impossible date of May
17th ; according to which a single day must have sufficed for Villars to send a
messenger to Paris and receive in return the answer of the king or his ministers.
See the full discussion in Court, Histoire des troubles des Cévennes, ii. 312-
321.

[2] See the lists in Louvreleuil, iii. 123-126 ; La Baume, 314-316 ; Court, ii. 322-
324.

isard leaders to copy his example, he met with unexpected difficulties.

In his haste to conclude an arrangement with a marshal of France, who flattered his vanity by treating with him almost as an equal, Cavalier seemed to forget that all of the four principal leaders of the Camisards, though of unequal strength, possessed, each in his own district, an authority independent of the others. If Cavalier, occupying, for the most part, the region of the plain from Uzès and Nismes to Sommières, had appeared to make himself most formidable to the intendant, and had won the most striking successes, it was he that had also encountered the most signal defeats. Roland, beyond Alais and Anduze, the chief gateways of the Cévennes, was scarcely less powerful, and gloried in his recent destruction of a good part of a royal regiment at Font Morte; while if La Roze, higher up in the north, and Joany, in the west, commanded smaller bands, they yielded to none in courage and resolution.[1] With all these leaders Cavalier experienced only rebuffs. Roland, in

Roland rebukes him.

particular, during the course of an interview with Cavalier, in the neighborhood of Anduze, was proof against arguments and entreaties. When Cavalier forgot himself so far as to assume a tone of superiority and menace, Roland did not hesitate to answer him frankly and defiantly: "Your head is turned," he said. "I am your senior in command. You ought to die of shame at betraying your cause. Since you have now become the marshal's ambassador, you may tell him, if you please, that I am resolved to die sword in hand unless the Edict of Nantes be restored to its full force. There will never be peace until entire liberty of conscience is conceded." The discussion grew so heated that, according to one account, the disputants might have come to blows had not friends interposed. Roland did indeed consent to send a messenger with Cavalier, to learn more precisely from the marshal's lips the terms upon which the Camisards might count. But Roland was not dazzled by the offer of a colonel's commission, and his envoy was the bearer of a letter couched in such terms as to leave no doubt respecting his determination. After expressing his joy

---

[1] See Aigaliers, 46, 47.

at learning that Villars had come to Languedoc in the spirit of gentleness, he assured him that for himself he asked nothing better than to enter the king's service. "But," said he, "my conscience does not permit me to lay down my arms before the re-establishment of the Edict of Nantes in every point; before the release of the prisoners, the recall of the exiles, the liberation of those sent to the galleys for religion's sake. Moreover, the Protestants must be freed of the intolerable imposts that crush them." [1]

Nor had Cavalier any greater success with his old comrades in arms. During the stay of the Camisards in Calvisson he intrusted the chief command to his lieutenant, Ravanel, and was himself absent a great part of the time, conferring with Villars and maturing the arrangements for the regiment that he was to lead. The secrecy of his movements bred curiosity, and curiosity bred suspicion and distrust. At length, upon his return, on Wednesday morning, the twenty-eighth of May, he was met with urgent demands to reveal the nature of the articles of peace that had been agreed upon. He would still have declined to give a direct reply, but Ravanel, Jonquet and others of the "elders," who, to the number of twelve, constituted his ordinary council, were in no mood to be put off any longer. At last Cavalier was forced to the admission that the Camisards, as the guerdon of their bravery, were to be permitted to go to fight the king's battles in Portugal, and that the tailors were at that moment busy making their red coats in the city of Nismes. "What a proposal," exclaims one of his dupes that was present, "what a proposal to lay before men that were expecting nothing less than the announcement of the grant of liberty of conscience to all the churches of France!" [2]

Cavalier is abandoned by his followers.

---

[1] La Baume gives a summary of this letter, pp. 318, 319. His account of the interview with Roland (p. 317) is confirmed and supplemented by that of Cavalier's Memoirs (p. 278), but the story of the latter, that Cavalier, having by this time become convinced of the treachery of the court, secretly confirmed Roland in his determination not to surrender, and that the apparent misunderstanding was the result of a secret arrangement between them, with the view of compelling the government to fulfil its promises, is one of the fictions that make of a book which should be our most valuable source of Camisard history an utterly untrustworthy production.

[2] Mémoires de Jacques Bonbonnoux, 38.

Amazement, indignation, contempt were depicted upon the countenances of all that heard, as the strange declaration was passed from a man to his neighbor. Ravanel was furious, but his protests and exhortations were scarcely needed to arouse the disgust of the common soldiers. With exclamations of "Coward!" "Traitor!" they turned their backs with one accord upon the man who had so long commanded them, and whose voice they had obeyed as implicitly as if it had been the voice of God,[1] and sorrowfully, but determinedly, made instant preparation to return to their favorite mountains. Cavalier, who, presuming upon the submission he had easily exacted on all previous occasions, looked for no trouble in enforcing his will at this critical juncture, found to his surprise that all his authority had vanished. "It would seem from the way in which you talk," he said to Ravanel, "that you are the master of the band." "Such I am in reality," replied the other, "as I shall convince you when you please. You may make peace as you judge proper; but we shall never lay down our arms save on the conditions we have proposed." And the great crowd of Camisards and assembled Protestants, in a voice terrible and menacing, took up the refrain, "No peace, brethren, no accommodation until we have our 'temples'!"[2]

In despair at seeing himself thus abandoned, Cavalier pursued the band on its march toward the Cévennes, and made a renewed trial of his powers of persuasion. He succeeded in bringing back with him not much over a score of his old followers.[3] Not that the rest had forgotten their past attachment

---

[1] "Que nous avions obéit à peu prez comme à Dieu lui-même." Mémoires de Jacques Bonbonnoux, ubi supra.

[2] "Point de paix, mes frères, point de raccommodement que nous n'ayons nos temples!" La Baume, 310. In the curious letter which Cavalier wrote the next day (May 29) to Basville, and which M. J. P. Hugues was so fortunate as to discover in the old archives of the ministry of war, he makes them express the same sentiments: "Ils ont répondu tous ouvertement qu'ils ne marcheroient pas, qu'ils n'eussent vu l'élargissement et la liberté au peuple de demeurer dans la tranquillité et permission de prier Dieu dans leur maison et au désert, après quoi ils ont proposé d'une même bouche qu'ils iroient tous où Sa Majesté leur ordonnera," etc. Bulletin de la Société de l'histoire du Prot. franç., ix. (1860), 81.

[3] Bonbonnoux says twenty-eight or twenty-nine, Aigaliers, fifty.

and confidence; for as he turned to leave them, at his exclamation "Let those that love me follow me!" "*Qui m'aime, me suive !*" the resolution of more than one Camisard began to waver, and numbers seemed about to join the standard of their former leader. At that moment a single voice broke the spell, and rendered the last appeal futile. It was that of the famous prophet Moïse, uttering the battle-cry heard on many a field of Huguenot combat—"*Vive l'Épée de l'Éternel !*" If the Gideon that so often had turned to flight the armies of the aliens had deserted them to make a delusive pact with the oppressor, the little band declined to partake in his fortunes and refused to abandon the cause which they deemed holy.[1]

Greatly chagrined by his inability to fulfil the promises which he had made to the marshal, Cavalier doubted whether Villars would consent to carry out the arrangements with the Camisards, but was reassured by Aigaliers, whom that officer sent to bring him back to Nismes. The small company of insurgents by whom Cavalier was accompanied were sent to the little island of Villabrègues upon the Rhone, to await their despatch to the frontiers.[2]

Loath to give up all hope of putting an end to the war by the milder method of negotiation, Villars now (on the first of June) formally prolonged the term of armistice for a few days, and, the more to impress the people with his preference for gentleness to cruelty, ordered that the scaffold and gallows which had been permanently erected at Nismes, as elsewhere, and had repeatedly witnessed the revolting but fruitless enforcement of the sanguinary resolve of the government to suppress the revolt at all hazards, should be taken down.[3] Another attempt was made to induce Roland, with whose band the com-

---

[1] See Bonbonnoux, 38–41 ; La Baume, 309–312 ; Court, ii. 329–335 ; Rossel d'Aigaliers, 50, 51.

[2] Rossel d'Aigaliers, 52 ; La Baume, 321. According to the latter, they were forty in number, with Duplan and the younger Cavalier at their head, and were paid, the two officers forty sous a day, the men ten sous. He adds the curious note that whenever the younger Cavalier made his appearance, all the men would rise to do him honor, and this was the signal for starting the singing of psalms.

[3] La Baume, 319, 321.

pany of Cavalier, now led by Ravanel, had united, to listen to proposals of peace and submission. The Baron of Aigaliers Aigaliers's was again employed to mediate. The Protestants of a new effort. number of villages were permitted or induced to send their delegates to Durfort to consult on measures of reconcilia- tion; but when these deputed some of their number to wait upon Roland and Ravanel, and threaten them with the loss of their support, if not with their active hostility, should they continue to hold out against the marshal's offers, they were met with hard words and dire threats. Roland told them plainly that they would be fired upon if they came again on such an errand, and Ravanel said that if they did not give the Cami- sards supplies the Camisards would know how to get them.[1] A little later, however, Roland showed a willingness to treat, if by any possibility the government might proffer such terms as men that had for two long years been battling for the sake of a principle, and for no personal ends, could accept. He invited the Baron d'Aigaliers to a conference, and was so favorably impressed with the roseate representations of that enthusiastic but misleading negotiator, that he consented to send two of his men, Malliet and Malplach, by name, to obtain from the mar- shal's own lips a statement of the advantages which they might hope for at his hands. On his side, Villars sent him two officers Villars of- as hostages—Montbel, who commanded a battalion of fers terms to the Cami- the galleys, and Maisonblanche, captain in one of the sards. regiments. The envoys were well received and are said to have brought back these favorable concessions : That Cavalier and Roland should each have a regiment to serve outside of the kingdom, and should be permitted to have a Protestant minister as chaplain ; that the prisoners should be set at liberty and the exiles recalled ; that the Protestants should be allowed to leave the kingdom with their effects ; that the Camisards that pre- ferred to remain might do so upon giving up their arms ; that those who were outside of the kingdom might return ; that no one should be disturbed in respect to his religion, provided he remained quiet at home ; that the indemnity for the expense of the war should be borne by the province, and that it should not

---

[1] Aigaliers, 52, 53.

be lawful to impose the contribution upon the Protestants in particular ; that there should be a general and unreserved amnesty. The Roman Catholic La Baume, the judge of the presidial court of Nismes, is our sole authority for the articles of this proposition.[1] He adds that M. de Montbel, one of the hostages, exceeded his authority, and is said to have promised on his own responsibility that those who were in the galleys for the matter of religion would be released, and that "the New Converts would be allowed to hold Calvinistic exercises." [2]

We may well believe that the two last articles did not emanate from the marshal, who had just repudiated with the utmost distinctness, in a proclamation purposely spread far and wide, any intention to offer religious liberty to the Protestants, as a thing utterly opposed to the will of the sovereign. But what shall be said of the sincerity of the greater part of the preceding articles, and the probability that they would have been carried out in good faith? The very edict by which Louis the Fourteenth revoked the Magna Charta of Huguenot liberties contained the very same stipulation that was here reiterated, to the effect that his Majesty's Protestant subjects might, until God were pleased to enlighten them, dwell unmolested for their religion's sake, pursue their usual trades, and enjoy their property in any part of the kingdom. But what had this assurance availed during the score of dreary years that ensued? The Dragonnades in every part of France and the brutal severity practised, under the name of "salutary compulsion," by the Abbé du Chayla and his fellows in the neighboring Cévennes, furnished a sufficient answer. Evidently the only safety of the Protestants of France, whether Camisards or not, lay in securing complete religious liberty of creed and profession. Every other assurance could only be, and was probably only meant to be, a snare for the unwary.

The envoys were accompanied upon their return by the Baron d'Aigaliers and by Cavalier. Roland met them at a short distance from Anduze. At first the two leaders greeted each

Their deceptive character.

---

[1] Relation historique de la révolte des fanatiques, 323, 324.   Court in his history, ii., 355, 356, does nothing but copy La Baume.
[2] La Baume, 322, 324.

other with reproaches, Roland blaming Cavalier for making his submission without consulting him, and Cavalier finding fault with Roland because he had not deferred to his advice; *Last interview between Cavalier and Roland and Ravanel.* but after this frank expression they embraced one another as brethren. Not so Ravanel, who was also present. He called Cavalier a traitor to his face, and, when he had warned Roland that all the information that came to him bade him beware of trusting himself to the power of the government, he declined to remain longer and went back to the band. Cavalier was a plausible speaker, and his persuasion, reinforced by the articles brought by the two envoys, seems nearly to have convinced Roland, against his better judgment, to follow the course to which he was invited, and to leave such as would remain with Ravanel upon the mountains. Thus much having been gained, the little group resolved to visit the main body of the Camisards, who, to the number of one thousand men or more, were two or three miles away, to lay before them the alternative and to give each man his choice. And now one of those incidents occurred which at a critical moment instantly change the course of events. Scarcely had Roland and his guests come in sight of the insurgents when they perceived a company of forty men posted as if to block their further progress. Aigaliers, at first sight, mistook them for a guard of honor, come to escort the visitors to the encampment; but he was soon undeceived. At their approach the Camisards threw themselves upon the new comers, while the loud cry went up from Ravanel at their head: "Brethren, here are the traitors that come to corrupt you! Let us defend the cause of the Almighty, even should we be cut to pieces!" Roland they forcibly drew to their band, as if to prevent his leaving them again. One of the two envoys was dragged from his horse and ignominiously stripped. The other scarcely escaped out of the hands of his assailants. Aigaliers, after enduring many menaces and some hard usage, was permitted to return to Anduze. The worst treatment had been reserved for Cavalier, who, happily, was somewhat in the rear, and, turning betimes, fled on his fleet horse, pursued by cries of "Traitor! traitor!"[1] It was the last

---

[1] Mémoires de Rossel d'Aigaliers, 53–55; La Baume, 324, 325.

scene in the attempt to negotiate. If, as is asserted, Roland sent word to Villars by the escaped envoy of his intention to come and make his submission within the prescribed time, and to bring with him those whom he could, to the number of at least one hundred and fifty, his unwise resolution was thwarted by the marshal's treachery in attacking and attempting to capture him before the expiration of the term of the truce. Roland barely escaped with his life. He had learned at his cost how much reliance could be placed upon the honor of a marshal of France.[1]

With Cavalier's final departure from Nismes, on the twenty-first of June, the connection of this remarkable adventurer with the affairs of French Protestantism ceases. In the minds of the adherents of the Reformed church his name had so recently been associated with the brave espousal of the cause of religious liberty that they could not see him go without testifying to their interest and good-will. A great crowd accompanied him a considerable distance from the city and loaded him with tokens of affection. Yet it cannot be denied that the admiration of which he was the object on the part of his contemporaries must in great part be withheld by the impartial verdict of posterity. Not that we can fail to recognize the military ability which, despite his youth and inexperience, enabled him, with an inconsiderable number of irregular troops, half-clad and exposed to every sort of hardship, to withstand and frequently to inflict deadly blows upon an enemy at all times greatly superior in numerical strength and in the appliances of war. But of heroic purpose and equally of deep conscientious conviction there was a strange lack in the leader who could so easily be persuaded to prefer personal safety, and the prospect of military advancement, to the continued support of a cause which, at the time he abandoned it, was certainly not more desperate than it had often been before—a leader who, in the long years he survived his expatriation, showed little or none of that religious zeal and fervor of which, as preacher and prophet, he had once made a cheap

---

[1] Rossel d'Aigaliers, ubi supra. La Baume, who relates the attempted surprise at the castle of Prades, near Thoiras, has nothing to say respecting the marshal's breach of faith.

but profitable display at the head of his troops.[1] His extreme
youth and the influence of the Baron d'Aigaliers over a person
so ignorant and unskilled as the baker's apprentice of Anduze,
must serve as the best, if not as a sufficient excuse for the unwise step into which Cavalier had now been led.

The next day Jean Cavalier embarked at Villabrègues on a boat
that was to take him up the Rhone in the direction of Alsace,
where he was directed to join the royal armies. About
one hundred Camisards accompanied him, a sorry
number in comparison with the regiment that he had
confidently expected to serve under him in the foreign wars.
Such as they were, the government was over glad to be well rid
of them, as is clearly evidenced by the list that has come down
to us, with a brief description set over against the name of each,
and with an occasional note of "*scélerat*," "*fanatique*," or
"*dangereux*" appended to the most conspicuous of the number.[2]
At Mâcon Cavalier received permission to leave his followers
for a few days, that he might proceed to court and lay before
the secretary of war an important communication.[3] His memoirs pretend, indeed, that he was granted an audience by the
king, and record the words that were used by Louis on that occasion. The truth seems to be, on the contrary, that although
Louis felt enough curiosity respecting the young man who had
given great trouble to his generals in Languedoc to induce him
to glance at Cavalier when passing near him on the grand stair-
case of the palace, his Majesty merely shrugged his shoulders
and did not vouchsafe to address the Camisard a single word.
Cavalier needed not this mark of the small consideration in

Cavalier leaves Languedoc.

---

[1] M. J. P. Hugues has, I think, justly emphasized the absence of interest exhibited by Cavalier, as governor of Jersey, in the welfare of the suffering Protestants in the Cévennes. Bulletin de la Société de l'histoire du Prot. franç., ix.
(1860) 77, 78.

[2] Estat des cens Camisards partis avec Cavalier, in Bulletin, etc., xxxiii. 235.

[3] Aigaliers makes no reference to any visit of Cavalier to court, but speaks
with warmth of the good treatment the Camisard leader and his followers received in a city where there were but few Protestant inhabitants. Cavalier held
public services for prayer, and they were frequented by the Roman Catholic
burgesses of the place. The baron ascribes the great friendliness shown to the
Camisards to "the hatred that is cherished pretty much everywhere for the
priests." Mémoires, p. 60.

which he was held to be undeceived. Long before he had approached the banks of the Rhine, he was well convinced that humiliation, if not a worse fate, was in store for him.

He escapes to Switzerland.

He communicated his suspicions to his companions, and they, taking advantage of a favorable moment, imitated his example, when, having reached the neighborhood of Montbéliard, he made good his escape over the French frontier into Switzerland.[1]

With the departure of Cavalier from Languedoc the importance of this singular man, at least so far as the interests of the French Protestants were concerned, came to an end. Not that the apprehensions of the French government on his account had vanished. Puisieux, his Majesty's ambassador, hastily addressed an arrogant letter to the magistrates of Berne, complaining in bitter terms of the asylum found by the "traitor" Cavalier and his followers at Lausanne. The reply of the Bernese was a firm and dignified production, worthy of the best days of the republic, whose hospitable neutrality it vindicated with a fearlessness that was all the more effective that it was set forth in terms strictly diplomatic.[2] Cavalier soon left Switzerland to enter the army of the Duke of Savoy, with the rank of colonel of a regiment of French refugees.

His subsequent fortunes.

Later he was invited to Holland to take part in organizing his exiled countrymen for service under the allies against Louis the Fourteenth. Crossing to England he was received with marked kindness by Queen Anne, a princess who showed deep interest in the welfare of the Huguenots. Under the younger Marquis of Ruvigny, now become Earl of Galway, he fought in Spain; and, in the disastrous battle of Almanza, led his Huguenot regiment against a French royalist regiment with such fury that, his soldiers being received by the enemy with equal animosity, both corps are said to have been almost annihilated.[3] Subsequently he became an officer in

---

[1] See Memoirs of the Wars of the Cévennes. 293–323. See Court, iii. 5–7.

[2] Cavalier reached Lausanne September 1, 1704. Puisieux wrote from Soleure just one week later, and the reply of Berne is dated on the 17th of the same month. The correspondence is given in full by Court, iii. 54–58.

[3] "La seule consolation qui me reste," writes Cavalier, "c'est que le régiment que j'ai eu l'honneur de commander n'a jamais regardé en arrière, et y a vendu sa

the English army, rising to the rank of general, and died thirty-
six years after his departure from Languedoc, royal governor
of the island of Jersey, and a major general in the British service.[1]

Meanwhile, Marshal Villars, disappointed at the meagre
results of a negotiation that had promised such great results,
divided his attention between measures of deportation, as cruel
as any that had disgraced his predecessor, and the fresh efforts put forth by the Baron d'Aigaliers to induce Roland to
accept the terms offered by the court. It would be needless to
give here in detail the story of the honest but mistaken efforts
of that visionary and unfortunate negotiator, born to be the un-
witting instrument in the overthrow of those whom he desired
to help. The curious may read it in full in the baron's own
picturesque and entertaining narrative. Aigaliers had a second
time visited Versailles, in the vain hope that he might secure
the only remedy for the disease in the body politic, "the re-
establishment of freedom of conscience, over which God has
reserved for Himself the sole authority." Secretary of war
Chamillart heard him patiently. Louis the Fourteenth
accorded him two audiences, repeatedly expressed his
satisfaction with the baron's exertions, and conde-
scended to tempt him to embrace the Roman Catholic
faith by hinting at the substantial favors and the honorable appointments to which he might in that case aspire. His majesty even listened without exhibiting anger when Aigaliers
told him of certain bishops in Languedoc who, instead of attracting the so-called "New Converts" by gentleness and good
examples, resorted to every form of persecution to show
them that God intended to punish their cowardice in abandoning a religion which they believed to be a good one, by giving
them over to religious shepherds that were intent on driving
them to despair. With more patience than might have been
expected, the monarch merely exclaimed: "That will do! Do

*Louis XIV.
gives audi-
ence to Ros-
sel d'Aiga-
liers.*

---

vie chèrement." Letter dated Genoa, July 10, 1707, printed in Bulletin, etc., vi.
70, from MS. in State Archives at the Hague.

[1] See La France Protestante, s. v., and the chapter devoted to his history by
Agnew, Protestant Exiles from France in the Reign of Louis XIV., 2d edition,
ii. 54-66. Cavalier died at Chelsea, May 17, 1740.

not speak any more about that matter!" But whatever concessions the baron secured—unfortunately he has not told us what the promises were—they certainly did not amount to anything like religious liberty, and probably were little more than the release of the prisoners and galley-slaves.

Meanwhile, before Aigaliers's return to Languedoc, the Camisards that were still under arms had been favored with a visit from an agent, sent by the English and Dutch envoys at Turin, to confer with the insurgents respecting the best methods for furnishing them assistance. If Tobie Rocayrol's mission proved barren of results, the account of his experiences, which he has left us, is both vivid and entertaining.[1] It was no easy matter to make his way to the haunts of the mountaineers; but the agent, disguised as a merchant, so cleverly contrived to fall into the hands of the roving party which was expecting him, that when he reappeared on the plains a few days later, he made out a plausible story of release from an involuntary captivity. His instructions were to explain the failures of the past, and give encouragement respecting the future. But the Camisards gave him clearly to understand that they could not in the nature of things come down from the Cévennes to welcome an auxiliary force from abroad upon the sea-shore. They would be cut to pieces before a junction could be effected. Nor were more men wanted, unless, with the men, the money necessary for their support were received. They now had, they informed him, three thousand foot and nearly two hundred horse; but they were destitute. Had they but twenty thousand francs at their disposal, they might readily increase their numbers to six thousand men, and in course of time to ten thousand. With these they would be able to set Marshal Villars at defiance. For, if their three thousand troops had been a match for twenty thousand of the enemy, much more would ten thousand mountaineers repulse thirty thousand. Nor was this strange, when of their opponents many were so friendly that for

Tobie Ro-cayrol's mis-sion to the Cévenols.

---

[1] It has been published in the Bulletin, xvi. (1867) 273, etc., under the title of Le Camp des Enfants de Dieu : Relation par Tobie Rocayrol de la mission dont MM. Hill et Vandermeer, envoyés d'Angleterre et de Hollande à Turin, l'avaient chargé aupres des Camisards.

a little money they were willing to sell the Camisards not only food, but the very munitions of war ; while others loudly protested against being constrained to fight against men who, they declared, did nothing else than pray to God. This description of the Camisards, according to Rocayrol, did not go beyond the truth.[1] Their preachers were able. One of the number, Jean Huc, of Genolhac, he had himself heard discourse on the lamentable cry of king Darius to the prophet Daniel, in so holy and touching a manner that he exclaims : "Would God that everybody had heard it ! There would be no one, whether little or great, that would not approve their conduct, and wish with all his heart to be able to relieve them." [2] So constantly did the Camisards sing the praises of the Almighty that there were men unable to read or write who, joining their band, had come to learn the psalms by heart, merely from hearing them sung by others. The exemplary life they led awakened the admiration of the beholder. Any of their number that were found guilty of profane swearing, after one or more admonitions, were flogged along the line ; and the thief or the rake, at his second offence, was remorselessly punished. All the soldiers called one another "Brother," from Roland himself down to the meanest private ; and for the most part they had all things in common. The ardent desire of their hearts was to obtain regularly ordained pastors. Meanwhile, their religious services were conducted according to the forms observed by the churches of Geneva and of the Pays de Vaud—that is, in the use of the liturgy of Calvin, the time-honored formulary of the Reformed Churches of France subsisting before the Revocation of the Edict of Nantes. Rocayrol was even able to assure those who had sent him that, in deference to the exhortations addressed to them from abroad, the Camisards had renounced the policy of burning churches or maltreating their sworn enemies the priests, and that it was notorious that none were now harmed save such as did them harm. The "Camisards Blancs " and those other licensed bandits, the "mique-

---

[1] His words are striking. "Ils prient Dieu sans cesse et avec un sy grand zèle qu'il semble *qu'ils soient collés à notre Seigneur Jésus-Christ*." Bulletin, xvi. (1867) 322.

[2] Ib., xvi. 280.

lets " from Roussillon, were the sole objects of their armed pursuit.[1]

The return of Baron d'Aigaliers to Languedoc was followed by a renewed attempt to bring the Camisards to submission. But as he could not offer them the only terms upon which men that had taken up arms to secure liberty of conscience could lay them down, it is not surprising that his failure was even more signal than before.[2] It was almost the last act in his singular career. Within a few days, for all reward of his patient and painstaking labors in the king's service, the baron received from the Secretary of War, Chamillart, a peremptory order of banishment. Retiring to Geneva, Aigaliers busied himself with the composition of the brief but valuable memoirs to which I have been indebted for many of the facts in the present narrative. Before he had quite completed his task a fresh hope to be of service to his country led him again to enter France; but having been discovered and arrested, he was thrown into the castle of Loches. Here he lost his life in an attempt to regain his liberty.[3]

End of Aigaliers.

Meantime, an event occurred that sealed the fate of the Camisard uprising; for the movement which had outlived the defection of Cavalier could not permanently recover from the loss it sustained in the death of Roland. The money lavished by Marshal Villars upon spies and traitors was not all expended in vain. Among the stanchest of the Protestants of the Lower Cévennes were the ladies of the noble family of Cornelly, who took their title from the castle, whose remains are yet to be seen, surrounded by a stately park, amid cascades and fountains, close to the town of La Salle.[4] These intrepid Huguenots, overcoming the natural timidity of their sex, had in the past braved peril by attending the assemblies held in the Desert by Brousson and Vivens. Since the Camisard revolt they had not proved themselves less courageous. They welcomed Roland to their home, both as preacher and as the valiant champion of their oppressed brethren in the

Death of Roland.

---

[1] Bulletin, xvi. (1867) 324, 325.
[2] See Mémoires de Rossel d'Aigaliers, 60–64.
[3] See Professor Frosterus's remarks, ibid., 66.
[4] See Joanne, Les Cévennes, 237.

faith.[1] He was, at the time to which I now refer, their guest in a house or castle not far from Castelnau. The secret had been sold by a traitor to M. de Parate, one of the most active of the Roman Catholic commanders, and the price paid was one hundred louis d'or. Parate lost not a moment in improving his opportunity. So rapid was the march to the spot, and so complete the surprise, that Roland had barely time to fly a few steps from the castle when he was overtaken by his pursuers. His firmness did not desert him even in the supreme moment. Resolutely posting himself with a tree at his back, he prepared to meet single-handed both the officer and the soldier who had caught up with him. But while these hesitated, disconcerted by the intrepidity of his bearing, a third enemy, by a well-directed shot, procured the Camisard hero what he most desired, an instantaneous death.[2] Five officers, his companions, were less fortunate. After their leader's death they gave up all hope, and suffered themselves to be taken without resistance. They paid the penalty of their discouragement by a most painful execution. Carried before the intendant at Nismes, they had, two days later, a quick trial and were sentenced to be broken upon the wheel. The same evening they endured the savage vengeance of the law, without showing any sign of weakness or fear. Their constancy and cheerfulness surprised all the spectators, but especially such as had never seen until now how a Camisard could die. They were not the least notable in the long list of sufferers at Nismes whom a contemporary, and perhaps an eye-witness, describes as talking and singing while stretched upon the wheel, and wearing as serene a countenance as if they had been in attendance upon a banquet.[3] Maillié,

---

[1] See note of J. Vielles to his edition of the Mémoires de Bonbonnoux, 118. No one accustomed to the reading of Brueys, Louvreleuil, and La Baume, and familiar with the readiness exhibited by these writers to accept as facts, and to incorporate in their histories every flying rumor to the disadvantage of the Camisard leaders and soldiers, will, I am sure, charge me with undue scepticism or partisanship, if I decline to give the slightest weight to their attempt to asperse the character of one or both of the ladies of Cornelly.

[2] Louvreleuil, iii. 193–195 ; Brueys, ii. 376–379 ; La Baume, 346–348 ; Court, iii. 40–42.

[3] Aigaliers, 65.

Roland's lieutenant, drew special attention to himself, and made a deep impression upon Villars. "The officers," writes the Maillié's con- marshal to the minister of war, with the scene yet stancy. fresh in his mind, "had been intended to serve as an example ; but the manner in which Maillié met death was much more suited to confirm in their religious views men whose heads were perverted, than to destroy them. He was a handsome young man, possessed of an intelligence above the common. He listened to the reading of his sentence with a smile, went through the city of Nismes with the same air, begging the priest not to torment him. The blows that he received did not change this air, nor wring from him a single cry. When the bones of his arms were broken, he still had strength enough to motion the priest to withdraw, and, so long as he retained the power of speech he cheered his companions. This made me think that, in the case of such people, the most expeditious death is always the most proper; that, above all, it is well not to give to a people that is already corrupted the spectacle of a priest that screams and a sufferer that treats him with scorn, and that we ought especially to base the sentence of the culprits rather upon their obstinacy in revolt than upon their religion." [3]

Five prelates of the Roman Catholic Church witnessed the execution. Their astonishment at the firm bearing of the Camisards was equalled only by the indecent joy they displayed that Languedoc was well rid of Roland and his most active supporters.[2] Nor was the dead leader neglected by the judges. After a formal procedure against his memory the mortal remains were duly attached by the neck to a cart, and drawn by oxen up and down the streets of the city. After which indignity the corpse was cast into the fire and burned. The ashes were cast to the wind.[3]

The loss of Roland was a death-blow to any reasonable hopes

---

[1] "Qu'il est surtout convenable de ne pas donner à un peuple gâté le spectacle d'un prêtre qui crie, et d'un patient qui le méprise," etc.   Marshal Villars to Chamillart, August 18, 1704, Mémoires de Villars, 142, 143.

[2] "Un officier, témoin de leur transport, m'a assuré qu'ils parurent indécens à bien des gens, qui n'étoient rien moins qu'amis des Camisards."   Court, iii. 43.

[3] La Baume, 348 ; Brueys, ii. 379 ; Louvreleuil, iii. 196.

that might still have been entertained regarding the ultimate success of the Camisards in securing for themselves and for their brethren in the faith some more tolerable terms of existence. No leader remained who could have gathered the scattered bands into a compact and formidable body. A great part of the insurgents recognized the fact. The next two months witnessed the submission of almost all the best leaders. In September, Castanet, Catinat, and Sauvage came in, taking advantage of the offer of a safe-conduct out of the kingdom. Early in October the fierce Joany surrendered with a band of forty-six braves. Later in the same month La Rose, Valette, La Foret, Salomon, Moulières, Salles, Abraham, and Marion gave up their arms. Some days after Fidel and Beulaugue followed their example.[1]

Successive surrenders of Camisard leaders.

Most of these found a refuge in Switzerland, where the insignificant appearance of the leaders, evidently men of low station and little education, only tended to enhance the general astonishment that, under adverse circumstances of the most formidable character, with troops altogether disproportionate to the number of disciplined soldiers brought against them, and in utter destitution of money for the purchase of clothing, shoes, and the very ammunitions of war, they had been able to cope with the generals of Louis the Fourteenth. Even now the apprehensions of the great king's advisers were not quieted. They insisted that the obscure peasants who had lately kept Languedoc and the Cévennes in commotion should not be permitted to remain in proximity to the frontier; and the great canton of Berne dared not refuse the demand of its powerful neighbor. It seemed, however, that, precisely now, when the revolt in France had been so thoroughly quelled that of all the chieftains only Ravanel remained in the mountains stubbornly refusing to accept any terms of submission, the interest of the outside world began to be aroused in behalf of the Camisards, and there was a prospect that the aid might be offered which a few months before might have been of some account.

Meanwhile, Marshal Villars, taking advantage of the appar-

[1] Louvreleuil, iii. 216–220; La Baume, 360, 361; Court, iii. 72.

ent suppression of the revolt, and longing for a wider field for the display of his military abilities, sought and obtained his recall from Languedoc. Before his departure (on the eighth of January, 1705) the provincial estates not only voted him their thanks for his services, but presented him with a voluntary gift of twelve thousand livres for himself and eight thousand for his wife.[1] The address made to him by the bishops was as flattering as the marshal could have desired. Greater honors awaited him at Versailles. There Louis the Fourteenth was pleased to confer upon him the collar of the royal order, and to lavish upon him some of those compliments more highly prized by courtiers than the most substantial of rewards.[2] He was replaced, in the military command of Languedoc, by the Duke of Berwick, an illegitimate son of James the Second of England, who was to win the marshal's baton by his services in completing the work of his predecessor, and later to gain the admiration of Europe by his success as a military commander in the great battle of Almanza.

Marshal Villars secures his recall, and is succeeded by the Duke of Berwick.

In previous years some funds had been furnished by the powers allied against France to foment the disturbances of Languedoc, but so unfaithful had proved the persons to whose hands they were intrusted that not a livre had reached the insurgents. The money which the agent Flottard gave in the name of Queen Anne to Marion and other Camisard chiefs, in the month of February, 1705, to encourage them to recommence the war, was therefore the first which the Protestants actually received from their foreign sympathizers, the great maritime states of Great Britain and the Netherlands.[3] The help so long held back was now inopportunely given, and ultimately produced more harm than good. The Camisard leaders that had availed themselves of Marshal Villars's offers, and were in a

---

[1] Letter of Fléchier, January 8, 1705, Œuvres complètes, x. 179.

[2] Court, iii. 97, 98.

[3] Antoine Court's statements are positive and incontrovertible. According to him, Hill, English envoy to the Duke of Savoy, wrote, November 19, 1704, in reference to the considerable remittances he had made to France, that he was at present persuaded that not a penny had ever reached those for whom they were intended. Histoire des troubles des Cévennes, iii. 101.

place of safcty beyond the Alps, were induced by the promise
of a substantial support, of which the present gift of money was
to be regarded only as an earnest, to steal back one by
one to the Cévennes, in order to renew under still

New executions in Languedoc.

greater discouragement a hopeless conflict. And thus
it was that, by the side of the name of Ravanel, the names of
Castanet and Valette, of Jonquet and Vilas, of Catinat and
others, who had made good their retreat to foreign lands, once
more figure in the long list of those upon whom the intendant Lamoignon de Basville, in the course of his bloody assizes,
was called upon, after a very brief trial, to pass the most atrocious of sentences. Some were caught upon the mountains,
arms in hand ; others were discovered through the treachery
of supposed friends, and arrested in Montpellier or Nismes,
whither they had resorted in disguise, for the purpose of obtaining provisions or of completing arrangements for carrying
out their plans of warfare. However diverse the modes of their
capture, there was a dreary uniformity in their fate. The punishment of death was meted out to all. Two wealthy merchants
of Nismes, found guilty of having acted as bankers to forward
the sums of money sent to the Camisards, shared the same end
as the humbler victims sprung from a lower class of society.
The armorer who was proved to have manufactured guns
for the Camisards, the innkeeper that had given them food, the
silk-dealer that had hidden them in his house, were visited with
as savage a penalty as the armed men whom they had befriended. A judge of the presidial court of Nismes informs us
that, in two of its sessions, this tribunal of justice condemned
not less than seventeen persons, whose names and occupations
he gives, either to the flames, or to the wheel, or to the gallows
—" a visible chastisement of heaven," he observes, "to teach
the people the obedience which it owes to its sovereign." "All
these scoundrels," he adds, " died with a surprising intrepidity.
Before their condemnation they seemed to despise the punishments with which they were threatened, and they endured these
punishments with a firmness that would deserve admiration had
not the cause for which they suffered them inspired every body
with horror. So true is it that, in crime as well as in virtue,
there is something extraordinary that is apt to deceive such

persons as are satisfied with the external appearance, and do not penetrate to the core of the action." [1]

In describing the constancy and misconstruing the character and end of these victims of intolerance, La Baume, the presidial judge, is outdone in severity by the priest Louvreleuil. " Men reap at death," observes the latter, " what they have sown in their lifetime. Inasmuch as these wicked persons had scattered broadcast the seed of blindness, impiety, and despair, they gathered its bitter fruit. They pursued the road which they had taken, they were paid by the master whom they had served. I mean that they fell into the hands of the devil, who recompensed with his black furies, his burning and his everlasting cruelties, the obedience they had rendered to his criminal suggestions." [2]

Fortunately we are not left entirely to the unfriendly pages of either Louvreleuil or La Baume for a record of the patience and Christian fortitude with which the victims of the sanguinary tribunal of Basville met death. The words and the actions of

Boeton. Boeton, whose unpardonable offence it was that at his house the plans had been concerted for a fresh uprising, were not unworthy of comparison with the most courageous utterances and deeds of the martyrs of the primitive church, or of those equally intrepid confessors of the truth in the times of the great Reformation. When he was stretched upon the rack not a syllable respecting the plans of the Protestants and their foreign allies could be wrung from his lips. Irritated by failure to obtain the information of which he stood greatly in need, the intendant Basville forgot every sentiment of generosity, and stooped to the dishonor of wantonly insulting a helpless prisoner. Whereupon Boeton, raising his eyes to heaven, exclaimed: "How long, O Lord, wilt Thou suffer the ungodly to triumph? How long wilt Thou permit him to shed the blood of the innocent? That blood cries before Thee for vengeance. Wilt Thou yet tarry long to execute justice therefor? Awaken Thine ancient jealousy, and remember Thy compassions!" On

---

[1] La Baume, 381, 382.

[2] L'Obstination confondue (the sequel to Le fanatisme renouvelé, of which it forms the fourth volume), 92, 93.

the way to the place of execution, seeing the emotion of one of his friends who burst into tears and hastily withdrew to a shop to hide himself from sight, Boeton asked permission to say a few words to him ; and, when the man was brought, "What!" he said, "do you flee from me because you see me clothed in the livery of Jesus Christ? Why do you weep, when He does me the favor to call me to Him and to the glory of sealing with my blood the defence of His cause?" He was no less constant and fearless when he came in sight of the platform erected upon the esplanade: "Be of good courage, my soul," he cried, "I see the scene of thy triumph. Soon released from thy painful bonds thou shalt enter the skies!" To a form of punishment that was always cruel were purposely added unusual and needless features of barbarity. After the prisoner had been extended upon the scaffold and the executioner of the law had successively broken with his ponderous hammer the bones both of the arms and of the legs of his victim, by an excess of malignity of which an African savage would scarcely have been guilty, Boeton was placed upon a wheel and allowed to languish full five hours, his broken limbs passed under his body and his head hanging down. Even then, despite the agony of his situation, despite the incessant roll of drums beaten for the purpose of drowning his voice, he did not cease for a moment to sing the dear old psalms of Marot and Beza, to pray with fervor to God, and to exhort and encourage such of his fellow-believers as were permitted to come near. In the end it was not pity, but policy, that induced Basville to give the order that the merciful blow should be struck that would deliver him from so much misery. A priest, the witness of the scene, had just warned him that, far from terrifying the Protestants, the sight of Boeton's slow death was only confirming them in their faith, as was evident from their tears and from the praise they lavished upon the champion of their religion. At that supreme moment, by an almost superhuman effort, the dying man raised his head, and, in cheerful tones, heard even above the deafening din which had not ceased for an instant, he uttered his farewell to his weeping friends: "My dear brethren," he said, "let my death be an example to you to maintain the purity of the Gospel, and be the faithful witnesses, testifying that I die belonging to the religion of Jesus Christ and of his holy Apostles."[1]

A few Camisards held out for several years in the Cévennes, too unimportant in numbers to deserve the name of a band, too weak to come into any engagement worthy of account with the royal troops. Their varied experiences, their hair-breadth escapes from the pursuers that were always upon their track, and the fate that from time to time befell some of them, constitute a theme of singular interest.[2] So desultory a warfare was sure to come to an end as soon as all hope of foreign assistance died out. Meantime some exploits of valor were performed worthy of the best days of Greece and Rome. The conflict of Justet, a prodigy of physical strength, alone and unarmed, against two grenadiers whom he held, giant-like, one in either hand, and slew in sight of their comrades by smiting them together, does not suffer by comparison with the deeds of prowess recorded of any hero of the band of Leonidas at Thermopylæ.[3]

End of the Camisard struggle.

Exploit of Justet.

It was in the month of July, 1709, and at a spot named Fontreal, in the mountains of Upper Vivarais, that for the last time any considerable number of Camisards came to blows with the troops of the king. Their dispersion and the capture and execution of several of their number virtually closed the hostilities.[4]

---

[1] Court, iii. 162–166.

[2] There is a peculiar charm in the unaffected story told by Jacques Bonbonnoux. Its marvels would scarcely be credible but for the evident good faith of the narrator. The Camisard's fertility of resource for the purpose of avoiding discovery was equalled only by his extraordinary good fortune. At one time he escaped the fate that overtook his two companions. by promptly climbing a tree, where happily the enemy never thought of looking for him. At another, he lay concealed in a small hogshead. On more than one occasion his hiding-place was little better than a rude excavation in the earth, protected from view by a heap of stones carelessly gathered about the opening. In describing the hardships of his life, which seemed to reach the climax when he fell sick of small-pox, the illiterate Cévenol, who at this time did not even know how to read, unconsciously falls into a train of thought reminding us of the words of one of Homer's heroes. "De tels contretemps auroient été funestes à quelqu'autre. Dieu voulut que je n'en mourusse pas, *il me réservoit encore pour d'autres aventures.*" (Page 93.) Cf. Odyssey. vi. 172, seq.

[3] Brueys, iii. 553; Court, iii 252. 253.

[4] Court, iii. 258, 259 ; Brueys, iii. 567, etc.

More than a year later, upon the esplanade of Montpellier, and almost in sight of a foreign fleet of over a score of foreign vessels of war that were hovering off the coast and could easily be descried from the city, the intendant Basville superintended in person the execution of two Camisard prisoners. They were hanged on the gallows. The more painful death by breaking on the wheel fell to the lot of Claris, the last leader of the dispersed Camisards, on the twenty-fifth of October in the same year (1710). The last exploit of Basville in the war was in the ensuing year (April, 1711), when having despatched his emissaries to Switzerland he succeeded in seizing one Saint Julieu, who had frequently acted as a bearer of despatches between the Dutch and English agents in Berne or Geneva and the Camisard leaders in the Cévennes. It mattered little to the redoubtable intendant that the capture was effected, contrary to the law of nations, on the waters of Lake Leman, opposite to Versoix, and within the jurisdiction of the Canton of Berne. None the less had he the satisfaction of trying the person whom he had kidnapped and executing him at Montpellier. With him ended the long list of those upon whom Basville wreaked vengeance during the course of the Camisard uprising.[1]

Respecting one of the last victims an interesting and pathetic story has come down to us. The extraordinary vigilance of Basville was rewarded, on the twenty-fifth of April, 1710, by the discovery and arrest, upon the old bridge of Alais, of a former Camisard and a preacher of some note, Salomon Sabatier, by name. What his fate would be was no matter of doubt; and, indeed, but four days elapsed before he was put to death at Montpellier. But, in the brief interval between his apprehension and his removal to the coast, several ladies of the city of Alais, some of them former Protestants, expressed to the officer into whose hands Sabatier had fallen a desire to hear the old Camisard preach one of those sermons of which they had heard so much. Monsieur de la Lande was too gallant a soldier to refuse a favor which he could so easily grant. Sabatier was sent for, and was informed that he might, if he pleased, repeat some stirring address which he had made before the as-

Salomon Sabatier.

---

[1] Brueys, iii. 636, 637 ; Court, iii. 303.

semblies of the Desert. The Cévenol preacher could not mistake the unworthy motive that prompted the invitation, nor ignore the indifference of some, at least, of his gentle hearers to the only truths which he felt at liberty to proclaim to them. None the less did he promptly and cheerfully comply with the general's request. First of all, however, he offered up a prayer "full of fire and zeal." For the text of his discourse he chose the first verse of the fifty-ninth chapter of Isaiah : "Behold the Lord's hand is not shortened, that it cannot save, nor His ear heavy, that it cannot hear." Availing himself of his rare opportunity, he became the spokesman of the Reformed churches of France. He set forth their deplorable condition, as the objects of unmerited persecution ; then passed on to the consideration of the joy which their misfortunes occasioned in the minds of their malicious and triumphant enemies. But over against this he drew a picture of the unshaken confidence felt by the Huguenots regarding their ultimate deliverance. Cast down they were, even to the earth, but not in despair. Speaking through a man destined within a few hours to end his days upon the wheel, the innocent objects of unparalleled oppression proclaimed unhesitatingly their certain expectation, founded upon the promises of Almighty God, upon His pity, upon His goodness, upon His power. The Lord's arm was not shortened : it would yet be outstretched for their rescue. His ear was not heavy : it was even now attentive to every sigh and groan of His children undergoing injury and outrage for His sake.

His sermon in the prison of Alais.

Again, as so often before in the history of the Christian church, it was the prisoner for righteousness' sake that assumed the place of conqueror, and triumphant Iniquity was forced to crouch at his feet, vanquished in the moral strife. As for the Camisard preacher's audience, those that had come to make sport of the misfortunes of a helpless captive were touched, were moved to tears, possibly began to doubt the justice of a cause which was compelled to resort to violence for its maintenance. Perceiving this, Monsieur de la Lande, annoyed at the unexpected issue of the ill-timed curiosity of his friends, and vexed with himself that he had complied with their request, abruptly ordered Sabatier to be silent and remanded him to his cell. "Ah, my friend," exclaimed one of his hearers as she took leave of the prisoner, "would that a cup of our blood might save you. Very gladly should we shed it in your behalf."[1]

The struggle was over. Had it been all in vain? Must the thousands of lives lost in the Cévennes, in the lowlands, in the Vaunage, be reckoned a wasteful sacrifice from which humanity, from which religion had derived no appreciable advantage? A dispassionate view will not lead us to this conclusion.

Results of the Camisard movement.

First of all, the Camisards demonstrated beyond controversy both to the crown and to the Roman Catholic people of France, that Protestantism, so far from being destroyed, was in fact indestructible. When Louis the Fourteenth based his revocatory edict upon the premiss that the greater and better part of the adherents of the so-called Reformed religion had been converted, we cannot, in the most charitable view of the case, suppose him to have been half convinced of the truth of the proposition which he was affirming. No doubt, however, he was determined to make it true. His advisers, especially the more intelligent men both of clergy and laity, while conceding that possibly the profession of Roman Catholicism which Protestant parents were constrained to make might be very wanting in candor and sincerity, maintained that it was quite practicable to educate the children in that faith from the start. The next generation, at any rate, would consist of trustworthy members of the established church. We have seen the measures adopted to compass this end. Laws at war with all the dictates of justice were pitilessly executed. Parents were compelled to send their children not only to a church which they detested, but to catechetical classes where they were taught doctrines which they loathed as not only false but pernicious. If the fines and punishments incurred by those who neglected this obligation were severe, they were still more cruel in the case of the father or mother

Protestantism indestructible.

---

[1] Mémoires de M. Corteis sur l'état de la religion réformée dans le Bas-Languedoc et Cévennes (ed. Baum), 16, 17. Antoine Court, Histoire des troubles des Cévennes, iii. 272, 273.

who was convicted, or even suspected, of counteracting by family instruction the priestly instruction given in the schools. The parent was thrown into prison, the children were torn from the home and placed in some convent, or school, to be educated at his expense, until such time as they might be sufficiently grounded in Roman Catholic doctrine to be suffered to return to the home. By these methods, and by other devices of a similar nature systematically pursued for a long course of years, it was confidently expected that Protestantism would soon be a thing of the past.[1]

The outbreak of the Camisard revolt roughly dispelled the unsubstantial dream. Bishop Fléchier, whose diocese was its theatre, begged the commiseration of his friends. He had lost, he said, the entire fruits of seventeen years of labor.[2] His astonishment is almost pitiful when he informs us that the Protestants, or, as he still persists in calling them, the New Converts of his diocese, whom he has "instructed, served, assisted, treated with great mildness and charity, have almost to a man been wholly perverted, and have instantly become the enemies of God, of the king, of the Catholics, and especially of the priests." [3]

Bishop Fléchier's lament.

Evidently there were just as many Protestants as there were so-called New Converts—all animated by a strong desire to profess the doctrines of the Reformation, all imbued with a violent hatred of the prevalent system, a hatred manifesting itself not merely in a wholesale abandonment of the parish church, but in deeds of violence, often savage and most unjustifiable, directed against members of the ecclesiastical establishment.

And it should be noted that the active participants in the warfare were, with few exceptions, young men. The Edict of Nantes had been revoked and Protestantism proscribed for seventeen years when the war broke out. Those who took the

---

[1] "The clergy shut up in convents and seminaries all their children of both sexes, in order to instruct them in their religion, hoping by that means that, when the old people were dead, the Protestant religion in France would be at an end." Memoirs of Cavalier, 9.

[2] "Nous voyons tout le fruit de nos travaux de dix-sept ans perdu." Letter of April 25, 1703. Œuvres, x. 121.

[3] Letter of April 27, 1704, ubi supra, x. 147.

most prominent part in it were twenty, twenty-five, rarely thirty years old. They were either infants or young children when the tolerant law of Henry the Great was recalled. Consequently their attachment to Protestantism was created at the very time when the clergy believed that, by their instructions, they were training the younger generation, the Protestant children, to become zealous Roman Catholics. Thus the uprising of the Camisards proved to their enemies the complete failure of the attempt to extirpate Protestantism.

It had a corresponding effect upon the Protestants themselves. It encouraged them to believe that there were better things in store for them ; that they had but to bide their time, and the monstrous fabric of persecution must crumble and fall. In the words of Holy Writ, which Sabatier so appropriately chose for the text of his discourse, the Lord's hand was not shortened that it could not save. Deliverance would yet come in God's appointed way.

But the experience of the war showed that this way was not to be through force of arms—not by the prowess of the Protestants themselves, nor by the interposition of foreigners or foreign states. On the one hand, hopes based upon the promised help of sympathizers abroad came to naught. On the other, the demoralizing effects of war discredited the recourse to the sword as the proper means of establishing a reign of peace and righteousness upon the earth. The excesses of the Camisards themselves, or of bands conveniently sheltering themselves beneath their name, were surpassed in cruelty only by the excesses of the *Cadets de la Croix* and the so-called *Camisards blancs*, and disgusted many even of those whose natural sympathies were on the side of religious toleration. Hence the collapse of a movement which, had it enlisted the undivided support of all the members of the Reformed communion, might have lasted, if not indefinitely, yet for a much longer period than that which it actually covered.

At the same time, if the Camisard war did not strike a death-blow at the enthusiastic frenzy of the Cévenol prophets, it hastened the extinction of that delusion. Pretended revelations from heaven contributed much to nerve the courage of the first Camisards. Persuaded that the road to victory was

Protestantism not to be re-established by force of arms.

distinctly pointed out by seers inspired of the Holy Ghost, men willingly undertook the most hazardous enterprises. As-

The approaching end of prophetic enthusiasm. sured that their bodies were invulnerable, they rushed into conflict with little thought of danger, not doubting that God would take care of His own children.

But as the war advanced, instances multiplied of the disappointment of hopes based upon private revelations, and while the illusion was not altogether dispelled, the faith of the multitude was shaken.

Thus it was that the Camisards made the path of Antoine Court less rugged when, about five years after the execution of Sabatier, he undertook to bring order out of the reigning confusion, and initiated that noble work of setting up again the ecclesiastical organization and discipline of his fellow-believers that has earned for him the enviable title of "the Restorer of French Protestantism."

The failure of the Camisard uprising was an important factor in the success of the Churches of the Desert.

BOOK SIXTH

THE DESERT AND THE RE-ESTABLISHMENT OF PROTES-
TANTISM (1715–1802)

BOOK SIXTH

THE DESERT AND THE RE-ESTABLISHMENT OF PROTESTANTISM (1715–1802)

CHAPTER XVIII

THE CHURCHES OF THE DESERT

THE death of Louis the Fourteenth marks the date of the greatest discouragement and gloom in the history of the Huguenots. Thirty years had passed since the king's signature was appended to the revocatory edict, and they were years of continued persecution. During an entire generation the exercises of Protestant worship had been proscribed. For so long a time the " temples," or churches, had been in ruins, and if any adventurous pastor or lay preacher undertook to confirm the languishing faith of his fellow-believers in conventicles secretly assembled on the mountains of the Cévennes or in some sequestered part of the plains, he did so with the full knowledge that he was exposing himself to the severest penalties of the law. The dying monarch himself supposed the religion of Calvin and Beza to be virtually extinct, and by this belief justified himself in his last and most savage act. On the eighth of March, 1715, being then in the seventy-seventh year of his age and the seventy-second of his reign, Louis the Fourteenth issued his final law respecting the Protestants, in the form of a Declaration which

The death of Louis XIV. an epoch in Huguenot history.

deserves to be regarded as a fitting capstone to the singular fabric of cruelty and proscription the rearing of which had occupied a great part of his time and thoughts during the latter half of his reign. The object of the new legislation was to make every Protestant, who in his last illness should refuse the sacraments of the Roman Catholic Church liable to the penalties pronounced upon persons that had relapsed into heresy. Their bodies were, therefore, liable to be thrown upon a hurdle, dragged through the streets, and finally consigned, as the refuse of the earth, to the filth of the common sewer. Their property was forfeited to the state. What were the reasons alleged for this treatment of a class of persons who had, in point of fact, never abjured, and therefore could not with any justice be said to have relapsed into heresy—a class of persons, moreover, to whom the assurance had been given in the revocatory edict itself that they might continue to reside safely and without molestation in their former homes? First, that it was difficult, and in many cases impossible, to obtain sufficient proof of abjuration ; and, in the second place, to use the king's own words, " that the sojourn which those who were of the so-called Reformed religion, or were born of Protestant parents, have made in our kingdom, since we abolished all exercise of the said religion therein, is proof more than sufficient that they have embraced the Roman Catholic and Apostolic religion, without which thing they would not have been suffered or tolerated therein." [1] It was the last reiteration by Louis the Fourteenth of the success of his persist-"Hæresis ent efforts to overthrow Protestantism—the sentiextincta." ment expressed upon one of the medals struck in honor of the Revocation, " *Hæresis extincta*," and the assertion of another medal which affirmed that two millions of Calvinists had been brought back into the bosom of the papal church. [2]

---

[1] Déclaration .   .   . qui ordonne que ceux de la R.P.R. qui dans leurs maladies auront refusé aux curés, vicaires ou autres prêtres, de recevoir les sacremens l'Église, et auront déclaré qu'ils veulent persister et mourir dans la R.P.R. soient reputez relaps. Édits, Déclarations et Arrests, 482–484.

[2] See the reproductions of these and other medals, in a plate in the first volume of E. Hugues, Les Synodes du Désert.

It is a strange circumstance that the publication of the most savage law against the Protestants remaining in France and the death of the monarch at whose hands they had for years been experiencing unparalleled rigor, should very nearly coincide in point of time with an event that constitutes an era in the religious regeneration of French Protestantism—the convocation of the first synod of the "churches of the Desert." This designation requires a word of explanation. The Protes-

The church in "the Desert." tants who, after the suppression of their places of public worship, began stealthily to gather, at first two or three in one place, afterward in increasing numbers, to read a few chapters of the Sacred Scriptures, to listen to some one repeating a sermon preached in happier days at Charenton or elsewhere, to pray to God for some alleviation of their sufferings, possibly to sing with suppressed voices their favorite psalms, sought out some spot remote from the habitations of men where they would be least exposed to discovery and violent interruption. To the minds of the men and women who had often come many weary miles to the place of meeting, men and women accustomed to Biblical thought and Biblical language, the spot presented striking analogies to the desert of the wandering, from which they too hoped in God's good time to reach the heavenly Canaan. The testimony which, in these quiet fields and on these mountain sides, they gave to truths which the tyranny of king and priest had exiled from the populous town, became to them "the voice crying in the wilderness," like to that of the great Forerunner who preached repentance and proclaimed the advent of his Master in the words : "Prepare ye the way of the Lord, make straight in the desert a highway for our God!" Nor did they forget the apocalyptic vision described by the seer on the isle of Patmos, of the woman clothed with the sun, who was persecuted by the dragon, and "fled into the wilderness, where she hath a place prepared of God." Before long a word which had originally been used in a metaphorical sense passed into current use and became a permanent name employed by friends and foes alike. The very minutes of the Protestant ecclesiastical bodies accepted the words "in the Desert" as a convenient and sufficient designation for places of meeting which it was unsafe to describe more narrowly. This

use of language occurred as early as in the acts of the synod of
Lower Languedoc and the Cévennes, in 1718. It survived the
publication of the Edict of Toleration and the end of legal persecution, being found in the proceedings of the synod of
Vivarais and Velay, in May, 1788. Even a legal document,
such as the sentence of the Parliament of Toulouse, which sent
to the gallows, in 1762, the brave François Rochette, the last
Huguenot pastor that died a martyr for his faith, accepts
the popular designation, and speaks of his offence of having
preached, baptized, celebrated the Lord's Supper, and performed marriage ceremonies " in assemblies designated by the
name of Desert." [1] As an equivalent for " the churches of
the Desert," the words " the churches under the Cross " sometimes appear; and the present calamitous period was referred
to by the first national synod, in 1726, as " the time of captivity."

To Antoine Court belongs the credit of having first conceived the idea of organizing the feeble and discouraged
churches. To him, therefore, more than to any other, properly
belongs, as was said in a previous chapter, the honorable title
of " the Restorer of French Protestantism."

Born of humble and obscure parents, in the village of Ville-
neuve de Berg, in Vivarais, in the year 1696, Antoine Court
seemed unlikely to be called to accomplish any important work either in church or in state. His parents
were Protestants and had devoted him, even before his
birth, to the Christian ministry. But his father died
while Antoine was only four or five years old, and his mother
was left with three small children and scanty means, in the
midst of a community unfriendly to Protestantism. There
was, however, in the boy himself that which made up for many
external disadvantages. He was quick and intent upon the
acquisition of knowledge, his memory was retentive, his aspirations all ran parallel with his parents' hopes, and he was ready
to endure any amount of contumely rather than swerve from a
consistent Protestantism. His autobiography gives us little of

Antoine Court, the restorer of French Protestant- ism.

---

[1] Text in Bulletin de la Société de l'histoire du Protestantisme français, ii.
184–186.

his inner religious life; of the record of spiritual experiences there is an entire absence. Possibly he did not deem such a record necessary in a sketch written with an apologetic purpose. But he does inform us that, as a boy, "he detested the mass with all his heart," while he freely concedes that prejudice had probably much more to do with his repugnance than had any intelligent convictions. He tells, in particular, of an instance

His child- in which his aversion was openly exhibited. Four
hood. of his Roman Catholic fellow-scholars, at one time, resolved to force him to go to mass, and to this end pursued him to his home, overtaking him before he had time to climb the stairs leading to his mother's rooms. If they were resolute, so was he. As they drew him down, he clung desperately to each successive step. He could not have fought more determinedly had his life depended on the issue of the struggle. In the end, his boyish assailants failed to accomplish their object; but Antoine Court had succeeded in making himself an object of universal dislike. Not only young children, but full-grown men, derisively shouted as he passed them on the street, "There goes Calvin's eldest son!" "*Au fils aîné de Calvin!*" It came at last to his being compelled to renounce attendance upon the schools. He would not conform to the practices of the established church, even for the sake of obtaining an education. But resoluteness supplied the lack of opportunity. With few books, even books of devotion, he contrived to accumulate a considerable store of knowledge, and the leaves of a tattered Bible enabled the lad to make himself "mighty in the Scriptures." A few women used to meet, with great precaution, for the worship of God. His mother was of the number, but fear had prevented her from revealing to her son the purpose of her clandestine walks. He suspected the secret, and, following her from the house on one occasion, insisted on accompanying her to the rendezvous. Not long after he was admitted to the gatherings at which some women, uniting in themselves the functions of prophet to those of preacher, were accustomed to hold forth. Finally, to his inexpressible joy, as he informs us, he enjoyed the privilege of hearing a veritable minister. It was Jacques Bonbonnoux, formerly a Camisard captain, now turned preacher; and his discourse was simply a printed sermon of

the celebrated Pierre Du Moulin which he had committed to memory. "But hunger for the word made men relish even that sort of preaching." A few months passed, and Antoine Court, at the age of seventeen, found himself preaching in conventicles, not the productions of others but sermons of his own composition, and this to the edification of many hearers.

He becomes a preacher at the age of seventeen years.

The boy-preacher had a more important work before him. For some time he had been becoming more and more suspicious of the pretended "revelations," then current, and had been verging upon the conviction that "if they could not be ascribed to fraud, it must at least be believed that the greater number of the persons that were styled 'inspired' were dupes of their own zeal and credulity."[1] An extended examination, into which he now entered, assured him that his surmises were well grounded. Before long he reached the settled judgment that the only hope for the rescue of French Protestantism from the double plague of confusion and fanaticism lay in the prompt and perfect organization of the small and imperfect communities of timid believers in regularly constituted churches. To the task of effecting this great change Antoine now directed all his energies.

The state of Protestantism in southern France is best narrated in the words of Court himself:

"My first circuits had Vivarais for their field. There the scaffolds and gibbets were still bloody by reason of the execution of a number of Protestants whom the spirit of fanaticism had drawn into the spirit of rebellion. Here there were to be found a few men and some fifteen women or girls who to the title of preachers joined that of prophets. I fear that I should not be believed were I to relate all the puerilities, all the speeches unworthy of religion and dishonoring religion uttered by these knavish or deluded people. I endeavored to convict the former of imposture, to undeceive the latter by my instructions. It was no rare thing to see in the meetings, small as they were, two or three women,

Fanaticism among the Protestants of the south.

---

[1] Mémoires d'Antoine Court (1696–1729), published for the first time in 1885, by Edmond Hugues, page 43.

and sometimes men, falling into a trance, and speaking all of them at once, like those Corinthians whom Saint Paul rebuked. Soon I passed, like another Elijah, for the scourge of the prophets, with this difference, that my zeal was not destructive, and that it was confined to convincing and instructing. 'He is fighting against God,' at first said all those who believed in inspiration. Yet my discourses were attended with the most encouraging success, and my progress was most rapid. In a short time fanaticism dared not show itself publicly. Those that were still tainted with it no longer indulged in it save secretly.

Court becomes "the scourge of the prophets."

"Meantime God shed not less of His blessing upon the efforts which I put forth to gather the people, to enlighten them, and to reanimate their almost extinct faith. The meetings were at the start infrequent and poorly attended. I did well if by dint of trouble and invitation I could induce six, ten, or a dozen persons in one place to follow me to some hollow in a rock, to some remote barn, or to the open fields, there to worship God and hear from me the pious exhortations which I addressed them. What a comfort was it, on the other hand, for me to be present, in 1744, at meetings of ten thousand souls, on the identical spots where, in the first years of my ministry, scarcely had I been able to bring together fifteen, thirty, sixty, or, at most, one hundred persons."

In relating Antoine Court's further efforts I shall have recourse to another narrative which he wrote many years later.

"Whatever success attended my first labors, I perceived that in order to extend them and make them more fruitful, it was absolutely necessary that I should at once apply myself to the re-establishment of discipline. I found that the prevailing disorder and the unfortunate affair of the Camisards, in conjunction with fanaticism, had so alienated the minds of the Protestants themselves and brought [religious matters] into such disrepute, that everybody and everything styled 'preacher' or 'assembly,' was viewed with a sort of horror; that, on the other hand, such was the freedom with which men made themselves preachers, that whoever conceived the idea of becoming a preacher could carry it out without hindrance; that men, women, in short everybody, caught up the trade; that such license must bring very bad people into the church; that it was, moreover, little calculated to remove the unfavorable opinions which the Protestants themselves had conceived regarding the preachers and the assemblies. What then, I said to myself, is more needful than to apply some cure to these disorders, and stop the progress of such great evils?

"To compass this end I called together, on the twenty-first of August, 1715, all the preachers that were to be found in the Cévennes and in Lower Languedoc. To this meeting I invited a few of the most enlightened laymen. I drew for them a vivid and touching picture of the state of affairs. I showed them the necessity of applying all the remedies in our power. One of the most effectual, next to the good example which every preacher was bound to set of the cleansing of the sanctuary from all fanaticism, was the restoration of discipline. I had myself come among them that day for the purpose of laying the foundations of this discipline. We must begin by electing a moderator and a secretary, the former to preside over our deliberations, the latter to reduce them to writing. All having acceded to my proposal, I was chosen by a majority of votes, not only to be president of the little meeting, but also to be its secretary.

"We began by conferring the office of elder upon the laymen that were present, and it was agreed that elders should be established in all places where preaching and preachers were welcomed. They were to be charged, first, with watching over the flocks in the absence of the pastors, and over the conduct of the pastors themselves; in the second place, with selecting suitable places for holding the meetings; thirdly, with gathering them with all possible prudence and secrecy; fourthly, with making collections to help the poor and prisoners; fifthly, with providing sure places of shelter for the preachers and furnishing them with guides to conduct them from one locality to another.

"I next submitted two resolutions: the first, that, according to Saint Paul's command, women should hereafter be forbidden to preach; the second, that it be ordained to hold to the Sacred Scriptures as the only rule of faith, and that, consequently, all the pretended revelations which were in vogue among us

The confer- ence, or "synod," of Mono- blet, Au- gust 21, 1715.

The estab- lishment of elders.

should be rejected, not only because they had no foundation in the Scriptures, but also because of the great abuses which they had created. These two articles were carried by a majority of the votes. The remainder of the day was spent in the examination of the manners and morals of all those who composed the little gathering. The fashion appeared to be a novel one. Two of the members, who in the sequel gave much trouble, and whom Providence in 1723 brought to a bad end, opposed it; but I showed them its necessity, and they submitted to it like the rest. The laws enacted by this little assembly, of which I took great care to have copies made and circulated abroad, made a great noise and produced an excellent effect. It was styled a *synod*, and it was followed by many others that bore the same name."[1]

Preaching of women and pretended revelations condemned.

Thus were quietly laid the foundations of the churches of the Desert. The place where the "synod" met was a deserted quarry near the village of Monoblet, in Lower Languedoc.[2] The seats of the members and the secretary's table were rude blocks of stone. The two elders set apart for their sacred office were members of the little knot of Protestants (no longer recognized as such by the government) in the village of Monoblet, which thus seems entitled to the honor of having had the first organized Protestant church after the Revocation of the Edict of Nantes. Nine persons in all constituted the little assembly, which, not for its numbers nor for the social or ecclesiastical standing of its members, but by reason of the weighty consequences of its acts, is rightly styled the first synod. Leaving out the elders, there were seven others—Antoine Court, Jacques Bonbonnoux, Jean Rouvière, Étienne Arnaud, Jean Vesson, Jean Huc, and Jean Couvet.[3] Pierre

The first organized church.

---

[1] This extended quotation is taken from a paper written by Antoine Court about thirty years after the events referred to (in 1744), and is somewhat more graphic than the account which he has left us in his Mémoires already referred to. Court MSS. in Charles Coquerel, Histoire des Églises du Désert, i. 26-29.

[2] On the southern slope of the Cévennes, midway between Anduze and Saint Hippolyte, and a little over twenty-five miles northwest of Nismes.

[3] Court MSS. in Picheral-Dardier, Paul Rabaut, ses lettres à Antoine Court, i. p. xvii.

Corteiz, more notable than any of the other preachers, save Court himself, was absent in foreign parts. Had he been pres-

No ordained ent, the gathering would have comprised, without excep-
pastors. tion, all the preachers in Languedoc and the Cévennes. Among them, however, there was not a single one upon whose head the hands of bishop or presbyter had been laid in ordination. They preached because the oppressed Protestants, deprived by violence of the opportunity of obtaining spiritual nourishment, hungered and thirsted for instruction, and because no others came forward able or willing to make the perilous attempt to satisfy in some measure that hunger and thirst. Of a regular call, even to the work of preaching, none could boast; for there had been no regularly organized churches to issue it. Moreover, according to the standards of the Reformed Church of France, the simple " proposant," or licentiate, had no authority to administer either of the sacraments, and no authority to celebrate marriage. It was indispensable that the churches of the Desert should have ordained pastors; but whence should they obtain them? Two men in the present corps of preachers stood forth pre-eminent, admitted on all sides to be fit for the sacred office. They were Antoine Court and Pierre Corteiz. Both could not be spared at the same time, to go and be set apart for the ministry in some country where freedom prevailed. Corteiz, therefore, as the older man, was first sent. He made his way, escaping the perils of the journey, to the city of Geneva. But that ancient citadel of liberty had lost somewhat of its pristine courage. Neither the venerable company of pastors, nor the syndics and council of the republic, were disposed to draw down upon themselves the anger of the court of Versailles by an act which might be construed as an affront to the French crown. Even Berne, the most powerful of the Swiss cantons, was reluctant, if it did not positively refuse, to ordain ministers whose intention it was to return at once and preach the Gospel in defiance of royal edicts, in contempt of tortures, gibbet, and wheel. Corteiz attained his object at the hands of the pastors of Zurich.[1] It had been arranged that on his return

---

[1] On the fifteenth of August, 1718, according to Corteiz's own narrative. Relation historique des principaux événements qui sont arrivés à la religion protes-

to Languedoc Court should follow his example, and resort to Switzerland. But the provincial synod interposed its authority to prevent Court from going. The season was too *Pierre Corteiz ordained* far advanced for him to enter upon a long journey; *at Zurich.* one ordained minister having been secured, he, it was said, could ordain a second; it was a dictate of prudence as well as economy not to go to a distance for the purpose of procuring what could as well be obtained near at hand; it would be to expose a preacher, upon whom the hopes of the churches seemed particularly to rest, to dangers that were great in themselves and that might have the most disastrous consequences— consequences so much the more to be avoided as neither the advantage of the church nor necessity called for the risk. Such, as Court tells us, were the arguments employed. Reluctantly did he yield to the pressure brought to bear upon him. In the presence of the synod he was examined at great length by Corteiz and Colom, "a venerable old man, distinguished for his piety and his intelligence," whom the synod selected for the purpose. The examination covered different points of theology, and especially the matters in dispute between the Protestant and Roman Catholic churches. That the candidate acquitted himself with credit was clear from the loud expressions of satisfaction that broke out on all sides. But the enthusiasm of *Antoine* the day was as nothing in comparison with the wild *Court examined and* joy of the evening, when in the joint meeting of sev*ordained.* eral neighboring churches gathered to witness the scene, the eloquent young preacher himself addressed an appreciative audience upon the duties of the office with which he was about to be invested, and praised Almighty God that, touched at length by the unhappy state of His church in France, He was raising up ministers for her at the very time when her enemies were most infuriated and most bent upon her destruction. The pious excitement reached its height when Court knelt before Corteiz, and the latter placing a copy of the Bible upon the candidate's head and laying on his clasped hands, conferred upon him, in the name of Jesus Christ, and by the authority of

tante depuis la révocation, etc. E. Hugues, Hist. de la Restauration du Protestantisme, i. 455. Ed. of Baum, 30.

the synod, the right to exercise all the functions of the ministry. Then did the gladness of the spectators burst forth, ex-
ceeding all bounds ; and, amid exclamations of praise and
thanksgiving, the whole assembly, at the suggestion of the revered examiner of the morning, joined in singing the words
of the one hundred and second psalm, of Theodore Beza's metrical version, so appropriate to the occasion :

> "En registre sera mise
> Une si grande entreprise,
> Pour en faire souvenir
> A ceux qui sont à venir.
> Et la gent à Dieu sacrée,
> Comme de nouveau creée,
> Lui chantera la louange
> De ce bienfait tant estrange."

The emotion manifested was extraordinary and striking.
But it was not strange nor misplaced. Since the Revocation
of the Edict of Nantes no similar event had taken place. Antoine Court was the first Protestant pastor ordained in France
since the proscription of the Reformed faith. The occurrence
was of good omen for the future. Antoine Court's fear—" that
his ministry might be rendered less fruitful because of the distinction which the people might draw between a call received
in a foreign academy and the call of a synod in which there
was but a single pastor"— was never realized. The lawfulness
of Court's ordination was never called in question.[1]

Meanwhile the long reign of Louis the Fourteenth had come
to an end and another protracted reign had begun. Louis the
Fifteenth, born on the fifteenth of February, 1710,
was a boy of five. His age was that of his great-
grandfather, the late king, at the accession of the latter, seventy-
two years before. The two reigns had therefore this in common, that both of necessity opened with a long minority, during
which the nominal prince exercised little or no influence,
and the course of events was shaped by the fortunate possessor
of the regency, or by the minister governing in the regent's
name. In the childhood of Louis the Fourteenth it had been

Accession of Louis XV.

---

[1] Mémoires d'Antoine Court, 149–153. Corteiz, Relation historique. Hugues,
ubi supra, i. 456.

Cardinal Mazarin that ruled, through the favor of the regent, Queen Anne of Austria. Now the regent was Philip, Duke of Orleans, son of that monarch's younger brother, and of the Princess Elizabeth Charlotte of the Palatinate.

It concerns us less, for the purpose of this history, to inquire into the other points of similarity or contrast between the two reigns, than to ascertain how the condition of the Huguenots under the great-grandson compared with their condition under the monarch that revoked the Edict of Nantes. Suffice it then to say at the outset, that the fifty-nine years of the reign of Louis the Fifteenth constitute, so far as the legislation affecting the Protestant religion is concerned, a period singularly dreary and monotonous. From the beginning to the end, that religion, with all its exercises of worship, lay under the ban of the law, being denied recognition as even existing in France. Throughout that long space of time the preaching of the gospel in assemblies, large or small, the administration of the sacraments, and the celebration of marriage according to the Reformed rites, were crimes of the first magnitude ; and every man, woman, and child was required, under severe penalties, to conform to the practices of the established church. From 1715 to 1774 the only conspicuous variations were found in the more or less rigid application and execution of the intolerant laws; the laws themselves were almost uniform in their severity from the accession to the death of Louis the Fifteenth.

Persecution throughout his reign— 1715–1774.

The king, the ministers of state with their subordinates, from the intendants and military commandants down to the local magistrates, and the clergy of the established church, from the prelates that convened every five years in general assembly at Paris or elsewhere, down to the priests, monks, and missionaries for the propagation of the faith—these constituted the powers arrayed against the revived Protestantism of the eighteenth century. Of these the king, nominally supreme, was distant and inaccessible to the Huguenots, for the most part indifferent to their welfare, always strangely ill informed of what concerned them, and certainly without sympathy. The kings of France have never been wont to study with thoroughness the history of their own realm. Louis the Fifteenth was no exception to the general ignorance of the royal house, and the delight which in his youth he took in inflicting suffering upon the lower animals did not augur well for the treatment which he would extend to his fellow-men in the years of his manhood. Posterity wonders that the Huguenots, who never received a single token of his compassion, should so far have deceived themselves as to give him credit for a kind heart. The licentious monarch, who found his highest enjoyment in the society of lewd women and in the *Parc aux cerfs*, had no sympathy to waste upon the persecuted Protestants of the Cévennes or of Dauphiny.

The ministry, the intendants, and the military commandants had different degrees of ardor for the work of the repression of the Huguenots, but were united, for the most part, in the persuasion that the policy to which Louis the Fourteenth had distinctly committed France must be upheld at all hazards. Not, however, that they did not tire from time to time of a task that could not but become more and more distasteful to men of ordinary humanity. Even a Lamoignon de Basville, we have seen, was not proof against a fatigue and disgust that occasionally found vent in reluctant admissions.

Behind king and ministers, behind intendants and military commandants, was the clergy—bishops, vicars-general, monks Activity of and nuns, parish priests and all—never wavering, the clergy. never tiring, but always alert, insistent, urging the civil power to the enforcement of every law against heresy. It was the clergy in its general assemblies that compelled the present monarch to persevere in the course of persecution and goaded the ministry on whenever their zeal seemed to flag ; for the grants of money, which the prelates could make or withhold, were as welcome in the eighteenth, as they had been in the seventeenth century. And it was the bishop in his diocese, and the curate in his parish, that were both the eyes of the civil and military authorities in the discovery of the places where the proscribed Huguenots held their secret conventicles, Its spies. and the brains that devised the methods for surprising and breaking up the conventicles and capturing the worshippers. Not only was every parish priest, in the very nature of the case, the bishop's agent to watch the movements of the New Converts of his diocese, but the bishop employed, if need be, a body of salaried spies who for efficiency compared favorably with those in the secret service of the government. Thus it was that, a few years before the close of the seventeenth century, the intendant Basville, writing to inform Fléchier that he was quite sure that one of the forbidden meetings of the Protestants had been held in the neighborhood of Nismes, and that Brousson or some other minister was in the region, said to the Bishop of Nismes: "You must stir up your spies and promise them new rewards." [1]

If the violence of persecution was remittent, it will generally be found that the cause was either the weariness of the civil

Why the persecution varied in intensity. authorities, to which I have referred, or their inability, or their fears. It was impracticable to dragoon a district, impracticable to march and countermarch over the mountains in quest of conventicles of New Converts, without a goodly number of regiments of soldiers at hand to do the work; and in time of foreign war those regiments were busy elsewhere. In time of foreign war, moreover, the Protestants must not be provoked by cruel treatment, either themselves to rise, or to lend an ear to the emissaries of the enemies of the king and favor the incursions or the landing of hostile forces. But the moment that fear was removed, the moment that the troops were once more at leisure, persecution was resumed, generally with greater vigor. Gratitude for Huguenot loyalty was an unknown virtue to the kings of the Bourbon line, successors of Henry the Fourth.

The eight years of the Regency (1715–1723) have often been represented as years of comparative toleration for the Hugue-

The Regency, 1715–1723. nots, under the unjust law of 1715. For unjust that law was admitted to be by no less a legal authority than the king's attorney in the Parliament of Paris: and he had taken the liberty to suggest that justice does not punish the accused on such simple presumptions as the law contemplated; it was not enough that the accused be reputed guilty,

---

[1] "Il faut éveiller vos espions et leur promettre de nouvelles récompenses." Basville to Fléchier, May, 1697, MSS. of Libr. of French Prot. Hist. Soc., apud Douen, Les Premiers Pasteurs du Désert, ii. 283.

he must be so indeed, in order to be condemned.[1] Far from
being a period of tranquillity to the Protestants, the rule of the
Duke of Orleans could scarcely be distinguished from that of
the late king.   The regent, whose undisguised immorality
shocked even the immoral age in which he lived, had little in
common with the Huguenots, even if he entertained no distinct
feeling of hatred for them.   It may be that that able and caustic person, his mother, who had never been able quite to disguise the fact that she was still a German and a Protestant at
heart, though she had professed to renounce her native country
and the religion in which she was born to become Philip's
wife, may have instilled into her son's mind a certain feeling
of pity for the victims of his uncle's cruelty.   It may be, too,
that, as the Duke of Saint Simon states, the regent, in his
hearing, not only gave utterance to that pity, but actually talked
of recalling the Huguenot fugitives and undoing the mischief
wrought by the Revocation of the Edict of Nantes.   If so,
however, Saint Simon experienced no great difficulty in deter-
ring him from the attempt by misrepresenting the Calvinists as
the authors of the disorders and civil wars of a previous age,
and by exaggerating the trouble which the undertaking must of
necessity entail.[2]

The Huguenots had conceived great hopes from the change
of government and from the accession to power of a nobleman
*The hopes
of the Hu-
guenots dis-
appointed.* supposed to be not unfriendly.   They were speedily
undeceived.   If the Duke of Orleans was not cruel
nor narrow-minded, neither had he the force of character necessary to enable him to withstand the pressure of the
clerical supporters of the policy of Louis the Fourteenth.   In
the first year of his regency a considerable number of Protestant
exiles returned to their native land, and in various places in
Poitou, Saintonge, Guyenne, and Languedoc, meetings for worship were held with a goodly attendance.   Some of these, es-

---

[1] See the interesting Lettre de M. d'Aguesseau, procureur-général du Parlement de Paris, du 26 mars 1715, written after the Declaration was signed by
the king, but before it was registered by parliament. MSS. Nat. Libr., apud
E. Hugues, Histoire de la Restauration du Protestantisme en France au XVIIIᵉ
siècle, i. (pièces inédits), 367–369.

[2] Mémoires du Duc de Saint Simon (Paris, 1853), xxvi. 182–189.

pecially in Guyenne, were broken up by the troops sent against them. It was discovered that the Huguenots had begun to gather by night for worship at Paris itself, in the faubourg Saint Antoine.[1] But the regent had no notion of tolerating so startling an innovation, and soon a placard appeared that struck a death-blow at the hopes of the Protestants. " His Majesty," so it ran, " being informed that certain persons, New Converts, have imagined without just grounds that assemblies might be permitted among them provided that arms were not carried, and have held some of them despite the ordinances passed in this regard, and desiring to make known his intentions on the point and to disabuse them of the chimerical ideas which ill-intentioned characters have suggested to them; by advice of the Duke of Orleans, regent, has declared that the edicts issued respecting the assemblies of the New Converts shall be executed with precision, all persons being forbidden to be found at any of them, on pain of punishment."[2] About the same time, or possibly a few weeks later, a longer placard was posted on the walls of all the towns and villages of Languedoc, still more explicitly defining the king's intention to prohibit every gathering of Protestants under pretext of prayers or worship of any kind, in any place, in any numbers, or on any other pretence whatsoever, and enumerating all the laws of Louis the Fourteenth bearing on the subject.[3]

French orders against conventicles.

Nor were these empty threats. The regent was greatly maligned by the Duke d'Antin, if he did not thoroughly approve of the severity of the sentence passed upon two men that were sent to row in the galleys for the simple crime of having worshipped with the Protestants who were surprised in the fields near Rouvière, and if he did not cheerfully acquiesce in inflicting the costs of the procedure and of the reward given to the informer upon the town of Florac and a neighboring commune, because some of their inhabitants were known to have been

---

[1] C. Coquerel, Histoire des Églises du Désert, i. 122.

[2] Placard dated May 10, 1716, apud C. Coquerel, Histoire des Églises du Désert. i. 127.

[3] E. Hugues, La Restauration du Protestantisme, i. 133.

present.[1] The only regret of the duke in this case was that the officiating minister had escaped capture.[2]

The government had been more fortunate in the case of another Protestant meeting, lately held in the neighborhood of Alais, and took great pleasure in hanging the preacher upon the gallows erected on the Place de la Maréchale at Montpellier.

Execution of the pastor Étienne Arnaud. The preacher was Étienne Arnaud, one of the small circle of ministers and elders that organized the church of the Desert, two or three years before, in their first meeting in the quarry of Monoblet. Young and ardently loved as he was, Arnaud's arrest aroused and excited the Protestants of the region, and a band was organized that might easily have effected his rescue from the hands of the small escort of soldiers on the road from Alais to Montpellier. But Antoine Court, his warm friend and colleague, on being informed, resolutely opposed the scheme and compelled its abandonment. "Better were it," he said, "that a brother should seal the truths he has preached by a death that may edify and be fruitful to the church, than that, by his rescue, blame should be drawn down upon the Protestant religion and disastrous consequences upon the province."[3]

The regent remained unmoved by the sufferings of the Huguenots to the very end of his days. Some months before the sudden death of the Duke of Orleans the veteran preacher Corteiz, having heard that Campredon, a royal officer at Barre, in the Cévennes, had openly promised to exert himself to the utmost to effect his arrest and execution, wrote him a long and touching letter in vindication of the Reformed religion and its supporters. Even at this distance of time the document can scarcely be read without emotion.[4]

The regent a persecutor to the end.

---

[1] " Le Régent approuve fort, Monsieur, le jugement que vous avez rendu en condamnant aux galères les deux hommes," etc. Letter of the Duke d'Antin, September 23, 1718, apud Corbière, Hist. de l'Église Réf. de Montpellier, 367.

[2] " Il ne restait qu'à pouvoir attraper le prédicant pour en faire un exemple." Ibid., ubi supra.

[3] Mémoires d'Antoine Court, 142. See, also, D. Bonnefon, Benjamin du Plan, gentilhomme d'Alais, député général des Synodes des Églises Réformées de France, 31.

[4] Lettre de Corteis à M. Campredoux, à Barre, en Cévennes. Bulletin de la Soc. de l'hist. du Prot. fr., xiii. 154–158. The letter is without a date ; but,

Campredon forwarded it to Bernage, intendant of Languedoc, by whom it was sent on to the Marquis of La Vrillière, the secretary of state. La Vrillière read it to the regent. What effect the appeal for justice and pity produced may be judged from the fact that La Vrillière returned this brief instruction to the intendant : " Sir, I have deferred answering the letter you took the trouble to write to me on the twenty-seventh of last month, until I might find time to read to My lord the Duke of Orleans the whole of the letter written to the Sieur Campredon by the preacher named Corteiz. His Royal Highness, who is more than ever convinced of the necessity of making sure of this man, has very highly approved the promise that has been made of three thousand *livres* to him who shall procure his capture. Thus you may cause steps to be the taken in conformity with it." [1]

Yet in spite of everything, in spite of the galleys and the halter for men and preachers, in spite of imprisonment in convents for

Progress of Protestant- ism.

women, in spite of significant warnings for those that were reported to eat meat on prohibited days, in spite of the carrying off of the children of such as would not rear them in a " Catholic " manner, in spite of fines and every species of annoyance, the churches of the Desert continued to grow. Parents began again to carry their children for baptism to the proscribed pastors ; young men and maidens to call upon those pastors to bless their nuptials. The " assemblies " multiplied apace. It was the Count of Saint Florentin, one of the ministers of state of Louis the Fifteenth, that wrote in 1721 : " I am advised that no traces are left of religion in certain provinces, in which the curates sometimes find themselves alone in their churches ; that the meetings of the Protestants are frequent and public, that the signal of the bell for the mass, on Sunday, serves to call together the meetings of the preachers, and that the priest when he leaves the altar frequently hears at the door of his church the singing of the psalms of Marot." [2]

---

as the writer refers in it to the death of Vesson and Huc, who were executed, the first, April 22, and the second, May 5, 1723 (see Hugues, ubi supra, i. 208, 209), it belongs to that year.

[1] La Vrillière to Bernage, Meudon, August 12, 1723. Bulletin, etc., xiii. 286.

[2] Archives of the Department of Hérault, apud E. Hugues, La Restauration du Protestantisme, i. 238.

It was no better two years later (1723), when the Bishop of
Alais sent to Paris a paper that was a bitter wail over the rise of
Protestantism and the decadence of Roman Catholi-
cism in the region of the Cévennes.   "The meetings
that previously were very rare and very secret have
become so frequent, public, and well attended that there have
been some of more than three thousand persons, and with as
many as four hundred horses at hand.   Baptism and the Lord's
Supper were administered, preachers were commissioned, and
the singing of psalms was heard as far as in the neighboring
villages, and, although men knew that the carrying of arms
made their meetings still more criminal, scarcely any were held
where there were not found a number of armed persons to
favor escape in case of surprise.   Our churches, which they
formerly frequented, at least out of regard for men, are at present forsaken ; there are large parishes in which there can
scarcely be found a single Catholic to wait upon the curates in
their ministry.   Parents cease to send their children to our
schools. . . .   The children whom we have reared with
great care in the doctrines of the church, soon fall into error
and succumb to the caresses or hard usage of their parents.
. . .   Within a few years we have perceived that a great
number of New Converts who appeared to have sincerely
returned to the Catholic faith and who persevered in it for a
long time, suddenly stopped attending our churches and plunged
into error and disorder.   But what touches us most keenly and
may have disastrous consequences, is the fall of many Old
Catholics who are being perverted.   There is scarcely a town
or village where sad examples of this cannot be seen, and the
number of such is increasing every day." [1]

The Bishop of Alais's account.

It was not in numbers alone that the churches of the Desert
were advancing ; they made progress also in the care they exercised for the morals of their members.   The reader
may smile when he learns that the provincial synod of
Lower Languedoc and the Cévennes, that met in May, 1721,
attempted to check some of the more common vices that passed

Protestant morals.

---

[1] Mémoire of the Bishop of Alais, now in the National Library, printed in
Hugues, Histoire de la Restauration, i. 246–250.

ınrebuked in the community, by pecuniary fines for the benefit
)f the poor. Persons that had sworn and blasphemed the
ıame of God, were to be condemned to give five sous for the
)oor; those that profaned the Lord's Day by games or other-
vise, must contribute a similar amount. For all foul language,
'or every false, slanderous, and mocking speech, and for the ut-
erance of words condemned in Holy Writ, the penalty was to
)e six deniers.[1] An incident for the truth of which Pierre Cor-
:eiz vouches in his autobiography, though in itself unimportant,
ınay serve to throw light on the manners of the day.

The Huguenots, anxious to test the virtue of their experiment,
were very particular, says the writer,[2] to exact payment of these
ñnes, extending them even to the person of a Roman Catholic
priest, the curate of Vialas, in the Cévennes. A stanch Prot-
ɔstant being in the company of the ecclesiastic, not long after
ɪhe meeting of the synod, and hearing him indulge in profane
ɜwearing, took the liberty of remarking: "We of the Reformed
religion, Sir, have agreed together, with the view of putting a
stop to bad language, that every one of us should for that
offence condemn himself to give something to the poor, and a
man could not give less than a six deniers piece." "That is
right," replíed the curé, "here is the six deniers piece." Thus
it was, whimsically observes the narrator, that a Roman Catholic priest shared in our discipline, to the honor of the Protestants.

The more severe and systematic persecution of the Huguenots

---

[1] Minutes of the Synod of Lower Languedoc and the Cévennes (1721), in Les
Synodes du Désert, i. 23.

[2] Baum edit., p. 40; Hugues, i. 463.—The very interesting and important
narrative of Pierre Corteiz is extant in two somewhat divergent forms.
Whether the variations are due to the author himself or were made by others,
possibly with the author's sanction (Corteiz being an illiterate man), I do not
know. Professor Baum published the document separately, in 1871, from a
manuscript in the archives of the French church of Zurich where Corteiz spent
the last years of his life. Mr. Edmond Hugues has printed it in the other form,
somewhat shorter, in the appendix of his Histoire de la Restauration du Prot.
au XVIIIᵉ siècle, with the title "Relation historique des principaux événements
qui sont arrivés à la religion protestante depuis la révocation des édits de Nantes,
l'an 1685, jusques à l'an présent 1728, par Corteiz." The manuscript of this is
in the Court collection of the Library of Geneva.

dates from the publication of the law of the fourteenth of May, 1724.

Even before the death of the regent, which occurred in 1723, there had been an attempt to summarize and co-ordinate the multitude of edicts, declarations, and orders in council issued against the Protestants with little regard either to justice or to method. It was a rare medley with which the lawyers had to do, the result of priestly suggestion, judicial caprice, and ministerial subserviency. The means of petty annoyance which happened to present itself to the mind of an inferior ecclesiastic had often been caught up by a royal officer and had taken shape in a judicial decision or an order in council. The order in council was presently transformed into an edict of universal application. Some laws bore upon their face that they were granted at the request of the bishops. A great number introduced new and iniquitous legislation of an unheard-of sort, under pretence of interpreting past statutes and explaining what the original lawgiver must have meant. Disorder and contradiction reigned everywhere. Apart from the laws that had been superseded and rendered inoperative by the sweeping provisions of the revocatory edict, there were, according to the statement of the distinguished attorney general of the Parliament of Paris, a good two hundred or more which were almost completely ignored.[1]

Royal Declaration of 1724.

Of the origin of the horrible law issued less than six months after the regent's death—for horrible indeed it was—it is enough to say that while Tressan, Bishop of Nantes, with the active assistance of Basville, late intendant of Languedoc, was the editor that threw it into shape, the clergy by their persistent efforts through many a year must be held to be the true authors.[2] Of course, I hold guiltless of this crime against human-

---

[1] "On songea alors (during the regency) à y remédier par une loi qui renfermerait la disposition de plus de deux cents édits, déclarations ou arrêts qui étaient presque ignorés. M. le chancelier d'Aguesseau y travailla." Joly de Fleury, apud Hugues, La Restauration du Protestantisme, i. 251.

[2] See Hugues, ubi supra, i. 263, who has discussed and shown the absurdity of the fanciful view of Malesherbes that Joly de Fleury drew it up for the purpose of laying a snare for the clergy, and the silliness of Rulhière's assertion that "the clergy, the intendants, and the tribunals of justice had neither asked for it nor foreseen it."

ity Louis the Fifteenth, a beardless boy of fourteen years and two months. Yet this beardless boy was made by the ministers that usurped his name to make such lying assertions as the statement contained in the second article, to the effect that there "had arisen and were daily arising in his kingdom a number of preachers who busied themselves solely in exciting the people to revolt, while diverting them from the exercises of the Roman Catholic and Apostolic religion." Louis himself may not have known that this was not so; but his advisers, thoroughly cognizant of the fact that the pastors and preachers of the Desert had cheerfully labored to thwart the efforts lately made by foreign emissaries, knew it full well.

There is no need that I should give even a sketch of the articles of the law of 1724, for it was not new legislation, but a repetition of the old with a view to more complete execution.[1] On only one point did a feeling of shame compel a slight alleviation. While re-enacting the pains against the person and memory of those who died as relapsed persons, the infliction upon the corpses of Huguenots of that inhuman treatment which had raised the indignation of civilized Europe was purposely omitted. The dead bodies of respectable men and women were no longer to be dragged naked through the streets of towns and villages upon a hurdle, flung into the common sewer, and there left to rot as worthless carrion.[2] But no more mercy was shown than heretofore to the living. Death remained the penalty for the Huguenot preacher. Indeed the clause was added that this penalty should not hereafter be regarded as *comminatory*, that is, a penalty that might be inflicted or not at the discretion of the judges.[3] The minister or preacher that fell into their hands must be sent to the gallows. Against the laymen that frequented the conventicles

A re-enactment of every severe law.

[1] Déclaration du Roy du 14 Mai 1724, concernant la Religion. Édits, Déclarations et Arrests, 534-550.

[2] This modification, however, was decently veiled under the words "pour être leur dite mémoire condamnée avec confiscation de leurs biens, dérogeant aux autres peines portées par la Déclaration du 29 Avril 1686, et à celle du 8 Mars 1715, lesquelles seront au surplus exécutées, en ce qui ne se trouvera contraire au présent Article." Article ix.

[3] "Les peines comminatoires ne sont encourues de plein droit, et peuvent n'être pas infligées." Dict. de l'Académie.

and those who harbored ministers the prescriptions were as heretofore—galleys for the men, shearing of the head and imprisonment for life for the women. In one important particular the condition of the Huguenots was aggravated. It was the first time that the civil status of the Protestants was distinctly attacked and the illegitimacy of their marriages was formally asserted.[1] Moreover, the education of the children of the Protestants in the doctrines of the Roman Catholic religion and the duty of their teachers to take them to attend mass was particularly emphasized.

It was something to be thankful for that the clerical hand that drew up the law almost always avoided or disdained the designation of the Protestants of France as "New Converts." They figure in its articles as " our subjects who heretofore made profession of the pretended Reformed religion," some of them " reunited with little sincerity to the Roman Catholic and Apostolic religion," or as " *Religionnaires ;* " in only a single instance are they spoken of as " our subjects recently reunited to the Catholic faith." They had won thus much at the hands of their enemies that they were not confounded with the mass of the Roman Catholic population, but occupied a place apart by themselves. It was a concession that Protestantism still existed.

Outside of the laws the same admission was made even more frankly. About this time Abbé Robert, provost of the cathedral of Nismes, did not hesitate to say that the interruption in the exercises of their religion for the space of forty years had not detached the Huguenots from it ; for parents impressed it upon the hearts of their children and found no difficulty in destroying the very first smattering of an education of a different kind that had been laboriously instilled into them.[2] Twelve years later the Abbé Maximin was ready to go much further. Doctor of the Sorbonne and Grand Vicar of Alais although he was, he admitted that, in the fifty years since the proscription of Calvinism, the Roman Catholic religion had lost more than it had gained. As to calling the "religionnaires " *new converts*, he made bold to say that no designation could be found that suited them less.[3]

The designation of " New Converts " admitted to be a misnomer.

---

[1] Hugues, ubi supra, i. 258, note.   [2] Ibid., i. 306.

[3] " Or, il n'y a point de nom qui leur convienne moins." Mémoire au sujet

Meanwhile, judicious men even among the Roman Catholics looked askance at the new law and doubted whereunto it would come. "There was published at the beginning of the present month," wrote a lawyer of the Parliament of Paris, in June, 1724, "a declaration of the fourteenth of May, and registered on the thirty-first, concerning religion. It contains eighteen very rigorous articles against the New Converts and about the education of their children. The old Catholics are involved also. This severity, which may degenerate into denunciation, is not regarded with approval, and it may well become the seed of trouble and civil war, from which may God defend us! The clergy would do far better to pay its annuities than give such counsels." [1]

Sensible Roman Catholics condemn the law.

For a few months after the publication of the law of 1724, great as was the disappointment and consternation of the Huguenots, there was little change in their outward relations ; but when, in 1726, the Cardinal Fleury displaced the Duke of Bourbon, whom three years before he had himself been instrumental in raising to the position of prime minister of the king, and was honored by the pope with a seat in the " sacred college," the fresh cloud of persecution which had so long been threatening burst forth in full force. For the crime of attendance upon Protestant assemblies or conventicles the procedure according to law, with its proverbial delays, was too dilatory. An order signed by the king directed that all persons taken in the very act should at once be condemned to the galleys or to lifelong imprisonment—penalties that should also be meted out, without other form or process of law, to any persons that might not indeed be caught on the spot but were known to have been there. [2]

Cardinal Fleury becomes prime minister— 1726.

---

des Religionnaires du Bas-Languedoc et des Cévennes présénté à la Cour par l'abbé de Saint-Maximin, docteur de Sorbonne, prévôt et grand vicaire d'Alais." This long and important document is found among the MSS. of the National Library of France, and is published in full by Hugues, ubi supra, ii. App. 423–439.

[1] Journal de Paris par Mathieu Marais, avocat au Parlement. In the Revue Rétrospective, xv. (1838) 242.

[2] Royal order to Marquis de La Fare, governor of Alais, etc., Fontainebleau, September 11, 1726. In C. Sagnier, La Tour de Constance et ses Prisonnières (Paris, 1880), Pièces justificatives, 113 et seq.

Now did the sombre Tour de Constance, at Aigues Mortes, begin to overflow with unfortunate Huguenot women, sent here when their fathers or husbands or brothers were condemned, for the same or similar offences, to serve in the galleys. Which had the harder lot, the men or the women, it is not easy to say. The sufferings of the wretched galley-slave have occupied our attention already, and were found to be terrible indeed. But, at least, the galley-slave lived out of doors and breathed the pure air of heaven. His eyes, not less than the captain's eyes, or the eyes of the cruel *comite* set over him as taskmaster, could take in the beauties of sea and land. If a shower of blows might any moment descend upon his naked back, and if an inhuman officer might occasionally exact an amount of toil at the oar almost beyond the power of mortal endurance, yet there were hours of rest and times when the variety and novelty of the surroundings gave fresh vigor to the jaded body. To the poor women that lingered out a dreary existence in the Tour de Constance during the greater part of the eighteenth century, there was a dreary monotony of scene and employment, each day being the precise counterpart of every other, and all days being alike destitute of hope.

The Tour de Constance a prison for Protestant women— 1708-1768.

There was Isabeau Menet, who, less than a year after her marriage, was surprised at a meeting held in a barn near Saint André de Bruzac. Fifteen years later they released her and gave her into her father's keeping ; she had lost her reason.

There was Marie Bereau, blind from her childhood. After thirty-one years' imprisonment she still languished in the tower, an old woman of fourscore. There, too, were Anne Gaussen, captured in 1723, and still in prison forty years later, and Marie Robert, who endured thirty-seven years of confinement. There was Marie Durand, destined to a little distinction above her unfortunate fellows. She was a young girl of fifteen when they immured her in these walls, for no other reason than that she had a brother who preached in the Desert. The king liberated her, of his great mercy, in 1768. She was then a prematurely old and infirm woman of fifty-three. Her brother, the Huguenot pastor, whom they caught in 1732, on the road to Vermoux, and hung at Montpellier that same year, had been dead a third of a century and

Marie Durand.

more. It would be hard to say why they had kept her for this long space, away from her kindred and friends, away from the light of day and the joys of social life, unless it be that she had remained firm in her Huguenot faith, and certainly that was not legally a crime in one that had broken the royal laws in no other respect. When Marie was arrested the king had also sent a *lettre de cachet* for the consignment to the fort of Brescou of a Protestant gentleman to whom she was betrothed. Among the letters that have come down to us from that age, not least in pathetic interest is a note which M. Serres, of St. Pierreville, found the means of forwarding to her, the more touching that the hope which he expressed of her speedy liberation and of their union was not destined ever to be fulfilled. These were two blighted lives among the many for which Louis the Fifteenth, like his predecessor, must bear the guilt.[1]

Visitors to the Tour de Constance may now see in the upper chamber a few characters scratched, as with some sharp instrument, upon the margin of the round hole that constitutes the only direct communication with the chamber beneath. The letters, rudely traced, form a single word, incorrectly spelled — RECISTEZ " — " *Resist !* " It is the tradition that it was Marie Durand who with her knitting-needle laboriously traced the letters upon the stone ; and the injunction she chose may well be taken as the appropriate motto of the long-enduring and patient adherents of the churches of the Desert, who by their steadfastness won the day at last for a faith exposed to persecutions calculated to try the fortitude of men and women above most persecutions.[2]

" Resistez !"
—a motto for
the perse-
cuted.

Not all these Christian women were so courageous as Marie

---

[1] The reader may see the note, dated from the place of the writer's incarceration, September 19, 1730, in Haag, La France Protestante, iv. 94, or in the admirable biography, Marie Durand, Prisonnière à la Tour de Constance, 1730–1768, by Daniel Benoit (Toulouse, 1884), 56.

[2] Mr. Charles Frossard, whose monograph, La Tour de Constance d'Aigues-Mortes, read before the French Protestant Historical Society in 1875, and published in the Society's Bulletin, xxiv. 173–182, is one of the most readable accounts of the buildings and its unhappy occupants, is right in regarding Marie Durand's motto for the Churches of the Desert as in nowise inferior to the " *Je maintiendrai* " of the Dutch Protestants.

Durand; but if they finally consented to make a pretence of abjuration, in order to purchase their deliverance, it was rarely, perhaps never, until years of hardship had broken down their spirit. Thus Anne Sabourin had been ten years incarcerated when the solicitations of the curate of Aigues Mortes at length prevailed upon her to make such concessions that he was able to certify that she had " of her pure and frank volition " entered the pale of the church, having forsworn the errors of Luther and Calvin—what errors they were he does not state— and that he had consequently granted her absolution. Great seems to have been the satisfaction of the court at the news, for the king at once sent an order by courier for her instant release. But the conversion was so evanescent that the moment Anne obtained her freedom she resumed the practices of her true religion, and when at her death, twenty-two years later, her brother sought and obtained the authority to bury her body, it was for an avowed Protestant that he demanded it.[1]

From about 1708, the last male prisoners having been removed from the Tour de Constance, shortly after the almost miraculous escape of Mazel and his companions, recorded on a previous page, until 1768,[2] when the dingy tower was transformed into a place of detention for ordinary criminals, the tower continued to be, not, indeed, the only place to which Huguenot women were consigned because of their devotion to their religion, but the most striking, and perhaps the most terrible. It was of the Tour de Constance that Monsieur de Boufflers, visiting it a year or two before it ceased to be a prison for Protestants, penned a description that has often been repeated. " I followed M. de Beauvau in a tour of inspection along the coasts of Languedoc. We arrived at Aigues Mortes, at the foot of the Tour de Constance. At the entrance we found an attentive doorkeeper, who after having conducted us by dark and tortuous staircases, opened with a loud noise a frightful door over which

Visit of M. de Boufflers.

---

[1] The best account of the prisoners is contained in the late Mr. Charles Sagnier's La Tour de Constance et ses Prisonnières. In the fourth volume of Haag, La France Protestante (2d edition), 83–99, s. v. Chassefière, the same writer has given as complete a list of the prisoners as was known in 1884.

[2] Sagnier, 13, 93.

one seemed to read Dante's inscription : *Lasciate ogni speranza, o voi ch' entrate.* Colors fail me to paint the horror of a view to which my eyes were so unaccustomed—a picture hideous and touching, at the same time, in which disgust added to the interest. We saw before us a spacious round chamber deprived of air and light. Fourteen women were languishing there in tears and wretchedness. The commandant had difficulty in containing his emotion ; and, doubtless for the first time, these unfortunate women read compassion on a human countenance. I can yet see them, at this sudden apparition, all of them falling at his feet, and bathing them with their tears, attempting to speak, but finding for words only sobs ; then, emboldened by our words of comfort, recounting all together their common sorrows. Alas ! their entire crime consisted in having been brought up in the same religion as Henry the Fourth. The youngest of these martyrs was older than fifty years : she was eight when arrested, going to the *prêche* with her mother, and the punishment lasted still ! " [1]

So ineffectual was the barbarous law of 1724 in preventing the celebration of baptisms and marriages " in the Desert," that it was precisely from the time when the strict enforcement of that law may be said to have commenced, that the practice of resorting to the proscribed conventicles for the purpose became more general than ever before.[2] In like manner the careful and minute provisions intended to compel parents to send their children to mass and to the Roman Catholic schools for religious instruction failed conspicuously of accomplishing their purpose. Not, however, but neglect or refusal entailed serious consequences. The fines imposed were a burden almost intolerable to a population like that of the Céven-

Fines for non-attendance of children at mass and school.

---

[1] I take this striking passage, which has so often been quoted, from the pages of E. B. D. Frossard, Tableau de Nismes et de ses Environs à vingt lieues à la ronde (Nismes, 1834–1838). ii. 217. The author of this work, who was a pastor of Nismes from 1825 to 1847, was not only an earnest theologian and a faithful preacher, but a writer of no little merit on historical and scientific subjects. The present book is written *con amore*, and the illustrations, from his own hand, are graphic and valuable. One of them is the only view I have seen of the interior of the Tour de Constance, of the upper chamber of which it gives a fair idea.

[2] Hugues, Hist. de la Restauration du Prot., ii. 15.

nes, poverty-stricken at best. A single example may serve to illustrate this. There is still preserved a statement made by the schoolmaster of the little village of Cassagnas, where almost the entire population of six or seven hundred souls appears to have been Protestant in the eighteenth century, as it is Protestant at the present day.[1] Over a score of families persistently declined to send the children to be taught doctrines and practices which the parents abhorred. The statement covers the single month of November, 1729, and shows that the parents of each child were fined ten sous for every time the child was absent from school or mass—in each case ten times in all. A father who had three children had to pay fifteen *livres tournois,* probably not far from his earnings for an entire week. For the whole twenty-seven children a sum of one hundred and thirty-five livres was assessed, for the payment of which the fathers, mothers, or guardians were condemned "to be constrained by the establishment of a military garrison (that is, by the quartering of soldiers), after a simple notice." [2]

Even more burdensome were the extraordinary and excessive fines laid upon entire communities of Huguenots, in conse-

Fines for conventicles.

quence of conventicles known to have been held within their bounds, and apportioned among the individual families whether they had attended the meetings or not. Not but that occasionally the money was collected with all Gallic politeness, and the observance of every point of etiquette. "I should be sorry," wrote one government agent to a gentleman of Montauban, in notifying him that his share of the fine laid by the intendant amounted to thirty-nine livres and a half, "I should be sorry to be constrained to have recourse to the methods

---

[1] The village of Cassagnas has, according to Gindre de Mancy, Dictionnaire des Communes, a population of 748 souls. The *parish* of Cassagnas, including, doubtless, a larger territory, contains a slightly larger Protestant population, having grown from 591, in 1802, to 850, in 1888. (Perrenoud, Étude hist. sur les progrès du Prot. en France, 241.) It is of interest to note that since 1840 it has not only had a consistorial church with a pastor and edifice for worship, but schools for boys and girls and a Sunday school. The fines under which the Huguenots groaned a century and a half ago have availed nothing for the overthrow of the Reformed faith in Cassagnas.

[2] See the curious document and table in the Bulletin de la Soc. de l'hist. du Prot. fr., xxxix. 318–320.

prescribed to me for the collection with which I am charged, and I hope that you will be so good as to avoid, by your exactness, the extreme pain I should have to resort to them and to see you exposed to the slightest expense." And he closed by signing himself, "very perfectly, your very humble and very obedient servant." [1]

Meantime, with the lapse of years the churches of the Desert developed gradually but steadily. It is appropriate that we should here glance at some of the more striking features of their internal growth. In the earliest stage, when the number of ordained ministers was extremely small, the synods and colloquies of the Desert were undoubtedly inclined to extend the right to administer the two sacraments of the church as far as possible. They did, indeed, altogether deny the right to the "proposant," or licentiate, to baptize or celebrate the Lord's Supper of his own authority; but they recognized the right of a regularly constituted eldership to empower him to administer these sacraments. A provincial synod declared "that all those that have received the approval of the elders to preach the Gospel, have the right to administer the sacrament of the Lord's Supper, and also that of Holy Baptism, upon the condition that the parents whose child is to be baptized shall promise to reply in the affirmative to the [Roman Catholic] priest, in case they be asked, whether the child has been baptized." [2] In full consistency with this action the Colloquy of the Cévennes, in December, 1720, disciplined the licentiate Jean Vesson, basing its sentence partly upon the fact that he had "administered the sacrament of Holy Baptism to children, without authority to do so, not having ordination or approbation of the elders elected and chosen by the faithful." "This," adds the colloquy, "is a grave offence and a gross irregularity. First, because there are ministers that have received all the forms requisite for the discharge of this sacred function; in the second place, because this is to revive the error of the Marcionites and to endorse that of

Marginal notes: Systematic development of the churches of the Desert. / The functions of the "proposants" restricted.

---

[1] Mr. Chateau to Mr. Bessy, former member of the king's guard, Montauban, June 15, 1747. Bulletin, etc., xxvi. 382.

[2] Synode du Languedoc et des Cévennes, le 7 février, 1718. Les Synodes du Désert, i. 11.

[the adherents of] the Romish church who imagine that necessity confers authority upon men and women, without any solid ground in support of their opinion. Whereas the Christian religion, which we are bound to profess, teaches us that those only who have received a lawful and ample call in a time of peace by an assembly of pastors and professors, can do so [*i.e.*, discharge ministerial functions] in a time of persecution, when there are no ministers or means of obtaining them. It is, indeed, allowable for elders elected by a majority of votes to select a man whom they know to possess qualifications requisite for the Holy Ministry, and confer upon him power and authority to discharge all the functions of a pastor. But the said sieur Vesson has not been established or inducted in any consistory of ministers, nor in any consistory of elders, as has already been stated. Wherefore he has no right to administer the aforesaid holy sacraments."[1]   As the number of pastors increased, the synods grew more strict. It became the rule that, under no circumstances whatsoever, should the "proposant," or licentiate, undertake anything beyond preaching the Gospel. Emphasizing this point, they adopted the custom of inserting in the certificate of licensure some such clause as we find in the following formula : " We have licensed him to discharge the functions of the Holy Ministry, excepting the celebration of marriage and the administration of the holy sacraments of Baptism and the Lord's Supper, which he cannot administer until he shall have received full and complete ordination."[2]

The acts of the synods and colloquies, so far as they have come down to us, give so distinct and interesting a picture of the churches of the Desert that I shall not hesitate to draw largely upon them for illustration of this phase of the religious life of France. Many of these records have, indeed, perished. The fragments of others that have come down to us, owe their preservation to some happy accident. Written upon a loose sheet, in a fine but legible hand, the solitary copy of the transactions of some important meeting, early in the eighteenth century, still bears the marks of the

Acts of the synods of the Desert.

---

[1] Les Synodes du Désert, i. 20.
[2] Synod of Lower Languedoc, May, 1736, ibid., i. 140.

care taken to conceal it from the eyes of prying soldiers or government agents. The tell-tale scrap, scarcely larger than a man's hand, which would have insured the incarceration, possibly the execution of him upon whose person it might have been found, was folded carefully and hidden in the pocket or wallet of the preacher who was interested, above all others, in the decisions it recorded. It is a marvel that so many such manuscripts have escaped the ravages of time and neglect, while destruction has overtaken many a carefully tended library of well-bound tomes.[1]

The administration of the churches was, from the first, both decorous and firm. Their judicatures were little, if at all, in-

Dignity of the church courts.

ferior in dignity to the ecclesiastical convocations held in the less troublous times under the Edict of Nantes. The synod might consist of a handful of ministers and elders, gathered in the mountains or in some lonely country-house; but, wherever convened, the rules of order were rigidly observed. It appointed its moderator and assistant moderator, its secretary and assistant secretary. The authority of the chair was enforced. The speakers were limited as to the number of times they might take the floor. The minister who was absent or late, the churches that neglected to send an elder or elders to the meeting, were censured by name, and the censure was duly recorded on the minutes. The founders, or, more properly, restorers of the discipline of the Protestant churches of France recognized the truth that, whatever may answer for a time of prosperity, nothing will serve so well in a time of persecution as a strong government. They magnified the office of the church courts, and they secured at

---

[1] The minutes of the synods of the Desert were in part accessible to Charles Coquerel, in the preparation of his history (published in 1841), and a few have been inserted in that work, in the Bulletin de la Société de l'histoire du Protestantisme français, etc. M. Edmond Hugues, however, has for the first time given a complete collection of all that are known in his Synodes du Désert. These stately quartos, of which the first volume appeared on the occasion of the Bicentenary of the Revocation, in 1885, contain the minutes of the national and provincial synods in the text, and those of the colloquies in the notes. In the abundance of illustrative notes and the beauty and value of the reproductions, by means of heliogravure, of rare engravings and fac-similes of documents, the work has few equals among recent historical publications.

once the respect which decision and firmness rarely fail to command. Once started in their career of patient, persistent effort for the recovery of the ground formerly occupied by the Reformation, the synods never flinched, never betrayed a sign of weakness or fear. It was a difficult work at all times; particularly difficult whenever persecution became, as it did become from time to time, more severe. Many pastors fell by the way, victims of the intolerance of their fellow-citizens; those that survived took no account of the dead, but pressed resolutely forward. In the minutes of the synods there is absolutely no bewailing of misfortunes, no lamentation over losses. The sufferings of the churches are rarely referred to, save as the marks of the Almighty's displeasure justly kindled against His people because of their sins. From time to time the name of some minister, perhaps a minister that has been frequently mentioned as moderator or secretary, drops out from the minutes and is read no more. We learn the cause from other sources. He was captured by a detachment of troops at such a place; he was hurriedly examined by such a judge; he was sentenced, hung, or broken on the wheel. His brethren in the synod never mention the execution, unless it be incidentally, when making provision for a slender pension to be paid annually to his necessitous widow and small children, or when appointing some one to take up the work he was compelled to lay down. In this there was nothing of insensibility. However much they might in private deplore the bereavement they had sustained, the former associates of the martyr felt they had quite another work before them when they were met in their synods. The blow had fallen upon their late comrade which might have fallen upon them. They were all men appointed to die. Their turn might come next. Whether it came or not, their time was better employed in labor for the good cause than in bemoaning the mishap of a Christian minister who, at the execution, so far from deeming himself unfortunate, rejoiced and pronounced his lot most blessed in the near approach of his crown and reward.

The scrupulous care taken to secure a ministry pious, exemplary, able, and learned is a noticeable feature of the action of the churches as recorded in the minutes. Not even the ur-

Firmness in the storm of persecution.

gent needs of the early years of the eighteenth century could induce the synods to swerve from the line of prudence. Min-

Care to se-
cure a well-
equipped
ministry.

isters found guilty of conduct immoral or scandalous were instantly deposed. No such persons could be restored until they had given long and convincing proof of penitence. Even then they could not return to the scene of their former labors, but must remove to some other and generally distant part of France.[1] Incompetent men, however well-meaning, were arrested in the midst of their course of preparation or of service, thanked for their labors or their good intentions, and recommended to enter some other occupation.[2] At every step the supervision was close, and, down to the time of the Revolution, the appointment of a commission to report upon the morals and studies of the candidates for the ministry was one of the standing orders of the provincial synods.

As a general thing, a promising youth was brought to the notice of the church by some pastor. Upon his recommendation

Ambulant
preparatory
schools.

the young man was placed upon the list of students and received an annual allowance for his support (unless his family was able to provide for that), while receiving preparatory instruction at the hands of the pastor who had introduced him or of some other.[3] The schools that thus grew up were very informal in their instruction; the teacher might at any moment receive tidings of the approach of troops sent to apprehend him, and the pupils might have to follow their master in his hasty retreat; the mountain-side was more frequented than the town, and there were no convenient halls furnished with maps and charts. But if the instructor happened to be an Antoine Court or a Paul Rabaut, the mere association with him was an education whose advantages were not inferior to those enjoyed in famous academies of learning.

---

[1] See, for example, the cases of Jean Bétrine and Étienne Defferre.

[2] So Grail in 1730, Bornac in 1744, Bénézet and Allud in 1749.

[3] A synodical meeting in which Languedoc and Vivarais were represented, October, 1731, decided upon the establishment, in each of the five synods then existing or projected, of a school designated as an *école ambulante*, because it would seem to have been intended that it should shift its quarters, attending the pastor to whose care it was confided.

Detailed pictures of this kind of scholastic life are rarely met with, but fortunately Antoine Court has left us one graphic sketch which may assist the imagination in drawing a more perfect representation. It portrays an incident in his own experience in the Desert.

"I had our field-beds laid out by a torrent," he says, "and underneath a rock. . . . Here we encamped nearly a week; this was our lecture-room, these were our grounds, these our rooms for study. In order that our time might not be wasted, and that our candidates might gain practice, I gave them a text of Sacred Scripture to comment upon. It was the first eleven verses of the fifth chapter of Saint Luke. They were permitted neither to communicate their views to one another, nor to use other helps than the Bible. In the hours of recreation I propounded to them now a doctrinal point to explain, now a passage of Scripture, or a moral precept; or I gave them passages to harmonize. And this is the method I employed. As soon as I had propounded the question, I asked the youngest for his opinion, and then the rest in turn until I reached the eldest. After each one had stated what he thought, I again addressed the youngest, asking him what objections he had to offer to the opinions of the rest, and so from one to the other. After all had argued, I gave them my own judgment respecting the matter propounded. When their exercises were ready, a pole was laid upon two forked stakes, and this, for the present occasion, served as a pulpit for preaching. When one of the young men had left it, I asked all to make remarks, observing the method above given." [1]

Open-air teaching.

In due time the young student came up for examination before the synod, and, if found to be competent, was admitted to the number of "proposants," or licentiates. He could now

---

[1] Court MSS., in Edmond Hugues, Histoire de la Restauration du Protestantisme in France au XVIII⁰ Siècle—Antoine Court, d'après des documents inédits, 4ᵉ édit. (Paris, 1875), i. 84, 85.—I owe to the kindness of M. Charles Dardier a copy of a monograph entitled La vie des Étudiants au Désert d'après la correspondance de l'un d'eux, Simon Lombard, 1756-1763 (Genève, 1893), published by him only a few months before his death. The collection of thirty-nine letters of the young student, with the valuable illustrative matter which the pamphlet contains, conveys a more complete notion of the life of the Desert, with its limitations and hardships, than I have seen elsewhere.

make trial of his abilities by assisting the pastors in their general work, and particularly by preaching in places which the
Care of the "propos-ants." pastors were unable to visit. Originally the licentiates were not expected to compose their own sermons. We have seen that the first religious discourse that Antoine Court ever heard was written by Du Moulin but preached by Jacques Bonbonnoux. An early synod of Lower Languedoc, indeed, prescribed that the "proposants" should use printed sermons, "or if they composed them themselves, they should submit them for examination to persons chosen by the synod, or else they should take no text."[1] A synod of Vivarais, a few years later, resolved: "It shall be left to the discretion of the preachers to preach sermons of good authors which they have learned by heart. If there be any who prefer to compose them for themselves, they shall not be allowed, after composing them, to deliver them in public until the discourses shall first have been examined by the commissioners named for the purpose."[2] So minute, indeed, was the supervision exercised over the candidates, at this stage of their preparation for active service, that we find a somewhat whimsical prohibition, intended, apparently, to check ostentation and conceit, to the effect that no "proposant" should be suffered to keep for his own use "a horse or other animal for riding."[3]

The licentiate whose ministrations proved acceptable to the churches generally applied, after a few years, to the synod
The theological school of Lausanne. within whose jurisdiction he labored, for a leave of absence, in order that he might go to Lausanne and perfect his theological education under the care of the "illustrious friends" of the French Protestants in that city.

The project of establishing on Swiss soil a seminary for the express purpose of training young Frenchmen for the ministry of the churches of the Desert, seems first to have occurred to the mind of Antoine Court, and by him it was carried into effect. It is doubtful, indeed, whether Protestantism is more indebted to

---

[1] Synod of September 30, 1719, E. Hugues, Les Synodes du Désert, i. 17.

[2] Synod of June 21, 1725, ibid., i. 47, 48.

[3] Synod of Vivarais, 1726, ibid., i. 67. Synod of the Lower Cévennes, 1747, ibid., i. 238.

him for having planned the restoration of its church organization and discipline, than for his indefatigable labors, extending
through about thirty years, to secure a proper theological education for its coming ministry.   It was in the summer of the
Court leaves year 1729 that Antoine Court reached the conclusion
France.   that the time had come for him to leave France.
There had been a large accession of pastors, and he could therefore be spared better than ever before.   On the other hand, so
persistent and determined were the efforts put forth to capture
him, to so high a sum had the price long since set upon his
head been lately raised, that there was, humanly speaking, little
prospect that he would long be able to escape arrest.   And arrest meant an end of all opportunity of further usefulness to
France.[1] Having reached Switzerland, Court appears to have
busied himself without delay in seeking from the persons
most interested in the regeneration of French Protestantism
the necessary funds for the establishment and endowment of
the seminary at Lausanne.   The institution began its work
about the year 1730.   No stately building was erected for its
accommodation.   The room is still pointed out, on the upper
An unpre-   story of a building near the Protestant cathedral,
tending es- where the lectures were given.   The professors were
tablishment,
             drawn from members of the faculty of the Acadé-
mie, or University, of the city, and they taught more from
love of the good cause than for any emolument, scanty at best,
which they could hope to derive from so poverty-stricken an
institution.   The scholars, in their coarse home-spun clothes
and with their awkward manners, were at as much of a disadvantage when compared with the well-to-do students of the

---

[1] Mémoires d'Antoine Court, 209, 210. This biographical sketch unfortunately closes at this point.—Court's decision to leave France, never to return,
with the exception of a brief visit, in 1744, to help in healing the schism caused
by Jacques Boyer, was openly condemned by some of his associates.   The secret disapproval of others betrayed itself, from time to time, in unguarded expressions. The judicious student of history will probably come to the conclusion that Antoine Court was, in the circumstances, fully justified in the course he
adopted. A reckless exposure of his person on the field of his former activity
might indeed have borne the appearance of manly courage, but it would have
been barren of the only results which the Huguenot minister had a right to consider.

Académie, sons of respectable families of the Pays de Vaud, as were the appointments of the seminary when contrasted with those of the Académie itself.[1] But the youth from Languedoc and Vivarais had a strange singleness of purpose, an uncompromising self-sacrifice, a heroism that might have invested even men of ruder speech and of more uncouth attire than theirs with the essential dignity of greatness of soul. For, as truly as in the case of any forlorn hope in garrison or in perilous defile, might it be said of them, that they were soon to sally forth in an expedition of which the grave was almost the certain goal.[2] And the seminary itself, to use the words of the most picturesque and striking of modern French historians, was " a strange school of death, which, while forbidding extravagant enthusiasm, with prosaic modesty never tired of sending forth martyrs and of furnishing food for the gallows to feed upon."[3]

<small>but a school of martyrs.</small>

The reason that the students of the churches of the Desert were not sent to the theological school established by Calvin in Geneva, or, if a new school was needed, that it was not founded within the bounds of that little republic, was doubtless the same that had prevented Pierre Corteiz from obtaining ordination at the hands of the Venerable Company of Pastors. Thus did Geneva lose the rare opportunity of adding to the lustre of its ancient glories; thus did the unpretending school of Lausanne win the distinction of becoming the savior of the Protestant churches of France in the eighteenth century.[4]

Much of the legislation of the synods of the Desert arose

---

[1] See the description in D. Benoit, Desubas, son ministère, son martyre, chapter iii.

[2] 'Ὡς τὴν ἐπὶ θανάτῳ ἔξοδον ποιεύμενοι. Herodotus, vii. 223.

[3] Michelet, Histoire de France. Louis XV., 74.

[4] "Ce fut en effet," truthfully remarks Charles Coquerel, " l'académie étrangère de Lausanne qui sauva cette fois les églises protestantes du pays." Histoire des Églises du Désert, i. 204.—The seminary founded by Antoine Court continued its useful career throughout the eighteenth century, and when closed by the Emperor Napoleon, in 1809, it was only after he had issed his decree of September 17, 1808, establishing the Theological Faculty of Montauban, which has thus become, as it were, the successor of the school of Lausanne. C. Coquerel, ubi supra, i. 205. Dardier, Ésaïe Gasc (Paris, 1876), 219 et seq. Léon Maury, Le Réveil religieux (Paris, 1892), i. 272 et seq.

directly from the extraordinary condition of the Protestants during the whole of this period. If persecution was not equally
active at all times, the relation of the so-called New Converts to
the established church did not change in the least. The hardships to which they were subjected did not consist primarily of
the compulsion exercised to wring from them a profession of
Roman Catholicism. The Dragonnades could not be maintained everywhere and for all time. If parents were fined for
neglecting to send their children to the schools taught by
monks and nuns, where attendance necessarily involved an attendance upon the mass also, many of the Protestants contrived
in some way to escape notice, and the unfortunate who did not
succeed in escaping notice were often assisted by the charitable
contributions of their brethren in the faith. The great trouble
was that, as Protestantism was, by a legal fiction, supposed to be
entirely extinct, its adherents had no standing in the sight of
the law. One could neither be born as a Protestant, nor be
baptized as a Protestant, nor be married as a Protestant, nor
be buried as a Protestant. With every civil act a profession of
Roman Catholicism was closely bound up. There could be no
wedlock recognized by the state, unless the marriage was performed by a priest of the Romish church ; and to obtain his intervention it was needful both to exhibit the evidence of baptism and to partake of the communion. Without such a ceremony the children that were the offspring of the union were
branded as bastards, and were incapable of succeeding to the
property of their parents. Certificates of baptism and marriage
" in the Desert " went for nothing ; in fact, they were to the
parents, in the one case, and to the husband and wife in the
other, *prima facie* evidence that they had rendered themselves
amenable to the laws prohibiting all " assemblies " for Protestant worship.

It was no easy task to persuade the laity to renounce the
easy-going policy of conformity into which the great majority
had fallen during the dark period of over a quarter of a century
following the Revocation. Yet to that task the synods of the
churches of the Desert applied themselves, and, by slow degrees, using firmness tempered with moderation and prudence,
they made steady, if not rapid, progress in checking the evil.

Reason was appealed to. Motives of Christian consistency were set forth. The resources of ecclesiastical discipline were drawn upon, with due consideration for human frailty.

The synods give tone to French Protestantism.

The ultimate result was that, as will be seen elsewhere, the lax practice, which had been almost universal at the death of Louis the Fourteenth, became less and less frequent, until, when Louis the Sixteenth, in 1787, published his edict of toleration, and provided therein for the registry of the marriages and baptisms celebrated in the Desert, there were tens of thousands in different parts of the country ready to avail themselves instantly of a privilege for which they had long been waiting.

The action of two synods, in one and the same year (1746), may suffice to illustrate the nature of an ecclesiastical legislation long and carefully considered, and reaching through more than fifty years. The synod of the Lower Cévennes and Rouergue placed upon its records the following article : " This body, after having maturely examined the conduct of the faithful of the province, enjoins upon the pastors, preachers, and consistories, to remonstrate in the most earnest and effective manner with the faithful under their direction who may get married or may have their children baptized in the Romish church, making known to them the enormity and atrocity of such conduct, which tends to extinguish every seed of religion and of the fidelity due to God. If, despite these reprimands, any person should be so wretched as to fall into either of these sins, or other sins related thereto, he is to be promptly suspended from participation in the Lord's Supper. This suspension shall be published in all the religious assemblies of the province, and greater penalties shall ensue in case they be needed." [1] The Synod of Lower Languedoc in like manner decided, "that those who have their children baptized in the Romish church shall be suspended from the Lord's Supper for one year. Those who, after having had one or more children baptized in the Desert, have another child baptized in the Romish church, shall be exposed to the same penalty for eighteen months. Those who, after having had their children baptized in the

---

[1] E. Hugues, Les Synodes du Désert, i. 219.

Desert, have them rebaptized by the priests, shall be suspended
from the Lord's Supper for two years. After the terms above
stated, the consistory shall judge of the contrition of the penitents, and shall abridge or lengthen the time of their punishment." [1]

Equal firmness was exhibited in dealing with another vexatious matter—the observance of Corpus Christi, or *La Fête Dieu.*
"La Fête Dieu." The festival had been instituted by Pope Urban IV.
in the second half of the thirteenth century, to attest
the belief of the church in the transmutation of the bread used
in the eucharist into the very body of Christ; and the Council
of Vienne, on the Rhone, in 1311, confirmed the papal action,
and secured to the "Feast of the Holy Sacrament" a wider
observance. Of how much annoyance and actual persecution
the "Fête Dieu" had been the occasion, the history of the
Huguenots during the two preceding centuries could abundantly testify. When, in a town or village, every house inhabited by Roman Catholics was gay with bright hangings, the
absence of decorations on the front of the houses of a few
Protestants became painfully conspicuous, and the occupants
found themselves the target for insult and abuse. On the other
hand, how could a Protestant drape his windows and doors
without signifying to the world, by the very act, his acceptance
of a doctrine against which the Reformation had made a solemn
protest? To meet this dilemma the Edict of Nantes, in the
third of its secret articles, had, indeed, relieved the Huguenots
of all constraint to adorn the front of their dwellings on such
occasions, but accompanied the concession with the require-
ment that they should permit their dwellings to be draped by
authority of the local officers. The Protestants were not to
contribute to the expense incurred. [2] Now, however, that the
kindly law of Henry the Fourth was overthrown, such of the
Protestants as declined to conform to the practice of their
Roman Catholic neighbors, and to obey the orders of the civil
authorities, were exposed not only to popular fury, but to

---

[1] E. Hugues, Les Synodes du Désert, i. 217.
[2] Édits, Déclarations et Arrests, p. lxi. Anquez, Histoire des Assemblées politiques des Réformés de France, 486.

heavy fines and to imprisonment. There were, of course, weak-kneed Protestants that promptly acquiesced in the custom, and some of these defended their conduct by maintaining that they were "compelled" to act as they did. But the synods made no account of such excuses. In their view no compulsion can justify an ungodly deed, short of "a violence which it is impossible to resist."[1] Consequently they protested against the "cowardice" of those "who, to avoid certain penalties, drape the front of their houses, sweep the streets or strew them with branches, on the day of the sacrament of the Romish Church; which is giving the creature external and religious marks of homage that belong to the Creator alone."[2] They objected even to the voluntary payment on the part of the Protestants of fines incurred by reason of the refusal to honor the Romish festival. A colloquy of Saintonge insisted that the faithful should withhold payment until execution was levied upon their property; but, at the same time, declared that inasmuch as the fines and the costs of execution would entail considerable charges, the churches should assume the expense.[3]

But if their desire to keep themselves clear of all participation in what they regarded as superstitious or blasphemous ceremonies, led the Protestants in certain matters to assume an attitude of antagonism to the clergy, and, indirectly, to the civil authority, their opposition went no further. Of malevolence toward the hierarchy of the Romish church there is no trace in the transactions of the synods of the eighteenth century. While it was notorious that all the vexations and persecutions that culminated in the recall of the Edict of Nantes were the immediate fruit of the periodical appeals of the clergy of France; while it was equally notorious that the great obstacle in the way of the renewed recognition of the civil rights of the Protestants lay in the nearly unanimous opposition of the same clergy, and in the fact that the parish priests

No malevolence toward the Roman Catholic clergy.

---

[1] Les Synodes du Désert, ii. 7.

[2] Synod of Béarn, July, 1758, ibid., ii. 150.

[3] Session of July 19, 1759, ibid., ii. 184.—It is interesting to note that the National Synod of 1758, probably in order to exhibit its aversion to the object of the institution of the *Fête Dieu*, appointed a solemn *fast* for that day! Ibid., ii. 159.

seemed to regard themselves as set apart, by virtue of their orders, to the congenial work of hunting, denouncing, and bringing to the gallows all Protestant pastors in France, it was more than strange that, in their synodical meetings these pastors dropped not a word in disparagement of their relentless enemies.

Toward the royal government the attitude of the Huguenots was equally remarkable. The most brutal severity never provoked them to retaliation, never prompted the utterance of harsh words respecting either the government at Versailles or the agents in the provinces. The very king, their persecutor, is referred to only with expressions of respect and love. " We have lost a good king," wrote Pomaret to a brother pastor, on the death of the monarch whose reign rivalled that of Louis the Fourteenth in the amount of suffering it entailed upon the Huguenots. " This good prince had his frailties, even his vices. What man has not? The hard and cruel man alone ought to be detested ; and Louis the Fifteenth was mildness, humanity, beneficence itself." [1] The proscribed Huguenots, not knowing but that the next moment their meetings might be fired upon by some detachment of troopers sent for the purpose, observed fasts when the king's health was enfeebled, or his arms met with reverses, or a foul conspiracy against his person was discovered. They offered solemn prayers for the continuation of the royal line, and sang the *Te Deum* over the marriage of the Dauphin. Nay, inspired by a loyalty to monarchical institutions with which a citizen of a free republic and a reader living in another century finds it hard to sympathize, the last National Synod of the churches of the Desert, in 1763, did not hesitate to reiterate the assertion made in 1659 by the last National Synod of the churches under the Edict, by the mouth of its moderator, the celebrated Jean Daillé, that "kings depend immediately upon God, and that there is no authority intermediate between theirs and that of omnipotence." [2]

(Loyalty to the crown.)

---

[1] Pomaret to Olivier Desmond, 1774, in Les Synodes du Désert, iii. 83, 84. Seventeen years earlier the Synod of Vivarais and Velay spoke of the same monarch as " the greatest and best of kings." Ibid., ii. 118.

[2] Aymon, Tous les Synodes nationaux des Églises Réformées de France, ii. 723 ; E. Hugues, Les Synodes du Désert, ii. 306.

Of doctrinal discussions the early records of the synods of the Desert have left us but scanty traces. The times in which they met were to the pastors and preachers of Languedoc and its neighboring provinces a period of intense activity. The Protestant ministers were not unintelligent spectators of the contests going on about them. Their letters betray in many places their interest in every new phase of religious controversy, but their own work was, until freedom of worship should be gained, of quite another kind. Through the whole of the century down to the Revolution, and especially during the earlier part, the influence of the standards adopted during what they loved to regard as the golden age of their history, restrained them from any pronounced departure from the creed of their fathers. Where any vital doctrine of the Reformed system was called in question, they did not fail to signify their displeasure at the innovation, even if certain considerations prevented them from distinctly stating their objections in writing. The National Synod of 1756, after expressing its high opinion of the usefulness of the Lausanne seminary, added to the thanks tendered to the friends that had directed the seminary's affairs, a very pointed request that they would more and more watch over the conduct of the students, and *always give them orthodox professors.*" [1] The last clause, which might at first sight seem unimportant enough, had its significance to those who were cognizant of recent events. Five years before, the synod of Lower Languedoc, whose ministers composed not far from one-third of the entire number of Protestant ministers in France, declined to send any of its licentiates to the seminary on the banks of Lake Leman. The elders might have been induced to consent to their going, but the ministers were unwilling that their young students should frequent an institution where an assistant professor or tutor, the pastor Bournet, held what they believed to be erroneous views respecting the divinity of our Lord Jesus Christ. Antoine Court, on being informed of the cause of the synod's action by Paul Rabaut, had

Margin notes: Doctrinal controversies. Trinitarian orthodoxy.

---

[1] " Et les prier de veiller de plus en plus sur la conduite de nos seminaristes et de leur donner toujours des professeurs orthodoxes." Les Synodes du Désert, ii. 86.

the offending instructor removed, and the temporary disaffection of the French pastors toward the seminary ceased.[1]

The belief and teaching of the pastors of the first half part of the eighteenth century would seem to have been in essential conformity with the standards of the French churches before the Revocation. This was certainly the case with the doctrinal views of Jacques Roger, the restorer of Protestantism in Dauphiny, whose labors in that province commenced some years before Antoine Court began to preach in Languedoc, and extended, as we shall see later, until his death on the scaffold in 1745. His most recent biographer has proved, from the entries in a note-book long hidden in the pastor's garden, which has barely escaped the tooth of time, that Roger was "an austere disciple of Calvin," "a reformer of the olden stamp with immovable convictions," one whom "the breath of the times had not reached." His tenets regarding the person of Jesus Christ, and the propitiatory and expiatory nature of His sufferings and death were those of the founders of French Protestantism.[2]

Gradually, however, the churches of the Desert developed an aversion to the strict Calvinism of the sixteenth century. This was evidenced by a marked preference for the cate-

Departure from strict Calvinism. chism of the well-known Swiss theologian Jean Fréderic Osterwald. The National Synod of 1744 enacted that the abridgment of this treatise should be used in all the provinces "as the most clear and methodical" manual of the kind ; while the Synod of Lower Languedoc, in 1771, went further and made it the duty of the elders of the churches to see to it that no other catechism than Osterwald's should be introduced into the public instruction of the youth. A grave incident that had just occurred in the southwest of France, explains the synod's action. Étienne Gibert, the pious and earnest pas-

---

[1] The references in the letter of Paul Rabaut to Court, March 17, 1751, are very guarded. Indeed the separate slip of paper which he had enclosed in his letter, and which he begged his correspondent to show to no one, has unfortunately been destroyed (as Rabaut intended that it should be). But Court's reply and hints dropped by others sufficiently explain the matter. See Paul Rabaut, ses lettres à Antoine Court, ii. 120, with M. Dardier's useful note.

[2] See D. Benoit's interesting volume, Jacques Roger, restaurateur du Protestantisme dans le Dauphiné (Toulouse, 1881), 234 et seq.

tor of Bordeaux,[1] dissatisfied both with Osterwald's catechism
and with that of Saurin, which enjoyed some currency among
the Protestants, was at the pains, without consulting the elders of his church, of printing an edition
of the Heidelberg catechism translated into French.[2]
This he intended to employ in the religious training of the
children; but he was met by the determined opposition of the
consistory. A warm and acrimonious discussion ensued. The
case was taken by appeal to the provincial synod. This body,
at its meeting of September, 1770, condemned Gibert's course
in introducing, without the knowledge of the elders, a new catechism, "albeit approved among the Protestant communions in
general." It further decided that "the consistory was in the
right, in view of the complaints made by several of the members
and by a large number of the faithful, when it directed the said
Sieur Gibert, as it did by its different resolutions, and particularly by those of the thirteenth of August last, to express himself, as well publicly as in private, respecting the matters of
grace, the spiritual inability of man, and the necessity of good
works, in the terms set forth in the aforesaid resolutions; inasmuch as this manner of expressing one's views does not seem to
the synod to impair orthodoxy in these matters, while it would
have prevented the aforesaid complaints, and put an end to the
unhappy divisions that have already occurred and may yet
arise."[3]

As may readily be seen, it was not so much the Calvinism
of Étienne Gibert, as the general character of his preaching
that offended his hearers. It is doubtful, indeed, how strong a

(marginal note: Étienne Gibert at Bordeaux.)

---

[1] Étienne Gibert was a younger brother of Jean Louis Gibert, also a pastor of
the Desert, who, in 1764, brought over to Charleston, S.C., a colony of one
hundred and thirty-eight Huguenots. They settled in a place (Abbeville County),
to which they gave the name of *New Bordeaux*. Jean Louis Gibert was accompanied or followed by his brother-in-law, the pastor Boutiton. Ramsay, History of South Carolina, i. 19, 20; Paper on the Huguenots of South Carolina
and their Churches, by Rev. Dr. C. S. Vedder, in Proceedings of the Huguenot
Society of America, i. 39.

[2] "The only catechism of that time, published in the French tongue, which
was squarely Trinitarian," says Dardier, in his Ésaïe Gasc, p. 332.

[3] Synod of Saintonge, Angoumois and Bordelais, in Les Synodes du Désert, ii.
497–499.

Calvinist the pastor of Bordeaux himself was. For, much as he admired the Genevese reformer, he preferred him little, if at all, to Zwingli, and of both reformers he could say that, when one can walk in the full brightness of the sun, one need not stop at any lesser lights. As for the doctrine of predestination, he clearly intimated that it was often treated in a manner that both affrighted and saddened him ; and he regarded it as out of place in the pulpit, where, above all things, the reassuring invitations of Jesus to the sinner were to be presented.[1] In point of fact, Gibert's intimacy with the Moravian brethren was one of the chief grounds of the fault that was found with him. A Protestant church and community with which religion had pretty much resolved itself into a code of morality, were scandalized at a style of preaching that disturbed the equanimity of the hearer, awakened him from his fancied security, and made him anxiously inquire what he must do to be saved. It was startling to church members, lethargic, if not spiritually dead, to be assured that "man can do nothing good before having faith," and "that philosophy is useless in the matter of religion ;" still more startling and disconcerting to discover that the statements impugned were explicitly taught in the old Confession of Faith held by the Reformed Churches and professed by them in the fires of persecution, from the day that they presented that confession to King Francis the Second, at Amboise, in 1560.[2] But when the consistory of Bordeaux gravely made it a principal charge against Gibert "that in his preaching he was always coming back to the same end, to Jesus Christ," its absurdity, not less than its entire misconception of Christianity, moves a recent historian, who has certainly never been accused of a leaning toward doctrinal orthodoxy, to exclaim : "A singular church, in truth, is this church of Bordeaux ! It cannot endure that its pastor should speak to it too much of Jesus Christ."[3] But

---

[1] See the remarkable letter of Étienne Gibert to Olivier Desmont, London, May 6, 1774. Bulletin, etc., xix. 70–73.

[2] See the ninth article of the Confession de Foy faite d'un commun accord par les François qui desirent vivre selon la pureté de l'Evangile de Nostre Seigneur Jesus Christ, in the Recueil des Choses Memorables faites et passées pour le faict de la Religion (Petits Mémoires de Condé), 1565, page 55.

[3] Charles Dardier, Ésaïe Gasc, 332.

perhaps even more singular than the attitude of the individual church of Bordeaux is the attitude of the synod, and, indeed, of a considerable number of prominent men in the churches, who condemned Gibert for disturbing the harmony of the churches, instead of applauding him for vindicating the purity and spirituality of their doctrine. Olivier Desmont hinted that Gibert would have done well not to recall too often "forgotten matters;" to which Gibert replied that if these were "forgotten matters," Christianity was in a sorry plight, for it was the doctrine of Saint Paul in brief that we are saved by grace, through faith, and that this comes not of ourselves but is the gift of God. "We are saved by grace alone," he added. "To forget the matter of grace is to forget the only way of salvation."[1] Paul Rabaut, it is said, was deeply grieved at the conduct of the consistory of Bordeaux, and would have had Gibert carry his cause up to the national synod by appeal; but many sympathized with Murat, of Montauban, who thought that Gibert "ought not to have embroiled himself with his consistory for points of so little importance and should have accommodated himself to the times!"[2]

The history of the churches of the Desert is to be studied rather in the minutes of the provincial than in those of the national synods. It was otherwise in the times previous to the Revocation of the Edict of Nantes. Then the national synods alone were of prime importance. After the Revocation there were held only eight synods claiming the designation of national, the latest being that of 1763. Far from seeking, as had at first been proposed, to call a national synod every year, the churches of the Desert early laid down the principle, distinctly enunciated in the "Discipline" drawn up, in 1739, by Barthélemy Claris, in pursuance of the instructions of the Synod of Lower Languedoc, that "the national synod shall

National synods rarely convoked.

---

[1] Letter of May 6, 1774, above quoted.

[2] See the full treatment of the incident in Mr. D. Benoit's interesting biography, Les Frères Gibert, 264–290. Gibert presents the main points of the controversy admirably in a letter to his church, dated October, 1770, of which copies seem to have been sent to various other churches, the church of Nismes among the rest. See Dardier, Ésaïe Gasc, pièces justif., 450–453, and Bulletin, etc., xxxi. 399–402.

convene only in case of very urgent need."[1] The reasons for this were, doubtless, the small number of the pastors, the long distances which they and the elders delegated by the churches must travel in order to reach the place of meeting, possibly in a distant part of France, the poverty of the laity who were ill able to defray the expense of the convocation, and, above all, the wholesale butchery to which the delegates exposed themselves in going to a meeting into the secret of which so many persons must necessarily be admitted long beforehand.[2] But if the general

Growth of the provincial synods.

synods lost, the provincial synods gained in importance. This was true, above all, of the Synod of Lower Languedoc. In 1719 it had but two ordained ministers. In 1789 it had forty ordained ministers, and sixty-eight churches, divided into the five colloquies of Nismes, Uzès, Sommières, Massillargues, and Montpellier. A body comparatively so large and so well equipped for work exerted a controlling influence in many ecclesiastical matters. Meantime the missionary spirit had been strongly developed. Districts but ill provided with ministers of the Gospel robbed themselves that they might "lend" one or more to the regions less favored. Thus it was at the price of self-denial and sacrifice that the Protestants of the Cévennes revived the Reformed religion among the descendants of those who had once been Protestants in Upper Languedoc. Thence the movement advanced southward into Foix, and westward into Guyenne and Béarn. Thus were Saintonge and Angoumois, reclaimed; thus, too, Aunis, the Isle de Ré, and the city of La Rochelle; thus Poitou, Normandy, Picardy, and other provinces. The progress was not always rapid, but it was steady. By the time of the National Synod of 1756, the number of ecclesiastical provinces had increased to ten, with forty-eight pastors and seventeen licentiates. In 1763 there were fourteen provinces, with sixty-two pastors and thirty-five licentiates. When the Edict of Tol-

---

[1] "Le synode national ne sera assemblé que dans une tres-grande necessité." Les Synodes du Désert, i. 367.

[2] "Cette assemblée rencontre de très grandes difficultés, et elle ne peut avoir lieu sans que la plupart des ministres du royaume s'exposent aux plus éminens perils." Paul Rabaut to Antoine Court, September 20, 1747. Lettres (Dardier), i. 279.

eration was signed, twenty-four years later, there were, if we
may judge from the known increase in certain synods, about
one hundred and twenty-five Protestant pastors in all
Protestant pastors in 1787. France. The increase of the professedly Protestant
laity was doubtless still greater in proportion. In some
districts of southern France the Huguenot families seemed to
be about as numerous as before the Revocation. It was a
grand work of resuscitation, and the instruments employed by
Providence in effecting it were a few devoted men, who compensated for their lack of numbers by their determination to
win back the ground which the Reformation had lost through
no fault of its own but as the result of merciless persecution.
To men like Paul Rabaut, who took for the motto on his seal,
" *Né à pâtir et mourir* "—" Born to suffer and die "—to men who
like him could playfully and fearlessly write, " I am worth more
than I was a while ago ; a sum of six thousand livres was the
price set on my head, now it is ten thousand ; and, instead of
the halter, I am now threatened with the wheel "—to such men
was it chiefly owing that the Revocation of the Edict of Nantes
proved in the end so complete a failure.

I have said that the ascendency of Cardinal Fleury began in
1726. It continued undiminished until his death in 1743. We
have seen that this period of seventeen years, if a period of
unabated persecution, was also a period of steady and surprising growth for the Protestant churches. In the accomplishment of this result the new generation of Huguenot pastors
that arose distinguished themselves—men who, not content
with building up and strengthening the works commenced by
others, boldly pushed westward and northward until the provinces that bordered the Bay of Biscay and the British Channel
began to vie with Languedoc and Dauphiny in the number and
promise of their religious communities. But among all that
illustrated this age and made their impress upon French Protestantism, down to the very times of returning toleration, no
Paul Rabaut. single name approaches in merited fame that of Paul
Rabaut, the typical Pastor of the Desert. Born of
Protestant parents at Bédarieux, on the twenty-ninth of January,
1718, and baptized, four days later, by the Roman Catholic curate
of the church of St. Alexandre, he was about twenty-two years

younger than his friend and great predecessor in the work, Antoine Court. Yet his career as a preacher was far longer than that of Court. For while the latter, after fifteen years of constant perils, turned aside to establish himself in a land of safety and thence exert his powers for the interest of the churches which he dearly loved, Paul Rabaut, beginning his labors as a preacher in 1738, when he was only twenty years of age, never forsook the field after having once entered it. At his death, on the twenty-fifth of September, 1794, in the midst of the French Revolution, he had abundantly earned the simple but grand title inscribed on the stone marking the place where he was quietly buried, in the cellar of the house he long inhabited at Nismes—now the asylum of the Orphan Girls of the Department of Gard—"The Apostle of the Desert." [1] He had outlived, as his dear churches had outlived, not only the long years of persecution but the Reign of Terror. His was, in truth, that wonderful devotion to principle which Antoine Court used to style "the spirit of the Desert," and which he defined as "a spirit of mortification, a spirit of reflection, of great wisdom, and especially of martyrdom, which as it teaches us to die daily to ourselves, to conquer and overcome our passions with their lusts, prepares and disposes us to lose our life courageously amid tortures and on the gallows, if Providence calls us thereto." [2] In fact, this spirit had inspired him from boyhood. Four years before he was permitted to preach, he sought of his own accord, and obtained, the dangerous privilege of attaching himself to a pastor, Jean Bétrine, whom he followed from place to place, exposing himself to the same extreme perils and hardships, that he might receive the training necessary for one who himself aspired to preach "under the cross." Of the possession of this spirit he gave evidence to the last. Whereas he had escaped imprisonment as a Protestant pastor for over half a century at the hands of a persecuting government claiming to be Christian, he incurred incarceration in the Fort of Nismes

---

[1] It was not until 1882 that search was made and the exact spot was discovered where Paul Rabaut's remains were laid. Since then a modest monument has been erected. See Charles Dardier's preface to his Paul Rabaut : ses lettres à Antoine Court, i. page lv.

[2] Dardier, ubi supra, xxviii.

by the order of the atheists of the Revolution for manfully refusing to renounce, at their dictation, his character of a Christian minister.[1]

Devoted with his whole soul to the work upon which he was
engaged, Paul Rabaut pursued it with unwavering fidelity. By
his disinterestedness, by the simplicity with which he preached
the fundamental doctrines of the Reformation, by a deportment
that was as gentle and conciliatory as it was resolute and fearless when occasion demanded, he gradually acquired an influence which his fellow-Protestants gladly acknowledged, which
those outside of his communion were not slow in recognizing,
and which the government itself was disposed to turn to advantage. For not only was he eloquent and persuasive as an
orator, but he had the secret of that manifest sincerity which
may render effective even words spoken badly. Hence it was
that over the whole of the broad parish that was confided to
his care, there was no one to whom the people listened with
greater pleasure, or to hear whom they came from greater distances and in greater numbers.

During the two years that immediately followed the death of
Cardinal Fleury (1743-1745) the era of comparative toleration
and of crowded conventicles seemed to have arrived.
Comparative toleration and crowded meetings, 1743-1745. Louis the Fifteenth, immersed in war and deprived
of the minister whom the clergy had found little dif-
ficulty in urging to the advocacy of severe measures,
apparently forgot the existence of the Huguenots.[2] Relieved
of the cardinal's pressure, the military commandant of Languedoc, the Duke of Richelieu, having no innate fondness for persecution, began to close his eyes to infractions of the laws against
the Protestants ; while Bernage, intendant of the same province, chafed at the spread of an evil which he declared was
growing daily to such a degree that for one Protestant converted there could be counted a hundred Catholics who had
apostatized.[3] On Sunday, the fourth of July, 1745, Paul Rabaut preached to a congregation consisting, " without exaggera-

---

[1] Dardier, ubi supra, liv.
[2] Hugues, La Restauration du Protestantisme, ii. 118.
[3] Hugues, ubi supra, ii. 119.

tion,"[1] of ten thousand souls. Large gatherings of the kind were the rule, not the exception. It happened the very next Sunday that, hearing that the great preacher of the Desert was holding a meeting in the neighborhood of Marsillargues, a great noble of Languedoc, the Marquis of Calvisson, who had just returned from Versailles, visited the Huguenot gathering for worship and listened to a good part of the sermon.[2] Not only so, but the marquis begged to have another meeting called in the vicinity of his possessions, and gave his peasants permission to be present. These came to a man. Not a Roman Catholic remained in the village of Calvisson, excepting the curate and his clerk.[3] The marquis and every other person present had incurred the penalty of the law. Such are the incongruities offered by an age of persecution !

It was at this auspicious time, as Paul Rabaut wrote, some years later, in the petition of whose romantic transmission to the government I shall soon have occasion to speak, that the greater number of the Protestants of Upper and Lower Languedoc opened their eyes to the crime and the danger of dissimulation and hypocrisy, and resolved to have their marriages blessed and their children baptized by their own ministers : I say expressly, the Protestants of Upper and Lower Languedoc, to distinguish them from those of the Cévennes and of Vivarais, who had for a long time been celebrating their marriages and baptisms according to the rites of their religion.[4]

But the respite enjoyed by the Huguenots was brief. From

---

[1] "Mes assemblées depuis quelque temps sont forts populeuses. Dimanche dernier il y avoit bien dix mille ames sans exageration." "Confions-nous toujours en Dieu," he adds. "Il n'abandonnera point son église ; il viendra quand il en sera tems." Paul Rabaut to Antoine Court, July 9, 1745. Lettres, i. 193.

[2] "Je fis dimanche dernier une assemblée près de Marsillargue. Le marquis de Calvisson y vint et entendit la moitié de mon sermon." The same to the same, July 14, 1745. Ibid., i. 196.

[3] "Le sermon fini, Mr. de Calvisson pria que l'on tînt une assemblée proche de sa terre, et il donna permission à ses paysans d'y aller, en sorte que du tems de cette assemblée, il ne resta pas un catholique dans le village, hormis le curé et son clerc." Court de Gébelin to his father, August 26, 1745. Ibid., i. 196, note.

[4] Supplément au mémoire dressé dans le mois de juin 1752 sur l'état des Protestans de la province du Languedoc. Bulletin de la Soc. de l'hist. du Prot. fr., xliv. (1895), 132.

comparative quiet the change was rapid to violent repression.
It was not that new laws were enacted, but that old laws which
had been held in abeyance, but had never been repealed, were again executed, and that, too, with increased malignity. The seven years from 1745 to
1752 may with propriety be styled *the Great Persecution.* This
persecution was the direct result of the solicitations of the
clergy. Never had the prelates of the Roman Catholic
church more distinctly betrayed their desires or dictated
their terms. One of the periodical assemblies general of the
Gallican church being held in 1745, there was a good opportunity for repeating every accusation by which royalty had
so often in the past been embittered against the Calvinists.
The Bishop of Saint Pons reiterated and enforced the sentiment that the Huguenots, of whose rapid growth he gave a
vivid and apparently truthful representation, would
never be good citizens except in so far as they were
constrained by fear.[1]   After which it is not surprising
that he was audacious enough to maintain, respecting the sermons of the pastors, " that they aimed less at inspiring the lis-
teners with Christian truth and Christian morality, than at incul-
cating a cruel and implacable hatred of the Catholic religion." [2]

The Archbishop of Tours was the mouthpiece of the clergy
in their " remonstrance " to the king, and the latter gave him
in answer the most gratifying assurances of his continued zeal
for the maintenance of the faith, the defence of the church, and
the extirpation of heresy.[3]

These were not vain words. In fact Louis had not waited to
be urged, for in February, the very month in which the assembly of the clergy convened, he had issued a proclamation of no doubtful import. To disabuse the
Protestants of any illusions respecting his intentions,
his Majesty gave notice that with regard both to
preachers and to persons attending the forbidden assemblies,
the full measure of punishment meted out by former ordinances

Marginal notes:
The Great Persecution, 1745-1752.

Solicitations of the prelates.

The laws against the Protestants to be en-forced.

---

[1] " Ils ne seront bons sujets qu'autant que la crainte les contiendra."

[2] See the extended extracts of the bishop's speech of April 7, 1745, in Hugues, La Restauration du Protestantisme, ii. 181-186.

[3] Ibid., ii. 187.

would be inflicted, and that men and women known to have
been present, even though not arrested on the spot, would be
sent, the former to the galleys, the latter to prison, "without
form or figure of trial." [1]

The results were not long delayed. The clergy did not spare
its urgent appeals. Some, at least, of the intendants, as Le

Pastors put Nain, in Languedoc, would seem to have required no
to death. urgency. Now came in rapid succession the arrest
and execution of several pastors. Never had the churches of
the Desert been subjected to such repeated losses. Dauphiny
suffered most. The Parliament of Grenoble, on the second of
March, sentenced Louis Ranc to be hung on the gallows at the
town of Die. Moreover, it ordered that his head should be cut
off and carried thence to Livron. At Livron it was to be exposed on a pole erected in front of the hostelry in which the

Louis Ranc. pastor had been arrested two weeks before. Ranc was
but twenty-six years of age. He was offered his life
if he would abjure ; but he died with as much fortitude as if he
were but sacrificing a brief remnant of his days. The martyrs'
psalm, " *La voici l'heureuse journée* " (Ps. cxviii.), was often upon
his lips as he went to his execution, but when he would have
addressed the people the roll of drums drowned his voice.
Neither state nor church opposed the ferocious populace when
the latter undertook to inflict upon his mutilated body, outrages not ordered by his sentence. [2] Indeed it is asserted that
the commandant and the grand vicar of the bishop themselves
caused the corpse to be dragged through the streets of Die and
cast into the common sewer. [3]

Far more important was the capture (on the twenty-ninth of
April) of the veteran Jacques Roger, who, as we have seen, had
for thirty years been the apostle of Protestantism in Dauphiny,
and who had built up a series of not less than sixty churches, [4]

---

[1] Royal ordinance of February 1, 1745. La Restauration du Protestantisme,
ii. 188.

[2] C. Coquerel, Histoire des Églises du Désert, i. 334, 335. The text of his
sentence is in the Bulletin de la Soc. de l'hist. du Prot. fr., xiii. 335.

[3] D. Benoit ; Jacques Roger et ses Compagnons d'œuvre (Toulouse, 1881), 209.

[4] Benoit gives the list, ubi supra, 288, 289 ; as does also Hugues, Restauration
du Protestantisme, ii. 151, 152.

monuments of his patient and unremitting labors. A contemporary of Court in his first undertakings, the career of Roger as a preacher antedated that of Court by five or six years. His success had been scarcely less brilliant than the success of Court. His arrest had been no less anxiously sought for by priests and intendants. He was now an old man of threescore and ten, and, unless his words and actions belied him, more than willing to finish his course, if so be that he might finish it with honor to his Master and joy to himself. His toils had been severe and unremitting. He had been subjected to continual hardship. The burden of the churches weighed heavily upon him. Calumny occasionally added to the burdens he had to bear. It was not a year since his enemies had circulated an absurd story that at a meeting which he held in the Desert, at Poyols, on the seventh of June, 1744, Roger read to the assembled worshippers a pretended edict of Louis the Fifteenth, just one month old, and bearing a seal which he represented to be that of his Majesty, granting to his subjects liberty of conscience and the right to come together for worship. Count Argenson, one of the secretaries of state, found it convenient to believe, or pretend to believe, the rumor, and wrote a letter to the first president of the Parliament of Dauphiny, denouncing the edict in question as a forgery, and inciting to renewed efforts for Roger's capture.[1] To this document, which was printed and scattered broadcast throughout the province, the pastor replied in a letter, firm but temperate in tone, which might serve both as a defence of himself and as a vindication of the loyalty of the maligned churches. Denying that the incident referred to had ever occurred, and that he had ever seen or heard of the pretended edict before reading the secretary's letter, he pronounced the whole matter a fabrication, intended by its authors to blacken the reputation of the Protestants and to render them odious in the king's eyes. He demanded that justice be done

Jacques Roger, the apostle of Dauphiny.

Calumnious stories and forgeries.

---

[1] The letter, printed as a broadside, bears the royal arms at the head, and the title "Copie de la lettre écrite par M. le comte d'Argenson, ministre et sécretaire d'état, à M. de Piolenc, premier président du Parlement de Dauphiné. Au camp devant Ypres, 22 juin 1744." In the Bulletin de la Soc. de l'hist. du Prot. fr., iii. 312.

as between the accuser and the accused.[1] It was a hopeless demand. Forgeries for the purpose of injuring the Huguenots were no novelty. Among others a disloyal song attributed to them about this time enjoyed a wide circulation. It was a prayer for the success of the arms of the English. The Huguenots, it was said, sang it in their meetings for worship. The song began (in imitation apparently of the first words of the fiftieth psalm of Clement Marot—"*Le Dieu, le Fort, l'Eternel parlera*")

> "O Dieu ! le Fort ! Arbitre de la guerre !
> Fais triompher les armes d'Angleterre,
> Donne puissance et victoire à son Roi,
> Le defenseur de ta divine loi."

The other seven verses were in the same strain. Paul Rabaut, learning that the poem had fallen into the hands of the Duke of Richelieu, wrote him an indignant letter in which he plainly intimated that the author was no Protestant but a Roman Catholic priest of Nismes.[2] It would have been a startling novelty had any genuine search been instituted for the authors and any honest attempt made to bring them to trial.

When at last Jacques Roger was betrayed into the hands of his enemies, he seemed not sorry that the end had come. The officer in command of the troops sent to apprehend him was not sure whether it was in truth the old preacher whom he met disguised as a peasant, and asked him his name. To whom Roger unhesitatingly replied : " I am the man whom you have been seeking these six-and-thirty years. It was high time that you found me." From that moment until the hour of his execution his emotions were joyful, not sad. It was with gladness that he announced to his fellow-Protestants confined with him for the sake of religion, that the happy day had come for him to seal with his blood the great truths which he had preached to them.[3]

---

[1] See Benoit, ubi supra, 179–182.

[2] Antoine Court printed both the poem and the letter in his Mémoire Apologétique en faveur des Protestans, and Rambach reprinted the former and translated the latter in his Schicksal der Protestanten in Frankreich (Halle, 1759), i. 310–314. See also the French text of the letter in Dardier : Lettres de Paul Rabaut à Antoine Court, i. 351. C. Coquerel, Hist. des Égl. du Désert, i. 352, etc.

[3] See Benoit, ubi supra, 222–231.

Jacques Roger was hung, and his lifeless body was flung into the waters of the river Isère.[1]

Other pastors there were that lost their lives whose names and whose valuable services I cannot stop to mention—men held in high esteem, men whom their devoted parishioners could scarcely bring themselves to give up. But the law as administered was merciless. When the pastor Matthieu Majal, better known by the surname which he had assumed of Desubas, was led a prisoner on the way to Vernoux, a small band of young men, who had heard him preach, in vain begged the officer in command to release him, and, showing too much eagerness to hold him, as though they would not let him go, received a volley of shot under which five of their number fell dead. It was still worse in Vernoux itself when a great crowd of Protestants—men, women, and children—that had come out to attend their religious meetings, excited, but unarmed, flocked into the place to call for the release of their minister. For all answer they were greeted with the discharge of musketry from the houses in front of which they passed. The " Massacre of Vernoux," as the incident came to be known, involved the death of some thirty Huguenots. Many more died of their wounds.[2]

Attempted rescue of Desubas.

Massacre of Vernoux, December 12, 1745.

Notwithstanding all the efforts of the wiser men, it was difficult for the people to contain their indignation when they saw the pastors whom they honored for their piety and self-sacrifice hurried away to be tried and executed as the vilest of malefactors. Antoine Court had scarcely persuaded the parishioners of Étienne Arnaud to desist from their purpose of snatching the latter from the hands of the paltry escort of fifty men that were to conduct him from Alais to Montpellier.[3] That was a quarter

---

[1] Paul Rabaut to Antoine Court, June 23, 1745. Lettres à A. Court, i. 185. I quote a characteristic passage from this letter : " Ce fut le 22ᵉ du mois dernier, qu'il receut cette glorieuse couronne *qu'il avoit tant desirée.* Peu de tems avant sa capture il avoit eu une maladie de laquelle il croyoit mourir ; et ce qui l'affligeoit extremement, c'étoit que Dieu ne lui fit pas l'honneur de l'appeler à signer de son sang la sainte doctrine qu'il avoit prechée. Le Seigneur voulut satisfaire à son desir ; aussi temoigna-t-il être fort content, qu'on lui lut la sentence par laquelle il étoit condamné à être pendu."

[2] C. Coquerel, Histoire des Églises du Désert, i. 378, 379.

[3] Mémoires d'Antoine Court, 142, and supra, p. 442.

of a century ago, and now that the Huguenots had grown in
numbers, and from time to time had seen the subordinate officers of government wink at their unauthorized meetings, they
were not disposed to submit tamely. Paul Rabaut himself
gives a picture of the effect produced upon Nismes and its environs when a rumor was circulated, on the day after Whitsunday (the seventh of June, 1745), that he was in danger. " A
detachment of soldiers was sent to Générac. We do not know
why it was that the Protestants took it into their heads that
these troops had been despatched to capture me. Somebody
confirmed the statement. At once three or four thousand persons from the single city of Nismes took the field.

*The Nis-
mois fly to
the succor
of their pas-
tor, Rabaut.*
Between a hundred and three hundred men started
from Milhau, and hastened to my succor. The whole
thing was done in an instant. One took an iron pitch-
fork, another a sickle, another a pistol, another a gun. Each
man took what he found most suitable for attack or defence.
Some walked, thus provided, with inconceivable speed to the
place where they had been told that the troops had invested
me. The others posted themselves at the crossings of the roads
that lead to the same spot, and all were fully resolved to sacrifice their lives to preserve the life of their pastor. Even the
women determined to have their share in the matter. Many of
them accompanied the troop of men, with stones in their
aprons, to overwhelm the soldiers ; and those who could not go
exhorted their husbands to go to my relief without loss of
time." [1]

Of incentives to exasperation, and even to retaliation, there
was no lack as the years passed on. For the persecution continued with little abatement. In 1746, it is true, the
*Temporary
abatement of
persecution.*
government thought fit to stop its ears to the unintermitting solicitations of the clergy. The fortunes of
war were not in favor of France. She had to contend against a
powerful coalition of Great Britain, Austria, and Savoy. What
if the Huguenots of the south should listen to the foreign emissaries that were said to be in the country urging them to revolt ? It was no time for a resort to extreme measures against

---

[1] Paul Rabaut to Antoine Court, June 23, 1745. Lettres, i. 189, 190.

Protestantism. The government in these circumstances found nothing more convenient than to disseminate an old letter, which the celebrated French pastor of Rotterdam, Jacques Basnage, had written nearly a quarter of a century before. The refugee pastor took such high ground regarding the obedience due from subjects to their sovereign, as to condemn the religious meet-

The government re- prints and circulates a Protestant letter on loyalty.

ings which the persecuted Protestants were holding in the Desert in disobedience to the commands of Louis the Fifteenth. Once before, immediately upon its publication, it had been reprinted in France, by express order of the Regent, and now a minister of state, the Count of Saint Florentin, caught up with delight the suggestion of a fresh issue. Strangely enough, the sermon now came out with a preface written by or under the supervision of Le Nain, the violent intendant of Languedoc. The tiger clothed himself for the nonce in sheep's clothing, the persecutor attempted to counterfeit the style of the persecuted. Needless to say, the " very dear brethren " whom he addressed were now styled members of the " Reformed," not of the " pretended Reformed," religion, and the " faithful," while the character and abilities of Basnage were lauded to the skies. He was one of God's ministers whose memory was greatly revered, one who had acquired the general veneration of Europe by his rare talents and still more by the purity of his morals, a wise and pious minister ever animated by that admirable solicitude which rendered him attentive to everything that could be of interest to his brethren the Protestants (religionnaires) of France. Afflicted by the disturbances which a false spirit of devotion had caused in the Cévennes, and the consequent acts of cruelty, he neglected nothing to make known, by learned and pious writings, how contrary is such conduct to the true Protestant religion itself and how opposed to the commandments of God. Le Nain's preface was a curiosity of literature, intended to deceive the very elect. It did deceive some Roman Catholic officials—the mayor of Mazamet, the Count of Caraman, the sub-intendant of Toulouse, even the first president of the parliament of that superstitious city itself. They looked with suspicion upon the tract of a Protestant pastor mysteriously deposited in the mail at Montauban and addressed to Protestants exclusively. Whether any Protestants were also deceived does not appear. Those of Castres, at any rate, suspected a trick of their enemies, and more than half of them declined even to take from the post-office the copies sent to their address.[1]

There was also a slight relaxation in the severity of the measures adopted against the Protestants after the conclusion of the Treaty of Aix-la-Chapelle (1748); but soon the old persecution was renewed with fresh energy. One need but peruse a diary of Paul Rabaut for the years 1750, 1751, and 1752, to form a conception of the intolerable burdens imposed upon conscientious Protestants and the still more fearful dangers that confronted them. For a time the uniform sequel of every conventicle was the arrest of prisoners. Two hundred persons were captured at Uzès. Five men were sent to the galleys, two women to the Tour de Constance, all for their entire lives. Thirty-eight men and women were sentenced to imprisonment at Nismes for six months. The experiment was made by the Huguenots of meeting on other days instead of Sunday; it was unsuccessful, for men could not leave their work. A meeting near Lezan was broken up by the advent of soldiers; all escaped save certain old men and children, to the number of nine. A few young men, distressed at the sight of the arrest of their relatives, followed the officer in command and begged for their release. When they became importunate the officer ordered his troops to fire on them, and three were killed. Fines were imposed upon parents that had had their children baptized in the Desert—five hundred livres for one child, a thousand for two children, fifteen hundred for three.[2] Bénézet, a student for the ministry, was captured at Le Vigan, and hung because he would not

Paul Rabaut's journal, 1750-1752.

Bénézet hung.

---

[1] The late M. J. P. Hugues, of Anduze, has given, from the archives of Montpellier, the secret and authentic history of this amusing episode of the fortunes of the Huguenots, in the Bulletin de la Soc. de l'hist. du Prot. fr., v. 192–210. The Preface of Le Nain is reproduced entire. In the same volume (v. 53–64) the Bulletin had already inserted an answer which Basnage's letter called forth from "the pastors of the Desert." It was dated July 30, 1719, and Antoine Court undoubtedly wrote it.

[2] The royal ordinance to this effect, of January 17, 1750, was iniquitously construed as retroactive. Claude d'Azémar, a Huguenot gentleman who traced his

abjure.[1] Presently the intendant undertook to compel parents to have their children rebaptized, ostensibly "to supplement the ceremonies of the church of Rome," and made use of dragoons to effect his purpose. Many families forsook their homes in consequence ; some of whom, solicited by relatives, returned, others made their escape to foreign lands. The number of fugitives from Nismes was large, and they were well received abroad. The Protestants of the banks of the Gard, seeing the cavalry stationed at Lédignan for the purpose of compelling

Retaliation on parish priests.
the rebaptism of children, thought it high time to arm themselves, gave the horsemen a fright, and shot the priests of Ners, Quillan, and Langrian, inflicting wounds of which two of the number died. "The cavalry, apprehending a like fate, decamped by order of the intendant, and, in virtue of the same order, restored the money they had already exacted from the Protestants."

At this juncture the Marquis Voyer d'Argenson de Paulmy, son of Marquis d'Argenson and nephew of Count d'Argenson

The Marquis of Paulmy comes to Languedoc,
—both of the latter secretaries of state—reached Languedoc. It was imagined that he would give rigorous orders against the Protestants, especially those of the vicinity of the river Gard ; "but, on the contrary," says Rabaut, "there was no longer a question of rebaptism or of anything else, and since his arrival we have been more tranquil than we have ever been since the Revocation of the Edict of Nantes." [2]

The marquis had a tender heart. Visiting the Tour de Constance at Aigues Mortes he could not contain his pity at the sight of the poor imprisoned women, and promised to intercede for them with the king. Before he left he gave them two

---

illustrious lineage back for many centuries, and belonged to the same family with the famous Counts Adhémar of the southeast of France (see La France Protestante, i. 38) was a victim. He had had two children baptized in the Desert *before* the publication of the law. See his most touching correspondence with the brutal intendant, Saint Priest, in the Bulletin, etc., x. 69–82.

[1] See the documents bearing upon his arrest and trial, in the Bulletin, etc., xxxiii. 543 et seq., and the "complainte" on his death, which took place March 27, 1752, ibid., xiv. 259.

[2] Journal de Paul Rabaut, Coquerel MSS. in the Library of the French Prot. Historical Society. Printed in its Bulletin, xxvii. 114 et seq.

louis d'or, and thrice asked them to pray to God for him. Two young girls ran after him, and, falling at his feet, begged him with tears to secure the release of their mothers, a request which, himself overcome by his emotions, he promised not to forget. "Were you not arrested for the matter of attending assemblies?" he asked the prisoners. "Yes, my lord," one of them replied, "and we do not believe that the king takes it amiss that people should gather to pray to God." "No, my child," the poor nobleman could not help replying.[1]

and visits the Tour de Constance.

On the nineteenth of September, 1752, the marquis was driving in his carriage not far from Nismes. It was seven o'clock in the evening when a group of five or six persons were descried in the distance apparently waiting for him. As soon as the marquis was near enough to see and hear them, one of their number dismounted, and, stepping forward, cried out that he had something to hand him. When Paulmy had bidden the driver stop, the man, short in stature and in the prime of life—he might be thirty-four or five years of age—approached the carriage-door and respectfully placed a sealed packet in the nobleman's own hands. The latter at once broke the seal, and without giving the stranger time to utter a word asked, "What is this?" "My lord," was the reply, "this is a memorial relating to another memorial drawn up in the month of June which you must have received. The persons whom this memorial concerns dare flatter themselves that they will experience the effects of that goodness and generosity which characterize your Excellency." Scarcely had he uttered these words, when, with an inclination of his head, the nobleman asked: "What is your name?" "My lord," answered the other, "I am Paul, to do you service." "Are you not Paul Rabaut?" was the curious rejoinder. "I am the same, my lord," replied the pastor, "to pay you my respects." "I have heard of you," the marquis said; then tried to read the memorial by the faint light of the moon, but, finding it impossible to do so, folded the paper and putting it in his pocket

The interview between the marquis and Paul Rabaut, September 19, 1752.

---

[1] Paul Rabaut to Antoine Court. Postscript of his letter of September 27, 1752. Lettres, ii. 228.

bowed low to the minister on whose head a price had for long years been set and thus courteously dismissed him. Paul Rabaut returned the salutation and bade him a prosperous journey. Then remounting his horse he returned home, praising God and praying Him to bless the pains which the Protestants had taken to secure the peace of their churches. Meantime the son of the secretary of state of Louis the Fifteenth rode on to the episcopal palace, where, in the hearing of more than one astonished grandee, he gave an account of his strange encounter with the famous preacher of the Desert. As the news spread far abroad in Languedoc and elsewhere, " the faithful were joyful, while their enemies gnashed their teeth and fancied that they already saw the temples of the Huguenots rebuilt."[1]

Paul Rabaut believed that the memorial which he handed, in this extraordinary interview, to the Marquis of Paulmy, and which was thus forced upon the notice of the king's advisers, drew attention to the piteous condition of the Huguenots and was a principal cause of the cessation of the greatest of the persecutions to which they were subjected in the eighteenth century. And certainly when cruelty had reached such extremes that the most intimate relations of life were interfered with, and bridegroom and bride were put asunder and imprisoned when their honeymoon was scarcely over, for the sole reason that they had been united in wedlock in the presence of a Protestant minister,[2] it was high time to call a halt. It may indeed be, I am sorry to say, that motives of pity influenced the government less than motives of expediency, and that the lack of soldiers to execute proscriptive laws[3] was even more potent a consideration than Paul Rabaut's elo-

End of "the great persecution."

---

[1] Paul Rabaut in his Journal (Bulletin, etc., xxvii. 122) briefly alludes to the incident as having occurred between Uchaud and Codognan, and states that the memorial was read at court, where it produced a very good effect. He gives a full and graphic account of it in a letter written to Antoine Court eight days later. Lettres à A. Court, ii. 226, 227.

[2] See the case of Louis Bousanquet, who died in prison. Bulletin, etc., xxx. 78 et seq.

[3] E. Hugues, Hist. de la Restauration du Prot. au xviiie siècle, ii. 231. This seems to be fully established by the letter of Saint Priest to the Count of Saint Florentin, November 13, 1752. Corbière, Hist. de l'Égl. réf. de Montpellier, pièces justif., 548–595.

quent and convincing appeal. None the less was the appeal, with its formidable and unanswerable array of facts, a mighty impeachment of the civilization of an age priding itself upon culture and refinement. And the unexpected discovery of the original of this now venerable document deserves to be regarded as one of the most interesting of very recent incidents in Huguenot historical research.[1]

The recognition of the existence and rights of Protestantism in France was yet distant. Thirty-five years were to intervene before that most rational solution of the perplexities in

Perplexity of the government. which the government confessedly found itself would be reached, and the clergy were still urgent for the enforcement of every severe law upon the statute-book

and for the enactment, if necessary, of new legislation. Yet there were not wanting signs of a coming change. Pressed by the priests, the government shrank from novel and untried expedients. Puechemille, a renegade student of the Lausanne seminary, who had now become a government spy, having proposed

A renegade's device for getting rid of ministers. as the most effectual means of compelling the pastors to leave France that their wives or parents should be placed under arrest as hostages for their departure,

the authorities positively declined to put the plan into execution. "The minister Court would be still in France," said the spy, "had not his wife been threatened with being sent to a convent. The minister Maroger, who is at present at Vevay, four leagues from Lausanne, would not have left France for foreign parts if his wife had not been shut up in the monastery of Lodève." [2] But the prudent intendant, knowing the reigning dearth and discontent, wrote to the secretary of state : " As to

---

[1] It is barely two months at the time I write these lines (April, 1895), since M. Weiss, in examining some old papers offered to him for purchase, came across the very petition which Rabaut handed to the Marquis of Paulmy on the 19th of September, 1752, a carefully written paper still neatly tied with its faded white and olive ribbons. M. Weiss promptly printed it in the Bulletin of the French Protestant Historical Society for March 15, 1895 (vol. xliv. 131–153).

[2] The curious " Mémoire " of Puechemille was published for the first time in the Bulletin de la Soc. de l'hist. du Prot. fr., vii. 39–43. The Count of Saint Florentin, in his despatch to the intendant Le Nain, May 28, 1750, expressed himself as quite disposed to adopt the suggestion. C. Coquerel, Hist. des Églises du Désert, ii. 29.

the imprisonment of the wives and parents of the pastors, it is impossible to take any risks in the present revolution." [1]

The very soldiers began to be restive when employed in hunting down Protestant ministers of the gospel. It is a Roman Catholic state paper, drawn up for the ex-press purpose of suggesting means of re-establishing order in matters of religion, that informs us of the "prejudice" the troops have against being made to disturb the adherents of the Protestant religion, and tells us that the regiment *de la Fé-ronnaye* in particular was extremely indignant with one of its captains, Chevalier de Pontual, for having arrested the minister Molines, acting, though the chevalier did, by order of Count de Moncau.[2] When it came to the matter of commanding the troops to fire upon a Huguenot meeting which might have been surprised, the author of the same important document, while not quite ready to give up this agreeable diversion, betrays the growing timidity in a suggestion that for the worshippers killed or sent to the galleys it was quite possible that some curates might have to pay the score with their lives.[3] The aggressors, whether soldiers or civil officers, were not unlikely to receive rough usage if they undertook to attempt to disperse a large Huguenot assembly of four thousand men, women, and children, gathered by night on a meadow skirted by woods in Saintonge; for a circle of two hundred mounted men was round about, who though apparently unarmed showed that they were there to protect their brethren. Occasionally, too, royal officers stum-bling upon a *prêche*, and ordering the worshippers in the king's name to disperse, were met with defiance or had guns pointed at them, with the significant remark: "Gentlemen, withdraw! It is not good for you to be here." [4]

Before long the Protestants of the west went further. To-ward the end of the year 1755, imagining that religious

The troops reluctant.

---

[1] Le Nain, apud D. Benoit, Les Frères Gibert (Toulouse, 1889), 22.

[2] Mémoire d'État pour rétablir l'ordre dans les matières de religion, 1753. MSS. Nat. Arch., printed in Bulletin, etc., x. 284–305.

[3] " Il ne seroit même point du tout surprenant qu'il y eût quelques curés as-sassinés." Ib., x. 289.

[4] Trois assemblées du Désert en Saintonge, 1749–1754. Bulletin, etc., xviii. 538–544.

liberty was about to be conceded to them, if indeed it was not already granted, the Protestants actually began the erection of a "temple" not far from Marennes, at the village of Arthouan.[1] The undertaking was, of course, premature, as a number of artisans learned at their cost, including Mesnard, the tailor of Marennes, who had brought the masons to the spot and set them at work, besides working at the building with his own hands. Mesnard, after a long imprisonment, was sentenced to banishment from the kingdom, and to the confiscation of half his goods by way of fine, the costs having been first deducted. The former part of the sentence was not carried into execution. Indeed, in vain did Mesnard demand his passport to enable him to go abroad. He could never get it. For eight years he insisted that either he must receive a safe conduct to go to another land with the half of his property that was left him, or he must be granted an official letter of rehabilitation, that he might remain undisturbed at home. No such letter was granted. He was compelled to content himself with an assurance from the superior magistrates of the province that, as his act had not been a crime, but only disobedience, he could remain in all safety. "There is no need," said they, "of the king's losing his subjects, and we regard you as a good citizen and a loyal subject."[2]

Huguenots bold in the west.

They undertake to build a temple.

---

[1] Arthouan, Artouan, or Arthuant, as it is indifferently called, is little better than a hamlet in the neighborhood of the village of Saint Just. On the great topographical map published by the French government it is represented as about six kilometres distant from Marennes, and half that distance from Saint Just.

[2] Les tristes peines, interrogations et confession de foy de Jean François Mesnard de Marennes. A la Rochelle, en 1756. Bulletin, etc., xix. 262 et seq. This is a very interesting account, given by Mesnard himself, and evidently circulated in manuscript among the faithful of the region for the purpose of encouraging and comforting them. Mesnard was a man of a strong character. Hear how indignantly he defends the validity of his marriage in the Desert against the insinuations of his examiner, Beaupreau, the lieutenant particulier in the presidial court of La Rochelle :

"D. Qui vous a épousé ? et en quel endroit avez-vous épousé ?

"R. C'est Monsieur Gibert, ministre, qui m'a épousé au Désert.

"D. Avez-vous votre certificat de mariage ?

"R. Monsieur, je ne l'ay point icy.

"D. Ah ! le bel adouage ! dit le rapporteur.

"R. Monsieur, je ne suis point adoué ; je suis fort bien épousé, en présence d'un nombre suffisant de bons témoins."

None the less did places of worship, from this time forward, begin to rise at many a point in the western provinces, and one

"Maisons d'oraison" arise.

who did not know better might have supposed that the day of persecution was quite passed. At first, if the case was flagrant and could not be overlooked, the magistrates made a great show of interference. But for the most part the plans were modest, and the "*maison d'oraison*," or "house of prayer," was neither so large nor so conspicuous, as needlessly to draw the attention of officers who did not care to see. Thus it was that between 1755 and 1763 there were built some twenty-eight edifices in the districts of Saintonge and Angoumois, while there were two in Perigord, and eleven in

Liberty in Foix.

the country of Foix.[1] Such in fact was the extent of the liberty allowed to the Protestants of the last-named district that they might well be pardoned for regarding the golden age as having returned. At Mas d'Azil their chapel (which they freely called a church) was erected in the very midst of the town, opposite to the cathedral, with only the market-place intervening. A man standing between the two places of worship could hear the psalms sung in French, on the one side, and in Latin on the other. Parents brought their children to the chapel at full noon for baptism.[2]

Yet so full of incongruities and inconsistencies was the practice—arising from the irreconcilable conflict between the unrepealed laws of the past and present monarchs respecting Protestantism and its adherents, and the growing spirit of equity in magistrates and people, that even while the *maisons d'oraison* were reared with little opposition on the part of any one in some provinces, the most barbarous sentences were rendered

Jean Fabre, "l'honnête criminel."

and the most savage executions were put into effect in other provinces. Men were still sent to row in the king's galleys for the simple crime of attending a conventicle. It was on the first of January, 1756, that occurred the incident of filial devotion that has made the name of Jean

---

[1] The detailed list was made out in connection with the minutes of the eighth national synod (1763). Les Synodes du Désert, ii. 324; Bulletin, etc., xxxiv. 124.

[2] Letter of the elders of Mas d'Azil to Paul Rabaut, November 10, 1763. Les Synodes du Désert, ii. 315.

Fabre famous for all time. That day a meeting of the Protestants in the immediate vicinity of Nismes was surprised by a detachment of soldiers. Among the persons captured was the aged father of Fabre. The younger man himself, alert and vigorous, experienced no difficulty in making good his escape. But learning the mishap that had befallen his father, the son returned full of grief and indignation, and offered himself as a substitute. The astonished sergeant at first declined to permit the exchange, but afterward gave his consent, doubtless regarding the king's service as gaining substantially by obtaining for a galley-slave a strong man of twenty-eight,[1] in place of an infirm old man of seventy-eight. Not so the father, who steadfastly refused until the son, throwing his arms around him, removed him by main force from the ranks of the prisoners and resolutely took his place. Friends led the former to his home, the soldiers conducted the latter to prison and trial. Sentenced to the galleys for life, Jean Fabre served out six years of his time before public sentiment compelled his tardy release. Not that the occurrence was unknown, but that a government which for meanness could scarcely find a parallel, sought to take advantage of his capture for its own ends. The Duke of Mirepoix, governor of Languedoc, offered to Fabre and to his Protestant fellow-convict, Jean Turges, a free release, on condition that their veteran pastor, Paul Rabaut, should leave France. The scheme failed utterly, as might have been anticipated. For even had the pastor been willing to forego his life of constant exposure to death, for the sake of releasing two fellow-believers of the many toiling at the oar, the man who had offered his liberty in exchange for that of his father could not have been induced to redeem it at the expense of the great interests of the church. He came out of the galleys to find himself celebrated. His magnanimity not only was in everybody's mouth, but furnished the subject of a dramatical piece, entitled " *L'honnête Criminel*," by Fenouillot de Falbaire, a work which was indeed of little merit, but which enjoyed, for

---

[1] Jean Fabre was born at Nismes, August 18, 1727. He died at Cette, May 31, 1797. His family was one of the most prominent of those engaged in trade, and professed the Protestant religion. Frossard, Tableau de Nismes et de ses environs, Supplément, 25, 26.

a time, a popularity quite disproportioned to its merits, and was honored by being played upon the stage at Versailles in the presence of Queen Marie Antoinette and at her express desire. The act of Jean Fabre was none the less meritorious because it had been paralleled, some time before, by that of a young man named Bareire, who, more unfortunate than Fabre, did not succeed in inducing his father's captors to consent to his substitution, and when he insisted beyond what they thought reasonable, was shot on the spot by an impatient soldier. Nor does it detract from the human interest of the incident to read in a letter that has come down to us, written by the galley-slave to his pastor, Paul Rabaut, expressions of repentance and mental anguish of an extraordinarily pungent character, called forth by the remembrance of the fact that, at the time of his arrest, he denied persistently that he had himself been in attendance upon the Protestant meeting.[1] His was a character of rare energy and simplicity, in which, as his recent biographer has pointed out, two forces predominate—the force of a love most devoted and unalterable for father, wife, and friend, and the force of a conscience whose inflexible severity proceeded from deep religious feeling.[2]

---

[1] Jean Fabre to Paul Rabaut, Toulon, May 25, 1757. Bulletin, etc., xiv. 90. Fabre wrote from the galleys.

[2] Athanase Coquerel fils, ubi supra, xiv. 86. Unable as I might be to endorse all the theological statements of the late M. Coquerel, a well-known representative of the liberal wing of the French Protestant Church of the nineteenth century, I cannot deny myself the pleasure of translating a passage of his address before the Société de l'histoire du Protestantisme français, as giving an interesting view of Fabre's attitude, and the attitude of many of whom he may serve as a type. "Those persons who expect to see Christian piety express itself at all periods in words very nearly similar, will be disappointed if they read the autobiography of the galley-slave condemned for his faith, his letter to Paul Rabaut, or the documents that concern him. . . We ourselves, quite inclined as we are to respect in every soul the free course and the spontaneity of faith, have regretted that we have not found a more pronounced evangelical character in the writings of Jean Fabre. Jesus Christ scarcely appears in them, and there seems established a strange alliance between the invincible faith of the Huguenots and the sentimental or moralizing language (*langage sentimental ou raisonneur*) of the eighteenth century. We have here a great lesson of toleration and equity. The same man whom we all revere as a Christian hero, and who suffered for the truth and his duty with marvellous fidelity, would certainly appear too little of a Christian to many persons, perhaps little capable of imitat-

Thus it will be seen that the growing disposition to overlook certain Protestant acts in certain parts of France did not prevent the government from continuing to send Huguenots remorselessly to the galleys, or from detaining them there for long years. This was certainly due, in part, to the influence of a capital enemy of the Protestants, the Count of Saint Florentin, secretary of state. Jean Fabre owed his liberation to the Duke of Choiseul; and not only was Saint Florentin unable to conceal his vexation when he heard of it, but he pursued the victim even after he had escaped his clutches, and effectually defeated a scheme which the benevolent had set on foot to raise a fund for the relief of his necessities.[1]

Nor did the altered state of things put an end to the perils incurred by the pastors of the Desert, who were still compelled to wander in disguise from place to place, under the ban of the law, and of whose personal appearance full descriptions were still circulated, for the purpose of facilitating the task of informers and traitors. In fact, the relentless pursuit of the ministers of the Reformed church did not come to an end until 1762, with the execution at Toulouse, on the nineteenth of February, of François Rochette, the last of the martyred pastors. The long list of noble confessors of the faith could not have closed with a worthier name than this.

Rochette was a young man, only twenty-six years of age. He had studied at Lausanne, and had been barely twenty months in the sacred office. When examined, he avowed with great frankness his profession, and the fact that he had preached, conducted public worship, and performed the ceremony of marriage. Great was the consternation in his great parish of Montauban at the news of his arrest, and great were the efforts put forth, without avail, for his release. Three young men, brothers, by the name

Execution of Rochette and the three "gentilshommes verriers," 1762.

---

ing him. Let us not ask Jean Fabre what his doctrinal views were. Like most of our co-religionists at the close of last century and the beginning of the present century, he would have found it very hard to answer such a question. None the less he knew, in all their simplicity and grandeur, those essential elements of the Christian life—faith, love, repentance, and humility."—The documents given by the Bulletin, vols. xiv. and xv., including Jean Fabre's autobiography, his letter to Paul Rabaut, etc., are of rare importance.

[1] See Fabre's autobiography, ubi supra.

of Grenier, known as "*les gentilshommes verriers*," from their honorable occupation,[1] were involved in his misfortunes. They had apparently conceived, but had not undertaken to execute, the plan of an armed rescue of their beloved pastor. Rochette was sentenced to be hung, the "*gentilshommes verriers*" to be beheaded, the two men who had served as the pastor's guides to be branded on the shoulder with the capital letters GAL (standing for *galérien*, or galley-slave) and sent to serve at the oar for a term of years.[2]   It was a part of Rochette's sentence that, clad in a simple shirt, with bare head and feet, kneeling, and holding in his hands a great yellow taper, and wearing both on his breast and on his back his accusation written in these words, MINISTER OF THE PRETENDED REFORMED CHURCH, he should "beg pardon of God, of the king, and of justice for his crimes and misdeeds."   This *amende honorable* was to take place in front of the great church of Saint Stephen.   We have seen that it was not the first time that, by an unintentional irony, the shrine of the great Christian protomartyr was chosen by the fanatical judges of the most fanatical city of France to witness outrages perpetrated in the name of religion.

It was on the Place du Salin that the scaffold was erected upon which the pastor and his friends were put to death. None of them, either before, or at the hour of the execution, displayed anything but the most firm faith in their Redeemer and the most joyful anticipations of blessedness with him. "My friend," said Rochette to one of the guards whom he saw overcome with grief for his prisoner's fate, "why do you, who are ready to die for the king, bewail me that I die for my God?" When forced against his will to descend from the tumbril in front of Saint Stephen's, he uttered these words aloud as he knelt, lest he should be thought to be abjuring his religion: "I beg pardon of God for all my sins, and I believe firmly that

---

[1] I have already noticed the circumstance that, according to French usage, the manufacture of glass was a business which was not regarded as derogating from the title of him that entered upon it to the rights of *noblesse*.   Hence the expression "*gentilhomme verrier*."

[2] Arrêt de la cour de parlement du 18 février 1762.   Printed from the registers of the Parliament of Toulouse, in C. Coquerel, Hist. des Égl. du Désert, ii. 284–286.

I am washed from them by the blood of Jesus Christ, who has redeemed us at a great price. I have no pardon to ask of the king. I have always honored him as the anointed of the Lord. I have always loved him as the father of his country. I have always been a good and faithful subject, and of this the judges seemed to me to be fully convinced. I have always preached to my flock patience, obedience, submission; and my sermons, which the authorities have in their hands, are, in brief, summed up in these words: 'Fear God, honor the king.' If I have violated his laws respecting religious meetings, it was because God commanded me to violate them. As to justice, I have not offended it, and I pray to God to forgive my judges." Such was Rochette's response to the order of the Parliament of Toulouse. It was also the answer of the pastors of the Desert to the calumnious accusation of impiety, disloyalty, and insubordination brought against them throughout an entire century. It was appropriate that the triumphant reply should be sealed in the blood of the last innocent victim offered up on the altar of intolerant hatred. And the last victim, like so many of his predecessors, died with words from the martyr's psalm upon his lips: "This is the day which the Lord hath made; we will rejoice and be glad in it!"

The three brothers, like their pastor, rejected every proffer of spiritual advice from the poor pestering monks who impertinently interrupted, if they could not prevent, their devotions. Like Rochette, they repudiated every suggestion of purchasing life by apostasy. Two of their number had been decapitated when the headsman paused in his work to say to the last of the "*gentilshommes verriers:*" "You have just seen your brothers perish. Change your religion, that you may not perish as they have perished." To which the youngest, with a quiet and proud air, only replied by the brief command, "Do your office." [1]

Toulouse, which in 1532 witnessed the death by slow fire of a lawyer of prominence, Jean de Caturce, one of the first Protestant martyrs of France,[2] had thus the unenviable distinction

---

[1] The affair of Rochette and the three "*gentilshommes verriers*" is exhaustively treated by C. Coquerel, Hist. des Égl. du Désert, ii. 269–291.

[2] The Rise of the Huguenots, i. 150.

of beholding, in the persons of Rochette and his companions, two
hundred and thirty years later, the last that suffered capitally
for their faith. If the government or the clergy expected to
strike consternation into the minds of the vast throng of spectators that had come to Toulouse even from a considerable distance, to the unprecedented sight of a pastor hung and three
gentlemen beheaded at once, they were disappointed. "The
Protestants are all of them proud of the greatness of soul of
these four persons," wrote an admiring spectator the next day.
" They liken them to the Maccabees." [1]

The faithful commemorated their end in verse. The " Complainte," or lament, over their death was the last and one of the
best, as it was probably the longest, of the series of popular
ballads composed and sung over the prominent ministers that
fell in the protracted struggle for the restoration of the Huguenot faith in France.[2]

The execution of Rochette and his companions took place at
the very time of the occurrence of the trial and judicial murder
of Jean Calas, which because of its important bearing upon the
establishment of toleration in France and the end of persecution, will occupy our attention in the following chapter.

Meanwhile we must notice the death, on the twelfth of June,
1760, of Antoine Court, the most prominent workman in rearing anew the fabric of Protestantism in France. The
last thirty years of his life, indeed, he had spent
abroad, mainly in Switzerland, and his activity had
taken a wide range. He had a passionate fondness for histori-

Death of Antoine Court, 1760.

---

[1] Copie de la lettre d'un étudiant en droit de Toulouse à son frère, abbé dans
le Velay. Bulletin, etc., xxiii. 279.

[2] The Complainte sur la mort du ministre Fr. Rochette et des trois frères de
Grenier (Bulletin, etc., xxiv. 31–44), composed to be sung to the "air des
commandements de Dieu," consists of not less than eighty-seven stanzas of four
lines each, and is throughout a song of triumph. The very hangman is apostrophized as the guide that leads to celestial victory. The pastor and each of
the brothers separately have their own portion in the joyful song, as have also
the church militant and the galley-slaves. The concluding stanza is a prayer:

" Seigneur, à de si beaux modèles
Attache nos yeux et nos cœurs,
Et fais qu' à toi toujeurs fidèles,
Nous mourions du monde vainqueurs."

There are other poems on the same subject in the Bulletin, etc., x. 422.

cal research, which he was able to indulge in a land of safety as
he could never have done amid the perils of his earlier labors.
He had accomplished much, especially, as we have seen, in connection with the defence of the cause of the much-abused Camisards. He had formed other literary plans, which illness and
death prevented him from carrying into effect. But these
studies never allured him from the work which had been and
which remained the chief object of his life—the general care of
the great interests of his persecuted brethren ; and it may be
His later   regarded as an incontrovertible truth that from his
services.   point of advantage outside of the dominions of Louis
the Fifteenth, he was enabled to accomplish far more than he
would have been likely to achieve for the churches of the Desert if he had remained in Languedoc, even had he been so
fortunate as to escape the hands of the enemy to the end of
his course.

Others, also, were entitled to the lasting gratitude of the
Protestants of France on kindred grounds. Benjamin du Plan,
Services of   a gentleman of Alais, discharged for many years the
Benjamin   onerous, and often thankless, duties of deputy-general
du Plan.   of the synods. Travelling through foreign lands, for
the most part at his own charges, he presented the claims of
the Huguenots upon the Christian liberality of such Protestant
rulers and peoples as could be induced to view the Huguenots
as sufferers for a common faith. It was Du Plan that spent
long years in endeavoring to interest in his plans the pious of
England, especially of London, and those of Holland, Germany,
Denmark, and Sweden. And it was Du Plan that was able by
his industry and persistent devotion to secure from sympathizing friends the large sums of money which, either as income or
as permanent funds, guaranteed the means for the support of
the professors and students of the theological school of the
churches of the Desert at Lausanne.[1] Noble and disinterested
men and women there were in almost every Protestant land

---

[1] I must refer the reader to the instructive volume of M. D. Bonnefon, pastor
of the Reformed church of Alais, entitled Benjamin du Plan, gentilhomme
d'Alais, Deputé général des Synodes des Églises réformées de France. 1688–
1763. (Paris, 1876.) It contains many details respecting matters into which,
in the nature of the case, I am unable to enter.

who, either individually or as members of committees, co-operated efficiently in the furtherance of the good work.

To Antoine Court succeeded his not less remarkable son, Court de Gébelin. With him unwavering affection for the

Court de Gébelin as general agent of the churches.

Protestant churches was associated with a breadth of historical and scientific acquirements which made him the marvel of his country and age. The greatness of these, however, must not lead us to underestimate his invaluable services to the Huguenot cause. The annoyances to which he submitted, with a good amount of patience and equanimity, for a score of years and more, during which he served the Protestants as their general agent, much of the time in Paris, would occupy more space than can be accorded to the recital. Scantily supported, irregularly paid, if paid at all, and having to contend with all manner of difficulties from the whims and vagaries of churches and of particular members of his own communion,[1] it was his misfortune, when he died, on the tenth of May, 1784, that his life was not spared long enough to permit him to see the promulgation of that tolerant law to advance which he labored so many years, and to whose ultimate enactment he, in fact, contributed greatly. It came three years later, in November, 1787. He was compelled to confront other difficulties, as well as dangers, coming from without. These he met with imperturbable courage and equanimity. A Protestant, and indeed known to be a Protestant minister, it was not without personal peril that he undertook to discharge the office of advocate at court for a proscribed people. Yet no sooner had he heard of a case of crying injustice, the carrying off of a Protestant child, the imprisonment of innocent men and women, or the imposition of crushing fines for the holding of a religious meeting or the celebration of a marriage in the Desert, than he set himself to the task of drawing up remonstrances and petitions. These he did not hesitate to present in person to ministers of state and others. At times his memorials were regarded as offensive, his requests treated as importunate. One day, we are told,

---

[1] See Eugène Arnaud's two articles: Court de Gébelin, ses tribulations comme agent général des Églises Réformées d'après la correspondance inédite des deux Chiron, in Bulletin, etc., xxxii., 269 et seq., 311 et seq.

he bearded the all-powerful minister of state, sworn enemy of
the Protestants, the Duke de la Vrillière, better known as
His intrepid- Count of Saint Florentin, to whom, in the distribution
ity.   of public affairs, matters relating to "those of the
pretended Reformed religion" were specially referred. Provoked beyond measure at Court de Gébelin's interference, the
"terrible" duke thundered out, "Do you know, Sir, that I am
going to have you hung?" "I know, my lord," Court replied,
unmoved by surprise or fear, "I know that you can do it; but
I also know that you are too just to do it, and I hope that you
will deign to hear me with kindness and to give some attention
to the memorial which I have the honor to present to you."
Astonished at his composure, Saint Florentin was mollified,
listened, and received the memorial. Indeed, he conceived from
that moment a certain esteem for him, and at a later time permitted Court de Gébelin to dedicate to him the first volume of
his great work.[1]

That work was a ponderous treatise, of which nine large
quarto volumes appeared under the title of "*Le Monde primitif.*"[2]
His "*Monde* A production of the highest rank, for the time at
Primitif." which it appeared, and wonderful by reason of the
erudition which it exhibited on the part of its author, this work
was full of suggestions of which succeeding writers have not
been slow to avail themselves.[3] Scholars greeted it with enthusiastic praise. The king subscribed for a hundred copies. His
example was followed by the ministers of state, by the intendants and by almost all the men of great influence. The Archbishop of Paris, M. de Beaumont, so far from scenting heresy in
the work of a Huguenot, the son of the pastor of the Desert,
Antoine Court, delighted the author's heart by subscribing for a
copy. The master of the seals, unsolicited, appointed Court de

---

[1] The incident is told, on the authority of a manuscript note of Charles de
Végobre, by my lamented friend, Mr. Charles Dardier, in the address on Court
de Gébelin, his life and writings, which he delivered in June, 1890, as president for the year of the Académie de Nîmes (page 9).

[2] Translated : "The Primitive World, analyzed and compared with the Modern
World, considered in the Natural History of Speech ; or, A Universal and Comparative Grammar."

[3] Ibid., 12.

Gébelin royal censor, and the French Academy accorded him a more appropriate, and, doubtless, more highly appreciated reward by voting to him, for two successive years, one of its highest honors, which D'Alembert, the permanent secretary, announced to him in the most flattering terms.[1] That he was able to accomplish successfully so great a task in the midst of daily occupations of a pressing character, was owing not more to an amazing capacity for sustained intellectual labor, than to rare powers of attention and great physical endurance. He composed and set down his thoughts with strange ease and rapidity. His singular The use of the pen entailed little or no fatigue. He quickness. wrote, says his friend Rabaut Saint Étienne, almost as fast as he could speak, and thought nothing of transcribing rare books which he could not purchase, or even entire dictionaries. Every moment of his time was filled. His correspondents were not surprised to receive letters which he had written while riding on horseback. In the matter of reading, an equal or a superior facility characterized him; he read a whole page at a single glance, and for the perusal of a book he required only the time necessary for turning the leaves.[2]

---

[1] Dardier, ubi supra, 13.

[2] Rabaut Saint Étienne's Lettre sur la vie et les écrits de M. Court de Gébelin, adressée au Musée de Paris. Œuvres (Paris, 1826), ii., 380, 381.

CHAPTER XIX

THE END OF PERSECUTION AND THE EDICT OF TOLERATION

NEARLY two-thirds of the eighteenth century had elapsed before the attention of the public mind in France was brought to a serious consideration of the advisability of suspending the sanguinary laws enacted against the Protestants. And it is a singular circumstance that the voice that first secured a hearing was neither the pitiful cry of one of the victims of intolerance, nor the charitable intercession of a minister of the established church, but the protest of a free-thinker whose caustic wit had been continuously directed for many years against all that was most sacred, a writer who, so far from holding that true and lofty conception of toleration which regards it as admirable only so far as it is founded upon, or coexists with, strong convictions,[1] laid it down as a principle that the fanaticism which has so desolated the world can be assuaged only by toleration, and that toleration can be brought about only by indifference.[2] While the persecuted pastors of the Desert failed to make their just claims audible at Paris and Versailles, and the hier-

Voltaire on intolerance.

archy of the Roman Catholic church showed no sign of relenting in its advocacy of severity, the appeal of Voltaire, the foremost writer of his age, commanded the ear of his contemporaries. If another quarter of a century was still to pass before the most obvious rights of the descendants of the old Huguenots were finally accorded, this was because the power of the clergy was so firmly entrenched that only a long and persistent effort could carry its works.

---

[1] " La tolérance n'est belle que dans ceux dont la croyance est forte." Cimber et Danjou, Archives curieuses, xiv. 7.

[2] " Le fanatisme, qui a tant désolé le monde, ne peut être adouci que par la tolérance, et la tolérance ne peut être amenée que par l'indifférence." Voltaire to the Count d'Argental, November 5, 1764. Œuvres complètes (Paris 1821), ix. 36.

Voltaire published his famous "Treatise on Toleration" in 1763. The occasion was the judicial murder of Jean Calas, at Toulouse, on the tenth of March of the preceding year.[1]

Jean Calas, a Protestant merchant, sixty-four years of age, had spent more than forty of those years in honorable trade, in the principal city of Languedoc, enjoying the reputa-

Jean Calas and his family. tion of an honest man and a good father. So far from being a bigoted Calvinist, he had made no strenuous opposition when his son Louis chose to become a Roman Catholic, and his only servant, who had lived in the family for thirty years, was a somewhat zealous adherent of the Roman Catholic church. Calas's wife and children were, with the exception just mentioned, professed Protestants.

One evening—it was the thirteenth of October, 1761—the eldest of the sons, Marc Antoine by name, was found to have hung himself upon an inner door of the store over which his parents lived, in the Rue des Filatiers. At the outcries made by the family when the lifeless corpse was discovered, the neighbors flocked to the house. A crowd was soon collected. Toulouse still retained the reputation it possessed two hundred years before, of being the most superstitious and the most fanatical of the cities of France, the most inimical to the Protestant faith. Within a few months there was to be celebrated the bicentenary of the frightful massacre of 1562, in which three thousand, some said four thousand, Huguenots were butchered in cold blood.[2] By inflammatory sermons in the churches and in other ways, priests and monks had already prepared the populace for the approaching commemoration. The minds of men were at the fever-heat of zeal and expectancy. It was not strange, therefore, that when some person in the throng gathered about

---

[1] Traité sur la Tolérance à l'occasion de la mort de Jean Calas. Œuvres complètes de Voltaire, xxix. 41–331.

[2] For an account of this event see the History of the Rise of the Huguenots of France, ii. 52, 53. I must refer the reader to that work for the enthusiastic description which Monseigneur Desprez, Archbishop of Toulouse, gave in 1862 of the centennial procession of 1762. It is encouraging to note that the government of Louis Napoleon refused to permit in the nineteenth century a disgraceful commemoration which the government of Louis XV. allowed in the eighteenth century.

the door of the Calas house, raised the cry that Jean had murdered his son in order to prevent him from becoming a Catholic,

Accused of
murdering
his son to
prevent his
conversion. the words were caught up with eagerness and repeated
by one and another.   Blind hatred of the Huguenots
magnified the story and soon filled in the details.
They were these : Marc Antoine was to have abjured
on the morrow.   His family and Lavaysse, a young friend
that had supped with them, had strangled him in hatred of the
Roman Catholic religion.   Protestants are such monsters, it was
said, that they make it a point to put their children out of the
way rather than let them be converted.   The Protestants of
Languedoc had met the day before, and had by a majority vote
decreed that Lavaysse should act as the executioner, or as an
assistant to Jean Calas, his wife, and his son Pierre in making
away with Marc Antoine.   One of the *capitouls* of Toulouse,
greedily accepting the truth of the accusation, ordered the arrest
of the unfortunate family, now prostrated by their sudden affliction.   As for the body of Marc Antoine, instead of being dragged
upon a hurdle as a suicide, it was ultimately carried by the
Confraternity of the White Penitents to the church of Saint
Étienne and buried in great pomp.   A magnificent *catafalque*
was reared, surmounted by a ghastly figure, in the shape of a
skeleton, representing the deceased, and bearing in the right
hand the martyr's palm, and in the left a scroll on which could
be read the words, " Abjuration of Heresy."   Nothing remained
for the poor suicide but canonization, and scarcely this.   For at
once he received the honors accorded to a saint.   His intercession was invoked.   Prayers were said at his tomb.   Relics of
his body were in demand.   Miracles were said to be wrought
by him.[1]

---

[1] Voltaire, Traité de la Tolérance, ubi supra, xxix. 55, 56.   Ath. Coquerel,
Jean Calas et sa famille (chap. v., Intervention ecclésiastique) 105, etc.—The
singularity of the worship before the tomb of a Protestant and a suicide (there
cannot be the slightest doubt that Marc Antoine Calas was both) is augmented
by the direct testimony of Chalier, an advocate of parliament.   He stated that
more than once the young man had told him that he thought seriously of going
to Geneva in order to prepare himself for the Protestant ministry ; a purpose
from which Chalier said he had as often dissuaded him by the remark that that
was a poor trade that led to a man's being hung for his pains—" que tout métier
qui faisoit pendre son homme ne valoit rien."   Coquerel, 53, **166.**

The fortunes of the living, however, interest us more than the fate of a corpse. On evidence almost too absurd and contradic-

He is tried by the Parliament of Toulouse and found guilty. tory for belief, the Parliament of Toulouse, to which the case was brought by appeal from the capitouls, found Jean Calas guilty of the murder of his son and rendered a sentence of extreme severity against him.
Torture was first to be applied—both the *question ordinaire* and the *question extraordinaire*—in order to extract a confession of his misdeeds. Next, he was to be carried in a tumbril to the door of the cathedral, and there, clad in a shirt and holding a great waxen taper, he was to perform the *amende honorable*, begging pardon of God, of the king, and of the judges. After this, upon a scaffold erected on the Place Saint Georges, the public hangman was successively to break "his arms, legs, thighs, and reins." Finally, he was to be placed upon a wheel, with face turned upward toward the sky, "there to live in pain and repentance for his aforesaid crimes and misdeeds, to serve as an example, and to inspire terror in the wicked, so long as it shall please God to vouchsafe him life."[1]

By the *retentum*, a secret clause in the sentence, Calas's sufferings upon the wheel were to be limited to precisely two

He bears his horrible sentence with Christian fortitude, March 10, 1762. hours. In every other respect the horrible judgment was executed to the letter. The victim endured it with unflinching fortitude and Christian composure. But a single cry escaped him, as limb after limb was broken by the iron bar held by the executioner. A momentary weakness would have involved other innocent lives; he yielded to no weakness, but persisted in the assertion of his own innocence and the innocence of his household. During the two hours that he languished on the wheel and awaited the tardy coming of death, no murmur, no expression of anger, no word of repining passed his lips. He prayed for his judges, that his death should not be laid to their charge, and added with touching simplicity: "No doubt they were deceived by false witnesses." An estimable Roman Catholic priest, Father Bourges, stood at his side, and, a few moments before death came, said to him affectionately: "My dear brother, you have but an instant

---

[1] Ath. Coquerel fils, Jean Calas et sa famille, 191.

to live. By that God whom you invoke, in whom you hope, and who died for you, I conjure you to give glory to the truth!" To whom he replied: "I have spoken the truth. I die innocent. But why should I complain? Jesus Christ, who was innocence itself, was pleased to die for me by a much more cruel anguish. I have no regret for a life whose end will, I hope, lead me to eternal blessedness." And he added with rare and touching thoughtfulness: "I pity my wife and my son; but that stranger, that son of Mr. Lavaysse, to whom I thought I was showing courtesy when I invited him to sup with me, ah! it is he that increases my regret still more." Such was the end of one who, however obscure his life would have remained but for its tragic close, was one of God's true noblemen.[1]

Were the judges of the criminal chamber of the Parliament of Toulouse in doubt respecting the guilt of the Calas family, or were they merely inconsistent with themselves? We know not. Certain it is that they condemned no one save the father to death. His unshaken firmness saved the rest. Pierre, indeed, was sentenced to perpetual banishment from the kingdom, on pain of death if he returned. The widow and young Lavaysse were also banished. A lettre de cachet was obtained from court to consign Jean Calas's two young daughters to a convent.

Inconsistencies of the judges.

It was a few weeks after the death of Jean Calas that the attention of Voltaire was drawn to the travesty of justice enacted at Toulouse. The horror and indignation inspired by the first recital were deepened by the interviews which he sought with the youngest of Calas's sons, who, from Nismes, where he had been living, had recently fled for safety to Geneva. Henceforth for three years Voltaire devoted himself, with a singleness of purpose rarely equalled, to the self-imposed task of securing the vindication of the victims

Voltaire's strenuous exertions for the Calas family.

---

[1] We have no portrait of Jean Calas. Ath. Coquerel has prefixed to the first chapter of the work in which he has gathered all available information respecting the family, a faithful representation of the house they inhabited (p. 19), and places at the close of the chapter devoted to Calas's execution (p. 211), a fac-simile of his firm and manly signature. I have based my account of the execution on the long and detailed official minute given, pages 192–199, and M. Coquerel's account, page 200 and following.

of the fanaticism of the *capitouls* and the Parliament of Toulouse. If anything could make one forget the outrages on the
cause of morality and religion committed by the philosopher of
Ferney, in his indecent stories and plays, and his sneers and
mockery directed against all things divine, it would be the ardor
of his new and benevolent undertaking.

To accomplish his object involved nothing less than a direct
attack upon the credit of one of the most influential and august
Difficulty of parliaments of France—the sovereign court of Tou-
his task. louse—and that parliament would not fail to resist to
the utmost of its power. It was necessary to form and stimulate public opinion, and to secure allies in Paris. Madame Calas must be brought from her obscure retreat to the capital, and
means must be found of gaining access for her to all the well-
disposed persons about the king, that she might tell the simple
but effective story of her wrongs. Able advocates, such as Élie
de Beaumont, must be secured, to plead her cause and the cause
of the memory of her husband, before the king's council which
alone could undertake to review the actions of a parliament.
Had France but possessed a monarch worthy of the name, the
task would have been easier ; but, in his intense selfishness,
Louis the Fifteenth was beyond the reach of appeals to justice
or compassion. Voltaire knew it well ; and he warned his correspondents against wasting their time and efforts in a fruitless
attempt. " Be persuaded," he said, " that his Majesty is the
man who exerts the least influence upon this affair in the kingdom ; he does not and he will not meddle with it." [1] " If a
hundred heads of families were to be broken on the wheel in
Languedoc," he wrote significantly elsewhere, " Versailles would
give itself little concern about the thing." [2] Still, though against
great opposition, the good work steadily, if slowly, advanced.
Voltaire was not discouraged. He did not indeed apparently
know, as we know, that one of the most powerful of the king's
ministers of state, the Count of Saint Florentin, was in full

[1] " Soyez persuadé que Sa Majesté est l'homme du royaume qui influe le
moins sur cette affaire ; il ne s'en mêle ni ne s'en mélera." Voltaire to Debrus,
in Coquerel, 241.

[2] " Quand on rouerait cent pères de famille dans le Languedoc, Versailles n'y
prendrait que très-peu de part." Ibid., ubi supra.

sympathy with the Toulouse judges and was chagrined when they were worsted.[1]   After all, it required a year to bring the king's council to demand of the Parliament of Toulouse the submission of all the papers in the case, including the grounds on which the sentence against Calas was based.   A second year was consumed in reaching a decision of the council annulling the parliament's sentence and referring the matter to a commission of *maîtres des requêtes* for ultimate decision.   The new judges were not less than forty in number, fourteen of them being intendants of provinces; but, when they finally rendered their verdict, they were unanimous. They cleared the living, and they rehabilitated the memory of the deceased.   They ordered that the names of Jean Calas and those associated with him in the case be stricken from the records of parliament, and that the new judgment be inscribed on the margin.   They gave the late accused full permission to sue for damages, and ordered the release of any that might be imprisoned.   The judges, by a singular conceit, chose as the day for rendering their decision the third anniversary of the condemnation of Jean Calas—the ninth of March, 1765.[2] Nor did they stop with declaring the innocence of the guiltless family.   Collectively they addressed a letter to the keeper of the seals, calling attention to the penury to which the Calas family had been reduced by the iniquitous treatment of which they had been the recipients, and received in reply the announcement of a gift of thirty thousand francs graciously granted to them by his Majesty.[3]

Voltaire assures us that he shed tears of joy at the news of the success of the efforts which he had set on foot.   We may well believe it.   Nor was his satisfaction diminished when he

Marginal note: The case re-tried and Calas's memory vindicated (1765).

---

[1] Powerful and arbitrary as he was, Saint Florentin feared the caustic pen of Voltaire; and Voltaire, shrewd as he was, was so deceived respecting the minister's sentiments as to write of him as "very well disposed." Ath. Coquerel has collected and published a number of secret despatches from Saint Florentin which prove the contrary. Ubi supra, 228, and pièces justificatives, Nos. xviii., xxiii., etc.

[2] Ath. Coquerel fils, Jean Calas et sa famille, 251.   The text of this interesting document may be read in the pièces justificatives, ibid., 366, 367.

[3] The correspondence is given by Coquerel, ibid., 254-256.

learned that the poor Huguenots throughout France had received great advantage from the decision, and that since its publication none of their number had been sent to the galleys for praying to Almighty God under the open sky.[1] It was a favorite thought with him that the good effects might extend to all the proscribed Protestants of France—a thought which the cynicism that had become a second nature with him would not allow him to express without a sneer rather affected than real. "I will say more," he wrote to a Protestant correspondent: "this affair is very likely to cause you Huguenots to obtain a toleration such as you have not enjoyed since the Revocation of the Edict of Nantes. I know very well that you will be sent to perdition in another world; but that is no reason for your being persecuted in this world."[2]

Incidentally the accusations raised against Jean Calas had been the occasion of calling forth a vehement defence of Protestantism from the pen of Paul Rabaut. Calm, placid in temperament, patient under the foul abuse to which, with his fellow-Huguenots, he had long been subjected, never does the devoted pastor of the Desert seem to have been so moved as at the present juncture. One step in the search which the prosecution had instituted to obtain damning evidence against Jean Calas, was the publication from all the pulpits of Toulouse, on three successive Sundays, of a "Monitory," as it was styled. Copies of the same document were also posted on the walls of houses along the public streets. Over the signature of the Abbé de Cambon, vicar-general of the archbishop, information was demanded of every one who, from hearsay or otherwise, was cognizant of certain words or deeds. This was a first step toward fulminating excommunication against all that withheld the knowledge desired. Specific facts were presupposed, all of them adverse to the Calas family, and evidence was sought to establish these facts, under the authority of the church. One article of the Monitory had a much wider range than the rest, since it assumed that a meeting, presumably of Protestants, had been held, in advance of the murder of Marc Antoine Calas, in a

The "Monitory" and its calumnious insinuations.

<hr>

[1] Ubi supra, 261.   [2] Letter to Debrus, ibid.

certain house of a parish designated by name, and that then
and there the murder was resolved upon. Those that witnessed the members of this council coming or going were
required to disclose the names.[1] The whole impression given
by the Monitory, the impression which its authors intended to
give, was that the Protestants of France were a body of Thugs
or Assassins, that were but carrying out the principles of their
pretended religion when they put out of the way any of their
adherents that might undertake to desert the ranks. The implication was too injurious to be passed over in silence, too
horrible to be treated with the contempt which it deserved. If
indignation was ever justifiable, it was justifiable under such
Paul Rabaut accusations; and indignation breathed in every line
refutes them. of Paul Rabaut's pamphlet. He entitled it "Calumny
Refuted; or, a Memoir in which is refuted a new Accusation
directed against the Protestants of the Province of Languedoc,
on the occasion of the matter of the Sieur Calas, detained in
the prisons of Toulouse." It bore the significant motto: " If
they have called the master of the house Beelzebub, how much
more shall they call them of his household ? " And though the
piece was anonymous, the author accompanied the copy which
he sent to the king's attorney in the Parliament of Toulouse,
with a manuscript note which he signed " Paul Rabaut, Minister of the Holy Gospel," and dated from Nismes, the fifth of
January, 1762.

The parliament replied to an unanswerable argument by
burning the pamphlet, with all due solemnities, in the court of
the prison wherein Jean Calas was confined. The
The Parlia- judges were even more incensed that the writer arro-
ment of
Toulouse gated to himself the office of Minister of the Word of
burns his
treatise. God, and thus set at defiance the royal ordinances
which, even before the Revocation of the Edict of Nantes and
the attempted annihilation of Protestantism, refused to allow
Protestant pastors to assume the title, than they were annoyed
at the contents of the paper. Yet the paper itself was certainly
firm and manly enough to exasperate such judges. Indeed, not

---

[1] The text of the Monitoire is given by Ath. Coquerel fils, Jean Calas et
sa famille, 94, 95. First granted October 17, on demand of the king's attorney,
it was renewed, December 11, and excommunication followed in due order.

a few weak-kneed Protestants thought it too strong. I cannot agree with them. The veteran apologist of the Protestant church of the Desert could not suppress his righteous resentment without a sacrifice of self-respect. His condemnation of the iniquity and the malevolence of Jean Calas's judges will stand as the verdict of history, from whose deliberate judgments there can be no appeal. For, in his own words : " That such atrocious statements should be disseminated in the midst of an ignorant people, and respecting a body of men but little known, might not furnish ground for astonishment. But, in an age so enlightened as ours, to load with accusations of the kind a church whose belief is that of one-half of Europe, for the magistrates to give occasion to them by a Monitory which tends to make us odious ; for the higher powers not to repress so cruel an outrage against citizens whom the law does not distinguish from the rest of the subjects—this amounts almost to giving us over to the fury of a credulous populace. We do not dissemble it : to ascribe such horrors to us is to attack us at the most sensitive point. Let our property be confiscated, send us to the galleys, let our ministers be placed on the gibbet, overwhelm us with insults and cruel punishments ; but, at least, let the maxims of a morality that has no other author than Jesus Christ be treated with respect. Punish us as bad logicians, or as transgressors of those penal laws which we cannot observe without violating more august laws ; but do not accuse us of being unnatural fathers, and of being such in virtue of the principles of a religion that is altogether holy ! " [1]

It may be doubted whether the treatise of the proscribed pastor of the Desert contributed much to advance the cause of religious toleration in France. Of greater influence was the formal plea of Voltaire, put forth a year later, to which I have already referred. Not the least interesting and effective part of this was a chapter wherein Vol-

Voltaire on the words, " Compel them to come in."

---

[1] Charles Dardier has inserted La Calomnie Confondue, in his second collection of Rabaut's Letters (Paul Rabaut : ses lettres à divers—1744–1794), i. 295–312. Rabaut's letter to the king's attorney, of January 5, 1762, ibid., i. 297 note. See, also, Ath. Coquerel fils, Jean Calas et sa famille, ch. viii., Paul Rabaut et les Protestants de France, pp. 170–188 ; and Charles Coquerel, Histoire des Églises du Désert, ii. 317–323.

taire, having turned biblical exegete, refuted with characteristic skill the interpretation, fashionable for the past century among Roman Catholic controversialists, which made of the urgency of the master of the house, in the Parable of the Great Supper, a justification for so-called " salutary constraint." " Clearly," said Voltaire, " a single servant cannot compel by force all whom he meets to come and sup with his lord ; and guests thus constrained would not make the meal a very agreeable one." "'Compel them to come in,' means, according to the most accredited commentators, nothing save ' pray,'' conjure,' ' urge,' ' prevail upon.' What connection, I should like to know, have this prayer and this supper with persecution ? " [1] He illustrated the meaning of the gospel by a reference to our Lord's command to " hate " father and mother. " Is there any one in the world," he indignantly asked, " so unnatural as to conclude that he must hate his parents, and do we not easily understand that these words mean, ' Do not hesitate between me and your dearest affections ? ' " And he concluded the discussion, conducted in no irreverent spirit, with the exhortation, " If you would resemble Jesus Christ, be martyrs and not hangmen." [2]

Three-quarters of a century before, Pierre Bayle had argued the same matter, at greater length and no less cogently, in a paper devoted exclusively to the theme ; [3] but the trenchant phrases of the learned author of the " *Dictionnaire Philosophique*," in the seventeenth century, produced little impression as compared with the less profound but more sprightly sentences of the most influential writer of the eighteenth.

The case of Jean Calas was not the only one of the kind in which Voltaire employed his pen and his personal efforts in behalf of persecuted Protestants. Shortly after, Paul Sirven, of The case of Castres, with his family, was nearly involved in as Paul Sirven. calamitous a fate, being falsely accused of having drowned his daughter in a well near Mazamet. More fortunate than Calas, he made good his escape, with those most dear to

---

[1] Traité sur la Tolérance. Œuvres complètes de Voltaire, xxix. 155.
[2] Ibid., xxix. 161.
[3] Commentaire philosophique sur ces paroles de Jesus-Christ, Contrains-les d'entrer. Œuvres de Pierre Bayle (La Haye, 1737), ii. 355-540.

him, through the snows of winter to the hospitable city of Geneva. There he met with friends and with an advocate who found no words too strong to denounce the persecuting spirit that still prevailed in the south of France. " It would appear," wrote Voltaire, " that there is in Languedoc a hellish Fury, introduced long ago by the inquisitors in the train of Simon de Montfort, and that, since then, she brandishes her torch from time to time." [1] Some years later (1772), it was to the iniquitous treatment of Protestants under the laws themselves that Voltaire directed public attention. He commented at length upon the flagrant injustice done to a Miss Camp,

The case of Miss Camp, 1772. daughter of a Protestant merchant of Montauban, who had been married " in the Desert " to an officer in the king's own regiment, one Viscount de Bombelles. The husband, subsequently tiring of his wife, took advantage of the circumstance that the law did not recognize the Protestant rites, to contract a new union with another woman. The first wife prosecuted him before the courts, but, in August, 1772, the judges not only decided against her claims, but, while allowing her damages, ordered that the child she had borne should be reared in the Roman Catholic religion. The incident afforded Voltaire a good opportunity for enforcing the need of putting an end to a system that rendered possible such violations of natural justice as this—a system of laws that, having robbed France of seven or eight hundred thousand useful citizens, still kept one hundred thousand families in constant uncertainty respecting themselves and their children.[2]

Far different from the conduct of Voltaire was that of his younger contemporary, Jean Jacques Rousseau. To him also

Paul Rabaut appeals to Jean Jacques Rousseau. an appeal was addressed, and that, too, earlier and more directly than to Voltaire. It was in 1761, and the occasion was the arrest and trial of François Rochette, for having preached " in the Desert," and of the three brothers, the " *gentilshommes verriers*," for having attempted the forci-

---

[1] Lettre de Voltaire à M. Damilaville, sur les Calas et les Sirvens, 1 mars, 1765. Œuvres complètes de Voltaire, xxix. 279–287. Avis au public sur les parricides imputés aux Calas et aux Sirvens. Ibid., xxix. 288–317.

[2] Reflexions philosophiques sur le procès de Mademoiselle Camp, 1772. Ibid., xxix. 572–579.

ble rescue of Rochette. This was a few weeks before the Calas incident. Rousseau was at the height of his fame. For more than ten years he had confessedly been regarded as one of the greatest writers of the age; while his attacks upon despotism, in his " Discourse on the Origin of Inequality among Men," seemed to pledge him in advance to the defence of the downtrodden. Moreover, he was by birth a Genevese and of a Protestant family. Upon the receipt of news of the peril in which Rochette and the three brothers stood, Paul Rabaut wrote to Rousseau an urgent letter. His appeal touched no responsive chord in the philosopher's breast. Ordinary courtesy required a reply, and ordinary humanity demanded an expression of sympathy: that expression was manifestly a pretence and nothing more. Rousseau did, indeed, profess to have seen with pain, mingled with indignation, the frightful treatment to which " our unfortunate brethren " were subjected in Languedoc ; but he was careful to avoid promising to lift a finger to render the lot of those brethren more tolerable. He seemed not to be quite sure that the minister Rochette and his three fellow-sufferers had not put them-

Rousseau makes paltry excuses. selves so far in the wrong as at least to furnish a pretext to their enemies. It is hard to be continually at the mercy of a cruel people and to be denied even the consolation of hearing the word of God. Yet that very word of God expressly enjoins the duty of obeying the laws of the king, and the prohibition of public gatherings is certainly within the king's rights. After all, these gatherings are not of the essence of Christianity ; so that a man may give them up without renouncing his faith. The attempt to snatch a man from the hands of justice, even if he be unjustly arrested, is an act of unjustifiable rebellion. There are vexations so severe as to try even the patience of the righteous ; but he that will be a Christian must learn to suffer. Rousseau feigned that he had but a very limited acquaintance with Malesherbes, in order to avoid complying with Rabaut's request that he should write to him. He had no influence with the ministry, who, he said, did not deign to answer his letters in case of a request, not for favors— he never asked favors—but for the clearest justice. " Every man has his calling in the world. Mine," says Rousseau, " is to tell the public truths that are hard, but useful. I have preached humanity, gentleness, toleration, so far as depended on me. It is not my fault if men have not listened to me. However, I have adopted as the rule of my conduct always to confine myself to general truths. I have composed neither libels nor satires. I attack not *a man* but *men*, not an act but a vice. I cannot go beyond that." The philosopher ended his letter by recommending Rabaut to apply elsewhere. A certain person whom he named could help mightily, should he undertake the cause of "our brethren." And he plaintively added: "My dear sir, the will is lacking with him, with me it is the ability; and meanwhile the righteous suffers. I see by your letter that, like me, you have learned to suffer in the school of poverty. Alas! poverty makes us sympathize in the misfortunes of others, but puts it out of our power to relieve them. Goodby, sir, I salute you with all my heart." [1]

A man so timid and cowardly as Rousseau here portrays himself deserved to be left to his own selfish devices. However, another appeal was made to his kind offices, three years later; but, as might be expected, with no better results. At fifty-two years of age Rousseau was as full of excuses for not doing what it was disagreeable to him to do, as he had been at forty-nine. He even showed a certain peevish impatience at being expected to do anything beyond what he pretended to have done already. "I like saying useful things," he replied to one correspondent, "but I do not like to repeat them; and those who must absolutely have restatements need only to provide themselves with several copies of the same written work. The Protestants of France are now enjoying a rest to which I may have contributed, not by vain declamations, as so many others have done, but by good political reasons well set forth; yet here they come and press me to write in their favor. This is making too much account of what I can do, or too little of what I have done. They admit that they are tranquil, but they want to be better off than well; and after I have served them with all my strength, they re-

He declines to write in favor of the Protestants.

[1] Jean Jacques Rousseau to Paul Rabaut, Montmorency, October 24, 1761. Bulletin de la Soc. de l'hist. du Prot. fr., ii. 363-365.

proach me for not serving them beyond my strength." [1] It
suited Jean Jacques Rousseau much better to pose as an aged
knight who had worn himself out in the tournament and was
quite willing to leave the lists open for other contestants to
enter, than to renew a fatiguing and possibly dangerous exhibition of his prowess. [2]

Of Rousseau Voltaire once significantly remarked : "Jean
Jacques writes only for the purpose of writing, and I write for
the purpose of acting." [3] Five years before he had exclaimed
in his indignation : "One would have to be a tiger not to protect these unfortunates (the Calas family), when the injustice of
their sentence has been demonstrated." [4]

In contrast with Rousseau's selfish indifference, the alacrity
of Voltaire in responding to the impulse of common humanity,
and the perseverance with which Voltaire devoted himself to
efforts for the relief of men in whose religious tenets he could
feel no great sympathy, earned for him the sincere and lasting
gratitude of the French Protestants. This was not strange.
They had received scant kindness from any quarter, either in
word or in deed, these many years ; and a friendly word or
act was welcome, no matter from what source it emanated. It
is somewhat startling, however, to see how far the expression
of their indebtedness to the good offices of their sceptical benefactor led them, not once, but many times. Of this a letter addressed to him, a year or two before his death, by the
worthy pastor of the church of Ganges, Gal-Pomaret,
is an interesting and amusing illustration. Very
tenderly does the Protestant minister call down the blessing of
Heaven upon the octogenarian, and pray that his last days may
also be his happiest days. Very kindly does he recall every-

A Protestant pastor's letter to Voltaire.

---

[1] Jean Jacques Rousseau to Jérémie de Pourtalès, Motiers, July 15, 1764.
Bulletin de la Soc. de l'hist. du Prot. fr., iii. 326. The whole correspondence
here given from the hitherto inedited letters that passed between Rousseau and
Pourtalès, of Neufchâtel, and Jean Foulquier, of Lausanne, is interesting.

[2] Ibid, ubi supra.

[3] "Jean Jacques n'écrit que pour écrire et moy j'écris pour agir." Letter,
apparently of 1767, quoted by Dardier, Ésaïe Gasc, 56.

[4] Voltaire to Ribote, August 13 (1762). Inedited letter in Bulletin, etc., xvii
399.

thing that Voltaire has done to lead men to cease butchering one another for opinion's sake, and bless God for having given Voltaire birth. But his charity goes far beyond this, and he sees in Voltaire a prospective heir of the Christian's crown and reward! " To contemplate the approach of death without fear, and meet it without agitation," he writes, " one must, in my opinion, believe the truths of the gospel; and I do not doubt that you believe them.[1] It is true that you have set forth many difficulties against them; but one may raise difficulties without being an unbeliever, and still more without being impious. When you were in the beautiful walks in which you found Numa, Pythagoras, Zoroaster, Socrates, and Jesus Christ, our Lord, you were told, sir, by the genius that led you, that the time when you were to know fully the last-named had not yet come. Well, that time will arrive for you, as for your fellow-men. You will see Jesus Christ in his glory, and you will share his blessedness. He pitied poor sinners, he sorrowed over their wretchedness, he hasted to deliver them. He showed himself harsh only toward hypocrites, and you were assuredly never a hypocrite." [2]

To which Voltaire replied courteously and with thanks for his correspondent's good wishes. " I am approaching the goal at which everything ends, and I shall finish my course regretting that I have gone so far without tasting the consolation of seeing you. I shall die near the region where died brave Zwingli, who thought that Numa, Socrates, and the others whom you name were all very honest people." [3]

After all, however, beyond the increasing aversion of the gov-

---

[1] " Pour voir approcher la mort sans crainte et la recevoir sans émotion, il faut être, selon moi, dans la croyance des vérités évangéliques ; et je ne doute pas que vous n'y soyez."

[2] Gal-Pomaret to Voltaire, March 8, 1776. Inedited letter published first in the Bulletin de la Soc. de l'hist. du Prot. fr., viii. (1859), 484, 485.—It will be remembered that Voltaire died May 30, 1778.

[3] " Je mourrai près du pays où mourut le brave Zwingle, qui pensait que les Numa, les Socrate, et les autres que vous nommez, étaient tous de fort honnêtes gens." Voltaire to Gal-Pomaret, April 8, 1776. Ibid., viii. 486 According to the Bulletin this is the true reading. The letter is printed, but incorrectly, in Voltaire's works, where instead of " les autres," etc., the reading is simply " l'autre," italicized. Œuvres complètes de Voltaire (Paris, 1832), xciv. 250.

ernment to execute to the letter the cruel laws still in force,
there were no immediate fruits from the efforts of Voltaire and
Toleration   other similar efforts.   It was, indeed, too late in the
deferred.   day to think of hanging or racking or burning men
for officiating, or even for being present at unauthorized religious assemblies; and, more and more, the king's ministers became accustomed not only to take for granted the existence of
Protestantism in France, but to look to the pastors of organized
Protestant churches as a security against disorder and commotion.   But it was still a great step to take, to admit that any
part of the legislation of Louis the Fourteenth was faulty; particularly that portion of it by which he believed that he had secured religious unity and earned imperishable merit in the sight
of heaven and endless renown among men.   The great king had
persuaded himself, or had been persuaded by others, that, at
the worst, the children of obdurate heretics would be brought
up from the cradle true subjects of mother holy church, com-
pensating by their sincerity for the enforced hypocrisy of their
parents.   How then could his successor bring himself to make
the humiliating confession of the truth—although all men of
sense knew it—that the grandchildren and the great-grand-
children of the contemporaries of the Revocation were as decided in their attachment to a proscribed religion as if that religion were still tolerated or established by law.   Had the monarch
been willing to make the admission, his clerical advisers would
not have permitted him to consent.   But Louis the Fifteenth
cared for none of these things.

At last, on the tenth of May, 1774, he closed his inglorious
reign of nearly threescore years.

With the accession of Louis the Sixteenth the cause of religious toleration bade fair to gain a speedy triumph.   In the
Turgot and   young king's first cabinet, two men of philosophic
Males-   minds and of known liberality of sentiment were called
herbes.   to power—Anne Robert Jacques Turgot and Chrétien
Guillaume de Lamoignon de Malesherbes.   If, in the end, the
latter was more directly concerned in the movement that secured the tardy recognition of the civil rights of the Protestants, to the former belongs the credit of an earlier and no less
important espousal of the same holy project.   With a mind

acute in detection the disastrous effects of the vices afflicting the body politic, and not less keen in the search for the remedies that might, if seasonably applied, forestall the fatal consequences, Turgot was equally interested in financial measures and in the reformation of a persecuting state. More than twenty years before the death of Louis the Fifteenth, and when barely twenty-six years of age, Turgot published his "Letters on Toleration,"

Turgot's "Letters on Toleration." which had a wide circulation and produced no little commotion among the opponents of religious liberty. He boldly took the ground that every man's interests are detached from those of every other man in the matter of his salvation, and that in his conscience he has God alone both as witness and as judge. No religion has a right to claim of the state anything beyond simple liberty. If the state chooses to protect any one religion, it must be on the ground that it is useful, not that it is true; and this protection should be limited to securing its perpetuity by giving each village a minister and assuring to that minister a pecuniary support. He denied that a king was competent to decide upon the truth, or upon the divine origin, of a particular form of religion, and asked with biting sarcasm, "Did Louis the Fourteenth know more about these matters than Le Clerc or Grotius?" He stigmatized the system which he attacked "as immoral and thoroughly impious." "Although society as a whole is greater than the individual man, it has not for that reason the right to oppress him. He has rights even against society. Intolerance is a form of tyranny. If the subjects of an intolerant king are in a condition to resist him, their revolt will be a just one; if they are too weak, they will be compelled to suffer, but God will avenge them. Such is the lot of men the moment they fail to regard religiously eternal justice as their fundamental law. The wars against the Albigenses, the establishment of the Inquisition in Languedoc, the Massacre of Saint Bartholomew's Day, the League, the Revocation of the Edict of Nantes, the vexatious treatment of the Jansenists—these are the fruits of the adoption of the axiom, 'One law, one faith, one king.'" "We have tolerant hearts; habit has made our minds fanatical. This way of thinking, which is too common in France, is, perhaps, the effect of the praise lavished upon the Revocation of the Edict

of Nantes : religion has been dishonored in order to flatter
Louis the Fourteenth." Turgot concluded with the assertion
that the revocatory edict was revolting to the men of his time,
and that the troops groaned in spirit whenever they were employed against the Protestants.[1]

The plea which Turgot so forcibly presented, when simply a
maître des requêtes, he had occasion to repeat, with more insist-
His effort to
change the
coronation
oath. ence, about a year after entering the young king's
cabinet. The ceremonial of coronation contained the
oath which, according to custom the monarch was
publicly to take, including the solemn promise that he would
exterminate the heretics from his dominions. Turgot wrote to
Louis the Sixteenth begging him to omit the objectionable
clause, and submitted to him more suitable forms to be employed on the august occasion. Louis, of whose kindly and
humane disposition no doubt could be entertained, was inclined to accept the suggestion ; but he was overborne by the
crafty arguments of the prime minister. Jealous of the ascendency which his younger colleague might gain if his advice were
accepted, Maurepas insisted upon the danger to which a young
prince would expose himself, if on the very threshold of his
reign, and when he had but just emerged from a popular storm
taking the shape of a bread-riot, he should introduce changes
which an older man might well shrink from attempting to effect in more peaceful times. Fanatics, said he, are more to be
feared than heretics. Old formulas, he added, which everybody
ignores, are no longer held to pledge one to anything.[2] But,
while the timid young king—he was not quite twenty-one years
of age when he received the anointing with oil from the *sainte*

---

[1] The first of the *Lettres sur la Tolérance* was written in 1753, the second, a
year later. Between the appearance of the two, Turgot wrote on the same subject two other letters, dated May 1 and May 8, 1754, under the title of *Le Con-
ciliateur*, publishing them in a small edition which he sent to the ministers and
councillors of state and to a few friends. The treatise was shown to Louis XV.
He read it and is said to have been convinced of the soundness of the views advanced, and to have ordered the suspension of the persecution of the Huguenots. I have in the text drawn upon both of the treatises. They may be read
in the Œuvres de Turgot (Paris, 1811) ii. 353–432.

[2] " Les vieilles formules, que tout le monde ignore, n'engagent plus à rien
dans l'opinion."

ampoule at Rheims, on the eleventh of June, 1775—yielded so far as to make no formal change in his coronation oath, he was careful not to pronounce the objectionable clause. Not only so, but in a low voice and blushing somewhat, he supplied its place with some other words which no one heard or understood. None the less did the official report make Louis the Sixteenth to have used the same persecuting formula as his predecessor.[1]

It is some satisfaction to know that, if Turgot's letter did not accomplish all that it was intended to effect, the writer did not abandon his effort to influence Louis. In a more extended paper, composed a few days later, he expressed his regret that the king had seen fit to take the oath to exterminate the heretics, and set forth the reasons why, should the monarch execute it, he would do violence to his duty to God, to his subjects, and to himself. He reminded him of the baneful fruits of intolerant fanaticism, the very spirit, the very doctrine, he said, that produced the hellish Saint Bartholomew and the detestable League, in turn putting the dagger in the hand of kings to butcher the people, and in the hand of the people to assassinate kings. No man, even be he a king, unless he has a direct commission from the Almighty, can exercise a right over men's consciences and over the matter of their salvation. Kings are not theologians. Respecting James the First of England, who attempted to be one, Europe came to the conclusion that he would have done better to employ his time in making himself a great king than a mediocre theologian. The writer asked his Majesty the pointed question: "Among all the monarchs of all time the history of whose lives you have read, is there one whom you would wish to consult on the choice of a religion? Yet almost all of them have imagined that they had the right to prescribe the religion of their subjects, to make laws and to punish men for no other crime than that they followed the dictates of their conscience. What is most surprising is that most of these princes violate in a thousand ways the precepts of their own religion, and associate the scandal of debauchery with the barbarity of persecution." He did not spare the memory of the author of the Revocation. "Louis the Fourteenth knew very

---

[1] Mémoires sur la vie de Turgot, Œuvres, i. 219, 220.

little. He candidly acknowledged that his education had been neglected. Yet, in spite of this admission, he dared to act as judge respecting the religion of his subjects. He believed that he had the right to deprive the Protestants of the liberty of conscience that had been solemnly guaranteed to them by Henry the Fourth, whose crown they had cemented with their blood. He reduced them to despair by a continued series of vexatious acts exercised in his name, the details of which make one shudder when reading them in the memoirs of the times ; and he visited with the greatest of punishments the faults which this despair led them to commit. Herein he believed himself to be performing a laudable and pious action." " The prince," added Turgot, " who orders his subject to profess the religion which the latter does not believe, or to renounce the religion which he does believe, commands him to commit a crime. The subject that yields obedience acts a lie, betrays his conscience, and does a thing which he believes to be forbidden him by God. The Protestant who, either from interest or from fear, becomes a Catholic, and the Catholic who, from the same motives, becomes a Protestant, are both of them guilty of the same crime ; for it is not the truth or the falsity of an assertion that constitutes the lie and the perjury." [1]

Truly the times had changed since Louis the Fourteenth set forth his own opinions, or those of his confessor, Père de la Chaise, as the absolute truth, to which he was entitled by divine right to require the unquestioning submission of all his subjects!

Only a month or two had elapsed, since the government itself had given to the world a pregnant proof of the altered condition of the Protestants, despite the survival of the proscriptive laws against them upon the pages of the statute-book.

Allusion has been made to the bread-riots that assumed portentous dimensions shortly before the coronation at Rheims. "La Guerre des Fa-rines." Among the most beneficent of the economic projects which Turgot had long since advocated in print, and which he undertook to carry into effect as soon as called into power, was the abolition of all legal impediments to the free interchange of grain between different parts of the

---

[1] Mémoire au Roi sur la Tolérance, Œuvres de Turgot, vii. 317–335.

kingdom. A measure so distinctly in the interest of the poor might have been expected to find favor with all except the friends of existing monopolies; but the latter so skilfully employed the means at their disposal as to excite and foment underhand a blind and unthinking discontent, and to direct it against the advocates of the very policy which would in the end secure cheaper food for the laboring classes. Soon accounts began to reach the court of mobs that plundered the markets and broke into the bakers' shops, in a number of places at no great distance from the capital. Before the end of April, 1775, Creil, Beaumont sur Oise, L'Isle Adam, and Pontoise had been successively visited. In the first few days of the next month Saint Germain was pillaged. Next Versailles was overrun by a mob that even threatened the castle. Then all the bakers of Paris were robbed, not a shop, however far out of the way it might be, being overlooked. Before the eleventh of May, according to the letter of an eye-witness, the wild frenzy had spread eastward and southward to Brie - Comte - Robert, to Meaux and Lagny, to Étampes, to Fontainebleau, to Nemours, and elsewhere. No resistance was instituted, the guards retired at the sight of the approaching crowd, whose extravagant actions and tumultuous outcries reminded the spectator of the unbridled gayety of young people making merry at a wedding.[1] Nothing could be more bold or more astonishing, save possibly the idea by which the marauders seemed to be possessed that when carrying off and wasting, or when occasionally burning or throwing into the rivers the precious stores of wheat which they discovered, or when ruining the mill-stones and destroying the machinery used to set them in motion, they were engaging in a laudable undertaking that must of itself lower the price of the necessaries of life.[2] The fury was not long-lived, but while it lasted the effects so closely resembled the events

---

[1] Letter of Court de Gébelin to Charles de Végobre, Paris, May 11, 1775, Court MSS. Public Lib. of Geneva, published in Charles Dardier, La Guerre des Farines et les Pasteurs de Nîmes et du Bas Languedoc, 1775 (Nismes, 1889), p. 7.

[2] See the statements of the government " Instruction," referred to on the next page, as well as the extract from the Gazette de Leyden, No. 36, given by Dardier, ubi supra, p. 14.

following in the wake of open hostilities that the people named it *La Guerre des Farines*. Nor was this episode of French history so insignificant as it would at first sight appear to have been, if, as the biographer of Turgot maintains, it was in some degree responsible for the horrors of the French Revolution! The loss of six weeks' time which it entailed, according to this authority, prevented the minister from being able to present to the king, at the proper moment, the financial scheme which he was maturing, and which, by equalizing the burdens of all classes, would have given such general contentment as to render the subsequent commotions improbable, if not impossible. The month of October was the annual period for the conclusion of the financial arrangements for the ensuing year. Before it came again Turgot was not in a position to propose the plans which he might have urged with success a year earlier.[1]

It was in the midst of the commotion arising from the "war" that the ministers took a step by which they formally recognized the existence of a faith which for ninety years had been proscribed and declared to be extinct, and called for the help of those Protestant pastors who, if arrested, could scarcely have escaped being hung or broken upon the wheel, without disregard for the prescriptions of the law.

The government seeks the support of the pastors of the Desert.

It was deemed advisable to address a circular letter to all the bishops and archbishops of the kingdom, and to accompany this with a letter of instructions to be forwarded by the prelates to every parish priest within their respective dioceses. The letter entered at considerable length into the nature of the existing commotion, set forth the absurdity of its alleged causes, recited some of the excesses that had been committed, and requested all the curates to emulate the wisdom of some of their own number, by seeking, from the pulpit and in every appropriate way, to impress upon the members of their flocks the good intentions of the government and to deter them from joining a movement as wicked and unreasonable as it was suicidal.[2]

---

[1] See Œuvres de Turgot, i. 191–193.

[2] Both letter and instruction were from the pen of Turgot, and may be read in his works, vii. 279–291. They are of the date of Versailles, May 9, 1775.

Turgot had entered the king's cabinet as secretary of the navy, but before many months (August, 1774) was transferred to the more congenial and important post of controller general of the finances, and was now at the head of the royal treasury. As controller he ordered the circular and the letter of instructions to be despatched to the Protestant pastors of the Desert at Nismes and elsewhere in Lower Languedoc. The copy addressed to the veteran Paul Rabaut is still to be seen in the rich collection of his papers, which constitutes one of the treasures of the library of the French Protestant Historical Society. Upon the blank leaf at its close, his son, Rabaut Saint Étienne, has added an extract from the proceedings of an extraordinary meeting of the delegates of the Protestant churches of Lower Languedoc called for the purpose of considering the communication from Versailles. In this minute, as well as in The Protestant reply. the answer which they sent to Turgot, the pastors of the Desert could proudly point to the inviolable fidelity of the French Protestants; while expressing "the hope which, under a government whereof justice and humanity are the basis, they venture to entertain, of the particular favors of a tender-hearted monarch who deigns to return to his people love for love." "These precious favors," they add, "which for a century have constituted the object of our prayers, we await with confidence, but with a respectful and submissive patience."[1]

The pastors of the Desert had no occasion to exert their influence in a practical manner. The "Guerre des Farines" died out in northern France without reaching southern France at all. Besides, as Rabaut Saint Étienne pithily observed, there was no Protestant *populace* at Montpellier,[2] and there could scarcely be supposed to exist in the other towns and villages of the region any unintelligent Protestant mob that could readily be stirred up to insane acts of rebellion and violence, as repugnant to the practice of the Protestants as

---

[1] See the minute of May 29, 1775, and the letter with which it was enclosed, apud Dardier, Guerre des Farines. pp. 18–21.

[2] "Cela est d'autant moins nécessaire à Montpellier (je veux dire de parler de cette émeute), que vous n'avez pas de populace protestante." Rabaut Saint Étienne, in a letter probably written to his brother, Rabaut Pomier. Dardier, ubi supra, p. 22.

opposed to the precepts of their oppressed religion. None the less did the pastors preach submission to the constituted authority. This, as they had signified to Turgot, they were enjoined by their church discipline to do at least once a year. Rabaut Saint Étienne, in particular, conducted, a fortnight after the king's coronation, a grand service in honor of that event. The principal features were a sermon on the text, "Render therefore unto Cæsar the things which are Cæsar's; and unto God the things that are God's," and the jubilant rendering of the *Te Deum*, sung alternately by the choir and by the congregation, while at each pause were read appropriate selections of the Holy Scriptures. Some thousands of Protestants and a few Roman Catholics were present at the meeting, which was held near the gates of the city. Every one, we are told, went home well pleased with the services.[1]

The incident of the "Guerre des Farines" did not stand alone as evidencing a disposition on the part of the government to recognize, and, when necessary, to avail itself of the help of the Protestant ministers. A month or two earlier, when many young men of Protestant families desired to bring proof that they had not reached the age at which they could be drawn for military service, they applied to their pastors for extracts from the church records giving the dates of their birth and baptism. And these certificates were, probably for the first time since the Revocation, accepted by the civil and military authorities as conclusive, the signature of the officiating minister having been duly attested by Paul Rabaut.[2] For to this venerable man, a patriarch in service rather than in age (for he was only fifty-seven years old) the government not unnaturally affected to concede a kind of official pre-eminence over his colleagues, secured to him by his great intellectual and moral superiority.

Protestant baptismal records officially recognized.

Meantime, philosophers and others continued to agitate the recall of the Protestants. Among others, that remarkable personage who figured at one time as *le chevalier* and at another as

---

[1] Paul Rabaut to Étienne Chiron, Nismes, June 26, 1775. Guerre des Farines, pp. 22, 23.

[2] Letter of Rabaut, April 5, 1775, ibid., p. 9.

la chevalière d'Eon, pleaded the cause of the Huguenots before
the royal council and denounced intolerance on the ground that,
while religion in the head of the *people* is the support of the
state, religion in the head of the *king* is the nation's scourge.
In the course of the argument the speaker used these words
of warning : "The recall of the Protestants may, at the present
moment, if not render impossible, at least delay yet more the
Revolution which we fear." [1]

Among the various means employed to force upon the public
attention the necessity of doing some justice to the remaining
Huguenots of France, fiction was not the least effective. In 1779 Rabaut Saint Étienne, the eldest son
of Paul Rabaut, and himself a pastor, published in
London his *Triomphe de l'intolérance,* to which, in a second
edition, brought out five years later, he gave the more characteristic title, *Le vieux Cévenol, ou Anecdotes de la vie d'Ambroise Borély, mort à Londres agé de 103 ans, 7 mois et 4 jours.*
The little book purported to record the personal experience of
a native of the south of France, whose birth in a family belonging to the Reformed religion was his great misfortune. In
connection with the adventures of his imaginary hero the author forcibly exhibited the unhappy situation of those whom
the absurd legislation of Louis the Fourteenth and his successor would neither suffer to expatriate themselves nor allow to
enjoy at home the ordinary and essential rights of men.

Marginal note: Rabaut Saint Étienne's "Le vieux Cévenol."

Born a few years before the Revocation of the Edict of Nantes, Ambroise witnesses in early childhood the ruin that was
wrought by the iniquitous edict of recall, in one of the many
Protestant homes of France. His father is put to death, with
scanty respect for the forms of law, on the mere suspicion of
having attended an unauthorized religious meeting. The home
of the family is visited and its furniture destroyed by the
ruthless dragoons. The mother, however, continues for years
to strive, in a humble way, to support her children, while secretly educating them in the religion of their forefathers.

At the age of fifteen Ambroise, reflecting that the time has

---

[1] Discours sur le rappel des Protestants prononcé au Conseil de France, in
1775. Bulletin de la Soc. de l'hist. du Prot. franç., xxxvi. 379-384.

come for him to prepare soon to become a bread-winner, applies to a lawyer of his acquaintance for permission to enter his office. To his consternation he is informed that there is no room for him in the legal profession ; for the king's ordinances expressly prohibit a Protestant from occupying any position, whether as judge, solicitor, advocate, or notary, or as the most insignificant functionary of the law.   The physician and the apothecary successively give him the unpalatable intelligence that he can have no hope of taking up the practice of medicine or the dispensing of drugs.   Borély finds it the same everywhere.   The Jesuits have gone so far as to procure from the crown a special edict to preclude a Protestant from giving lessons in horsemanship. These fathers having never frequented riding-schools, apparently suppose that the masters are profound theologians who would argue with their pupils while teaching them how to turn or to start off at the right pace.   When Borély thinks of enlisting in the army, he finds, indeed, that his Majesty will permit a subject who is not a Roman Catholic to enter the service, but expressly warns any such person that he is to expect no favors, that is to say, no promotion, at his hands.   Moreover, he remembers that, in the course of his military duties, it is not improbable that he may some day be called upon to enforce in the case of his innocent fellow believers orders such as have brought disaster to his own kindred, orders from obedience to which his whole nature will recoil, but to no purpose.   In short, no career is open to him but trade.   He engages in this, and before long, being both industrious and intelligent, his efforts are crowned with a good degree of prosperity.

Meanwhile, Ambroise is a witness in his own family to the wretchedness of those whose loss of civil rights could scarcely be more complete.   An informer, significantly named Claude Hypocris, not content with making filthy lucre by securing his share of many successive fines inflicted upon the widowed mother of Ambroise for her neglect to send her children to school, takes advantage of a royal edict that deprives Protestant wives of "new converts," and even Protestant widows, of the disposal of their dower and of all privileges accorded to them by their husbands, unless they become converted to the Roman Catholic faith within a month after the publication of the law.

Ambroise's mother is reduced to the necessity of living upon a scanty allowance reluctantly doled out to her to keep her from absolute starvation; while her enemy obtains the administration of the property rightfully hers. New disasters follow. The daughters are carried off to convents. The Benjamin of the family, a boy of only seven years of age, is converted to Roman Catholicism by the offer of pictures and sweetmeats. Borély witnesses the barbarous treatment inflicted upon the remains of a " new convert," who in his last hours refused the ministrations of a priest of the Roman Catholic church, and was therefore, after death, dragged naked upon a hurdle, subjected to every form of insult and contumely at the hands of the hooting populace, and flung, as something unworthy of Christian burial, into the common sewer. The young Cévenol resolves to flee from a land where such barbarity can be practised. In his attempt to reach Switzerland he is arrested, and, in company with others, is driven to the seaboard, borne down by the weight of his ponderous chain. Instead, however, of the service in the galleys which he expects, he is sentenced to the more frightful punishment of transportation to America. He is put on board a leaky vessel, purposely selected for its unseaworthiness. When two or three days out from port the captain carries out his instructions, scuttles the ship, and taking to his gig with the crew, leaves his Protestant passengers to drown in the waves. A few of these, more fortunate than the rest, cling to spars and are picked up by a passing vessel. Ambroise is of the number. The British cruiser, for such it proves to be, carries him to London. He becomes naturalized, engages in trade, and in the course of a number of years, by industry and application, accumulates a fortune. But a man never forgets his birthplace. Ambroise conceives an unconquerable longing to revisit the sunny fields of Languedoc. Of all his relatives he finds only his two sisters alive. The one has been persuaded to become a nun; the other, having made profession of Roman Catholicism, is in possession of the family inheritance. She supposes that Ambroise, who purposely avoids giving any intimation of his newly acquired wealth, has returned to claim his share of the family patrimony, and plainly informs him that he may spare himself the trouble of contesting her title, inasmuch as the law protects the Roman Catholic heir, as against any Protestant brother or sister. When she discovers her mistake, Ambroise's sister would gladly recall her words, but he will have nothing to do with her and prepares in disgust to leave France for ever. He has not, however, yet learned the full extent of the decay of natural affection for which the monstrous legislation of his native country is directly responsible. A pretty face adjourns his departure. He falls in love with Sophie Robinel, the daughter of a Roman Catholic of the region, who readily consents to give her hand to the rich Englishman. A Protestant minister performs the nuptial service. After a year of happy married life Sophie dies, leaving her husband a son, the fruit of their wedlock. Within a few days Ambroise is surprised in the midst of his sorrow by the receipt of a document served upon him with all the forms of law. It proves to be a summons " to surrender the goods and chattels left by the late Sophie Robinel, of whom he falsely asserts himself to have been the husband, seeing she was but a concubine with whom he has led a scandalous life," with other words to the like effect. The action at law is in the name of the father and mother of the deceased. Borély resolves to defend the rights of his infant son, not less than the honor and good name of her whom he called wife. The legal counsel whom he consults candidly informs him that the law, as Louis the Fourteenth and Louis the Fifteenth have made it, pronounces the nullity of marriages celebrated by Protestant ministers, and the consequent bastardy of the offspring of such marriages. Despite this, he contests the case in the courts. His lawyer makes a vigorous plea for the rights of nature, which are older than, and superior to, all written statutes. It is all to no purpose. Sophie's infant son is declared incapable of succeeding to her property. The judges have little to say by way of justification, when privately interrogated as to the reasons why, while conveniently relaxing the strict observance of the proscriptive legislation at some points, they still persist in a partial enforcement of it, especially in a direction where it comes into manifest conflict with the dictates of natural justice. One of them, however, sagely gives his opinion of the present state of things in these words: " The Protestants are as well off as they need be.

If you except the liberty of their conscience, the freedom to dispose of their property, the security of their condition, the undisturbed possession of their children, and the choice of trades and professions, they are treated just about in the same way as the rest of the king's subjects." Borély, possibly esteeming the exceptions named to be of more consequence than they are in the judge's estimation, hastens to get beyond the frontiers. He shows the more alacrity to do so at learning that his complacent interlocutor has already applied to the king for a *lettre de cachet* for the arrest of Ambroise, and that even an Englishman does not enjoy immunity from the operation of this instrument of arbitrary oppression. Once safe in a free country he renounces all desire to venture again into a land where the most sacred rights of man are set at naught.

But better times were near at hand for the Protestants.

The same enlightened nobleman whose labors in behalf of American independence have endeared his name for all time to the citizens of the great western republic, may be said to have exerted a decisive influence in securing to the Huguenots of France a tardy recognition of their rights. The Marquis of Lafayette returned to his native land fully resolved to accomplish this object. It will perhaps strike the reader who knows that in 1785 the outbreak of a mighty political revolution, that would in the end hurl the monarchy into the dust, was only four years distant, as a singular circumstance that, even so late as this, it was unsafe to write and send through the mail a letter alluding to the projected reform in the stern legislation of Louis the Fourteenth. Yet such was the case, and Lafayette, in communicating with Washington not only intrusted his letter to "young Mr. Adams" to tell him of things of which, said he, "I should not be willing to treat through the medium of the French post-office;" but requested his correspondent to make none but the most cautious reply. "The Protestants in France," he wrote, "are subjected to an intolerable despotism. Although there is at present no open persecution, they are dependent on the caprice of the king, of the queen, of parliament, or of a minister. Their marriages are not legal; their wills have no force in the sight of the law; their children are regarded as bastards, their persons as worthy of the halter. I desire to bring about a change in their situation. For this purpose I am going, under certain pretexts, and with the consent of M. de Castries and another [probably Malesherbes] to visit their principal seats. I shall afterward attempt to obtain the support of M. de Vergennes and of parliament, together with that of the keeper of the seals, who is acting as chancellor. It is a work that demands time and is not free from some inconvenience to me, for the reason that no one would give me a word in writing or any support whatsoever. I shall take my chances. Only M. de Castries [one of the ministers] could be let into my secret, this matter not being in his department. Do not return me any answer, except that you have received my letter in cipher brought by Mr. Adams. But when, in the course of the autumn or winter, you learn that something has been accomplished in this matter, I wish you to know that I contributed to it." [1]

Leaving court ostensibly for the purpose of visiting his native home in Auvergne, Lafayette shortly reached the city of Nismes. It was here that he sought out and found the patriarch of the Desert, and with youthful ardor laid before the veteran pastor the plans he had conceived to effect

He visits Paul Rabaut at Nismes. the legal restoration of the proscribed churches, for the spiritual restoration of which the other had been patiently working for forty-four years. Lafayette was not yet twenty-eight years old. Paul Rabaut was over sixty-seven, and yet he was bowed down, not so much under the burden of age as under the weight of incessant labors, perils, and anxieties. As truly as Saint Paul, in the first century, and John Calvin, in the sixteenth, he could point to the overwhelming pressure of matters that came upon him daily, the care of all the churches. It was a startling interview, in which the foremost of the younger nobles of France, the scion of one of its most illustrious families, a hero of the American Revolutionary War, communicated to a Protestant minister, whom the government had repeatedly done its best to apprehend, and whose marvellous escapes in disguise were on every man's lips, his hopes, now

---

[1] Marq. de Lafayette to Gen. Washington, May 11, 1785. Mémoires, correspondance et manuscrits du général Lafayette, publiés par sa famille (Bruxelles, 1837), i. 200.

apparently soon to be realized. It is said that Paul Rabaut reverently thanked God, using the words of the aged Simeon : "Lord, now lettest thou thy servant depart in peace, according to thy word : for mine eyes have seen thy salvation." [1] It will be remembered that just one hundred years before, Chancellor Le Tellier devoutly repeated the same words upon his death-bed, in his joy at being permitted to set the great seal of France to the edict for the Revocation of the Edict of Nantes. History is not called upon to pronounce upon the comparative sincerity with which the *Nunc dimittis* was said upon two such different occasions and by two such different men ; but History can safely be trusted to render a true verdict concerning the comparative merit of the measures that respectively called forth the joy of two aged men, each of whom was nearing the end of his earthly course.

Lafayette judged it indispensable that either Paul Rabaut or his son, Rabaut Saint Étienne, should come to the capital to labor directly for the good cause. The age of the father made the choice fall upon the younger man. Himself a Prot-estant pastor, and therefore under the ban of the law, Rabaut Saint Étienne's liberty, if not his life, was exposed to great danger when from Nismes he sought the vicinity of the court. Protestant committees at Nismes, at Montpellier, and at Bor-deaux charged themselves with the duty of supplying the very moderate sum necessary to defray his travelling expenses and support ; but so great was the need of secrecy that even these com-mittees were scantily informed of his movements. A specious pretext was sought for the journey. It was given out to the pub-lic that Saint Étienne had gone to consult learned men in Paris and to print a book which he had recently written on the primi-tive history of Greece.[2] Even so, however, his steps were the object of continual espionage, and he was compelled to use the utmost circumspection both in his actions and in his corre-spondence.[3]

Rabaut Saint Étienne in-vited to court.

---

[1] Mémoires, etc., de Lafayette, i. 219.

[2] Lettre à M. Bailly sur l'histoire primitive de la Grèce, 1786. It was dedicated by the author to his father.

[3] Besides the interesting letters that passed between Lafayette, Paul Rabaut, Rabaut Saint Étienne, and De Poitevin, published in the Bulletin of the French

The difficulties were great. Louis the Sixteenth was not hard-hearted. Tolerant measures were naturally welcome to him, but he was timid and irresolute. Moreover, he had been brought up under priestly influence. When, a year later, the condition of the Protestants was about to come before the council for discussion, he was reported to have made up his mind to do them justice, but he still felt need of support and encouragement from without. Queen Marie Antoinette became interested in the new projects and spoke to her husband with warmth. Whereupon the latter took both her hands in his own and affectionately said: "You give me great pleasure when you express these views. Talk to me often about the matter, so as to sustain me in this mood."[1] Yet he was reluctant to break with the traditions of the past. In 1783—and it was probably the same in 1785—he still clung to the practice of Louis the Fourteenth and paid missionaries to labor, in the way in which we know they labored, for the conversion of the Protestants of Poitou.[2]

Difficulties.

Timidity of Louis XVI.

Public opinion was, indeed, favorable to toleration, and few cultured men could be found that would deliberately espouse the defence of the sanguinary laws still held in suspense over the heads of the Protestants. But the Protestants themselves were objects of aversion in and about the court. Particularly was this the case with the Protestant ministers, whose portrait had never been drawn save by the hand of enemies. The unmerited reproach with which the law covered them was held by men disposed to look at every-

Prejudice against the Protestants.

Protestant Historical Society, ii. 330, etc., under the title Les Promoteurs de l'Édit de 1787, I refer the reader particularly to the long report made by Rabaut Saint Étienne to the Bordeaux Committee, under date of Paris, February 12, 1788. This important document is in manuscript in the archives of the Consistory of the church of Nismes, but has recently been printed for the first time, I believe, in Charles Dardier's Paul Rabaut: ses lettres à divers (Paris, 1892), ii. 393–416.

[1] "A la fin de l'été de 1786, j'eus la certitude que le Conseil allait s'occuper de notre affaire. Le roi était décidé, la reine s'y intéressait ; elle en parla avec chaleur au roi, qui lui répondit en lui prenant affectueusement les mains : Vous me faites grand plaisir de penser ainsi ; parlez-m'en souvent, afin de m'entretenir dans ces dispositions." Ibid., ii. 399.

[2] It was a New-Year's gift. See the order signed by Louis XVI., January 1, 1783. Bulletin de la Soc. de l'hist. du Prot. fr., ii. 368.

thing superficially to justify contempt on the part of all sensible persons. A timid cabinet took account of this prejudice, if indeed it did not share it, and was indisposed to advocate any measure that would not meet universal approval and that might endanger the popularity of the cabinet officer who proposed it. Moreover, there was not a little reason to fear that the Protestants, when once the smaller part of their rights was conceded, would raise their demands and claim the remainder with importunate urgency.[1]

What was most embarrassing was that, as I have already hinted, even the most friendly of the king's advisers dared take no position resembling an attempt to demolish any portion of the structure reared by "the great monarch" at so vast an expenditure of time, trouble, and blood. Malesherbes himself, in a memoir which he handed in to the Council this very year (1785), " On the Marriage of the Protestants," was careful to impress upon the king's mind the idea, which was simple and easy for him to grasp, that in providing for this difficult matter he would but be completing what Louis the Fourteenth had intended to do, but for some reason had held in suspense. It was the same in Malesherbes's second memoir on the same subject, submitted a year later. "Thus it is," observes the Protestant agent, "that we are grieved to see subsisting that frightful phantom of the shade of Louis the Fourteenth; but that phantom is still venerated in the neighborhood of the throne, and be it religion, habit, mental indolence, national self-love, or prejudice, it would have been impossible to overthrow this colossus, and to lay down a simple law on the immutable principles of natural justice." [2]

"The phantom of the shade of Louis XIV."

The circumstances therefore were peculiar and not devoid of a certain interest. It was not the general public that had to be convinced of the equity of according to the Protestants of France—be they less than one million souls, as some asserted, or over two millions, as others maintained with no less positiveness—full civil rights, or an equality with the rest of the citizens. It was a narrow circle, and, especially the king himself, that must be persuaded that a few of the most essential preroga-

[1] Bulletin de la Soc. de l'hist. du Prot. fr., ii. 395.   [2] Ibid., ii. 397.

tives of man might safely be conceded without disturbing institutions viewed with almost superstitious awe. What therefore at first sight appear to be signal defects, the result of contracted views, historically incorrect—both in the important " *Éclaircissements historiques*," composed by Rulhière at the direction of Baron Breteuil, to which I have in the preceding pages had frequent occasion to refer, and in the memoirs of Malesherbes—are, in point of fact, indications of a clear comprehension of what, in the circumstances, was possible and what was impossible of attainment.

The report of Rabaut Saint Étienne to the committee of Protestants at Bordeaux sheds a flood of light on the situation of affairs. He tells us that the memoirs of Malesherbes, which were subsequently published, were published not to form public opinion, but to induce the Parliament of Paris to consent to the registration of the edict, by showing that all its difficulties had been anticipated. They were composed for the king's council, and it is as read *there* that they must now be read and judged. Their author was a skilful fencer who parried prejudices which he could not destroy; a legislator who spoke as calmly and with as entire an absence of passion as the law itself. An eloquent phrase would have spoiled everything. To avoid eloquence in treating a subject that is calculated to excite the feelings, and when the writer is one of the most eloquent orators in the kingdom, is proof of great intellectual strength. An ordinary man would not have failed to grow animated and indulge in figures of speech—and he would have ruined his case. For if eloquence be necessary in forming popular opinion, in questions of administration it excites distrust and renders him an object of suspicion who seems desirous of forcing opinion and gaining votes. One must consequently transport one's self to the council in which the memoirs were read, that council in which were present not only the king, but M. de Vergennes, Minister of Foreign Affairs, whose principles were those of the politician, and who clothed with harshness his narrow and contracted views, and M. de Miromesnil, the keeper of the seals, of whose opposition no one was ignorant, and who wanted no law made by any one else than himself.

The adroitness of Malesherbes.

The reigning belief was that the Revocation of the Edict of Nantes was the work of a consummate policy and the fruit of a system planned long since. It was necessary to prove in the council itself that neither Louis the Fourteenth nor his council had ever had any system, that there were Protestants in France, and that that monarch had the intention of preserving their rights as citizens.

Such is the picture drawn by Rabaut Saint Étienne which I have reproduced substantially in his own words.[1]

Many months passed before success crowned the persevering exertions put forth by Malesherbes and his faithful coadjutors.

Ineffectual attempt of the Parliament of Paris. Among the singularities of the history of the struggle was the circumstance that the same Parliament of Paris which, a few months later, strenuously opposed the registration of the Edict of Toleration, at this point disclosed an ambition to assume legislative functions, and actually petitioned Louis the Sixteenth to restore to the Protestants the most important of the rights of which they had for a whole century been deprived; thereby annoying the monarch, who was far from relishing an attempt on the part of the judges to dictate to him the course which he was himself intending to pursue.[2] The resolution which parliament adopted, after listening to the noble plea made by one of its own judges, Robert de Saint Vincent, before the united chambers (on the ninth of February, 1787), directed the first president to present himself before the king, for the purpose of begging his Majesty "to weigh, in his wisdom, the means of giving a civil status to the Protestants."[3] It has been conjectured, not without probabil-

---

[1] Lettre-Rapport de Rabaut Saint Étienne à messieurs les membres du comité de Bordeaux, Paris, February 12, 1788. Lettres de Rabaut à divers, ii. 397, 398.

[2] " Ce corps qui commençait à avoir la fantaisie, qu'il a tout à fait annoncée dépuis, de faire le législateur, délibéra de demander au roi l'état civil pour les protestants ; et le roi trouva mauvais que le parlement lui dictât ce que lui-même avait dessein de faire." Rabaut Saint Étienne, ubi supra, ii. 400.

[3] " Il a été arrêté qu'il sera fait registre du récit d'un de messieurs et que M. le premier président sera chargé de se retirer par devant le roi, à l'effet de supplier ledit seigneur roi de peser, dans sa sagesse, les moyens de donner un état civil aux protestants." Anquez, De l'état civil des réformés de France (Paris, 1868), 199.

ity, that parliament, which was at this time far more likely to
be moved by considerations of interest or vanity than by moral
principle, had no higher motive in its hasty action on the present occasion than to deprive the Assembly of Notables, which
was soon to convene, and from which a solemn demonstration in
favor of the Protestants was expected, of the honor of taking
the initiative.[1]

For the Marquis of Lafayette was reserved the honorable
duty of bringing the repeal of Protestant disabilities before the
Notables, at their session of the twenty-third of May,
1787. That body had met at Versailles two months
before (on the twenty-second of February), and was
on the eve of concluding its long and unsatisfactory
sessions. Whatever discord and acrimonious debate had been
aroused by the unpalatable proposals of Calonne to extricate
the kingdom from its desperate financial straits, the project of
Lafayette commended itself so strongly to the enlightened
judgment and humanity of the members that it passed without
opposition. The Count of Artois, who presided over the "second bureau" of the Notables, in which the motion was made,
alone objected that the matter, being foreign to the ends for
which the Notables were summoned, did not fall within the
powers of the body, but consented to report it to his brother
the king, if such was their desire. From a learned and upright
prelate of the Roman Catholic church the Marquis of Lafayette
received hearty and loyal assistance.[2] The Bishop of Langres
spoke with admirable tact. "I support the request of M. de
Lafayette," said he, "from different motives from his. He has
spoken as a philosopher; I shall speak as a bishop, and say
that I prefer 'temples' to 'preachings' and 'ministers' to
'preachers.'"[3]

Lafayette's address was short and simple. It admitted that
the object to which the king's attention was invited was foreign

*Lafayette's
motion at
the Assem-
bly of the
Notables,
May, 1787.*

---

[1] Anquez, De l'état civil des réformés de France, ubi supra.

[2] " J'ai été libéralement secondé par un savant et vertueux prélat, l'évêque de
Langres, qui a parlé admirablement sur la motion religieuse que j'avais intro-
duite." Lafayette to John Jay. May 3, 1787. Mémoires de Lafayette, i. 227.

[3] "Je dirai que j'aime mieux des temples que des prêches et des ministres
que des prédicants." Anquez, De l'état civil des réformés de France, 207.

to the petitioners' labors, but insisted upon its importance to humanity. A part of their fellow-citizens, who had not the happiness of professing the Catholic religion, found themselves smitten with a species of civil death. The petitioners knew too well the king's heart not to be persuaded that he desired to cause the true religion to be beloved by all his subjects, of whom he was the common father. His Majesty knew that Truth sustains herself by her own strength, that Error alone needs to use constraint, and his Majesty united the dispositions of a beneficent tolerance to all the virtues that had earned for him the love of the nation. The petitioners therefore eagerly presented to the king their solicitations that this portion of his subjects might cease to groan under a *régime* of proscription contrary alike to the general interests of the population, to the national industries, and to all the dictates of morality and of expediency.[1]

The Notables struck out but one sentence. Lafayette had written : "The clergy, penetrated by the grand principles which the fathers of the church honored themselves with professing, will doubtless applaud this act of justice." The words seemed to some to sound like covert irony. They recalled the fact that the assemblies of the clergy, even when these were presided over by prelates that were avowed infidels, like the Archbishops of Toulouse and Narbonne, had never ceased to demand the rigorous execution of the cruel ordinances enacted against the Protestants during the last two reigns.[2]

The Count of Artois duly presented the petition of the Notables to Louis the Sixteenth. The latter received it graciously.[3]

If six months more elapsed before the desire, thus clearly expressed, was gratified, the reason is to be found in the desperate resistance of the clergy. From the prelates down to the humblest parish priest, it sometimes looked as if the clergy had learned nothing, had forgotten nothing. There were, of course,

---

[1] See the text in the Mémoires de Lafayette, i. 218, and in Anquez, De l'état civil des réformés de France, 205, 206.

[2] Mémoires de Lafayette, i. 218.

[3] "Elle a été presentée au roi par le comte d'Artois, notre président, et gracieusement reçue." Lafayette to John Jay, May 3, 1787. Ibid., i. 227.

many exceptions; but, as a body, the ecclesiastics appeared unconscious that they were no longer living in the times of Louis
the Fourteenth, and kept up a system of espionage as petty,
and at times as annoying, as it was a century before.[1] That
they would contest the progress of toleration when it threatened to make so decided a gain as was now proposed, might
reasonably have been apprehended. But even those that knew
them well were startled at the virulence of a pamphlet that now
appeared, under the title of a "Discourse to be read at the
Council, in the King's presence, by a Patriot Minister, on the
Project to accord a Civil Status to the Protestants." The
"patriot minister" was a Jesuit. Some suspected him to be
the Abbé L'Enfant, reputed the foremost preacher of his order.
More probably he was the less prominent Father Bonnaud.
But whoever wrote the document, certain it is that it fully met
the approval of the party in whose interests it was put forth.[2]

On the nineteenth of November, 1787, Louis the Sixteenth,
attended by his brothers the Count of Provence and the Count

Louis XVI.
visits the
Parliament
of Paris,
November
19, 1787.

of Artois, two future kings of France, entered the
hall in which the Parliament of Paris was awaiting
him. He had been preceded by the law officers of the
crown who laid before the judges two important bills.
When the king took his seat, Lamoignon, keeper of the seals,
explained the nature of the two measures. With the first—a
law providing for a loan of four hundred and eighty million
livres to meet the pressing needs of the treasury—we have nothing to do. Unpopular in itself, it was rendered doubly odious
by the arbitrary course of Louis, who, after listening for some
hours to a discussion of its merits, was so ill-advised as summarily to stop the debate by ordering that it be entered at once
upon the parliamentary records, as registered in the monarch's
presence, in a *lit de justice*, and by his Majesty's most express
command. The second measure, which was next submitted, be-

---

[1] See the *certificate*, signed by Martin, curate of Mezières, July 14, 1785, to
the effect that a recent convert to the Roman Catholic religion was infrequent
in his attendance upon mass, etc. Bulletin de la Soc. de l'hist. du Prot. fr.,
xxxii. 239.

[2] See the monograph of M. Charles Read, in the Bulletin de la Soc. de l'hist.
du Prot. fr. (1892), xli. 449–465.

fore the murmurs of discontent on the part of the offended counsellors had ceased to make themselves heard, and which Louis left to be discussed after he had retired from the hall, was the EDICT OF TOLERATION.[1]

By this law, after having for one hundred and two years been denied a legal existence within the realm of France, the Huguenots were at length to be recognized as human beings actually breathing the same air as their Roman Catholic fellow-citizens, and entitled to the most obvious rights of humanity. The statute by which the change was effected is so important and contains such singular admissions as to deserve careful consideration.

The Edict of Toleration.

The authors of the edict were confronted, as we have seen, with the difficult problem, how to reverse the legislation and the practice of a full century, without condemning in express terms the iniquitous acts of the reigning monarch's ancestors, and, most of all, the revocatory edict of Louis the Fourteenth. Their task was, however, rendered less arduous by the circumstance that the new measure, being but a first step toward the rehabilitation of Protestantism, did not give back to the adherents of that form of religion the right of public worship. Neither openly nor in private were they to assemble for the service of God, and their sermons continued in theory to be as illegal as their celebrations of the sacraments or of marriage. The legislator confined himself to a recognition of the claim of dissidents to certain privileges which were undeniably involved in the admission of the fact that Protestantism had never been thoroughly extirpated from French soil.

Thanks to this, the honor of Louis the Fourteenth could be guarded, and the just concessions made to the persecuted Huguenots could be represented as being virtually the very provision which that monarch had intended to establish for their benefit but had been prevented by circumstances from effecting. " When Louis the Fourteenth solemnly forbade in all the lands subject to his authority the public exercise of any other religion than the Catholic, the hope of bringing his people to so desirable a unity in the same worship, founded upon deceptive

---

[1] See the account in Anquez, De l'état civil des réformés de France, 211, 212.

appearances of conversions, prevented that great king from carrying out the plan which he had formed in his councils, of legally establishing the civil status of those of his subjects who
could not be admitted to the sacraments of the church." Such
is the beginning of the preamble, in which, while professing as
ardent a purpose as any of his predecessors to promote every
proper effort to bring his subjects to the faith which he holds,
the king repudiates, as contrary to reason and humanity not less
than to the true spirit of Christianity, any recourse to violent
measures for the sake of compassing this end. Long experience, he affirms, has demonstrated the inefficacy of rigorous
methods of conversion. He cannot longer suffer the laws needlessly to punish men for the misfortune of their birth, by depriving them of rights which nature itself does not cease to demand in their behalf.

In consequence of the difficult attitude of the monarch he
studiously avoids designating those whose hardships he is endeavoring to alleviate any more definitely than as " those of our
subjects that profess another religion than the Catholic." The
word " Protestants " does not occur in the body of the edict.[1]
The solitary instance in which Louis is betrayed into using
it occurs in the preamble, where he admits that " the Protestants,
thus despoiled of all legal existence, were placed in the unavoid-
able alternative either of profaning the sacraments by feigned
conversions, or of compromising the status of their children by
contracting marriages declared in advance to be null and void
by the legislation of the realm." [2]

Yet the edict does not spare the errors of the past. The as-
sumption of the royal ordinances that there were none but
Catholics in France is styled a fiction which can no longer be
admitted.[3] It is alleged that principles so contrary to the public prosperity and tranquillity would have greatly increased the

---

[1] And therefore Louis considered himself warranted in saying to the three
presidents of parliament whom he had summoned: " Avant la révocation de
l'édit de Nantes, les protestants avaient une existence religieuse ; mon édit ne
leur en donne aucune ; les protestants n'y sont pas même nommés." Anquez,
ubi supra, 234.

[2] " Nous avous considéré que les Protestants ainsi dépouillés," etc.

[3] " Cette fiction, aujourd'hui inadmissible."

emigration from the realm and excited continual troubles in families, had not the crown provisionally taken advantage of the powers of the courts of law to set aside grasping collateral heirs who strove to wrest from children the inheritance of their parents. "Such an order of things," Louis frankly admits, "long since called upon us to interpose our authority and put an end to these dangerous contradictions between the rights of nature and the provisions of the law. We had purposed to proceed to the investigation with all the mature deliberation demanded by the importance of the decision. Our resolution had already been agreed upon in our councils, and we intended to reflect still further for some time respecting the legal form ; but circumstances have appeared to us adapted to multiply the advantages which we hope to derive from our new law, and have determined us to hasten the time of its publication. If it be not in our power to prevent that there should be different sects in our states, we shall never suffer them to be therein a source of discord among our subjects. We have adopted the most effectual measure to forestall disastrous associations. The Catholic religion, which we have the good fortune to profess, will alone enjoy in our realm the rights and honors of public worship ; while our other non-Catholic subjects, deprived of all influence upon the order established in our states, declared in advance and forever incapable of forming one body in our realm, subjected to the ordinary regulations for the observance of feast-days, will obtain from the law only what natural justice does not permit us to deny to them—namely, the authentication of their births, marriages, and deaths—in order that they may, like all the rest of our subjects, enjoy the civil effects that result therefrom."

This preamble, at least, was candid. The law to which it was prefixed was honest. Unlike the mendacious revocatory law of Louis the Fourteenth, which while it purposed to render the residence of Protestants in France impossible, offered them a delusive assurance of protection so long as they refrained from disturbing the peace, the Edict of Toleration of Louis the Sixteenth accorded only a small part of what the Protestants could justly demand, but gave assurance of a conscientious execution of its promises, and permitted the beneficiaries to hope for still better things in the near future. On some points the new

edict seemed to be less liberal than the occasional practice of
the government had of late been ; for it distinctly forbade the
judges, or any other persons, to take account of the certificates
of births, marriages, or deaths that might be presented to them
attested by the signatures of ministers or pastors not of the Roman Catholic religion.[1] Nor did it relieve the Protestants from
any duties of respect, from any burdens of a pecuniary character exacted of the Roman Catholics. But, with a sincerity
which none could doubt, it promised them a safe and undisturbed abode in France, and it provided for their enjoyment of
the most essential rights of citizenship. For the future, Protestants desiring to be united in matrimony might elect to go before the Roman Catholic curate or his vicar, or, as they would
be more likely to prefer doing, to present themselves before the
civil judge of the place. In the latter case, the publication of
the bans was to be made by the clerk of the court, at the doors of
the parish church and at the conclusion of the mass. But more
important than any arrangements for the future was the provision whereby all the marriages heretofore celebrated in the
Desert could be rendered legitimate, and the children that were
the offspring of such unions were relieved of the stigma and the
disabilities of bastardy. To this effect it was only necessary
that, within a year from the publication of the edict, the husband and wife should appear, accompanied by four witnesses,
before the curate or the royal judge, and make declaration of
their marriage, giving proof of its date, and of the number,
age, and sex of their children. Thus attested, the record was
to be entered upon the same registers with the marriages of
the Roman Catholics. The curate or vicar that refused to admit it subjected himself to the penalties he would have incurred had the parties belonged to the established church.
Similar arrangements were made for the attestation of births
and deaths. The troublesome matter of the burial of Protestants received special attention. If the Protestants were debarred from the privilege of laying the bodies of their deceased

---

[1] Article 4, l.c.: "Leur défendons spécialement de s'ingérer à délivrer aucuns
certificats de mariages, naissances ou décés, lesquels nous déclarons dés à présent nuls et de nul effet, sans qu'en aucuns cas nos juges ni autres puissent y
avoir égard."

friends in state in front of their houses, as was customary with those who died in the communion of the Roman Catholic church, this and the prohibition to sing or to recite prayers with a loud voice while carrying the remains to their last resting-place, were restraints not likely to be regarded as of much moment by the men who, in the hour when kindly sympathy is most welcome, had long been accustomed not only to every form of lawless violence and popular abuse, but to the legal barbarity of a code which accorded a Protestant a burial little better than that of a dog.

Like the Edict of Nantes, in 1598, and like the revocatory edict of Louis the Fourteenth, in 1685, Louis the Sixteenth's Edict of Toleration, of November, 1787, was declared to be a " perpetual and irrevocable edict." [1]

Another perpetual and irrevocable edict.

Notwithstanding the known desire of the monarch, and the reiterated statements of his purpose to have the law promptly recorded, the Parliament of Paris did not finally enter it upon its registers until the twenty-ninth of January, 1788.[2] Other parliaments of France, to which, according to usage, it was not submitted until it had been approved by the highest judicature of the realm, did not register it until months after. These delays furnished a new opportunity for the manifestation of opposition, as fruitless as the opposition which had preceded the enactment of the edict. One of the members of the Parliament of Paris, Duval d'Eprémenil, an enthusiast who believed that he had heard the voice of the blessed Virgin bidding him to speak against the Protestants, denounced the law as a violation of the oath taken by Louis at his coronation, and in a highly dramatic period, pointing to a crucifix hanging on the walls of the " grand '

The law registered by Parliament, January 29, 1788.

---

[1] The Edict of Toleration is given by Isambert, Recueil des anciennes lois françaises, xxviii. 472–482, and by Le Code Protestant, in the Almanach des Réformés et Protestans pour l'an 1808, pp. 73–92. In both the text is that of the law as modified and registered by Parliament. A subsequent royal declaration extended the term within which the Protestants must apply for the authentication of their marriages to January 1, 1790. Isambert, xxviii. 634.

[2] " Le vingt-neuf cette compagnie enrégistra enfin l'édit si paternel de Louis XVI., qui rendait aux protestans l'exercice de leurs droits civils." Mémoires de Louis XVIII., recueillis et mis en ordre par le duc de D. (Paris, 1832), iii. 315.

chambre," exclaimed : " Will you crucify Him afresh ? " [1]   And, near the end of December, the Archbishop of Paris, with fifteen other members of the episcopal order, begged the monarch in vain, at an audience which he had granted them, to defer the law until the coming assembly of the clergy of France might have the opportunity of remonstrating.   But Louis stood firm to his purpose.[2]

His resoluteness was the more commendable that he lacked the undivided support of his own immediate family.   The clergy in its persistent opposition had succeeded in enlisting in the advocacy of intolerance the championship of the king's youngest brother.   Charles, Count of Artois, a slave to his superstitious fears, was induced to endeavor to dissuade the king from prosecuting his purpose.   Artois's weakness and bigotry only rendered the Count of Provence more indignant than before at the presumption of the hierarchy, which had long shaped the policy of the realm to suit its own narrow views. He mercilessly attacked the Count of Artois for his singular conduct.   For all reply the latter could only say, apologetically, that he wished to save his soul.   " In that case," tartly retorted the future Louis the Eighteenth, " it may be well for you to show yourself less an admirer of the ladies and to diminish the number of your creditors." [3]

From every part of enlightened Europe save one there came to Louis the Sixteenth loud expressions of approval of his course.   The court of Rome alone, we are told, gave him clearly to understand that he had signed his spiritual death-warrant, unless he addressed himself to the pope and confessed the fault he had committed.   " I shall do better," replied Louis ; " for I shall address myself to God." [4]

---

[1] " Voulez-vous le crucifier une seconde fois ? "   Anquez, ubi supra, 220. " On sait," say the Mémoires of Lafayette (i. 219) " quelles résistances cet édit éprouva dans le parlement de Paris, et combien l'allocution fanatique de d'Esprémenil au crucifix de la grand' chambre trouvait encore d'approbateurs."

[2] See the full and valuable account of the action of the parliaments, etc., in Anquez, De l'état civil des réformés de France, 219–249.

[3] " Je le querellai sans pitié, et il me répondit qu'il voulait sauver son âme. Dans ce cas, lui dis-je, montrez-vous moins admirateur des dames, et diminuez le nombre de vos créanciers."   Mémoires de Louis XVIII., iii. 315, 316.

[4] Louis XVIII., who vouches for the truth of this interesting story, remarks:

In the final appeal to France, which was prepared five or six years later, to be issued in the name of Louis the Sixteenth, he was made to lay stress on the Edict of Toleration. "Notwithstanding these private annoyances," said the unfortunate monarch, "I did not desist from my beneficent plans, of which nothing was to suspend the effect. There was one, above all, which had for a long time aroused my feelings. I believed that the time had come to disclose it. I was pained at the injustice exercised for so many years against the adherents of the Reformed religion *(Religionnaires)*, and I regarded it as my duty to repair the severity of the edict of 1685, by giving back to the Protestants the civil status of which they had been deprived for more than a century, and by restoring them to human fellowship *(à la société)*. Accordingly, in the month of November, 1787, I issued my edict in favor of those who did not profess the Catholic religion." [1]

"Ce mot, plein d'esprit et de sens, resta dans l'intérieur de la famille, et je suis bien aise de le rappeler ici." Mémoires, iii. 316.

[1] The Revue Rétrospective, xiv. 323–414, and xv. 1–125, published the full text of the Appel de Louis XVI., roi de France, à la Nation. Paris, 1793. When, according to the Review, it seemed probable that the king would be condemned, Malesherbes instructed Grouber de Groubentall, advocate in the Parliament of Paris, to prepare an appeal in favor of his Majesty. When Louis's sentence was pronounced, and his demand to have recourse to the Nation was rejected, Groubentall promptly destroyed every copy of his work in his possession, with the exception of a single one, which was subsequently presented to Louis XVIII. Its fate is unknown. The printer, however, had preserved the last revised proof, and from this the reprint in the review is said to have been made.

CHAPTER XX

THE FULL RECOGNITION OF PROTESTANTISM

INADEQUATE to their wants as was the Edict of Toleration, the Protestants, now no longer viewed by the law as New Converts, but rejoicing in the recognition of their right to exist, hailed the law as the harbinger of still greater liberality, and hastened to avail themselves of whatever it contained of advantage. The joy expressed in their religious assemblies in the Desert, which no officious servant of government now dreamed of disturbing, was equalled only by the gladness experienced in ten thousand homes. As soon as the welcome tidings of the registry of the beneficent ordinance by the Parliament of Paris reached any district peopled by the descendants of the old Huguenots, a novel scene presented itself to the eye. From many a hamlet, men and women of every station and of every stage in life, from youth to extreme old age, might be seen hastening to the residence of the royal judge, to claim the privilege of securing the sanction of law for a union which, in some cases, had been contracted many years before, and had been hallowed only by the blessing of a proscribed minister of the Desert. There were, among these couples, men and women so far advanced on the journey of life that they were seeking to obtain, along with the official record of their own marriages, the record of the marriage not only of their children, but even of their grandchildren. It was the happy day for whose advent they had long been straining their eyes.[1] Throughout the year the stream continued to pour in the direction of the seats of the courts of justice. Far

Joy created by the Edict of Toleration.

---

[1] See Aperçu de la situation des chrétiens réformés en France, depuis la révocation de l'Édit de Nantes jusqu'à ce jour, in the Almanach des réformés et protestans de l'empire français pour l'an 1808 (Paris, 1808), 12, 13.

from diminishing, it only increased as the season of grace drew toward its close. Some were unavoidably delayed. The infirm, in remote districts, whom the state of their health threatened to preclude from availing themselves of their privilege, were almost in despair, and needed all the encouragement of their more favored brethren. Yet the assurances freely given by the royal keeper of the seals, to the effect that the terms of the law would not be construed too literally, were surely unnecessary. For did not common-sense itself suggest that the monarch could not leave one-half of his Protestant subjects without the legal benefits which the other half alone had been in a situation to accept?[1] Thus wrote Rabaut Saint Étienne to a pastor whose sick and bedridden Cévenol parishioners doubtless deemed their apprehensions not ill-founded; for may they not have remembered that for well nigh a hundred and fifty years it had been an established principle of French jurisprudence that, where the Huguenots were concerned, the terms of edicts must be construed strictly, and that a religion existing only by sufferance was not to be reckoned among "favorable things" for which the terms of law are wont to be graciously interpreted and extended?[2]

No wonder that Huguenot ministers preached joyful sermons. No wonder that with Rabaut Pomier, at Montpellier, in the excess of their delight, they cried out: "Happy am I, if I inspire your hearts and lead you all with me to exclaim, 'O frightful Intolerance! thou that a thousand times hast reddened the earth with blood, thou that art fit only to lay waste kingdoms, where is thy triumph? Thanks be to Reason, to Justice, and to Humanity, which have dashed all thy weapons

---

[1] A recently discovered letter of Rabaut Saint Étienne to Bruguier, pastor at Ners, near Boucoiran, and dated February 8, 1789, contains interesting practical suggestions respecting the course to be pursued under the circumstances. See an article, "Quatre lettres inédits de Rabaut Saint Étienne," in Bulletin de la Soc. de l'hist. du Prot. fr., xxxiv. (1885) 214–227; and the hitherto inedited document, entitled Observations de Rabaut Saint Étienne sur l'édit de Louis XVI. restituant l'état civil aux non-Catholiques, in the same Bulletin, xiii. (1864) 342–352.

[2] The reader will recognize the opinion given by Omer Talon at the Grands Jours de Poitiers, in 1634, to which I have referred above, in Chapter VII., Vol. I., page 357.

to pieces! Heaven grant that thou shalt never again be able to exercise thy rage!'"[1]

Nor was the rejoicing over the new order of things confined to the members of the Reformed communion. The Marquis of Lafayette wrote to his old comrade in arms, General Washington, on the fourth of February, 1788: "The edict that gives a civil status to the king's non-Catholic subjects has been registered. You will easily imagine how much pleasure I had, last Sunday, in presenting at a ministerial board the first Protestant clergyman who has been permitted to make his appearance at Versailles since the Revocation of 1685."[2]   And from the other side of the Atlantic Ocean the aged philanthropist, Benjamin Franklin, sympathetically wrote from Philadelphia: "The *arrêt* in favor of the non-Catholiques gives great pleasure here, not only from its present advantages, but as it is a good step toward general toleration, and to the abolishing, in time, all party spirit among Christians, and the mischiefs that have so long attended it.   Thank God, the world is growing wiser and wiser, and as by degrees men are convinced of the folly of wars for religion, for dominion, or for commerce, they will be happier and happier."[3]

Satisfaction of Lafayette and Franklin.

Yet the law was very incomplete. It by no means satisfied the Protestants. If it allowed them to be born, baptized, married, and, when they died, buried as human, indeed, almost as Christian beings, the lawgiver ostentatiously admitted the fact that he merely conceded to non-Catholics what were their natural rights and what he could no longer deny them.[4] But this very statement seemed to hint that should the Huguenots take it into their heads to gather for divine worship, not in the retirement of the Desert, but near the haunts of men—even, where popular fanaticism was not too

Public worship in the capital.

---

[1] Discours fait à l'occasion de l'édit du roi qui regarde les Protestants, published for the first time in the Bulletin de la Soc. de l'hist. du Prot. fr., xxxvi. (1887) 596–604.

[2] E. Hugues, Les Synodes du Désert, iii. 540.

[3] Letter to M. Le Veillard, Philadelphia, June 8, 1788. Works of Benjamin Franklin, edited by John Bigelow, ix. 481.

[4] "Nos autres sujets non-Catholiques . . . ne tiendront de la loi que ce que le droit naturel ne nous permet pas de leur refuser." Preamble of the edict.

strong, in the crowded towns and cities—they might count upon being unmolested. As yet, however, the government was only willing to wink at a violation of the public ordinances against Protestant worship. It would grant no formal permission; and when the Huguenots of the capital committed the blunder of asking for one, in a long and doubtless very able petition, presented to the minister of the king's house, they received a distinct refusal. They were informed, however, that there were a number of foreign embassies at Paris where they could, doubtless, worship if they so pleased.[1] They were the very embassies, it may be remarked, which Louis the Fourteenth and Louis the Fifteenth had strictly forbidden their subjects to visit for purposes of worship, the very embassies to which spies had often been sent by the police to watch whether any Frenchmen were in attendance. I have before me a list of not less than six special ordinances, issued between the years 1719 and 1740, and directed against such of the king's subjects as should venture to frequent them—the embassies of England and the Netherlands in particular—the penalty being summary arrest.[2] Yet the number of Huguenots that had been willing to incur the risk was not small. The Dutch chaplain, on one occasion, makes the apparently extravagant statement that it would have required an edifice twice as large as Notre Dame de Paris to contain all that applied for admission, and, in 1720, two services were held in his chapel every Lord's day—the one at seven and the other at eleven—for their express accommodation.[3]

A few months now altered the face of the world. Before men realized the momentous change that was taking place, the French Revolution had fairly begun. On the fifth of May, 1789, the States General were convoked at Versailles. It was the first time that the representatives had gathered since the impotent sessions at Paris in the winter of 1614 and 1615. The Protestants of the capital barely waited until the deputies from

---

[1] Armand Lods, L'Église réformée à Paris de la Révocation à la Révolution, 1685–1789, in Bulletin de la Soc. de l'hist. du Prot. fr., xxxviii. (1889) 309.

[2] Ibid., ubi supra, xxxvii. 307. O. Douen, La Révocation de l'Édit de Nantes à Paris, ii. 547.

[3] "Il faudrait deux fois la Notre Dame de Paris." Bulletin, ubi supra.

all parts of France had taken their seats, to secure a place of worship and to begin to conduct regular services—not at Ablon, nor even at Charenton, dear as Charenton had been to their fathers, but in the very heart of Paris. It was on the seventh of June, 1789, that Paul Henri Marron, a former chaplain of the Dutch ambassador, who had been chosen to the office of pastor, first preached from the pulpit in a hall of the Rue de Mondétour (now Rue Turbigo) to a congregation that sat with open doors. The worshippers judged aright that they would not be disturbed by the police. Within two years the hall was exchanged for the old church of Saint Louis, situated within the court of the Louvre, where now stands the Pavillon Mollien. In 1811, when this church, in turn, was torn down, in the work of extending the castle of the Louvre, the Protestants obtained in its stead the large and commodious church of the Oratoire.[1]

The Oratoire and the monument of Coligny. From behind the apsis of this structure the statue of Gaspard de Coligny, recently erected by the descendants of the Huguenots, with the approval and co-operation of the government of republican France, now looks out —a monument of retributive justice—toward the neighboring spot where, three centuries ago, the great Protestant admiral was wounded in front of the cloisters of St. Germain l'Auxerrois, as well as toward that other spot, a house in the old Rue de Béthisy, where, two days later, the brave old warrior was murdered in his room by hired assassins.[2]

Meanwhile, events of national importance pressed hard upon one another. On the fourteenth of July, 1789, the Fall of the Bastile took place, a date from which the French Revolution

---

[1] Armand Lods, ubi supra, xxxviii. 310, 311.

[2] The French government contributed one-third of the expense of the Coligny monument. The municipal council of Paris gave the ground between the apsis of the church and the Place du Louvre, the most suitable site in Paris for such a monument. Private gifts from France, from Great Britain, and, I am happy to say, from some of the descendants of the Huguenots in the United States, paid the remainder of the expense of the monument and provided for the changes in the exterior of the church rendered necessary by its erection. See Bulletin de la Soc. de l'hist. du Prot. fr., xxxii. (1883) 142, 143. A good representation of the striking statue of the admiral, with the two statues of the Fatherland and of Religion, seated below on either side, may be seen in the Bulletin, xxxviii. (1889) 505.

may justly be reckoned. Soon the National Assembly was
busy with the consideration of the Declaration of the Rights
of Man. One of the articles adopted enunciated the

Beginning of
the French
Revolution.

principle, which has ever since been accepted in French
jurisprudence, that all citizens being equal in the eyes
of the law, are equally admissible to all public offices and trusts.
More than any other Frenchmen, the Protestants were deeply
concerned in the provisions of this important document.
Among the most prominent and influential members of the assembly, was Rabaut Saint Étienne, who later was chosen to

Rabaut Saint
Étienne,
President of
the Nation-
al Assem-
bly.

preside over the body, and who on that occasion wrote
to his aged father, Paul Rabaut, exulting in the startling fact that for the first time a Protestant had been
placed in so honorable a post of government: "My
father, the President of the National Assembly is at your
feet!"[1] As a member representing Nismes, at this time the
leading city of French Protestantism, Rabaut Saint Étienne
sought and obtained, on the twenty-third of August, 1789,
permission to express his sentiments on a cardinal point. It
was the first time that a Huguenot had enjoyed the opportunity to make himself heard in the assertion of the perfect equality with the rest of the population to which his long down-
trodden fellow Protestants distinctly laid claim. He spoke to
oppose a restriction which the enemies of full religious liberty
strove to affix to the recognition of the right of public expression of opinion and of religious worship. No man, said the
authors of the Declaration, shall be molested for his religious
opinions nor disturbed in the exercise of his worship. But the
Curé du Vieux Poussange offered an amendment, in the words:
"Provided their manifestation shall not disturb the public order

His speech
on tolera-
tion and lib-
erty.

established by law." This addition Rabaut Saint
Étienne denounced. When he told the Assembly that
his instructions from his constituents directed him to
secure liberty of worship for non-Catholics, a great number of
his colleagues cried out that their own *cahiers* contained the

---

[1] Hugues, Les Synodes du Désert, iii. 571. Rabaut Saint Étienne was the
twenty-first president of the Constituent Assembly, and held office from March
13 to March 28, 1790. See the list in Stephens, History of the French Revolution, i. 532, 533.

same demands, and many others called out "All! All!" He claimed that the non-Catholics had, as the Edict of November, 1787, itself admitted, gained only what could no longer be denied them. That law he styled "more celebrated than just." He demanded, he said, in behalf of two million Protestants, not toleration but their rights as Frenchmen. "Gentlemen," he exclaimed, "it is not *toleration* that I claim, but *liberty*. 'Toleration,' 'sufferance,' 'pardon,' 'clemency'—these are ideas supremely unjust toward dissenters, so long as it shall remain true that difference of opinion is not a crime. 'Toleration!' I demand that 'Toleration' in its turn be proscribed. And it shall be proscribed—that unjust word which presents us only as citizens deserving of pity, as culprits to whom pardon is accorded, as men whom frequently accident and education have led to think otherwise than we do. Error, gentlemen, is not a crime. He that professes it takes it for the truth. It is the truth for him. He is bound to profess it, and no man, no association of men, has the right to forbid him." Speaking in the name of a great *sénéchaussée*, with three hundred and sixty thousand inhabitants, more than one hundred and twenty thousand of whom were Protestants, he begged the National Assembly of France to cast their eyes on the other side of the ocean, and learn a lesson from the inhabitants of the young republic of the New World. "If examples may be cited," he said, "imitate the example of those generous Americans that have placed at the head of their civil code the sacred maxim of universal religious freedom; of those Pennsylvanians who have declared that all who adore one God, in whatever manner they adore Him, shall enjoy every right of citizenship; of those gentle and wise inhabitants of Philadelphia who see all forms of worship established in their city, with twenty different churches, and who perchance owe to this profound acquaintance with liberty the liberty which they have won for themselves." [1]

The effect of the Protestant pastor's speech was mingled sur-

---

[1] Œuvres de Rabaut Saint Étienne (Paris, 1826), ii. 137–150. For an interesting account of the discussion of the bill of rights I must refer to M. Weiss's monograph entitled Les séances des 22 et 23 Août 1789 à l'assemblée nationale, in the Bulletin de la Soc. de l'Hist. du Prot. franç., xxxviii. (1889) 561–575.

prise and admiration of his powers. The *Moniteur* declared that he was "made to be a legislator in the eighteenth century." For a time his reputation seemed to surpass that of Mirabeau himself.[1] Unhappily his eloquence did not avail to induce the Assembly to reject the ill-advised addition to the article of the Declaration of the Rights of Man. It was destined to be fruitful of evil for many a year.

Meanwhile, the recovery of a recognized position in the sight of the law, and even the recovery of full religious liberty, including the right of public worship and admission to offices of trust and emolument, did not satisfy all the claims of the Huguenots. Their goods had been stolen, and they demanded restitution.

When Louis the Fourteenth undertook to strip the Huguenots, his subjects, of that right of expatriation which nature has given to every man, and few even among tyrants have *The confisca-* been audacious enough to challenge or deny, he also *ted property of the Hu-* issued edicts that were intended to rob all successful *guenots.* fugitives of the property which they left behind them. In this way, according to Barère de Vieuzac, the government found itself, as early as in 1689, in possession of the inheritance of over one hundred thousand French citizens. Possibly entertaining scruples as to the propriety of appropriating the riches thus sequestered for his own advantage, the monarch covered the iniquity of the proceeding by devoting the funds to *pious* ends. A portion was given to the "New Converts" to quicken their zeal. Another part fell to the lot of informers and other secret favorites of the men in power. The remainder was intrusted to farmers and administrators of the royal finances, until such time as the government should determine its ultimate destination.[2]

At the end of one hundred years there still remained no inconsiderable part of this fund in the hands of the government. In fact there had been some accessions from property of Protestants subsequently seized on the ground of the illegitimacy of the

---

[1] Weiss, ubi supra, xxxviii. 568.

[2] Report presented to the National Assembly, December 9, 1790, by the Comité des Domaines. Moniteur universel of December 11, 1790.

holders, the offspring of parents whose marriage having been celebrated not before the curate, but by some preacher of the Desert, was viewed as invalid. In the single *sénéchaussée* of Nismes, at the outbreak of the French Revolution, the fund yielded an annual revenue of one hundred and ten thousand livres. The *tiers état* of this sénéchaussée inserted in its petition to the National Assembly, a demand that the confiscated property be restored to the families of the former possessors, on proof of their descent, and even to heirs born in foreign lands, on condition that they returned and took up their abode in France. The noblesse instructed their representatives to adopt similar action in favor of the nearest of kin resident in the kingdom, whether Catholic or non-Catholic.[1]

In obedience to such appeals the National Assembly, on the tenth of July, 1790, passed a decree to the effect that the property of non-Catholics still in the hands of the farmers of the fund should be restored to the heirs, successors, or assigns of the fugitives, and instructed the committee on the public domains to bring forward a plan for the execution of this decision.[2] The committee reported, five months later (on the ninth of December, 1790), a well matured and equitable scheme, which was adopted with applause by the National Assembly. Again was Barère the spokesman, and well did he exhibit the difficulty, amounting in many cases to an impossibility, that would confront the Protestants if they should be compelled to furnish documentary proof of their rights such as, in other circumstances, might properly be demanded of them. " Go back for an instant," said he, " to those unhappy times when superstitious and bloody laws tyrannized over the conscience and branded the persons of men, made a crime of the indefeasible and natural right of emigration, and adjudged to informers, courtiers, or fanatics the goods, even to the very clothes, of emigrants surprised or arrested in their flight. What title-deeds could

Its restoration decreed by the National Assembly.

The appeal of Barère de Vieuzac.

[1] F. Rouvière, Les Religionnaires des diocèses de Nîmes, Alais et Uzès et la Révolution française, 6, 7.
[2] Moniteur universel of July 11, 1790 (original edition p. 788). The motion was made, on behalf of the committee on the domains, by Marsanne Font Julianne, and was adopted after " une légère discussion."

these unfortunates carry with them, and what proofs or family papers could go with these beings who sought only to escape proscriptive laws? What precautions can you suppose to have been taken by men who could neither be born, nor marry, nor live, nor die under the forms prescribed by the laws? Without civil calling though citizens, without wives though married, without heirs though fathers, how should they have busied themselves with getting together and preserving those compacts of union, those titles to succession, those agreements which scarcely preserve the traces of prosperous families? . . . These unfortunate fugitives have left no traces but on the sand of a terrible country that swallowed up their children; and Time has added its ravages to those of religious persecution." [1]

Thus eloquently and successfully were urged the claims of the Huguenots by one of the ablest, but most treacherous, of those that were destined to take part in the horrors of the Reign of Terror. For it was one of the singularities of the fortunes of the Protestants, in this most singular of periods, that as, shortly after the middle of the century they had had, in the matter of toleration, the advocacy of a celebrated freethinker whose views on religious matters were as opposite as possible to theirs, so, near its close, they were materially helped in the recovery of their property by an unprincipled adventurer, destined to pass into history as equally bloodthirsty with Robespierre, and, for his cowardice, even more deserving of the contempt and execration of all honest men.

New perils awaited the Protestant faith, and a religion which had weathered a century of proscription seemed likely to make shipwreck on the rock of infidelity. The triumph of atheism in the new French republic, in the year 1793, is familiar to every reader of general history. To Chaumette and Hébert the deism professed by Robespierre and Saint Just was itself too moderate a creed. They were not content until the worship of Reason had taken the place of the

The triumph of atheism.

---

[1] Barère's speech fills several columns of the Moniteur universel of December 11, 1790 (original edition, pp. 1424, 1425), which also gives the text of the decree itself, which was adopted almost without discussion. M. Rouvière has reprinted a good part of the former and the whole of the latter (pages 8, 9, and 11–17).

worship of God. At the suggestion of Chaumette, the commune banished the Roman Catholic religion from the public
view, forbidding all ministers of religion to perform any act of
worship outside of the edifices erected for the purpose. Pictures and images of the Virgin and saints were removed from
the streets. Funeral processions ceased. The cross and every
other Christian emblem disappeared from the gate of the cemetery, and, in their stead, a statue of Sleep was reared as an emblem of the state of endless unconsciousness that had overtaken
the dead. "Reason" reigned supreme. On the seventh of
November, 1793, Gobel, "constitutional" archbishop

Archbishop
Gobel lays
down his
mitre and
crosier.

of Paris, came with a retinue of inferior clergy to the
hall of the National Convention, and laid down his
mitre, his crosier, and his episcopal ring. If he did
not formally abjure his faith and declare that he had all his
life been deceiving men, he gave his hearers to understand that,
as he became bishop at a time when the people wanted bishops,
so he now ceased to be a bishop when the people wanted
bishops no longer. Other ecclesiastics went farther than Gobel,
and, together with their certificates of priesthood, boldly renounced their faith, which they stigmatized as fanaticism.[1]

The flood-tide that swept Gobel and others from their moor-
ings also bore some Protestants along in its resistless course.
A few days before the scene to which I have just referred was
enacted, the council of the newly re-established Protestant
church of Paris adopted a resolution that divine worship should
henceforth (from the twenty-first of October onward) be held
on the *décadi*—the tenth day, recently set apart as a public
holiday in place of the weekly Christian day of rest. It was
not at first the intention of the council to dispense with all exercises on the Lord's day; but less than a fortnight elapsed
before a new resolution was passed to give up all services except
those held on the décadi. The mover, strange to say, was the
Protestant pastor himself, Paul Henri Marron. A minister
who, through fear, could adopt so cowardly a course was sure
to go farther; and it may surprise us less than it otherwise
might, that, on the thirteenth of November (or six days after

---

[1] Thiers, Hist. de la Révolution française (Paris, 1834) v. 435–443.

Gobel's public renunciation of his office), Marron appeared before the municipal officers of the commune of Paris, and offered Paul Henri Marron offers to the Convention the chalices of the Protestant church. up the four silver cups used by his church at the celebration of the holy communion, the only pieces of plate in its possession. All ranks of society, said he, without discrimination, used to drink, from these cups, Equality, Fraternity, inseparable associates of Liberty. It was a system worthy of respect, which at last the daylight of Reason, long eclipsed by the clouds of Superstition and Fanaticism, now gilded with the most brilliant splendor. As for himself, his ministry had always aimed at propagating this system. His conscientious views had undergone no change. His was an ardent love for the Revolution, and the fortunes of no one had been more closely bound to the Revolution than had his. He had no letters of priesthood to sacrifice upon the altar of Truth. He had never received any. Such absurd diplomas were unknown in the land of his birth (Holland). " But receive, citizens," he added, " my inviolable oath to co-operate, with a zeal eager not to lag behind yours, in extending the kingdom of Reason, and in establishing upon laws that cannot be shaken the august sway of Liberty, Equality, and Fraternity. Hatred to all those structures of lies and puerilities which Ignorance and Dishonesty have dignified with the pompous name of Theology ! Homage to good sense, to virtue, to the eternal and immortal principles of Evidence and Morality ! *Vive la République !* "

Such was the unworthy address of the minister of a religion which, but six years before, had won the first concessions of a freedom long the object of its highest aspirations. If not an explicit surrender of the whole body of truth for which the Protestant martyrs of three centuries in great numbers had cheerfully laid down life, the words of Marron, to say the least, cast wanton dishonor on the mode in which those witnesses for the truth had delighted to set forth their views. And the minister who had so shamefully lowered the standard of his conviction amply merited the cynical remarks with which the president of the commune replied : " Under the reign of Philosophy prejudices disappear, truth shines forth, and, by an irresistible impulse, men hasten to abjure their error. If any religion could be preserved, it would be that one in which all the citizens used to drink from a single cup ; but reason rules and the people drives far from it all that has to do with superstition, all that can obscure its genius.   Hereafter let men have no other worship than that of Liberty and Equality !   May sound morality take the place of fanaticism !   May the pulpit of falsehood become the pulpit of truth, and then we shall be truly free and worthy of being free ! " [1]

It is affirmed that the sentiments uttered by Marron were not his real convictions, and that men knew that they were not. However this may be, it is some satisfaction that his poltroonery did not avail to save the recreant pastor from suspicion and arrest.   It would not have saved him from the guillotine had not the fall of Robespierre and the end of the Reign of Terror opportunely intervened.[2]

As in the case of Archbishop Gobel there were Roman Catholic ecclesiastics that went beyond him and openly published Some priests   their hypocrisy, so also there were Protestant pastors and pastors   who, not content with the cowardly pretences of Mar-
abjure.   ron, seemed to glory in proclaiming their own shame. The pastor of Condé gave up his religious services, declaring to his parishioners that he did not believe a word of what he had been preaching to them for the last twenty years.[3]   Others, not so outspoken, showed with equal clearness that they were entirely devoid of principle.   I am not able to state the number of the ministers of either religion that apostatized under the influence of mingled fear and desire of popular applause.   It was doubtless considerable.[4]

---

[1] Unfortunately this discreditable incident rests upon the best of documentary evidence—detached leaves of the minutes of the consistory of the church of Paris, forming part of the important Collection Coquerel (xxvi. 225 et seq.), now in the library of the Bibliothèque du Protestantisme Français.   See Bulletin de la Soc. de l'hist. de Prot. fr., xxxviii. (1889) 363–365.

[2] Ibid., xxxviii. 367, 368.

[3] Léon Maury, Le Réveil religieux (Paris, 1892), i. 407.

[4] Francisque Mège, in his interesting book, Le Puy de Dôme en 1793 et le proconsulat de Couthon (Paris, 1877), 334 et seq., says that he cannot state accurately the whole number of Roman Catholic priests that renounced their orders in the diocese of Clermont, but that there were about seventy in the single district of Ambert.   There was a curious variety in their procedure.   Some merely

Happily there was a large number of ministers of both communions who, while forced by the Reign of Terror to be silent and suspend for the time their religious functions, were far from acquiescing in the impious course of the commune, and watched their opportunity to bring the people back from their mad frenzy. Of this number was Jean Frédéric Oberlin, the philanthropic pastor of the villages of the Ban de la Roche, in Alsace. To resist openly the absurd innovations of the commune and the National Convention would have been sheer madness; but, as we shall shortly see, Oberlin, by his tact, was able to direct the course of the stream which would have overwhelmed him had he undertaken to stand in its way.

For the observance of the worship of Reason and of the *décadi* devoted to this purpose was formally instituted at the capital and quickly spread to every other part of France. In the great metropolitan church of Notre Dame de Paris, a young woman was enthroned at the grand altar as the living representation of the Goddess of Reason. That same day—it was the twentieth day of Brumaire, or the tenth of November, 1793—Chaumette announced to the National Convention the arrival of the new goddess to the halls of legislation. A group of young musicians opened the way, followed by orphan girls, children of defenders of their country who had laid down life in its defence, singing a patriotic hymn. A motley crowd of citizens wearing the red liberty cap next entered shouting " *Vive la République! Vive la Montagne!* " After them a military band filled the air with the cherished airs of the republic. They preceded a bevy of young women dressed in white, with a girdle of red, white, and blue, and crowned with flowers. Behind them came the goddess herself, a handsome woman, borne aloft in an armchair by four men, a liberty cap on her head, a blue cloak above her white

[margin note:] Worship of the Goddess of Reason.

---

submitted. Some asserted that they had acted hitherto in all good faith, but that now, being better instructed " by the torch that directs the republicans," they recognized their error. Others posed as thinkers and made a profession of a philosophical creed. The curé of Novacelles told the members of his district that he was a priest contrary to his will, and that he came to ask of them his regeneration and to take refuge in the ark of the *sans-culotterie*, out of which he agreed that there was no salvation!

dress, and in her hands a pike supporting a blue ensign on which the word " Reason " was inscribed. Then it was that, as the strange divinity that was to take the place of the old, paused in front of the chair of the presiding officer, Chaumette again addressed the legislators of France. " Fanaticism," he said, " has lost its hold. It has abandoned the place it occupied to reason, justice, and truth. . . . To-day all the people of Paris has gone beneath the Gothic arches, so long resounding only with the voice of error, which for the first time have echoed the cry of truth. . . . We have not offered our sacrifices to vain images, to inanimate idols. No, it is a masterpiece of nature that we have chosen for the purpose of representing her (Reason), and this sacred image has inflamed all hearts. One single wish, one single cry made itself heard on every side. The people said : ' No more priests ! No more gods save those that nature offers us ! ' " Whereupon, on the motion of Chabot, Notre Dame was voted to be the Temple of Reason for all future time ; and on the motion of another, the living goddess was admitted to sit beside the president of the National Convention, where, amid rapturous applause, she was saluted by him and by the secretaries with a fraternal kiss. The meeting broke up that its members and the citizens of Paris, in a promiscuous band, might go to the Temple of Reason, there to sing the hymn to Liberty.[1]

Thus it was that, boasting of freedom, in the midst of a popular tyranny under the reign of which no man's life or liberty was safe for an hour, men fancied themselves to have reached a pinnacle of enlightenment at the wild vagaries and irrational antics of whom posterity scarcely knows whether to laugh in derision or to shed the tear of pity.

If the provinces could not emulate the pomp with which the practice of the strange cult was inaugurated at the capital, none the less did the minor towns and villages undertake to establish

---

[1] See the graphic account, which I have followed, in the columns, otherwise dreary enough, of the Moniteur Universel, of November 13, 1793.—The representation of the scene in Notre Dame, from the brush of C. L. Muller, of which Charles d'Hericault gives a fine reproduction in his magnificent work La Révolution 1789–1882 (Paris, 1883), represents the " goddess " as trampling under foot a crucifix. One of the crowd brandishes a wine-bottle.

and maintain meetings on every *décadi*, at which all the virtues, collectively and severally, were descanted upon by the popular orators to their hearts' content, if not to any great satisfaction on the part of the people. For soon the poor travesty of worship was found to be a very meagre substitute for a religion, the meetings becoming for the most part the object of general derision, the sensible avoiding them as much as possible from the beginning, and their neighbors speedily following their example.[1]

Oberlin had greeted the advent of the Revolution with ardent hopes, and he was not disconcerted by the decree of the National Convention ordering the suppression of all religious worship. The new law bade every commune elect a president. This president was instructed to designate some one to be the orator of the clubs, and as such to deliver an address on some moral and patriotic subject. Oberlin forthwith convened the inhabitants of his commune and laid before them the Convention's decree. The commune without delay made choice of the schoolmaster to be president, and the schoolmaster appointed Oberlin orator. His nomination was welcomed and confirmed by the loud acclamation of the people. Thus invested with authority, he found no trouble in inducing his former parishioners to hold their meetings under the new order of things in the church, this being the only building suited to be a place of assembly. His first address was a sufficient indication of his plan, as it was also an evidence of his sound judgment. " According to the decree of the Convention," he said, by way of exordium, " I am to speak against tyrants, and we are to concern ourselves with their destruction." Then,

Oberlin's tact.

---

[1] According to Francisque Mège, in his book Le Puy de Dôme en 1793, page 339, the proconsul Couthon instituted popular societies in the department of Puy de Dôme, under the name of *comités d'instruction publique*, and these sent out missionaries to preach on *décadi* days upon the rights and duties of the people. The missionaries had little success in securing an audience. Some flatly refused to come to hear persons to whom they applied such uncomplimentary epithets as "*canaille*" or "*damnés d'huguenots.*" Thereupon constraint was resorted to for the purpose of enforcing the attendance of the reluctant hearers. It was a new and startling illustration of the once current exegesis of the " *Compelle intrare* " of the parable.

after explaining what is ordinarily meant by the word "tyrant," he added : "Here, in our peaceful Ban de la Roche, we assuredly have no tyrants of this sort, and it would be superfluous to speak against them. But I can name and describe to you other tyrants that dwell not only in Ban de la Roche, but in your houses and even in your hearts. They are your sins, and the only means of overcoming and destroying them is faith in Jesus Christ." At the close of his address he asked his hearers to sing a psalm. Thus it was that, under another name, he reinstituted the exercises of divine worship and maintained them through the perilous days of the new proscription at the hands of intolerant infidelity.[1]

The Reign of Terror did not pass without depriving the Protestants of France of some of their best men, and among these losses not the least was that of Rabaut Saint Étienne. This excellent pastor was not only the most effective worker in securing the Edict of Toleration of 1787. He was also, perhaps, from the beginning the man who entertained the most intelligent views of the true scope and possibilities of the Revolution. It was he who, anticipating by a year the Abbé Sieyès's famous definition of the *Tiers État*,[2] gave to the world, or at least to the French, the first intelligent view of the position of the people in the body politic : "The third estate is the nation, minus the noblesse and the clergy. The clergy is not the nation ; it is an aggregate of two hundred thousand nobles or commoners, devoted to the worship of the altars or of religion. The noblesse is not the nation, but the part of the nation that is honored with titles. It is a certain number of Frenchmen to whom are accorded certain hereditary honors and prerogatives. Cut off, let us suppose, the two hundred thousand ecclesiastics that there may be in France, and you still have the nation. Cut off in like manner all the noblesse, you still have the nation ; for to-morrow a thousand nobles can

Rabaut Saint Étienne put to death.

---

[1] I have followed the narrative of Léon Maury, Le Réveil religieux, i. 264, 265. Two ladies by the name of Berckheim have left a graphic description of a visit which they made to Oberlin's services at this critical period. It is reproduced in Dr. Maury's appendix, ii. 393-396.

[2] "Qu'est-ce que le Tiers État ? Tout.—Qu'a-t-il été jusqu' ici ? Rien.—Que demande-t-il ? Devenir quelque chose."

be created, as was done at the return from the Crusades. But if you cut off the twenty-four millions of Frenchmen known by the name of the 'Third Estate,' what will remain? Nobles and ecclesiastics. But there will no longer be a nation. Therefore it is evident that the Third Estate is the nation, minus the noblesse and clergy." [1]

So intelligent, upright, and patriotic a man as Rabaut Saint Étienne must needs have renounced all participation in public affairs to avoid death at the hands of the reckless pilots who had made themselves masters of the ship of state. Rabaut Saint Étienne's particular offence was that he was a member of a commission of twelve, which ordered the arrest of the infamous Hébert. Called upon to justify himself and his associates, he stood in the Convention for two hours, vainly attempting to speak, and interrupted at every sentence by Marat, Bazire, and others. Two days after he was placed under arrest, but made his escape only to be discovered and executed some six months later.[2]

It may interest the reader to know that it was as the friend and representative of the man whom America honors above all other Frenchmen, for his participation in the War of American Independence, that Rabaut Saint Étienne was most heartily hated. The address which the deputation of twenty-seven sections of Paris presented to the Convention denouncing Rabaut, began thus : " An unjust and arbitrary commission oppresses the patriots and throws them into irons. The traitor Lafayette is not in the dungeons of Berlin ; the priest Rabaut, his apologist, the editor of four poisonous journals—this four-salaried legislator reigns within our walls, and Lafayette triumphs. He sees the blood of the patriots flow, he is going to walk over their dead bodies. Arrest him!" [3]

---

[1] Considérations très importantes sur les intérêts du Tiers État (1788), in Dardier, Lettres de Paul Rabaut à divers, ii. 374, 375.

[2] Collin de Plancy, Notice sur Rabaut Saint Étienne, prefixed to Œuvres (Paris, 1826), i. p. xi. R.'s speech, of May 31, 1793, with the rude interruptions, ibid., ii. 230–233, and in the Moniteur Universel for Sunday, June 2, 1793.

[3] Moniteur Universel for Saturday, June 1, 1793, giving the minutes of the session of the preceding Thursday.

Even before the fall of Robespierre the undisputed reign of atheism had been broken. On the motion of Chaumette, the commune, fearful of the revulsion which its extreme measures would certainly arouse, declared that, by its action closing all the churches, it had not intended to interfere with religious liberty, and that it did not forbid the adherents of any religion from gathering together in places of worship paid for and supported at their own expense. The National Convention took a similar course, and, in addition, forbade that the plate still remaining in the churches should be touched, as the treasury had no farther need of it. From this time, we are told, the indecent farces in which the people had engaged in Paris and the pomps connected with the worship of Reason were abolished.[1] Chaumette was sent to the guillotine on the thirteenth of April, 1794. Little more than a month elapsed before it was proposed by Robespierre himself that the republic should recognize the existence and lend the sanction of law to the worship of a Supreme Being. "In the eyes of the law-giver," he said, "everything that is useful for the world and that is good in practice is the truth. The idea of the Supreme Being and of the immortality of the soul is a continual call to justice ; it is therefore social and republican. . . . Who has given you the mission to proclaim to the people that the Deity does not exist, you that have a passion for this arid doctrine, and have never had a passion for your native land ? What advantage do you find in persuading man that a blind force presides over his destiny and smites at random crime and virtue, that his soul is but a light breath that is extinguished at the portals of the grave ? Will the notion of his nothingness inspire him with purer and loftier sentiments than the notion of his immortality ? Will it inspire him with more respect for his kind and for himself, more devotion for fatherland, more boldness in braving tyranny, more contempt for death or for pleasure ? "

Thus it was that, in his speech of the eighteenth Floréal (the seventh of May, 1794), Robespierre urged a return from atheism as a sound political measure, and secured, amid universal

End of the reign of atheism.

Robespierre proposes the recognition of the Supreme Being.

---

[1] Thiers, Révolution française, vi. 25.

acclamation, the adoption of a decree whose articles asserted that the French people recognized the existence of the Supreme Being and the immortality of the soul, declared that it regarded the practice of man's duties as the worship most worthy of the Supreme Being, and instituted celebrations, on all the successive days of *décadi*, in honor of great thoughts and virtues, the celebration of the Supreme Being being at the head of the long list.

The decree, it must be noticed, contained a new proclamation of the right of freedom of worship.[1]

A pompous service in honor of the Supreme Being followed on the twentieth of Prairial (the eighth of June, 1794), and soon from the fronts of the church buildings throughout France on which the words "À LA RAISON" had so recently been inscribed, the former dedication was erased, to make room for a new one, À L'ÊTRE SUPRÊME."[2] In place of Reason, the Supreme Being and Virtue were on every man's lips; and everybody believed himself both virtuous and religious.

On the ninth of Thermidor (the twenty-seventh of July, 1794) Robespierre was overthrown. On the morrow he paid the penalty of his detestable crimes by the forfeit of his life. It was a day of deliverance and happiness for all France.[3]

End of the Reign of Terror.

The principle of religious liberty was endorsed by the constitution of 1795 (Year III.), which provided that all forms of worship should be free, although not recognized by the state nor supported at public expense.[4] Sustained by the popular vote, practically unanimous throughout France, this gave an assurance to Protestants, as well as to Roman Catholics, that they might count upon protection in their rights for the future. Accordingly, no sooner was the law promulgated than all the Protestant pastors hastened to

Religious worship is resumed.

---

[1] The Moniteur Universel of Nonidi, 19 Floréal An II. (Thursday May 8, 1794), giving an account of the meeting of the previous day, at which Carnot presided. The full text of Robespierre's speech, "in the name of the Committee of Public Safety," is given.

[2] Thiers, Révolution française, vi. 258–262.

[3] Aperçu de la situation des chrétiens réformés en France, 16.

[4] Thiers, Révolution française, viii. 16.

make the declaration which was required of them recognizing the sovereignty of the French people and promising submission and obedience to the laws of the republic. In a number of departments the consistories began to secure buildings for public worship. Many Protestant churches, however, unable to procure for themselves suitable edifices, continued to hold their services, as they had long held them during the prevalence of persecution, in the open fields, or, as men still continued to express themselves, from long practice, in the Desert. This state of things continued for the next six or seven years, or until the publication of the law of the eighteenth of Germinal of the Year X. (the seventh of April, 1802), of which I shall shortly speak, and which constitutes the natural term of this history.[1] It was a period of gradual reconstruction. The work had now to be undertaken which the Huguenots had not, since the removal of the ban under which they had lain for a century, had the time seriously to commence. For within less than two years after the signing of the Edict of Toleration, and scarcely more than a twelvemonth from the registration by the Parliament of Paris, the great Revolution broke out. Since then the thoughts of men had taken an entirely different direction, leaving no opportunity for the further exercise of that wonderful recuperative power which the churches of the Desert put forth. More than this, the storm with which the cult of reason and atheism swept over the land was not without its temporary blighting effects. It required time and patience to recover from them.

No sooner had Napoleon Bonaparte, as first consul, firmly grasped the reins of government, than he turned his thoughts The Concordat with Pope Pius VII. 1801. seriously to a definite adjustment of the relations of France with the pope and the Roman Catholic Church. By the Concordat with Pius the Seventh, made on the fifteenth of July, 1801, Napoleon readmitted the former established religion to its ancient position of honor and influence, not, indeed, as the sole religion of France, but as the religion of the majority of the French people. In return for the benefit

---

[1] Aperçu de la situation des chrétiens réformés en France, 16. See, also, De Félice, 557.

thus conferred, the Roman pontiff was willing to grant to the
new ruler larger prerogatives in ecclesiastical matters than had
been enjoyed by any previous king. Pius freely divested himself of the right of appointment of all future bishops and archbishops, merely reserving for himself and his successors the,
barren privilege of giving canonical investiture. He went so
far as to recognize as valid the sale of church lands and houses
by the revolutionary government, accepting in lieu of all endowment for the support of the clergy the generous provision
which the government pledged from the public revenues.

The very arrangement made for the maintenance and control of the religion of the majority of the French people im-
plied a suitable, and, so far as might be, similarly ad-
vantageous arrangement in favor of the dissidents
constituting a recognized minority. This was not long
in coming. Portalis, later Minister of Public Worship, a man of
intelligence, probity, and energy, took the chief part in effecting
it. The report which he presented to the first consul, and which
has recently been published for the first time,[1] testifies to his
enlightened sentiments and his equipoise of judgment. In matters general and common, such as civil and political laws, their
constitution and forms, the will of the majority, said Portalis, is
binding upon the minority. It is otherwise with worship, its
rites and its dogmas, which are matters special and voluntary.
Protestantism, therefore, though the religion of the smaller
number, is entitled to independence and to protection. Moreover, Protestantism merits special marks of consideration and
kindness. Its founders were the first to spread throughout
Europe liberal maxims of government. They have advanced
morals, philosophy, the sciences, and the liberal arts. In recent
times they have been the first to place themselves under the
flag of liberty, and they have never deserted it. It is therefore
the duty of the government to assure its protection to the
peaceable gatherings of this enlightened and generous minority
of citizens who assemble in their churches with the laudable

Report of Portalis to the first consul.

---

[1] Rapport inédit présenté au premier consul sur l'organisation des cultes
protestans. An X. in the Bulletin de la Soc. de l'hist. du Prot. franç., xxxviii.
(1889) 413-416.

purpose of learning and practising the precepts of the religion
of Christ.

One thing alone ought, according to Portalis, to distinguish
the Protestant minority from the Roman Catholic majority.
While equally independent, the Protestants should be
left to support their religion at their own expense. In
justification of this exception three reasons were alleged : First, the use of the public funds belongs to
the category of general and common matters, in which
the numerical minority of the citizens is subject to the majority.
Second, the application of the national funds to the support of
the Roman Catholic worship is not, under present circumstances, a gratuitous gift of munificence.   Third, in the Concordat the obligation assumed by the state is compensated by the
right acquired by the government to exercise a direct influence
upon the administration of the church, in determining its
bounds, in determining the bounds of the dioceses and parishes,
in nominating the bishops, and in giving or refusing its approval of the nomination of the inferior ministers.

He proposes to leave the Protestant pastors without salary from the state.

I have been thus particular in respect to the last point, for
the reason that the wise suggestions of Portalis were thwarted
through the ill-advised and short-sighted views of
Protestants of influence.   The yoke of slavery to the
civil government, from which Portalis would have
freed the Protestants, in the interest of their independence, was placed upon their neck by the request of some of
their own number, in the interest of the fancied strength and
stability of their position.   A church possessed of the authority to elect all its future ministers, a church whose ministers
were merely required, before entering upon their functions, to
obtain the approval of the government, and to take an oath "of
submission to the laws and obedience to the government instituted by the constitution of the republic "—such a church might,
indeed, claim to enjoy almost perfect independence.   But was
not this independence purchased at the expense of constant
exposure to perils such as had but recently been experienced ?
Was it not better to sacrifice something in order to obtain
security under the protection of the civil power ?   The "notable " Protestants of Paris answered these questions in the

His plan thwarted by the Protes- tants of Paris.

affirmative, and demanded a union of the Reformed and Lutheran churches with the state.[1] They had done better to trust
to the working of the well-regulated system of synodical government of their fathers, and to the generous support
of the members of their own communion. For, if they
secured from the state an annual grantof money for the
support of their ministers, too large to be willingly renounced,
while too niggardly to suffice for their decent maintenance, they
reduced those ministers at the same time to the position of paid
officials. The first consul, soon to become emperor of France,
desired nothing better than to extend to the Protestant churches
the control which he already exercised over the Roman Catholic Church. In accepting the desire expressed by the notable
Protestants of Paris, and drawing up the law that went into
effect, Portalis bluntly stated it to the first consul, as a recommendation of the measure, that, by paying the pastors, the government placed them "in immediate dependence and could easily stop, suspend, or withhold the salary of such or such a
pastor and assure itself of the submission and obedience of
all."[2]

Results of this mistake.

The organic law for the Protestant churches of France was
dated the eighteenth of Germinal of the tenth year of the Republic, or the seventh of April, 1802.

The first section applies equally to the Reformed churches
and to the churches of the Confession of Augsburg, or the
Lutheran churches. It defines in detail the relations
of both to the state. None but a Frenchman can
officiate in public worship. Neither ministers nor
churches can enter into relations with foreign powers
or authorities. Prayers must be offered for the prosperity of
the republic and of the consuls. No doctrinal decision or confession of faith may be promulgated or taught, and no change in

Provisions of the law of the 18th Ger-minal (April 7, 1802).

---

[1] Armand Lods, L'Église réformée de Paris pendant la révolution, in the
Bulletin de la Soc. de l'hist. du Prot. franç., xxxviii. (1889) 467.

[2] Report of Portalis, 22 Brumaire, An XII. (November 12, 1803), in Lods, ubi
supra, xxxviii. 469.—"Leurs pasteurs," says the author of the Aperçu de la
situation des chrétiens réformés en France (p. 20), "devinrent des fonction-
naires publies salariés par le gouvernement et confirmés par lui dans leurs
charges."

discipline may be made, until authorized by the government. Provision shall be made for the salary of the pastors of consistorial churches. There shall be two academies or theological seminaries in the eastern part of France for the training of ministers for the Lutheran churches, and one, at Geneva, for that of ministers of the Reformed churches.[1] All professors will be appointed by the first consul. A definite time of study at these seminaries, and a certificate from them, will be exacted of all persons before they can be elected pastors in either of the Protestant communions. The regulations adopted for the management of the seminaries, the number and quality of the professors, the method and subjects of instruction, and the certificates given, are all to be approved by the government. The supervision could scarcely have been more complete.

The second section of the law applies particularly to the Reformed churches. These churches are to have pastors, local consistories, and synods. There is to be one consistorial church for six thousand souls belonging to the Reformed communion, and five consistorial churches will form the territory of a synod. Each consistory shall be composed of the pastor or pastors of the individual church and the elders or notable laymen—not less than six nor more than twelve in number—chosen from among the citizens paying the largest direct taxes to the state. To this body is intrusted the maintenance of discipline, the administration of the finances, and the distribution of the alms given by the people. It is to elect all future pastors and to remove them for cause, but neither election nor removal is to take effect without the approval of government. No extraordinary

---

[1] It will be remembered that the old republic of Geneva had been forcibly annexed to France, with scarcely a semblance of popular consent, April 15, 1798. This was in the time of the Directory. A. Daguet, Histoire de la Confédération suisse, 488. The extraordinary commission which had been elected to deliberate on the relations of the republic to France met on the afternoon of the day on which sixteen hundred French troops had entered the city by three different gates, and it reluctantly voted in favor of the union, in the hope that the conditions would be less hard. See the excellent chapter on the subject in Charles Dardier's work, Ésaïe Gasc, citoyen de Genève (Paris, 1876), and especially pages 205-209.—The modern Protestant Theological Faculty of Montauban was established, as we have seen, by the imperial decree of September 17, 1808. Ibid., 219.

meeting can be held without express permission of the subprefect or mayor. The permission of the government is required for the assembling of the synods, each of which consists of one pastor and one elder or notable from each of the five churches within its bounds. All matters that are to come before it must be submitted in advance to the councillor of state charged with affairs respecting public worship. Every session must be held in the presence of the prefect or subprefect of the department, who shall forward the minutes of the deliberations to the councillor of state aforementioned. The latter is enjoined to report thereupon as speedily as possible to the government. Six days are set down as the extreme limit of the duration of the synod's sessions.[1]

Such was the plan of organization under which the Reformed churches were reconstituted by Napoleon Bonaparte. It has remained in force, essentially unchanged, up to the present day. Without provision for anything above a meeting of five adjacent churches, to be convened at irregular intervals and then only by permission of the civil authorities, the law of the eighteenth of Germinal, while taking the Reformed churches under its protection, held forth no prospect of the re-establishment of that orderly system of self-government by colloquies and provincial and national synods which had once been their pride and constituted their strength. Nor was it until the year 1872, or after the lapse of full seventy years, that the government was induced to authorize the convocation of a general or national synod, the first held since 1659. Even this synod has as yet had no successor, the government deeming it prudent, in view of divergencies developed in that assembly, to protect the minority by declining to convene a body which might give to the views of the greater number the sanction of law. This inconvenience the churches have attempted to remedy, not without success, by the shrewd device of instituting a system of national and particular synods, differing from those which they desired in little save that their decisions are binding only upon those who choose to accept them. The synod in each case is, to use French terms, *officieux* and not *officiel.*

---

[1] The Loi du 18 Germinal An X., Articles organiques des cultes protestans may be read in the Almanach des Réformés et Protestans pour 1808, pages 27–37.

With the promulgation of the law of the eighteenth of Germinal, the history of the Huguenots and the Revocation of the Edict of Nantes properly ends.   So far as legislation could effect that result, the mischief wrought by the act of Louis the Fourteenth, so cruel to the Huguenots, so pernicious to France entire, might be said, not without truth, to be fully repaired.[1]   The Revocation was based upon a false opinion that Protestantism, thanks to the measures put into operation for that end, had almost, if not quite, ceased to exist ; the new law not only admitted its existence, but made provision for its perpetuity.   The Revocation proscribed the Reformed worship ; the new law took this worship under the protection of the state.   The Revocation ordered the Huguenot ministers to leave France within a fortnight, commanding them on pain of the galleys to abstain, meanwhile, from preaching or exercising any other function of their office ; the new law pledged them a salary to be paid by the public treasury.   The Revocation closed every school of every grade ; the new law declared that there should be a seminary in the city of Calvin for the systematic training of young men for the ministry, and ordained that no person should be elected minister or pastor of a Reformed church without having studied in that seminary and without bringing a certificate of study from its professors.

Louis the Sixteenth in his Edict of Toleration, fifteen years before, had restored to the Huguenots an existence in the eyes of the law, avowedly conceding only those rights which it was impossible longer to deny ; but he had given them no freedom of worship.   Later, the National Assembly invested non-Catholics with all the rights enjoyed by the rest of the population, and forbade that any person should be molested because of his opinions.   The same body, in 1790, made provision for the restoration of the property of Protestant refugees to their lawful heirs.   But it remained for the law of the eighteenth of Germinal to set the capstone of this monument of religious liberty, by

The law closes the history of the Huguenots and the Revocation.

---

[1] " Ce ne fut qu' à cette époque du 18 Germinal qu'il leur rendit les droits qu'ils avaient à son attention et à son intérêt, et que la révocation de l'édit de Nantes, si malheureuse pour eux et pour toute la France, fut entièrement réparée."   Aperçu de la situation, etc., p. 20.

formally re-establishing the public worship of a long proscribed faith.

It was therefore with perfect sincerity that the deputies of the Protestants, a few months later, on the occasion of the coronation of Napoleon Bonaparte as emperor, rendered him thanks for the engagements which he had taken and which he had just confirmed by an oath. To whom the emperor replied : " I see with pleasure the pastors of the Reformed churches of France here gathered together. I eagerly embrace this oppor-

Napoleon Bonaparte on religious lib- erty. tunity to testify to them how well satisfied I have al- ways been with everything reported to me of the loy- alty and the good conduct of the pastors and citizens of the different Protestant communions. I am desirous that it should be known that my intention and my firm purpose are to maintain religious liberty. The domain of law ends where begins the indefinite domain of conscience. The law and the monarch can do nothing against that liberty. Such are my principles and the principles of the nation ; and if some one of those of my blood, succeeding me, were to forget the oath I have taken, and, deceived by the suggestion of a perverted con- science, should go so far as to violate it, I devote him to public animadversion, and I authorize you to give him the name of Nero." [1]

Nearly three centuries had elapsed since Jacques Lefèvre d'Étaples discovered in the Holy Scriptures the long neglected doctrine of justification by faith, the cardinal doctrine of the Reformation, and grasping by the hand his pupil Farel, uttered in impressive tones the prediction : " Guillaume, the world is about to be renewed, and you will behold it ! " To the story of that renovation and of the brave people who in France es- poused the religious views promulgated by Lefèvre and others of like mind that came after him, the volumes now given to the public and the volumes that preceded them have been devoted.

The sixteenth century witnessed the rise and rapid growth of the religious and political party that came to be known

---

[1] The address of M. Martin, of Geneva, in behalf of the Protestants, and the reply of Bonaparte, are given in the Almanach des Réformés et Protestans pour 1808, 21-23.

by the name of the Huguenots. The bloody persecutions, culminating in the Massacre of Saint Bartholomew's Day, proved powerless to exterminate its adherents. Equally impotent was the warfare of Henry the Third and of the League; and the Edict of Nantes, voluntarily accorded to the Huguenots by their former ally and companion-in-arms, Henry of Navarre, now become Henry the Fourth of France, was but the acknowledgment of the patent fact that Protestantism in France had won an established position. These events I have set forth in my earlier histories. In the present work I have treated of the attempt to undo the work of the great Henry, from the gradual encroachments under Louis the Thirteenth to the more rapid and more violent measures that prepared the way for the formal Revocation of the Edict by Louis the Fourteenth. I have also pointed out the consequences of the recall in the great emigration, the suppression of Protestant worship save in the proscribed conventicles of the Desert, and the war of the Camisards, into which fanaticism was driven by cruel intolerance. Finally, I have delineated the gradual recovery by the oppressed Huguenots of their ecclesiastical organization and of the civil and religious rights from which they had been long debarred, until, after being barely tolerated, they were at last fully recognized by the civil government.

The theme can scarcely have failed to impress itself upon the reader as well worthy of close study. Had they no moral to convey, the startling vicissitudes of the Huguenots would yet be entitled to rank among the most interesting and important of human experiences. But the story has a message of surpassing value to impart in the lesson that, in the wise providence of Almighty God, truth and right never sustain crushing defeat, never succumb to ultimate disaster. Correctly viewed, the history of the Huguenots is in no sense the history of a lost cause. It is the record of the miserable failure of persecution to destroy freedom of thought. What a contemporary of the Revocation erroneously described as "the last Efforts of Afflicted Innocence" were, in reality, the prelude of final triumph.

The history of the Huguenots not the history of a lost cause.

I do not forget the diminution in numbers sustained by the Huguenots, through the defection of many driven from their ranks, temporarily or permanently, by the intolerable oppression of Louis the Fourteenth and Louis the Fifteenth. In the process of winnowing, the corn is certainly lessened in bulk. But the emigration of the Huguenots, while to France it proved an injury that has not even yet been fully made up, must be viewed in the larger relations of world-history, wherein the advantages accruing to the Netherlands, to Switzerland, to Germany, to England, to the United States, and to other countries, far more than offset the damage received by the land which the fugitives forsook. It may be true that there are fewer Huguenots in France than there were before the effort to secure uniformity of religious belief; but the men and women who in almost every part of Christendom boast the Huguenot blood running in their veins doubtless far exceed in number the original victims of royal tyranny. And, in fact, the descendants of the Huguenots in France itself, proud of their ancestral faith and of their history, have within our own days awakened to a new consciousness of their powers and of their mission, regarding it their duty and their privilege to renew the struggle to win for their religious views a country which they bade fair to gain over, in the sixteenth century, when their ambitious efforts were thwarted by the violence of persecution.

Meanwhile, exerting an influence out of all proportion to their numbers, the descendants of the Huguenots shape, to no inconsiderable extent, the policy of a nation that scarcely appreciates as yet the service which those men of firm and loyal principle rendered to France in the past, or the service which their successors are capable of rendering to France in the future. During the course of the very year in which these lines are written (1895), it has been made the occasion of a public attack upon Protestantism in the city of Paris, that the adherents of this religion, although constituting, as is asserted, but one million out of the thirty-seven millions of Frenchmen, give the law to, and, in a sense, govern the other thirty-six millions. They have been styled "an oppressive minority," and it has been alleged in proof of the appropriateness of this designation that there are places in the department of Tarn et Garonne which have but a single Protestant inhabitant, and this Protestant is the mayor of the commune. If the statement be correct, the fact is, on a small scale, as significant as the larger national fact that in the first cabinet of a truly Republican character, after the fall of President MacMahon, in 1879, a majority of the ministers—five out of nine—were Protestants, and that from that time to this the Protestant representation in the chief councils of the nation has never been small. It has, indeed, been urged as a grievance that in those branches of the administration that specially call for high intellectual culture Protestants have appropriated a share to which they are not entitled —that a Protestant is the director of the normal school, that Protestants are at the head of primary and secondary instruction, that a Protestant woman presides over the school of Sèvres, that Protestant generals direct the polytechnic school and the school of Versailles, and that there are a host of Protestants in the courts of law, as judges, counsellors, and officers. But the charge, instead of a reproach, is in reality a tribute to the stanch integrity, the superior type of manhood, and the intelligent attachment to free institutions that characterize a body of men whose ancestors always deserved well of their country.

A minority that by virtue of its own excellence can so maintain itself, far from being " oppressive," is entitled to be regarded with profound respect and genuine admiration. The cause which that minority represents may almost be said to have won the victory already by anticipation ; for it has been demonstrated that the principles for which the Huguenots battled are not only elevated and ennobling, but imperishable.

INDEX

A.

ants of police, justice, and finances, i.
429, seq.; issues the severe law of April
2, 1666, i. 448, seq., which Abbé Caveyrac
styles a first essay of the Revocation, i.
449, 450 ; his reply to the great elector,
i. 451, seq.; he gives audience to Pierre
du Bosc, whose eloquence he eulogizes,
i. 457-459; nevertheless he suppresses
the Chambers of the Edict, January,
1669, i. 460 ; recalls his edict of 1666
(February, 1669), and thus irritates the
clergy, i. 463 ; proposes to allow another
national synod of the Protestants to
meet, i. 465, seq.; is entreated to slay the
Hydra of Heresy, i. 469 ; he orders that
Protestant girls be not *forced* to see
their parents before abjuring, i. 470,
471 ; he establishes, at Pélisson's suggestion, a fund for purchasing the conversion of Protestants, i. 473, seq.; concludes
the Peace of Nimeguen, and begins a
more systematic assault upon the rights
of the Huguenots (August, 1678), i. 477 ;
on the resignation of the elder Marquis
of Ruvigny, appoints the son deputy
general of the Huguenots, i. 478 ; suppresses the "chambres mi-parties," i.
482 ; his Jesuit confessor, Père de la
Chaise, i. 483 ; he restricts pastoral visitation, and forbids that a Protestant
should be a midwife, i. 484; his personal
activity in conversions, i. 489, 490 ;
grants or denies justice at his mere good
pleasure, i. 490, seq.; declares himself superior to the Edict of Nantes, i. 491 ;
enacts a law permitting Huguenot children of seven years of age to renounce
the religion of their parents (June 17,
1681), i. 494 ; his reply to Ruvigny's intercession, i. 501 ; he would cut off one
of his hands to secure the extirpation of
heresy, i. 502 ; his brutal denial of the
Huguenot petition, ib.; approves Marillac's use of the dragoons in Poitou, i.
507; was he ignorant of the latter's inhumanity ? i. 508 ; orders the clergy's Pastoral Admonition to be read to all Protestant consistories, i. 517; he rejects an
absurd proposal, i. 523 ; but excludes
Protestants from judicial offices, ib.; and
instructs judges to withhold justice from
Protestants, ib.; transfers Protestant
trust funds to Roman Catholic hospitals,
i. 525 ; orders that "fief" churches shall
be attended only by residents, i. 529 ;
commands that no pastor remain over
three years in one place, i. 547 ; indications of a change in his purpose, ib.; he
approves the plans of Foucault for re-
stricting the public services of the Huguenots in Béarn, i. 551 ; he rejoices over
the conversions effected by Foucault, i.
556 ; his piety praised by Cosnac and others, ii. 7, 8 ; his advisers in the recall of
the Edict of Nantes, ii. 10, seq.; he
marries Madame de Maintenon, ii. 18 ;

he signs the Revocation of the Edict of
Nantes, October 17, 1685, ii. 25 ; which is
registered by parliament and published
October 22, 1685, ii. 30 ; his feverish anxiety, ii. 35 ; interprets the treacherous
article of the revocatory edict, ii. 38 ;
forfeits his word most solemnly given,
ii. 39 ; receives a congratulatory brief
from the pope, ii. 64 ; refuses to allow
the mails to be tampered with, ii. 79 ;
suffers a few Protestants of distinction
to emigrate, ii. 103, seq.; makes death
the penalty for attendance on conventicles, July, 1686, ii. 157 ; issues a Declaration to secure the instruction of
Protestant children in the Roman Catholic religion, December, 1698, ii. 223 ;
authorizes the devastation of the Cévennes, ii. 313, seq.; issues laws against
Protestants frequenting Orange for
worship, ii. 337 ; again seizes Orange,
ii. 339 ; sees Cavalier at Versailles, ii.
404 ; his Declaration of March 8, 1715,
inflicting the penalties of the relapsed
on all Huguenots refusing the last sacraments of the church, ii. 425, seq.; the
"phantom of his shade," ii. 537.
Louis XV., accession of, ii. 436 ; persecution throughout his reign, ii. 437, seq.;
his Declaration of 1724, ii. 446 ; which
re-enacts every severe law, ii. 447, seq.;
his selfish indifference, ii. 509 ; his
death, ii. 520.
Louis XVI., his accession, May 10, 1774,
ii. 520 ; how he takes the coronation
oath, ii. 522, 523 ; he is timid respecting
the attempt to do justice to the Protestants, but is encouraged by Marie Antoinette, ii. 536 ; receives graciously the
petition of the notables in behalf of
the Protestants, ii. 541 ; issues the Edict
of Toleration, November 19, 1787, ii.
542, seq.; and disregards clerical opposition, ii. 548, 549.
Louvois, François Michel Le Tellier, Marquis of, minister of war, i. 506 ; his instructions to Marillac, i. 507 ; reproves
and finally recalls Marillac from Poitou,
i. 509 ; i. 549 ; encourages Foucault in
dragooning Béarn, i. 556 ; gives the order for the great Dragonnades, i. 558 ;
his affected surprise at the reported
treatment of the Huguenots, ii. 5 ; he
drops the mask, ii. 6 ; ii. 10 ; his character, ii. 12, 13, 14 ; ii. 18, 25 ; instructs
the dragoons to commit the greatest
possible disorder, ii. 42 ; ii. 58, 159, 160,
175.
Louvreleuil, ii. 226, 301, 317, 318, 327,
414.
Loyalty, excessive expressions of, i. 113,
156-158, 178, 276.
Lyons, riot at, i. 203 ; losses of, through
Huguenot emigration, ii. 78.
Luynes, Duke of, afterward Constable of
France, i. 126, 146, 147, 154, 167, 180,

504; his untiring exertions in behalf of the family of Jean Calas, ii. 508, seq.; he secures a retrial of the case and a vindication of Calas's memory, ii. 510; his hopes for the Huguenots, ii., 511; his interpretation of the words, "Compel them to come in," ii. 513, seq.; exerts himself for Paul Sirven and his family, ii. 514, 515; for Miss Camp, ii. 515; his opinion of Rousseau, ii. 518; gratitude of the Protestants, ib.; his correspondence with a Protestant pastor, ii. 518, 519.

W.

Waldenses of Piedmont, their "Glorious Recovery," ii. 192.

Wars. First Huguenot War (1621–1622), i. 175–231; Second Huguenot War (1625–1626), i. 251–270; Third Huguenot War, (1626–1629), i. 283–346; Camisard War (1702–1710), ii. 213–422.

William of Orange commissions Jean Claude to write the "Plaintes," ii. 90; his assurances, ii. 202; his death, ii. 338.

Wine-casks, escape of children in, ii. 72.

Worship, Protestant, proscribed, ii. 28.

Würtemberg, ii. 83.

Z.

Zorzi, Zorzo, Venetian ambassador, his estimate of Marie de' Medici, i. 16; of Cardinal Richelieu, i. 346.